STUDY GUIDE

STUDY GUIDE

Richard O. Straub
University of Michigan, Dearborn

with
**Focus on Vocabulary and Language
by *Cornelius Rea***
Douglas College, British Columbia

to accompany

David G. Myers
Exploring Psychology
Sixth Edition

WORTH PUBLISHERS

Study Guide
by Richard O. Straub
to accompany
Myers: **Exploring Psychology**, Sixth Edition

Printed in the United States of America

ISBN: 0-7167-8672-9 (EAN: 9780716786726)

Third printing

Worth Publishers
41 Madison Avenue
New York, New York 10010
www.worthpublishers.com

Contents

Preface   vii

How to Manage Your Time Efficiently and
Study More Effectively   ix

CHAPTER 1
Thinking Critically With Psychological Science   1

CHAPTER 2
Neuroscience and Behavior   34

CHAPTER 3
The Nature and Nurture of Behavior   66

CHAPTER 4
The Developing Person   89

CHAPTER 5
Sensation and Perception   123

CHAPTER 6
States of Consciousness   159

CHAPTER 7
Learning   187

CHAPTER 8
Memory   216

CHAPTER 9
Thinking, Language, and Intelligence   244

CHAPTER 10
Motivation   278

CHAPTER 11
Emotions, Stress, and Health   306

CHAPTER 12
Personality   345

CHAPTER 13
Psychological Disorders   378

CHAPTER 14
Therapy   405

CHAPTER 15
Social Psychology   431

APPENDIX A
Statistical Reasoning in Everyday Life   462

APPENDIX B
Psychology at Work   477

Preface

This Study Guide is designed for use with *Exploring Psychology*, Sixth Edition, by David G. Myers. It is intended to help you to learn material in the textbook, to evaluate your understanding of that material, and then to review any problem areas. Beginning on page ix, "How to Manage Your Time Efficiently and Study More Effectively" provides detailed instructions on how to use the textbook and this Study Guide for maximum benefit. It also offers additional study suggestions based on principles of time management, effective notetaking, evaluation of exam performance, and an effective program for improving your comprehension while studying from textbooks.

The sixth edition of this Study Guide offers many useful features. Each chapter includes three review tests: In addition to the two Progress Tests that focus on facts and definitions, there is a Review and Reflect test that evaluates your understanding of the text chapter's broader conceptual material and its application to real-world situations. This test contains at least 20 multiple-choice questions and an essay question. For all three review tests, the correct answers are given, followed by textbook page references (so you can easily go back and reread the material). In addition, complete explanations are given not only of why the answer is correct but also of why the other choices are incorrect.

The chapter review is organized by major text section. Each section includes a Section Preview—the objectives for that section—and Stepping Through the Section—detailed questions about the topics covered. The detailed guidelines provided for the objectives are useful for a section-by-section review of each textbook chapter and as a source of additional essay questions. Some chapters include a Cross-Check, which provides an engaging crossword puzzle review of chapter terms and concepts. Other chapters include fill-in-the-blank flow charts, which promote a deeper understanding of the conceptual relationships among chapter issues. In addition, each chapter includes Focus on Vocabulary and Language, written by Cornelius Rea of Douglas College, British Columbia. This section provides brief, clear explanations of some of the idioms and expressions used by David Myers that may be unfamiliar to some students. They are first listed in the relevant section preceding the Section Preview, then explained at the back of the chapter.

General Internet Resources

To obtain general information about psychology-related topics, you might want to consult some of the following Web sites. Russ Dewey's Psych Web is an effort to compile a great deal of information for psychology students and teachers, including self-quizzes, lists of psychology journals on the Web, self-help resources, tip sheets for psychology majors, and psychology departments on the Web. Psych Web is available at the site:

http://www.psychwww.com

Deborah Kelley-Milburn and Michael A. Milburn's "Cyberspace: Resources for Psychologists on the Internet" (*Psychological Science*, [1995, July], Volume 6, pp. 203–211) provides another excellent resource. This feature review provides helpful information on Listservs, Usenet groups, electronic journals and newsletters, databases, grant and job information, and library catalogues.

Both the American Psychological Association (APA) and the American Psychological Society (APS) have Internet services. These services provide not only information about their organizations but also selected articles from their main journals, information about current research in the discipline, and links to other science-related sites on the Internet. Their locations are as follows:

APA: http://www.apa.org/ and APS: http://www.psychologicalscience.org

Finally, and perhaps most important, is Psychtalk, a list for students interested in discussion topics and controversies related to psychology. Topics that have been discussed over the past few years include child abuse, the nature-nurture issue, homosexuality, and pornography. To subscribe, send a message to:

psychtalk-request@fre.fsu.umd.edu

The message should read "subscribe psychtalk (your name)."

Acknowledgments

I would like to thank all the students and instructors who used this Study Guide in its previous editions and provided such insightful and useful suggestions. Special thanks are also due to Betty Shapiro Probert for her extraordinary editorial contributions and to Don Probert for his skill and efficiency in the composition of this guide. I would also like to thank Andrea Musick and Stacey Alexander of Worth Publishers for their dedication and energy in skillfully coordinating various aspects of production. Most important, I want to thank Jeremy, Rebecca, Melissa, and Pam for their enduring love and patience.

Richard O. Straub
February 2004

How to Manage Your Time Efficiently and Study More Effectively

How effectively do you study? Good study habits make the job of being a college student much easier. Many students, who *could* succeed in college, fail or drop out because they have never learned to manage their time efficiently. Even the best students can usually benefit from an in-depth evaluation of their current study habits.

There are many ways to achieve academic success, of course, but your approach may not be the most effective or efficient. Are you sacrificing your social life or your physical or mental health in order to get A's on your exams? Good study habits result in better grades *and* more time for other activities.

Evaluate Your Current Study Habits

To improve your study habits, you must first have an accurate picture of how you currently spend your time. Begin by putting together a profile of your present living and studying habits. Answer the following questions by writing *yes* or *no* on each line.

_____ 1. Do you usually set up a schedule to budget your time for studying, recreation, and other activities?

_____ 2. Do you often put off studying until time pressures force you to cram?

_____ 3. Do other students seem to study less than you do, but get better grades?

_____ 4. Do you usually spend hours at a time studying one subject, rather than dividing that time between several subjects?

_____ 5. Do you often have trouble remembering what you have just read in a textbook?

_____ 6. Before reading a chapter in a textbook, do you skim through it and read the section headings?

_____ 7. Do you try to predict exam questions from your lecture notes and reading?

_____ 8. Do you usually attempt to paraphrase or summarize what you have just finished reading?

_____ 9. Do you find it difficult to concentrate very long when you study?

_____ 10. Do you often feel that you studied the wrong material for an exam?

Thousands of college students have participated in similar surveys. Students who are fully realizing their academic potential usually respond as follows: (1) yes, (2) no, (3) no, (4) no, (5) no, (6) yes, (7) yes, (8) yes, (9) no, (10) no.

Compare your responses to those of successful students. The greater the discrepancy, the more you could benefit from a program to improve your study habits. The questions are designed to identify areas of weakness. Once you have identified your weaknesses, you will be able to set specific goals for improvement and implement a program for reaching them.

Manage Your Time

Do you often feel frustrated because there isn't enough time to do all the things you must and want to do? Take heart. Even the most productive and successful people feel this way at times. But they establish priorities for their activities and they learn to budget time for each of them. There's much in the saying "If you want something done, ask a busy person to do it." A busy person knows how to get things done.

If you don't now have a system for budgeting your time, develop one. Not only will your academic accomplishments increase, but you will actually find more time in your schedule for other activities. And you won't have to feel guilty about "taking time off," because all your obligations will be covered.

Establish a Baseline

As a first step in preparing to budget your time, keep a diary for a few days to establish a summary, or baseline, of the time you spend in studying, socializing, working, and so on. If you are like many students, much of your "study" time is nonproductive; you may sit at your desk and leaf through a book, but the time is actually wasted. Or you may procrastinate. You are always getting ready to study, but you rarely do.

Besides revealing where you waste time, your diary will give you a realistic picture of how much time you need to allot for meals, commuting, and other fixed activities. In addition, careful records should indicate the times of the day when you are consistently most productive. A sample time-management diary is shown in Table 1.

Plan the Term

Having established and evaluated your baseline, you are ready to devise a more efficient schedule. Buy a calendar that covers the entire school term and has ample space for each day. Using the course outlines provided by your instructors, enter the dates of all exams, term paper deadlines, and other important academic obligations. If you have any long-range personal plans (concerts, weekend trips, etc.), enter the dates on the calendar as well. Keep your calendar up to date and refer to it often. I recommend carrying it with you at all times.

Develop a Weekly Calendar

Now that you have a general picture of the school term, develop a weekly schedule that includes all of your activities. Aim for a schedule that you can live with for the entire school term. A sample weekly schedule, incorporating the following guidelines, is shown in Table 2.

1. Enter your class times, work hours, and any other fixed obligations first. *Be thorough.* Using information from your time-management diary, allow plenty of time for such things as commuting, meals, laundry, and the like.

Table 1   Sample Time-Management Diary

	Monday	
Behavior	Time Completed	Duration Hours: Minutes
Sleep	7:00	7:30
Dressing	7:25	:25
Breakfast	7:45	:20
Commute	8:20	:35
Coffee	9:00	:40
French	10:00	1:00
Socialize	10:15	:15
Video game	10:35	:20
Coffee	11:00	:25
Psychology	12:00	1:00
Lunch	12:25	:25
Study Lab	1:00	:35
Psych. Lab	4:00	3:00
Work	5:30	1:30
Commute	6:10	:40
Dinner	6:45	:35
TV	7:30	:45
Study Psych.	10:00	2:30
Socialize	11:30	1:30
Sleep		

Prepare a similar chart for each day of the week. When you finish an activity, note it on the chart and write down the time it was completed. Then determine its duration by subtracting the time the previous activity was finished from the newly entered time.

2. Set up a study schedule for each of your courses. The study habits survey and your time-management diary will help direct you. The following guidelines should also be useful.

(a) Establish regular study times for each course. The 4 hours needed to study one subject, for example, are most profitable when divided into shorter periods spaced over several days. If you cram your studying into one 4-hour block, what you attempt to learn in the third or fourth hour will interfere with what you studied in the first 2 hours. Newly acquired knowledge is like wet cement. It needs some time to "harden" to become memory.

(b) Alternate subjects. The type of interference just mentioned is greatest between similar topics. Set up a schedule in which you spend time on several *different* courses during each study session. Besides reducing the potential for interference, alternating subjects will help to prevent mental fatigue with one topic.

(c) Set weekly goals to determine the amount of study time you need to do well in each course. This will depend on, among other things, the difficulty of your courses and the effectiveness of your methods. Many

Table 2   Sample Weekly Schedule

Time	Mon.	Tues.	Wed.	Thurs.	Fri.	Sat.
7–8	Dress Eat	Dress Eat	Dress Eat	Dress Eat	Dress Eat	
8–9	Psych.	Study Psych.	Psych.	Study Psych.	Psych.	Dress Eat
9–10	Eng.	Study Eng.	Eng.	Study Eng.	Eng.	Study Eng.
10–11	Study French	Free	Study French	Open Study	Study French	Study Stats.
11–12	French	Study Psych. Lab	French	Open Study	French	Study Stats.
12–1	Lunch	Lunch	Lunch	Lunch	Lunch	Lunch
1–2	Stats.	Psych. Lab	Stats.	Study or Free	Stats.	Free
2–3	Bio.	Psych. Lab	Bio.	Free	Bio.	Free
3–4	Free	Psych.	Free	Free	Free	Free
4–5	Job	Job	Job	Job	Job	Free
5–6	Job	Job	Job	Job	Job	Free
6–7	Dinner	Dinner	Dinner	Dinner	Dinner	Dinner
7–8	Study Bio.	Study Bio.	Study Bio.	Study Bio.	Free	Free
8–9	Study Eng.	Study Stats.	Study Psych.	Open Study	Open Study	Free
9–10	Open Study	Open Study	Open Study	Open Study	Free	Free

This is a sample schedule for a student with a 16-credit load and a 10-hour-per-week part-time job. Using this chart as an illustration, make up a weekly schedule, following the guidelines outlined here.

professors recommend studying at least 1 to 2 hours for each hour in class. If your time-management diary indicates that you presently study less time than that, do not plan to jump immediately to a much higher level. Increase study time from your baseline by setting weekly goals [see (4)] that will gradually bring you up to the desired level. As an initial schedule, for example, you might set aside an amount of study time for each course that matches class time.

(d) Schedule for maximum effectiveness. Tailor your schedule to meet the demands of each course. For the course that emphasizes lecture notes, schedule time for a daily review soon after the class. This will give you a chance to revise your notes and clean up any hard-to-decipher shorthand while the material is still fresh in your mind. If you are evaluated for class participation (for example, in a language course), allow time for a review just *before* the class meets. Schedule study time for your most difficult (or least motivating) courses during hours when you are the most alert and distractions are fewest.

(e) Schedule open study time. Emergencies, additional obligations, and the like could throw off your

schedule. And you may simply need some extra time periodically for a project or for review in one of your courses. Schedule several hours each week for such purposes.

3. After you have budgeted time for studying, fill in slots for recreation, hobbies, relaxation, household errands, and the like.

4. Set specific goals. Before each study session, make a list of specific goals. The simple note "7–8 PM: study psychology" is too broad to ensure the most effective use of the time. Formulate your daily goals according to what you know you must accomplish during the term. If you have course outlines with advance assignments, set systematic daily goals that will allow you, for example, to cover fifteen chapters before the exam. And be realistic: Can you actually expect to cover a 78-page chapter in one session? Divide large tasks into smaller units; stop at the most logical resting points. When you complete a specific goal, take a 5- or 10-minute break before tackling the next goal.

5. Evaluate how successful or unsuccessful your studying has been on a daily or weekly basis. Did you reach most of your goals? If so, reward yourself immediately. You might even make a list of five to ten rewards to choose from. If you have trouble studying regularly, you may be able to motivate yourself by making such rewards contingent on completing specific goals.

6. Finally, until you have lived with your schedule for several weeks, don't hesitate to revise it. You may need to allow more time for chemistry, for example, and less for some other course. If you are trying to study regularly for the first time and are feeling burned out, you probably have set your initial goals too high. Don't let failure cause you to despair and abandon the program. Accept your limitations and revise your schedule so that you are studying only 15 to 20 minutes more each evening than you are used to. The point is to *identify a regular schedule with which you can achieve some success.* Time management, like any skill, must be practiced to become effective.

Techniques for Effective Study

Knowing how to put study time to best use is, of course, as important as finding a place for it in your schedule. Here are some suggestions that should enable you to increase your reading comprehension and improve your notetaking. A few study tips are included as well.

Using SQ3R to Increase Reading Comprehension

How do you study from a textbook? If you are like many students, you simply read and reread in a *passive* manner. Studies have shown, however, that most students who simply read a textbook cannot remember more than half the material ten minutes after they have finished. Often, what is retained is the unessential material rather than the important points upon which exam questions will be based.

This Study Guide employs a program known as SQ3R (*Survey, Question, Read, Rehearse,* and *Review*) to facilitate, and allow you to assess, your comprehension of the important facts and concepts in *Exploring Psychology,* Sixth Edition, by David G. Myers.

Research has shown that students using SQ3R achieve significantly greater comprehension of texts than students reading in the more traditional passive manner. Once you have learned this program, you can improve your comprehension of any textbook.

Survey Before you read a text chapter, determine whether the text or the study guide has an outline or list of objectives. Read this material and the summary at the end of the chapter. Next, read the textbook chapter fairly quickly, paying special attention to the major headings and subheadings. This survey will give you an idea of the chapter's contents and organization. You will then be able to divide the chapter into logical sections in order to formulate specific goals for a more careful reading of the chapter.

In this Study Guide, the *Chapter Overview* summarizes the major topics of the textbook chapter. This section also provides a few suggestions for approaching topics you may find difficult.

Question You will retain material longer when you have a use for it. If you look up a word's definition in order to solve a crossword puzzle, for example, you will remember it longer than if you merely fill in the letters as a result of putting other words in. Previewing the chapter will allow you to generate important questions that the chapter will proceed to answer. These questions correspond to "mental files" into which knowledge will be sorted for easy access.

As you survey, jot down several questions for each chapter section. One simple technique is to generate questions by rephrasing a section heading. For example, the "Preoperational Thought" head could be turned into "What is preoperational thought?" Good questions will allow you to focus on the important points in the text. Examples of good questions are those that begin as follows: "List two examples of . . . ." "What is the function of . . .?" "What is the significance of . . .?" Such questions give a purpose to your reading. Similarly, you can formulate questions based on the chapter outline.

The *Section Previews* of this Study Guide provide the types of questions you might formulate while surveying each chapter. This section is a detailed set of objectives covering the points made in the text. Guidelines for answers to these objectives are provided at the end of each chapter.

Read When you have established "files" for each section of the chapter, review your first question, begin reading, and continue until you have discovered its answer. If you come to material that seems to answer an important question you don't have a file for, stop and write down the question.

Using this Study Guide, read the chapter one section at a time. First, preview the section by skimming it, noting headings and boldface items. Next, study the appropriate section objectives in the *Section Preview.* Then, as you read the chapter section, search for the answer to each objective.

Be sure to read everything. Don't skip photo or art captions, graphs, or marginal notes. In some cases, what may seem vague in reading will be made clear by a simple graph. Keep in mind that test questions are sometimes drawn from illustrations and charts.

Rehearse When you have found the answer to a question, close your eyes and mentally recite the question and its answer. Then *write* the answer next to the question. It is important that you recite an answer in your own words rather than the author's. Don't rely on your short-term memory to repeat the author's words verbatim.

In responding to the objectives, pay close attention to what is called for. If you are asked to identify or list, do just that. If asked to compare, contrast, or do both, you should focus on the similarities (compare) and differences (contrast) between the concepts or theories. Answering the objectives carefully not only will help you to focus your attention on the important concepts of the text but also will provide excellent practice for essay exams.

Rehearsal is an extremely effective study technique, recommended by many learning experts. In addition to increasing reading comprehension, it is useful for review. Trying to explain something in your own words clarifies your knowledge, often by revealing aspects of your answer that are vague or incomplete. If you repeatedly rely upon "I know" in recitation, you really *may not know.*

Rehearsal has the additional advantage of simulating an exam, especially an essay exam; the same skills are required in both cases. Too often students study without ever putting the book and notes aside, which makes it easy for them to develop false confidence in their knowledge. When the material is in front of you, you may be able to *recognize* an answer, but will you be able to *recall* it later, when you take an exam that does not provide these retrieval cues?

After you have recited and written your answer, continue with your next question. Read, recite, and so on.

Review When you have answered the last question on the material you have designated as a study goal, go back and review. Read over each question and your written answer to it. Your review might also include a brief written summary that integrates all of your questions and answers. This review need not take longer than a few minutes, but it is important. It will help you retain the material longer and will greatly facilitate a final review of each chapter before the exam.

In this Study Guide, *Stepping Through the Section* contains fill-in and brief essay questions for you to complete after you have finished reading the section and have written answers to the objectives. The correct answers are given at the end of the chapter. Gen-

erally, your answer to a fill-in question should match exactly (as in the case of important terms, theories, or people). In some cases, the answer is not a term or name, so a word close in meaning will suffice. You should answer these questions several times before taking an exam, so it is a good idea to mentally fill in the answers until you are ready for a final pretest review. Textbook page references are provided with each section title, in case you need to reread any of the material.

Also provided to facilitate your review are two *Progress Tests* that include multiple-choice questions and, where appropriate, matching or true–false questions. These tests are *not* to be taken until you have read the chapter, written answers to the objectives, and completed the *Chapter Review.* Correct answers, along with explanations of why each alternative is correct or incorrect, are provided at the end of the chapter. The relevant text page numbers for each question are also given. If you miss a question, read these explanations and, if necessary, review the text pages to further understand why. The *Progress Tests* do not test every aspect of a concept, so you should treat an incorrect answer as an indication that you need to review the concept.

Following the two *Progress Tests* is a *Review and Reflect* test, which should be taken just prior to an exam. It includes questions that test your ability to analyze, integrate, and apply the concepts in the chapter. Each *Review and Reflect* test includes an essay question dealing with a major concept covered in the chapter. As with the *Progress Tests,* answers for the *Review and Reflect* test are provided at the end of each chapter, along with relevant page numbers.

In most cases, the core of the chapter concludes with *Key Terms.* For chapters that contain many new technical terms, this section includes not only a list of key terms but also a crossword puzzle. *Writing Definitions* requires that you write definitions of all key terms on a separate piece of paper. *Cross-Check* reverses the process, asking you to complete a crossword puzzle by filling in the terms that apply to the definitions provided. As with the *Section Preview* objectives, it is important that these answers be written from memory, and in your own words. The *Answers* section at the end of the chapter gives a definition of each term, sometimes along with an example of its usage and/or a tip to help you remember its meaning. It also includes answers to the crossword puzzle.

Where appropriate, *Key Terms* is followed by *Summing Up,* one or two fill-in-the-blank flow charts. These charts are designed to help you integrate and apply major concepts described in the chapter.

Following the answers is a list of potentially unfamiliar idioms, words, and expressions (*Focus on Vocabulary and Language*), ordered by text page number and accompanied by definitions and examples.

One final suggestion: Incorporate SQ3R into your time-management calendar. Set specific goals for completing SQ3R with each assigned chapter. Keep a record of chapters completed, and reward yourself for being conscientious. Initially, it takes more time and effort to "read" using SQ3R, but with practice, the steps will become automatic. More important, you will comprehend significantly more material and retain what you have learned longer than passive readers do.

Taking Lecture Notes

Are your class notes as useful as they might be? One way to determine their worth is to compare them with those taken by other good students. Are yours as thorough? Do they provide you with a comprehensible outline of each lecture? If not, then the following suggestions might increase the effectiveness of your notetaking.

1. Keep a separate notebook for each course. Use $8\frac{1}{2} \times 11$-inch pages. Consider using a ring binder, which would allow you to revise and insert notes while still preserving lecture order.

2. Take notes in the format of a lecture outline. Use roman numerals for major points, letters for supporting arguments, and so on. Some instructors will make this easy by delivering organized lectures and, in some cases, by outlining their lectures on the board. If a lecture is disorganized, you will probably want to reorganize your notes soon after the class.

3. As you take notes in class, leave a wide margin on one side of each page. After the lecture, expand or clarify any shorthand notes while the material is fresh in your mind. Use this time to write important questions in the margin next to notes that answer them. This will facilitate later review and will allow you to anticipate similar exam questions.

Evaluate Your Exam Performance

How often have you received a grade on an exam that did not do justice to the effort you spent preparing for the exam? This is a common experience that can leave one feeling bewildered and abused. "What do I have to do to get an A?" "The test was unfair!" "I studied the wrong material!"

The chances of this happening are greatly reduced if you have an effective time-management schedule and use the study techniques described here. But it can happen to the best-prepared student and is most likely to occur on your first exam with a new professor.

Remember that there are two main reasons for studying. One is to learn for your own general academic development. Many people believe that such knowledge is all that really matters. Of course, it is possible, though unlikely, to be an expert on a topic without achieving commensurate grades, just as one can, occasionally, earn an excellent grade without truly mastering the course material. During a job interview or in the workplace, however, your A in Cobol won't mean much if you can't actually program a computer.

In order to keep career options open after you graduate, you must know the material and maintain competitive grades. In the short run, this means performing well on exams, which is the second main objective in studying.

Probably the single best piece of advice to keep in mind when studying for exams is to *try to predict exam questions*. This means ignoring the trivia and focusing on the important questions and their answers (with your instructor's emphasis in mind).

A second point is obvious. How well you do on exams is determined by your mastery of *both* lecture and textbook material. Many students (partly because of poor time management) concentrate too much on one at the expense of the other.

To evaluate how well you are learning lecture and textbook material, analyze the questions you missed on the first exam. If your instructor does not review exams during class, you can easily do it yourself. Divide the questions into two categories: those drawn primarily from lectures and those drawn primarily from the textbook. Determine the percentage of questions you missed in each category. If your errors are evenly distributed and you are satisfied with your grade, you have no problem. If you are weaker in one area, you will need to set future goals for increasing and/or improving your study of that area.

Similarly, note the percentage of test questions drawn from each category. Although exams in most courses cover *both* lecture notes and the textbook, the relative emphasis of each may vary from instructor to instructor. While your instructors may not be entirely consistent in making up future exams, you may be able to tailor your studying for each course by placing *additional* emphasis on the appropriate area.

Exam evaluation will also point out the types of questions your instructor prefers. Does the exam consist primarily of multiple-choice, true–false, or essay questions? You may also discover that an instructor is fond of wording questions in certain ways. For example, an instructor may rely heavily on questions that require you to draw an analogy between a theory or concept and a real-world example. Evaluate both your instructor's style and how well you do with each format. Use this information to guide your future exam preparation.

Important aids, not only in studying for exams but also in determining how well prepared you are, are the *Progress* and *Thinking Critically Tests* provided in this Study Guide. If these tests don't include all of the types of questions your instructor typically writes, make up your own practice exam questions. Spend extra time testing yourself with question formats that are most difficult for you. There is no better way to evaluate your preparation for an upcoming exam than by testing yourself under the conditions most likely to be in effect during the actual test.

A Few Practical Tips

Even the best intentions for studying sometimes fail. Some of these failures occur because students attempt to work under conditions that are simply not conducive to concentrated study. To help ensure the success of your time-management program, here are a few suggestions that should assist you in reducing the possibility of procrastination or distraction.

1. If you have set up a schedule for studying, make your roommate, family, and friends aware of this commitment, and ask them to honor your quiet study time. Close your door and post a "Do Not Disturb" sign.

2. Set up a place to study that minimizes potential distractions. Use a desk or table, not your bed or an extremely comfortable chair. Keep your desk and the walls around it free from clutter. If you need a place other than your room, find one that meets as many of the above requirements as possible—for example, in the library stacks.

3. Do nothing but study in this place. It should become associated with studying so that it "triggers" this activity, just as a mouth-watering aroma elicits an appetite.

4. Never study with the television on or with other distracting noises present. If you must have music in the background in order to mask outside noise, for example, play soft instrumental music. Don't pick vocal selections; your mind will be drawn to the lyrics.

5. Study by yourself. Other students can be distracting or can break the pace at which *your* learning is most efficient. In addition, there is always the possibility that group studying will become a social gathering. Reserve that for its own place in your schedule.

If you continue to have difficulty concentrating for very long, try the following suggestions.

6. Study your most difficult or most challenging subjects first, when you are most alert.

7. Start with relatively short periods of concentrated study, with breaks in between. If your attention starts to wander, get up immediately and take a break. It is better to study effectively for 15 minutes and then take a break than to fritter away 45 minutes out of an hour. Gradually increase the length of study periods, using your attention span as an indicator of successful pacing.

Some Closing Thoughts

I hope that these suggestions help make you more successful academically, and that they enhance the quality of your college life in general. Having the necessary skills makes any job a lot easier and more pleasant. Let me repeat my warning not to attempt to make too drastic a change in your life-style immediately. Good habits require time and self-discipline to develop. Once established, they can last a lifetime.

chapter 1

Thinking Critically With Psychological Science

Chapter Overview

Psychology's historical development and current activities lead us to define the field as the science of behavior and mental processes. Chapter 1 discusses the development of psychology from ancient times until today and the range of behaviors and mental processes being investigated by psychologists in each of the various specialty areas. In addition, it describes the seven major perspectives from which psychologists work. This is followed by an overview of the diverse subfields in which psychologists conduct research and provide professional services.

The next section explains the limits of intuition and common sense in reasoning about behavior and mental processes. To counteract our human tendency toward faulty reasoning, psychologists adopt a scientific attitude that is based on curiosity, skepticism, humility, and critical thinking. Using the scientific method, they employ the research strategies of description, correlation, and experimentation in order to objectively describe, predict, and explain behavior.

The chapter then discusses several questions people often ask about psychology, including why animal research is relevant, whether laboratory experiments are ethical, whether behavior varies with culture and gender, and whether psychology's principles don't have the potential for misuse.

The chapter concludes by explaining how to get your study of psychology off on the right foot by learning (and pledging to follow!) the SQ3R study method. This study method is also discussed in the essay at the beginning of this Study Guide.

Chapter 1 introduces a number of concepts and issues that will play an important role in later chapters. Pay particular attention to the strengths and weaknesses of descriptive and correlational research. In addition, make sure that you understand the method of experimentation, especially the importance of control conditions and the difference between independent and dependent variables. Finally, you should be able to discuss three important principles concerning populations and samples, as well as the concept of significance in testing difference.

NOTE: Answer guidelines for all Chapter 1 questions begin on page 19.

What Is Psychology? (pp. 1–10)

> David Myers at times uses idioms that are unfamiliar to some readers. If you do not know the meaning of any of the following words, phrases, or expressions in the introduction to this chapter and in this section, refer to pages 30–31 for an explanation: *to remedy their woes; peekaboo; grist for psychology's mill; down-to-earth; wise-cracking; "Magellans of the mind"; unpack this definition; sift opinions and evaluate ideas; hunches; mushrooming; wrestled with some issues; rekindled the debate; nature-nurture tension dissolves; "red in the face"; "hot under the collar"; But there is a payoff.*

Section Preview

First, skim this section, noting headings and boldface items. Then read the following objectives and, as you read the section, search for the information that will enable you to meet each objective. Answer guidelines are provided on page 19.

1. Trace the roots of psychology.

2. Describe the formal beginnings of the field of psychology.

3. Define psychology and identify several of its pioneers.

4. Identify and briefly describe the different perspectives of psychology.

5. Explain how psychology's different perspectives contribute to a complete view of human behavior.

6. Identify the major subfields of psychology.

Stepping Through the Section

After you have read the section, complete the sentences and answer the questions. As you proceed, evaluate your performance by consulting the answers beginning on page 19. Do not continue with the next section until you understand each answer. If you need to, review or reread the section in the textbook before continuing.

1. In the prescientific era, scholars such as
_____ in India and _____ in China pondered the relationship between mind and body.

2. The Greek philosophers _____ and
_____ viewed mind and body as
_____ (inseparable/separable) and assumed that knowledge is _____ (inherited/learned). The Greek philosopher who argued that all knowledge comes from experiences stored in memories is _____ .

3. In the 1600s, the views of the Greek philosophers were revived by _____ , who believed that some ideas are innate; by Englishman _____ , who became one of the founders of modern science; and _____ , who believed knowledge originates in experience. This idea, along with the principle that science flourishes through observation and experiment, is called _____ .

4. The first psychological laboratory was founded in 1879 by Wilhelm _____ . His student, _____ , introduced the school of _____ , which used the method of _____ to explore the basic elements of the mind. This method proved _____ (reliable/unreliable), and psychologist _____ introduced the school of

_____ , which focused on the adaptive significance of mental and behavioral processes. James was also the author of an 1890 textbook that introduced psychology to the educated public.

5. The first female president of the American Psychological Association was _____ . The first woman to receive a Ph.D. in psychology was _____ .

6. The historical roots of psychology include the fields of _____ and _____ .

7. Some early psychologists included Ivan Pavlov, who pioneered the study of _____ ; the personality theorist _____ ; and Jean Piaget, who studied _____ .

8. In its earliest years, psychology was defined as the science of _____ life. From the 1920s into the 1960s, psychology in America was redefined as the science of _____ behavior. The text author defines psychology as the science of _____ and _____ processes.

9. In this definition, "behavior" refers to any action that we can _____ and _____ , and "mental processes" refers to the internal _____ _____ we can _____ from behavior.

10. As a science, psychology is less a set of findings than a way of _____ _____ .

11. The controversy over the relative contributions of biology and experience on behavior is called the _____-_____ issue.

12. (Table 1.1) Psychologists who study how the body and brain enable emotions, memories, and sensory experiences are working within the _____ perspective.

13. (Table 1.1) Psychologists who study how natural selection influences behavior tendencies are working within the _____ perspective, whereas those concerned with the relative influences of genes and environment on individual differences are working within the _____ _____ perspective.

14. (Table 1.1) Psychologists who believe that behavior springs from unconscious drives and conflicts are working from the _____ perspective.

15. (Table 1.1) Psychologists who study the mechanisms by which observable responses are acquired and changed are working within the _____ perspective.

16. (Table 1.1) The _____ perspective explores how our minds encode, process, store, and retrieve information.

17. (Table 1.1) Psychologists who study how thinking and behavior vary in different situations are working within the _____-_____ perspective.

18. The different perspectives on the big issues _____ (contradict/complement) one another.

19. Psychologists may be involved in conducting _____ _____ , which builds psychology's knowledge base, or _____ _____ , which seeks solutions to practical problems.

20. Psychologists who study, assess, and treat troubled people are called _____ psychologists.

21. Medical doctors who provide psychotherapy and treat physical causes of psychological disorders are called _____ .

Why Do Psychology? (pp. 11–15)

> If you do not know the meaning of any of the following words, phrases, or expressions in the context in which they appear in the introduction to this chapter and in this section, refer to pages 31–32 for an explanation: *dresses it in jargon; we outsmart the smartest computers; bull's eye; out of sight, out of mind; absence makes the heart grow fonder; familiarity breeds contempt; drop a course; hard-headed curiosity; leap of faith; the proof is in the pudding; auras; crazy-sounding ideas; arena of competing ideas; so much the worse for our ideas; "the rat is always right"; the spectacles of our preconceived ideas; gut feelings; debunked; "play the tape."*

Section Preview

Answer guidelines are provided on page 20.

1. Identify two pitfalls in thinking that make intuition and common sense untrustworthy.

2. Discuss the attitudes that characterize scientific inquiry, and explain the nature of critical thinking.

Stepping Through the Section

Answers are provided on page 20.

1. The tendency to perceive an outcome that has occurred as being obvious and predictable is called the _____ _____ .

2. Our everyday thinking is also limited by _____ in what we think we know.

3. The scientific approach is characterized by the attitudes of _____ , _____ , and _____ .

4. Reasoning that examines assumptions, discerns hidden values, evaluates evidence, and assesses conclusions is called _____ _____ .

How Do Psychologists Ask and Answer Questions? (pp. 15–27)

> If you do not know the meaning of any of the following words, phrases, or expressions in the context in which they appear in the text, refer to pages 32–33 for an explanation: *handful of case studies; numbers are numbing; anecdotes are often more startling; snapshot of the opinions; having affairs; laypeople; flipped a coin; hot and cold streaks; recap.*

Section Preview

Answer guidelines begin on page 20.

1. Explain the importance of theories, hypotheses, operational definitions, and replication of research in psychology.

2. Discuss the descriptive research strategies.

3. Discuss the limitations and possible pitfalls of descriptive research.

7. Discuss the importance of random assignment and control techniques in research.

4. Describe the types of correlation, and discuss why correlation enables prediction but not explanation.

5. Explain the nature and significance of illusory correlations.

6. Describe the nature and advantages of experimentation.

Stepping Through the Section

Answers are provided on page 21.

1. An explanation using an integrated set of principles that organizes and predicts observable behaviors or events is a _____ . Testable predictions that allow a scientist to evaluate a theory are called _____ .

2. In order to prevent theoretical biases from influencing scientific observations, research must be reported precisely—using clear _____ _____ of all concepts—so that others can _____ the findings.

3. The research strategy in which one or more individuals is studied in depth in order to reveal universal principles of behavior is the

_____ _____ .

A potential problem with this method is that any given individual may be _____ .

4. The method in which a group of people is questioned about their attitudes or behavior is the _____ method.

5. An important factor in the validity of survey research is the _____ of questions.

6. Surveys try to obtain a _____ sample, one that will be representative of the _____ being studied. In such a sample, every person _____ (does/does not) have a chance of being included.

7. Large, representative samples _____ (are/are not) better than small ones.

8. The research strategy in which people or animals are directly observed in their natural environments is called _____

_____ .

9. Case studies, surveys, and naturalistic observation do not explain behavior; they simply _____ it.

10. Using naturalistic observation of walking speed and the accuracy of public clocks, researchers have concluded that the pace of life _____ (varies/does not vary) from one culture to another. Researchers have also found that people are more likely to laugh in _____ situations than in _____ situations.

11. When changes in one factor are accompanied by changes in another, the two factors are said to be _____ , and one is thus able to _____ the other. If the factors increase or decrease together, they are

_____ _____ .

If, however, one decreases as the other increases, they are _____ _____ .

12. Correlation does not prove _____ ; rather, it merely indicates the possibility of a

_____ -_____

relationship.

13. A perceived correlation that does not really exist is an _____

_____ . This error in thinking helps explain many _____ beliefs.

If your level of test anxiety goes down as your time spent studying for the exam goes up, would you say these events are positively or negatively correlated? Explain your reasoning.

14. Another common tendency is to perceive order in _____ _____ .

15. (Thinking Critically) Basketball players and fans mistakenly believe that players are _____ (no more likely/more likely) to score after having just made the last two or three shots. However, we need to remember that our _____ often misleads us.

16. Research studies have found that breast-fed infants _____ (do/do not) grow up with higher intelligence scores than those of infants who are bottle-fed with cow's milk. To study cause-effect relationships, psychologists conduct _____ . Using this method, a researcher _____ the factor of interest, while _____ _____ other factors.

17. Researchers sometimes give certain participants a pseudotreatment, called a _____ , and compare their behavior with that of subjects who receive the actual treatment. When merely thinking that one is receiving a treatment produces results, a _____ _____ is said to occur.

18. When neither the subjects nor the person collecting the data knows which condition a subject is in, the researcher is making use of the

_____ -_____

_____ .

19. An experiment must involve at least two conditions: the _____ condition, in which the experimental treatment is absent, and the _____ condition, in which it is present.

20. Experimenters rely on the _____ _____ of individuals to experimental and control groups.

21. The factor that is being manipulated in an experiment is called the _____ variable.

The measurable factor that may change as a result of these manipulations is called the _____ variable.

Explain at least one advantage of the experiment as a research strategy.

Frequently Asked Questions About Psychology (pp. 27–31)

> If you do not know the meaning of any of the following words, phrases, or expressions in the context in which they appear in the text, refer to page 33 for an explanation: *plunge in; To understand how a combustion engine works . . . .; ethics committee; color "the facts."*

Section Preview

Answer guidelines begin on page 21.

1. Discuss questions regarding the artificiality of experimentation and whether psychological principles are culture- or gender-free.

2. Explain why psychologists study animals, and discuss the ethics of experimentation.

3. Describe how psychologists' values influence their work, and discuss whether psychology is potentially dangerous.

Stepping Through the Section

Answers are provided on page 22.

1. Laboratory experiments in psychology are sometimes criticized as being _____. However, psychologists' concern is not with the specific behaviors but with the underlying theoretical _____.

2. Culture refers to shared _____, _____, _____, and _____ that one generation passes on to the next.

3. Although specific attitudes and behaviors vary across cultures, the underlying _____ are the same. For instance, throughout the world people diagnosed with _____ exhibit the same _____ malfunction.

4. Some people question whether experiments with animals are _____. They wonder whether it is right to place the _____ of humans over those of animals.

Describe the goals of the ethical guidelines for psychological research.

5. Psychologists' values _____ (do/ do not) influence their theories, observations, and professional advice.

Tips for Studying Psychology (pp. 31–32)

> If you do not know the meaning of the following expression in the context in which it appears in the text, refer to page 33 for an explanation: *spaced practice*.

Section Preview

Answer guidelines are provided on page 22.

1. Explain the SQ3R study method.

Stepping Through the Section

Answers are provided on page 22.

1. In order to master any subject, you must _____ process it.

2. The _____ study method incorporates five steps: **a.** _____ , **b.** _____ , **c.** _____ **d.** _____ , and **e.** _____ .

List five additional study tips identified in the text.

a. _____

b. _____

c. _____

d. _____

e. _____

Progress Test 1

Multiple-Choice Questions

Circle your answers to the following questions and check them with the answers beginning on page 22. If your answer is incorrect, read the explanation for why it is incorrect and then consult the appropriate pages of the text (in parentheses following the correct answer).

1. In its earliest days, psychology was defined as the:
   a. science of mental life.
   b. study of conscious and unconscious activity.
   c. science of observable behavior.
   d. science of behavior and mental processes.

2. Who would be most likely to agree with the statement, "Psychology should investigate only behaviors that can be observed"?
   a. Wilhelm Wundt
   b. Sigmund Freud
   c. John B. Watson
   d. William James

3. Today, psychology is defined as the:
   a. study of mental phenomena.
   b. study of conscious and unconscious activity.
   c. study of behavior.
   d. science of behavior and mental processes.

4. Who introduced the early school of structuralism?
   a. Edward Titchener
   b. Wilhelm Wundt
   c. William James
   d. Mary Whiton Calkins

5. Who wrote a psychology textbook published in 1890?
   a. Wilhelm Wundt   d. William James
   b. Ivan Pavlov   e. Sigmund Freud
   c. Jean Piaget

6. Psychologists who study the degree to which genes influence our personality are working within the _____ perspective.
   a. behavioral   d. neuroscience
   b. evolutionary   e. cognitive
   c. behavior genetics

7. Which of the following exemplifies the issue of the relative importance of nature and nurture on our behavior?
   a. the issue of the relative influence of biology and experience on behavior
   b. the issue of the relative influence of rewards and punishments on behavior
   c. the debate as to the relative importance of heredity and instinct in determining behavior
   d. the debate as to whether mental processes are a legitimate area of scientific study

8. The seventeenth-century philosopher who believed that the mind is blank at birth and that most knowledge comes through sensory experience is:
   a. Plato.
   b. Aristotle.
   c. Descartes.
   d. Locke.

9. Which seventeenth-century philosopher believed that some ideas are innate?
   a. Aristotle
   b. Plato
   c. Descartes
   d. Locke

10. Which psychological perspective emphasizes the interaction of the brain and body in behavior?
   a. neuroscience
   b. cognitive
   c. behavioral
   d. behavior genetics
   e. evolutionary

11. After detailed study of a gunshot wound victim, a psychologist concludes that the brain region destroyed is likely to be important for memory functions. Which research strategy did the psychologist use to deduce this?
   a. the case study
   b. a survey
   c. correlation
   d. experimentation

12. A psychologist who conducts experiments solely intended to build psychology's knowledge base is engaged in:
   a. basic research.
   b. applied research.
   c. industrial-organizational research.
   d. clinical research.

13. Psychologists who study, assess, and treat troubled people are called:
   a. basic researchers.
   b. applied psychologists.
   c. clinical psychologists.
   d. psychiatrists.

14. Today, psychology is a discipline that:
   a. connects with a diversity of other fields.
   b. is largely independent of other disciplines.
   c. is focused primarily on basic research.
   d. is focused primarily on applied research.

15. In an experiment to determine the effects of exercise on motivation, exercise is the:
   a. control condition.
   b. intervening variable.
   c. independent variable.
   d. dependent variable.

16. Francis Bacon's ideas led most directly to the scholarly view known as:
   a. functionalism.
   b. structuralism.
   c. empiricism.
   d. introspection.

17. In order to determine the effects of a new drug on memory, one group of people is given a pill that contains the drug. A second group is given a sugar pill that does not contain the drug. This second group constitutes the:
   a. random sample.   c. control group.
   b. experimental group.   d. test group.

18. A psychologist who explores how Asian and North American definitions of attractiveness differ is working within the _____ perspective.
   a. behavioral   c. cognitive
   b. evolutionary   d. social-cultural

19. Theories are defined as:
   a. testable propositions.
   b. factors that may change in response to manipulation.
   c. statistical indexes.
   d. principles that help to organize, predict, and explain facts.

20. In order, the sequence of steps in the SQ3R method is:
   a. preview, survey, review, think critically, read.
   b. plan, read, take notes, rehearse, review.
   c. survey, question, read, rehearse, review.
   d. plan, review, take notes, rehearse, read.

21. A psychologist studies the play behavior of third-grade children by watching groups during recess at school. Which research strategy is being used?
   a. correlation
   b. case study
   c. experimentation
   d. naturalistic observation

22. To ensure that other researchers can repeat their work, psychologists use:
   a. control groups.
   b. random assignment.
   c. double-blind procedures.
   d. operational definitions.

23. The scientific attitude of skepticism is based on the belief that:
   a. people are rarely candid in revealing their thoughts.
   b. mental processes can't be studied objectively.
   c. the scientist's intuition about behavior is usually correct.
   d. ideas need to be tested against observable evidence.

24. Which of the following is *not* a basic research strategy used by psychologists?
   a. description
   b. replication
   c. experimentation
   d. correlation

25. Psychologists' personal values:
   a. have little influence on how their experiments are conducted.
   b. do not influence the interpretation of experimental results because of the use of statistical techniques that guard against subjective bias.
   c. can bias both scientific observation and interpretation of data.
   d. have little influence on investigative methods but a significant effect on interpretation.

26. If shoe size and IQ are negatively correlated, which of the following is true?
   a. People with large feet tend to have high IQs.
   b. People with small feet tend to have high IQs.
   c. People with small feet tend to have low IQs.
   d. IQ is unpredictable based on a person's shoe size.

27. Which of the following research strategies would be best for determining whether alcohol impairs memory?
   a. case study   **c.** survey
   b. naturalistic observation   **d.** experiment

28. Well-done surveys measure attitudes in a representative subset, or _____ , of an entire group, or _____ .
   a. population; random sample
   b. control group; experimental group
   c. experimental group; control group
   d. random sample; population

Matching Items

Match each term or concept with its definition or description.

Terms

_____ 1. neuroscience perspective
_____ 2. social-cultural perspective
_____ 3. psychiatry
_____ 4. clinical psychology
_____ 5. behavior genetics perspective
_____ 6. behavioral perspective
_____ 7. industrial-organizational psychology
_____ 8. cognitive perspective
_____ 9. basic research
_____ 10. applied research
_____ 11. evolutionary perspective
_____ 12. psychodynamic perspective
_____ 13. structuralism
_____ 14. functionalism
_____ 15. empiricism
_____ 16. culture
_____ 17. placebo
_____ 18. hindsight bias
_____ 19. critical thinking
_____ 20. illusory correlation

Definitions or Descriptions

a. behavior in the workplace
b. how people differ as products of different environments
c. the study of practical problems
d. an early school of psychology that used introspection to explore the contents of the mind
e. the mechanisms by which observable responses are acquired and changed
f. how the body and brain create emotions, memories, and sensations
g. how the mind processes, stores, and retrieves information
h. the view that science flourishes through observation and experimentation
i. how natural selection favors traits that promote the perpetuation of one's genes
j. the study, assessment, and treatment of troubled people
k. the medical treatment of psychological disorders
l. the disguised effects of unfulfilled wishes and childhood traumas
m. adds to psychology's knowledge base
n. an early school of psychology that focused on the adaptive value of thoughts and behaviors
o. how much genes and environment contribute to individual differences
p. shared ideas and behaviors passed from one generation to the next
q. "I-knew-it-all-along" phenomenon
r. reasoning that does not blindly accept arguments
s. chemically inert substance
t. false perception of a relationship between two variables

Progress Test 2

Progress Test 2 should be completed during a final chapter review. Answer the following questions after you thoroughly understand the correct answers for the section reviews and Progress Test 1.

Multiple-Choice Questions

1. The first psychology laboratory was established by _____ in the year _____ .
   a. Wundt; 1879   c. Freud; 1900
   b. James; 1890   d. Watson; 1913

2. Who would be most likely to agree with the statement, "Psychology is the science of mental life"?
   a. Wilhelm Wundt
   b. John Watson
   c. Ivan Pavlov
   d. virtually any American psychologist during the 1960s

3. In psychology, "behavior" is best defined as:
   a. anything a person says, does, or feels.
   b. any action we can observe and record.
   c. any action, whether observable or not.
   d. anything we can infer from a person's actions.

4. Which of the following research methods does *not* belong with the others?
   a. case study
   b. survey
   c. naturalistic observation
   d. experiment

5. In the experiment on subliminal perception, students listened for five weeks to tapes they thought would enhance their memory or self-esteem. At the end of the experiment:
   a. students who thought they had a memory tape believed their memories had improved, but, in fact, there was no improvement.
   a. self-esteem, but not memory, improved.
   c. memory, but not self-esteem, improved.
   d. both self-esteem and memory improved over the course of the experiment.

6. Two historical roots of psychology are the disciplines of:
   a. philosophy and chemistry.
   b. physiology and chemistry.
   c. philosophy and biology.
   d. philosophy and physics.

7. The Greek philosopher who believed that intelligence was inherited was:
   a. Aristotle.
   b. Plato.
   c. Descartes.
   d. Simonides.

8. The way the mind encodes, processes, stores, and retrieves information is the primary concern of the _____ perspective.
   a. neuroscience
   b. evolutionary
   c. social-cultural
   d. behavioral
   e. cognitive

9. Which of the following individuals is also a physician?
   a. clinical psychologist
   b. experimental psychologist
   c. psychiatrist
   d. biological psychologist

10. Dr. Jones' research centers on the relationship between changes in our thinking over the life span and changes in moral reasoning. Dr. Jones is most likely a:
    a. clinical psychologist.
    b. personality psychologist.
    c. psychiatrist.
    d. developmental psychologist.

11. Which subfield is most directly concerned with studying human behavior in the workplace?
    a. clinical psychology
    b. personality psychology
    c. industrial-organizational psychology
    d. psychiatry

12. Dr. Ernst explains behavior in terms of different situations. Dr. Ernst is working within the _____ perspective.
    a. behavioral
    b. evolutionary
    c. social-cultural
    d. cognitive

13. Which perspective emphasizes the learning of observable responses?
    a. behavioral
    b. social-cultural
    c. neuroscience
    d. cognitive

14. A psychologist who studies how worker productivity might be increased by changing office layout is engaged in _____ research.
    a. applied
    b. basic
    c. clinical
    d. developmental

15. A major principle underlying the SQ3R study method is that:
    a. people learn and remember material best when they actively process it.
    b. many students overestimate their mastery of text and lecture material.
    c. study time should be spaced over time rather than crammed into one session.
    d. "overlearning" disrupts efficient retention.

16. Which statement about the ethics of experimentation with people and animals is false?
    a. Only a small percentage of animal experiments use shock.
    b. Allegations that psychologists routinely subject animals to pain, starvation, and other inhumane conditions have been proven untrue.
    c. The American Psychological Association and the British Psychological Society have set strict guidelines for the care and treatment of human and animal subjects.
    d. Animals are used as subjects in almost 25 percent of all psychology experiments.

17. In an experiment to determine the effects of attention on memory, memory is the:
    a. control condition.
    b. intervening variable.
    c. independent variable.
    d. dependent variable.

18. Which of the following *best* describes the hindsight bias?
    a. Events seem more predictable before they have occurred.
    b. Events seem more predictable after they have occurred.
    c. A person's intuition is usually correct.
    d. A person's intuition is usually not correct.

19. The procedure designed to ensure that the experimental and control groups do not differ in any way that might affect the experiment's results is called:
    a. variable controlling.
    b. random assignment.
    c. representative sampling.
    d. stratification.

20. Illusory correlation refers to:
    a. the perception that two negatively correlated variables are positively correlated.
    b. the perception of a correlation between two unrelated variables.
    c. an insignificant correlation.
    d. a correlation that equals –1.0.

21. In generalizing from a sample to the population, it is important that:
    a. the sample be representative.
    b. the sample be nonrandom.
    c. the sample not be too large.
    d. all of the above be true.

22. Which of the following is true, according to the text?
    a. Because laboratory experiments are artificial, any principles discovered cannot be applied to everyday behaviors.
    b. No psychological theory can be considered true until tested.
    c. Psychology's theories reflect common sense.
    d. Psychology has few ties to other disciplines.

23. Which type of research strategy would allow you to determine whether students' college grades accurately predict later income?
    a. case study
    b. naturalistic observation
    c. experimentation
    d. correlation

24. In a test of the effects of air pollution, groups of students performed a reaction-time task in a polluted or an unpolluted room. To what condition were students in the unpolluted room exposed?
    a. experimental   c. randomly assigned
    b. control   d. dependent

25. In order to study the effects of lighting on mood, Dr. Cooper had students fill out questionnaires in brightly lit or dimly lit rooms. In this study, the independent variable consisted of:
    a. the number of students assigned to each group.
    b. the students' responses to the questionnaire.
    c. the room lighting.
    d. the subject matter of the questions asked.

26. In defining psychology, the text notes that psychology is most accurately described as a:
    a. way of asking and answering questions.
    b. field engaged in solving applied problems.
    c. set of findings related to behavior and mental processes.
    d. nonscientific approach to the study of mental disorders.

True–False Items

Place a *T* (*True*) or an *F* (*False*) in the blank next to each statement.

_____ 1. Worldwide, the number of psychologists has been decreasing.
_____ 2. The primary research tool of the first psychologists was the experiment.
_____ 3. The subject matter of psychology has changed over the history of the field.
_____ 4. Every psychological event is simultaneously a biological event.
_____ 5. Today, most psychologists work within the behavioral perspective.
_____ 6. The major perspectives in psychology contradict one another.
_____ 7. "Spaced practice" promotes better retention than "massed practice."
_____ 8. "Overlearning" hinders retention.
_____ 9. A major goal of psychology is to teach us how to ask important questions and to think critically as we evaluate competing ideas.
_____ 10. One reason the school of structuralism fell from favor is that the method of introspection was unreliable.
_____ 11. Our preconceptions can bias our observations.
_____ 12. Men and women are more different than they are similar.

_____ 13. Life is slower paced in Japan and Western Europe.

_____ 14. Descartes believed that all knowledge comes from experience.

_____ 15. The placebo effect is well documented with pain, depression, and anxiety.

Review and Reflect

Answer these questions the day before an exam as a final check on your understanding of the chapter's terms and concepts.

Multiple-Choice Questions

1. Psychology is defined as the "science of behavior and mental processes." Wilhelm Wundt would have omitted which of the following words from this definition?
   a. science
   b. behavior and
   c. and mental processes
   d. Wundt would have agreed with the definition as stated.

2. Jawan believes that psychologists should go back to using introspection as a research tool. This technique is based on:
   a. survey methodology.
   b. experimentation.
   c. self-examination of mental processes.
   d. the study of observable behavior.

3. Dharma's term paper on the history of American psychology notes that:
   a. psychology began as the science of mental life.
   b. from the 1920s into the 1960s, psychology was defined as the science of observable behavior.
   c. contemporary psychologists study both overt behavior and covert thoughts.
   d. all of the above are true.

4. Sensations, dreams, beliefs, and feelings are:
   a. examples of behavior.
   b. examples of subjective experiences.
   c. not considered appropriate subject matter for psychology today.
   d. b. and c.

5. The philosophical views of John Locke are to those of René Descartes as _____ is to _____ .
   a. nature; nurture
   b. nurture; nature
   c. rationality; irrationality
   d. irrationality; rationality

6. To say that "psychology is a science" means that:
   a. psychologists study only observable behaviors.
   b. psychologists approach the study of thoughts and actions with careful observation and rigorous analysis.
   c. psychological research should be free of value judgments.
   d. all of the above are true.

7. In concluding her report on the "nature-nurture debate in contemporary psychology," Karen notes that:
   a. most psychologists believe that nature is a more important influence on the development of most human traits.
   b. most psychologists believe that nurture is more influential.
   c. the issue is more heatedly debated than ever before.
   d. nurture works on what nature endows.

8. Dr. Waung investigates how a person's interpretation of a situation affects his or her reaction. Evidently, Dr. Waung is working within the _____ perspective.
   a. neuroscience   c. cognitive
   b. behavioral   d. social-cultural

9. Dr. Aswad is studying people's enduring inner traits. Dr. Aswad is most likely a(n):
   a. clinical psychologist.
   b. psychiatrist.
   c. personality psychologist.
   d. industrial-organizational psychologist.

10. The psychological perspective that places the most emphasis on how observable responses are learned is the _____ perspective.
    a. behavioral   c. behavior genetics
    b. cognitive   d. evolutionary

11. During a dinner conversation, a friend says that the cognitive and behavioral perspectives are quite similar. You disagree and point out that the cognitive perspective emphasizes _____, whereas the behavioral perspective emphasizes _____.
    a. conscious processes; observable responses
    b. unconscious processes; conscious processes
    c. overt behaviors; covert behaviors
    d. introspection; experimentation

12. Concerning the major psychological perspectives on behavior, the text author suggests that:
    a. researchers should work within the framework of only one of the perspectives.
    b. only those perspectives that emphasize objective measurement of behavior are useful.
    c. the different perspectives often complement one another; together, they provide a fuller understanding of behavior than provided by any single perspective.
    d. psychologists should avoid all of these traditional perspectives.

13. Your roommate announces that her schedule permits her to devote three hours to studying for an upcoming quiz. You advise her to:
    a. spend most of her time reading and rereading the text material.
    b. focus primarily on her lecture notes.
    c. space study time over several short sessions.
    d. cram for three hours just before the quiz.

14. A fraternity brother rationalizes the fact that he spends very little time studying by saying that he "doesn't want to peak too soon and have the test material become stale." You tell him that:
    a. he is probably overestimating his knowledge of the material.
    b. if he devotes extra time to studying, his retention of the material will be improved.
    c. the more often students review material, the better their exam scores.
    d. all of the above are true.

15. The psychological views of William James are to those of Edward Titchener as _____ is to _____.
    a. nature; nurture
    b. nurture; nature
    c. structuralism; functionalism
    d. functionalism; structuralism

16. You decide to test your belief that men drink more soft drinks than women by finding out whether more soft drinks are consumed per day in the men's dorm than in the women's dorm. Your belief is a(n) _____, and your research prediction is a(n) _____.
    a. hypothesis; theory
    b. theory; hypothesis
    c. independent variable; dependent variable
    d. dependent variable; independent variable

17. Your roommate is conducting a survey to learn how many hours the typical college student studies each day. She plans to pass out her questionnaire to the members of her sorority. You point out that her findings will be flawed because:
    a. she has not specified an independent variable.
    b. she has not specified a dependent variable.
    c. the sample will probably not be representative of the population of interest.
    d. of all the above reasons.

18. The concept of control is important in psychological research because:
    a. without control over independent and dependent variables, researchers cannot describe, predict, or explain behavior.
    b. experimental control allows researchers to study the influence of one or two independent variables on a dependent variable while holding other potential influences constant.
    c. without experimental control, results cannot be generalized from a sample to a population.
    d. of all the above reasons.

19. Martina believes that high doses of caffeine slow a person's reaction time. In order to test this belief, she has five friends each drink three 8-ounce cups of coffee and then measures their reaction time on a learning task. What is wrong with Martina's research strategy?
    a. No independent variable is specified.
    b. No dependent variable is specified.
    c. There is no control condition.
    d. There is no provision for replication of the findings.

20. A researcher was interested in determining whether her students' test performance could be predicted from their proximity to the front of the classroom. So she matched her students' scores on a math test with their seating position. This study is an example of:
    a. experimentation.
    b. correlational research.
    c. a survey.
    d. naturalistic observation.

21. Your best friend criticizes psychological research for being artificial and having no relevance to behavior in real life. In defense of psychology's use of laboratory experiments you point out that:
    a. psychologists make every attempt to avoid artificiality by setting up experiments that closely simulate real-world environments.
    b. psychologists who conduct basic research are not concerned with the applicability of their findings to the real world.
    c. most psychological research is not conducted in a laboratory environment.
    d. psychologists intentionally study behavior in simplified environments in order to gain greater control over variables and to test general principles that help to explain many behaviors.

22. A professor constructs a questionnaire to determine how students at the university feel about nuclear disarmament. Which of the following techniques should be used in order to survey a random sample of the student body?
    a. Every student should be sent the questionnaire.
    b. Only students majoring in psychology should be asked to complete the questionnaire.
    c. Only students living on campus should be asked to complete the questionnaire.
    d. From an alphabetical listing of all students, every tenth (or fifteenth, e.g.) student should be asked to complete the questionnaire.

23. If eating saturated fat and the likelihood of contracting cancer are positively correlated, which of the following is true?
    a. Saturated fat causes cancer.
    b. People who are prone to develop cancer prefer foods containing saturated fat.
    c. A separate factor links the consumption of saturated fat to cancer.
    d. None of the above is necessarily true.

24. Rashad, who is participating in a psychology experiment on the effects of alcohol on perception, is truthfully told by the experimenter that he has been assigned to the "high-dose condition." What is wrong with this experiment?
    a. There is no control condition.
    b. Rashad's expectations concerning the effects of "high doses" of alcohol on perception may influence his performance.
    c. Knowing that Rashad is in the "high-dose" condition may influence the experimenter's interpretations of Rashad's results.
    d. Both b. and c. are correct.

25. A friend majoring in anthropology is critical of psychological research because it often ignores the influence of culture on thoughts and actions. You point out that:
    a. there is very little evidence that cultural diversity has a significant effect on specific behaviors and attitudes.
    b. most researchers assign subjects to experimental and control conditions in such a way as to fairly represent the cultural diversity of the population under study.
    c. it is impossible for psychologists to control for every possible variable that might influence research participants.
    d. even when specific thoughts and actions vary across cultures, as they often do, the underlying processes are much the same.

26. The scientific attitude of humility is based on the idea that:
    a. researchers must evaluate new ideas and theories objectively rather than accept them blindly.
    b. scientific theories must be testable.
    c. simple explanations of behavior make better theories than do complex explanations.
    d. researchers must be prepared to reject their own ideas in the face of conflicting evidence.

27. Which of the following procedures is an example of the use of a placebo?
    a. In a test of the effects of a drug on memory, a participant is led to believe that a harmless pill actually contains an active drug.
    b. A participant in an experiment is led to believe that a pill, which actually contains an active drug, is harmless.
    c. Participants in an experiment are not told which treatment condition is in effect.
    d. Neither the participants nor the experimenter knows which treatment condition is in effect.

28. If height and body weight are positively correlated, which of the following is true?
    a. There is a cause-effect relationship between height and weight.
    b. As height increases, weight decreases.
    c. Knowing a person's height, one can predict his or her weight.
    d. All of the above are true.

29. Joe believes that his basketball game is always best when he wears his old gray athletic socks. Joe is a victim of the phenomenon called:
    a. statistical significance.
    b. overconfidence.
    c. illusory correlation.
    d. hindsight bias.

Essay Questions

1. Explain how researchers working from each of psychology's major perspective might investigate an emotion such as love. (Use the space below to list the points you want to make, and organize them. Then write the essay on a separate piece of paper.)

2. Elio has a theory that regular exercise can improve thinking. Help him design an experiment evaluating this theory. (Use the space below to list the points you want to make, and organize them. Then write the essay on a separate piece of paper.)

Key Terms

Writing Definitions

Using your own words, on a separate piece of paper write a brief definition or explanation of each of the following.

1. empiricism
2. structuralism
3. functionalism
4. psychology
5. nature-nurture issue
6. basic research
7. applied research
8. clinical psychology
9. psychiatry
10. hindsight bias
11. critical thinking
12. theory
13. hypothesis

14. operational definition
15. replication
16. case study
17. survey
18. population
19. random sample
20. naturalistic observation
21. correlation coefficient
22. illusory correlation
23. experiment

24. placebo
25. double-blind procedure
26. placebo effect
27. experimental condition
28. control condition
29. random assignment
30. independent variable
31. dependent variable
32. culture
33. SQ3R

Cross-Check

As you learned in this chapter, reviewing and overlearning of material are important to the learning process. After you have written the definitions of the key terms in this chapter, you should complete the crossword puzzle to ensure that you can reverse the process—recognize the term, given the definition.

ACROSS

1. In SQ3R, reading over your notes and the text.
8. Pioneer in the study of learning.
9. Perspective that explores how our minds process, store, and retrieve information.
10. In SQ3R, using your own words to test yourself on the material to be learned.
12. Another term for biology's influence on behavior and mental processes.
13. An inert substance or condition in an experiment.
15. The condition in an experiment in which the independent variable is withheld.
16. Pioneer in personality theory.
20. A testable proposition.
21. The variable in an experiment that is being manipulated by the investigator.
22. Type of research that seeks only to advance psychology's knowledge base.
23. Type of research that includes case studies, surveys, and naturalistic observation.

DOWN

2. Defined psychology as the "science of observable behavior."
3. _____ definitions specify the procedures used to define independent and dependent variables.
4. Perspective concerned with how natural selection influences our behavior.
5. Research strategy that seeks to uncover predictable relationships between variables.
6. Perspective concerned with the extent to which our genes and our environment influence our individual differences.

7. The tendency to overestimate the extent to which others share our beliefs and behaviors.

9. Thinking that does not blindly accept arguments and conclusions.

11. After-the-fact belief that you would have known the outcome.

13. Medical doctors who provide psychotherapy.

14. Enduring behaviors, ideas, attitudes, and traditions shared by a large group of people and transmitted from one generation to the next.

17. An explanation using an integrated set of principles that organizes and predicts observations.

18. Type of research that aims to solve specific problems.

Answers

What Is Psychology?

Section Preview

1. Psychology's ancestors date back to the world's first scholars, including Buddha and Confucius, who considered the origin of ideas; the ancient Hebrews, who linked mind and emotion to the body; and Socrates and Plato, who viewed knowledge as inborn. The Greek naturalist and philosopher Aristotle emphasized the power of careful observation and saw knowledge as coming from the experiences stored in our memories. In the 1600s, Francis Bacon, John Locke, and René Descartes revived the controversy, with Bacon and Locke arguing that knowledge depends on experience and Descartes maintaining that some knowledge is inborn. Bacon and Locke's legacy helped shape modern science and its emphasis on empiricism.

2. Wilhelm Wundt founded the first psychology laboratory in 1879. Wundt's student, Edward Titchener, introduced structuralism and its use of introspection to pinpoint the elemental structure of the mind. Under the influence of Charles Darwin, who introduced the idea of evolutionary psychology, William James introduced functionalism, with its emphasis on how behavior and mental processes enable organisms to adapt and survive. Two early women pioneers were Mary Calkins, who became the first female president of APA, and Margaret Washburn, who was the first woman to receive a Ph.D. in psychology.

3. The young science of psychology evolved from philosophy and biology. Ivan Pavlov, who pioneered the study of learning, was a Russian physiologist. Jean Piaget, the most influential observer of children, was a Swiss biologist, and Sigmund Freud was an Austrian physician. Psychology is the science of behavior and mental processes. It began as the science of mental life, with Wilhelm Wundt's focus on inner sensations, feelings, and images. From the 1920s into the 1960s, psychology in the United States was most influenced by John Watson and others who redefined it as the "science of observable behavior." In the 1960s, psychology began to recapture its interest in mental processes so that today psychology encompasses the scientific study of both overt behavior and covert thoughts and feelings.

4. Psychologists who work from a neuroscience perspective study how the body and brain create behavior and mental processes. Psychologists who work from an evolutionary perspective study how natural selection favors traits that promote the perpetuation of one's genes. Behavior geneticists study how genes and environment contribute to individual differences. The behavioral perspective emphasizes how observable behaviors are learned. Psychologists who work from a psychodynamic perspective believe that behavior springs from unconscious drives and conflicts. The cognitive perspective explores how people encode, process, store, and retrieve information. The social-cultural perspective calls attention to the importance of each person's social and cultural environment in shaping his or her thoughts, emotions, and behaviors.

5. Psychology's different perspectives need not contradict one another. In fact, they usually complement one another. Each perspective has its questions and its limits. Together, they provide a complete picture.

6. Some psychologists conduct basic research that builds psychology's knowledge base. Biological psychologists explore the links between brain and mind, developmental psychologists study our changing abilities, and personality psychologists investigate our inner traits. Others conduct applied research to solve practical problems. Industrial-organizational psychologists, for example, study and advise on behavior in the workplace. Still others provide professional services. Clinical psychologists study, assess, and treat troubled people. Psychiatrists are physicians who treat the physical causes of psychological disorders.

Stepping Through the Section

1. Buddha; Confucius

2. Socrates; Plato; separable; inherited; Aristotle

3. René Descartes; Francis Bacon; John Locke; empiricism

4. Wundt; Edward Titchener; structuralism; introspection; unreliable; William James; functionalism

5. Mary Calkins; Margaret Washburn

6. biology; philosophy

7. learning; Sigmund Freud; children

8. mental; observable; behavior; mental

9. observe; record; subjective experiences; infer

10. asking and answering questions

11. nature-nurture

12. neuroscience

13. evolutionary; behavior genetics

14. psychodynamic

15. behavioral

16. cognitive

17. social-cultural

18. complement

19. basic research; applied research

20. clinical

21. psychiatrists

Why Do Psychology?

Section Preview

1. Two reliable phenomena—hindsight bias and overconfidence—make intuition and common sense untrustworthy. Hindsight bias is the tendency to perceive an outcome that has already occurred as being obvious and predictable. Overconfidence is the tendency to think we know more about an issue than we actually do and to overestimate the accuracy of that knowledge.

2. As scientists, psychologists attempt to study thoughts and actions with an attitude of curiosity and skepticism. Scientists must also possess an attitude of humility because they may have to reject their ideas in the light of new evidence. Whether applied to reading news reports or listening to a lecture, critical thinking examines assumptions, discerns hidden values, evaluates evidence, and assesses conclusions.

Stepping Through the Section

1. hindsight bias

2. overconfidence

3. curiosity; skepticism; humility

4. critical thinking

How Do Psychologists Ask and Answer Questions?

Section Preview

1. Scientists rely on theories to explain, organize, and predict the behaviors or events under study. Good theories give direction to research by generating testable predictions, called hypotheses. Operational definitions specify the procedures used to define and measure research variables. Such definitions prevent ambiguity by providing an exactness of meaning that allows other scientists to replicate (repeat) the study.

2. The simplest research strategy is description; examples include case studies, surveys, and naturalistic observation. In the case study, one or more individuals is studied in great depth in the hope of revealing general principles underlying the behavior of all people. Surveys measure the self-reported attitudes or behaviors of a randomly selected representative sample of an entire group, or population. Naturalistic observation seeks to observe and record the behavior of organisms (including humans) in their natural environments.

3. Although descriptive research can suggest hypotheses for further study, it is limited to describing behavior and cannot reveal predictive or cause-effect relationships. One possible pitfall of case studies is that any given individual may be atypical, making the case misleading. Survey results may be misleading because even subtle changes in the order or wording of questions can influence responses. And the samples on which surveys are based may not be representative of the populations from which they are drawn. Like the case study and survey methods, naturalistic observation does not explain behavior.

4. A correlation is a statistical measure of relationship, revealing how accurately one event predicts another. Correlations are often graphically represented as scatterplots. A positive correlation indicates a *direct* relationship in which two things increase or decrease together. A negative correlation indicates an *inverse* relationship in which one thing increases as the other decreases. A correlation between two events or behaviors means only that one event can be predicted from the other. Because two events may both be caused by some other event, a correlation between the two events does not mean that one caused the other. Correlation thus does not enable explanation.

5. A perceived correlation that does not really exist is an illusory correlation. Illusory correlations help explain superstitious beliefs; they arise from

our eagerness to perceive order in events, even those that are random.

6. Conducting experiments allows psychologists to explain behaviors in terms of cause-effect relationships. This is because experiments allow researchers to manipulate one or more experimental factors (the independent variables) while holding all other potential independent variables constant. If a subject's behavior (the dependent variable) changes, the change can be attributed to the influence of the independent variable under study. In the typical experiment, participants are randomly assigned to either a control condition, in which the experimental treatment is absent, or an experimental condition, in which the treatment of interest is present.

7. Researchers randomly assign research participants to the experimental and control conditions of experiments in order to minimize any pre-existing differences between the groups. Two other control techniques involve use of a placebo and the double-blind procedure. These help ensure that any changes in the dependent variable that occur are due to the independent variable rather than to researchers' or participants' expectations.

Stepping Through the Section

1. theory; hypotheses
2. operational definitions; replicate
3. case study; atypical
4. survey
5. wording
6. random; population; does
7. are
8. naturalistic observation
9. describe
10. varies; social; solitary
11. correlated; predict; positively correlated; negatively correlated
12. causation; cause-effect
13. illusory correlation; superstitious

This is an example of a negative correlation. As one factor (time spent studying) increases, the other factor (anxiety level) decreases.

14. random events
15. more likely; intuition
16. do; experiments; manipulates; holding constant
17. placebo; placebo effect

18. double-blind procedure
19. control; experimental
20. random assignment
21. independent; dependent

Experimentation has the advantage of increasing the investigator's control of both relevant and irrelevant variables that might influence behavior. Experiments also permit the investigator to go beyond observation and description to uncover cause-effect relationships in behavior.

Frequently Asked Questions About Psychology

Section Preview

1. Psychologists intentionally conduct experiments on simplified behaviors in an artificial laboratory environment in order to gain control over the numerous independent and dependent variables present in more complex behaviors and the "real world." By studying simplified behaviors under controlled circumstances psychologists are able to test general principles of behavior that also operate in the real world.

   For similar reasons, psychologists often apply their findings from psychological studies of people from one culture to people in general and from one gender to the other. Although attitudes and behaviors vary greatly from culture to culture and the genders are different in many ways, the underlying principles are much the same.

2. Some psychologists study animals simply to understand animal behavior. For the same reasons that psychologists investigate human behavior in simplified laboratory environments before attempting to understand more complex everyday behaviors, other psychologists attempt to learn more about human behavior by studying simpler, yet similar, behaviors in animals.

   Although animals in psychological research rarely experience pain, opposition to animal experimentation raises two important issues: (1) whether it is morally right to place the well-being of humans above that of animals, and (2) what safeguards should protect the well-being of animals.

   Ethical standards developed by the American Psychological Association and the British Psychological Society provide strict guidelines regarding the treatment of people and animals in psychology experiments.

3. No science, including psychology, is value-free. Psychologists' values influence their choice of

research topics, their observations, and their interpretations of research findings. Psychological knowledge is a power that, like all powers, can be used for good or evil. Many psychologists conduct research aimed at solving some of the world's most serious problems, including war, prejudice, overpopulation, and crime.

Stepping Through the Section

1. artificial; principles

2. ideas; behaviors; attitudes; traditions

3. principles or processes; dyslexia; brain

4. ethical; well-being

Ethical guidelines require investigators to (1) obtain informed consent from potential participants, (2) protect them from harm and discomfort, (3) treat information obtained from participants confidentially, and (4) fully explain the research afterward.

5. do

Tips for Studying Psychology

Section Preview

1. The SQ3R study method incorporates the idea that mastery of a subject requires active processing of it. SQ3R stands for the five steps of the method: Survey, Question, Read, Rehearse, and Review. The text and this study guide are organized to facilitate use of the SQ3R method.

Stepping Through the Section

1. actively

2. SQ3R; a. Survey; b. Question; c. Read; d. Rehearse; e. Review
   a. Distribute study time.
   b. Learn to think critically
   c. Listen actively in class.
   d. Overlearn material.
   e. Be a smart test-taker.

Progress Test 1

Multiple-Choice Questions

1. **a.** is the answer. (p. 6)
   b. Psychology has never been defined in terms of conscious and unconscious activity.
   c. From the 1920s into the 1960s, psychology was defined as the science of observable behavior.
   d. Psychology today is defined as the science of behavior and mental processes. In its earliest

days, however, psychology focused exclusively on mental phenomena.

2. **c.** is the answer. (p. 6)
   a. Wilhelm Wundt, the founder of the first psychology laboratory, used the method of introspection to study mental phenomena.
   b. Sigmund Freud developed an influential theory of personality that focused on unconscious processes.
   d. William James, author of a psychology textbook in 1890, was a philosopher and was more interested in mental phenomena than observable behavior.

3. **d.** is the answer. (p. 6)
   a. In its earliest days psychology was defined as the science of mental phenomena.
   b. Psychology has never been defined in terms of conscious and unconscious activity.
   c. From the 1920s into the 1960s, psychology was defined as the science of behavior.

4. **a.** is the answer. (p. 3)

5. **d.** is the answer (p. 5)
   a. Wilhelm Wundt founded the first psychology laboratory.
   b. Ivan Pavlov pioneered the study of learning.
   c. Jean Piaget was this century's most influential observer of children.
   e. Sigmund Freud, as noted later in the text, wrote *The Interpretation of Dreams* in 1900.

6. **c.** is the answer. (p. 8)

7. **a.** is the answer. Biology and experience are internal and external influences, respectively. (p. 7)
   b. Rewards and punishments are both external influences on behavior.
   c. Heredity and instinct are both internal influences on behavior.
   d. The legitimacy of the study of mental processes does not relate to the internal/external issue.

8. **d.** is the answer. For Locke, the mind at birth was a blank tablet. (p. 3)
   a. Plato assumed that much of intelligence is inherited and therefore present at birth. Moreover, he was a philosopher of ancient Greece.
   b. Aristotle held essentially the same viewpoint as Locke, but he lived in the fourth century B.C.
   c. Descartes believed that knowledge does not depend on experience.

9. **c.** is the answer. (p. 2)
   a. Aristotle was a philosopher in ancient Greece who would have agreed with Locke that knowledge comes from experience.
   b. Plato assumed that character and intelligence are inherited.

d. Locke believed that the mind is a blank slate at birth.

10. **a.** is the answer. (p. 8)

    b. The cognitive perspective is concerned with how we encode, process, store, and retrieve information.

    c. The behavioral perspective studies the mechanisms by which observable responses are acquired and changed.

    d. The behavior genetics perspective focuses on the relative contributions of genes and environment to individual differences.

    e. The evolutionary perspective studies how natural selection favors traits that promote the perpetuation of one's genes.

11. **a.** is the answer. In a case study one subject is studied in depth. (p. 16)

    b. In survey research a group of people is interviewed.

    c. Correlations identify whether two factors are related.

    d. In an experiment an investigator manipulates one variable to observe its effect on another.

12. **a.** is the answer. (p. 9)

    b. & **c.** Applied and industrial-organizational psychologists tackle practical problems.

    d. Clinical psychologists (and researchers) focus on treating troubled people.

13. **c.** is the answer. (p. 10)

    d. Psychiatrists are medical doctors rather than psychologists.

14. **a.** is the answer. (p. 10)

    c. & **d.** Psychologists are widely involved in both basic and applied research.

15. **c.** is the answer. Exercise is the variable being manipulated in the experiment. (p. 25)

    a. A control condition for this experiment would be a group of people not permitted to exercise.

    b. An intervening variable is a variable other than those being manipulated that may influence behavior.

    d. The dependent variable is the behavior measured by the experimenter—in this case, the effects of exercise.

16. **c.** is the answer. (p. 3)

    a. & **b.** Bacon emphasized the importance of orderly observation and experimentation, neither of which was a focal point of these early schools of psychology.

    d. This is a research method used by the early structural psychologists, not a scholarly viewpoint.

17. **c.** is the answer. The control condition is that for which the experimental treatment (the new drug)

is absent. (p. 25)

a. A random sample is a subset of a population in which every person has an equal chance of being selected.

b. The experimental condition is the group for which the experimental treatment (the new drug) is present.

d. "Test group" is an ambiguous term; both the experimental and control group are tested.

18. **d.** is the answer. (p. 8)

    a. Behavioral psychologists investigate how learned behaviors are acquired. They generally do not focus on subjective opinions, such as attractiveness.

    b. The evolutionary perspective studies how natural selection favors traits that promote the perpetuation of one's genes.

    c. Cognitive psychologists study the mechanisms of thinking and memory, and generally do not investigate attitudes. Also, because the question specifies that the psychologist is interested in comparing two cultures, d. is the best answer.

19. **d.** is the answer. (p. 15)

    a. Hypotheses are testable propositions.

    b. Dependent variables are factors that may change in response to manipulated independent variables.

    c. Statistical indexes may be used to test specific hypotheses (and therefore as indirect tests of theories), but they are merely mathematical tools, not general principles, as are theories.

20. **c.** is the answer. (p. 32)

21. **d.** is the answer. In this case, the children are being observed in their normal environment rather than in a laboratory. (p. 18)

    a. Correlational research measures relationships between two factors. The psychologist may later want to determine whether there are correlations between the variables studied under natural conditions.

    b. In a case study, one subject is studied in depth.

    c. This is not an experiment because the psychologist is not directly controlling the variables being studied.

22. **d.** is the answer. (p. 15)

23. **d.** is the answer. (pp. 13–14)

24. **b.** is the answer. Replication is the repetition of an experiment in order to determine whether its findings are reliable. It is not a research strategy. (p. 15)

25. **c.** is the answer. (p. 30)

a., b., & d. Psychologists' personal values can influence all of these.

26. **b.** is the answer. (p. 19)

   a. & c. These answers would have been correct had the question stated that there is a *positive* correlation between shoe size and IQ. Actually, there is probably no correlation at all!

27. **d.** is the answer. In an experiment, it would be possible to manipulate alcohol consumption and observe the effects, if any, on memory. (p. 24)

   a., b., & c. These answers are incorrect because only by directly controlling the variables of interest can a researcher uncover cause-effect relationships.

28. **d.** is the answer. (p. 18)

   a. A sample is a subset of a population.

   b. & c. Control and experimental groups are used in experimentation, not in survey research.

Matching Items

1. f (p. 8)
2. b (p. 8)
3. k (p. 10)
4. j (p. 10)
5. o (p. 8)
6. e (p. 8)
7. a (p. 9)
8. g (p. 8)
9. m (p. 9)
10. c (p. 9)
11. i (p. 8)
12. l (p. 8)
13. d (p. 3)
14. n (p. 4)
15. h (p. 3)
16. p (p. 28)
17. s (p. 25)
18. q (p. 11)
19. r (p. 14)
20. t (p. 21)

Progress Test 2

Multiple-Choice Questions

1. **a.** is the answer. (p. 3)

2. **a.** is the answer. (p. 3)

   b. & d. John Watson, like many American psychologists during this time, believed that psychology should focus on the study of observable behavior.

   c. Because he pioneered the study of learning, Pavlov focused on observable behavior and would certainly have disagreed with this statement.

3. **b.** is the answer. (p. 6)

4. **d.** is the answer. Only experiments can reveal cause-effect relationships; the other methods can only *describe* relationships. (p. 24)

5. **a.** is the answer. (p. 26)

   b., c., & d. There was no actual improvement in memory or self-esteem in this experiment.

6. **c.** is the answer. (p. 5)

7. **b.** is the answer. (p. 2)

   a. Aristotle believed that all knowledge originates with sensory experience.

c. Descartes was a philosopher of the seventeenth century.

d. Simonides was a well-known Greek orator.

8. **e.** is the answer. (p. 8)

   a. The neuroscience perspective studies the biological bases for a range of psychological phenomena.

   b. The evolutionary perspective studies how natural selection favors traits that promote the perpetuation of one's genes.

   c. The social-cultural perspective is concerned with variations in behavior across situations and cultures.

   d. The behavioral perspective studies the mechanisms by which observable responses are acquired and modified in particular environments.

9. **c.** is the answer. After earning their M.D. degrees, psychiatrists specialize in the diagnosis and treatment of mental health disorders. (p. 10)

   a., b., & d. These psychologists generally earn a Ph.D. rather than an M.D.

10. **d.** is the answer. The emphasis on change during the life span indicates that Dr. Jones is most likely a developmental psychologist. (p. 10)

   a. Clinical psychologists study, assess, and treat people who are psychologically troubled.

   b. Personality psychologists study our inner traits.

   c. Psychiatrists are medical doctors.

11. **c.** is the answer. (p. 9)

   a. Clinical psychologists study, assess, and treat people with psychological disorders.

   b. & d. Personality psychologists and psychiatrists do not usually study people in work situations.

12. **c.** is the answer. (p. 8)

   a. Psychologists who follow the behavioral perspective emphasize observable, external influences on behavior.

   b. The evolutionary perspective focuses on how natural selection favors traits that promote the perpetuation of one's genes.

   d. The cognitive perspective places emphasis on conscious, rather than unconscious, processes.

13. **a.** is the answer. (p. 8)

14. **a.** is the answer. The research is addressing a practical issue. (p. 9)

   b. Basic research is aimed at contributing to the base of knowledge in a given field, not at resolving particular practical problems.

   c. & d. Clinical and developmental research would focus on issues relating to psychological disorders and life-span changes, respectively.

15. **a.** is the answer. (p. 31)
    b. & c. Although each of these is true, SQ3R is based on the more general principle of active learning.
    d. In fact, just the opposite is true.

16. **d.** is the answer. Only about 7 percent of all psychological experiments involve animals. (p. 29)

17. **d.** is the answer. (p. 25)
    a. The control condition is the comparison group, in which the experimental treatment (the treatment of interest) is absent.
    b. Memory is a directly observed and measured dependent variable in this experiment.
    c. Attention is the independent variable, which is being manipulated.

18. **b.** is the answer. (p. 11)
    c. This refers to overconfidence.

19. **b.** is the answer. (p. 25)
    a. The phenomenon is related to hindsight rather than foresight.
    c. & d. The phenomenon doesn't involve whether or not the intuitions are correct but rather people's attitude that they had the correct intuition.

20. **b.** is the answer. (p. 21)

21. **a.** is the answer. (pp. 17–18)
    b. & c. Large, random samples are more likely to be representative of the populations from which they are drawn.

22. **b.** is the answer. (p. 16)
    a. In fact, the artificiality of experiments is part of an intentional attempt to create a controlled environment in which to test theoretical principles that are applicable to all behaviors.
    c. Some psychological theories go against what we consider common sense; furthermore, on many issues that psychology addresses, it's far from clear what the "common sense" position is.
    d. Psychology has always had ties to other disciplines, and in recent times, these ties have been increasing.

23. **d.** is the answer. Correlations show how well one factor can be predicted from another. (p. 19)
    a. Because a case study focuses in great detail on the behavior of an individual, it's probably not useful in showing whether predictions are possible.
    b. Naturalistic observation is a method of describing, rather than predicting, behavior.
    c. In experimental research the effects of manipulated independent variables on dependent variables are measured. It is not clear how an ex-

periment could help determine whether IQ tests predict academic success.

24. **b.** is the answer. The control condition is the one in which the treatment—in this case, pollution—is absent. (p. 25)
    a. Students in the polluted room would be in the experimental condition.
    c. Presumably, all students in both conditions were randomly assigned to their groups. Random assignment is a method for establishing groups, rather than a condition.
    d. The word *dependent* refers to a kind of variable in experiments; conditions are either experimental or control.

25. **c.** is the answer. The lighting is the factor being manipulated. (p. 25)
    a. & d. These answers are incorrect because they involve aspects of the experiment other than the variables.
    b. This answer is the dependent, not the independent, variable.

26. **a.** is the answer. (p. 8)
    b. Psychology is equally involved in basic research.
    c. Psychology's knowledge base is constantly expanding.
    d. Psychology is the *science* of behavior and mental processes.

True–False Items

1. F (p. 7)	**6.** F (p. 8)	**11.** T (p. 30)
2. F (p. 3)	**7.** T (p. 32)	**12.** F (p. 28)
3. T (pp. 5–6)	**8.** F (p. 32)	**13.** F (p. 19)
4. T (p. 7)	**9.** T (p. 14)	**14.** F (p. 2)
5. F (p. 7)	**10.** T (p. 4)	**15.** T (p. 25)

Review and Reflect

Multiple-Choice Questions

1. **b.** is the answer. (p. 3)
   a. As the founder of the first psychology laboratory, Wundt certainly based his research on the scientific method.
   c. The earliest psychologists, including Wilhelm Wundt, focused on the self-examination of covert thoughts, feelings, and other mental processes.

2. **c.** is the answer. (p. 3)

3. **d.** is the answer. (pp. 5–6)

4. **b.** is the answer. (p. 6)
   a., c., & d. Psychologists today study both overt and covert behavior.

5. **b.** is the answer. Locke believed that all knowledge comes from experience (nurture). Descartes believed that some ideas are innate (nature). (pp. 2, 3)
   c. & d. The text does not discuss the views of these philosophers regarding this issue.

6. **b.** is the answer. (p. 6)
   a. Psychologists study both overt (observable) behaviors and covert thoughts and feelings.
   c. Psychologists' values definitely do influence their research.

7. **d.** is the answer. Because both nature and nurture influence most traits and behaviors, the tension surrounding this issue has dissolved. (p. 7)

8. **c.** is the answer. (p. 8)
   a. This perspective emphasizes the influences of physiology on behavior.
   b. This perspective emphasizes environmental influences on observable behavior.
   d. This perspective emphasizes how behavior and thinking vary across situations and cultures.

9. **c.** is the answer. (p. 9)
   a. Clinical psychology is concerned with the study and treatment of psychological disorders.
   b. Psychiatry is the branch of medicine concerned with the physical diagnosis and treatment of psychological disorders.
   d. Industrial-organizational psychologists study behavior in the workplace.

10. **a.** is the answer. (p. 8)

11. **a.** is the answer. (p. 8)
    b. Neither perspective places any special emphasis on unconscious processes.
    c. Neither perspective emphasizes covert behaviors.
    d. Introspection was a research method used by the earliest psychologists, not those working from the cognitive perspective.

12. **c.** is the answer. (p. 9)
    a. The text suggests just the opposite: By studying behavior from several perspectives, psychologists gain a fuller understanding.
    b. & d. Each perspective is useful in that it calls researchers' attention to different aspects of behavior. This is equally true of those perspectives that do not emphasize objective measurement.

13. **c.** is the answer. (p. 32)

a. To be effective, study must be active rather than passive in nature.
b. Most exams are based on lecture and textbook material.
d. Cramming hinders retention.

14. **d.** is the answer. (p. 32)

15. **d.** is the answer. James emphasized the adaptive value of our thoughts and behaviors (functionalism). Titchener used the method of introspection to examine the basic contents of the mind (structuralism). (pp. 3, 4)
    a. & b. The text does not discuss the views of these psychologists regarding the nature-nurture issue.

16. **b.** is the answer. A general belief such as this one is a theory; it helps organize, explain, and generate testable predictions (called hypotheses) such as "men drink more soft drinks than women." (p. 15)
    c. & d. Independent and dependent variables are experimental treatments and behaviors, respectively. Beliefs and predictions may involve such variables, but are not themselves those variables.

17. **c.** is the answer. The members of one sorority are likely to share more interests, traits, and attitudes than will the members of a random sample of college students. (pp. 17–18)
    a. & b. Unlike experiments, surveys do not specify or directly manipulate independent and dependent variables. In a sense, survey questions are independent variables, and the answers, dependent variables.

18. **b.** is the answer. (p. 25)
    a. Although the descriptive methods of case studies, surveys, naturalistic observation, and correlational research do not involve control of variables, they nevertheless enable researchers to describe and predict behavior.
    c. Whether or not a sample is representative of a population, rather than control over variables, determines whether results can be generalized from a sample to a population.

19. **c.** is the answer. In order to determine the effects of caffeine on reaction time, Martina needs to measure reaction time in a control, or comparison, group that does not receive caffeine. (p. 25)
    a. Caffeine is the independent variable.
    b. Reaction time is the dependent variable.
    d. Whether or not Martina's experiment can be replicated is determined by the precision with which she reports her procedures, which is not an aspect of research strategy.

20. **b.** is the answer. (p. 19)

a. This is not an experiment because the researcher is not manipulating the independent variable (seating position); she is merely measuring whether variation in this factor predicts test performance.

c. If the study were based entirely on students' self-reported responses, this would be a survey.

d. This study goes beyond naturalistic observation, which merely describes behavior as it occurs, to determine if test scores can be predicted from students' seating position.

21. **d.** is the answer. (p. 27)

22. **d.** is the answer. Selecting every tenth person would probably result in a representative sample of the entire population of students at the university. (p. 18)

a. It would be difficult, if not impossible, to survey every student on campus.

b. Psychology students are not representative of the entire student population.

c. This answer is incorrect for the same reason as b. This would constitute a biased sample.

23. **d.** is the answer. (pp. 19–20)

a. Correlation does not imply causality.

b. Again, a positive correlation simply means that two factors tend to increase or decrease together; further relationships are not implied.

c. A separate factor may or may not be involved. That the two factors are correlated does not imply a separate factor. There may, for example, be a direct causal relationship between the two factors themselves.

24. **d.** is the answer. (p. 25)

a. The low-dose comparison group is the control group.

25. **d.** is the answer. (p. 28)

a. In fact, just the opposite is true.

b. Actually, psychological experiments tend to use the most readily available subjects, often white North American college students.

c. Although this may be true, psychological experiments remain important because they help explain underlying processes of human behavior everywhere. Therefore, d. is a much better response than c.

26. **d.** is the answer. (p. 14)

a. This follows from the attitude of skepticism, rather than humility.

b. & c. Although both of these are true of the scientific method, neither has anything to do with humility.

27. **a.** is the answer. (p. 25)

b. Use of a placebo tests whether the behavior of a research participant, who mistakenly believes

that a treatment (such as a drug) is in effect, is the same as it would be if the treatment were actually present.

c. & d. These are examples of "blind" and "double-blind" control procedures.

28. **c.** is the answer. If height and weight are positively correlated, increased height is associated with increased weight. Thus, one can predict a person's weight from his or her height. (p. 19)

a. Correlation does not imply causality.

b. This situation depicts a negative correlation between height and weight.

29. **c.** is the answer. A correlation that is perceived but doesn't actually exist, as in the example, is known as an illusory correlation. (p. 21)

a. Statistical significance is a statement of how likely it is that an obtained result occurred by chance.

b. Overconfidence is the tendency to think we are more right than we actually are.

d. Hindsight bias is the tendency to believe, after learning an outcome, that one would have foreseen it.

Essay Questions

1. A psychologist working from the neuroscience perspective might study the brain circuits and body chemistry that trigger attraction and sexual arousal. A psychologist working from the evolutionary perspective might analyze how love has facilitated the survival of our species. A psychologist working from the behavior genetics perspective might attempt to compare the extent to which the emotion is attributable to our genes and the extent to which it is attributable to our environment. A psychologist working from the psychodynamic perspective might search for evidence that a person's particular emotional feelings are disguised effects of unfulfilled wishes. A psychologist working from the behavioral perspective might study the external stimuli, such as body language, that elicit and reward approach behaviors toward another person. A psychologist working from a cognitive perspective might study how our thought processes, attitudes, and beliefs foster attachment to loved ones, and a psychologist working from a social-cultural perspective might explore situational influences on attraction and how the development and expression of love vary across cultural groups.

2. Elio's hypothesis is that daily aerobic exercise for one month will improve memory. Exercise is the independent variable. The dependent variable is

memory. Exercise could be manipulated by having people in an experimental group jog for 30 minutes each day. Memory could be measured by comparing the number of words they recall from a test list studied before the exercise experiment begins, and again afterward. A control group that does not exercise *is* needed so that any improvement in the experimental group's memory can be attributed to exercise, and not to some other factor, such as the passage of one month's time or familiarity with the memory test. The control group should engage in some nonexercise activity for the same amount of time each day that the experimental group exercises. The participants should be randomly selected from the population at large, and then randomly assigned to the experimental and control groups.

Key Terms

Writing Definitions

1. **Empiricism** is the twofold view that (a) knowledge comes from the senses (rather than being inborn), and (b) observation and experimentation are the basis of science. (p. 3)

2. Introduced by Edward Titchener, **structuralism** is the early school of psychology that used self-reflection (introspection) to examine the basic structure of the mind. (p. 3)

3. Introduced by William James, **functionalism** is the early school of psychology that emphasized the adaptive significance of behavior and mental processes. (p. 4)

4. **Psychology** is the science of behavior and mental processes. (p. 6)

5. The **nature-nurture issue** is the controversy over the relative contributions that genes (nature) and experience (nurture) make to the development of psychological traits and behaviors. (p. 7)

6. **Basic research** is pure science that aims to increase psychology's scientific knowledge base rather than to solve practical problems. (p. 9)

7. **Applied research** is scientific study that aims to solve practical problems. (p. 9)

8. **Clinical psychology** is the branch of psychology concerned with the study, assessment, and treatment of people with psychological disorders. (p. 10)

9. **Psychiatry** is the branch of medicine concerned with the physical diagnosis and treatment of psychological disorders. (p. 10)

10. **Hindsight bias** refers to the tendency to believe, after learning an outcome—including a psycho-

logical research finding—that one would have foreseen it. (p. 11)

11. **Critical thinking** is careful reasoning that examines assumptions, discerns hidden values, evaluates evidence, and assesses conclusions. (p. 14)

12. A **theory** is an explanation using an integrated set of principles that organizes and predicts observations. (p. 15)

13. A **hypothesis** is a testable prediction, often implied by a theory; testing the hypothesis helps scientists to test the theory. (p. 15)

   Example: In order to test his theory of why people conform, Solomon Asch formulated the testable **hypothesis** that an individual would be more likely to go along with the majority opinion of a large group than with that of a smaller group.

14. **Operational definitions** are precise statements of the procedures (operations) used to define independent and dependent variables. (p. 15)

15. **Replication** is the process of repeating the essence of a research study, often with different participants and in different situations, to see whether the basic finding generalizes to other people and circumstances. (p. 15)

16. The **case study** is a descriptive research strategy in which one person is studied in great depth, often with the intention of revealing universal principles. (p. 16)

17. The **survey** is a descriptive research strategy in which a representative, random sample of people is questioned about attitudes or behaviors. (p. 17)

18. A **population** consists of all the members of a group being studied. (p. 18)

19. A **random sample** is one that is representative because every member of the population has an equal chance of being included. (p. 18)

20. **Naturalistic observation** involves observing and recording behavior in a naturally occurring situation without trying to manipulate or control the situation. (p. 18)

21. The **correlation coefficient** is a statistical measure that indicates the extent to which two factors vary together, and thus how well one factor can be predicted from the other. Correlations can be positive or negative. (p. 19)

   Example: If there is a **positive correlation** between air temperature and ice cream sales, the warmer (higher) it is, the more ice cream is sold. If there is a **negative correlation** between air temperature and sales of cocoa, the cooler (lower) it is, the more cocoa is sold.

22. Illusory correlation is the false perception of a relationship between two events when none exists. (p. 21)

23. An **experiment** is a research strategy in which a researcher directly manipulates one or more factors (independent variables) in order to observe their effect on some behavior or mental process (the dependent variable); experiments therefore make it possible to establish cause-effect relationships. (p. 24)

24. A **placebo** is an inert substance or condition that is administered as a test of whether an experimental participant, who mistakenly thinks a treatment is in effect, behaves the same as he or she would if the treatment were actually present. (p. 25)

25. A **double-blind procedure** is a control procedure in which neither the experimenter nor the research participants are aware of which condition is in effect. It is used to prevent experimenters' and participants' expectations from influencing the results of an experiment. (p. 25)

26. The **placebo effect** is any effect on behavior caused by a placebo. (p. 25)

27. The **experimental condition** of an experiment is one in which participants are exposed to the independent variable being studied. (p. 25)

Example: In the study of the effects of a new drug on reaction time, participants in the **experimental condition** would actually receive the drug being tested.

28. The **control condition** of an experiment is one in which the treatment of interest, or independent variable, is withheld so that comparison to the experimental condition can be made. (p. 25)

Example: The **control condition** for an experiment testing the effects of a new drug on reaction time would be a group of participants given a placebo (inactive drug or sugar pill) instead of the drug being tested.

29. Random assignment is the procedure of assigning participants to the experimental and control conditions by chance in order to minimize preexisting differences between the groups. (p. 25)

30. The **independent variable** of an experiment is the factor being manipulated and tested by the investigator. (p. 25)

Example: In the study of the effects of a new drug on reaction time, the drug is the **independent variable**.

31. The **dependent variable** of an experiment is the factor being measured by the investigator. (p. 25)

Example: In the study of the effects of a new drug on reaction time, the participants' reaction time is the **dependent variable**.

32. Culture is the enduring behaviors, ideas, attitudes, and traditions shared by a large group of people and transmitted from one generation to the next. (p. 28)

33. SQ3R is a method of active studying that incorporates five steps: Survey, Question, Read, Rehearse, Review. (p. 31)

Cross-Check

ACROSS	DOWN
1. review	2. Watson
8. Pavlov	3. operational
9. cognitive	4. evolutionary
10. rehearse	5. correlational
12. nature	6. behavior genetics
13. placebo	7. false consensus
15. control	9. critical thinking
16. Freud	11. hindsight bias
20. hypothesis	13. psychiatrists
21. independent	14. culture
22. basic	17. theory
23. descriptive	18. applied

FOCUS ON VOCABULARY AND LANGUAGE

Page 1: . . . to remedy their own woes, millions turn to "psychology." In order to alleviate or fix (*remedy*) their misery, anxiety, grief, pain, and suffering (*woes*), people seek help from "psychology." (Psychology is in quotes because Myers wants to point out that not everything you think of as "psychology" is part of scientific psychology.)

Page 1: Have you ever played *peekaboo* with a 6-month-old infant . . . ? Peekaboo is a game played in most cultures where a person hides or pretends to hide from a child and then reappears saying "PEEK-ABOO!" The important question for psychologists is, why do infants all over the world react similarly to this game; what are they actually feeling, perceiving, and thinking?

Page 1: Such questions provide *grist for psychology's mill* . . . . The expression "*provide grist for the mill*" derives from the practice in the past where farmers brought their grain (*grist*) to the *mill* (a building with machinery for grinding grain into flour). Today the expression means that a greater volume of work (*grist*) does not present a problem; in fact, it is welcomed. The amount of grain (*grist*) is analogous to the variety of questions asked, and the research conducted to answer them is like the *mill* producing flour from the grist. Thus, psychology is a science that thrives on attempting to answer a variety of questions about how we think, feel, and act through scientific methodology (research).

What Is Psychology?

Page 2: . . . down-to-earth . . . This means to be straightforward and practical. In Britain, scientists such as Francis Bacon (1561–1626) were concerned with experimentation, experience, and common-sense judgment (they took a *down-to-earth* approach).

Page 4: . . . wise-cracking . . . William James was well-known for joking and making witty remarks (*wise-cracking*) during his lectures on psychology. He also showed great courage (*displayed spunk*) by admitting Mary Calkins into his graduate seminar despite the objections of Harvard's president.

Page 5: This list of pioneering psychologists . . . "*Magellans of the mind*" . . . . Ferdinand Magellan (1489–1521) was a famous Portuguese navigator who made many discoveries and explored areas of the world previously unknown to his fellow Europeans. Because early psychologists made exciting

discoveries and explored unknown frontiers, they are "*Magellans of the mind.*"

Page 6: Let's *unpack* this definition. *Unpack* here means to take apart or disassemble. So psychology, defined as the science of behavior and mental processes, is broken down into overt behavior (i.e., observable events) and covert processes (i.e., events hidden within, such as thoughts, feelings, perceptions, beliefs, and so on) and is studied using the scientific or empirical method.

Page 6: . . . psychology attempts to *sift* opinions and evaluate ideas . . . . Literally, *sift* means to separate the finer particles from the coarser ones by passing material through a sieve. Myers uses the word *sift* to explain how psychology examines or evaluates ideas, opinions, facts, and concepts and separates those that are useful and worthwhile from those that are not. (Be sure you understand the word *sift*, because Myers uses it quite often.)

Page 6: . . . psychological science welcomes *hunches* and plausible-sounding theories. In popular usage a *hunch* is an intuitive feeling about a situation or event. Psychology can use subjective ideas to help formulate hypotheses or predictions which can then be tested empirically or scientifically.

Page 7: . . . mushrooming . . . Membership in psychological societies is growing at a rapid rate (*mushrooming*), and psychology is becoming more and more international (*globalizing*).

Page 7: . . . psychology has *wrestled* with some issues . . . . Psychology has struggled (*wrestled*) with a number of issues, particularly those of stability-change, rationality-irrationality, and nature-nurture, and these issues may be perceived differently by the various perspectives in the discipline (i.e., several issues *cut across* modern psychology). Myers points out that these different views may be complementary or compatible rather than antagonistic or opposite.

Page 7: Locke and Descartes *rekindled* the debate [nature-nurture] in the 1600s. *Rekindled* means to restart as in to restart a fire (*rekindle*). John Locke in the 1600s repeated what Aristotle had said 2000 years before—that humans are born without any knowledge (i.e., that we are blank slates, or blank paper, at birth) and that all knowledge comes from experience (*nurture*). Plato and, later, René Descartes argued that we are born with some innate knowledge (*nature*).

Page 7: Yet over and over again we will see that in contemporary science the nature-nurture *tension dis-*

solves. The main point is that both sides of the debate have something to offer: Each contributes to the search for the truth. Thus, in modern science the strained relations (*tension*) over this issue diminish (*dissolve*).

Page 8: "Red in the face" and *"hot under the collar"* refer to the physical changes that often accompany emotional arousal (e.g., anger). A person's face may become red due to blood rushing to it (blushing), and he or she may feel hot and perspire (*hot under the collar*). Different perspectives (neuroscience, evolutionary, behavior genetics, psychodynamic, behavioral, cognitive, and social-cultural) view the same event (emotional change) from different points of view (see Table 2, p. 8). Myers points out that these different perspectives are not necessarily in opposition to each other but, rather, are complementary; that is, each helps to complete the puzzle of why the event occurs by supplying answers from different points of view (*perspectives*).

Page 9: But there is a *payoff:* Psychology is a *meeting ground* for different disciplines, and is thus a *perfect home* for those with *wide-ranging* interests. Myers points out that there is much diversity in the discipline of psychology (i.e., it lacks unity), but this is beneficial (a *payoff*) because it is a nice place (area) to work in (a *perfect home*) for those who have broad or diverse (*wide-ranging*) interests. Thus, psychology is the ideal meeting place or *meeting ground* for different disciplines.

Why Do Psychology?

Page 11: Although in some ways we *outsmart* the smartest computers, our *intuition* often goes *awry.* The main point is that humans are in many ways superior to computers (*we outsmart them*), but our beliefs, feelings, and perceptions (*intuition*) can often lead us astray (*awry*) or away from the truth. To be human means we can, and do, make mistakes (*to err is human*).

Page 11: Some say psychology merely *documents* what people already know and *dresses it in jargon.* Some people criticize psychology, saying that it simply reports (*documents*) common sense, or what's obvious to everyone. Instead of stating something plainly, the critics suggest, psychology translates the information into the specialized and obscure vocabulary of the discipline (*dresses it up in jargon*). Myers makes it very clear with some good examples that this criticism is not justified and points out that our intuitions about reality can often be very mistaken.

Page 11: How easy it is to seem *astute* when *drawing the bull's eye after the arrow has struck.* In the sport of

archery the task is to shoot the arrow at the red circle in the center of the target (the *bull's eye*). If we first shoot an arrow, then draw the target so that the arrow is in the center (in the *bull's eye*), we can appear to be very accurate. Myers uses this analogy to illustrate how the hindsight bias can lead us to believe that we are shrewd (*astute*) and would have been able to predict outcomes that we have learned after-the-fact.

Page 11: "Out of sight, out of mind" and *"Absence makes the heart grow fonder."* These two sayings, or expressions, about romantic love have opposite meanings. The first one suggests that when couples are apart (*out of sight*) they are less likely to think about each other (*out of mind*) than when they are together. The second saying makes the point that being separated (*absence*) increases the feelings of love the couple shares (*makes the heart grow fonder*). People who are told that the results of a study support the first expression (*out of sight, out of mind*) see this as mere common sense. People told that the results support the second expression (*absence makes the heart grow fonder*) also say this is obviously true. There is clearly a problem here; relying on common sense can lead to opposite conclusions.

Page 12: . . . our intuition may tell us that *familiarity breeds contempt. . . .* This expression and others are based on many casual observations but are often wrong. For example, is it true that the better you know someone (*familiarity*), the more likely it is that you will dislike the person (have *contempt*)? In fact, research shows that the opposite is probably true. (Your text, again and again, will emphasize the fact that our common sense and intuition do not always provide us with reliable evidence.)

Page 13: . . . drop a course . . . This means to stop going to class and to have your name removed from the class list.

Page 13: Underlying all science is, first, a *hard-headed curiosity . . . Hard-headed* here means to be practical, uncompromising, realistic, or unswayed by sentiment. All science, including psychology, is guided by this realistic desire to know (*curiosity*) about nature and life.

Page 13: . . . leap of faith. This is a belief in something in the absence of demonstrated proof. Some questions—about the existence of God or life after death, for example—cannot be answered by science and cannot be scientifically proved or disproved; if a person believes, then it is on the basis of trust and confidence alone (*leap of faith*).

Page 13: . . . the *proof is in the pudding.* This comes from the expression *"the proof of the pudding is in the eating."* A *pudding* is a sweet dessert. We can test (or prove) the quality of the dessert (*pudding*) by trying it (*eating*). Likewise, many questions, even if they appear to make little sense (*crazy-sounding ideas*—p. 13), can be tested using the scientific method.

Page 13: . . . *auras* . . . An *aura* is a bright glow surrounding a figure or an object. Some believe that humans have auras which only those with extrasensory abilities can see. The magician James Randi proposed a simple test of this claim, but nobody who is alleged to have this magical power (*aura-seer*) has taken the test.

Page 13: More often, science relegates *crazy-sounding ideas* to the *mountain* of forgotten claims. . . . The use of scientific inquiry can get rid of or dispose of (*relegate*) non-sensible concepts (*crazy-sounding ideas*) to the large stack or pile (*mountain*) of ridiculous claims no longer remembered.

Page 13: In the *arena* of competing ideas . . . An *arena* is an area where games, sports, and competitions take place. Myers is suggesting that in an area (*arena*) where there is a contest between ideas (*competing ideas*), skeptical testing can help discover the truth.

Page 14: . . . *then so much the worse for our ideas.* This means that we have to give up, or get rid of, our ideas if they are shown to be wrong (*so much the worse for them*). We have to be humble (i.e., have humility).

Page 14: *"The rat is always right."* This early *motto* (a phrase used as a maxim or guiding principle) comes from the fact that for most of the first half of the twentieth century psychology used animals in its research (especially in the study of learning). The *rat* became a symbol of this research, and its behavior or performance in experiments demonstrated the truth. If the truth, as shown by the rat, is contrary to the prediction or hypothesis, then one has to be humble about it and try another way.

Page 14: We all view nature through the *spectacles* of our *preconceived ideas.* This means that what we already believe (*our preconceived ideas*) influences, and to some extent determines, what we look for and actually see or discover in nature. It's as though the type of eyeglasses (*spectacles*) we wear limits what we can see.

Page 14: . . . *gut feelings* . . . This refers to basic intuitive reactions or responses. Critical thinking requires determining whether a conclusion is based simply on a subjective opinion (*gut feeling*) or anecdote (a story someone tells) or on reliable scientific evidence.

Page 14: . . . *debunked* . . . This means to remove glamor or credibility from established ideas, persons, and traditions. Myers points out that scientific evidence and critical inquiry have indeed discredited (*debunked*) many popular presumptions.

Page 14: . . . one *cannot* simply *"play the tape"* and relive long-buried or *repressed* memories. . . . This is an example of a discredited (*debunked*) idea that hidden (*repressed*) memories can be accurately and reliably retrieved (*brought back*) intact and complete in the same way that *playing a tape* on a VCR allows us to watch exactly the same show over and over again.

How Do Psychologists Ask and Answer Questions?

Page 16: Sigmund Freud constructed his theory of personality from *a handful of case studies.* A *handful* means a very small number. Freud published only about 12 (*a handful of*) in-depth investigations of individuals (*case studies*).

Page 17: Numbers can be numbing . . . *Anecdotes are often more startling.* . . . We are often overwhelmed and our senses deadened (*numbed*) by the sometimes inappropriate use of statistics and numbers. We are also alarmed or frightened (*startled*) by the strange stories people tell (*anecdotes*).

Page 18: . . . 1500 randomly sampled people, drawn from all areas of a country, provide a remarkably accurate *snapshot* of the opinions of a nation. A *snapshot* is a picture taken with a camera, and it captures what people are doing at a given moment in time. A good survey (*1500 randomly selected representative people*) gives an accurate picture (*snapshot*) of the opinions of the whole population of interest (the *target group*).

Page 18: . . . *having affairs* . . . Myers points out that the results of a large, nonrandom, nonrepresentative sample of married women which suggested that a large percentage (70 percent) were having sexual relations with someone other than their spouse (*having affairs or love affairs*) were not valid or reliable. A better study, using a smaller but a more representative and random sample, showed that the figure was actually closer to 10 percent. (Note: The word *affair* has other meanings. For example, in the phrase *"applying science to human affairs,"* the word *affairs* refers to human concerns or business.)

Page 20: . . . *laypeople* . . . refers to people who do not belong to a particular profession. Both professionals and nonprofessionals (*laypeople*) mistakenly assume that correlation proves causation. It does not. Correlation means that one variable goes along with (predicts) another variable. For growing children, shoe size goes along with cognitive ability, but obviously one variable does not *cause* the other.

Page 21: If someone *flipped a coin* six times, which of the following sequences of heads (H) and tails (T) would be most likely: HHHTTT or HTTHTH or HHHHHH? *Flipping a coin* means throwing or tossing the coin into the air and observing which side is facing up when it lands. (The side of the coin that usually has the imprint of the face of a famous person on it—e.g., the president or the queen—is called *heads* (H) and the other side is called *tails* (T). By the way, all of the above sequences are equally likely, but most people pick HTTHTH. Likewise, any series of five playing cards (e.g., a bridge or poker hand in a game of cards) is just as likely as any other hand.

Page 23: Thinking critically about: *Hot and cold streaks in Basketball and the Stock Market*. Players who have *"hot hands"* can't seem to miss. Those who have *"cold"* ones can't find the center of the hoop. In this context, *hot* and *cold* do not refer to temperature. Here, being *hot* means doing well, and doing well consistently is *having a hot streak*. Having a run of poor luck is a *cold streak*. The crucial point, however, is that our intuition about sequences of events (*streaks*) often deceives us. Random sequences often are not what we think they should be, so when we think we're doing well (*hot*), we're not.

Page 25: Let's *Recap*. Recap is an abbreviation of *recapitulate*, which means to repeat or go over briefly, to summarize. Myers summarizes (*recaps*) the important points in each section of the chapter.

Frequently Asked Questions About Psychology

Page 27: . . . *plunge in*. In this context, *plunge in* means to move ahead quickly with the discussion. (Simi-

larly, when you dive into a swimming pool [*plunge in*], you do so quickly.) Before going on with the discussion of psychology (*plunging in*), Myers addresses some important issues and questions.

Page 29: To understand how a combustion engine works, you would do better to study *the engine of a lawn mower than that of a Mercedes*. A *Mercedes* is a very complex luxury car, and a *lawn mower* (a machine for cutting grass in the garden) has a very simple engine. To understand the principles underlying both machines, it is easier to study the simpler one. Likewise, when trying to understand the nervous system, it is better to study a simple one (e.g., sea slugs) than a complex one (humans).

Page 30: . . . most universities today screen research proposals through an *ethics committee*. . . . *Ethics committees* (groups of people concerned with moral behavior and acceptable standards of conduct) subject research proposals to rigorous tests (*screen them*) to ensure that they are fair and reasonable and that they do not harm the participants' well-being.

Page 30: *Values* can even *color* "the facts." Our values (what we believe is right and true) can influence (*color*) our observations, interpretations, and conclusions ("the facts").

Tips for Studying Psychology

Page 32: One of psychology's oldest findings is that *spaced practice* promotes better retention than *massed practice*. *Spaced practice* refers to studying over a longer period of time, say 2 hours a day over 5 days rather than 10 hours on one day (*massed practice* or cramming). Distributing your study time is much better for learning and retention than one long study period (a *blitz*).

chapter 2

Neuroscience and Behavior

Chapter Overview

Chapter 2 is concerned with the functions of the brain and its component neural systems, which provide the basis for all human behavior. Under the direction of the brain, the nervous and endocrine systems coordinate a variety of voluntary and involuntary behaviors and serve as the body's mechanisms for communication with the external environment.

The brain consists of the brainstem, the thalamus, the cerebellum, the limbic system, and the cerebral cortex. Knowledge of the workings of the brain has increased with advances in neuroscientific methods. Studies of split-brain patients have also given researchers a great deal of information about the specialized functions of the brain's right and left hemispheres.

Many students find the technical material in this chapter difficult to master. Not only are there many terms for you to remember, but you must also know the organization and function of the various divisions of the nervous system. Learning this material will require a great deal of rehearsal. Working the chapter review several times, drawing and labeling brain diagrams, and mentally reciting terms are all useful techniques for rehearsing this type of material.

NOTE: Answer guidelines for all Chapter 2 questions begin on page 51.

Introduction Preview

First, skim the introduction. Then read the following objective and, as you read, search for the information that will enable you to meet each objective. Answer guidelines are provided on page 51.

1. Explain why psychologists are concerned with human biology.

Stepping Through the Introduction

After you have read this material, complete the sentences and answer the questions. As you proceed, evaluate your performance by consulting the answers on page 51. Do not continue with the next section until you understand each answer. If you need to, review or reread the text material before continuing.

1. In the most basic sense, every idea, mood, memory, and behavior that an individual has ever experienced is a _____ phenomenon.

2. The theory that linked our mental abilities to bumps on the skull was _____ .

3. Researchers who study the links between biology and behavior are called _____

   _____ .

Neural Communication (pp. 38–43)

> David Myers at times uses idioms that are unfamiliar to some readers. If you do not know the meaning of any of the following words, phrases, or expressions in the context in which they appear in the text, refer to pages 62–63 for an explanation: *to shoot a basketball; an ill-fated theory; a wrongheaded theory; happy fact of nature; building blocks; a sluggish 2 miles per hour to . . . a breakneck 200 or more miles; somewhat like pushing a neuron's accelerator . . . more like pushing its brake; How do we distinguish a gentle touch from a big hug; "protoplasmic kisses"; runner's high; They trigger unpleasant, lingering aftereffects; Agonists excite . . . Antagonists inhibit; some chemicals don't have the right shape to slither through this barrier.*

Section Preview

Answer guidelines are provided on page 51.

1. Describe the structure of a neuron and the process by which an action potential is triggered.

2. Describe how nerve cells communicate, and discuss the importance of neurotransmitters for human behavior.

3. Discuss the significance of endorphins, and explain how drugs influence neurotransmitters.

Stepping Through the Section

Answers begin on page 51.

1. Our body's neural system is built from billions of nerve cells, or _____ .

2. The extensions of a neuron that receive messages from other neurons are the _____ .

3. The extensions of a neuron that transmit information to other neurons are the

   _____ ; some of these extensions are insulated by a layer of fatty cells called the

   _____ _____ , which helps speed the neuron's impulses.

4. Identify the major parts of the neuron diagrammed below:

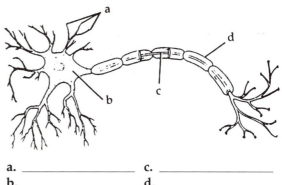

   a. _____   c. _____
   b. _____   d. _____

5. The neural impulse, or _____

   _____ , is a brief electrical charge that travels down a(n) _____ .

6. In order to trigger a neural impulse,

   _____ signals minus

   _____ signals must exceed a certain intensity, called the _____ .

Increasing a stimulus above this level _____ (will/will not) increase the neural impulse's intensity. This phenomenon is called an _____ -

_____ -_____ response.

Outline the sequence of reactions that occur when a neural impulse is generated and transmitted from one neuron to another.

7. The strength of a stimulus _____ (does/does not) affect the speed of a neural impulse.

8. The junction between two neurons is called a _____ , and the gap is called the

_____ _____ .

9. The chemical messengers that convey information across the gaps between neurons are called _____ . These chemicals unlock tiny channels on receptor sites, allowing electrically charged _____ to enter the neuron.

10. Neurotransmitters influence neurons either by _____ or _____ their readiness to fire. Excess neurotransmitters are reabsorbed by the sending neuron in a process called _____ .

11. Among the neurotransmitters that researchers have pinpointed are _____ , which

enables muscle action, learning, and memory; _____ , which influences movement, learning, attention, and emotion; _____ , which affects mood, hunger, sleep, and arousal; _____ , which helps control alertness and arousal; _____ , which is an inhibitory neurotransmitter whose undersupply is linked to seizures, tremors, and insomnia; and _____ , which is involved in memory.

12. A neurotransmitter that is important in muscle contraction is _____ . The poison _____ produces paralysis by blocking the activity of this neurotransmitter.

13. Naturally occurring opiatelike neurotransmitters that are present in the brain are called _____ . When the brain is flooded with drugs such as _____ or _____ , it may stop producing these neurotransmitters.

14. Drugs that produce their effects by mimicking neurotransmitters are called _____ . Drugs that block the effects of neurotransmitters by occupying their _____ _____ are called

_____ .

15. The molecular shape of some drugs prevents them from passing through the

_____ -_____ _____ by which the brain fences out unwanted chemicals.

16. The tremors of _____ disease are due to the death of neurons that produce the neurotransmitter _____ . People with this condition can be helped to regain control over their muscles by taking

_____ .

The Nervous System (pp. 43–46)

> If you do not know the meaning of any of the following words, phrases, or expressions in the context in which they appear in the text, refer to page 63 for an explanation: *Like an automatic pilot, it may sometimes be consciously overridden; yield an ever-changing wiring diagram that dwarfs a powerful computer; work groups; information highway; The knee-jerk response . . . a headless warm body could do it.*

Section Preview

Answer guidelines are provided on page 52.

1. Identify the major divisions of the nervous system and their primary functions, and describe the neurons that carry information throughout the system.

2. Describe the operation of reflexes in the spinal cord.

Stepping Through the Section

Answers are provided on page 52.

1. Taken altogether, the neurons of the body form the _____ _____ .

2. The brain and spinal cord comprise the _____ nervous system. The neurons that link the brain and spinal cord to the body's sense receptors, muscles, and glands form the _____ nervous system.

3. Sensory and motor axons are bundled into electrical cables called _____ .

4. Information arriving in the central nervous system from the body travels in _____ neurons. The neurons that enable internal communication within the central nervous system are called _____ .

5. The central nervous system sends instructions to the body's tissues by means of _____ neurons. The cells that support nerve cells by guiding neural connections, providing nutrients and insulating myelin, and mopping up debris are called

_____ _____ .

6. The division of the peripheral nervous system that transmits sensory input to the central nervous system and directs the movements of the skeletal muscles is the _____ nervous system.

7. Involuntary, self-regulating responses—those of the glands and muscles of internal organs—are controlled by the _____ nervous system.

8. The body is made ready for defensive action by the _____ division of the autonomic nervous system.

9. The _____ division of the autonomic nervous system produces calming effects.

Describe and explain the sequence of physical reactions that occur in the body as an emergency is confronted and then passes.

10. To perform complex computations, neurons in the brain cluster into work groups called

    _____ _____ .

11. Automatic responses to stimuli, called

    _____ , illustrate the work of the

    _____ _____ . Simple

    pathways such as these are involved in the

    _____-_____

    response and in the _____ reflex.

Beginning with the sensory receptors in the skin, trace the course of a spinal reflex as a person reflexively jerks his or her hand away from an unexpectedly hot burner on a stove.

The Brain (pp. 46–58)

> If you do not know the meaning of any of the following words, phrases, or expressions in the context in which they appear in the text, refer to pages 63–64 for an explanation: *we live in our heads; This peculiar cross-wiring is but one of many surprises the brain has to offer; . . . what London is to England's trains; the right side of the body is wired to . . .; snoop on; Other new windows into the brain . . . Supermanlike; snapshots of the brain's activity provide . . . divides its labor; a doughnut-shaped neural system; magnificent mistake; wrinkled organ, shaped somewhat like the meat of an oversized walnut; Being human takes a lot of nerve; eyes in the back of our head; most widespread falsehoods; frontal lobes ruptured; Gage's moral compass; What you experience as . . . the visible tip of the information-processing iceberg.*

Section Preview

Answer guidelines begin on page 52.

1. Describe the functions of structures within the brainstem, as well as those of the thalamus and the cerebellum.

2. (Close-Up) Identify and explain the methods used in studying the brain.

3. Describe the functions of the structures in the limbic system.

4. Describe the structure and functions of the cerebral cortex.

5. Discuss how damage to one of several different cortical areas can impair language functioning, and outline the process by which the brain directs reading aloud.

Stepping Through the Section

Answers begin on page 53.

1. According to neuroscientists, the mind is

   _____ .

2. The oldest and innermost region of the brain is

   the _____ .

3. At the base of the brainstem, where the spinal cord enters the skull, lies the _____ , which controls _____ and _____ .

4. Nerves from each side of the brain cross over to connect with the body's opposite side in the _____ .

5. The _____ _____ is contained inside the brainstem and helps control _____ . Electrically stimulating this area will produce an _____ animal. Lesioning this area will cause an animal to lapse into a _____ .

6. At the top of the brainstem sits the _____ , which serves as the brain's sensory switchboard.

7. At the rear of the brainstem lies the _____ . It influences one type of _____ _____ and memory, but its major function is coordination of _____ _____ and balance.

8. The lower brain functions occur without _____ effort, indicating that our brains process most information _____ (inside/outside) of our awareness.

9. (Close-Up) Researchers sometimes study brain function by producing _____ or by selectively destroying brain cells. The oldest technique for studying the brain involves _____ _____ of patients with brain injuries or diseases.

10. (Close-Up) The _____ is a recording of the electrical activity of the whole brain.

11. (Close-Up) The technique depicting the level of activity of brain areas by measuring the brain's consumption of glucose is called the _____ _____ .

(Close-Up) Briefly explain the purpose of the PET scan.

12. (Close-Up) A technique that produces clearer images of the brain by using magnetic fields and radio waves is known as _____ . By taking pictures less than a second apart, the _____ _____ detects blood rushing to the part of the cortex thought to control the bodily activity being studied.

13. Between the brainstem and cerebral hemispheres is the _____ system. One component of this system that processes memory is the _____ .

14. Aggression or fear will result from stimulation of different regions of the _____ .

15. Below the thalamus is the _____ , which regulates bodily maintenance behaviors such as _____ , _____ , and _____ _____ . The hypothalamus also regulates behavior chemically through its influence on the _____ gland. Olds and Milner discovered that this region also contains _____ centers, which animals will work hard to have stimulated.

16. Some researchers believe that alcoholism, drug abuse, binge eating, and other _____ disorders may stem from a genetic _____ _____ _____ in the natural brain systems for pleasure.

17. The most complex functions of human behavior are linked to the most developed part of the brain, the _____ _____ .

18. The human cortex has a _____ (smooth/wrinkled) surface. This _____ (increases/decreases) the overall surface area of our brains.

19. List the four lobes of the brain.

    a. _____   c. _____

    b. _____   d. _____

20. Electrical stimulation of one side of the _____ cortex, an arch-shaped region at the back of the _____ lobe, will produce movement on the opposite side of the body. Research findings from studies in which recording electrodes are implanted in this area of animals' brains raise hopes that people who are _____ may one day be able to control machines directly with their _____ .

21. At the front of the parietal lobes lies the _____ cortex, which, when stimulated, elicits a sensation of _____ .

22. The more sensitive a body region, the greater the area of _____ _____ devoted to it.

23. Visual information is received in the _____ lobes, whereas auditory information is received in the _____ lobes.

24. Areas of the brain that don't receive sensory information or direct movement but, rather, integrate and interpret information received by other regions are known as _____ . Approximately _____ of the human cortex is of this type. Such areas in the _____ lobe are involved in making judgments and carrying out plans and in some aspects of personality. An area on the underside of the _____ lobe enables us to recognize faces.

25. Brain injuries may produce an impairment in language use called _____ . Studies of people with such impairments have shown that _____ _____ is involved in producing speech, _____ _____ is involved in understanding speech, and the _____ _____ is involved in recoding printed words into auditory form.

26. Although the mind's subsystems are localized in particular brain regions, the brain acts as a _____ _____ .

Brain Reorganization (pp. 58–62)

> If you do not know the meaning of any of the following words, phrases, or expressions in the context in which they appear in the text, refer to pages 64–65 for an explanation: *hard-wired; one patient even managed to quip that he had a "splitting headache"; When the "two minds" are at odds; look alike to the naked eye . . . harmony of the whole.*

Section Preview

Answer guidelines are provided on page 54.

1. Discuss brain plasticity and what it reveals about brain reorganization.

2. Describe research on divided and undivided brains, and discuss what it reveals regarding normal brain functioning.

Stepping Through the Section

Answers are provided on page 54.

1. The quality of the brain that makes it possible for undamaged brain areas to take over the functions of damaged regions is known as

   _____ .

2. Although most severed neurons _____ (will/will not) regenerate, neural tissue can _____ in response to damage. Humans _____ (can/cannot) generate new brain cells. The brains of young children _____ (are/are no) more plastic than those of adults.

3. Because damage to it will impair language and understanding, the _____ hemisphere came to be known as the _____ hemisphere.

4. In treating several patients with severe epilepsy, Vogel and Bogen separated the two hemispheres of the brain by cutting the _____ _____ . When this structure is severed, the result is referred to as a

   _____ _____ .

5. In a split-brain patient, only the _____ hemisphere will be aware of an unseen object held in the left hand. In this case, the person would not be able to _____ the object. When different words are shown in the left and right visual fields, if the patient fixates on a point on the center line between the fields, the patient will be able to say only the word shown on the

   _____ .

Explain why a split-brain patient would be able to read aloud the word *pencil* flashed to his or her right visual field, but would be unable to identify a pencil by touch using only the left hand.

6. Researchers studying undivided brains _____ (have/have not) found evidence of hemispheric specialization. For example, pictures are recognized more rapidly when they are flashed to the _____ (right/left) hemisphere, whereas words are recognized faster and more accurately when flashed to the _____ (right/left) hemisphere. Babies _____ (demonstrate/do not demonstrate) cerebral specialization, as revealed by their tendency to _____

   _____ .

The Endocrine System (pp. 63–64)

> If you do not know the meaning of any of the following words, phrases, or expressions in the context in which they appear in the text, refer to page 65 for an explanation: *kindred systems; Conducting and coordinating this whole electrochemical orchestra is that maestro we call the brain; dwarfs.*

Section Preview

Answer guidelines are provided on page 54.

1. Discuss the functioning of the endocrine system.

2. Identify two important endocrine glands, and specify their functions.

Stepping Through the Section

Answers are provided on page 54.

1. The body's chemical communication network is called the _____ _____ . This system transmits information through chemical messengers called _____ at a much _____ (faster/slower) rate than the nervous system.

2. In a moment of danger, the _____ glands release _____ and _____ .

3. The most influential gland is the _____ , which, under the control of the brain area called the _____ , helps regulate _____ and the release of hormones by other endocrine glands.

Write a paragraph describing the feedback system that links the nervous and endocrine systems.

Progress Test 1

Multiple-Choice Questions

Circle your answers to the following questions and check them with the answers beginning on page 54. If your answer is incorrect, read the explanation for why it is incorrect and then consult the appropriate pages of the text (in parentheses following the correct answer).

1. The axons of certain neurons are covered by a layer of fatty tissue that helps speed neural transmission. This tissue is:
    a. the glial cells.
    b. the myelin sheath.
    c. acetylcholine.
    d. an endorphin.

2. Heartbeat, digestion, and other self-regulating bodily functions are governed by the:
    a. voluntary nervous system.
    b. autonomic nervous system.
    c. sympathetic division of the autonomic nervous system.
    d. somatic nervous system.
    e. central nervous system.

3. A strong stimulus can increase the:
    a. speed of the impulse the neuron fires.
    b. intensity of the impulse the neuron fires.
    c. number of times the neuron fires.
    d. threshold that must be reached before the neuron fires.

4. The pain of heroin withdrawal may be attributable to the fact that:
    a. under the influence of heroin the brain ceases production of endorphins.
    b. under the influence of heroin the brain ceases production of all neurotransmitters.
    c. during heroin withdrawal the brain's production of all neurotransmitters is greatly increased.
    d. heroin destroys endorphin receptors in the brain.

5. The brain research technique that involves monitoring the brain's usage of glucose is called (in abbreviated form) the:
    a. PET scan.   c. EEG.
    b. fMRI.   d. MRI.

6. Agonist is to antagonist as:
    a. excitation is to inhibition.
    b. inhibition is to excitation.
    c. lock is to key.
    d. key is to lock.

7. Though there is no single "control center" for emotions, their regulation is primarily attributed to the brain region known as the:
    a. limbic system.   c. brainstem.
    b. reticular formation.   d. cerebral cortex.

8. Which is the correct sequence in the transmission of a simple reflex?
    a. sensory neuron → interneuron → sensory neuron
    b. interneuron → motor neuron → sensory neuron
    c. sensory neuron → interneuron → motor neuron
    d. interneuron → sensory neuron → motor neuron

9. Damage to _____ will usually cause a person to lose the ability to comprehend language.
   a. the angular gyrus
   b. Broca's area
   c. Wernicke's area
   d. frontal lobe association areas

10. Which of the following is typically controlled by the right hemisphere?
    a. language
    b. learned voluntary movements
    c. arithmetic reasoning
    d. perceptual tasks

11. Dr. Hernandez is studying neurotransmitter abnormalities in depressed patients. She would most likely describe herself as a:
    a. psychiatrist.
    b. clinical psychologist.
    c. psychoanalyst.
    d. biological psychologist.

12. The increasing complexity of animals' behavior is accompanied by a(n):
    a. increase in the size of the brainstem.
    b. decrease in the ratio of brain to body weight.
    c. increase in the size of the frontal lobes.
    d. increase in the amount of association area.

13. Voluntary movements, such as writing with a pencil, are directed by the:
    a. sympathetic nervous system.
    b. somatic nervous system.
    c. parasympathetic nervous system.
    d. autonomic nervous system.

14. A neuron will generate action potentials more often when it:
    a. remains below its threshold.
    b. receives an excitatory input.
    c. receives more excitatory than inhibitory inputs.
    d. is stimulated by a neurotransmitter.
    e. is stimulated by a hormone.

15. Which is the correct sequence in the transmission of a neural impulse?
    a. axon → dendrite → cell body → synapse
    b. dendrite → axon → cell body → synapse
    c. synapse → axon → dendrite → cell body
    d. axon → synapse → cell body → dendrite
    e. dendrite → cell body → axon → synapse

16. Chemical messengers produced by endocrine glands are called:
    a. agonists.
    b. neurotransmitters.
    c. hormones.
    d. enzymes.

17. Following a head injury, a person has ongoing difficulties staying awake. Most likely, the damage occurred to the:
    a. thalamus.
    b. corpus callosum.
    c. reticular formation.
    d. cerebellum.

18. Based on research, which of the following seems true about the specialized functions of the right and left hemispheres?
    a. They are more clear-cut in men than in women.
    b. They are more clear-cut in women than in men.
    c. Most complex tasks emerge from the activity of one or the other hemisphere.
    d. Most complex activities emerge from the integrated activity of both hemispheres.

19. Cortical areas that are not primarily concerned with sensory, motor, or language functions are:
    a. called projection areas.
    b. called association areas.
    c. located mostly in the parietal lobe.
    d. located mostly in the temporal lobe.

20. In the brain, learning, feeling, and thinking are enabled by cell work groups called:
    a. action potentials.
    b. neural networks.
    c. endocrine systems.
    d. dendrites.
    e. synaptic gaps.

Matching Items

Match each structure with its corresponding function or description.

Structures

_____ 1. hypothalamus
_____ 2. lesion
_____ 3. EEG
_____ 4. PET scan
_____ 5. reticular formation
_____ 6. MRI
_____ 7. thalamus
_____ 8. corpus callosum
_____ 9. cerebellum
_____ 10. amygdala
_____ 11. medulla

Functions or Descriptions

a. amplified recording of brain waves
b. technique that uses radio waves and magnetic fields to image the brain
c. serves as sensory switchboard
d. contains reward centers
e. tissue destruction
f. a technique that traces the brain's consumption of a radioactive form of glucose
g. helps control arousal
h. links the cerebral hemispheres
i. influences rage and fear
j. regulates breathing and heartbeat
k. enables coordinated movement

Progress Test 2

Progress Test 2 should be completed during a final chapter review. Answer the following questions after you thoroughly understand the correct answers for the section reviews and Progress Test 1.

Multiple-Choice Questions

1. The visual cortex is located in the:
   a. occipital lobe.
   c. frontal lobe.
   b. temporal lobe.
   d. parietal lobe.

2. Which of the following is typically controlled by the left hemisphere?
   a. spatial reasoning
   b. word recognition
   c. the left side of the body
   d. perceptual skills

3. When Sandy scalded her toe in a tub of hot water, the pain message was carried to her spinal cord by the _____ nervous system.
   a. somatic
   c. parasympathetic
   b. sympathetic
   d. central

4. Which of the following are/is governed by the simplest neural pathways?
   a. emotions
   b. physiological drives, such as hunger
   c. reflexes
   d. movements, such as walking
   e. balance

5. Melissa has just completed running a marathon. She is so elated that she feels little fatigue or discomfort. Her lack of pain is probably the result of the release of:
   a. ACh.
   d. norepinephrine.
   b. endorphins.
   e. acetylcholine.
   c. dopamine.

6. Parkinson's disease involves:
   a. the death of nerve cells that produce a vital neurotransmitter.
   b. impaired function in the right hemisphere only.
   c. impaired function in the left hemisphere only.
   d. excess production of the neurotransmitters dopamine and acetylcholine.

7. The technique that uses magnetic fields and radio waves to produce computer images of structures within the brain is called:
   a. the EEG.
   c. a PET scan.
   b. a lesion.
   d. MRI.

8. The myelin sheath that is on some neurons:
   a. increases the speed of neural transmission.
   b. slows neural transmission.
   c. regulates the release of neurotransmitters.
   d. does a. and c.
   e. does b. and c.

9. The theory of phrenology, which was proposed by _____ , maintains that _____ .
   a. Pert; the brain has receptors for naturally occurring opiates
   b. Ramón y Cajal; neurons are separated from one another by small gaps
   c. Sherrington; a strong stimulus can trigger more neurons to fire than a weak stimulus can
   d. Gall; bumps on the skull reveal personality traits

10. The neurotransmitter acetylcholine (ACh) is most likely to be found:
    a. at the junction between sensory neurons and muscle fibers.
    b. at the junction between motor neurons and muscle fibers.
    c. at junctions between interneurons.
    d. in all of the above locations.

11. The gland that regulates body growth is the:
    a. adrenal.   d. pituitary.
    b. thyroid.   e. hyperthyroid.
    c. hypothalamus.

12. Epinephrine and norepinephrine are _____ that are released by the _____ gland.
    a. neurotransmitters; pituitary
    b. hormones; pituitary
    c. neurotransmitters; adrenal
    d. hormones; adrenal
    e. hormones; thyroid

13. Jessica experienced difficulty keeping her balance after receiving a blow to the back of her head. It is likely that she injured her:
    a. medulla.   d. cerebellum.
    b. thalamus.   e. cerebrum.
    c. hypothalamus.

14. Moruzzi and Magoun caused a cat to lapse into a coma by severing neural connections between the cortex and the:
    a. reticular formation.   d. cerebellum.
    b. hypothalamus.   e. medulla.
    c. thalamus.

15. Research has found that the amount of representation in the motor cortex reflects the:
    a. size of the body parts.
    b. degree of precise control required by each of the parts.

c. sensitivity of the body region.
d. area of the occipital lobe being stimulated by the environment.

16. The effect of a drug that is an agonist is to:
    a. cause the brain to stop producing certain neurotransmitters.
    b. mimic a particular neurotransmitter.
    c. block a particular neurotransmitter.
    d. disrupt a neuron's all-or-none firing pattern.

17. The nerve fibers that enable communication between the right and left cerebral hemispheres and that have been severed in split-brain patients form a structure called the:
    a. reticular formation.   d. parietal lobes.
    b. association areas.   e. limbic system.
    c. corpus callosum.

18. Beginning at the front of the brain and working backward then down and around, which of the following is the correct order of the cortical regions?
    a. occipital lobe; temporal lobe; parietal lobe; frontal lobe
    b. temporal lobe; frontal lobe; parietal lobe; occipital lobe
    c. frontal lobe; occipital lobe; temporal lobe; parietal lobe
    d. frontal lobe; parietal lobe; occipital lobe; temporal lobe
    e. occipital lobe; parietal lobe; temporal lobe; frontal lobe

19. Following a gunshot wound to his head, Jack became more uninhibited, irritable, and profane. It is likely that his personality change was the result of injury to his:
    a. parietal lobe.   d. frontal lobe.
    b. temporal lobe.   e. endocrine system.
    c. occipital lobe.

20. Three-year-old Marco suffered damage to the speech area of the brain's left hemisphere when he fell from a swing. Research suggests that:
    a. he will never speak again.
    b. his motor abilities will improve so that he can easily use sign language.
    c. his right hemisphere will take over much of the language function.
    d. his earlier experience with speech will enable him to continue speaking.

Matching Items

Match each structure or term with its corresponding function or description.

Structures or Terms

_____ 1. right hemisphere
_____ 2. brainstem
_____ 3. adrenal
_____ 4. aphasia
_____ 5. plasticity
_____ 6. Broca's area
_____ 7. Wernicke's area
_____ 8. limbic system
_____ 9. association areas
_____ 10. left hemisphere
_____ 11. angular gyrus

Functions or Descriptions

a. controls speech production
b. specializes in rationalizing reactions
c. translates writing into speech
d. specializes in spatial relations
e. glands that produce epinephrine and norepinephrine
f. language disorder
g. oldest part of the brain
h. regulates emotion
i. the brain's capacity for modification
j. responsible for language comprehension
k. brain areas involved in higher mental functions

In the diagrams to the right, the numbers refer to brain locations that have been damaged. Match each location with its probable effect on behavior.

Location

_____ 1.
_____ 2.
_____ 3.
_____ 4.
_____ 5.
_____ 6.
_____ 7.
_____ 8.
_____ 9.

Behavioral Effect

a. vision disorder
b. insensitivity to touch
c. motor paralysis
d. hearing problem
e. lack of coordination
f. abnormal hunger
g. split brain
h. sleep/arousal disorder
i. altered personality

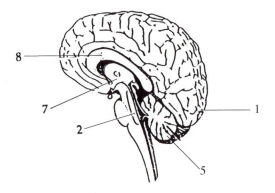

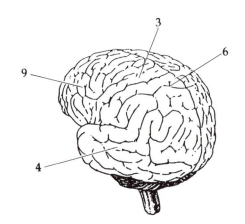

Review and Reflect

Answer these questions the day before an exam as a final check on your understanding of the chapter's terms and concepts.

Multiple-Choice Questions

1. A biological psychologist would be *more* likely to study:
   a. how you learn to express emotions.
   b. how to help people overcome emotional disorders.
   c. life-span changes in the expression of emotion.
   d. the chemical changes that accompany emotions.

2. The part of the human brain that is most like that of a fish is the:
   a. cortex.
   b. limbic system.
   c. brainstem.
   d. right hemisphere.
   e. corpus callosum.

3. You are able to pull your hand quickly away from hot water before pain is felt because:
   a. movement of the hand is a reflex that involves intervention of the spinal cord only.
   b. movement of the hand does not require intervention by the central nervous system.
   c. the brain reacts quickly to prevent severe injury.
   d. the autonomic division of the peripheral nervous system intervenes to speed contraction of the muscles of the hand.

4. In order to pinpoint the location of a tumor, a neurosurgeon electrically stimulated parts of the patient's sensory cortex. If the patient was conscious during the procedure, which of the following was probably experienced?
   a. "hearing" faint sounds
   b. "seeing" random visual patterns
   c. movement of the arms or legs
   d. a sense of having the skin touched

5. If Dr. Rogers wishes to conduct an experiment on the effects of stimulating the reward centers of a rat's brain, he should insert an electrode into the:
   a. thalamus.
   b. sensory cortex.
   c. hypothalamus.
   d. corpus callosum.

6. A split-brain patient has a picture of a knife flashed to her left hemisphere and that of a fork to her right hemisphere. She will be able to:
   a. identify the fork using her left hand.
   b. identify a knife using her left hand.
   c. identify a knife using either hand.
   d. identify a fork using either hand.

7. Which of the following is *not* a correct description of a brain research technique?
   a. using a PET scan to examine the brain's structure
   b. using the EEG to record the brain's electrical activity
   c. using MRI to examine the brain's structure
   d. using an fMRI to examine the brain's structure

8. Following Jayshree's near-fatal car accident, her physician noticed that the pupillary reflex of her eyes was abnormal. This *may* indicate that Jayshree's _____ was damaged in the accident.
   a. occipital cortex
   b. autonomic nervous system
   c. left temporal lobe
   d. cerebellum
   e. brainstem

9. Anton is applying for a technician's job with a neurosurgeon. In trying to impress his potential employer with his knowledge of the brain, he says, "After my father's stroke I knew immediately that the blood clot had affected his left cerebral hemisphere because he no longer recognized his friend." Should Anton be hired?
   a. Yes. Anton obviously understands brain structure and function.
   b. No. The right hemisphere, not the left, specializes in facial recognition.
   c. Yes. Although blood clots never form in the left hemisphere, Anton should be rewarded for recognizing the left hemisphere's role in facial recognition.
   d. No. Blood clots never form in the left hemisphere, and the right hemisphere is more involved than the left in recognizing faces.

10. A person with a damaged angular gyrus would most likely have difficulty:
    a. speaking.
    b. comprehending other people's words.
    c. reading aloud from a newspaper.
    d. hearing.

11. Dr. Johnson briefly flashed a picture of a key in the right visual field of a split-brain patient. The patient could probably:
    a. verbally report that a key was seen.
    b. write the word *key* using the left hand.
    c. draw a picture of a key using the left hand.
    d. do none of the above.

12. In primitive vertebrate animals, the brain primarily regulates _____ ; in lower mammals, the brain enables _____ .
    a. emotion; memory
    b. memory; emotion
    c. survival functions; emotion
    d. reproduction; emotion
    e. reproduction; memory

13. Since Malcolm has been taking a drug prescribed by his doctor, he no longer enjoys the little pleasures of life, such as eating and drinking. His doctor explains that this is because the drug:
    a. triggers release of dopamine.
    b. inhibits release of dopamine.
    c. triggers release of ACh.
    d. inhibits release of ACh.

14. A scientist from another planet wishes to study the simplest brain mechanisms underlying emotion and memory. You recommend that the scientist study the:
    a. brainstem of a frog.
    b. limbic system of a dog.
    c. cortex of a monkey.
    d. cortex of a human.
    e. brainstem of a dog.

15. Which of the following was a major problem with phrenology?
    a. It was "ahead of its time" and no one believed it could be true.
    b. The brain is not neatly organized into structures that correspond to our categories of behavior.
    c. The brains of humans and animals are much less similar than the theory implied.
    d. All of the above were problems with phrenology.

16. I am a relatively slow-acting (but long-lasting) chemical messenger carried throughout the body by the bloodstream. What am I?
    a. a hormone
    b. a neurotransmitter
    c. acetylcholine
    d. dopamine

17. Your brother has been taking prescription medicine and experiencing a number of unpleasant side effects, including unusually rapid heartbeat and excessive perspiration. It is likely that the medicine is exaggerating activity in the:
    a. reticular formation.
    b. sympathetic nervous system.
    c. parasympathetic nervous system.
    d. amygdala.

18. Dr. Frankenstein made a mistake during neurosurgery on his monster. After the operation, the monster "saw" with his ears and "heard" with his eyes. It is likely that Dr. Frankenstein "rewired" neural connections in the monster's:
    a. hypothalamus.
    b. cerebellum.
    c. amygdala.
    d. thalamus.
    e. hippocampus.

19. A bodybuilder friend suddenly seems to have grown several inches in height. You suspect that your friend's growth spurt has occurred because he has been using drugs that affect the:
    a. pituitary gland.
    b. thalamus.
    c. adrenal glands.
    d. medulla.
    e. cerebellum.

20. Raccoons have much more precise control of their paws than dogs. You would expect that raccoons have more cortical space dedicated to "paw control" in the _____ of their brains.
    a. frontal lobes
    b. parietal lobes
    c. temporal lobes
    d. occipital lobes

Essay Question

Discuss how the endocrine and nervous systems become involved when a student feels stress—such as that associated with an upcoming final exam. (Use the space below to list the points you want to make, and organize them. Then write the essay on a separate sheet of paper.)

Key Terms

Writing Definitions

Using your own words, on a piece of paper write a brief definition or explanation of each of the following terms.

1. biological psychology
2. neuron
3. dendrites
4. axon
5. action potential
6. myelin sheath
7. threshold
8. synapse
9. neurotransmitters
10. endorphins
11. nervous system
12. central nervous system (CNS)
13. peripheral nervous system (PNS)
14. nerves
15. sensory neurons
16. interneurons
17. motor neurons
18. somatic nervous system
19. autonomic nervous system
20. sympathetic nervous system
21. parasympathetic nervous system
22. reflex
23. brainstem
24. medulla
25. reticular formation
26. thalamus
27. lesion
28. electroencephalogram (EEG)
29. PET (positron emission tomography) scan
30. cerebellum
31. MRI (magnetic resonance imaging)
32. limbic system
33. amygdala
34. hypothalamus
35. cerebral cortex
36. frontal lobes
37. parietal lobes
38. occipital lobes
39. temporal lobes
40. motor cortex
41. sensory cortex
42. association areas
43. aphasia
44. Broca's area
45. Wernicke's area
46. plasticity
47. corpus callosum
48. split brain
49. endocrine system
50. hormones
51. adrenal glands
52. pituitary gland

Cross-Check

As you learned in Chapter 1, reviewing and overlearning of material are important to the learning process. After you have written the definitions of the key terms in this chapter, you should complete the crossword puzzle to ensure that you can reverse the process—recognize the term, given the definition.

ACROSS

3. The division of the nervous system that connects the brain and spinal cord to the body's sense receptors, muscles, and glands.
6. Located on the sides of the brain, these lobes contain the auditory areas, which receive information from the ears.
7. Located at the back of the frontal lobe, the part of the cortex that controls voluntary movement.
9. Located just behind the forehead, these lobes are involved in speaking and muscle movements and in making plans and judgments.
12. Glands that produce the hormones epinephrine and norepinephrine.
14. Located in the brainstem, this structure controls breathing and heartbeat.
15. The thin outer covering of the cerebral hemispheres.
16. Junction between the axon tip of the sending neuron and the dendrite or cell body of the receiving neuron.
17. Amplified recording of the waves of electrical activity of the brain.
19. Destruction of tissue.
20. Technique that uses magnetic fields and radio waves to produce computer-generated images of brain structures.
22. Located at the back and base of the brain, these lobes contain the visual cortex, which receives information from the eyes.
23. The part of the limbic system involved in regulation of the emotions of fear and rage.
26. Situated between the frontal and occipital lobes, these lobes contain the sensory cortex.

DOWN

1. Limbic system structure that regulates hunger, thirst, and body temperature and contains the so-called reward centers of the brain.
2. Large band of neural fibers that links the right and left hemispheres.
3. Technique that measures the levels of activity of different areas of the brain by tracing their consumption of a radioactive form of glucose.
4. Neural impulse generated by the movement of positively charged atoms in and out of channels in the axon's membrane.
5. Neurotransmitter that triggers muscle contractions.
8. Simple, automatic, inborn response to a sensory stimulus.
10. Doughnut-shaped neural system that plays an important role in the regulation of emotions and basic physiological drives.
11. Natural opiatelike neurotransmitters linked to pain control and to pleasure.
13. Division of the peripheral nervous system that controls the glands and the muscles of internal organs.

17. The body's slower chemical communication system, consisting of glands that secrete hormones into the bloodstream.

18. The brain and spinal cord, collectively, are the _____ nervous system.

21. An impairment of language as a result of damage to any of several cortical areas.

24. More numerous than cortical neurons, these cells of the brain guide neural connections and provide nutrients and insulating myelin.

25. Extension of a neuron that sends impulses to other nerve cells or to muscles or glands.

Answers

Introduction

Introduction Preview

1. Biological processes underlie every aspect of our behavior and mental processes. By studying the links between biology and psychology, biological psychologists achieve a greater understanding of such behaviors as sleep, hunger, sex, stress and disease, depression, and other human conditions.

Stepping Through the Introduction

1. biological

2. phrenology

3. biological psychologists

Neural Communication

Section Preview

1. Each neuron consists of a cell body, branching fibers called dendrites that receive information from other neurons, and an extension fiber called an axon through which the neuron passes information to other neurons or to muscles or glands. Some axons are insulated with a myelin sheath, which helps speed neural impulses.

   A neural impulse, or action potential, occurs if the excitatory signals minus the inhibitory signals received by the neuron on its dendrites or cell body exceeds the neuron's threshold. This leads to the electrical charge that travels down the axon into junctions with other neurons and with the muscles and glands of the body.

2. When an action potential reaches the end of the axon, chemical messengers called neurotransmitters are released into the synaptic gap between the sending and receiving neuron. This junction is called a synapse. Neurotransmitter molecules bind to receptor sites on the receiving neuron and have either an excitatory or inhibitory influence on that neuron's tendency to generate its own action potential. If the receiving neuron receives more excitatory than inhibitory inputs, more neural impulses are generated.

   A particular neural pathway may use only one or two neurotransmitters, each of which may have a specific effect on behavior and emotions. Acetylcholine, for example, is the neurotransmitter at every synapse between a motor neuron and a skeletal muscle. Other known neurotransmitters include dopamine, which influences movement, learning, attention, and emotion; serotonin, which affects mood, hunger, sleep, and arousal; norepinephrine, which helps control alertness and arousal; gamma-aminobutyric acid (GABA), which is an inhibitory neurotransmitter whose undersupply is linked to seizures, tremors, and insomnia; and glutamate, an excitatory neurotransmitter involved in memory.

3. Endorphins are opiatelike neurotransmitters found in the brain that are released in response to pain and vigorous exercise. The existence of endorphins may help explain good feelings such as the "runner's high," the pain-killing effects of acupuncture, and the indifference to pain in some injured people.

   Drugs have a number of different effects on neurotransmitters. Some (agonists) mimic a particular neurotransmitter or interfere with the reuptake of the neurotransmitter; others (antagonists) block a particular neurotransmitter. Opiate drugs, for example, may cause the brain to stop producing endorphins.

Stepping Through the Section

1. neurons

2. dendrites

3. axons; myelin sheath

4. **a.** dendrites
   b. cell body
   c. axon
   d. myelin sheath

5. action potential; axon

6. excitatory; inhibitory; threshold; will not; all-or-none

A neural impulse is generated by excitatory signals minus inhibitory signals exceeding a certain threshold. The stimuli are received through the dendrites, combined in the cell body, and electrically transmitted in an all-or-none fashion down the length of the axon. When the combined signal reaches the end of the axon, chemical messengers called neurotransmitters are released into the synaptic cleft, or gap, between two neurons. Neurotransmitter molecules bind to receptor sites on the dendrites of neighboring neurons and have either an excitatory or inhibitory influence on that neuron's tendency to generate its own neural impulse.

7. does not

8. synapse; synaptic cleft (gap)

9. neurotransmitters; atoms

10. exciting; inhibiting; reuptake

11. acetylcholine; dopamine; serotonin; norepinephrine; GABA (gamma-aminobutyric acid); glutamate

12. acetylcholine (ACh); curare

13. endorphins; heroin; morphine

14. agonists; receptor sites; antagonists

15. blood-brain barrier

16. Parkinson's; dopamine; L-dopa

The Nervous System

Section Preview

1. The central nervous system includes all the neurons in the brain and spinal cord. The peripheral nervous system, which links the central nervous system with the body's sense receptors, muscles, and glands, has two divisions: somatic and autonomic. The somatic nervous system controls the voluntary movements of the skeletal muscles.

   The autonomic nervous system, which influences the glands and muscles of our internal organs, also is a dual system. The sympathetic nervous system arouses the body during emergencies by accelerating heartbeat, slowing digestion, raising blood sugar, dilating arteries, and creating perspiration. When the emergency has passed, the parasympathetic nervous system relaxes the body by producing the opposite effects.

   Sensory neurons relay information from the body's tissues and sensory organs to the brain and spinal cord. Interneurons of the brain and spinal cord (the central nervous system) are involved in processing this information from the sensory neurons. The central nervous system then sends instructions to the body's tissues by means of the motor neurons.

2. Reflexes, which are automatic responses to stimuli, are governed by the simplest neural connections. In response to a painful stimulus to the fingertips, for example, a sensory neuron conveys the message to an interneuron in the spinal cord. The interneuron triggers an action potential in motor neurons that cause muscles of your arm to jerk your hand away.

Stepping Through the Section

1. nervous system

2. central; peripheral

3. nerves

4. sensory; interneurons

5. motor; glial cells

6. somatic

7. autonomic

8. sympathetic

9. parasympathetic

The sympathetic division of the autonomic nervous system becomes aroused in response to an emergency. The physiological changes that occur include accelerated heartbeat, elevated blood sugar, dilation of arteries, slowing of digestion, and increased perspiration to cool the body. When the emergency is over, the parasympathetic nervous system produces the opposite physical reactions.

10. neural networks

11. reflexes; spinal cord; knee-jerk; pain

From sensory receptors in the skin the message travels via sensory neurons to an interneuron in the spinal cord, which in turn activates a motor neuron. This motor neuron causes the muscles in the hand to contract, and the person jerks his or her hand away from the heat.

The Brain

Section Preview

1. The brainstem is the oldest and innermost region of the brain. It begins where the spinal cord enters the skull and is the point where nerves to and from each side of the brain cross over to connect with the opposite side of the body. It contains the medulla and reticular formation. The medulla controls breathing and heartbeat, and the reticular formation helps control arousal. The thalamus serves as the brain's sensory switchboard, routing information from sensory neurons to higher brain regions dealing with seeing, hearing, tasting, and touching. The cerebellum enables one type of nonverbal learning and memory; its most obvious function is coordinating voluntary movement.

2. The oldest method of studying the brain is by observing the effects of brain disease and injuries. More recently, electrical, chemical, or magnetic stimulation in humans and surgical lesions of brain tissue in animals have been used to study the brain. The electroencephalogram (EEG) is a

recording of the brain's electrical activity from electrodes placed on its surface. Scientists also examine the brain with PET (positron emission tomography) scans and magnetic resonance imaging (an MRI or a functional MRI). Although the text discusses the use of scanning and imaging on the brain only, these techniques are also used to diagnose problems elsewhere in the body.

3. In the limbic system, the hippocampus processes memory. The amygdala influences aggression and fear. When this region is surgically lesioned, aggressive behavior in animals is diminished. When one region of the amygdala is electrically stimulated, a normally placid domestic animal will behave aggressively; when another area is stimulated, the animal will display signs of fear.

The hypothalamus contains neurons that regulate hunger, thirst, body temperature, and sexual behavior; it also contains the so-called reward centers. The hypothalamus also secretes hormones that control the pituitary gland, which influences hormone release by other glands, which the hypothalamus monitors.

4. The cerebral cortex is a thin surface layer of nerve cells. It covers the left and right cerebral hemispheres. Each hemisphere is divided into four regions called lobes: frontal, parietal, temporal, and occipital. The frontal lobes control movement through the motor cortex and contain association areas that are involved in making plans and judgments. When specific parts of the motor cortex in the left and right hemispheres are electrically stimulated, movement is triggered in specific body parts on the opposite side of the body.

The parietal lobes house the sensory cortex which, when electrically stimulated, triggers a sense of a particular body part having been touched. The more sensitive a body region, the greater the area of sensory cortex devoted to it.

The temporal lobes receive auditory information primarily from the opposite ear, and the occipital lobes similarly receive input from the eyes.

Approximately three-fourths of the cortex consists of uncommitted association areas that communicate with one another and with neurons of the sensory and motor areas. Association areas influence personality, learning, remembering, and many other "higher" mental abilities.

5. Damage to any one of several areas of the cortex can cause aphasia, an impaired use of language. Damage to Broca's area in the left frontal lobe dis-rupts speaking. Damage to Wernicke's area in the left temporal lobe disrupts language comprehension and leaves people able to speak words but in a meaningless way. Damage to the angular gyrus will disrupt the ability to read aloud.

When you read aloud, words are registered in the visual area of the cortex and then relayed to the angular gyrus, which transforms the words into an auditory code. This code is comprehended by Wernicke's area and then sent to Broca's area, which directs the motor cortex to produce speech.

Stepping Through the Section

1. what the brain does

2. brainstem

3. medulla; breathing; heartbeat

4. brainstem

5. reticular formation; arousal; alert (awake); coma

6. thalamus

7. cerebellum; nonverbal learning; voluntary movement

8. conscious; outside

9. lesions; clinical observation

10. electroencephalogram (EEG)

11. PET scan

By depicting the brain's consumption of radioactively labeled glucose, the PET scan allows researchers to see which brain areas are most active as a person performs various tasks. This provides additional information on the specialized functions of various regions of the brain.

12. MRI (magnetic resonance imaging); functional MRI

13. limbic; hippocampus

14. amygdala

15. hypothalamus; hunger, thirst, body temperature (or sex); pituitary; reward

16. addictive; reward deficiency syndrome

17. cerebral cortex

18. more wrinkled; increases

19. a. frontal lobe
    b. parietal lobe
    c. occipital lobe
    d. temporal lobe

20. motor; frontal; paralyzed; thoughts (or brains)

21. sensory; touch

22. sensory cortex
23. occipital; temporal
24. association areas; three-fourths; frontal; right temporal
25. aphasia; Broca's area; Wernicke's area; angular gyrus
26. unified whole

Brain Reorganization

Section Preview

1. When a particular area of the brain is damaged, such as occurs following a stroke, other areas may in time reorganize and assume its functions (plasticity). Neurons that are near damaged ones compensate for the damage by making new neural connections to replace the damaged ones. The brains of young children, in which functions are not yet regionally fixed, exhibit the greatest plasticity. Humans can generate new brain cells.

2. In order to control severe epileptic seizures, surgeons sometimes sever the wide band of fibers (the corpus callosum) that connects the two hemispheres of the brain.

    Sperry and Gazzaniga studied such split-brain patients, revealing that the left and right hemispheres each have specialized functions. In a person with an intact brain, information in the left or right side of our field of vision of both eyes projects directly to the opposite hemisphere of the brain and is quickly passed to the other hemisphere through the corpus callosum. In the split-brain patient, however, a briefly flashed image on the subject's right, for example, will be perceived only in the left hemisphere. By flashing images in this way, researchers are able to send information to either the left or right hemisphere and thereby determine its capabilities.

    Using the latest tools for studying the brain, researchers have also found evidence of hemispheric specialization in the *intact* (undivided) brain. These experiments demonstrate that the right hemisphere is superior to the left at recognizing faces, perceiving differences, perceiving emotions, and expressing emotions. The left hemisphere is more logical and verbal. Despite these specialized functions, the two hemispheres work together in an integrated manner during most activities.

Stepping Through the Section

1. plasticity
2. will not; reorganize; can; are
3. left; dominant (major)
4. corpus callosum; split brain
5. right; name; right

The word *pencil* when flashed to a split-brain patient's right visual field would project only to the opposite, or left, hemisphere of the patient's brain. Because the left hemisphere contains the language control centers of the brain, the patient would be able to read the word aloud. The left hand is controlled by the right hemisphere of the brain. Because the right hemisphere would not be aware of the word, it would not be able to guide the left hand in identifying a pencil by touch.

6. have; right; left; demonstrate; favor the left side of their mouth when beginning a smile and the right side when using baby language

The Endocrine System

Section Preview

1. The endocrine system is a relatively slow-acting chemical communication system of glands that secrete hormones influencing growth, reproduction, metabolism, mood, and reactions to stress.

2. The adrenal glands release epinephrine (adrenaline) and norepinephrine (noradrenaline) during emergencies. These hormones provide a source of energy by increasing heart rate, blood pressure, and blood sugar. The pituitary gland, located in the base of the brain, releases hormones that influence growth and the release of hormones by other glands. It forms an elaborate feedback system with the brain (the hypothalamus) in its influence on behavior.

Stepping Through the Section

1. endocrine system; hormones; slower
2. adrenal; epinephrine; norepinephrine
3. pituitary; hypothalamus; growth

The hypothalamus in the brain influences secretions by the pituitary. The pituitary regulates other endocrine glands, which release hormones that influence behavior. The hypothalamus monitors these changes in blood chemistry and thereby adjusts its inputs to the pituitary.

Progress Test 1

Multiple-Choice Questions

1. **b.** is the answer. (p. 38)
   a. Glial cells support and nourish nerve cells.
   c. Acetylcholine is a neurotransmitter that triggers muscle contraction.
   d. Endorphins are opiatelike neurotransmitters linked to pain control and to pleasure.

2. **b.** is the answer. The autonomic nervous system controls internal functioning, including heartbeat, digestion, and glandular activity. (p. 44)
   a. The functions mentioned are all automatic, not voluntary, so this answer cannot be correct.
   c. This answer is incorrect because most organs are affected by both divisions of the autonomic nervous system.
   d. The somatic nervous system transmits sensory input to the central nervous system and directs the movements of skeletal muscles.
   e. The central nervous system need not be involved in automatic activities.

3. **c.** is the answer. Stimulus strength can affect only the number of times a neuron fires or the number of neurons that fire. (p. 39)
   a., b., & d. These answers are incorrect because firing is an all-or-none response, so intensity remains the same regardless of stimulus strength. Nor can stimulus strength change the neuronal threshold or the impulse speed.

4. **a.** is the answer. Endorphins are neurotransmitters that function as natural painkillers. When the body has a supply of artificial painkillers such as heroin, endorphin production stops. (p. 42)
   b. The production of neurotransmitters other than endorphins does not cease.
   c. Neurotransmitter production does not increase during withdrawal.
   d. Heroin makes use of the same receptor sites as endorphins.

5. **a.** is the answer. The PET scan measures glucose consumption in different areas of the brain to determine their levels of activity. (pp. 48–49)
   b. & d. The fMRI and MRI use magnetic fields and radio waves to produce computer-generated images of soft tissues of the body.
   c. The EEG is a measure of electrical activity in the brain.

6. **a.** is the answer. (p. 42)

7. **a.** is the answer. (p. 50)
   b. The reticular formation is linked to arousal.

   c. The brainstem governs the mechanisms of basic survival—heartbeat and breathing, for example—and has many other roles.
   d. The cerebral cortex governs the "higher" functions of the brain.

8. **c.** is the answer. In a simple reflex, a sensory neuron carries the message that a sensory receptor has been stimulated to an interneuron in the spinal cord. The interneuron responds by activating motor neurons that will enable the appropriate response. (p. 45)

9. **c.** is the answer. Wernicke's area is involved in comprehension, and aphasics with damage to Wernicke's area are unable to understand what is said to them. (p. 56)
   a. The angular gyrus translates printed words into speech sounds; damage would result in the inability to read aloud.
   b. Broca's area is involved in the physical production of speech; damage would result in the inability to speak fluently.
   d. The cortex's association areas are involved in, among other things, processing language; damage to these areas wouldn't specifically affect comprehension.

10. **d.** is the answer. (p. 61)
    a. In most persons, language is primarily a left hemisphere function.
    b. Learned movements are unrelated to hemispheric specialization.
    c. Arithmetic reasoning is generally a left hemisphere function.

11. **d.** is the answer. Biological psychologists study the links between biology (in this case, neurotransmitters) and psychology (depression, in this example). (p. 37)
    a., b., & c. These mental health professionals are more involved in the *treatment* of troubled behavior than in research.

12. **d.** is the answer. As animals increase in complexity, there is an increase in the amount of association areas. (p. 55)
    a. The brainstem controls basic survival functions and is not related to the complexity of an animal's behavior.
    b. The ratio of body and brain weight is a poor predictor of behavior complexity.
    c. The frontal lobe is concerned with personality, planning, and other mental functions, but its size is unrelated to intelligence or the complexity of behavior.

13. **b.** is the answer. (p. 44)

a., c., & d. The autonomic nervous system, which is divided into the sympathetic and parasympathetic divisions, is concerned with regulating basic bodily maintenance functions.

14. **c.** is the answer. (p. 39)
    a. An action potential will occur only when the neuron's threshold is *exceeded*.
    b. An excitatory input that does not reach the neuron's threshold will not trigger an action potential.
    d. This answer is incorrect because some neurotransmitters inhibit a neuron's readiness to fire.
    e. Hormones are produced by the glands of the endocrine system.

15. **e.** is the answer. A neuron receives incoming stimuli on its dendrites and cell body. These electrochemical signals are combined in the cell body, generating an impulse that travels down the axon, causing the release of neurotransmitter substances into the synaptic cleft or gap. (pp. 38–39)

16. **c.** is the answer. (p. 63)
    a. Agonists are drugs that excite neural firing by mimicking a particular neurotransmitter.
    b. Neurotransmitters are the chemicals involved in synaptic transmission in the nervous system.
    d. Enzymes are chemicals that facilitate various chemical reactions throughout the body but are not involved in communication within the endocrine system.

17. **c.** is the answer. The reticular formation plays an important role in arousal. (p. 47)
    a. The thalamus relays sensory input.
    b. The corpus callosum links the two cerebral hemispheres.
    d. The cerebellum is involved in coordination of voluntary movement.

18. **d.** is the answer. (p. 62)

19. **b.** is the answer. Association areas interpret, integrate, and act on information from other areas of the cortex. (p. 55)

20. **b.** is the answer. (p. 45)
    a. Action potentials are neural impulses that occur in all forms of communication in the nervous system.
    c. The endocrine system is the body's glandular system of chemical communication.
    d. Dendrites are the branching extensions of neurons that receive messages from other nerve cells.
    e. Synaptic gaps are the spaces between neurons.

Matching Items

1. d (p. 51)	**5.** g (p. 47)	**9.** k (p. 48)
2. e (p. 48)	**6.** b (p. 49)	**10.** i (p. 50)
3. a (p. 48)	**7.** c (p. 47)	**11.** j (p. 47)
4. f (p. 48)	**8.** h (p. 59)	

Progress Test 2

Multiple-Choice Questions

1. **a.** is the answer. The visual cortex is located at the very back of the brain. (p. 53)

2. **b.** is the answer. (p. 61)
   a., c., & d. Spatial reasoning, perceptual skills, and the left side of the body are primarily influenced by the right hemisphere.

3. **a.** is the answer. Sensory neurons in the somatic nervous system relay such messages. (p. 44)
   b. & c. These divisions of the autonomic nervous system are concerned with the regulation of bodily maintenance functions such as heartbeat, digestion, and glandular activity.
   d. The spinal cord itself is part of the central nervous system, but the message is carried to the spinal cord by the somatic division of the peripheral nervous system.

4. **c.** is the answer. As automatic responses to stimuli, reflexes are the simplest complete units of behavior and require only simple neural pathways. (p. 45)
   a., b., & d. Emotions, drives, and voluntary movements are all behaviors that are much more complex than reflexes and therefore involve much more complicated neural pathways.
   e. Balance is regulated by the cerebellum.

5. **b.** is the answer. Endorphins are neurotransmitters that function as natural painkillers and are evidently involved in the "runner's high" and other situations in which discomfort or fatigue is expected but not experienced. (p. 41)
   a. ACh is a neurotransmitter involved in muscular control.
   c. Dopamine is a neurotransmitter involved in, among other things, motor control.
   d. Norepinephrine is an adrenal hormone released to help us respond in moments of danger.
   e. Acetylcholine is the complete name of ACh.

6. **a.** is the answer. Parkinson's disease causes the death of brain tissue that produces dopamine. (p. 43
   b. & c. This disease affects both hemispheres of the cortex.
   d. This disease causes insufficient production of the neurotransmitters.

7. **d.** is the answer. (p. 49)
   a. The EEG is an amplified recording of the brain's electrical activity.
   b. A lesion is tissue destruction.

c. The PET scan is a visual display of brain activity that detects the movement of a radioactive form of glucose as the brain performs a task.

8. **a.** is the answer. (p. 38)
c., d., & e. Myelin sheaths are not involved in regulating the release of neurotransmitters.

9. **d.** is the answer. (p. 37)

10. **b.** is the answer. ACh is a neurotransmitter that causes the contraction of muscle fibers when stimulated by motor neurons. This function explains its location. (p. 41)
a. & c. Sensory neurons and interneurons do not directly stimulate muscle fibers.

11. **d.** is the answer. The pituitary regulates body growth, and some of its secretions regulate the release of hormones from other glands. (p. 64)
a. The adrenal glands are stimulated by the autonomic nervous system to release epinephrine and norepinephrine.
b. The thyroid gland produces a hormone that controls the rates of various chemical reactions in the body.
c. The hypothalamus regulates the pituitary but does not itself directly regulate growth.
e. There is no such gland. Hyperthyroidism is a *condition* in which the thyroid gland is overactive.

12. **d.** is the answer. Also known as adrenaline and noradrenaline, epinephrine and norepinephrine are hormones released by the adrenal glands. (p. 63)

13. **d.** is the answer. The cerebellum is involved in the coordination of voluntary muscular movements. (p. 48)
a. The medulla regulates breathing and heartbeat.
b. The thalamus relays sensory inputs to the appropriate higher centers of the brain.
c. The hypothalamus is concerned with the regulation of basic drives and emotions.
e. The cerebrum is the center of all complex activities.

14. **a.** is the answer. The reticular formation controls arousal via its connections to the cortex. Thus, separating the two produces a coma. (p. 48)
b., c., d., & e. None of these structures controls arousal. The hypothalamus regulates hunger, thirst, sexual behavior, and other basic drives; the thalamus is a sensory relay station; the cerebellum is involved in the coordination of voluntary movement; and the medulla controls heartbeat and breathing.

15. **b.** is the answer. (pp. 53–54)
c. & d. These refer to the sensory cortex.

16. **b.** is the answer. (p. 42)
a. Abuse of certain drugs, such as heroin, may have this effect.
c. This describes the effect of an antagonist.
d. Drugs do not have this effect on neurons.

17. **c.** is the answer. The corpus callosum is a large band of neural fibers linking the right and left cerebral hemispheres. To sever the corpus callosum is in effect to split the brain. (p. 59)

18. **d.** is the answer. The frontal lobe is in the front of the brain. Just behind is the parietal lobe. The occipital lobe is located at the very back of the head and just below the parietal lobe. Next to the occipital lobe and toward the front of the head is the temporal lobe. (p. 53)

19. **d.** is the answer. As demonstrated in the case of Phineas Gage, injury to the frontal lobe may produce such changes in personality. (pp. 55–56)
a. Damage to the parietal lobe might disrupt functions involving the sensory cortex.
b. Damage to the temporal lobe might impair hearing.
c. Occipital damage might impair vision.
e. The endocrine system is the body's slower chemical communication system that transmits hormones through the bloodstream from tissue to tissue.

20. **c.** is the answer. (pp. 58–59)

Matching Items

1. d (p. 61)	**5.** i (p. 58)	**9.** k (p. 55)
2. g (p. 47)	**6.** a (p. 56)	**10.** b (p. 61)
3. e (p. 63)	**7.** j (p. 56)	**11.** c (p. 56)
4. f (p. 56)	**8.** h (p. 50)	

Brain Damage Diagram (pp. 46–60)

1. a	**4.** d	**7.** f
2. h	**5.** e	**8.** g
3. c	**6.** b	**9.** i

Review and Reflect

Multiple-Choice Questions

1. **d.** is the answer. Biological psychologists study the links between biology (chemical changes in this example) and behavior (emotions in this example). (p. 37)
a., b., & c. Experimental, clinical, and developmental psychologists would be more concerned with the learning of emotional expressions, the treatment of emotional disorders, and life-span changes in emotions, respectively.

2. **c.** is the answer. The brainstem is the oldest and most primitive region of the brain. It is found in

lower vertebrates, such as fish, as well as in humans and other mammals. The structures mentioned in the other choices are associated with stages of brain evolution beyond that seen in the fish. (pp. 46, 47)

3. **a.** is the answer. Since this reflex is an automatic response and involves only the spinal cord, the hand is jerked away before the brain has even received the information that causes the sensation of pain. (p. 45)
b. The spinal cord, which organizes simple reflexes such as this one, is part of the central nervous system.
c. The brain is not involved in directing spinal reflexes.
d. The autonomic nervous system controls the glands and the muscles of the internal organs; it does not influence the skeletal muscles controlling the hand.

4. **d.** is the answer. Stimulation of the sensory cortex elicits a sense of touch, as the experiments of Penfield demonstrated. (p. 54)
a., b., & c. Hearing, seeing, or movement might be expected if the temporal, occipital, and motor regions of the cortex, respectively, were stimulated.

5. **c.** is the answer. As Olds and Milner discovered, electrical stimulation of the hypothalamus is a highly reinforcing event because it is the location of the animal's reward centers. The other brain regions mentioned are not associated with reward centers. (p. 51)

6. **a.** is the answer. The left hand, controlled by the right hemisphere, would be able to identify the fork, the picture of which is flashed to the right hemisphere. (p. 60)

7. **a.** is the answer. The PET scan, which traces the brain's use of a radioactive form of glucose, measures brain *activity* in various regions. It does not reveal anything about structure. (pp. 48–49)
b., c., & d. Each of these techniques is utilized to study the structure or activity of the brain.

8. **b.** is the answer. Simple reflexes, such as this one, are governed by activity in the autonomic nervous system. (p. 44)
a. The occipital lobes process sensory messages from the eyes; they play no role in the reflexive response of the pupils to light.
c. The left temporal lobe specializes in processing language.
d. The cerebellum specializes in coordinating movement.
e. The brainstem is the oldest and innermost region of the brain.

9. **b.** is the answer. (p. 61)
a., c., & d. The left hemisphere does not specialize in facial recognition. And blood clots can form anywhere in the brain.

10. **c.** is the answer. (p. 56)
a. This would be true of someone who has damage in Broca's area.
b. This would be true of someone who has damage in Wernicke's area.
d. This would be true of someone who has damage in the auditory cortex.

11. **a.** is the answer. The right visual field projects directly to the verbal left hemisphere. (p. 60)
b. & c. The left hand is controlled by the right hemisphere, which, in this situation, would be unaware of the word since the picture has been flashed to the left hemisphere.

12. **c.** is the answer. (p. 46)
d. & e. Reproduction is only one of the basic survival functions the brain regulates.

13. **b.** is the answer. (pp. 42, 51)
a. By triggering release of dopamine, such a drug would probably *enhance* Malcolm's enjoyment of the pleasures of life.
c. & d. ACh is the neurotransmitter at synapses between motor neurons and muscle fibers.

14. **b.** is the answer. The hippocampus of the limbic system is involved in processing memory. The amygdala of the limbic system influences fear and anger. (p. 50)
a. & e. The brainstem controls vital functions such as breathing and heartbeat; it is not directly involved in either emotion or memory.
c. & d. These answers are incorrect because the limbic system is an older brain structure than the cortex. Its involvement in emotions and memory is therefore more basic than that of the cortex.

15. **b.** is the answer. (p. 37)
a. "Ahead of its time" implies the theory had merit, which later research clearly showed it did not. Moreover, phrenology *was* accepted as an accurate theory of brain organization by many scientists.
c. Phrenology said nothing about the similarities of human and animal brains.

16. **a.** is the answer. (p. 63)
b., c., & d. Acetylcholine and dopamine are fast-acting neurotransmitters released at synapses, not in the bloodstream.

17. **b.** is the answer. Sympathetic arousal produces several effects, including accelerated heartbeat and excessive perspiration. (p. 44)

a. Stimulation of the reticular formation increases alertness, but would not necessarily accelerate heartbeat or cause excessive perspiration.

c. Arousal of the parasympathetic nervous system would have effects opposite to those stated.

d. If the medication were affecting his amygdala, your brother might experience emotions such as anger or fear at illogical times.

18. **d.** is the answer. The thalamus relays sensory messages from the eyes, ears, and other receptors to the appropriate projection areas of the cortex. "Rewiring" the thalamus, theoretically, could have the effects stated in this question. (p. 47)

    a., b., c., & e. These brain structures are not directly involved in brain processes related to sensation or perception.

19. **a.** is the answer. Hormones of the pituitary gland regulate body growth. (p. 64)

    b., d., & e. Because they are not endocrine glands, the thalamus, medulla, and cerebellum are not influenced by hormones.

    c. The adrenal glands produce hormones that provide energy during emergencies; they are not involved in regulating body growth.

20. **a.** is the answer. The motor cortex, which determines the precision with which various parts of the body can be moved, is located in the frontal lobes. (p. 53)

    b. The parietal lobes contain the sensory cortex, which controls sensitivity to touch.

    c. The temporal lobes contain the primary projection areas for hearing and, on the left side, are also involved in language use.

    d. The occipital lobes contain the primary projection areas for vision.

Essay Question

The body's response to stress is regulated by the nervous system. As the date of the exam approaches, the stressed student's cerebral cortex activates the hypothalamus, triggering the release of hormones that in turn activate the sympathetic branch of the autonomic nervous system and the endocrine system. The autonomic nervous system controls involuntary bodily responses such as breathing, heartbeat, and digestion. The endocrine system contains glands that secrete hormones into the bloodstream that regulate the functions of body organs.

In response to activation by the hypothalamus, the student's pituitary gland would secrete a hormone which in turn triggers the release of epinephrine, norepinephrine, and other stress hormones from the adrenal glands. These hormones would help the student's body manage stress by making nutrients available to meet the increased demands for energy stores the body often faces in coping with stress. As these hormones activate the sympathetic division of the autonomic system, the body's fight-or-flight response occurs, including increased heart rate, breathing, and blood pressure and the suppression of digestion. After the exam date has passed, the student's body would attempt to restore its normal, pre-stress state. The parasympathetic branch of the autonomic system would slow the student's heartbeat and breathing and digestive processes would no longer be suppressed, perhaps causing the student to feel hungry.

Key Terms

Writing Definitions

1. **Biological psychology** is the study of the links between biology and behavior. (p. 37)

2. The **neuron**, or nerve cell, is the basic building block of the nervous system. (p. 38)

3. The **dendrites** of a neuron are the bushy, branching extensions that receive messages from other nerve cells and conduct impulses toward the cell body. (p. 38)

4. The **axon** of a neuron is the extension that sends impulses to other nerve cells or to muscles or glands. (p. 38)

5. An **action potential** is a neural impulse generated by the movement of positively charged atoms in and out of channels in the axon's membrane. (p. 38)

6. The **myelin sheath** is a layer of fatty tissue that covers many axons and helps speed neural impulses. (p. 38)

7. A neuron's **threshold** is the level of stimulation that must be exceeded in order for the neuron to fire, or generate an electrical impulse. (p. 39)

8. A **synapse** is the junction between the axon tip of the sending neuron and the dendrite or cell body of the receiving neuron. The tiny gap at this junction is called the synaptic cleft or gap. (p. 39)

9. **Neurotransmitters** are chemicals that are released into synaptic gaps and so transmit neural messages from neuron to neuron. (p. 39)

10. **Endorphins** are natural, opiatelike neurotransmitters linked to pain control and to pleasure. (p. 41)

    Memory aid: <u>End</u>orphins *end* pain.

11. The **nervous system** is the speedy, electrochemical communication system, consisting of all the

nerve cells in the peripheral and central nervous systems. (p. 43)

12. The **central nervous system** consists of the brain and spinal cord; it is located at the *center*, or internal core, of the body. (p. 43)

13. The **peripheral nervous system** connects the central nervous system to the body's sense receptors, muscles, and glands; it is at the *periphery* of the body relative to the brain and spinal cord. (p. 43)

14. **Nerves** are bundles of neural axons that connect the central nervous system with muscles, glands, and sense organs. (p. 43)

15. **Sensory neurons** carry information from the sense receptors to the central nervous system for processing. (p. 44)

16. **Interneurons** are the neurons of the central nervous system that link the sensory and motor neurons in the transmission of sensory inputs and motor outputs. (p. 44)

17. **Motor neurons** carry information and instructions for action from the central nervous system to muscles and glands. (p. 44)

18. The **somatic nervous system** is the division of the peripheral nervous system that controls voluntary movements of the skeletal muscles. (p. 44)

19. The **autonomic nervous system** is the division of the peripheral nervous system that controls the glands and the muscles of internal organs and thereby controls internal functioning; it regulates the *automatic* behaviors necessary for survival. (p. 44)

20. The **sympathetic nervous system** is the division of the autonomic nervous system that arouses the body, mobilizing its energy in stressful situations. (p. 44)

21. The **parasympathetic nervous system** is the division of the autonomic nervous system that calms the body, conserving its energy. (p. 45)

22. A **reflex** is a simple, automatic, inborn response to a sensory stimulus; it is governed by a very simple neural pathway. (p. 45)

23. The **brainstem**, the oldest and innermost region of the brain, is an extension of the spinal cord and is the central core of the brain; its structures direct automatic survival functions. (p. 47)

24. Located in the brainstem, the **medulla** controls breathing and heartbeat. (p. 47)

25. Also part of the brainstem, the **reticular formation** is a nerve network that plays an important role in controlling arousal. (p. 47)

26. Located atop the brainstem, the **thalamus** routes incoming messages to the appropriate cortical centers and transmits replies to the medulla and cerebellum. (p. 47)

27. A **lesion** is destruction of tissue; studying the consequences of lesions in different regions of the brain—both surgically produced in animals and naturally occurring—helps researchers to determine the normal functions of these regions. (p. 48)

28. An **electroencephalogram (EEG)** is an amplified recording of the waves of electrical activity of the brain. *Encephalo* comes from a Greek word meaning "related to the brain." (p. 48)

29. The **PET (positron emission tomography) scan** measures the levels of activity of different areas of the brain by tracing their consumption of a radioactive form of glucose, the brain's fuel. (p. 48)

30. The **cerebellum** assists in balance and the coordination of voluntary movement. (p. 48)

31. **MRI (magnetic resonance imaging)** uses magnetic fields and radio waves to produce computer-generated images that show brain structures more clearly. (p. 49)

32. A doughnut-shaped neural system, the **limbic system** plays an important role in the regulation of emotions and basic physiological drives. (p. 50)

    Memory aid: Its name comes from the Latin word *limbus*, meaning "border"; the **limbic system** is at the border of the brainstem and cerebral hemispheres.

33. The **amygdala** is part of the limbic system and is involved in regulation of the emotions of fear and rage. (p. 50)

34. Also part of the limbic system, the **hypothalamus** regulates hunger, thirst, body temperature, and sex and contains the so-called reward centers of the brain. (p. 51)

35. The **cerebral cortex** is the thin outer covering of the cerebral hemispheres. The seat of information processing, the cortex is responsible for those complex functions that make us distinctively human. (p. 52)

    Memory aid: Cortex in Latin means "bark." As bark covers a tree, the **cerebral cortex** is the "bark of the brain."

36. Located at the front of the brain, just behind the forehead, the **frontal lobes** are involved in speaking and muscle movements and in making plans and judgments. (p. 53)

37. Situated between the frontal and occipital lobes, the **parietal lobes** contain the sensory cortex. (p. 53)

38. Located at the back and base of the brain, the **occipital lobes** contain the visual cortex, which receives information from the eyes. (p. 53)

39. Located on the sides of the brain, the **temporal lobes** contain the auditory areas, which receive information from the ears. (p. 53)

    Memory aid: The **temporal lobes** are located near the *temples.*

40. Located at the back of the frontal lobe, the **motor cortex** controls voluntary movement. (p. 53)

41. The **sensory cortex** is located at the front of the parietal lobes, just behind the motor cortex. It registers and processes body sensations. (p. 54)

42. Located throughout the cortex, **association areas** of the brain are involved in higher mental functions, such as learning, remembering, and abstract thinking. (p. 55)

    Memory aid: Among their other functions, **association areas** of the cortex are involved in integrating, or *associating*, information from different areas of the brain.

43. **Aphasia** is an impairment of language as a result of damage to any of several cortical areas, including Broca's area and Wernicke's area. (p. 56)

44. **Broca's area**, located in the left frontal lobe, is involved in controlling the motor ability to produce speech. (p. 56)

45. **Wernicke's area,** located in the left temporal lobe, is involved in language comprehension. (p. 56)

46. **Plasticity** is the brain's capacity for modification, as evidenced by brain reorganization following damage (especially in children). (p. 58)

47. The **corpus callosum** is a large band of neural fibers that links the right and left cerebral hemispheres. Without this band of nerve fibers, the two hemispheres could not interact. (p. 59)

48. **Split brain** is a condition in which the major connections between the two cerebral hemispheres (the corpus callosum) are severed, literally resulting in a split brain. (p. 60)

49. The **endocrine system**, the body's "slower" chemical communication system, consists of glands that secrete hormones into the bloodstream. (p. 63)

50. **Hormones** are chemical messengers, mostly those manufactured by the endocrine system, that are produced in one tissue and circulate through the bloodstream to their target tissues, on which they have specific effects. (p. 63)

51. The **adrenal glands** produce epinephrine and norepinephrine, hormones that prepare the body to deal with emergencies or stress. (p. 63)

52. The **pituitary gland**, under the influence of the hypothalamus, regulates growth and controls other endocrine glands; sometimes called the "master gland." (p. 64)

Cross-Check

ACROSS	DOWN
3. peripheral	**1.** hypothalamus
6. temporal	**2.** corpus callosum
7. motor	**3.** PET scan
9. frontal	**4.** action potential
12. adrenal	**5.** acetylcholine
14. medulla	**8.** reflex
15. cortex	**10.** limbic system
16. synapse	**11.** endorphins
17. EEG	**13.** autonomic
19. lesion	**17.** endocrine
20. MRI	**18.** central
22. occipital	**21.** aphasia
23. amygdala	**24.** glial
26. parietal	**25.** axon

FOCUS ON VOCABULARY AND LANGUAGE

Page 37: . . . to shoot a basketball. . . . This means to throw the ball, in the game of basketball, through the hoop. Science today is intensely focused on (*riveted on*) research involving the brain and how it accomplishes a wide variety of mental and physical tasks.

Page 37: . . . an ill-fated theory. . . . Myers is referring to the theory that bumps or lumps on the skull could reveal our personality (*phrenology*). It was a theory destined for failure (*ill-fated*), despite its popularity during the early 1800s.

Page 37 (caption): A wrongheaded theory. Even though phrenology was without any scientific merit (*wrongheaded*), it did suggest the idea that different parts of the brain influence a variety of functions and behaviors.

Neural Communication

Page 38: For scientists, it is a *happy fact of nature* that the information systems of humans and other animals operate similarly. . . The structure and function of neurons are very similar in humans and other animals (e.g., squids and sea slugs) and this is a good thing (*a happy fact of nature*) for those researching the nervous system. Myers makes the important point about this similarity, noting that it would not be possible to tell the difference between a small piece of your brain tissue and that of a monkey.

Page 38: Its *building blocks* are **neurons,** or nerve cells. Building blocks are the basic or fundamental parts (e.g., bricks) that make up a structure (e.g., a house). The structure of our nervous system, or neural information system, is made up of neurons (*its building blocks*) .

Page 39: . . . the neural impulse travels at speeds ranging from a *sluggish* 2 miles per hour to, in some myelinated fibers, a *breakneck* 200 or more miles per hour. The speed of the neural impulse ranges from extremely slow (*sluggish*) to very fast (a *breakneck* speed). Compared to the speed of electricity or sophisticated electronics systems your neural impulses travel at a relatively slow pace.

Page 39: Some of these signals are *excitatory, somewhat like pushing a neuron's accelerator.* Other signals are *inhibitory, more like pushing its brake.* Myers is making a comparison between the effect of a neuron firing and the effect of speeding up a car when accelerating (*excitatory effect*) or slowing it down by applying the brake (*inhibitory effect*). He also likens excitatory signals to those who love social gatherings (*party animals*), and inhibitory signals to those who do not (*party poopers*); if those who want to have a party outvote those who don't, then the party (*action potential*) will happen.

Page 39: How do we distinguish a gentle touch from a big hug? This question is concerned with how we become aware of the magnitude of a stimulus, from a soft stroke or pat (*gentle touch*) to a strong embrace (*big hug*). The answer is that the intensity of the stimulus is a function of the number and frequency of neurons firing. A strong stimulus (*big hug*) does not initiate (*trigger*) a more powerful or faster impulse than a weak stimulus (*gentle touch*); rather, it triggers more neurons to fire, and to fire more often.

Page 39: . . . these near-unions of neurons—"*protoplasmic kisses*". . . were another of nature's marvels. The reference here is to the fact that the axon terminal of one neuron is separated from the receiving neuron by a tiny space called the synaptic gap. Protoplasm is the material that constitutes all living cells, and the communication between cells is likened to a kiss between cells. The transmission between sender and receiver is via chemicals called neurotransmitters. The cells don't actually touch but send messages across the synaptic gap.

Page 41: . . . "runner's high" . . . This refers to the feeling of emotional well-being or euphoria (*high*) following vigorous exercise such as running or jogging and is the result of the release of opiatelike substances called endorphins.

Page 42: They *trigger* unpleasant, *lingering aftereffects.* For suppressing the body's own neurotransmitter production, *nature charges a price.* Mood-altering drugs, such as alcohol, nicotine, heroin, and morphine, all initiate (*trigger*) disagreeable changes that persist for a long period of time (*lingering aftereffects*). When flooded with these opiates, the brain stops producing its own endorphins (i.e., they suppress production), and for the addict who stops taking the drugs the cost may be a great deal of pain and agony (*nature charges a price*).

Page 42: Agonists excite. An agonist molecule may be similar enough to the neurotransmitter to *mimic* its effects, or it may block the neurotransmitter's reuptake. *Antagonists* inhibit. An *agonist* drug molecule is enough like the neurotransmitter to imitate (*mimic*) its effects (for example, by producing a temporary euphoric feeling—a "high"). An *antagonist* drug molecule is enough like the neurotransmitter to stop (*block*) its effects (for example, some toxins, such as curare, may cause muscle paralysis by blocking acetylcholine receptors).

Page 43: . . . some *chemicals* don't have the right shape to *slither* through this [*blood-brain*] *barrier* . . . Some neurotransmitter substances (*chemicals*) such as dopamine do not work when given to patients because they can't slide or slip smoothly (*slither*) through the *blood-brain barrier* since they are the wrong shape. The *blood-brain barrier* is a system that blocks or obstructs unwanted chemicals circulating in the blood from getting into the brain (the brain *fences them out*).

The Nervous System

Page 44: Like an *automatic pilot*, this system may be consciously *overridden*. The autonomic nervous system automatically takes care of the operation of our internal organs much as a plane can be flown by the automatic (*or mechanical/computerized*) pilot. The system can, however, be consciously taken over (*overridden*) in the same way that the real pilot can take over flying the plane.

Page 45: Tens of billions of neurons, each communicating with thousands of other neurons, *yield an ever-changing wiring diagram that dwarfs a powerful computer*. The complexity of the central nervous system, which allows or makes possible (*enables*) our thinking, feeling, and behavior, is similar to the electronic circuitry (*wiring diagrams)* of the best computer, except, by comparison, the computer would appear to be extremely tiny or small (*dwarfed by*) and the brain's wiring would seem to be constantly modifying or altering itself (*ever-changing*).

Page 45: Neurons cluster into *work groups* called *neural networks*. Myers points out that the brain works much like a computer making many simultaneous computations. This is accomplished by neural networks which are clusters of interconnected neurons (*work groups*). Neurons work with nearby neurons for much the same reason people live in cities—it is easier for brief, quick interactions.

Page 45: . . . *information highway*. . . . The spinal cord is similar to the freeway (*highway*), but instead of cars moving up and down, sensory and motor messages (*information*) travel between the peripheral nervous system and the brain. This information moves either up to the brain (*ascending*) or down from the brain (*descending*).

Page 45: The *knee-jerk response*, for example, involves one such simple pathway; *a headless warm body could do it*. When the patellar tendon of a bent knee is struck, the whole leg reflexively straightens out (*the knee-jerk response*). This automatic reaction is a function of a simple spinal reflex pathway so it does not require mediation by the brain (*a headless warm* [live] *body could do it*).

The Brain

Page 46: . . . *we live in our heads*. What this means is that you subjectively feel that the essence of your being, your mind, resides in your brain, which is inside your head. The brain in our head allows us to function psychologically as well as physically: *the mind is what the brain does*.

Page 47: *This peculiar cross-wiring is but one of many surprises the brain has to offer.* In the brainstem most nerves from the left side of the body connect to the right side of the brain and those from the right connect to the left side of the brain. This strange (*peculiar*) traverse of nerves from one side to the other (*cross-wiring*) is one of the many marvels or astonishing findings (*surprises*) about the brain.

Page 47: Think of the thalamus as being to sensory input what *London is to England's trains*. London is the relay center for trains going to all parts of the country just as Chicago is the hub or relay center for many airlines flying to different parts of the United States. Myers uses this as an analogy for the thalamus, which receives messages from sensory neurons and sends them on, or relays them to higher brain areas.

Page 48: . . . the right side of the body is *wired* to the brain's left side, and *vice versa*. This means that the functions of one side of the body are controlled by (*wired to*) the opposite side of the brain. The right side of the body is controlled by the left hemisphere, and the other way is also true (*vice versa*): the left side of the body is controlled by the brain's right side.

Page 48: We can also *snoop on* the *mass action* of billions of neurons as their electrical activity *sweeps in regular waves* across the brain. With today's technology it is possible to unobtrusively view or spy on (*snoop on*) single nerve cells as well graphically depict the collective behavior (*mass action*) of millions and millions of neurons as their electrical activity undulates (*sweeps in waves*) over the surface of the brain.

Page 48: Other *new windows into the brain* give us a *Supermanlike* ability to see inside the brain without *lesioning it*. Modern technological means of viewing the brain (*new windows into the brain*), such as the CT and the PET scans, provide us with a greater than normal (*Supermanlike*) ability to look inside the cortex without destroying tissue (*lesioning it*). (*Note:* Superman is a comic-book, TV, and movie character with x-ray vision which allows him to see through solid matter.)

Page 49: Such *snapshots* of the brain's *activity* provide new insights into how the brain *divides its labor*. The MRI technique allows pictures (*snapshots*) to be taken of different brain areas at work (the brain *divides its labor*) while a person is carrying out various mental tasks.

Page 50: . . . a *doughnut-shaped* neural system, the **limbic system**. This system is in the shape of a ring (*doughnut-shaped*) and has three components: the **hippocampus,** which is involved in forming (*laying down*) new memories; the **amygdala,** which influences aggression and fear; and the **hypothalamus,** which regulates hunger, thirst, body temperature, and sexuality.

Page 51: . . . they made *a magnificent mistake*. Olds and Milner accidentally discovered (*stumbled upon*) a brain area that provides a pleasurable reward and then went on to find other similar areas which they called *"pleasure centers"* (which we now call *reward centers*). Myers calls this a splendid and spectacular error (*a magnificent mistake*). When rats are allowed to stimulate these areas by pressing a bar or lever (*pedal*) they seem to prefer this to any other activity and will continue at a very rapid rate (*feverish pace*) until they are too tired to go on (*until they drop from exhaustion*).

Page 52: If you opened a human skull, exposing the brain, you would see a *wrinkled* organ, shaped somewhat like the *meat of an oversized walnut*. The human brain has a convoluted (*wrinkled*) surface, and the cerebral cortex is divided into two halves or hemispheres just like the two lobes of the edible portion (*the meat or seed*) in the shell of a very large (*oversized*) walnut.

Page 53: Being human *takes a lot of nerve*. Myers is using humor here to make an important point. The expression "it takes a lot of nerve" means to be brave or courageous (another expression, "it takes a lot of guts" means the same thing!). Thus, when he states that being human takes a lot of nerve, the literal meaning in this context is that humans are made up of many, many nerves (the humor is derived from the double meaning).

Page 54: In a sense, we *do* have *eyes in the back of our head!* The reference here is to the visual cortex (or occipital lobes) which processes visual information and is located at the rear of the brain. So, in a way seeing is not just done with the eyes but also involves specialized areas at the back of the brain.

Page 55: . . . one of pop psychology's most widespread *falsehoods:* that we ordinarily *use only 10 percent of our brains*. Research into the association areas of the brain showed that they don't have specific functions but rather are involved in many different operations such as interpreting, integrating, and acting on information processed by the sensory areas. The incorrect notion (*falsehood*) that *we use only 10 percent of our brains* may have arisen because early researchers were unsure about the function of the association areas. Remember, we use all of our brain, all the time. Damage to the frontal lobes (association areas) would result in very serious deficits.

Page 56: With his frontal lobes *ruptured,* Gage's *moral compass* became disconnected from his behavior. Phineas Gage's frontal lobes were severely damaged (*ruptured*) when the tamping iron shot through his head (much as meat is pierced by a skewer for a shish-kebab). As a result, he lost many of his normal inhibitions which caused him to veer away from his previous honest ways (he lost his *moral compass*).

Page 56: What you experience as a continuous, indivisible stream of perception is actually but the visible tip of the information-processing iceberg, most of which lies beneath the surface of your conscious awareness. Myers is making an analogy here. Most of the important functions that allow you to see the world as a whole are not part of conscious experience, but, like most of the mass of an iceberg, are below the surface and out of awareness.

Brain Reorganization

Page 58: Thus, the brain may not be as *"hard-wired"* as once thought. Myers is noting a comparison that used to be made between the brain's neural networks and the fixed circuits of computer hardware. We now know that the brain is much more flexible—it is not *"hard-wired."* Myers uses the term *plastic* or *brain plasticity* to describe this malleability or adaptability.

Page 60: Waking from the surgery, one patient even managed to *quip* that he had a *"splitting headache"* . . . . People have had their corpus callosum severed or cut in order to control epileptic seizures. Despite such a major operation this patient managed to joke (*quip*) that he had a very bad headache (*a splitting headache*). Personality and intellectual functioning were not affected by this procedure, and you would not be able to detect anything unusual if you were having a casual conversation with a split-brain patient.

Page 61: When the "two minds" are at odds, the left hemisphere seems to act as *the brain's press agent,* doing *mental gymnastics* to *rationalize* reactions it does not understand. In split-brain patients, if information or commands are delivered to the right hemisphere (which does not have language), then the left hemisphere, which can talk, would not be aware of what was requested. So if the patient carried out the command to do something (e.g., "walk" or "clap"), the left hemisphere will go through all kinds of contortions (*mental gymnastics*) to make up some plausible story (*rationalize*); in this way it acts to make sense of and explain behavior, much as *press agents* do for the company or person they represent.

Page 62: From simply looking at the two hemispheres, which *appear alike* to the *naked eye,* who would suppose that they contribute so uniquely to *the harmony of the whole?* Myers points out that research with split-brain people and normal people shows that we have unified brains with different parts that have specialized functions. Thus, if we observe the two hemispheres without optical aids (*with the naked eye*), they may appear to be the same (*appear alike*); however, their differential functioning combines to produce an integrated unit (*the harmony of the whole*).

The Endocrine System

Page 63: The endocrine system and nervous system are therefore *kindred* systems. These two systems are very similar and have a close relationship (*kindred systems*). The hormones of the endocrine system are chemically equivalent to neurotransmitters, but operate at a much slower speed. Messages in the nervous system move very rapidly (they zip along as fast as e-mail) compared to endocrine system messages which move relatively slowly (they trudge along like regular or "snail" mail).

Page 64: Conducting and coordinating this whole *electrochemical orchestra* is that *maestro* we call the brain. Myers is comparing the functioning of the neurotransmitters and hormones to a large group of musicians (*electrochemical orchestra*) whose movements and actions are directed by the conductor or master (*maestro*), the brain.

Page 64: Yet what is unknown still *dwarfs* what is known. This means that all that has been discovered so far is very, very small (*dwarfed*) compared to what yet remains to be discovered.

chapter 3

The Nature and Nurture of Behavior

Chapter Overview

Chapter 3 is concerned with the ways in which our biological heritage, or nature, interacts with our individual experiences, or nurture, to shape who we are. After a brief explanation of basic terminology, the chapter discusses psychology's use of evolutionary principles to answer universal questions about human behavior. The next section explores the field of behavior genetics, which studies twins and adopted children to weigh genetic and environmental influences on behaviors.

The third section of the chapter shifts the spotlight to focus on environmental influences on behavior. The impact of parents, the prenatal environment, early experience, peers, and culture on the development of the brain and behavior are each discussed in depth. The final section of the chapter explores how genes and environment interact to shape both the biological and social aspects of our gender. In the end, the message is clear: our genes and our experience together form who we are.

NOTE: Answer guidelines for all Chapter 3 questions begin on page 79.

Genes: Our Biological Blueprint (pp. 69–70)

> David Myers at times uses idioms that are unfamiliar to some readers. If you do not know the meaning of the following word in the context in which it appears in the text, refer to page 86 for an explanation: *blueprint*.

Section Preview

First, skim this section, noting headings and boldface items. Then read the following objectives and, as you read the section, search for the information that will enable you to meet each objective. Answer guidelines are provided on page 79.

1. Identify the mechanisms of heredity.

2. Explain why geneticists and psychologists are interested in the commonalities and variations in our genetic makeup.

Stepping Through the Section

After you have read the section, complete the sentences and answer the questions. As you proceed, evaluate your performance by consulting the answers on page 80. Do not continue with the next section until you understand each answer. If you need to, review or reread the section in the textbook before continuing.

1. A fundamental question in psychology deals with the extent to which we are shaped by our heredity, called our _____ , and by our life history, called our _____ .

2. The master plans for development are stored in the _____ . In number, each person inherits _____ of these structures, _____ from each parent. Each is composed of a coiled chain of the molecule _____ .

3. If chromosomes are the "books" of heredity, the "words" that make each of us a distinctive human being are called _____ ; these segments are self-replicating units capable of synthesizing _____ . The sequence of these words is _____ (very different/virtually the same) from person to person.

4. Human traits are influenced by many genes acting together in _____ _____ .

Evolutionary Psychology: Maximizing Fitness
(pp. 70–75)

If you do not know the meaning of any of the following words, phrases, or expressions in the context in which they appear in the text, refer to page 86 for an explanation: *cash-strapped; tight genetic leash; In our ancestral history, females most often sent their genes into the future by pairing wisely, men by pairing widely; stick-around dads over likely cads; mobile gene machines.*

Section Preview

Answer guidelines are provided on page 80.

1. Explain the scope of evolutionary psychology, focusing on the importance of the concept of natural selection.

2. Discuss gender differences in sexuality, and outline the evolutionary explanation for these differences.

3. Identify several criticisms of evolutionary explanations of gender differences in sexuality.

Stepping Through the Section

Answers are provided on page 80.

1. According to the principle of _____ _____ , traits that contribute to reproduction and survival will be most likely to be passed on to succeeding generations.

2. Genetic _____ are random errors in genetic replication that are the source of all genetic _____ .

3. Genetic constraints on human behavior are generally _____ (tighter/looser) than those on animal behavior. The human species' adaptive _____ in responding to different _____ contributes to our _____ , defined as our ability to _____ and _____ .

4. Researchers who study natural selection and the adaptive nature of human behavior are called _____ _____ . The principles of natural selection favor behaviors that spread one's _____ .

5. Compared to females, males are _____ (equally/more/less) likely to desire more sex, and they are _____ (equally/more/less) likely to initiate sexual activity. This is an example of a _____ difference. These differences _____ (also characterize/do not characterize) homosexual people.

6. The _____ explanation of gender differences in attitudes toward sex is based on differences in the optimal strategy by which women and men pass on their _____ . According to this view, males and females _____ (are/are not) selected for different patterns of sexuality.

7. Cross-cultural research reveals that men judge women as more attractive if they have a _____ appearance, whereas women judge men who appear _____ , _____ , _____ , and _____ as more attractive.

8. Critics of the evolutionary explanation of the gender sexuality difference argue that it often works _____ (forward/backward) to propose a _____ explanation. Another critique is that gender differences in sexuality vary with _____ expectations and social and family structures. Gender differences in mate preferences are largest in cultures characterized by greater gender _____ (equality/inequality).

Behavior Genetics: Predicting Individual Differences (pp. 75–81)

> If you do not know the meaning of any of the following words, phrases, or expressions in the context in which they appear in the text, refer to pages 86–87 for an explanation: *To disentangle the threads of heredity and environment, behavior geneticists often use two sets of tweezers; blue-collar families; startling twin similarity stories; Genes-R-Us; the area of a field is more the result of its length or width.*

Section Preview

Answer guidelines are provided on page 80.

1. Describe the focus of behavior genetics, and explain why researchers use twin and adoption studies to study individual differences.

2. Discuss the origins of temperament, and explain the concept of gene-environment interaction.

Stepping Through the Section

Answers begin on page 80.

1. Researchers who specifically study the effects of genes on behavior are called _____ _____ . As used by these researchers, the term *environment* refers to every _____ influence.

2. To study the power and limits of genetic influences on behavior, researchers use _____ and _____ studies.

3. Twins who developed from a single egg are genetically _____. Twins who developed from different fertilized eggs are no more genetically alike than siblings and are called _____ twins. In terms of the personality traits of extraversion and neuroticism, identical twins are _____ (more/no more) alike than are fraternal twins.

4. Through research on identical twins raised apart, psychologists are able to study the influence of the _____ .

5. Studies tend to show that the personalities of adopted children _____ (do/do not) closely resemble those of their adoptive parents. Still, adoption studies show that parenting _____ (does/does not) matter. For example, adoptive children often score _____ (higher/lower) than their biological parents on intelligence tests.

6. The term that refers to the inborn personality, especially the child's emotional excitability, is _____ , which _____ (does/does not) endure over time.

7. Faced with a new or strange situation, high-strung infants become _____ (more/less) physiologically aroused than less excitable infants.

8. Our biologically rooted temperament helps form our enduring _____ .

9. Heritable individual differences _____ (imply/need not imply) heritable group differences.

10. For _____ traits, human differences are nearly always the result of both _____ and _____ influences.

11. Throughout life, we are the product of the _____ of our _____ predispositions and our surrounding _____ .

Environmental Influence (pp. 82–89)

> If you do not know the meaning of any of the following words, phrases, or expressions in the context in which they appear in the text, refer to pages 87–88 for an explanation: *as a potter molds clay; while the excess connections are still on call; pathways through a forest; wiring of Eric Clapton's brain; shuffle their gene decks; cerebral hard drive . . . cultural software; norms grease the social machinery; cultures collide.*

Section Preview

Answer guidelines are provided on page 81.

1. Discuss the effect of parental behavior and the prenatal environment on person-to-person differences in children's personalities.

2. Describe the role of experience on brain development and the socializing influence of peers on children and youth.

3. Discuss the effect of culture on behavior and child-rearing practices.

Stepping Through the Section

Answers are provided on page 81.

1. Genetic influences explain about _____ percent of individual variations in many personality traits.

2. Children's shared environmental influences—including the same home influences—typically account for less than _____ percent of their personality differences.

3. Environmental influences begin during the period of _____ development. Even identical twins may differ in this respect, because they may or may not share the same

   _____ .

4. Rosenzweig and Krech discovered that rats raised from a young age in enriched environments had _____ (thicker/thinner) cortexes than animals raised in isolation.

Describe the effects of sensory stimulation on neural development.

5. Experiences with _____ have a powerful effect on how children develop, partly as a result of a "_____ effect" by which kids seek out others with similar attitudes and interests.

6. The enduring behaviors, ideas, attitudes, and traditions of a group of people and transmitted from one generation to the next defines the group's

   _____ .

7. All cultural groups evolve their own rules for expected behavior, called _____ . For example, one such rule involves the buffer zone that people maintain around their bodies, called _____ _____ .

Identify several cultural differences in personal space, expressiveness, and pace of life.

8. Whereas most Western parents place more emphasis on _____ (emotional closeness/independence) in their children, many Asian and African parents focus on cultivating _____ (emotional closeness/independence).

9. Most Westernized cultures are noted for their _____ , whereas many Asian, African, and Central and South American countries favor _____ .

10. In general, differences between groups are _____ (smaller/larger) than person-to-person differences within groups. Differences sometimes attributed to _____ may actually result from other factors.

The Nature and Nurture of Gender and Postscript: Reflections on Nature and Nurture (pp. 90–95)

If you do not know the meaning of any of the following words, phrases, or expressions in the context in which they appear in the text, refer to page 88 for an explanation: *throws a master switch; initiated dates . . . picked up the check; With the flick of an apron; won the day; boggles the mind.*

Section Preview

Answer guidelines begin on page 81.

1. Explain how nature defines our gender.

2. Explain how gender is also socially constructed.

3. Summarize the results and implications of research on the nature/nurture issue.

Stepping Through the Section

Answers are provided on page 82.

1. The twenty-third pair of chromosomes determines the developing person's _____ . The mother always contributes a(n) _____ chromosome. When the father contributes a(n) _____ chromosome, the testes begin producing the hormone _____ . Females _____ (do/do not) also have this hormone. At about the _____ (what week?), this hormone initiates the development of external male sex organs.

2. Different brain-wiring patterns for males and females develop during the _____ (what number?) prenatal months.

3. Our expectations about the way men and women behave define our culture's _____ _____ .

4. Gender roles _____ (are/are not) rigidly fixed by evolution, as evidenced by the fact that they vary across _____ and over _____ . For instance, in _____ societies there tends to be minimal division of labor by sex; by contrast, in _____ societies, women remain close to home while men roam freely, herding cattle or sheep.

5. Our individual sense of being male or female is called our _____ _____ . The degree to which we exhibit traditionally male or female traits and interests is called _____-_____ .

6. According to _____ _____ theory, children learn gender-linked behaviors by observing others and being rewarded or punished. When their families discourage traditional gender-typing, children _____ (do/do not) organize themselves into "boy worlds" and "girl worlds."

7. A later version of this theory, called _____-_____ theory, recognizes the importance of children's developing gender _____ .

8. So, too, does _____ _____ theory, which combines _____ _____ theory with _____ . According to this theory, children learn from their _____ what it means to be male or female and adjust their behavior accordingly.

Progress Test 1

Multiple-Choice Questions

Circle your answers to the following questions and check them with the answers beginning on page 82. If your answer is incorrect, read the explanation for why it is incorrect and then consult the appropriate pages of the text (in parentheses following the correct answer).

1. Dr. Ross believes that principles of natural selection help explain why infants come to fear strangers about the time they become mobile. Dr. Ross is most likely a(n):
   a. behavior geneticist.
   b. molecular geneticist.
   c. evolutionary psychologist.
   d. molecular biologist.

2. A pair of adopted children or identical twins reared in the same home are most likely to have similar:
   a. temperaments.
   b. personalities.
   c. religious beliefs.
   d. emotional reactivity.

3. The sequence of genes and DNA:
   a. is virtually the same in all humans.
   b. is virtually the same throughout the animal kingdom.
   c. varies from race to race.
   d. is more similar among females than among males.

4. If a fraternal twin becomes schizophrenic, the likelihood of the other twin developing serious mental illness is much lower than with identical twins. This suggests that:
   a. schizophrenia is caused by genes.
   b. schizophrenia is influenced by genes.
   c. environment is unimportant in the development of schizophrenia.
   d. identical twins are especially vulnerable to mental disorders.

5. Of the following, the best way to separate the effects of genes and environment in research is to study:
   a. fraternal twins.
   b. identical twins.
   c. adopted children and their adoptive parents.
   d. identical twins raised in different environments.

6. Through natural selection, the traits that are most likely to be passed on to succeeding generations are those that contribute to:
   a. reproduction.   d. a. and b.
   b. survival.   e. a., b., and c.
   c. aggressiveness.

7. Which of the following is *not* true regarding gender and sexuality?
   a. Men more often than women make sacrifices to gain sex.
   b. Women are more likely than men to cite affection as a reason for first intercourse.
   c. Men are more likely than females to initiate sexual activity.
   d. Gender differences in sexuality are noticeably absent among gay men and lesbian women.

8. Evolutionary psychologists attribute gender differences in sexuality to the fact that women have:
   a. greater reproductive potential than do men.
   b. lower reproductive potential than do men.
   c. weaker sex drives than men.
   d. stronger sex drives than men.

9. According to evolutionary psychology, men are drawn sexually to women who seem _____ , while women are attracted to men who seem _____ .
   a. nurturing; youthful
   b. youthful and fertile; mature and affluent
   c. slender; muscular
   d. exciting; dominant

10. Unlike _____ twins, who develop from a single fertilized egg, _____ twins develop from separate fertilized eggs.
    a. fraternal; identical
    b. identical; fraternal
    c. placental; nonplacental
    d. nonplacental; placental

11. Temperament refers to a person's characteristic:
    a. emotional reactivity and intensity.
    b. attitudes.
    c. behaviors.
    d. role-related traits.

12. When evolutionary psychologists use the word "fitness," they are specifically referring to:
    a. an animal's ability to adapt to changing environments.
    b. the diversity of a species' gene pool.
    c. the total number of members of the species currently alive.
    d. our ability to survive and reproduce.

13. In a hypothetical world where all schools are of uniform quality, all families equally loving, and all neighborhoods equally healthy, the heritability of person-to-person differences would be:
    a. large.
    b. small.
    c. zero.
    d. unpredictable.

14. Westernized cultures such as that of the United States are noted for:
    a. individualism.
    b. collectivism.
    c. interdependence.
    d. all of the above.

15. Which of the following most accurately expresses the extent of parental influence on personality?
    a. It is more extensive than most people believe.
    b. It is weaker today than in the past.
    c. It is more limited than popular psychology supposes.
    d. It is almost completely unpredictable.

16. Gender refers to:
    a. the biological and social definition of male and female.
    b. the biological definition of male and female.
    c. one's sense of being male or female.
    d. the extent to which one exhibits traditionally male or female traits.

17. The fertilized egg will develop into a boy if, at conception:
    a. the sperm contributes an X chromosome.
    b. the sperm contributes a Y chromosome.
    c. the egg contributes an X chromosome.
    d. the egg contributes a Y chromosome.

18. Which theory states that gender becomes a lens through which children view their experiences?
    a. social learning theory
    b. Vygotsky's sociocultural theory
    c. Piaget's theory
    d. gender schema theory

19. The hormone testosterone:
    a. is found only in females.
    b. determines the sex of the developing person.
    c. stimulates growth of the female sex organs.
    d. stimulates growth of the male sex organs.

20. Research studies have found that when infant rats and premature human babies are regularly touched or massaged, they:
    a. gain weight more rapidly.
    b. develop faster neurologically.
    c. have more agreeable temperaments.
    d. do a. and b.
    e. do a., b., and c.

Matching Items

Match each term with its corresponding definition or description.

Terms

_____ 1. X chromosome
_____ 2. chromosomes
_____ 3. fraternal
_____ 4. genes
_____ 5. DNA
_____ 6. identical
_____ 7. Y chromosome
_____ 8. gender role
_____ 9. gender identity
_____ 10. gender-typing
_____ 11. gender

Functions or Descriptions

a. the biochemical units of heredity
b. twins that develop from a single egg
c. one's personal sense of being female or male
d. a set of expected behaviors for males and females
e. twins that develop from separate eggs
f. threadlike structures made of DNA
g. biological and social characteristics by which people define male and female
h. the sex chromosome found in both women and men
i. the acquisition of a traditional gender role
j. a complex molecule containing the genetic information that makes up the chromosomes
k. the sex chromosome found only in men

Progress Test 2

Progress Test 2 should be completed during a final chapter review. Answer the following questions after you thoroughly understand the correct answers for the section reviews and Progress Test 1.

Multiple-Choice Questions

1. Each cell of the human body has a total of:
   a. 23 chromosomes.
   b. 23 genes.
   c. 46 chromosomes.
   d. 46 genes.

2. Genes direct our physical development by synthesizing:
   a. nucleotides.
   b. proteins.
   c. DNA.
   d. chromosomes.

3. Taking off street shoes when entering a house in Japan and using only the fingers of your right hand when eating in South Asia are examples of:
   a. norms.
   b. roles.
   c. typing.
   d. schemas.

4. Most human traits are:
   a. learned.
   b. determined by a single gene.
   c. influenced by many genes acting together.
   d. unpredictable.

5. Mutations are random errors in _____ replication that lead to a genetic change.
   a. gene
   b. chromosome
   c. DNA
   d. protein

6. Casual sex is most frequent among:
   a. males with high circulating levels of testosterone.
   b. a majority of males but a minority of females.
   c. females and males who are weakly gender-typed.
   d. females and males who are strongly gender-typed.

7. Evolutionary explanations of gender differences in sexuality have been criticized because:
   a. they offer "after-the-fact" explanations.
   b. standards of attractiveness vary with time and place.
   c. they underestimate cultural influences on sexuality.
   d. of all of the above reasons.

8. Several studies of long-separated identical twins have found that these twins:
   a. have little in common, due to the different environments in which they were raised.
   b. have many similarities, in everything from medical histories to personalities.
   c. have similar personalities, but very different likes, dislikes, and life-styles.
   d. are no more similar than are fraternal twins reared apart.

9. Adoption studies show that the personalities of adopted children:
   a. closely match those of their adoptive parents.
   b. bear more similarities to their biological parents than to their adoptive parents.
   c. closely match those of the biological children of their adoptive parents.
   d. closely match those of other children reared in the same home, whether or not they are biologically related.

10. Of the following, parents are most likely to influence their children's:
    a. temperament.
    b. personality.
    c. faith.
    d. emotional reactivity.

11. Chromosomes are composed of small segments of _____ called _____ .
    a. DNA; genes
    b. DNA; neurotransmitters
    c. genes; DNA
    d. DNA; enzymes

12. When the effect of one factor (such as environment) depends on another (such as heredity), we say there is a(n) _____ between the two factors.
    a. norm
    b. positive correlation
    c. negative correlation
    d. interaction

13. Compared to children raised in Western societies, those raised in communal societies, such as Japan or China:
  a. grow up with a stronger integration of the sense of family into their self-concepts.
  b. exhibit greater shyness toward strangers.
  c. exhibit greater concern for loyalty and social harmony.
  d. have all of the above characteristics.
  e. have none of the above characteristics.

14. The "selection effect" in peer influence refers to the tendency of children and youth to:
  a. naturally separate into same-sex playgroups.
  b. establish large, fluid circles of friends.
  c. seek out friends with similar interests and attitudes.
  d. do all of the above.

15. Which of the following is *not* true regarding cultural diversity?
  a. Culture influences emotional expressiveness.
  b. Culture influences personal space.
  c. Culture does not have a strong influence on how strictly social roles are defined.
  d. All cultures evolve their own norms.

16. Women and men are most likely to be attracted to strongly gender-typed mates in cultures characterized by:
  a. gender inequality.
  b. gender equality.
  c. flexible gender roles.
  d. few norms.

17. An evolutionary psychologist would be most interested in studying:
  a. why most parents are so passionately devoted to their children.
  b. hereditary influences on skin color.
  c. why certain diseases are more common among certain age groups.
  d. genetic differences in personality.

18. Children who are raised by parents who discourage traditional gender-typing:
  a. are less likely to display gender-typed behaviors themselves.
  b. often become confused and develop an ambiguous gender identity.
  c. nevertheless organize themselves into "girl worlds" and "boy worlds."
  d. display excessively masculine and feminine traits as adults.

19. Brain-wiring patterns for males and females undergo a significant period of differentiation during which months of prenatal development?
  a. first and second
  b. fourth and fifth
  c. sixth and seventh
  d. eighth and ninth

20. Providing a child with a stimulating educational environment during early childhood is likely to:
  a. ensure the formation of a strong attachment with parents.
  b. foster the development of a calm, easygoing temperament.
  c. prevent neural connections from degenerating.
  d. do all of the above.

True–False Items

Indicate whether each statement is true or false by placing *T* (*True*) or *F* (*False*) in the blank next to the item.

_____ 1. Gender differences in mate preferences vary widely from one culture to another.

_____ 2. The most emotionally reactive newborns tend to be the most restrained 9-month-olds.

_____ 3. As environments become less similar, heredity as a source of differences becomes more important.

_____ 4. Compared to identical twins reared in different families, fraternal twins recall their early family life more differently.

_____ 5. Parents have a stronger influence than do peers on whether a youth starts smoking.

_____ 6. Nature selects behavior tendencies that increase the likelihood of sending one's genes into the future.

_____ 7. Genetic influences explain roughly 40 to 50 percent of our individual variations in many personality traits.

_____ 8. Parental influence on personality is more limited than popular psychology supposes.

_____ 9. North Americans prefer more personal space than do Latin Americans.

_____ 10. Lacking any exposure to language before adolescence, a person will never master any language.

Review and Reflect

Answer these questions the day before an exam as a final check on your understanding of the chapter's terms and concepts.

Multiple-Choice Questions

1. If chromosomes are the _____ of heredity, the "words" are the _____ .

   a. books; genes
   b. words; genes
   c. letters; DNA
   d. words; DNA

2. Like other Asian women, Noriko is most likely to feel attracted to men who seem:

   a. healthy and fertile.
   b. healthy, mature, and dominant.
   c. youthful.
   d. any of the above; it is impossible to predict the features that attract one person to another.

3. After comparing divorce rates among identical and fraternal twins, Dr. Alexander has concluded that genes do play a role. Dr. Alexander is most likely a(n):

   a. evolutionary psychologist.
   b. behavior geneticist.
   c. social learning theorist.
   d. divorcee.

4. Despite growing up in the same home environment, Karen and her brother John have personalities as different from each other as two people selected randomly from the population. Why is this so?

   a. Personality is inherited. Because Karen and John are not identical twins, it is not surprising they have very different personalities.
   b. Gender is the most important factor in personality. If Karen had a sister, the two of them would probably be much more alike.
   c. The interaction of their individual genes and nonshared experiences accounts for the common finding that children in the same family are usually very different.
   d. Their case is unusual; children in the same family usually have similar personalities.

5. I am a rat whose cortex is lighter and thinner than my litter mates. What happened to me?

   a. You were born prematurely.
   b. You suffer from fetal alcohol syndrome.
   c. You were raised in an enriched environment.

   d. You were raised in a deprived environment.
   e. You did not imprint during the critical period.

6. Chad, who grew up in the United States, is more likely to encourage _____ in his future children than Asian-born Hidiyaki, who is more likely to encourage _____ in his future children.

   a. obedience; independence
   b. independence; emotional closeness
   c. emotional closeness; obedience
   d. loyalty; emotional closeness

7. One of the best ways to distinguish how much genetic and environmental factors affect behavior is to compare children who have:

   a. the same genes and environments.
   b. different genes and environments.
   c. similar genes and environments.
   d. similar genes and similar families.
   e. the same genes but different environments.

8. My sibling and I developed from a single fertilized egg. Who are we?

   a. opposite sex identical twins.
   b. same-sex identical twins.
   c. opposite sex fraternal twins.
   d. same-sex fraternal twins.

9. A psychologist working from the evolutionary perspective is likely to suggest that people are biologically predisposed to:

   a. protect their offspring.
   b. fear heights.
   c. be attracted to fertile-appearing members of the opposite sex.
   d. do all of the above.

10. Shay, who is an impulsive and aggressive young man, probably had an infant temperament characterized by:

    a. emotional inhibition.
    b. fear.
    c. emotional reactivity.
    d. any of the above; it is impossible to predict.

11. Concluding her presentation on gender roles, Marla notes that:

    a. gender roles are fixed by evolution.
    b. in nomadic societies of food-gathering people, there is minimal division of labor by sex.
    c. in agricultural societieis, boys and girls receive much the same upbringing.
    d. all of the above are true.

12. Of the relatively few genetic differences among humans _____ are differences among races.
    a. less than 1 percent
    b. less than 10 percent
    c. approximately 25 percent
    d. approximately 40 to 50 percent

13. Responding to the argument that gender differences are often by-products of a culture's social and family structures, an evolutionary psychologist is most likely to point to:
    a. our great human capacity for learning.
    b. the tendency of cultural arguments to reinforce traditional gender inequalities.
    c. the infallibility of "hindsight" explanations.
    d. all of the above.

14. A person whose twin has Alzheimer's disease has _____ risk of sharing the disease if they are identical twins than if they are fraternal twins.
    a. less
    b. about the same
    c. much greater
    d. an unpredictable amount of

15. Which of the following is an example of an interaction?
    a. Swimmers swim fastest during competition against other swimmers.
    b. Swimmers with certain personality traits swim fastest during competition, while those with other personality traits swim fastest during solo time trials.
    c. As the average daily temperature increases, sales of ice cream decrease.
    d. As the average daily temperature increases, sales of lemonade increase.

16. Which of the following most accurately summarizes the findings of the 40-year fox-breeding study described in the text?
    a. Wild wolves cannot be domesticated.
    b. "Survival of the fittest" seems to operate only when animals live in their natural habitats.
    c. By mating aggressive and unaggressive foxes, the researchers created a mutant species.
    d. By selecting and mating the tamest males and females, the researchers have produced affectionate, unaggressive offspring.

17. Compared to men, women are more likely to:
    a. be concerned with their partner's physical attractiveness.
    b. initiate sexual activity.

    c. cite "liking one another" as a justification for having sex in a new relationship.
    d. be less accepting of casual sex.

18. When his son cries because another child has taken his favorite toy, Brandon admonishes him by saying, "Big boys don't cry." Evidently, Brandon is an advocate of _____ in accounting for the development of gender-linked behaviors.
    a. gender schema theory
    b. gender identity theory
    c. gender-typing theory
    d. social learning theory

19. The fact that after age 2, language forces children to begin organizing their worlds on the basis of gender is most consistent with which theory of how gender-linked behaviors develop?
    a. gender schema theory
    b. gender identity theory
    c. gender-typing theory
    d. social learning theory

20. Three-year-old Jack is inhibited and shy. As an adult, Jack is likely to be:
    a. cautious and unassertive.
    b. spontaneous and fearless.
    c. socially assertive.
    d. Who knows? This aspect of personality is not very stable over the life span.

Essay Question

Lakia's new boyfriend has been pressuring her to become more sexually intimate than she wants to at this early stage in their relationship. Strongly gender-typed and "macho" in attitude, Jerome is becoming increasingly frustrated with Lakia's hesitation, while Lakia is starting to wonder if a long-term relationship with this type of man is what she really wants. In light of your understanding of the evolutionary explanation of gender differences in sexuality, explain why the tension between Lakia and Jerome would be considered understandable. (Use the space below to list the points you want to make, and organize them. Then write the essay on a separate sheet of paper.)

Key Terms

Writing Definitions

Using your own words, on a piece of paper write a brief definition or explanation of each of the following terms.

1. chromosomes

2. DNA

3. genes

4. natural selection

5. mutation

6. evolutionary psychology

7. gender

8. behavior genetics

9. environment

10. identical twins

11. fraternal twins

12. temperament

13. interaction

14. culture

15. norm

16. personal space

17. X chromosome

18. Y chromosome

19. testosterone

20. role

21. gender role

22. gender identity

23. gender-typing

24. social learning theory

25. gender schema theory

Cross-Check

As you learned in the Prologue, reviewing and overlearning of material are important to the learning process. After you have written the definitions of the key terms in this chapter, you should complete the crossword puzzle to ensure that you can reverse the process—recognize the term, given the definition.

ACROSS

6. Parents whose personalities bear little relevance to their children's personalities.
7. Complex molecule containing the genetic information that makes up the chromosomes.
9. Set of expected behaviors for those who occupy a particular social position.
10. An understood rule for expected and accepted behavior.
11. The biological and social characteristics by which people define male and female.
12. The enduring behaviors, ideas, attitudes, and traditions shared by a large group of people.
13. Environmental influences on behavior.
14. According to the evolutionary perspective, women are drawn to healthy-looking men who are also _____ .
15. Behavior geneticists often compare the traits of adopted children to those of their _____ parents.
16. Source of all genetic diversity.
19. Threadlike structure made up largely of DNA molecules.

DOWN

1. The study of the relative power and limits of genetic and environmental influences on behavior.
2. Subfield of psychology that uses principles of natural selection to explore human traits and behaviors.
3. When the effect of one factor depends on another factor.
4. Any nongenetic influence.
5. A lens through which children organize their understanding of being male or female.
8. One's personal sense of being female or male.

17. Another word for heredity.
18. Segments of DNA capable of synthesizing proteins.

Answers

Genes: Our Biological Blueprint

Section Preview

1. When a mature egg is fertilized by a sperm, the 23 chromosomes carried in the egg pair up with the 23 chromosomes of the sperm. Each chromosome is composed of long threads of a DNA molecule; DNA is made of thousands of genes that determine development by directing the synthesis of proteins.

2. Geneticists and psychologists are interested in our genetic commonalities and variations because they tell them why one person has a disease and another does not, why one person is short and another is tall. Knowing why, they may find ways to treat physical and psychological problems.

Stepping Through the Section

1. nature; nurture
2. chromosomes; 46; 23; DNA
3. genes; proteins; virtually the same
4. gene complexes

Evolutionary Psychology: Maximizing Fitness

Section Preview

1. Evolutionary psychologists study how natural selection favors behavioral tendencies and thinking and learning capacities that contributed to the survival and spread of our ancestors' genes. Natural selection works on random errors in gene replication (mutations), which are the basis of genetic diversity.

2. Throughout the world, gender differences in sexuality are apparent. Men are more likely than females to initiate sexual activity, they are more accepting of casual sex, and they report thinking about sex more often than women do. According to evolutionary psychologists, these differences may be grounded in biology. Because sperm are much more plentiful than eggs, natural selection may have favored different mating strategies and attitudes toward sex in males and females. As support for this argument, they suggest that while men are drawn to healthy, fertile-appearing women, women feel attracted to men who seem mature, dominant, bold, and affluent.

3. Critics of evolutionary explanations of human behavior note that such explanations often start with an effect (such as the gender sexuality difference) and work backward to propose an explanation. Critics also point to the fact that standards of attractiveness vary with time and place, indicating that cultural expectations also shape sexuality. Finally, gender differences in mate preferences are larger in cultures with gender inequality than in those characterized by gender equality.

Stepping Through the Section

1. natural selection
2. mutations; diversity
3. looser; flexibility; environments; fitness; survive; reproduce
4. evolutionary psychologists; genes
5. more; more; gender; also characterize
6. evolutionary; genes; are
7. youthful; mature; dominant; bold; affluent
8. backward; hindsight; cultural; inequality

Behavior Genetics: Predicting Individual Differences

Section Preview

1. Behavior geneticists focus on our individual differences and the extent to which they are shaped by genetic and environmental influences. Because identical twins are genetically identical, the findings that they are more similar in a trait than fraternal twins or other siblings suggest that there is a substantial genetic influence on that trait. Studies of identical twins who were separated and raised by different families reinforce this point. In this way, twin studies provide psychologists with a greater understanding of the role of genes in our behaviors. Critics of twin studies contend that twin similarities may merely be coincidental rather than a reflection of heredity. Moreover, because adoption agencies tend to place separated twins in similar homes, critics argue that similarities in traits may reflect the impact of similar experiences rather than heredity alone.

   Adoption studies enable psychologists to determine the relative influence of nature and nurture on development by asking whether adopted children are more like their biological parents, who contribute their genes, or their adoptive parents, who contribute a home environment. Such studies show that, although the personalities of adopted children do not much resemble their adoptive parents, parents do influence children's attitudes, values, manners, faith, and politics.

2. Temperament refers to a person's characteristic emotional reactivity and intensity. Research studies with both humans and animals demonstrate that heredity seems to predispose differences in temperament. Anxious, high-strung infants become more physiologically aroused when facing new or strange situations. Moreover, identical twins are more likely to have similar temperaments.

   Because genes and experience interact in influencing development, it is incorrect to say that a certain trait is x percent due to genes and y percent due to experience. It is also incorrect to interpret heritable individual differences in specific traits as evidence of heritable group differences in those traits.

Stepping Through the Section

1. behavior geneticists; nongenetic
2. twin; adoption
3. identical; fraternal; more

4. environment

5. do not; does; higher

6. temperament; does

7. more

8. personality

9. need not imply

10. psychological; genetic; environmental

11. interaction; genetic; environment

Environmental Influence

Section Preview

1. A widely held belief is that parental nurture is as important as genetic influences in shaping a child's personality. However, behavior geneticists have repeatedly found that shared environmental influences, including the home environment that siblings share, typically account for less than 10 percent of their personality differences. To some developmental psychologists, this implies that parents should be given less credit (and less blame) for the way their kids turn out.

   Another early environmental influence that researchers are investigating is the prenatal environment. Because some twins have separate placentas, even those who are genetically identical may develop in environments that vary in nourishment and protection against viruses. These differences may partly explain later differences in their psychological traits.

2. Sights, smells, touches, and other experiences foster the development of neural connections within the brain. In a classic study, rats who were raised in an enriched environment developed heavier and thicker brain cortexes than did those raised in an impoverished environment. Other studies have found that premature infants and laboratory animals who receive extra handling and a variety of experiences develop faster neurologically than those raised in deprived environments.

   Experiences with peers powerfully socialize children and youth, in part as a result of a "selection effect," in which kids seek out peers with similar attitudes and interests.

3. A culture is the enduring traditions, behaviors, ideas, and attitudes shared by a group of people and passed from one generation to the next. All cultural groups evolve their own norms for acceptable and expected behavior. Because of differing norms for personal space, expressiveness, and pace of life, for example, misunderstandings are commonplace. Cultural differences in child-rearing are another case in point. Unlike most Westerners, who now raise their children to be independent, many Asians and Africans live in communal cultures that focus on cultivating social harmony and emotional closeness.

   Cultural norms change over time. Today, parents in Western societies place more emphasis on raising independent children than they did several generations earlier. Despite variations across culture and time, however, we must not lose sight of our human kinship. Compared with person-to-person differences within groups, the differences between groups are small.

Stepping Through the Section

1. 40 to 50

2. 10

3. prenatal; placenta

4. thicker

Research has shown that infant rats and premature babies given extra sensory stimulation gain weight more rapidly and develop faster neurologically. Throughout life, sensory stimulation activates and strengthens particular neural connections, while other connections weaken with disuse. In this way, our experiences shape the very structure of the neural pathways that process those experiences.

5. peers; selection

6. culture

7. norms; personal space

Most North Americans, the British, and Scandinavians prefer more personal space than do Latin Americans, Arabs, and the French. Cultural differences in expressiveness and the pace of life often create misunderstandings. For example, people with northern European roots may perceive people from Mediterranean cultures as warm and charming but inefficient, while Mediterraneans may see the northern Europeans as efficient but emotionally cold.

8. independence; emotional closeness

9. individualism; collectivism

10. smaller; race

The Nature and Nurture of Gender and Postscript: Reflections on Nature and Nurture

Section Preview

1. Our biological sex is determined by the twenty-third pair of chromosomes, the sex chromosomes, one of which comes from each parent. The mother always contributes an X chromosome. The father's sperm contributes an X or a Y chromo-

some; with an X chromosome, the developing person becomes a girl; with a Y chromosome, a boy develops. The Y chromosome contains a single gene that triggers the testes to develop and produce the principal male hormone, testosterone, which, at about the seventh week, starts the development of external male organs.

2. Gender is also socially constructed; gender roles are our expectations about the way men and women behave. Gender identity is our personal sense of being male or female. Gender-typing, which refers to the acquisition of a traditional masculine or feminine role, has been alternatively explained by social learning theory and by gender schema theory. According to social learning theory, children acquire gender-linked behaviors by observing and imitating others and by being rewarded or punished. Gender schema theory assumes that the child's culture transmits a copy of what it means to be male or female. The child then adjusts his or her behavior to fit the concept.

3. While it is true that genes form us, it is also true that our experiences in families and social relationships teach us ways of thinking and acting. Moreover, differences initiated by our nature may be amplified by our nurture, as, for example, when cultural norms regarding masculinity and femininity encourage men and women to act differently. It is equally true that humans are an open system. Although genes and culture are pervasive influences, they are not immutable forces.

Stepping Through the Section

1. sex; X; Y; testosterone; do; seventh
2. fourth and fifth
3. gender roles
4. are not; cultures; time; nomadic; agricultural
5. gender identity; gender-typing
6. social learning; do
7. social-cognitive; conceptions
8. gender schema; social learning; cognition; schemas

Progress Test 1

Multiple-Choice Questions

1. **c.** is the answer. (p. 71)
   a. & d. Whereas evolutionary psychologists attempt to explain universal human tendencies, these researchers investigate genetic differences among individuals.

   b. Molecular genetics was not discussed in the text.

2. **c.** is the answer. Research has not shown a strong parental influence on personality, temperament, or emotional reactivity. (p. 79)

3. **a.** is the answer. (p. 70)
   b. The text does not address this issue.
   c. & d. More than 99.9 percent of our DNA matches that of all other humans, regardless of race and gender.

4. **b.** is the answer. (p. 76)
   a. & c. Although an identical twin is at increased risk, the relationship is far from perfect. Mental disorders, like all psychological traits, are influenced by *both* nature and nurture.
   d. This is not at all implied by the evidence from twin studies.

5. **d.** is the answer. (p. 77)
   a., b., & c. In order to pinpoint the influence of one of the two factors (genes and environment), it is necessary to hold one of the factors constant.

6. **d.** is the answer. (pp. 71–72)
   c. Natural selection favors traits that send one's genes into the future, such as surviving longer and reproducing more often. Aggression does not necessarily promote either.

7. **d.** is the answer. Such gender differences characterize both heterosexual and homosexual people. (p. 73)

8. **b.** is the answer. Women can incubate only one infant at a time. (p. 73)
   c. & d. The text does not suggest that there is a gender difference in the strength of the sex drive.

9. **b.** is the answer. (p. 73)
   a. According to this perspective, women prefer mates with the potential for long-term nurturing investment in their joint offspring.
   c. While men are drawn to women whose waists are roughly a third narrower than their hips, the text does not suggest that women equate muscularity with fertility.
   d. Excitement was not mentioned as a criterion for mating.

10. **b.** is the answer. (p. 76)
    c. & d. There are no such things as "placental" or "nonplacental"" twins. All twins have a placenta during prenatal development.

11. **a.** is the answer. (p. 79)

12. **d.** is the answer. (p. 71)
    a. Survival ability is only one aspect of fitness.
    b. & c. Neither of these is related to fitness.

13. **a.** is the answer. (p. 80)

b., c., & d. This hypothetical world is one in which there is no environmental variation. Therefore, any individual differences are predictably due to genes.

14. **a.** is the answer. (p. 88)
    c. Interdependence is emphasized in cultures characterized by collectivism.

15. **c.** is the answer. (p. 82)

16. **a.** is the answer. (p. 72)
    c. This defines gender identity.
    d. This defines gender-typing.

17. **b.** is the answer. (p. 90)
    a. In this case, a female would develop.
    c. & d. The egg can contribute only an X chromosome. Thus, the sex of the child is determined by which chromosome the sperm contributes.

18. **d.** is the answer. (p. 92)
    a. According to social learning theory, gender-typing evolves through imitation and reinforcement.
    b. & c. Neither theorist is discussed in this chapter. Moreover, neither proposed a theory of gender-typing.

19. **d.** is the answer. (p. 90)
    a. Although testosterone is the principal male hormone, it is present in both females and males.
    b. This is determined by the sex chromosomes.
    c. In the absence of testosterone, female sex organs will develop.

20. **d.** is the answer. (p. 84)

Matching Items

1. h (p. 90)   5. j (p. 69)   9. c (p. 92)
2. f (p. 69)   6. b (p. 76)   10. i (p. 92)
3. e (p. 76)   7. k (p. 90)   11. g (p. 72)
4. a (p. 69)   8. d (p. 90)

Progress Test 2

Multiple-Choice Questions

1. **c.** is the answer. (p. 69)
   b. & d. Each cell of the human body contains hundreds of genes.

2. **b.** is the answer. (p. 69)
   a., c., & d. Nucleotides define DNA, segments of which comprise genes and chromosomes.

3. **a.** is the answer. (p. 87)

4. **c.** is the answer. (p. 70)

5. **a.** is the answer. (p. 71)

6. **b.** is the answer. (p. 72)

a. Testosterone levels have not been linked to the frequency of casual sex.
c. & d. Males are far more accepting of casual sex than are females.

7. **d.** is the answer. (pp. 74–75)

8. **b.** is the answer. (pp. 76–77)
   a., c., & d. Despite being raised in different environments, long-separated identical twins often have much in common, including likes, dislikes, and life-styles. This indicates the significant heritability of many traits.

9. **b.** is the answer. (p. 78)
   a., c., & d. The personalities of adopted children do not much resemble those of their adoptive parents (therefore, not a.) or other children reared in the same home (therefore, not c. or d.).

10. **c.** is the answer. (p. 82)
    a. & d. Temperament, which refers to a person's emotional reactivity, is determined primarily by genes.
    b. Genes limit parents' influence on their children's personalities.

11. **a.** is the answer. (p. 69)
    b. Neurotransmitters are the chemicals involved in synaptic transmission in the nervous system.
    d. Enzymes are chemicals that facilitate various chemical reactions throughout the body but are not involved in heredity.

12. **d.** is the answer. (p. 81)
    a. A norm is a culturally determined set of expected behaviors for a particular role, such as a gender role.
    b. & c. When two factors are correlated, it means either that increases in one factor are accompanied by increases in the other (positive correlation) or increases in one factor are accompanied by decreases in the other (negative correlation).

13. **d.** is the answer. (p. 88)

14. **c.** is the answer. (p. 85)

15. **c.** is the answer. (pp. 86–87)

16. **a.** is the answer. (p. 75)
    b. In such cultures gender differences in mate preferences tend to be much smaller.
    c. Although flexibility in gender roles was not discussed per se, it is likely that greater flexibility would equate with greater equality in gender roles.
    d. All cultures develop norms.

17. **a.** is the answer. This is an example of a trait that contributes to survival of the human species and the perpetuation of one's genes. (pp. 71–72)
    b., c., & d. These traits and issues would likely be of greater interest to a behavior geneticist, since

they concern the influence of specific genes on behavior.

18. **c.** is the answer. (p. 92)
b. & d. There is no evidence that being raised in a "gender neutral" home confuses children or fosters a backlash of excessive gender-typing.

19. **b** is the answer. (p. 90)

20. **c.** is the answer. (p. 83)
a. Although early experiences are a factor in the development of attachment (discussed in a later chapter), educational stimulation is probably less important than warmth and nurturance.
b. Because temperament appears to be a strongly genetic trait, it is unlikely that early educational experiences would affect its nature.

True–False Items

1. F (p. 73)	**5.** F (p. 85)	**9.** T (p. 87)
2. F (p. 79)	**6.** T (p. 71)	**10.** T (p. 84)
3. F (p. 80)	**7.** T (p. 82)	
4. T (p. 81)	**8.** T (p. 82)	

Review and Reflect

Multiple-Choice Questions

1. **a.** is the answer. (p. 69)

2. **b.** is the answer. (p. 73)
a. & c. These are characteristics of women that are most likely to attract men.

3. **b.** is the answer. (p. 75)
a. Evolutionary psychologists study the evolution of behavior using the principles of natural selection.
c. Social learning theorists focus on the effect of the environment on behavior.
d. Who knows?

4. **c.** is the answer. (pp. 80–81)
a. Although heredity does influence certain traits, such as outgoingness and emotional instability, it is the interaction of heredity and experience that ultimately molds personality.
b. There is no single "most important factor" in personality. Moreover, for the same reason two sisters or brothers often have dissimilar personalities, a sister and brother may be very much alike.
d. Karen and John's case is not at all unusual.

5. **d.** is the answer. (p. 83)
a. & b. Premature birth and fetal alcohol syndrome (discussed in a later chapter) usually do not have this effect on the developing brain.

c. If the question had stated "I have a heavier and thicker cortex," this answer would be correct.
e. Imprinting, which is discussed in the next chapter, has no effect on brain cells.

6. **b.** is the answer. Although parental values differ from one time and place to another, studies reveal that Western parents today want their children to think for themselves, while Asian and African parents place greater value on emotional closeness. (p. 88)
d. Both of these values are more typical of Asian than Western cultures.

7. **e.** is the answer. To separate the influences of heredity and experience on behavior, one of the two must be held constant. (p. 77)
a., b., c., & d. These situations would not allow one to separate the contributions of heredity and environment.

8. **b.** is the answer. (p. 76)
a. Because they are genetically the same, identical twins are always of the same sex.
c. & d. Fraternal twins develop from two fertilized eggs.

9. **d.** is the answer. (pp. 71, 73)

10. **c.** is the answer. (p. 79)

11. **b.** is the answer. (p. 91)

12. **b.** is the answer. Actually, only 6 percent are differences among races. (p. 71)

13. **a.** is the answer. (p. 71)
b. & c. In fact, these are typical criticisms of evolutionary psychology.

14. **c.** is the answer. (p. 76)

15. **b.** is the answer. (p. 81)
a. An interaction requires at least two variables; in this example there is only one (competition).
c. This is an example of a negative correlation.
d. This is an example of a positive correlation.

16. **d.** is the answer. (pp. 70–71)

17. **d.** is the answer. (p. 72)
a., b., & c. These are typical male attitudes and behaviors.

18. **d.** is the answer. Following social learning theory, Brandon is using verbal punishment to discourage what he believes to be an inappropriate gender-linked behavior in his son. (p. 92)
a. Gender schema theory maintains that children adjust their behaviors to match their cultural concept of gender. In this example, we have only the father's behavior on which to base our answer.
b. & c. No such theories were discussed.

19. **a.** is the answer. Many aspects of language, including masculine and feminine pronouns, provide children with schemas through which they begin organizing their worlds on the basis of gender. (p. 92)

20. **a.** is the answer. (p. 79)

    b., c., & d. Temperament is one of the most stable personality traits.

Essay Question

Evolutionary psychologists would not be surprised by the tension between Lakia and Jerome and would see it as a reflection of women's more relational and men's more recreational approach to sex. Since eggs are expensive, compared with sperm, women prefer mates with the potential for long-term investment in their joint offspring. According to this perspective, this may be why Lakia is not in a hurry to become sexually intimate with Jerome. Men, on the other hand, are selected for "pairing widely" but not necessarily wisely in order to maximize the spreading of their genes. This is especially true of men like Jerome, who have traditional masculine attitudes.

Key Terms

Writing Definitions

1. **Chromosomes** are threadlike structures made of DNA molecules, which contain the genes. In conception, the 23 chromosomes in the egg are paired with the 23 chromosomes in the sperm. (p. 69)

2. **DNA** (deoxyribonucleic acid) is a complex molecule containing the genetic information that makes up the chromosomes. (p. 69)

3. **Genes** are the biochemical units of heredity that make up the chromosomes; they are segments of the DNA molecules capable of synthesizing a protein. (p. 69)

4. **Natural selection** is the evolutionary principle that traits that contribute to reproduction and survival are the most likely to be passed on to succeeding generations. (p. 71)

5. **Mutations** are random errors in gene replication that are the source of genetic diversity within a species. (p. 71)

6. **Evolutionary psychology** is the study of the evolution of behavior using the principles of natural selection. (p. 71)

7. **Gender** refers to the biological and social characteristics by which people define male and female. (p. 72)

8. **Behavior genetics** is the study of genetic and environmental influences on specific behaviors. (p. 75)

9. In behavior genetics, **environment** refers to every nongenetic, or external, influence on our traits and behaviors. (p. 75)

10. **Identical twins** develop from a single fertilized egg that splits in two and therefore are genetically identical. (p. 76)

11. **Fraternal twins** develop from two separate eggs fertilized by different sperm and therefore are no more genetically similar than ordinary siblings. (p. 76)

12. **Temperament** refers to a person's characteristic emotional reactivity and intensity. (p. 79)

13. An **interaction** occurs when the effects of one factor (such as heredity) depend on another factor (such as environment). (p. 81)

    Example: Because the way people react to us (an environmental factor) depends on our genetically influenced temperament (a genetic factor), there is an **interaction** between environment and heredity.

14. A **culture** is the enduring behaviors, ideas, attitudes, and traditions shared by a large group of people and transmitted from one generation to the next. (p. 86)

15. **Norms** are understood social prescriptions, or rules, for accepted and expected behavior. (p. 87)

16. **Personal space** refers to the buffer zone, or mobile territory, that people like to maintain around their bodies. (p. 87)

17. The **X chromosome** is the sex chromosome found in both men and women. Females inherit an X chromosome from each parent. (p. 90)

18. The **Y chromosome** is the sex chromosome found only in men. Males inherit an X chromosome from their mothers and a Y chromosome from their fathers. (p. 90)

19. **Testosterone** is the principal male sex hormone. During prenatal development, testosterone stimulates the development of the external male sex organs. (p. 90)

20. A **role** is a culturally prescribed set of behaviors expected of those who occupy a particular social position. (p. 90)

21. A **gender role** is a culturally prescribed set of behaviors for males and females. (p. 90)

22. **Gender identity** is one's personal sense of being male or female. (p. 92)

23. **Gender-typing** is the acquisition of a traditional feminine or masculine gender role. (p. 92)

24. According to **social learning theory**, people learn social behavior (such as gender roles) by observing and imitating and by being rewarded or punished. (p. 92)

25. According to **gender schema theory**, children acquire a cultural concept of what it means to be female or male and adjust their behavior accordingly. (p. 92)

Cross-Check

ACROSS	DOWN
6. adoptive	1. behavior genetics
7. DNA	2. evolutionary
9. role	3. interaction
10. norm	4. environment
11. gender	5. gender schema
12. culture	8. gender identity
13. nurture	17. nature
14. affluent	18. genes
15. biological	
16. mutation	
19. chromosome	

FOCUS ON VOCABULARY AND LANGUAGE

Genes: Our Biological Blueprint

Page 69: . . . *blueprint* . . . Blueprint is an architectural term for a copy of an original diagram or plan used as a working drawing for creating the building or structure. Myers notes that the 46 chromosomes in each body cell (23 from the egg and 23 from the sperm) contain the master plan (*blueprint*) in the form of genes that ultimately makes each of us a unique human being.

Evolutionary Psychology: Maximizing Fitness

Page 71: cash-strapped . . . This means to be in desperate need of money (*strapped for cash*). Russian researchers selectively bred only the tamest and friendliest foxes from each of 30 generations over a 40-year period. The present breed of foxes are affectionate, docile, and eager to please; in order to raise funds for the financially destitute (*cash-strapped*) institute, they are being marketed as house pets.

Page 71: But the tight genetic *leash* . . . is looser on humans. Just as a dog is restrained or held in check by a strap or cord (*leash*), genes generally determine the behaviors of many animals. In humans, however, genes are less influential; thus, the usually strong genetic constraints (*tight genetic leash*) operate in a less determined way (*are looser*).

Page 73: In our *ancestral history*, women most often sent their genes into the future by *pairing wisely*, men by *pairing widely*. Evolutionary psychologists note that our normal desires (*natural yearnings*) help perpetuate our genes. In our evolutionary past (*ancestral history*) females accomplished this best by being selective in their choice of mate (*pairing wisely*) and men by more promiscuous behavior (*pairing widely*). Myers points out, however, that environmental factors, such as cultural expectations, can alter or shape how sexual behavior is expressed by both males and females (*can bend the genders*).

Page 74: They (women) prefer *stick-around dads over likely cads*. Women tend to prefer males who show the promise of becoming and remaining good fathers for their joint offspring (*stick-around dads*) rather than males who indicate little or no willingness to make such a co-parenting commitment (*likely cads*).

Page 74: As *mobile gene machines*, we are predisposed to prefer whatever worked for our ancestors. Evolutionary psychologists believe that behavioral tendencies that increase the probability of getting one's genes into the future have been selected for over the course of evolution. Humans who actively seek out mates and successfully procreate (*mobile gene machines*) are passing on inherited tendencies to behave in certain ways (*our natural yearnings*) because these behaviors were adaptive for our ancestors.

Behavior Genetics: Predicting Individual Differences

Page 75: To *disentangle the threads* of heredity and environment, behavior geneticists often use *two sets of tweezers*: twin studies and adoption studies. Myers is using an analogy here: To separate out (*disentangle*) two different strings (*threads*) that are tightly intertwined, you can use a small pincers (*tweezers*). Similarly, in an attempt to discover and separate out (*tease apart*) the differential effects of the environment and genes (*threads that are entangled*), behavior geneticists use two approaches (*two sets of tweezers*): twin studies and adoption studies.

Page 77: blue-collar families . . . This phrase refers to a social category based on the type of work people do. Traditionally, manual workers wore blue (denim) work shirts (*blue-collar workers*) in contrast to office workers, managers, etc., who wore white shirts (*white-collar workers*). The identical twins (both named Jim) were adopted by similar working-class (*blue-collar*) families.

Page 77: The *startling twin similarity stories* do not impress Bouchard's critics. Bouchard's investigation into the similarities between separated twins suggests that genes influence many behaviors, such as career choices, TV-watching habits, and food likes and dislikes (*startling stories*). The critics point out that any two strangers of the same sex and age would probably have many coincidental things in common if they were to spend hours comparing their behaviors and life histories.

Page 78: Genes-R-Us The name of a large retail chain, Toys-R-Us, is an abbreviated version of the idea that the company makes and sells only toys (*toys are us*). Myers is indicating something similar when he says *Genes-R-Us*; genes make and shape who we are.

Page 80: Thus, asking whether your personality is more a product of your genes or environment is like asking. . . whether *the area of a field is more the result of its length or width*. The area of a space, such as a soccer field or a football field, is determined by multiplying the length by the width. Obviously, you cannot find the area of the field without both length and width. Likewise, we do not become who we are without both nature and nurture. As Myers notes, from conception onward, we are the result of a large number (*a cascade*) of interactions between our genetic tendencies and environmental influences.

Environmental Influence

Page 82: And society reinforces such parent-blaming: Believing that parents shape their children as a *potter molds clay*, people readily praise parents for their children's virtues and blame them for their children's vices. Myers suggests that, because some factors that affect development are under the parent's control and others are not, it is not appropriate to be judgmental. We should be slower to praise parents for their children's achievements (children's virtues) and slower yet to be critical when the children do not perform up to our expectations (chil-

dren's vices). Children are not simply formed by their parents' child-rearing abilities (*as a potter molds clay*) but rather are influenced by many factors beyond their control.

Page 84: During early childhood—while the excess connections are *still on call*— . . . . To *be on call* means to be ready and available for use. Thus, during the early childhood years while there are many neural connections ready for use (*still on call*), an enriched and stimulating environment is extremely important for intellectual, perceptual, and social development. As Myers puts it, ". . . use it or lose it."

Page 84: Similar to *pathways* through a forest, less traveled paths gradually disappear, *popular paths* are broadened. This analogy suggests that brain development goes on throughout life. Neural connections (*pathways*) that are frequently used (*popular paths*) are widened and more clearly defined, while those connections that are seldom used (*in disuse*) become weakened and may eventually disappear.

Page 84: The *wiring of Eric Clapton's brain* reflects the thousands of hours he has spent playing the guitar. Repeated experience or practice will strengthen the neural pathways or connections (the *wiring*) in the brain. Eric Clapton is a very famous pop musician, and his expertise at playing the guitar is a function of many, many hours of practice and performing.

Page 85: In procreation, a woman and a man *shuffle their gene decks and deal a life-forming hand* to their child-to-be . . . The idea here is that just as cards are randomly interspersed (*shuffled*) and then passed on (*dealt*) to the players, a man and a woman intermingle their genes (*shuffle their gene decks*) and conceive offspring (*deal a life-forming hand to their child-to-be*). The child is then exposed to numerous environmental factors beyond parental control that limit how much the parents influence the child's development (*children are not formless blobs sculpted by parental nurture*).

Page 86: We come equipped with a huge *cerebral hard drive ready to receive many gigabytes of cultural software*. Myers is comparing our capacity to learn and adapt through cultural transmission to that of a computer's operating system (*cerebral hard drive*) which, like a human, is capable of receiving very large amounts of information through programming (*gigabytes of cultural software*).

Page 87: Yet, norms *grease the social machinery*. Every society has its own rules and regulations about accepted and appropriate modes of conduct (social norms), and these standards differ from culture to culture. These proscriptions may sometimes seem unjust or senseless, but because they are known and practiced by most people, they serve the function of helping society run smoothly (*they grease the social machinery*).

Page 87:   When cultures collide, their differing norms often *befuddle*. When people from different cultures meet, the interaction can be confusing (*befuddling*). Personal space (the distance we like to have between us and others) varies; someone who prefers more space may end up constantly retreating (*backpedaling*) from someone who needs to be close in order to have a comfortable conversation.

The Nature and Nurture of Gender

Page 90:   The Y chromosome includes a single gene that *throws a master switch* triggering the testes to develop and produce the principal male hormone, testosterone. . . . We all get an X chromosome from our mothers and either an X (you'll be a girl) or a Y (you'll be a boy) from our fathers. Thus, the Y chromosome is crucial to making males, and a single gene is responsible for initiating the process (*it throws the switch*) that activates (*triggers*) the production of testosterone by the testes.

Page 90: Traditionally, men have *initiated dates*, driven the car, and *picked up the check*; women have decorated the home, bought and cared for the children's clothes, and selected the wedding gifts. Gender roles are a culture's expectations for male and female

behaviors, but these behaviors change over time and across cultures. Historically, males ask females to go out (*initiate dates*) and pay for the meal and entertainment (*pick up the check*) and women look after the domestic concerns.

Page 91: With the *flick of an apron*, the number of U.S. college women hoping to be full-time homemakers *plunged* during the late 1960s and early 1970s. Over time, gender roles have changed. Within a relatively brief period of time (*with the flick of an apron*), the number of women engaged in the traditional female role (full-time homemaker) declined rapidly (*plunged*) and the number of women in the work force increased substantially, especially in traditional male fields such as medicine, law, and engineering.

Page 94: won the day . . . Galileo's theory that the Earth revolved around the Sun, and not the other way around (vice-versa), was eventually accepted (*it won the day*). His explanation was a coherent account (*it hung together*) of the way the solar system actually works.

Page 95: It **boggles** the mind—the entire universe *popping out of a single point* some 14 billion years ago. . . When something is startling, unexpected, or hard to comprehend, we say that "it *boggles* the mind." The idea that the entire universe arose from a singularity (*popped out of a single point*) approximately 14 billion years ago is one such "mind-boggling" idea.

chapter 4

The Developing Person

Chapter Overview

Developmental psychologists study the life cycle, from conception to death, examining how we develop physically, mentally, and socially. Chapter 4 covers physical, cognitive, and social development over the life span and introduces three major issues in developmental psychology: (1) the relative impact of genes and experience on behavior, (2) whether development is best described as gradual and continuous or as a discontinuous sequence of stages, and (3) whether the individual's personality remains stable or changes over the life span.

Although there are not too many terms to learn in this chapter, there are a number of important research findings to remember. Pay particular attention to the stage theories of Piaget, Kohlberg, and Erikson, as well as to the discussion regarding intellectual stability during adulthood. Writing carefully prepared answers to the section preview items should be especially helpful in mastering the material in this chapter.

Note: Answer guidelines for all Chapter 4 questions begin on page 107.

Introducing the Developing Person (p. 99)

> David Myers at times uses idioms that are unfamiliar to some readers. If you do not know the meaning of the following phrase in the context in which it appears in the text, refer to page 119 for an explanation: . . . *journey through life from womb to tomb.*

Introduction Preview

First, skim the introduction. Then read the following objectives and, as you read the text, search for the information that will enable you to meet each objective. Answer guidelines are provided on page 107.

1. Briefly describe the work of developmental psychologists.

2. Identify and briefly describe three major issues that pervade developmental psychology.

Stepping Through the Introduction

After you have read the introduction, complete the sentences and answer the questions. As you proceed, evaluate your performance by consulting the answers on page 107. Do not continue with the next section until you understand each answer. If you need to, review or reread the section in the textbook before continuing.

1. Scientists who study physical, mental, and social changes throughout the life cycle are called

    _____ _____ .

2. One of the major issues in developmental psychology concerns the relative importance of genes and experience in determining behavior; this is called the _____ /

    _____ issue.

3. A second developmental issue,

    _____ / _____ ,

    concerns whether developmental changes are gradual or abrupt.

4. A third controversial issue concerns the consistency of personality and whether development is characterized more by _____ over time or by change.

Prenatal Development and the Newborn
(pp. 99–102)

Section Preview

Answer guidelines are provided on page 107.

1. Describe conception, and outline the course of prenatal development.

2. Discuss the possible effects of teratogens on the developing embryo and fetus.

3. Describe the capacities of the newborn.

4. (Close-Up) Explain how psychologists are able to study infant thinking.

Stepping Through the Section

Answers are provided on page 108.

Describe the moment of conception and the beginning of prenatal development.

1. Fertilized human eggs are called

    _____ . During the first week, the cells in this cluster begin to specialize in structure and function, that is, they begin to

    _____ . From about 2 until 8 weeks of age the developing human is called a(n)

    _____ . During the final stage of prenatal development, the developing human is called a(n) _____ .

2. Along with nutrients, a range of harmful substances known as _____ can pass through the placenta.

3. Moderate consumption of alcohol during pregnancy _____ (usually does not affect/can affect) the fetal brain. If a mother

drinks heavily, her baby is at risk for the birth defects and mental retardation that accompany _____

_____ _____ .

4. When an infant's cheek is touched, it will vigorously search for a nipple, a response known as the _____ _____ .

Give some evidence supporting the claim that a newborn's sensory equipment is biologically prewired to facilitate social responsiveness.

5. (Close-Up) To study infants' thinking, developmental researchers have focused on a simple form of learning called _____ , which involves a _____ in responding with repeated stimulation. Using this procedure, researchers have found that infants can discriminate _____ ,

_____ , and _____ ; they also understand some basic concepts of _____ and _____ .

Infancy and Childhood (pp. 103–115)

> If you do not know the meaning of any of the following words, phrases, or expressions in the context in which they appear in the text, refer to pages 119–120 for an explanation: *toddler; wild growth spurt; fruitless; double take; breathing wind-up dolls; it gets high marks; cognitive milestones; concrete demonstrations . . . think for themselves; pit the drawing power; gosling; "Mere exposure"; mobile sperm banks; footprints on the brain; parenting styles . . . lax; heed this caution.*

Section Preview

Answer guidelines begin on page 108.

1. Describe the brain development that occurs from infancy through childhood, including its impact on memory.

2. Describe the roles of nature and nurture in motor development through infancy and childhood.

3. Discuss Piaget's view of how the mind develops, and describe his cognitive stages.

4. Discuss the development of theory of mind and the nature of autism.

5. Discuss current views of Piaget's theory of cognitive development.

6. Discuss the origins and effects of early attachment and the roles of familiarity and parenting in the development of attachment.

7. Discuss how disruptions in attachment affect child development.

8. Discuss the possible effects of different parenting styles on children.

Stepping Through the Section

Answers begin on page 109.

1. At birth the human nervous system _____ (is/is not) fully mature. After puberty, a process of _____ shuts down some neural connections and strengthens others.

2. Biological growth processes that enable orderly changes in behavior are called _____ .

3. The lack of neural connections helps explain why our earliest memories do not occur before age _____ . The average age of earliest conscious memory is _____ years.

4. Infants pass the milestones of _____ development at different rates, but the basic _____ of stages is fixed. Genes play a _____ (major/minor) role in motor development. Until the necessary muscular and neural maturation is complete, experience has a _____ (large/small) effect on behavior.

5. The first researcher to show that the thought processes of adults and children are very different was _____ .

6. To organize and interpret his or her experiences, the developing child constructs cognitive concepts called _____ .

7. The interpretation of new experiences in terms of existing ideas is called _____ . The adaptation of existing ideas to fit new experiences is called _____ .

8. The term for all the mental activities associated with thinking, remembering, communicating, and knowing is _____ .

9. In Piaget's first stage of development, the _____ stage, children experience the world through their motor and sensory interactions with objects. This stage occurs between infancy and nearly age _____ .

10. The awareness that things continue to exist even when they are removed from view is called _____ _____ . This awareness begins to develop at about _____ months of age.

11. Researchers see development as more _____ than Piaget did. For instance, babies have a head for _____ , as Karen Wynn demonstrated.

12. According to Piaget, during the preschool years and up to age _____ , children are in the _____ stage.

13. The principle that the quantity of a substance remains the same even when the shape of its container changes is called _____ . Piaget believed that preschoolers _____ (have/have not) developed this concept.

14. Preschoolers are often unable to perceive things from another person's point of view. This inability is called _____ .

15. The child's growing ability to take another's perspective is evidence that the child is acquiring a _____ _____ _____ . Between 3¹/₂ and 4, children come to realize that others may hold _____ _____ .

16. The disorder characterized by deficient _____ and _____ interaction is _____ . This disorder is related to malfunctions of brain areas that enable _____ .

17. Piaget believed that children acquire the mental abilities needed to comprehend mathematical transformations and conservation by about _____ years of age. At this time, they enter the _____ _____ stage.

18. In Piaget's final stage, the _____ _____ stage, reasoning expands from the purely concrete to encompass _____ thinking. Piaget believed most children begin to enter this stage by age _____ .

Explain briefly how contemporary researchers view Piaget's theory.

19. By about _____ months of age, soon after object permanence emerges and children become mobile, a new fear, called _____ _____ , emerges.

20. The development of a strong emotional bond between infant and parent is called _____ .

21. Harlow's studies of monkeys have shown that mother-infant attachment does not depend on the mother providing nourishment as much as it does on her providing the comfort of _____ _____ . Another key to attachment is _____ .

22. In some animals attachment will occur only during a restricted time called a _____ _____ .

Konrad Lorenz discovered that young birds would follow almost any object if it were the first moving thing they observed. This phenomenon is called _____ .

23. Human infants _____ (do/do not) have a precise critical period for becoming attached.

24. Placed in a strange play situation, children show one of two patterns of attachment: _____ attachment or _____ attachment.

Contrast the responses of securely and insecurely attached infants to strange situations.

Discuss the effect of responsive parenting on infant attachment.

25. A child's characteristic emotional reactivity and intensity is called the child's _____ . This tendency _____ (is/is not) influenced by genes.

26. A father's love and acceptance for his children are _____ (comparable to/less important than) a mother's love in predicting their children's health and well-being

27. According to Erikson, securely attached infants approach life with a sense of

    _____ _____ .

28. Separation anxiety peaks in infants around _____ months, then _____ (gradually declines/remains constant for about a year). This is true of children _____ (in North America/throughout the world).

29. Harlow found that when monkeys reared in social isolation are placed with other monkeys, they reacted with either fear or _____ .

30. Most abused children _____ (do/do not) later become abusive parents.

31. Although most children who grow up under adversity are _____ and become normal adults, early abuse may produce changes in the brain chemical _____ .

32. Parents who impose rules and expect obedience are exhibiting a(n) _____ style of parenting.

33. Parents who make few demands of their children and tend to submit to their children's desires are identified as _____ parents.

34. Setting and enforcing standards after discussion with their children is the approach taken by _____ parents.

35. Studies have shown that there tends to be a correlation between high self-esteem on the part of the child and the _____ style of parenting. This may be because this parenting style gives children the greatest sense of _____ over their lives.

Explain why the correlation between authoritative parenting and social competence does not necessarily reveal cause and effect.

Adolescence (pp. 115–123)

If you do not know the meaning of any of the following words, phrases, or expressions in the context in which they appear in the text, refer to pages 120–121 for an explanation: *pays dividends; out of sync; intellectual summit; character—the psychological muscles for controlling impulses; moral ladder; "psychosocial" task; forge their identity; surfaces early.*

Section Preview

Answer guidelines are provided on page 110.

1. Identify the major physical changes that occur in adolescence.

2. Describe developments in cognitive and moral reasoning during adolescence, focusing on Kohlberg's theory and its criticisms.

3. Describe how Erikson viewed adolescence and the nature of social relationships during adolescence, and explain adolescents' changing relationships with parents and peers.

Stepping Through the Section

Answers begin on page 110.

1. The "storm and stress" view of adolescence is credited to _____ , one of the first American psychologists to describe adolescence.

2. Adolescence begins with the time of developing sexual maturity known as _____ . A two-year period of rapid physical development begins in girls at about the age of _____ and in boys at about the age of _____ . This growth spurt is marked by the development of the reproductive organs and external genitalia, or _____ _____ characteristics, as well as by the development of traits such as pubic hair and enlarged breasts in females and facial hair in males. These nonreproductive traits are known as _____ _____ characteristics.

3. Girls who are _____ and those without _____ are prone to earlier puberty. Evolutionary psychologists suggest that early reproduction "makes sense" when _____ _____ can support pregnancy and when _____-_____ bonds are weak.

4. The first menstrual period, called _____ , occurs by about age _____ . In boys, the first ejaculation occurs by about age _____ .

5. The _____ (timing/sequence) of pubertal changes is more predictable than their _____ (timing/sequence).

6. Boys who mature _____ (early/late) tend to be more popular, self-assured, and independent; they also are at increased risk for _____ _____ . For girls, _____ (early/late) maturation can be stressful, especially when their bodies are out of sync with their _____ _____ .

7. The adolescent brain undergoes a selective _____ of unused connections. Also, teens' occasional impulsiveness and risky behaviors may be due, in part, to the fact that development in the brain's _____ _____ lags behind that of the _____ _____ .

8. During the early teen years, reasoning is often _____ , as adolescents often feel their experiences are unique.

9. Piaget's final stage of cognitive development is the stage of _____ _____ . The adolescent in this stage is capable of thinking logically about _____ as well as concrete propositions.

10. The theorist who proposed that moral thought progresses through stages is _____ . These stages are divided into three basic levels: _____ , _____ , and _____ .

11. In the preconventional stages of morality, characteristic of children, the emphasis is on obeying rules in order to avoid _____ or gain _____ .

12. Conventional morality usually emerges by early _____ . The emphasis is on gaining social _____ or upholding the social _____ .

13. Individuals who base moral judgments on their own perceptions of basic ethical principles are said by Kohlberg to employ _____ morality.

Summarize the criticisms of Kohlberg's theory of moral development.

14. The idea that children progress from preconventional to conventional moral reasoning _____ (has/has not) been confirmed. Postconventional reasoning appears mostly among educated, _____-class members of cultures that prize _____ .

15. Today's character education programs teach children _____ for others' feelings.

16. Children who learn to delay _____ become more socially responsible, academically successful, and productive.

Complete the missing information in the following table of Erikson's stages of psychosocial development.

Group Age	Psychosocial Stage
Infancy	_____
_____	Autonomy vs. shame and doubt
Preschooler	_____
_____	Competence vs. inferiority
Adolescence	_____
_____	Intimacy vs. isolation
Middle adulthood	_____
_____	Integrity vs. despair

17. According to Erikson, the task of adolescence is to develop a clear sense of self, or _____ . Erikson saw this development as a prerequisite for the development of _____ in young adulthood.

18. During the early to mid-teen years, self-esteem generally _____ (rises/falls/remains stable). During the late teens and twenties, self-esteem generally _____ (rises/falls/remains stable).

19. Gilligan believes that females are _____ (more/less) concerned than males with establishing individualistic identities.

20. Girls play in _____ (smaller/larger) groups than boys. Girls' play also is less _____ than boys' play and is more likely to imitate _____ _____ .

21. Gender differences in connectedness peak in _____ _____ .

Compare the genders in terms of social connectedness.

22. Adolescence is typically a time of increasing influence from one's _____ and decreasing influence from _____ ; most adolescents report that they _____ (do/do not) get along with their parents.

23. With improved _____ , sexual maturation is beginning _____ (earlier/later) than in the past, and, influenced by compulsory _____ , adult independence is occurring _____ (earlier/later).

Adulthood (pp. 124–134)

> If you do not know the meaning of any of the following words, phrases, or expressions in the context in which they appear in the text, refer to page 121 for an explanation: *stairs get steeper, the print gets smaller, and people seem to mumble more; levies a tax; Use it or lose it; myth . . . laid to rest; "Pair-bonding is a trademark of the human animal"; test-driving life together.*

Section Preview

Answer guidelines begin on page 111.

1. Identify the major physical changes that occur in middle adulthood and later life.

2. Describe the major cognitive changes that occur in adulthood and old age.

3. Explain why stage theories of adult social development are controversial.

4. Discuss the importance of family and career commitments in adult development, and describe the sense of well-being across the life span.

Stepping Through the Section

Answers are provided on page 112.

1. During adulthood, age _____ (is/is not) a very good predictor of people's traits.

2. The mid-twenties are the peak years for

    _____ _____ ,

    _____ _____ ,

    _____ _____ , and

    _____ _____ . Because

    they mature earlier, _____ (women/men) also peak earlier.

3. During early and middle adulthood, physical vigor has less to do with _____ than with a person's _____ and _____ habits.

4. The cessation of the menstrual cycle, known as _____ , occurs within a few years of _____ . This biological change results from lowered levels of the hormone _____ . A woman's experience during this time depends largely on her _____ and _____ .

5. Although men experience no equivalent to menopause, they do experience a more gradual decline in _____ count, level of the hormone _____ , and speed of erection and ejaculation during later life.

6. With age, the eye's pupil _____ (shrinks/enlarges) and its lens becomes _____ (more/less) transparent. As a

result, the amount of light that reaches the retina is _____ (increased/reduced).

7. Although older adults are _____ (more/less) susceptible to life-threatening ailments, they suffer from short-term ailments such as flu _____ (more/less) often than younger adults.

8. Aging _____ (slows/speeds/has no effect on) neural processing and causes a gradual loss of _____

_____ .

9. Aging may proceed more slowly in _____ (men/women); also, their brains shrink _____ (more/less) slowly than those of the other gender.

10. Physical exercise stimulates _____ _____ development, thanks to increased _____ and nutrient flow.

11. Studies of developmental changes in learning and memory show that during adulthood there is a decline in the ability to _____ (recall/recognize) new information but not in the ability to _____ (recall/recognize) such information.

12. One factor that influences memory in the elderly is the _____ of material.

13. A research study in which people of various ages are compared with one another is called a

_____-_____

study. A research study in which the same people are retested over a period of years is called a _____ study. The first kind of study found evidence of intellectual _____ during adulthood; the second found evidence of intellectual

_____ .

Explain why studies of intellectual decline and aging yielded conflicting results.

14. The accumulation of stored information that comes with education and experience is called _____ intelligence, which tends to _____ with age.

15. The ability to reason abstractly is referred to as _____ intelligence, which tends to _____ with age.

16. Contrary to popular opinion, job and marital dissatisfaction do not surge during the forties, thus suggesting that a midlife _____ need not occur.

17. The term used to refer to the culturally preferred timing for leaving home, getting a job, marrying, and so on is the _____

_____ . Today, the timing of such life events is becoming _____ (more/less) predictable. More important than age are _____ _____ .

18. According to Erikson, the two basic tasks of adulthood are achieving _____ and _____ . According to Freud, the healthy adult is one who can _____ and _____ .

19. Human societies have nearly always included a relatively _____ bond between men and women. Marriage bonds are usually lasting when couples marry after age _____ and are _____

_____ .

20. Marriages today are _____ (half/twice) as likely to end in divorce as they were in 1960. Couples who live together before marrying have a _____ (higher/lower) divorce rate than those who do not.

21. Of those who divorce, _____ (how many?) eventually remarry. Marriage is a predictor of _____ , _____

_____ , _____ , and

_____ .

22. Neighborhoods with high marriage rates typically have low rates of _____

_____ .

23. As children begin to absorb time and energy, satisfaction with the marriage itself _____ (increases/decreases). This is particularly true among _____ women, who shoulder most of the burden.

24. For most couples, the children's leaving home produces a(n) _____ (increase/decrease) in marital satisfaction.

25. Research studies of women who are or are not employed have found that a woman's satisfaction in life depends on the _____ of her experience in her life's role.

26. According to studies, older people _____ (do/do not) report as much happiness and satisfaction with life as younger people do.

27. Grief over a loved one's death is especially severe when it comes _____ .

28. Reactions to a loved one's death _____ (do/do not) vary according to cultural norms. Those who express the strongest grief immediately _____ (do/do not) purge their grief more quickly.

29. Immediately after losing a spouse, _____ (women/men) are more at risk for ill health than those of the other gender.

30. Terminally ill and bereaved people _____ (do/do not) go through predictable stages.

31. According to Erikson, the final task of adulthood is to achieve a sense of _____ .

Reflections on Two Major Developmental Issues (pp. 134–136)

> If you do not know the meaning of any of the following words, phrases, or expressions in the context in which they appear in the text, refer to pages 121–122 for an explanation: *as a giant redwood differs from its seedling; goof-off.*

Section Preview

Answer guidelines are provided on page 112.

1. State current views of psychologists on the continuity versus stages issue.

2. State current views of psychologists on the stability versus change issue.

Stepping Through the Section

Answers are provided on page 112.

1. Stage theories that have been considered include the theory of cognitive development proposed by _____ , the theory of moral development proposed by _____ , and the theory of psychosocial development proposed by _____ .

2. Although research casts doubt on the idea that life proceeds through age-linked _____ , there are spurts of _____ growth during childhood and puberty that correspond roughly to the stages proposed by _____ .

3. The first two years of life _____ (do/do not) provide a good basis for predicting a person's eventual traits.

4. Research on the consistency of personality shows that some traits, such as those related to _____ , are more stable than others, such as social attitudes.

Progress Test 1

Circle your answers to the following questions and check them with the answers beginning on page 112. If your answer is incorrect, read the explanation for why it is incorrect and then consult the appropriate pages of the text (in parentheses following the correct answer).

Multiple-Choice Questions

1. Dr. Joan Goodman is studying how memory changes as people get older. She is most likely a(n) _____ psychologist.
   a. social
   b. cognitive
   c. developmental
   d. experimental

2. In Piaget's stage of concrete operational intelligence, the child acquires an understanding of the principle of:
   a. conservation.
   b. deduction.
   c. attachment.
   d. object permanence.

3. Piaget held that egocentrism is characteristic of the:
   a. sensorimotor stage.
   b. preoperational stage.
   c. concrete operational stage.
   d. formal operational stage.

4. During which stage of cognitive development do children acquire object permanence?
   a. sensorimotor
   b. preoperational
   c. concrete operational
   d. formal operational

5. The rooting reflex occurs when a:
   a. newborn's foot is tickled.
   b. newborn's cheek is touched.
   c. newborn hears a loud noise.
   d. newborn makes eye contact with his or her caregiver.
   e. newborn hears his or her mother's voice.

6. Harlow's studies of attachment in monkeys showed that:
   a. provision of nourishment was the single most important factor motivating attachment.
   b. a cloth mother produced the greatest attachment response.
   c. whether a cloth or wire mother was present mattered less than the presence or absence of other infants.
   d. attachment in monkeys is based on imprinting.

7. When psychologists discuss maturation, they are referring to stages of growth that are *not* influenced by:
   a. conservation.
   b. nature.
   c. nurture.
   d. continuity.

8. The developmental theorist who suggested that securely attached children develop an attitude of basic trust is:
   a. Piaget.
   b. Harlow.
   c. Vygotsky.
   d. Freud.
   e. Erikson.

9. Research findings on infant motor development are consistent with the idea that:
   a. cognitive development lags significantly behind motor skills development.
   b. maturation of physical skills is relatively unaffected by experience.
   c. in the absence of relevant earlier learning experiences, the emergence of motor skills will be slowed.
   d. in humans, the process of maturation may be significantly altered by cultural factors.

10. According to Erikson, the central psychological challenges pertaining to adolescence, young adulthood, and middle age, respectively, are:
    a. identity formation; intimacy; generativity.
    b. intimacy; identity formation; generativity.
    c. generativity; intimacy; identity formation.
    d. intimacy; generativity; identity formation.
    e. identity formation; generativity; intimacy.

11. In preconventional morality, the person:
    a. obeys out of a sense of social duty.
    b. conforms to gain social approval.
    c. obeys to avoid punishment or to gain concrete rewards.
    d. follows the dictates of his or her conscience.

12. Which of the following is correct?
    a. Early maturation places both boys and girls at a distinct social advantage.
    b. Early maturing girls are more popular and self-assured than girls who mature late.
    c. Early maturation places both boys and girls at a distinct social disadvantage.
    d. Early maturing boys are more popular and self-assured than boys who mature late.

13. A person's general ability to think abstractly is called _____ intelligence. This ability generally _____ with age.
    a. fluid; increases
    b. fluid; decreases
    c. crystallized; decreases
    d. crystallized; increases

14. Among the hallmarks of growing up are a boy's first ejaculation and a girl's first menstrual period, which also is called:
    a. puberty.
    b. menopause.
    c. menarche.
    d. generativity.

15. An elderly person who can look back on life with satisfaction and reminisce with a sense of completion has attained Erikson's stage of:
    a. generativity.
    b. intimacy.
    c. isolation.
    d. acceptance.
    e. integrity.

16. According to Piaget, the ability to think logically about abstract propositions is indicative of the stage of:
    a. preoperational thought.
    b. concrete operations.
    c. formal operations.
    d. fluid intelligence.

17. The cognitive ability that has been shown to decline during adulthood is the ability to:
    a. recall new information.
    b. recognize new information.
    c. learn meaningful new material.
    d. use judgment in dealing with daily life problems.

18. Which of the following statements concerning the effects of aging is true?
    a. Aging almost inevitably leads to memory loss if the individual lives long enough.
    b. Aging increases susceptibility to short-term ailments such as the flu.
    c. Significant increases in life satisfaction are associated with aging.
    d. The aging process can be significantly affected by the individual's activity patterns.

19. Longitudinal tests:
    a. compare people of different ages.
    b. study the same people at different times.
    c. usually involve a larger sample than do cross-sectional tests.
    d. usually involve a smaller sample than do cross-sectional tests.

    e. are less informative than cross-sectional tests.

20. The average age at which puberty begins is _____ in boys; in girls, it is _____ .
    a. 14; 13   c. 11; 10
    b. 13; 11   d. 10; 9

21. After puberty, the self-concept usually becomes:
    a. more positive in boys.
    b. more positive in girls.
    c. more positive in both boys and girls.
    d. more negative in both boys and girls.

22. Adolescence is marked by the onset of:
    a. an identity crisis.
    b. parent-child conflict.
    c. the concrete operational stage.
    d. puberty.

23. The end of menstruation is called:
    a. menarche.
    b. menopause.
    c. the midlife crisis.
    d. generativity.

24. The popular idea that terminally ill and bereaved people go through predictable stages, such as denial, anger, and so forth:
    a. is widely supported by research.
    b. more accurately describes grieving in some cultures than others.
    c. is true of women but not men.
    d. is not supported by research studies.

True–False Items

Indicate whether each statement is true or false by placing *T* (*True*) or *F* (*False*) in the blank next to the item.

_____ 1. Most abused children later become abusive parents.

_____ 2. At birth, the brain and nervous system of a healthy child are fully developed.

_____ 3. The sequence in which children develop motor skills varies from one culture to another.

_____ 4. Research shows that development is more continuous than Piaget believed.

_____ 5. The process of grieving is much the same throughout the world.

_____ 6. Sexual maturity is beginning earlier today than in the past.

_____ 7. During adulthood, age only moderately correlates with people's traits.

_____ 8. Intelligence declines throughout adulthood.

_____ **9.** By the age of 50, most adults have experienced a "midlife crisis."

_____ **10.** Compared to those who are younger, elderly people are more susceptible to short-term ailments such as flu and cold viruses.

_____ **11.** Grieving spouses who talk often with others adjust better than those who grieve privately.

Progress Test 2

Progress Test 2 should be completed during a final chapter review. Answer the following questions after you thoroughly understand the correct answers for the section reviews and Progress Test 1.

1. Stranger anxiety develops soon after:
 a. the concept of conservation.
 b. egocentrism.
 c. a theory of mind.
 d. the concept of object permanence.

2. Before Piaget, people were more likely to believe that:
 a. the child's mind is a miniature model of the adult's.
 b. children think about the world in radically different ways from adults.
 c. the child's mind develops through a series of stages.
 d. children interpret their experiences in terms of their current understandings.

3. Which is the correct sequence of stages in Piaget's theory of cognitive development?
 a. sensorimotor, preoperational, concrete operational, formal operational
 b. sensorimotor, preoperational, formal operational, concrete operational
 c. preoperational, sensorimotor, concrete operational, formal operational
 d. preoperational, sensorimotor, formal operational, concrete operational
 e. sensorimotor, concrete operational, preoperational, formal operational

4. A child can be born a drug addict because:
 a. drugs used by the mother will pass into the child's bloodstream.
 b. addiction is an inherited personality trait.
 c. drugs used by the mother create genetic defects in her chromosomes.
 d. the fetus's blood has not yet developed a resistance to drugs.

5. A child whose mother drank heavily when she was pregnant is at heightened risk of:
 a. being emotionally excitable during childhood.
 b. becoming insecurely attached.
 c. being born with the physical and cognitive abnormalities of fetal alcohol syndrome.
 d. addiction to a range of drugs throughout life.

6. Which is the correct order of stages of prenatal development?
 a. zygote, fetus, embryo
 b. zygote, embryo, fetus
 c. embryo, zygote, fetus
 d. embryo, fetus, zygote
 e. fetus, embryo, zygote

7. The term *critical period* refers to:
 a. prenatal development.
 b. the initial 2 hours after a child's birth.
 c. the preoperational stage.
 d. a restricted time for learning.

8. Which of the following was *not* found by Harlow in socially deprived monkeys?
 a. They had difficulty mating.
 b. They showed extreme fear or aggression when first seeing other monkeys.
 c. They showed abnormal physical development.
 d. The females were abusive mothers.

9. Shay and Jared are planning to have children, but first they want to move to a neighborhood that is likely to have few social pathologies. You advise them to look for a neighborhood that has:
 a. many children.
 b. few teenagers.
 c. a high marriage rate.
 d. a high average socioeconomic level.

10. Most people's earliest memories do not predate _____ of age.
 a. 6 months   **d.** 3 years
 b. 1 year   **e.** 6 years
 c. 2 years

11. Insecurely attached infants who are left by their mothers in an unfamiliar setting often will:
 a. hold fast to their mothers on their return.
 b. explore the new surroundings confidently.
 c. be indifferent toward their mothers on their return.
 d. display little emotion at any time.

12. Whose stage theory of moral development was based on how people reasoned about ethical dilemmas?
    a. Erikson
    b. Piaget
    c. Levinson
    d. Kohlberg
    e. Kübler-Ross

13. The cross-sectional method:
    a. compares people of different ages with one another.
    b. studies the same group of people at different times.
    c. tends to paint too favorable a picture of the effects of aging on intelligence.
    d. is more appropriate than the longitudinal method for studying intellectual change over the life span.

14. The social clock refers to:
    a. an individual or society's distribution of work and leisure time.
    b. adulthood responsibilities.
    c. typical ages for starting a career, marrying, and so on.
    d. age-related changes in one's circle of friends.

15. To which of Kohlberg's levels would moral reasoning based on the existence of fundamental human rights pertain?
    a. preconventional morality
    b. conventional morality
    c. postconventional morality
    d. generative morality

16. In Erikson's theory, individuals generally focus on developing _____ during adolescence and then _____ during young adulthood.
    a. identity; intimacy
    b. intimacy; identity
    c. basic trust; identity
    d. identity; basic trust

17. After menopause, most women:
    a. experience anxiety and a sense of worthlessness.
    b. experience hot flashes.
    c. secrete unusually high levels of estrogen.
    d. gain a lot of weight.
    e. feel a new sense of freedom.

18. Notable achievements in fields such as _____ are often made by younger adults in their late twenties or early thirties, when _____ intelligence is at its peak.
    a. mathematics; fluid
    b. philosophy; fluid

    c. science; crystallized
    d. literature; crystallized
    e. history; crystallized

19. After their grown children have left home, most couples experience:
    a. the distress of the "empty nest syndrome."
    b. increased strain in their marital relationship.
    c. both a. and b.
    d. greater happiness and enjoyment in their relationship.

20. Compared with men, women:
    a. use conversation to communicate solutions.
    b. emphasize freedom and self-reliance.
    c. talk more openly
    d. do all of the above.

21. A person's accumulation of stored information, called _____ intelligence, generally _____ with age.
    a. fluid; decreases
    b. fluid; increases
    c. crystallized; decreases
    d. crystallized; increases

22. In terms of incidence, susceptibility to short-term illnesses _____ with age and susceptibility to long-term ailments _____ with age.
    a. decreases; increases
    b. increases; decreases
    c. increases; increases
    d. decreases; decreases

23. Stage theories have been criticized because they fail to consider that development may be significantly affected by:
    a. variations in the social clock.
    b. each individual's experiences.
    c. each individual's historical and cultural setting.
    d. all of the above.

24. Research on the American family indicates that:
    a. fewer than 23 percent of unmarried adults, but nearly 40 percent of married adults, report being "very happy" with life.
    b. the divorce rate is now one-half the marriage rate.
    c. of those who divorce, 3 in 4 remarry.
    d. all of the above are true.

Review and Reflect

Answer these questions the day before an exam as a final check on your understanding of the chapter's terms and concepts.

Multiple-Choice Questions

1. Calvin, who is trying to impress his psychology professor with his knowledge of infant motor development, asks why some infants learn to roll over before they lift their heads from a prone position, while others develop these skills in the opposite order. What should Calvin's professor conclude from this question?
   a. Calvin clearly understands that the sequence of motor development is not the same for all infants.
   b. Calvin doesn't know what he's talking about. Although some infants reach these developmental milestones ahead of others, the order is the same for all infants.
   c. Calvin needs to be reminded that rolling over is an inherited reflex, not a learned skill.
   d. Calvin understands an important principle: motor development is unpredictable.

2. Deborah is a mathematician and Willie is a philosopher. Considering their professions:
   a. Deborah will make her most significant career accomplishments at an earlier age than Willie will.
   b. Deborah will make her most significant career accomplishments at a later age than Willie will.
   c. Deborah will make her most significant career accomplishments at about the same time as Willie.
   d. there is still not enough information for predicting such accomplishments.

3. Based on the text discussion of maturation and popularity, who among the following is probably the most popular sixth grader?
   a. Jessica, the most physically mature girl in the class
   b. Roger, the most intellectually mature boy in the class
   c. Rob, the tallest, most physically mature boy in the class
   d. Cindy, who is average in physical development and is on the school debating team

4. As a child observes, liquid is transferred from a tall, thin tube into a short, wide jar. The child is asked if there is now less liquid in order to determine if she has mastered:
   a. the schema for liquids.
   b. the concept of object permanence.
   c. the concept of conservation.
   d. the ability to reason abstractly.

5. I am 14 months old and fearful of strangers. I am in Piaget's _____ stage of cognitive development.
   a. sensorimotor
   b. preoperational
   c. concrete operational
   d. formal operational

6. I am 3 years old, can use language, and have trouble taking another person's perspective. I am in Piaget's ____ stage of cognitive development.
   a. sensorimotor
   b. preoperational
   c. concrete operational
   d. formal operational

7. In Piaget's theory, conservation is to egocentrism as the _____ stage is to the _____ stage.
   a. sensorimotor; formal operational
   b. formal operational; sensorimotor
   c. preoperational; sensorimotor
   d. concrete operational; preoperational

8. Four-year-old Jamail has a younger sister. When asked if he has a sister, he is likely to answer _____ ; when asked if his sister has a brother, Jamail is likely to answer _____ .
   a. yes; yes
   b. no; no
   c. yes; no
   d. no; yes

9. In a 1998 movie, a young girl finds that a gaggle of geese follow her wherever she goes because she was the first "object" they saw after they were born. This is an example of:
   a. conservation.
   b. imprinting.
   c. egocentrism.
   d. basic trust.

10. Joshua and Ann Bishop have a 13-month-old boy. According to Erikson, the Bishops' sensitive, loving care of their child contributes to:
    a. the child's sense of basic trust.
    b. the child's secure attachment.
    c. the child's sense of control.
    d. a. and b. only.

11. Fourteen-year-old Cassandra feels freer and more open with her friends than with her family. Knowing this is the case, Cassandra's parents should:
    a. be concerned, because deteriorating parent-adolescent relationships, such as this one, are often followed by a range of problem behaviors.
    b. encourage Cassandra to find new friends.
    c. seek family counseling.
    d. not worry, since adolescence is typically a time of growing peer influence and diminishing parental influence.
    e. ask *their* friends to suggest ways to communicate with Cassandra.

12. Thirteen-year-old Irene has no trouble defeating her 11-year-old brother at a detective game that requires following clues in order to deduce the perpetrator of a crime. How might Piaget explain Irene's superiority at the game?
    a. Being older, Irene has had more years of schooling.
    b. Girls develop intellectually at a faster rate than boys.
    c. Being an adolescent, Irene is beginning to develop abstract reasoning skills.
    d. Girls typically have more experience than boys at playing games.

13. Which of the following was *not* mentioned in the text as a criticism of Kohlberg's theory of moral development?
    a. It does not account for the fact that the development of moral reasoning is culture-specific.
    b. Postconventional morality appears mostly in educated, middle-class persons.
    c. The theory is biased against the moral reasoning of people in communal societies such as China.
    d. The theory is biased in favor of moral reasoning in men.

14. Compared with her teenage brother, 14-year-old Samantha is likely to play in groups that are:
    a. larger and less competitive.
    b. larger and more competitive.
    c. smaller and less competitive.
    d. smaller and more competitive.

15. Sixty-five-year-old Calvin cannot reason as well as he could when he was younger. More than likely, Calvin's _____ intelligence has declined.
    a. analytic
    b. crystallized
    c. fluid
    d. both b. and c.

16. Cross-sectional studies of intelligence are potentially misleading because:
    a. they are typically based on a very small and unrepresentative sample of people.
    b. retesting the same people over a period of years allows test performance to be influenced by practice.
    c. they compare people who are not only different in age, but of different eras, education levels, and affluence.
    d. of all the above reasons.

17. Which statement illustrates cognitive development during the course of adult life?
    a. Adults in their forties have better recognition memory than do adults in their seventies.
    b. Recall and recognition memory both remain strong throughout life.
    c. Recognition memory decreases sharply at midlife.
    d. Recall memory remains strong until very late in life.
    e. Adults in their forties have better recall memory than adults in their seventies.

18. Given the text discussion of life satisfaction patterns, which of the following people is likely to report the greatest life satisfaction?
    a. Billy, a 7-year-old second-grader
    b. Kathy, a 17-year-old high-school senior
    c. Alan, a 30-year-old accountant
    d. Mildred, a 70-year-old retired teacher
    e. too little information to tell

19. Which of the following statements is consistent with the current thinking of developmental psychologists?
    a. Development occurs in a series of sharply defined stages.
    b. The first two years are the most crucial in determining the individual's personality.
    c. The consistency of personality in most people tends to increase over the life span.
    d. Social and emotional style are among the characteristics that show the least stability over the life span.

20. Sam, a junior in high school, regularly attends church because his family and friends think he should. Which stage of moral reasoning is Sam in?
    a. preconventional
    b. conventional
    c. postconventional
    d. too little information to tell

21. Research on social relationships between parents and their adolescent children shows that:
    a. parental influence on children increases during adolescence.
    b. high school girls who have the most affectionate relationships with their mothers tend to enjoy the most intimate friendships with girlfriends.
    c. high school boys who have the most affectionate relationships with their fathers tend to enjoy the most intimate friendships with friends.
    d. most teens are strongly influenced by parents in matters of personal taste.
    e. parent-adolescent conflict is most common between mothers and daughters.

22. Most contemporary developmental psychologists believe that:
    a. personality is essentially formed by the end of infancy.
    b. personality continues to be formed until adolescence.
    c. the shaping of personality continues during adolescence and well beyond.
    d. adolescent development has very little impact on adult personality.

23. After a series of unfulfilling relationships, 30-year-old Carlos tells a friend that he doesn't want to marry because he is afraid of losing his freedom and independence. Erikson would say that Carlos is having difficulty with the psychosocial task of:
    a. trust versus mistrust.
    b. autonomy versus doubt.
    c. intimacy versus isolation.
    d. identity versus role confusion.
    e. generativity versus stagnation.

24. Research on the relationship between self-reported happiness and employment in American women has revealed that:
    a. women who work tend to be happier.
    b. women who do not work tend to be happier.
    c. women today are happier than in the past, whether they are working or not.
    d. the quality of a woman's experience in her various roles is more predictive of happiness than the presence or absence of a given role.

Essay Question

Sheryl is 12 years old and in the sixth grade. Describe the developmental changes she is likely to be experiencing according to Piaget, Kohlberg, and Erikson. (Use the space below to list the points you want to make, and organize them. Then write the essay on a separate sheet of paper.)

Key Terms

Using your own words, on a piece of paper write a brief definition or explanation of each of the following terms.

1. developmental psychology
2. zygote
3. embryo
4. fetus
5. teratogens
6. fetal alcohol syndrome (FAS)
7. rooting reflex
8. habituation
9. maturation
10. schema
11. assimilation
12. accommodation
13. cognition
14. sensorimotor stage
15. object permanence
16. preoperational stage
17. conservation
18. egocentrism

19. theory of mind

20. concrete operational stage

21. formal operational stage

22. stranger anxiety

23. attachment

24. critical period

25. imprinting

26. basic trust

27. adolescence

28. puberty

29. primary sex characteristics

30. secondary sex characteristics

31. menarche

32. identity

33. intimacy

34. menopause

35. cross-sectional study

36. longitudinal study

37. crystallized intelligence

38. fluid intelligence

39. social clock

Answers

Introducing the Developing Person

Introduction Preview

1. Developmental psychologists study physical, mental, and social commonalities and changes throughout the human life cycle.

2. The nature/nurture issue is concerned with how much development is influenced by heredity and how much by experience. The continuity or stages issue concerns whether development is a gradual, continuous process or a sequence of separate stages. The stability or change issue asks whether individual traits persist over the life span or people become different persons as they age.

Stepping Through the Introduction

1. developmental psychologists

2. nature/nurture

3. continuity/stages

4. stability

Prenatal Development and the Newborn

Section Preview

1. A woman's ovary releases a mature egg. The few sperm from the man that reach the egg release digestive enzymes that eat away the egg's protective covering. As soon as one sperm penetrates the egg, the egg's surface blocks out all other sperm. The egg and sperm nuclei fuse and become one.

   Prenatal development is divided into three stages: zygote (from conception to 2 weeks); embryo (2 weeks through 8 weeks); and fetus (9 weeks to birth).

   During the period of the zygote, cell division is the primary task. Within two weeks of conception the increasingly numerous cells begin to differentiate—to specialize in structure and function. At this time the zygote's outer part attaches to the mother's uterine wall, becoming the placenta. During the period of the embryo, body organs begin to form and function. By the end of the sixth month the fetus's internal organs have become sufficiently functional to allow a premature fetus a chance of survival.

2. Teratogens are damaging agents such as chemicals and viruses that pass through the placenta into the embryo or fetus. Teratogens may result in a variety of physical and cognitive abnormalities in the developing child. For example, mothers who are heavy smokers often give birth to underweight infants. Mothers addicted to drugs such as heroin give birth to addicted newborns. If a mother is a heavy alcohol drinker, her infant may suffer from fetal alcohol syndrome, which is characterized by small, misproportioned heads and brain abnormalities, which lead to mental retardation.

3. Newborns are born with a variety of reflexes that help ensure their survival. When touched on its cheek, for example, a baby will open its mouth and search for food (rooting reflex).

   The newborn's sensory capabilities facilitate social responsiveness. Newborns prefer human voices and drawings of human faces. Within days of birth, babies can distinguish their mother's odor and voice.

4. Psychologists use habituation, decreasing responsiveness with repeated stimulation, to study infant thinking. Infants respond to a novel stimulus with interest, but the more the stimulus is presented, the less the infant responds. If an infant responds when a new stimulus is presented, the researcher knows that the infant recognizes that the stimulus is different.

Stepping Through the Section

An egg has been released by the ovary; during intercourse, millions of sperm are deposited and travel toward the egg. At the moment of conception, those few sperm that reach the egg release digestive enzymes that eat away the egg's protective coating, allowing one sperm to penetrate. The fertilizing sperm is drawn into the egg, where the egg nucleus and sperm nucleus fuse.

1. zygotes; differentiate; embryo; fetus

2. teratogens

3. can affect; fetal alcohol syndrome

4. rooting reflex

Newborns reflexively turn their heads in the direction of human voices. They gaze longer at a drawing of a human face than at a bull's-eye pattern. They focus best on objects about 8 to 12 inches away, which is about the distance between a nursing infant's eyes and the mother's.

5. habituation; decrease; colors, shapes, sounds; numbers; physics

Infancy and Childhood

Section Preview

1. Most of the brain cells a person will ever have are present at birth. However, the neural connections that enable walking, talking, and memory are only beginning to form. This neural immaturity may explain why we have no memories of events before 3 years of age. After puberty, a process of pruning shuts down some neural connections and strengthens others.

2. While nurture may play a role in motor development, nature plays a major role. Before biological maturation creates a readiness to develop a particular skill, experience has a limited effect.

   Although the age at which infants sit, stand, walk, and control bowel and bladder varies from child to child, the sequence in which babies develop these abilities is universal.

3. Piaget believed that children actively construct their understanding of the world in radically different ways from adults. He further believed that children's minds develop through a series of stages in which they form increasingly complex schemas that organize their past experiences and provide a framework for understanding future experiences.

   In the sensorimotor stage, from birth to about 2 years, children experience their world through their senses and actions. During this stage, object permanence (and, shortly after, stranger anxiety) develop.

   In the preoperational stage, from about 2 to 6 or 7 years, children are able to use language but lack logical reasoning. During this stage, egocentrism develops, along with the rudiments of a theory of mind.

   In the concrete operational stage, from about 6 or 7 to 11 years, children are able to think logically about concrete events and perform mathematical operations. Conservation also develops during this stage.

   The formal operational stage, from age 12 through adulthood, is characterized by abstract and systematic reasoning, as well as by the potential for mature moral reasoning.

4. Although preschoolers remain egocentric, they begin forming a theory of mind as their ideas about their own and others' feelings and thoughts develop. Between 3.5 and 4, children begin to realize that others may hold false beliefs. A preschooler's growing ability to tease, empathize, and persuade others stems from a growing ability to take another's perspective (theory of mind).

   Autism is a childhood disorder marked by deficient communication and social interaction, an impaired theory of mind, and malfunctions in brain areas that enable attending to others.

5. Today's researchers see development as more continuous than Piaget did. By detecting the beginnings of each type of thinking at earlier ages, they have revealed conceptual abilities Piaget missed. Moreover, they see formal logic as a smaller part of cognition then he did.

   In many ways, however, Piaget's theory continues to receive support. Despite variations in the rate at which children develop, research reveals that human cognition everywhere unfolds in the basic sequence he proposed.

6. Harlow's research with monkeys reveals that attachment usually grows from body contact with parents, rather than by association with feeding. In many animals, attachment is also based on familiarity and forms during a critical period shortly after hatching or birth (a process called *imprinting*). Although human infants prefer faces and objects with which they are familiar, they do not have a critical period for forming attachments.

   Responsive parenting is also a factor. Sensitive, responsive mothers tend to have infants who become securely attached. Insensitive, unresponsive mothers often have insecurely attached infants.

7. Erik Erikson believed that infants with sensitive, loving caregivers form a lifelong attitude of basic trust—a sense that the world is predictable and reliable. Children who suffer parental neglect or abuse may form lasting scars—nightmares, depression, a troubled adolescence, and a greater tendency to later abuse their own children.

   Babies reared in institutions without nurturing care are often withdrawn, frightened, even speechless. Fortunately, most infants recover from disruptions of attachment if placed in a more positive and stable environment. Although most children who grow up under adversity are resilient and become normal adults, early abuse may alter the brain chemical serotonin.

8. Three parenting styles have been identified. Authoritarian parents impose rules and expect their children to be obedient. Authoritative parents are demanding, yet more responsive to their children. They set and enforce rules but also are willing to explain and discuss the reasoning behind rules. Permissive parents make few demands of their children and submit to their wishes. Children with the highest self-esteem, self-reliance, and social competence usually have authoritative parents, perhaps because their parents provide them with the greatest sense of self-control.

Stepping Through the Section

1. is not; pruning
2. maturation
3. 3; 3.5
4. motor; sequence; major; small
5. Piaget
6. schemas
7. assimilation; accommodation
8. cognition
9. sensorimotor; 2
10. object permanence; 8
11. continuous; numbers
12. 6 or 7; preoperational
13. conservation; have not
14. egocentrism
15. theory of mind; false beliefs
16. communication; social; autism; attending to others
17. 6 or 7; concrete operational

18. formal operational; abstract; 12

Contemporary researchers see development as more continuous than did Piaget. By detecting the beginnings of each type of thinking at earlier ages, they have revealed conceptual abilities that Piaget missed. They also see formal logic as a smaller part of cognition than Piaget did. Despite these revisions to Piaget's theory, studies support the basic idea that cognitive development unfolds as a sequence of distinct stages.

19. 8; stranger anxiety
20. attachment
21. body contact; familiarity
22. critical period; imprinting
23. do not
24. secure; insecure

Placed in a strange situation, securely attached infants play comfortably, happily exploring their new environment. In contrast, insecurely attached infants are less likely to explore their surroundings and may even cling to their mothers. When separated from their mothers, insecurely attached infants are much more distressed than securely attached infants. When reunited with their mothers, insecurely attached infants may be indifferent.

Research studies conducted by Mary Ainsworth have revealed that sensitive, responsive mothers tend to have securely attached infants, whereas insensitive, unresponsive mothers often have insecurely attached infants. Other studies have found that temperamentally difficult infants whose mothers receive training in responsive parenting are more likely to become securely attached than are control infants.

25. temperament; is
26. comparable to
27. basic trust
28. 13; gradually declines; throughout the world
29. aggression
30. do not
31. resilient; serotonin
32. authoritarian
33. permissive
34. authoritative
35. authoritative; control

There are at least three possible explanations for the correlation between authoritative parenting and social competence in children. (1) Parenting may foster children's competence. (2) Children's competence may promote authoritative parenting. (3) A third factor, such as heredity or parental education or socioeconomic status, may foster both authoritative parenting and child competence.

Adolescence

Section Preview

1. Adolescence begins with puberty, a two-year period of rapid development that begins in girls at about age 11 and in boys at about age 13. Girls who are obese and those without biological fathers at home are prone to earlier puberty. Evolutionary psychologists suggest that early reproduction "makes sense" when body fat can support pregnancy and when parent-child bonds are weak. During the growth spurt, sexual maturation occurs, as the primary sex characteristics (reproductive organs) and secondary sex characteristics (nonreproductive traits) develop dramatically.

   The hallmarks of puberty are the first ejaculation in boys at about age 14 and the first menstrual period, called menarche, in girls at about age 13. As in earlier life stages, the sequence of physical changes is more predictable than their timing.

   Teens' occasional impulsiveness and risky behaviors may be due, in part, to the fact that development in the brain's frontal lobe lags behind that in the limbic system.

2. During the early teen years, reasoning tends to be self-focused. Eventually, however, most adolescents attain Piaget's stage of formal operations and become capable of abstract, logical thinking.

   Kohlberg believed that moral reasoning builds on cognitive development and proceeds through as many as six stages. Before age 9, most children obey rules either to avoid punishment or to gain rewards (preconventional morality). By early adolescence, they develop the conventional morality of abiding by laws simply because "those are the rules." Postconventional morality, which is achieved by those who develop the abstract reasoning of formal operations, affirms people's agreed-upon rights or follows a personal code of ethics.

   Critics contend that the postconventional level appears mostly in the educated middle class of countries that value individualism. Others contend that Kohlberg's stages reflect a male bias, and that for women, moral maturity is less a matter of abstract justice than it is an ethic of caring relationships.

3. According to Erikson, the primary task of adolescence is the formation of identity. Many adolescents try out different "selves" by playing different roles in various situations until their sense of identity becomes clearer.

   Once adolescents have formed a sense of who they are, said Erikson, they focus on developing close relationships. Carol Gilligan believes that females are less concerned than males with developing a sense of identity as separate individuals *before* they strive to form close relationships.

   This gender difference in connectedness carries into adulthood. Women emphasize caring more than men and have closer, more intimate relationships.

   Despite popular belief, only a very small percentage of teenagers report not getting along with their parents at all. However, adolescence is a time of growing peer influence and diminishing parental influence, especially on matters of personal taste and life-style.

Stepping Through the Section

1. G. Stanley Hall
2. puberty; 11; 13; primary sex; secondary sex
3. overweight or obese; biological fathers at home; body fat; parent-child
4. menarche; 13; 14
5. sequence; timing
6. early; alcohol use and premature sexual activity; early; emotional maturity
7. pruning; frontal lobe; limbic system
8. self-focused
9. formal operations; abstract
10. Kohlberg; preconventional; conventional; postconventional
11. punishment; rewards
12. adolescence; approval; order
13. postconventional

Critics of Kohlberg's theory argue that the perception of postconventional moral reasoning as the highest level of moral development reflects a Western middle-class bias. Others have argued that for women, morality is less a matter of abstract, impersonal justice and more an ethic of caring relationships.

14. has; middle; individualism
15. empathy
16. gratification

Erikson's stages of psychosocial development

Group Age	Psychosocial Stage
Infancy	**Trust vs. mistrust**
Toddlerhood	Autonomy vs. shame and doubt
Preschooler	**Initiative vs. guilt**
Elementary school	Competence vs. inferiority
Adolescence	**Identity vs. role confusion**
Young adulthood	Intimacy vs. isolation
Middle adulthood	**Generativity vs. stagnation**
Late adulthood	Integrity vs. despair

17. identity; intimacy

18. falls; rises

19. less

20. smaller; competitive; social relationships

21. late adolescence

Women provide most of the care to the very young and the very old. They also have closer, more intimate relationships, especially with other women.

22. peers; parents; do

23. nutrition; earlier; education; later

Adulthood

Section Preview

1. Muscular strength, reaction time, sensory keenness, and cardiac output all peak by the mid-twenties and begin to decline thereafter. Health and exercise habits are important factors in the rate of physical decline.

   For women, menopause is the foremost biological change related to aging. Despite popular belief, menopause usually does not create psychological problems for women. Men experience a gradual decline in sperm count, testosterone level, and speed of erection and ejaculation as they get older.

   Decline in the functioning of the body's disease-fighting immune system makes the elderly more susceptible to life-threatening ailments such as cancer and pneumonia. Older people suffer short-term ailments, such as colds and the flu, less often, however.

   Aging also slows neural processing and results in a small, gradual net loss of brain cells. The birth of new cells and the proliferation of neural connections helps compensate for the cell loss.

2. Typically, the ability to recall (but not to recognize) new information, particularly material that is not meaningful to the individual, declines. Longitudinal studies of intelligence have laid to rest the myth that intelligence sharply declines with age. Whether intelligent performance on a task increases or decreases with age depends largely on the task. Tests of accumulated knowledge reveal that crystallized intelligence increases up to old age. Tests measuring one's ability to reason abstractly reveal that fluid intelligence decreases with age. These differences help explain why people in different professions produce their most notable work at different ages.

3. Some psychologists have suggested that the early forties are a time of emotional instability, when a "midlife transition," or crisis, is likely. Research has not found, however, that emotional distress of this kind peaks at any particular age.

   Researchers are skeptical of stage theories of adult social development for several reasons. For one, the settings of the *social clock* prescribing "proper" ages for various life events vary from culture to culture and from era to era. Even more important than one's age in defining new life stages are life events such as marriage, parenthood, job changes, divorce, and retirement. Increasingly, events such as these are occurring at unpredictable ages.

4. According to Erikson, the tasks of forming close relationships (intimacy) and being productive and supporting future generations (generativity) dominate adulthood. Freud expressed the same viewpoint in saying that the healthy adult is one who can love and work.

   Despite the rising divorce rate, most married Europeans and North Americans generally feel happier than those who are unmarried, especially those who are separated or divorced. Although having a child is for most people a happy event, as children begin to absorb time, money, and emotional energy, satisfaction with marriage often declines.

   Despite the popular belief that the departure of adult children usually causes parents to feel great distress and a loss of purpose, research reveals that those whose nest has emptied generally report greater happiness and enjoyment of their marriage.

   Studies of the relationship between happiness and having a career have compared employed and unemployed women. The results of these studies reveal that what matters is not which role(s) a woman occupies—as worker, wife, and/or mother—but the quality of her experience in each. People of all ages report similar feelings of happiness and satisfaction with life.

Stepping Through the Section

1. is not

2. muscular strength, reaction time, sensory keenness, cardiac output; women

3. age; health; exercise

4. menopause; 50; estrogen; expectations; attitude

5. sperm; testosterone

6. shrinks; less; reduced

7. more; less

8. slows; brain cells

9. women; less

10. brain cell; oxygen

11. recall; recognize

12. meaningfulness

13. cross-sectional; longitudinal; decline; stability

Because cross-sectional studies compare people not only of different ages but also of different eras, education levels, family size, and affluence, it is not surprising that such studies reveal cognitive decline with age. In contrast, longitudinal studies test one group over a span of years. However, because those who survive to the end of longitudinal studies may be the brightest and healthiest, these studies may underestimate the average decline in intelligence. Research is also complicated by the fact that certain tests measure only one type of intelligence. Tests that measure fluid intelligence reveal decline with age; tests that measure crystallized intelligence reveal just the opposite.

14. crystallized; increase

15. fluid; decrease

16. crisis (transition)

17. social clock; less; life events

18. intimacy; generativity; love; work

19. monogamous; 20; well educated

20. twice; higher

21. 3 out of 4; happiness; sexual satisfaction; health; income

22. social pathologies such as crime, delinquency, and emotional disorders among children

23. decreases; employed

24. increase

25. quality

26. do

27. suddenly and before its expected time on the social clock

28. do; do not

29. men

30. do not

31. integrity

Reflections on the Major Developmental Issues

Section Preview

1. Although research casts doubt on the idea that life proceeds through neatly defined, age-linked stages of cognitive, moral, and social development, the concept of stages remains useful. Stage theories show the order in which abilities develop and help focus awareness on how people of one age think and act differently when they arrive at a later age.

2. Research has revealed that there is a consistency to personality due to an underlying stability in basic social and emotional styles. Although the first two years of life provide a poor basis for predicting eventual traits, as people grow older dispositions become quite stable and attitudes much more predictable.

Stepping Through the Section

1. Piaget; Kohlberg; Erikson

2. stages; brain; Piaget

3. do not

4. temperament

Progress Test 1

Multiple-Choice Questions

1. **c.** is the answer. Developmental psychologists study physical, cognitive (memory, in this example), and social change throughout the life span. (p. 99)
   a. Social psychologists study how people influence and are influenced by others.
   b. Cognitive psychologists *do* study memory; because Dr. Goodman is interested in life-span *changes* in memory, she is more likely a developmental psychologist.
   d. Experimental psychologists study physiology, sensation, perception, learning, and other aspects of behavior. Only developmental psychologists focus on developmental changes in behavior and mental processes.

2. **a.** is the answer. (p. 108)
   b. Deduction, or deductive reasoning, is a formal operational ability.
   c. Piaget's theory is not concerned with attachment.

d. Attaining object permanence is the hallmark of sensorimotor thought.

3. **b.** is the answer. The preoperational child sees the world from his or her own vantage point. (p. 107)
a. As immature as egocentrism is, it represents a significant cognitive advance over the sensorimotor child, who knows the world only through senses and actions. Even simple self-awareness takes a while to develop.
c. & d. As children attain the operational stages, they become more able to see the world through the eyes of others.

4. **a.** is the answer. Before object permanence is attained, "out of sight" is truly "out of mind." (p. 105)
b., c., & d. Developments that occur during the preoperational, concrete operational, and formal operational stages include language use, conservation, and abstract reasoning, respectively.

5. **b.** is the answer. The infant turns its head and begins sucking when its cheek is stroked. (p. 101)
a., c., & d. These stimuli produce other reflexes in the newborn.
e. The mother's voice causes the newborn to turn toward the sound; no touch is involved.

6. **b.** is the answer. (p. 110)
a. When given the choice between a wire mother with a bottle and a cloth mother without, the monkeys preferred the cloth mother.
c. The presence of other infants made no difference.
d. Imprinting plays no role in the attachment of higher primates.

7. **c.** is the answer. Through maturation—an orderly sequence of biological growth processes that are relatively unaffected by experience—all humans develop. (p. 103)
a. Conservation is the cognitive awareness that objects do not change with changes in shape.
b. The forces of nature *are* those that direct maturation.
d. The continuity/stages debate has to do with whether development is a gradual and continuous process or a discontinuous, stagelike process. Those who emphasize maturation see development as occurring in stages, not continuously.

8. **e.** is the answer. Erikson proposed that development occurs in a series of stages, in the first of which the child develops an attitude of either basic trust or mistrust. (p. 112)
a. Piaget's theory is concerned with cognitive development.

b. Harlow conducted research on attachment and deprivation.
c. Vygotsky focused on the influence of sociocultural factors on development.
d. Freud's theory is concerned with personality development.

9. **b.** is the answer. (p. 104)

10. **a.** is the answer. (p. 120)

11. **c.** is the answer. At the preconventional level, moral reasoning centers on self-interest, whether this means obtaining rewards or avoiding punishment. (p. 118)
a. & b. Moral reasoning based on a sense of social duty or a desire to gain social approval is associated with the conventional level of moral development.
d. Reasoning based on ethical principles is characteristic of the postconventional level of moral development.

12. **d.** is the answer. Boys who show early physical maturation are generally stronger and more athletic than boys who mature late; these qualities may lead to greater popularity and self-assurance. (p. 117)
a. & c. Early maturation tends to be socially advantageous for boys but not for girls.
b. Early-maturing girls often suffer embarrassment and are objects of teasing.

13. **b.** is the answer. (p. 128)
a. Fluid intelligence tends to decrease with age.
c. & d. Crystallized intelligence refers to the accumulation of facts and general knowledge that takes place during a person's life. Crystallized intelligence generally *increases* with age.

14. **c.** is the answer. (p. 117)
a. Puberty refers to the early adolescent period during which accelerated growth and sexual maturation occur, not to the first menstrual period.
b. Menopause is the cessation of menstruation, which typically occurs in the early fifties.
d. In Erikson's theory, generativity, or the sense of contributing and being productive, is the task of middle adulthood.

15. **e.** is the answer. (p. 133)
a. Generativity is associated with middle adulthood.
b. & c. Intimacy and isolation are associated with young adulthood.
d. The term *acceptance* is not associated with Erikson's theory.

16. **c.** is the answer. Once formal operational thought has been attained, thinking is no longer limited to concrete propositions. (p. 108)

a. & b. Preoperational thought and concrete operational thought emerge before, and do not include, the ability to think logically about abstract propositions.

d. Fluid intelligence refers to abstract reasoning abilities; however, it is unrelated to Piaget's theory and stages.

17. **a.** is the answer. (pp. 127–128)

    b., c., & d. These cognitive abilities remain essentially unchanged as the person ages.

18. **d.** is the answer. "Use it or lose it" seems to be the rule: Often, changes in activity patterns contribute significantly to problems regarded as being part of usual aging. (p. 126)

    a. Elderly people do not necessarily have substantial memory loss; it depends on their activity level.

    b. Although the elderly are more subject to long-term ailments than younger adults, they actually suffer fewer short-term ailments.

    c. People of all ages report equal happiness or satisfaction with life.

19. **b.** is the answer. (p. 128)

    a. This answer describes cross-sectional research.

    c. & d. Sample size does not distinguish cross-sectional from longitudinal research.

    e. Just the opposite is true.

20. **b.** is the answer. (p. 115)

21. **c.** is the answer. Because the late teen years provide many new opportunities for trying out possible roles, adolescents' identities typically incorporate an increasingly positive self-concept. (p. 120)

22. **d.** is the answer. The physical changes of puberty mark the onset of adolescence. (p. 115)

    a. & b. An identity crisis or parent-child conflict may or may not occur during adolescence; neither of these formally marks its onset.

    c. Formal operational thought, rather than concrete reasoning, typically develops in adolescence.

23. **b.** is the answer. (p. 125)

    a. Menarche refers to the onset of menstruation.

    c. When it does occur, the midlife crisis is a psychological, rather than biological, phenomenon.

    d. Generativity is Erikson's term for productivity during middle adulthood.

24. **d.** is the answer. (p. 133)

True–False Items

1. F (p. 113)	**5.** F (p. 133)	**9.** F (p. 124)
2. F (p. 103)	**6.** T (p. 116)	**10.** F (p. 126)
3. F (p. 104)	**7.** T (p. 124)	**11.** F (p. 133)
4. T (p. 109)	**8.** F (p. 128)	

Progress Test 2

1. **d.** is the answer. With object permanence, a child develops schemas for familiar objects, including faces, and may become upset by a stranger who does not fit any of these schemas. (pp. 105, 110)

    a. The concept of conservation develops during the concrete operational stage, whereas stranger anxiety develops during the sensorimotor stage.

    b. & c. Egocentrism and a theory of mind both develop during the preoperational stage. This follows the sensorimotor stage, during which stranger anxiety develops.

2. **a.** is the answer. (p. 104)

    b., c., & d. Each of these is an understanding developed by Piaget.

3. **a.** is the answer. (p. 106)

4. **a.** is the answer. Any drug taken by the mother passes through the placenta and enters the child's bloodstream. (p. 100)

    b. Addiction cannot be inherited; it requires exposure to an addictive drug.

    c. Drugs may disrupt the mechanisms of heredity, but there is no evidence that such changes promote addiction.

    d. This answer is incorrect because at no age does the blood "resist" drugs.

5. **c.** is the answer. (p. 101)

    a., b., & d. A child's emotional temperament, attachment, and addiction have not been linked to the mother's drinking while pregnant.

6. **b.** is the answer. (p. 100)

7. **d.** is the answer. A critical period is a restricted time during which an organism must be exposed to certain influences or experiences for a particular kind of learning to occur. (p. 111)

    a. Critical periods refer to developmental periods after birth.

    b. Critical periods vary from behavior to behavior, but they are not confined to the hours following birth.

    c. Critical periods are not specifically associated with the preoperational period.

8. **c.** is the answer. Deprived monkeys were impaired in their social behaviors but not in their physical development. (p. 113)

a., b., & d. Each of these was found in socially deprived monkeys.

9. **c.** is the answer. (p. 131)

10. **d.** is the answer. This is because of a lack of neural connections before that age. (p. 103)

11. **c.** is the answer. (p. 111)

a. Insecurely attached infants often cling to their mothers when placed in a new situation; yet, when the mother returns after an absence, the infant's reaction tends to be one of indifference.

b. These behaviors are characteristic of securely attached infants.

d. Insecurely attached infants in unfamiliar surroundings will often exhibit a range of emotional behaviors.

12. **d.** is the answer. (p. 118)

a. Erikson is known for his theory of psychosocial development.

b. Piaget is known for his theory of cognitive development.

c. & e. These theorists were not discussed.

13. **a.** is the answer. (p. 128)

b. This answer describes the longitudinal research method.

c. & d. Cross-sectional studies have tended to exaggerate the negative effects of aging on intellectual functioning; for this reason they may not be the most appropriate method for studying lifespan development.

14. **c.** is the answer. Different societies and eras have somewhat different ideas about the age at which major life events should ideally occur. (p. 129)

15. **c.** is the answer. (p. 118)

a. Preconventional morality is based on avoiding punishment and obtaining rewards.

b. Conventional morality is based on gaining the approval of others and/or on following the law and social convention.

d. There is no such thing as generative morality.

16. **a.** is the answer. (pp. 119–121)

b. According to Erikson, identity develops before intimacy.

c. & d. The formation of basic trust is the task of infancy.

17. **e.** is the answer. (p. 125)

a. Most women do not experience anxiety and distress following menopause; moreover, the woman's experience will depend largely on her expectations and attitude.

b. Only 4 or 5 in 10 postmenopausal Canadian and U.S. women and 1 in 7 postmenopausal Japanese women experience hot flashes.

c. Menopause is caused by a *reduction* in estrogen.

d. This was not mentioned in the text.

18. **a.** is the answer. A mathematician's skills are likely to reflect abstract reasoning, or fluid intelligence, which declines with age. (p. 128)

b., d., & e. Philosophy, literature, and history are fields in which individuals often do their most notable work later in life, after more experiential knowledge (crystallized intelligence) has accumulated.

c. Scientific achievements generally reflect fluid, rather than crystallized, intelligence.

19. **d.** is the answer. (p. 131)

a., b., & c. Most couples do not feel a loss of purpose or marital strain following the departure of grown children.

20. **c.** is the answer. (p. 121)

a. & b. In fact, just the opposite is true.

21. **d.** is the answer. (p. 128)

a. & b. Fluid intelligence, which decreases with age, refers to the ability to reason abstractly.

c. Crystallized intelligence increases with age.

22. **a.** is the answer. (p. 126)

23. **d.** is the answer. (p. 135)

24. **d.** is the answer. (p. 131)

Review and Reflect

Multiple-Choice Questions

1. **b.** is the answer. (p. 104)

a. & d. Although the rate of motor development varies from child to child, the basic sequence is universal and, therefore, predictable.

c. Rolling over and head lifting are both learned.

2. **a.** is the answer. Mathematical and philosophical reasoning involve fluid and crystallized intelligence, respectively. Because fluid intelligence generally declines with age while crystallized intelligence increases, it is likely that significant mathematical accomplishments will occur at an earlier age than philosophical accomplishments. (pp. 128–129)

3. **c.** is the answer. Early maturing boys tend to be more popular. (p. 117)

a. Early maturing girls may temporarily suffer embarrassment and be the objects of teasing.

b. & d. The social benefits of early or late maturation are based on physical development, not on cognitive skills.

4. **c.** is the answer. This test is designed to determine if the child understands that the quantity of liquid is conserved, despite the shift to a container that is different in shape. (p. 107)

   a. These are general processes related to concept building.

   b. Object permanence is the concept that an object continues to exist even when not perceived; in this case, the water is perceived throughout the experiment.

   d. This experiment does not require abstract reasoning, only the ability to reason logically about the concrete.

5. **a.** is the answer. This child's age and stranger anxiety clearly place him within Piaget's sensorimotor stage. (pp. 105, 110)

6. **b.** is the answer. This child's age, ability to use language, and egocentrism clearly place her within Piaget's preoperational stage. (p. 107)

7. **d.** is the answer. Conservation is a hallmark of the concrete operational stage; egocentrism is a hallmark of the preoperational stage. (pp. 107, 108)

8. **c.** is the answer. Being 4 years old, Jamail would be in Piaget's preoperational stage. Preoperational thinking is egocentric, which means Jamail would find it difficult to "put himself in his sister's shoes" and perceive that she has a brother. (p. 146)

9. **b.** is the answer. (p. 111)

   a. Conservation is the ability to realize that the amount of an object does not change even if its shape changes.

   c. Egocentrism is the inability to take another person's perspective.

   d. According to Erikson, basic trust is feeling that the world is safe as a result of sensitive, loving caregivers.

10. **a.** is the answer. Although loving parents will also produce securely attached children, Erikson's theory deals with trust or mistrust. (p. 112)

    c. Control is not a factor in this stage of Erikson's theory.

11. **d.** is the answer. (p. 122)

    a. This description of Cassandra's feelings does not suggest that her relationship with her parents is deteriorating. Cassandra's social development, like that of most adolescents, is coming under increasing peer influence and diminishing parental influence.

    b. & c. Because Cassandra's feelings are normal, there is no reason for her to change her circle of friends or for her parents to seek counseling.

    e. Her parents' friends are probably in the same situation.

12. **c.** is the answer. (p. 118)

    a., b., & d. Piaget did not link cognitive ability to amount of schooling, gender, or differences in how boys and girls are socialized.

13. **a.** is the answer. Children in various cultures do seem to progress through Kohlberg's preconventional and conventional levels, which indicates that some aspects of the development of moral reasoning are universal. (p. 119)

14. **c.** is the answer. (p. 121)

15. **c.** is the answer. Reasoning is based on fluid intelligence. (p. 128)

    a. There is no such thing as "analytic" intelligence.

    b. Crystallized intelligence increases up to old age.

16. **c.** is the answer. Because several variables (education, affluence, etc.) generally distinguish the various groups in a cross-sectional study, it is impossible to rule out that one or more of these, rather than aging, is the cause of the measured intellectual decrease. (p. 128)

    a. Small sample size and unrepresentativeness generally are not limitations of cross-sectional research.

    b. This refers to longitudinal research.

17. **e.** is the answer. (p. 127)

    a. & c. In tests of recognition memory, the performance of older persons shows little decline.

    b. & d. The ability to recall material, especially meaningless material, declines with age.

18. **e.** is the answer. Research has not uncovered a tendency for people of any particular age group to report greater feelings of satisfaction or well-being. (p. 132)

19. **c.** is the answer. Although some researchers emphasize consistency and others emphasize potential for change, they all agree that consistency increases over the life span. (p. 135)

    a. One criticism of stage theories is that development does not occur in sharply defined stages.

    b. Research has shown that individuals' adult personalities cannot be predicted from their first two years.

    d. Social and emotional style are two of the most stable traits.

20. **b.** is the answer. Conventional morality is based in part on a desire to gain others' approval. (p. 118)

a. Preconventional reasoning is based on external incentives such as gaining a reward or avoiding punishment.

c. Postconventional morality reflects an affirmation of agreed-upon rights or universal ethical principles.

d. Fear of others' disapproval is one of the bases of conventional moral reasoning.

21. **b.** is the answer. (p. 122)
    a. In fact, just the opposite is true: Parental influence on children *decreases* during adolescence.
    d. Teens reflect their parents' social, political, and religious views, but rely on peers for matters of personal taste.
    e. The text does not mention this.

22. **c.** is the answer. (pp. 135–136)

23. **c.** is the answer. Carlos' age and struggle to form a close relationship place him squarely in this stage. (p. 121)
    a. Trust versus mistrust is the psychosocial task of infancy.
    b. Autonomy versus doubt is the psychosocial task of toddlerhood.
    d. Identity versus role confusion is the psychosocial task of adolescence.
    e. Generativity versus stagnation is the task of middle adulthood.

24. **d.** is the answer. (p. 132)

Essay Question

Sheryl's age would place her at the threshold of Piaget's stage of formal operations. Although her thinking is probably still somewhat self-focused, Sheryl is becoming capable of abstract, logical thought. This will increasingly allow her to reason hypothetically and deductively. Because her logical thinking also enables her to detect inconsistencies in others' reasoning and between their ideals and actions, Sheryl and her parents may be having some heated debates about now.

According to Kohlberg, Sheryl is probably at the threshold of postconventional morality. When she was younger, Sheryl probably abided by rules in order to gain social approval, or simply because "rules are rules" (conventional morality). Now that she is older, Sheryl's moral reasoning will increasingly be based on her own personal code of ethics and an affirmation of people's agreed-upon rights. Because she is a woman, her morality may be more concerned with caring about relationships.

According to Erikson, psychosocial development occurs in eight stages, each of which focuses on a particular task. As an adolescent, Sheryl's psychosocial task is to develop a sense of self by testing roles, then integrating them to form a single identity. Erikson called this stage "identity versus role confusion."

Key Terms

1. **Developmental psychology** is the branch of psychology concerned with physical, cognitive, and social change throughout the life span. (p. 99)

2. The **zygote** (a term derived from the Greek word for "joint") is the fertilized egg, that is, the cluster of cells formed during conception by the union of sperm and egg. (p. 100)

3. The **embryo** is the developing prenatal organism from about 2 weeks through 2 months after conception. (p. 100)

4. The **fetus** is the developing prenatal human from 9 weeks after conception to birth. (p. 100)

5. **Teratogens** (literally, poisons) are any drugs, viruses, or other substances that cross the mother's placenta and can harm the developing embryo or fetus. (p. 100)

6. The **fetal alcohol syndrome (FAS)** refers to the physical and cognitive abnormalities that heavy drinking by a pregnant woman may cause in the developing child. (p. 101)

7. The **rooting reflex** is the newborn's tendency, when his or her cheek is stroked, to orient toward the stimulus and begin sucking. (p. 101)

8. A simple form of learning used to study infant cognition, **habituation** is decreasing responsiveness to a stimulus that is repeatedly presented. (p. 102)

9. **Maturation** refers to the biological growth processes that enable orderly changes in behavior and are relatively uninfluenced by experience or other environmental factors. (p. 103)
   Example: The ability to walk depends on a certain level of neural and muscular **maturation**. For this reason, until the toddler's body is physically ready to walk, practice "walking" has little effect.

10. In Piaget's theory of cognitive development, **schemas** are mental concepts or frameworks that organize and interpret information. (p. 105)

11. In Piaget's theory, **assimilation** refers to interpreting a new experience in terms of an existing schema. (p. 105)

12. In Piaget's theory, **accommodation** refers to changing an existing schema to incorporate new information that cannot be assimilated. (p. 105)

13. **Cognition** refers to all the mental processes asso-

ciated with thinking, knowing, remembering, and communicating. (p. 105)

14. In Piaget's theory of cognitive stages, the **sensorimotor stage** lasts from birth to about age 2. During this stage, infants gain knowledge of the world through their senses and their motor activities. (p. 105)

15. **Object permanence,** which develops during the sensorimotor stage, is the awareness that things do not cease to exist when not perceived. (p. 105)

16. In Piaget's theory, the **preoperational stage** lasts from about 2 to 6 or 7 years of age. During this stage, language development is rapid, but the child is unable to understand the mental operations of concrete logic. (p. 107)

17. **Conservation** is the principle that properties such as number, volume, and mass remain constant despite changes in the forms of objects; it is acquired during the concrete operational stage. (p. 107)

18. In Piaget's theory, **egocentrism** refers to the difficulty that preoperational children have in considering another's viewpoint. "Ego" means "self," and "centrism" indicates "in the center"; the preoperational child is "self-centered." (p. 107)

19. Our ideas about our own and others' thoughts, feelings, and perceptions and the behaviors these might predict constitute our **theory of mind.** (p. 107)

20. During the **concrete operational stage,** lasting from about ages 6 or 7 to 11, children can think logically about concrete events and objects. (p. 108)

21. In Piaget's theory, the **formal operational stage** normally begins about age 12. During this stage people begin to think logically about abstract concepts. (p. 108)

    Memory aid: To help differentiate Piaget's stages remember that "operations" are mental transformations. *Pre*operational children, who lack the ability to perform transformations, are "before" this developmental milestone. Concrete operational children can operate on real, or concrete, objects. Formal operational children can perform logical transformations on abstract concepts.

22. **Stranger anxiety** is the fear of strangers that infants begin to display at about 8 months of age. (p. 110)

23. **Attachment** is an emotional tie with another person, shown in young children by their seeking closeness to a caregiver and showing distress on separation. (p. 110)

24. A **critical period** is a limited time shortly after birth during which an organism must be exposed to certain experiences or influences if it is to develop properly. (p. 111)

25. **Imprinting** is the process by which certain animals form attachments during a limited critical period early in life. (p. 111)

26. According to Erikson, **basic trust** is a sense that the world is predictable and trustworthy—a concept that infants form if their needs are met by responsive caregiving. (p. 112)

27. **Adolescence** refers to the life stage from puberty to independent adulthood, denoted physically by a growth spurt and maturation of primary and secondary sex characteristics, cognitively by the onset of formal operational thought, and socially by the formation of identity. (p. 115)

28. **Puberty** is the early adolescent period of sexual maturation, during which a person becomes capable of reproduction. (p. 115)

29. The **primary sex characteristics** are the body structures (ovaries, testes, and external genitalia) that enable reproduction. (pp. 115–116)

30. The **secondary sex characteristics** are the nonreproductive sexual characteristics, for example, female breasts, male voice quality, and body hair. (p. 116)

31. **Menarche** is the first menstrual period. (p. 117)

32. In Erikson's theory, establishing an **identity,** or one's sense of self, is the primary task of adolescence. (p. 119)

33. In Erikson's theory, **intimacy,** or the ability to establish close, loving relationships, is the primary task of late adolescence and early adulthood. (p. 121)

34. **Menopause** is the cessation of menstruation and typically occurs in the early fifties. It also refers to the biological and psychological changes experienced during a woman's years of declining ability to reproduce. (p. 125)

35. In a **cross-sectional study,** people of different ages are compared with one another. (p. 128)

36. In a **longitudinal study,** the same people are tested and retested over a period of years. (p. 128)

37. **Crystallized intelligence** refers to those aspects of intellectual ability, such as vocabulary and general knowledge, that reflect accumulated

learning. Crystallized intelligence tends to increase with age. (p. 128)

38. **Fluid intelligence** refers to a person's ability to reason speedily and abstractly. Fluid intelligence tends to decline with age. (p. 128)

39. The **social clock** refers to the culturally preferred timing of social events, such as leaving home, marrying, having children, and retiring. (p. 129)

FOCUS ON VOCABULARY AND LANGUAGE

Page 99: As we *journey* through life—from *womb to tomb*—when, how, and why do we develop? In the process of becoming who we are, and as we travel (*journey*) through life, from conception to death (*womb to tomb*) we change and mature physically, psychologically, and socially. (Another humorous expression describing the life span or life cycle is from "sperm to worm.")

Infancy and Childhood

Page 103: . . . toddler . . . This describes a child who is beginning to learn to walk and who walks with short, uneven steps.

Page 103: After birth, the neural networks that eventually enabled you to walk, talk, and remember had a *wild growth spurt.* Myers points out that when you were born, you had all the brain cells that you will ever have. But after birth there is a very rapid development (*a wild growth spurt*) in the number of connections between neurons.

Page 105: . . . fruitless . . . This word means to be unproductive or useless (like a tree that does not produce fruit). It is pointless (*fruitless*), according to Piaget's theory, to try to teach a child who is in the preoperational stage of development how to use abstract logic to solve a complex problem (formal operational reasoning).

Pages 106: When she lifted the screen, the infants sometimes *did a double take,* staring longer when shown a wrong number of objects. In this experiment with 5-month-old infants, Karen Wynn showed that these very young children were capable of conceptual thinking. She did this by measuring their reaction time to expected and unexpected outcomes. Shown an impossible outcome, infants stared longer (*they did a double take*) and they also demonstrated a mental capacity for detecting changes or differences in the frequency of events (*they have a head for numbers*).

Page 107: Rather than thinking of people as *breathing wind-up dolls . . .* Preschoolers gradually begin to understand that other people are not just living mechanical toys or automatons (*breathing wind-up dolls*) but have mental capacities, intentions, motivations, etc. (children form a theory of mind). This is illustrated when the young girl in the children's story *Little Red Riding Hood* recognizes that the big bad wolf (disguised as her grandmother) has very bad intentions toward her and quickly escapes (*races away*).

Page 109: Piaget's stage theory is controversial. For some things it gets high marks. Piaget's theory has its supporters and its critics (*it is controversial*). Cross-cultural research supports the basic stages he proposed (*it gets high marks*), but most researchers believe that development is more continuous than Piaget thought. Children have more conceptual abilities at earlier periods than his theory suggested.

Page 109: . . . cognitive milestones . . . A milestone is an event of significance or importance. (Originally, a milestone was a large stone by the roadside inscribed with the distance in miles to nearby towns.) Myers notes that the age at which children usually succeed at important mental tasks (*cognitive milestones*) is of less relevance than the developmental order or sequence in which these abilities appear.

Page 109: Teachers would do better to *build on* what children already know, engaging them in *concrete demonstrations* and stimulating them to *think for themselves.* Preschool and elementary school children think differently from adults. In order for them to become independent thinkers (*think for themselves*), Piaget recommends that they be given specific, tangible examples (*concrete demonstrations*) that utilize (*build on*) their existing knowledge.

Page 110: To pit the drawing power of a food source against the contact comfort of the blanket, Harlow created two artificial mothers. Harlow's experiment was designed to test whether food or nourishment was more rewarding than the comfort of a soft terry cloth. Thus, when he tested the attraction (*pitted the drawing power*) of the artificial mother who supplied food against the soft comfort of the terry cloth mother (*contact comfort*), he was surprised that they preferred the cloth mother. They used "her" as a *secure base* from which to explore and a safe place (*safe haven*) to return to when frightened or anxious.

Page 111: The first moving object a *gosling, duckling, or chick* sees during the hours shortly after *hatching* is normally its mother. A *gosling* is a young goose, a *duckling* a young duck, and a *chick* a young chicken. What all these young fowl have in common is a tendency to follow, or trail after, the first larger moving object they see shortly after they emerge (*hatch*) from the eggshell. This attachment process is called **imprinting**.

Page 111: "*Mere exposure*" to people and things fosters *fondness*. Children do not imprint in the same way that ducklings and other animals do; nevertheless, repeated encounters with (or *exposure to*) other humans and objects encourage or promote liking and attachment (*fosters fondness*). As Myers puts it, "familiarity breeds content." This is a twist on the old saying "familiarity breeds contempt" and suggests that intimacy creates (*breeds*) satisfaction (*contentment*) rather than scorn (*contempt*).

Page 112: But evidence increasingly indicates that fathers are more than just *mobile sperm banks*. A *sperm bank* is where donated sperm is stored until it is used for artificial insemination. More and more research shows that fathers are not simply sperm producers who can move around (*mobile sperm banks*) and get mothers pregnant. Rather, evidence suggests they are capable caregivers who may interact with their babies much as mothers do.

Page 113: . . . can leave *footprints* on the brain. Traumatic experiences that occur early in development can have an effect on brain functioning; metaphorically, they can leave impressions (*footprints*) on the brain. The production of neurotransmitters such as serotonin, which calms aggressive impulses, is slower (*sluggish*) in abused children who become aggressive teens and adults.

Page 114: Parenting styles vary. Some parents *spank*, some *reason*. Some are *strict* and some are *lax*. When it comes to child-rearing practices (*parenting styles*), there is much variability: (a) some parents use strict controls and physical punishment (*spanking*); (b) others talk and discuss problems and issues with their children (*reason with them*); and (c) still others allow the children to do what they want and make few demands of them (*they are lax*). Myers identifies these parenting styles as (a) *authoritarian*, (b) *authoritative*, and (c) *permissive*.

Page 114: Before jumping to conclusions about the results of different parenting styles, *heed this caution*. Myers is suggesting that we must be careful (*heed a caution*) before quickly deciding (*jumping to conclusions*) about the merits of various parenting styles. He points out that the evidence is correlational and does not imply cause and effect. Thus, there may be other factors that are causally involved (e.g., some children may, because of their temperament, engender [elicit] greater trust and warmth from their parents).

Adolescence

Page 117: Early maturation *pays dividends* for boys. If onset of puberty occurs before the expected or usual time (*early maturation*), it will be much less stressful for boys than for girls. In general, for boys in their early teen years, being stronger and more athletic leads to more self-assurance, greater popularity, and greater independence (*it pays dividends*).

Page 117: If a young girl's body is *out of sync* with her own emotional maturity and her friends' physical development and experiences, she may begin associating with older adolescents or may suffer teasing or sexual harassment. *Sync* is an abbreviation of *synchronize*, which means to occur at the same time. So, if a girl's biological development is not proceeding at the same rate (*out of sync*) with her emotional and social development, she may start fraternizing (*associating*) with and imitating the behavior of older girls. Thus, early maturation can be a problem for girls, especially if the people around them react in an inappropriate or suggestive manner to their physical development (*sexual harassment*) or make fun of them (*tease them*).

Page 118: Gradually, though, most achieve the *intellectual summit* that Piaget called *formal operations*. The *formal operational* stage is the highest level in Piaget's theory of cognitive development (*intellectual summit*). Most adolescents reach this stage and are capable of logical and abstract reasoning. For example, many think about (*ponder*) and discuss (*debate*) such issues as good and evil, truth and justice, and other abstract topics about human nature.

Page 118: A crucial task of childhood and adolescence is discerning right from wrong and developing *character—the psychological muscles for controlling impulses*. *Character* refers to the total qualities a person possesses, including attitudes, beliefs, interests, actions, and a philosophy of life. By developing *character*, adolescents learn to have the intellectual strength (*psychological muscles*) to refrain from acting immorally (*controlling impulses*). Kohlberg proposed a controversial stage theory of moral development which has three levels: preconventional, conventional, and postconventional.

Page 119: Kohlberg's claim was that these levels form a *moral ladder* . . . In Kohlberg's view children have to go through each of the three stages (preconventional, conventional, and postconventional) in succession much as a person climbs a ladder, one rung at a time, from bottom to top. The lowest rung on this *moral ladder* involves self-interest and avoidance of punishment; the highest rung, which often develops during and after adolescence, is concerned with personal ethical principles and universal justice. Critics contend that the theory has cultural and gender biases.

Page 119: . . . *"psychosocial" task* . . . According to Erikson, each stage of life involves a dilemma (*crisis*) that has to be resolved before we can move on to the next stage. These tasks involve interactions between ourselves, our surroundings, and other people; thus, they are *social* in nature. The psychosocial assignment (*psychosocial task*) of adolescence involves *role confusion vs. forming an identity.* (This is sometimes called an **identity crisis**).

Page 120: Erikson noticed that some adolescents *forge* their identity early, simply by taking on their parents' values and expectations. *Forge* literally means to form or shape by heating and hammering metal. Erikson observed that some young people form (*forge*) their identities early, while others never quite appear to acquire a strong feeling of who they are (i.e., they don't *find themselves*).

Page 121: These gender differences *surface early,* in children's play. Males and females differ in their feelings of belonging (*connectedness*), a disparity that is noticeable from a young age (*surfaces early*). When playing, boys tend to engage in competitive group activity without much close, confidential, or affectionate dialogue. Girls typically are more intimate with each other and play in smaller groups, frequently with one friend, and they are less competitive and more supportive and empathic.

Page 123: That *gap*—the years spent *morphing* from child to adult—is adolescence. The time period (*gap*) between the end of childhood and the beginning of adulthood involves many social and biological changes; the person is transformed (*morphed*) from one type of entity (a child) to something quite different (an adult).

Adulthood

Page 125: In later life, the stairs get steeper, the print gets smaller, and people seem to *mumble* more. This is not meant to be taken literally. Myers is pointing out that as we become older, our sensory and perceptual abilities change so that our reaction time and our ability to see and hear decline. Thus, the stairs *appear* steeper, the print *seems* smaller, and people do not appear to be speaking clearly (*they mumble*).

Page 126: Aging *levies a tax* on the brain by slowing our neural processing. Myers is pointing out that aging is accompanied by a decrease in some perceptual and cognitive abilities. Just as you have less money after taxes have been assessed (*levied*) on your income, there are some losses in the brain's ability to function optimally due to the aging process.

Page 126: We are more likely to *rust from disuse than to wear out from overuse.* "Use it or lose it" is sound advice. When adults remain active physically, sexually, and mentally (they *"use it"*), they are less likely to become inactive later in life (*"lose it"*). If we follow sedentary life-styles, we will be like unused pieces of metal machinery that suffer from rust; on the other hand, keeping active will not do us any harm (*we won't wear out from overuse*); instead, we may benefit both mentally and physically.

Page 128: According to this more optimistic view, the *myth* that intelligence sharply declines with age is *laid to rest.* The false idea (*myth*) that our intellectual abilities decrease as we get older has been destroyed or buried (*laid to rest*) by recent **longitudinal research**. This research tests the same group of people over many years and may give more accurate results than testing many groups of people (each group having a different age range) at one period in time (**cross-sectional research**). However, both research methods have their own problems (*pitfalls*).

Page 130: "Pair-bonding is a trademark of the human animal," observed anthropologist Helen Fisher (1993). *Pair-bonding* refers to the monogamous attachment formed between one person and another, such as with a marriage partner, and this affiliation is characteristic (*a trademark*) of human beings.

Page 131: Might *test-driving life together* in a "trial marriage" minimize divorce risk? Does premarital cohabitation or a "trial marriage" (*test-driving life together*) increase the probability of a successful later marriage and reduce the likelihood of divorce (*minimize divorce risk*)? The research suggests it does not.

Those who live together before marriage are more likely to get divorced than those who don't. (These findings are correlational and Myers warns against making causal inferences.)

Reflections on the Major Developmental Issues

Page 134: But do they differ as a giant redwood differs from its seedling . . . or . . . as a butterfly differs from a caterpillar . . . ? The giant redwood is a large coniferous tree that grows in a continuous, cumulative way from seedling to mature tree. On the other hand, the butterfly emerges as a different creature after passing through a stage as a caterpillar. The question developmental psychologists ask is: Are changes throughout the life span (from infant to adult) due to a slow, continuous shaping process (like the tree), or do we go through a series of genetically preprogrammed stages (like the butterfly)?

Page 136: Many a 20-year-old *goof-off* has matured into a 40-year-old business or cultural leader. To *goof off* means to avoid work and act in a lazy manner; a person who behaves this way is called a *goof-off*. Some traits, such as temperament, are relatively stable over time, but everyone changes in some way with age. Thus, a lazy youth (*20-year-old goof-off*) may develop (*mature*) into a more productive adult (*40-year-old leader*).

chapter 5

Sensation and Perception

Chapter Overview

Chapter 5 explores the processes by which our sense receptors and nervous system represent our external environment (sensation), as well as how we mentally organize and interpret this information (perception). The senses of vision, hearing, taste, touch, smell, kinesthesis, and the vestibular sense are described, along with the ways in which we organize the stimuli reaching these senses in order to perceive form; depth; and constant shape, size, and lightness. To enhance your understanding of these processes, the chapter also discusses research findings from studies of subliminal stimulation, sensory restriction, recovery from blindness, adaptation to distorted environments, perceptual set, and extrasensory perception.

In this chapter there are many terms to learn and several theories you must understand. Many of the terms are related to the structure of the eye, ear, and other sensory receptors. Doing the chapter review several times, labeling the diagrams, and rehearsing the material frequently will help you to memorize these structures and their functions. The theories discussed include the Young-Helmholtz three-color and opponent-process theories of color vision and the Gestalt theory of form perception. As you study these theories, concentrate on understanding the strengths and weaknesses (if any) of each.

NOTE: Answer guidelines for all Chapter 5 questions begin on page 141.

Introducing Sensation and Perception
(p. 141)

> David Myers at times uses idioms that are unfamiliar to some readers. If you do not know the meaning of the following phrase in the context in which it appears in the text, refer to page 155 for an explanation: . . . *in a mirror, she is again stumped.*

Introduction Preview

First, skim the introduction. Then read the following objectives and, as you read the text, search for the information that will enable you to meet each objective. Answer guidelines begin on page 141.

1. Contrast the processes of sensation and perception.

Stepping Through the Introduction

After you have read the introduction, complete the sentences and answer the questions. As you proceed, evaluate your performance by consulting the answers on page 142. Do not continue with the next section until you understand each answer. If you need to, review or reread the section in the textbook before continuing.

1. The process by which we detect physical energy from the environment and encode it as neural signals is _____ .

The process by which sensations are selected, organized, and interpreted is

_____ .

2. Sensory analysis, which starts at the entry level and works up, is called _____-

_____ _____ .

Perceptual analysis, which works from our experience and expectations, is called

_____-_____

_____ .

3. The perceptual disorder in which a person has lost the ability to recognize familiar faces is

_____ .

Sensing the World: Some Basic Principles (pp. 142–146)

> If you do not know the meaning of any of the following words, phrases, or expressions in the context in which they appear in the text, refer to page 155 for an explanation: *A frog could starve to death knee-deep in motionless flies; The shades on our own senses are open just a crack; "satanic messages"; hucksters; price hike . . . to raise the eyebrows; everywhere that Mary looks the scene is sure to go.*

Section Preview

Answer guidelines are provided on page 142.

1. Distinguish between absolute and difference thresholds.

2. Discuss whether subliminal stimuli are sensed, and whether they are persuasive.

3. Describe the phenomenon of sensory adaptation, and show how it focuses our attention on changing stimulation.

Stepping Through the Section

Answers are provided on page 142.

1. The study of relationships between the physical characteristics of stimuli and our psychological experience of them is _____ .

2. The _____ _____ refers to the minimum stimulation necessary for a stimulus to be detected _____ percent of the time.

3. Some weak stimuli may trigger in our sense receptors a response that is processed by the brain, even though the response doesn't cross the threshold into _____ awareness.

4. Some entrepreneurs claim that exposure to "below threshold," or _____ , stimuli can be persuasive, but their claims are probably unwarranted.

5. The minimum difference required to distinguish two stimuli 50 percent of the time is called the

_____ _____ .

Another term for this value is the

_____ _____

_____ .

6. The principle that the difference threshold is not a constant amount, but a constant proportion, is known as _____

_____ . The proportion depends on the _____ .

7. After constant exposure to an unchanging stimulus, the receptor cells of our senses begin to fire less vigorously; this phenomenon is called

_____ _____ .

Explain why sensory adaptation is beneficial.

Vision (pp. 146–156)

> If you do not know the meaning of any of the following words, phrases, or expressions in the context in which they appear in the text, refer to pages 155–156 for an explanation: *This was baffling; blind spot; Holy Grail; blindsight; Color, like all aspects of vision, . . . the theater of our brains.*

Section Preview

Answer guidelines begin on page 142.

1. Explain the visual process, including the stimulus input, the structure of the eye, and the transduction (transformation) of light energy.

2. Discuss how visual information is processed in parallel (through the eye's retina and the brain) and at increasingly abstract levels.

3. Discuss how both the Young-Helmholtz and the opponent-process theories contribute to our understanding of color vision.

4. Explain color constancy, and discuss its significance to our understanding of vision.

Stepping Through the Section

Answers are provided on page 143.

1. The visible spectrum of light is a small portion of the larger spectrum of _____ radiation.

2. The distance from one light wave peak to the next is called _____ . This value determines the wave's color, or

   _____ .

3. The amount of energy in light waves, or _____ , determined by a wave's _____ , or height, influences the _____ of a light.

4. Light enters the eye through the transparent _____ , then passes through a small opening called the _____ ; the size of this opening is controlled by the colored _____ .

5. By changing its curvature, the _____ can focus the image of an object onto the _____ , the light-sensitive inner surface of the eye.

6. The process by which the lens changes shape to focus light is called _____ .

7. The retina's receptor cells are the _____ and _____ .

8. The neural signals produced in the rods and cones activate the neighboring _____ cells, then activate a network of _____ cells. The axons of ganglion cells converge to form the

   _____ _____ ,

   which carries the visual information to the

   _____ .

9. Where this nerve leaves the eye, there are no receptors; thus the area is called the

   _____ _____ .

10. It is the _____ (rods/cones) of the eye that permit the perception of color.

11. Unlike cones, in dim light the rods are _____ (sensitive/insensitive).

    Adapting to a darkened room will take the retina approximately _____ minutes.

12. Hubel and Wiesel discovered that certain neurons in the_____
_____ of the brain respond only to specific features of what is viewed. They called these neurons _____
_____ .

13. Feature detectors in the visual cortex pass their information to higher-level brain cells in the _____ and _____ cortex, which respond to specific visual scenes. Research has shown that in monkey brains such cells specialize in responding to a specific

_____ , _____
_____ , _____ , or
_____ _____ .

Other supercell clusters _____ this information.

14. The brain achieves its remarkable speed in visual perception by processing several subdivisions of a stimulus _____ (simultaneously/sequentially). This procedure, called

_____ _____ , may explain why people who have suffered a stroke may lose just one aspect of vision. Other brain-damaged people may demonstrate _____ by responding to a stimulus that is not consciously perceived. "Sight unseen" describes the brain's two visual systems—one that gives us our _____ _____ and one that
_____ .

15. An object appears to be red in color because it _____ the long wavelengths of red and because of our mental _____ of the color.

16. One out of every 50 people is color deficient; this is usually a male because the defect is genetically _____-_____ .

17. According to the Young-Helmholtz trichromatic theory, the eyes have three types of color receptors: one reacts most strongly to _____ , one to _____ , and one to _____ .

18. After staring at a green square for a while, you will see the color red, its _____ color, as an _____ .

19. Hering's theory of color vision is called the
_____ -_____
theory. According to this theory, after visual information leaves the receptors it is analyzed in terms of pairs of opposing colors:
_____ versus
_____ , _____
versus _____ , and
_____ versus
_____ .

Summarize the two stages of color processing.

20. The experience of color depends on the _____ in which an object is seen.

21. In an unvarying context, a familiar object will be perceived as having consistent color, even as the light changes. This phenomenon is called

_____ _____ .

The Other Senses (pp. 154–162)

If you do not know the meaning of any of the following words, phrases, or expressions in the context in which they appear in the text, refer to page 156 for an explanation: *sensitive to faint sounds; A piccolo produces much shorter, faster sound waves than does a tuba; If a car to the right honks. . . . ; we yearn to touch—to kiss, to stroke, to snuggle; Rubbing the area around your stubbed toe; A well-trained nurse may distract needle-shy patients by chatting with them; there is more to taste than meets the tongue; bathing your nostrils in a stream of scent-laden molecules; biological gyroscopes.*

Section Preview

Answer guidelines begin on page 143.

1. Explain the auditory process, including the stimulus input, the structure and function of the ear, and how sounds are located.

2. Describe the sense of touch.

3. Explain how pain is a property of the senses, and describe the gate-control theory of pain.

4. Describe taste, smell, kinesthesis, and the vestibular sense. Comment on the nature of sensory interaction.

Stepping Through the Section

Answers are provided on page 144.

1. The tendency of vision to dominate the other senses is referred to as _____ _____ .

2. The stimulus for hearing, or _____ , is sound waves, created by the compression and expansion of _____ _____ .

3. The amplitude of a sound wave determines the sound's _____ . The pitch of a sound is derived from the _____ of its wave.

4. Sound energy is measured in units called _____ . The absolute threshold for hearing is arbitrarily defined as _____ such units.

5. The ear is divided into three main parts: the _____ ear, the _____ ear, and the _____ ear.

6. The outer ear channels sound waves toward the _____ , a membrane that then vibrates.

7. The middle ear transmits the vibrations through a piston made of three small bones: the _____ , _____ , and _____ .

8. In the inner ear, a coiled tube called the _____ contains the receptor cells for hearing. The incoming vibrations cause the _____ _____ to vibrate the fluid that fills the tube, which causes ripples in the _____ _____ , which is lined with _____ _____ , whose movement triggers impulses in adjacent nerve fibers that converge to form the auditory nerve. As a general rule, a noise is potentially harmful if you can't _____ .

9. We locate a sound by sensing differences in the _____ and _____ with which it reaches our ears.

10. A sound that comes from directly ahead will be _____ (easier/harder) to locate than a sound that comes from off to one side.

11. The sense of touch is a mixture of at least four senses: _____ , _____ , _____ , and _____ . Only the sense of _____ has identifiable receptors. Other skin sensations, such as tickle, itch, hot, and wetness, are _____ of the basic ones.

12. Pain is a property of the _____ as well as of the _____ .

13. A sensation of pain in an amputated leg is referred to as a _____ _____ sensation.

14. The pain system _____ (is/is not) triggered by one specific type of physical energy. The body _____ (does/does not) have specialized receptor cells for pain.

15. Melzack and Wall have proposed a theory of pain called the _____-_____ theory, which proposes that there is a neurological _____ in the _____ _____ that blocks pain signals or lets them through. It may be opened by activation of _____ (small/large) nerve fibers and closed by activation of _____ (small/large) fibers or by information from the _____ .

List some pain control techniques used in the Lamaze method of prepared childbirth.

16. The basic taste sensations are _____ , _____ , _____ , _____ , and a possible fifth taste of _____ .

17. Taste, which is a _____ sense, is enabled by the 200 or more _____ _____ on the top and sides of the tongue. Each contains a _____ that catches food chemicals.

18. Taste receptors reproduce themselves every _____ .

19. When the sense of smell is blocked, as when we have a cold, foods do not taste the same; this illustrates the principle of _____ _____ .

20. Like taste, smell (or _____) is a _____ sense. Unlike light, an odor _____ (can/cannot) be separated into more elemental odors.

21. There is a direct connection between brain areas that receive information from the nose and the brain's _____ centers associated with _____ and _____ .

22. The system for sensing the position and movement of body parts is called _____ . The receptors for this sense are located in the _____ , _____ , and _____ of the body.

23. The sense that monitors the position and movement of the head (and thus the body) is the _____ _____ . The receptors for this sense are located in the _____ _____ and _____ _____ of the inner ear.

Perceptual Organization (pp. 165–175)

> If you do not know the meaning of any of the following words, phrases, or expressions in the context in which they appear in the text, refer to page 157 for an explanation: *There is far more to perception than meets the senses; Sometimes, however, they can lead us astray; mothers then coaxed them to crawl out on the glass; The floating finger sausage; As we move, objects that are actually stable may appear to move; through a paper tube.*

Section Preview

Answer guidelines begin on page 144.

1. Discuss Gestalt psychology's contribution to our understanding of perception, including the figure-ground relationship and principles of perceptual grouping in form perception.

2. Discuss research on depth perception involving the use of the visual cliff.

3. Explain how 3-D movies are made, and describe the binocular and monocular cues in depth perception.

4. Describe the perceptual constancies, and show how they operate in visual illusions.

Stepping Through the Section

Answers are provided on page 145.

1. According to the _____ school of psychology, we tend to organize a cluster of sensations into a _____ , or form. This tendency can be illustrated using a figure called a _____ cube.

2. When we view a scene, we see the central object, or _____ , as distinct from surrounding stimuli, or the _____ .

Identify the major contributions of Gestalt psychology to our understanding of perception.

3. Proximity, similarity, closure, continuity, and connectedness are examples of Gestalt rules of _____ .

4. The principle that we organize stimuli into smooth, continuous patterns is called _____ . The principle that we fill in gaps to create a complete, whole object is _____ . The grouping of items that are close to each other is the principle of _____ ; the grouping of items that look alike is the principle of _____ . The tendency to perceive uniform or attached items as a single unit is the principle of _____ .

5. The ability to see objects in three dimensions despite their two-dimensional representations on our retinas is called _____ .

6. Gibson and Walk developed the _____ _____ to test depth perception in infants. By _____ (what age?) infants demonstrate that they are using Gestalt perception principles.

Summarize the results of Gibson and Walk's studies of depth perception.

For questions 7–16, identify the depth perception cue that is defined.

7. Any cue that requires both eyes: _____ .

8. Any cue that requires either eye alone: _____ .

9. The greater the difference between the images received by the two eyes, the nearer the object: _____ _____

3-D movies simulate this cue by photographing each scene with _____ (how many?) cameras. This chapter's fundamental lesson is that our _____ are the constructions of our _____ .

10. The more our eyes focus inward when we view an object, the nearer the object: _____ .

11. If two objects are presumed to be the same size, the one that casts a smaller retinal image is perceived as farther away: _____ _____ .

12. An object partially covered by another is seen as farther away: _____ .

13. Objects lower in the visual field are seen as nearer: _____ _____ .

14. As we move, objects at different distances appear to move at different rates: _____ _____ .

15. Parallel lines appear to converge in the distance: _____ _____ .

16. Dimmer, or shaded, objects seem farther away: _____ _____ _____ .

17. Our tendency to see objects as unchanging while the stimuli from them change in size, shape, and lightness is called _____ _____ .

18. Several illusions, including the _____ and _____ illusions, are explained by the interplay between perceived _____ and perceived _____ . When distance cues are removed, these illusions are _____ (diminished/strengthened).

Explain how the size-distance relationship accounts for the moon illusion.

19. The brain computes an object's brightness _____ (relative to/independent of) surrounding objects. The amount of light an object reflects relative to its surroundings is called _____ _____ .

Perceptual Interpretation (pp. 175–182)

> If you do not know the meaning of any of the following words, phrases, or expressions in the context in which they appear in the text, refer to pages 157–158 for an explanation: *Ping-Pong ball; we may feel slightly disoriented, even dizzy; to see is to believe . . . to believe is to see; a "monster" in Scotland's Loch Ness; from what's behind our eyes and between our ears; in the eyes of their beholders; uncanny; one more dashed hope.*

Section Preview

Answer guidelines begin on page 145.

1. Briefly describe the nature-nurture debate on the origins of perception.

2. Discuss research findings on sensory deprivation and restored vision.

3. Explain what the use of distorting goggles indicates regarding the adaptability of perception.

4. Discuss the effects of experiences, assumptions, expectations, and contexts on our perceptions.

5. (Thinking Critically) State the claims of ESP, and explain why most research psychologists remain skeptical.

Stepping Through the Section

Answers are provided on page 146.

1. The idea that knowledge comes from inborn ways of organizing sensory experiences was proposed by the philosopher _____ .

2. On the other side was the philosopher who maintained that we learn to perceive the world by experiencing it, namely, _____ .

3. Studies of cases in which vision has been restored to a person who was blind from birth show that, upon *seeing* tactilely familiar objects for the first time, the person _____ (can/cannot) recognize them.

4. Studies of sensory restriction demonstrate that visual experiences during _____ are crucial for perceptual development. Such experiences suggest that there is a

_____ _____ for normal sensory and perceptual development. For this reason, human infants born with an opaque lens, called a _____ , typically have corrective surgery right away.

5. Humans given glasses that shift or invert the visual field _____ (will/will not)

adapt to the distorted perception. This is called

_____ _____ .

6. A mental predisposition that influences perception is called a _____

_____ .

7. How a stimulus is perceived depends on the _____ in which it is experienced, which may be colored by _____ about gender or culture.

8. (Thinking Critically) Perception outside the range of normal sensation is called _____

_____ .

9. (Thinking Critically) Psychologists who study ESP are called _____ .

10. (Thinking Critically) The form of ESP in which people claim to be capable of reading others' minds is called _____ . A person who "senses" that a friend is in danger might claim to have the ESP ability of

_____ . An ability to "see" into the future is called _____ . A person who claims to be able to levitate and move objects is claiming the power of _____ .

11. (Thinking Critically) Analyses of psychic visions and premonitions reveal _____ (high/chance-level) accuracy. Nevertheless, some people continue to believe in their accuracy, because vague predictions often are later _____ to match events that have already occurred. In addition, people are more likely to recall or _____ dreams that seem to have come true.

12. (Thinking Critically) Critics point out that a major difficulty for parapsychology is that ESP phenomena are not consistently

_____ .

13. (Thinking Critically) Researchers Bem and Honorton used the _____ procedure to reduce external distractions between a "sender" and a "receiver" in an ESP experiment. Although these researchers reported performance levels that _____ (beat/did not beat) chance levels, a more recent analysis of 30 follow-up studies found _____ (no effect/a reliable effect). .

Progress Test 1

Multiple-Choice Questions

Circle your answers to the following questions and check them with the answers beginning on page 146. If your answer is incorrect, read the explanation for why it is incorrect and then consult the appropriate pages of the text (in parentheses following the correct answer).

1. If you can just notice the difference between 10- and 11-pound weights, which of the following weights could you differentiate from a 100-pound weight?
   a. 101-pound weight
   b. 105-pound weight
   c. 110-pound weight
   d. There is no basis for prediction.

2. A decrease in sensory responsiveness accompanying an unchanging stimulus is called:
   a. sensory fatigue.
   b. accommodation.
   c. sensory deprivation.
   d. sensory adaptation.
   e. sensory interaction.

3. The size of the pupil is controlled by the:
   a. lens.
   b. retina.
   c. cornea.
   d. iris.

4. The process by which the lens changes its curvature is:
   a. accommodation.
   b. sensory adaptation.
   c. focusing.
   d. transduction.

5. The receptor of the eye that functions best in dim light is the:
   a. iris.
   b. ganglion cell.
   c. cone.
   d. bipolar cell.
   e. rod.

6. The Young-Helmholtz theory proposes that:
   a. there are three different types of color-sensitive cones.
   b. retinal cells are excited by one color and inhibited by its complementary color.
   c. there are four different types of cones.
   d. rod, not cone, vision accounts for our ability to detect fine visual detail.

7. Frequency is to pitch as _____ is to _____ .
   a. wavelength; loudness
   b. amplitude; loudness
   c. wavelength; intensity
   d. amplitude; intensity

8. The receptors for hearing are located in:
   a. the outer ear.
   b. the middle ear.
   c. the inner ear.
   d. all parts of the ear.

9. According to the gate-control theory, a way to alleviate chronic pain would be to stimulate the _____ nerve fibers that _____ the spinal gate.
   a. small; open
   b. small; close
   c. large; open
   d. large; close

10. The brain breaks vision into separate dimensions such as color, depth, movement, and form and works on each aspect simultaneously. This is called:
    a. feature detection.
    b. parallel processing.
    c. accommodation.
    d. opponent processing.

11. Kinesthesis involves:
    a. the bones of the middle ear.
    b. information from the muscles, tendons, and joints.
    c. membranes within the cochlea.
    d. the body's sense of balance.

12. One light may appear reddish and another greenish if they differ in:
    a. wavelength.
    b. amplitude.
    c. opponent processes.
    d. brightness.

13. Which of the following explains why a rose appears equally red in bright and dim light?
    a. the Young-Helmholtz theory
    b. the opponent-process theory
    c. feature detection
    d. color constancy

14. The historical movement associated with the statement "The whole may exceed the sum of its parts" is:
    a. parapsychology.
    b. behavioral psychology.
    c. functional psychology.
    d. Gestalt psychology.

15. Figures tend to be perceived as whole, complete objects, even if spaces or gaps exist in the representation, thus demonstrating the principle of:
    a. connectedness.
    b. similarity.
    c. continuity.
    d. proximity.
    e. closure.

16. The figure-ground relationship has demonstrated that:
    a. perception is largely innate.
    b. perception is simply a point-for-point representation of sensation.
    c. the same stimulus can trigger more than one perception.
    d. different people see different things when viewing a scene.

17. As we move, viewed objects cast changing shapes on our retinas, although we do not perceive the objects as changing. This is part of the phenomenon of:
    a. perceptual constancy. c. linear perspective.
    b. relative motion.   d. continuity.

18. Which of the following illustrates the principle of visual capture?
    a. We tend to form first impressions of other people on the basis of appearance.
    b. Because visual processing is automatic, we can pay attention to a visual image and any other sensation at the same time.
    c. We cannot simultaneously attend to a visual image and another sensation.
    d. When there is a conflict between visual information and that from another sense, vision tends to dominate.

19. Which philosopher maintained that knowledge comes from inborn ways of organizing our sensory experiences?
    a. Locke   c. Gibson
    b. Kant   d. Walk

20. (Thinking Critically) Which of the following was *not* mentioned in the text as a criticism of parapsychology?
    a. ESP effects have not been consistently reproducible.
    b. Parapsychology has suffered from a number of frauds and hoaxes.

c. The tendency of people to recall only events that confirm their expectations accounts for much of the belief in ESP.
    d. There have been no laboratory-controlled studies of ESP.

21. _____ processing refers to how the physical characteristics of stimuli influence their interpretation.
    a. Top-down   c. Parapsychological
    b. Bottom-up   d. Extrasensory

22. Adults who are born blind but later have their vision restored:
    a. are almost immediately able to recognize familiar objects.
    b. typically fail to recognize familiar objects.
    c. are unable to follow moving objects with their eyes.
    d. have excellent eye-hand coordination.

23. The moon illusion occurs in part because distance cues at the horizon make the moon seem:
    a. farther away and therefore larger.
    b. closer and therefore larger.
    c. farther away and therefore smaller.
    d. closer and therefore smaller.

24. Figure is to ground as _____ is to _____ .
    a. night; day
    b. top; bottom
    c. cloud; sky
    d. sensation; perception

25. (Thinking Critically) Using the ganzfeld procedure to investigate telepathy, researchers have found that:
    a. when external distractions are reduced, both the "sender" and the "receiver" become much more accurate in demonstrating ESP.
    b. only "senders" become much more accurate.
    c. only "receivers" become much more accurate.
    d. over many studies, none of the above occur.

Matching Items

Match each of the structures with its function or description.

Structures or Conditions

_____ 1. lens
_____ 2. iris
_____ 3. pupil
_____ 4. rods
_____ 5. cones
_____ 6. middle ear
_____ 7. inner ear
_____ 8. large nerve fiber
_____ 9. small nerve fiber
_____ 10. semicircular canals
_____ 11. sensors in joints

Functions or Descriptions

a. amplifies sounds
b. closes pain gate
c. vestibular sense
d. controls pupil
e. accommodation
f. opens pain gate
g. admits light
h. vision in dim light
i. contains basilar membrane
j. kinesthesis
k. color vision

Progress Test 2

Progress Test 2 should be completed during a final chapter review. Answer the following questions after you thoroughly understand the correct answers for the Chapter Review and Progress Test 1.

Multiple-Choice Questions

1. The inner ear contains receptors for:
   a. audition and kinesthesis.
   b. kinesthesis and the vestibular sense.
   c. audition and the vestibular sense.
   d. audition, kinesthesis, and the vestibular sense.

2. According to the opponent-process theory:
   a. there are three types of color-sensitive cones.
   b. the process of color vision begins in the cortex.
   c. neurons involved in color vision are stimulated by one color's wavelength and inhibited by another's.
   d. all of the above are true.

3. What enables you to feel yourself wiggling your toes even with your eyes closed?
   a. vestibular sense
   b. sense of kinesthesis
   c. the skin senses
   d. sensory interaction

4. Hubel and Wiesel discovered feature detectors in the _____ of a monkey's visual system.
   a. lens   d. cortex
   b. optic nerve   e. retina
   c. iris

5. Weber's law states that:
   a. the absolute threshold for any stimulus is a constant.
   b. the jnd for any stimulus is a constant.
   c. the absolute threshold for any stimulus is a constant percentage.
   d. the jnd for any stimulus is a constant percentage.

6. The principle that one sense may influence another is:
   a. sensory restriction.   c. Weber's law.
   b. sensory adaptation.   d. sensory interaction.

7. Which of the following is the correct order of the structures through which light passes after entering the eye?
   a. lens, pupil, cornea, retina
   b. pupil, cornea, lens, retina
   c. pupil, lens, cornea, retina
   d. cornea, retina, pupil, lens
   e. cornea, pupil, lens, retina

8. In the opponent-process theory, the three pairs of processes are:
   a. red-green, blue-yellow, black-white.
   b. red-blue, green-yellow, black-white.
   c. red-yellow, blue-green, black-white.
   d. dependent upon the individual's past experience.

9. Wavelength is to _____ as _____ is to brightness.
   a. hue; intensity
   b. intensity; hue
   c. frequency; amplitude
   d. brightness; hue

10. Concerning the evidence for subliminal stimulation, which of the following is the best answer?
    a. The brain processes some information without our awareness.
    b. Stimuli too weak to cross our thresholds for awareness may trigger a response in our sense receptors.
    c. Although we process some stimuli outside of conscious awareness, our behavior is not usually influenced by these stimuli.
    d. All of the above are true.

11. Which of the following is the most accurate description of how we process color?
    a. Throughout the visual system, color processing is divided into separate red, green, and blue systems.
    b. Red-green, blue-yellow, and black-white opponent processes operate throughout the visual system.
    c. Color processing occurs in two stages: (1) a three-color system in the retina and (2) opponent-process cells en route to the visual cortex.
    d. Color processing occurs in two stages: (1) an opponent-process system in the retina and (2) a three-color system en route to the visual cortex.

12. Given normal sensory ability, a person can hear a watch ticking in a silent room from 20 feet away. This is a description of hearing's:
    a. difference threshold.
    b. jnd.
    c. absolute threshold.
    d. subliminal stimulation.

13. The tendency to organize stimuli into smooth, uninterrupted patterns is called:
    a. closure.   d. proximity.
    b. continuity.   e. connectedness.
    c. similarity.

14. Which of the following is a monocular depth cue?
    a. relative size
    b. convergence
    c. retinal disparity
    d. All of the above are monocular depth cues.

15. Which of the following statements is consistent with the Gestalt theory of perception?
    a. Perception develops largely through learning.
    b. Perception is the product of heredity.
    c. The mind organizes sensations into meaningful perceptions.
    d. Perception results directly from sensation.

16. Experiments with distorted visual environments demonstrate that:
    a. adaptation rarely takes place.
    b. animals adapt readily, but humans do not.
    c. humans adapt readily, while certain lower animals typically do not.
    d. adaptation is possible during a critical period in infancy but not thereafter.

17. The phenomenon that refers to the ways in which an individual's expectations influence perception is called:
    a. perceptual set.   c. convergence.
    b. retinal disparity.   d. visual capture.

18. Jack claims that he often has dreams that predict future events. He claims to have the power of:
    a. telepathy.   c. precognition.
    b. clairvoyance.   d. psychokinesis.

19. According to the philosopher _____ , we learn to perceive the world.
    a. Locke   c. Gibson
    b. Kant   d. Walk

20. The phenomenon of size constancy is based upon the close connection between an object's perceived _____ and its perceived _____ .
    a. size; shape   d. shape; distance
    b. size; distance   e. shape; brightness
    c. size; brightness

21. Which of the following statements best describes the effects of sensory deprivation?
    a. It produces functional blindness when experienced for any length of time at any age.
    b. It has greater effects on humans than on animals.
    c. It has more damaging effects when experienced during infancy.
    d. It has greater effects on adults than on children.

22. (Thinking Critically) Which of the following statements concerning ESP is true?
    a. Most ESP researchers are quacks.
    b. There have been a large number of reliable demonstrations of ESP.
    c. Most research psychologists are skeptical of the claims of defenders of ESP.
    d. There have been reliable laboratory demonstrations of ESP, but the results are no different from those that would occur by chance.

23. Each time you see your car, it projects a different image on the retinas of your eyes, yet you do not perceive it as changing. This is because of:
    a. perceptual set.
    b. retinal disparity.
    c. perceptual constancy.
    d. convergence.

24. Studies of the visual cliff have provided evidence that much of depth perception is:
    a. innate.
    b. learned.
    c. innate in lower animals, learned in humans.
    d. innate in humans, learned in lower animals.

●-● ●-● ●-●

25. You probably perceive the diagram above as three separate objects due to the principle of:
    a. proximity.   c. closure.
    b. continuity.   d. connectedness.

Review and Reflect

Answer these questions the day before an exam as a final check on your understanding of the chapter's terms and concepts.

Multiple-Choice Questions

1. In shopping for a new stereo, you discover that you cannot differentiate between the sounds of models X and Y. The difference between X and Y is below your:
   a. absolute threshold.
   b. sensory adaptation level.
   c. receptor threshold.
   d. difference threshold.

2. The phantom limb sensation indicates that:
   a. pain is a purely sensory phenomenon.
   b. the central nervous system plays only a minor role in the experience of pain.
   c. pain involves the brain's interpretation of neural activity.
   d. all of the above are true.

3. While competing in the Olympic trials, marathoner Kirsten O'Brien suffered a stress fracture in her left leg. That she did not experience significant pain until the race was over is probably attributable to the fact that during the race:
   a. the pain gate in her spinal cord was closed by information coming from her brain.
   b. her body's production of endorphins decreased.
   c. an increase in the activity of small pain fibers closed the pain gate.
   d. a decrease in the activity of large pain fibers closed the pain gate.
   e. a decrease in the activity of large pain fibers opened the pain gate.

4. Which of the following is an example of sensory interaction?
   a. finding that despite its delicious aroma, a weird-looking meal tastes awful
   b. finding that food tastes bland when you have a bad cold
   c. finding it difficult to maintain your balance when you have an ear infection
   d. All of the above are examples.

5. In comparing the human eye to a camera, the film would be analogous to the eye's:
   a. pupil.   c. cornea.
   b. lens.   d. retina.

6. Sensation is to _____ as perception is to
   _____ .
   a. recognizing a stimulus; interpreting a stimulus
   b. detecting a stimulus; recognizing a stimulus
   c. interpreting a stimulus; detecting a stimulus
   d. seeing; hearing

7. I am a cell in the thalamus that is excited by red and inhibited by green. I am a(n):
   a. feature detector.
   b. cone.
   c. bipolar cell.
   d. opponent-process cell.
   e. rod.

8. Which of the following correctly lists the order of structures through which sound travels after entering the ear?
   a. auditory canal, eardrum, middle ear, cochlea
   b. eardrum, auditory canal, middle ear, cochlea
   c. eardrum, middle ear, cochlea, auditory canal
   d. cochlea, eardrum, middle ear, auditory canal
   e. auditory canal, middle ear, eardrum, cochlea

9. Assuming that the visual systems of humans and other mammals function similarly, you would expect that the retina of a nocturnal mammal (one active only at night) would contain:
   a. mostly cones.
   b. mostly rods.
   c. an equal number of rods and cones.
   d. more bipolar cells than an animal active only during the day.

10. As the football game continued into the night, LeVar noticed that he was having difficulty distinguishing the colors of the players' uniforms. This is because the _____ , which enable color vision, have a _____ absolute threshold for brightness than the available light intensity.
    a. rods; higher
    b. cones; higher
    c. rods; lower
    d. cones; lower

11. After staring at a very intense red stimulus for a few minutes, Carrie shifted her gaze to a beige wall and "saw" the color _____ . Carrie's experience provides support for the _____ theory.
    a. green; trichromatic
    b. blue; opponent-process
    c. green; opponent-process
    d. blue; trichromatic

12. How does pain differ from other senses?
    a. It has no identifiable receptors.
    b. It has no single stimulus.
    c. It is influenced by both physical and psychological phenomena.
    d. All the above are true.

13. Tamiko hates the bitter taste of her cough syrup. Which of the following would she find most helpful in minimizing the syrup's bad taste?
    a. tasting something very sweet before taking the cough syrup
    b. keeping the syrup in her mouth for several seconds before swallowing it
    c. holding her nose while taking the cough syrup
    d. gulping the cough syrup so that it misses her tongue

14. Although carpenter Smith perceived a briefly viewed object as a screwdriver, police officer Wesson perceived the same object as a knife. This illustrates that perception is guided by:
    a. linear perspective.
    b. shape constancy.
    c. retinal disparity.
    d. perceptual set.
    e. convergence.

15. The fact that a white object under dim illumination appears lighter than a gray object under bright illumination is called:
    a. relative luminance.
    b. perceptual adaptation.
    c. color contrast.
    d. lightness constancy.

16. When two familiar objects of equal size cast unequal retinal images, the object that casts the smaller retinal image will be perceived as being:
    a. closer than the other object.
    b. more distant than the other object.
    c. larger than the other object.
    d. smaller than the other object.

17. If you slowly bring your finger toward your face until it eventually touches your nose, eye-muscle cues called _____ convey depth information to your brain.
    a. retinal disparity
    b. interposition
    c. continuity
    d. proximity
    e. convergence

18. As her friend Milo walks toward her, Noriko perceives his size as remaining constant because his perceived distance _____ at the same time that her retinal image of him _____ .
    a. increases; decreases
    b. increases; increases
    c. decreases; decreases
    d. decreases; increases

19. The illusion that the St. Louis Gateway arch appears taller than it is wide (even though its height and width are equal) is based on our sensitivity to which monocular depth cue?
    a. relative size
    b. interposition
    c. relative height
    d. retinal disparity

20. How do we perceive a pole that partially covers a bush?
    a. as farther away
    b. as nearer
    c. as larger
    d. There is not enough information to determine the object's size or distance.

21. An artist paints a tree orchard so that the parallel rows of trees converge at the top of the canvas. Which cue has the artist used to convey distance?
    a. interposition
    b. relative size
    c. linear perspective
    d. light and shadow

22. Objects higher in our field of vision are perceived as _____ due to the principle of _____ .
    a. nearer; relative height
    b. nearer; linear perspective
    c. farther away; relative height
    d. farther away; linear perspective

23. Regina claims that she can bend spoons, levitate furniture, and perform many other "mind over matter" feats. Regina apparently believes that she has the power of:
    a. telepathy.
    b. clairvoyance.
    c. precognition.
    d. psychokinesis.

24. When the traffic light changed from red to green, the drivers on both sides of Leon's vehicle pulled quickly forward, giving Leon the disorienting feeling that his car was rolling backward. Which principle explains Leon's misperception?
    a. relative motion
    b. continuity
    c. visual capture
    d. proximity

25. While studying the road map before her trip, Colleen had no trouble following the route of the highway she planned to travel. Colleen's ability illustrates the principle of:
    a. closure.
    b. similarity.
    c. continuity.
    d. proximity.
    e. connectedness.

Essay Question

A dancer in a chorus line uses many sensory cues when performing. Discuss three sensory cues that dancers rely on, and explain why each is important. (Use the space below to list the points you want to make, and organize them. Then write the essay on a separate sheet of paper.)

Summing Up

Use the diagrams to identify the parts of the eye and
ear (p. 140), then list them in the order in which they
contribute to vision and hearing. Also, briefly explain
the role of each structure.

The Eye

1. _____

_____

2. _____

_____

3. _____

_____

4. _____

_____

5. _____

_____

6. _____

_____

7. _____

_____

_____

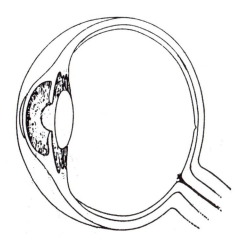

The Ear

1. _____
   _____

2. _____
   _____

3. _____
   _____

4. _____
   _____

5. _____
   _____

6. _____
   _____

7. _____
   _____

8. _____
   _____

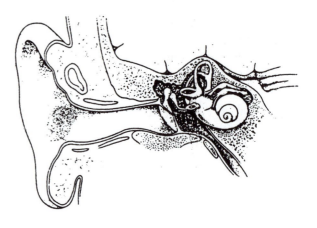

Key Terms

Writing Definitions

Using your own words, on a piece of paper write a brief definition or explanation of each of the following terms.

1. sensation

2. perception

3. bottom-up processing

4. top-down processing

5. psychophysics

6. absolute threshold

7. subliminal

8. difference threshold (jnd)

9. Weber's law

10. sensory adaptation

11. wavelength and hue

12. intensity

13. accommodation

14. retina

15. rods and cones

16. optic nerve

17. blind spot

18. feature detectors

19. parallel processing

20. Young-Helmholtz   trichromatic   (three-color) theory

21. opponent-process theory

22. color constancy

23. visual capture

24. audition

25. pitch and frequency

26. middle ear

27. inner ear

28. cochlea

29. gate-control theory

30. sensory interaction

31. kinesthesis

32. vestibular sense

33. gestalt

34. figure-ground

35. grouping

36. depth perception

37. visual cliff

38. binocular cues

39. monocular cues

40. retinal disparity

41. convergence

42. perceptual constancy

43. perceptual adaptation

44. perceptual set

45. extrasensory perception (ESP)

46. parapsychology

Cross-Check

As you learned in Chapter 1, reviewing and overlearning of material are important to the learning process. After you have written the definitions of the key terms in this chapter, you should complete the crossword puzzle to ensure that you can reverse the process—recognize the term, given the definition.

ACROSS

4. Psychological characteristic of a sound that is determined by its frequency.
7. Part of the ear in which sounds are converted to nerve impulses.
9. In the ear, the membrane that is lined with hair cells.
11. Study of the relationship between the physical characteristics of stimuli and our psychological experience of them.
13. Grouping principle that we fill in gaps in visual stimuli to create a complete, whole image.
14. Psychological characteristic of light that is determined by wavelength.
15. Receptors that enable color vision.
16. Information processing in which several aspects of a problem are processed simultaneously.
17. Minimum stimulation needed to detect a stimulus 50 percent of the time is the _____ threshold.
19. Another term for the difference threshold (abbreviation).
20. Snail-like structure of the inner ear that contains the receptors for hearing.
21. Collective term for clairvoyance, telepathy, and precognition (abbreviation).
22. A binocular cue for perceiving depth.

DOWN

1. Number of complete wavelengths that pass a given point in a given time.
2. Part of the eye that contains the rods and cones.
3. Monocular cue for perceiving distance that involves the convergence of parallel lines.
4. The study of ESP.
5. Monocular depth cue in which we perceive an object that partially blocks our view of another object as closer.
6. The sense of the position and movement of the parts of the body.
8. Grouping principle by which we perceive uniform and linked spots, lines, or areas as a single unit.
10. The organization of the visual field into two parts is referred to as the _____ relationship.
12. Binocular cue in which the eyes turn inward.
18. Visual receptors that concentrated in the periphery of the retina.

Answers

Introducing Sensation and Perception

Introducing Sensation and Perception Preview

1. Sensation refers to how we detect physical energy from the environment and encode it as neural signals. Perception refers to how we select, organize, and interpret sensory information. Sensory

analysis, which works at the entry level, is called "bottom-up" processing. Perception, which draws on our experience and expectations, is called "top-down" processing.

Stepping Through the Introduction

1. sensation; perception
2. bottom-up processing; top-down processing
3. prosopagnosia

Sensing the World: Some Basic Principles

Section Preview

1. An absolute threshold is the minimum stimulation necessary to detect a particular environmental stimulus 50 percent of the time. A difference threshold, or just noticeable difference (jnd), is the minimum difference a person can detect between any two stimuli 50 percent of the time. Weber's law states that the difference threshold is a constant proportion of the stimulus.

2. Stimuli at or above the "absolute" threshold are detected half the time; subliminal stimuli, which are below the absolute threshold, are therefore detected less than half the time. Experiments show that under certain conditions, a weak stimulus may reach a part of the brain where it evokes a feeling but not conscious awareness. Claims that subliminal stimulation may lead to thought persuasion have not been supported, however. While subliminal messages may have a fleeting effect on thinking, they do not have an enduring effect on behavior.

3. Sensory adaptation refers to our diminishing sensitivity to an unchanging stimulus. By allowing us to focus our attention on informative changes in the environment, it keeps us from being distracted by the uninformative, constant stimulation of unchanging stimuli.

Stepping Through the Section

1. psychophysics
2. absolute threshold; 50
3. conscious
4. subliminal
5. difference threshold; just noticeable difference
6. Weber's law; stimulus
7. sensory adaptation

Although sensory adaptation reduces our sensitivity, it enables us to focus our attention on informative changes in the environment without being distracted

by the uninformative, constant stimulation that bombards our senses.

Vision

Section Preview

1. Visible light is a small portion of the larger spectrum of electromagnetic radiation. Light can be described by two physical characteristics, wavelength, which determines hue, and intensity, which influences brightness.

   Vision begins when light enters the eye through the opening in the iris called the pupil. Light passes through the lens, which changes its curvature (accommodation) in order to focus light on the retina. Within the retina are the rods and cones, which are responsible for the transduction (transformation) of light energy into neural impulses. The optic nerve carries neural impulses from the retina to visual processing centers in the brain.

2. The lowest level of visual information processing—the encoding and analyzing of sensory information—is at the retina. As we view a scene, the rods and cones of the retina transduce the reflected light into neural impulses that are relayed to bipolar and ganglion cells and then sent to the brain via the optic nerve. The brain—the source of most information processing—processes these visual stimuli relatively quickly by breaking them down into various subdimensions and working on each simultaneously (parallel processing). Thus, feature detectors break the image into bars, edges, angles, and movements. Higher-level brain cells in the parietal and temporal lobes respond to specific visual scenes and then compare the resulting image with previously stored images until a match, and therefore recognition, occurs.

3. The Young-Helmholtz trichromatic (three-color) theory states that the retina has three types of color receptors, each sensitive to one of three colors: red, green, or blue. To "see" other hues, such as yellow, there must be a unique combination of activity in two or three of these color receptors (red and green, in this case). This theory explains color processing at the level of the retina.

   According to the opponent-process theory, some cells in the retina and in the thalamus of the brain analyze visual information in terms of the opponent colors red and green, blue and yellow, and black and white. This theory explains why we see afterimages following intense stimulation with a particular color.

4. Color constancy refers to the fact that, in an unvarying context, the color of an object remains roughly constant despite changes in lighting. If the context in which an object is viewed changes, the perceived color of the object changes. This demonstrates that the experience of color results not only from the light waves reflected from an object, but also from the light waves reflected by an object relative to surrounding objects.

Stepping Through the Section

1. electromagnetic
2. wavelength; hue
3. intensity; amplitude; brightness
4. cornea; pupil; iris
5. lens; retina
6. accommodation
7. rods; cones
8. bipolar; ganglion; optic nerve; brain
9. blind spot
10. cones
11. sensitive; 20
12. visual cortex; feature detectors
13. parietal; temporal; gaze; head angle; posture; body movement; integrate
14. simultaneously; parallel processing; blindsight; conscious perceptions; guides our actions
15. reflects; construction
16. sex-linked
17. red; green; blue
18. opponent; afterimage
19. opponent-process; red; green; yellow; blue; black; white

In the first stage of color processing, the retina's red, green, and blue cones respond in varying degrees to different color stimuli, as suggested by the three-color theory. The resulting signals are then processed by red-green, blue-yellow, and black-white opponent-process cells, which are stimulated by one wavelength and inhibited by its opponent.

20. context
21. color constancy

The Other Senses

Section Preview

1. The stimulus energy for hearing is the sound waves of compressed and expanded air that are created by vibrating objects. The strength, or amplitude, of sound waves determines loudness; their length, or frequency, determines their pitch. Decibels are the measuring unit for sound energy. The absolute threshold for hearing is arbitrarily defined as 0 decibels.

   Hearing begins when the outer ear channels sound waves through the auditory canal to the eardrum. The middle ear transmits the eardrum's vibrations over three tiny bones (hammer, anvil, and stirrup) to the membrane entrance (oval window) of the fluid-filled cochlea of the inner ear. These vibrations cause ripples in the basilar membrane, which is lined with the hair cell receptors for audition. Movements of the basilar membrane cause the hair cells to bend, triggering impulses in the adjacent nerve fibers, which converge to form the auditory nerve. Because of the distance between the two ears, a sound coming from one side of the body will arrive sooner at one ear and be slightly louder. That differences in loudness and arrival time are used in locating sounds is demonstrated by the difficulty we have in locating a sound that comes from directly ahead, behind, overhead, or beneath us. Such sounds strike the two ears simultaneously and with equal intensity.

2. The sense of touch is a mixture of at least four skin senses—pressure, warmth, cold, and pain. Of these, only pressure has identifiable neural receptors. Other skin sensations, such as tickle, itch, wetness, and hot, are variations of the four basic ones.

3. Pain is a property of the senses and the brain. Unlike other senses, pain has neither a single stimulus nor specialized receptors. According to the gate-control theory, the spinal cord contains a neural "gate" that either opens to permit pain signals to reach the brain or closes to prevent them from reaching the brain. This may explain why electrical stimulation, massage, and acupuncture relieve chronic pain—by triggering "gate-closing" activity in the spinal cord.

   The gate-control theory also suggests that the pain gate can be closed by information from the brain. This may explain why thought distraction, hypnosis, and other psychological influences on pain are powerful.

4. Taste is a chemical sense that mostly involves four basic sensations—sweet, sour, salty, and bitter. Mixtures of these basic sensations give rise to other tastes. The receptors for taste (taste buds) are unevenly distributed so that different regions of the tongue are especially sensitive to one or more specific tastes. Although the taste buds

reproduce themselves every week or two, their number decreases with aging, smoking, and the use of alcohol.

Smell (olfaction) occurs when air-carried molecules of a substance reach receptor cells in the nasal cavity. Unlike other senses, olfaction is not based on a small set of basic odors from which all other odors derive. Exactly how the olfactory receptors work remains a mystery.

Sensors in the muscles, tendons, and joints of the body provide the brain with information about the position and movement of body parts (kinesthesis).

Receptors in the semicircular canals and the vestibular sacs of the inner ear monitor the position and movement of the whole body and enable us to maintain balance (the vestibular sense).

Sensory interaction is the principle that one sense may influence another. An example of sensory interaction is the enhancement of a food's taste that occurs when it smells delicious, or conversely the loss of taste when one has a cold.

Stepping Through the Section

1. visual capture
2. audition; air molecules
3. loudness; frequency
4. decibels; 0
5. outer; middle; inner
6. eardrum
7. hammer; anvil; stirrup
8. cochlea; oval window; basilar membrane; hair cells; talk over it
9. speed (timing); loudness
10. harder
11. pressure; warmth; cold; pain; pressure; variations
12. senses; brain
13. phantom limb
14. is not; does not
15. gate-control; gate; spinal cord; small; large; brain

The Lamaze method of prepared childbirth combines several pain control techniques, including distraction, deep breathing and muscle relaxation, and counterstimulation through gentle massage.

16. sweet; sour; salty; bitter; umami
17. chemical; taste buds; pore
18. week or two
19. sensory interaction
20. olfaction; chemical; cannot
21. limbic; memory; emotion
22. kinesthesis; muscles; tendons; joints
23. vestibular sense; semicircular canals; vestibular sacs

Perceptual Organization

Section Preview

1. The Gestalt psychologists demonstrated that perception involves the organization of sensations into meaningful wholes, or gestalts, that may exceed the sum of their individual parts and be regrouped into more than one perception. They also showed that to recognize an object, we must first perceive it as a figure distinct from its surrounding stimuli, or ground. The Gestalt psychologists identified several principles by which sensations are organized into meaningful perceptions; these include proximity, similarity, continuity, closure, and connectedness.

2. The visual cliff is a miniature cliff with an apparent drop-off on one side of a table. Gibson and Walk found that infants as young as 6 months of age refused to crawl out on the glass, despite their mother's coaxing. Newborn animals with virtually no visual experience respond similarly, thus indicating that the ability to perceive depth is at least partly innate.

3. Three-dimensional movies create the impression of depth by simulating retinal disparity. Each scene is photographed with two cameras placed a few inches apart. Viewers wear spectacles that allow each eye to see only the image from one camera. The perceived depth occurs as each eye focuses on one of the two-dimensional images and the brain integrates them in a single 3-D image.

    The binocular (two-eye) cues to depth include retinal disparity and convergence, and the monocular (one-eye) cues to depth include relative size, interposition, relative height, relative motion, linear perspective, and light and shadow.

4. Thanks to perceptual constancy we perceive familiar objects as having a constant form (shape constancy), size (size constancy), and brightness (lightness or brightness constancy), even when our retinal images of them change.

    There is a close interplay between an object's perceived size and its distance. As the retinal image of a familiar object decreases, we perceive its distance as increasing rather than its size as changing. This size-distance relationship partially explains the "moon illusion": Cues to objects' distances at the horizon make the moon behind them seem farther away, and seemingly larger, than when high in the sky.

Stepping Through the Section

1. Gestalt; whole; Necker
2. figure; ground

The Gestalt psychologists described some key principles of perceptual organization and, in so doing, demonstrated that perception is far more than a simple sensory process. The reversible figure-ground relationship, for example, demonstrates that a single stimulus can trigger more than one perception. As Gestalt psychologists showed, we continually filter sensory information and construct our perceptions in ways that make sense to us.

3. grouping
4. continuity; closure; proximity; similarity; connectedness
5. depth perception
6. visual cliff; 3 months

Research on the visual cliff suggests that in many species the ability to perceive depth is present at, or very shortly after, birth.

7. binocular
8. monocular
9. retinal disparity; two; perceptions; brains
10. convergence
11. relative size
12. interposition
13. relative height
14. relative motion (motion parallax)
15. linear perspective
16. light and shadow
17. perceptual constancy
18. moon; Ponzo; size; distance; diminished

A partial reason for the illusion that the moon at the horizon appears up to 50 percent larger than the moon directly overhead is that cues to the distance of objects at the horizon make the moon, behind them, seem farther away and therefore larger. When we see the moon overhead in the sky, these misleading cues are lacking.

19. relative to; relative luminance

Perceptual Interpretation

Section Preview

1. On one side of the nature-nurture debate, the German philosopher Immanuel Kant maintained that knowledge comes from our inborn ways of organizing sensory experiences. On the other side, the British philosopher John Locke argued that we learn how to perceive the world through our experiences of it.

2. In both humans and animals, infancy is a critical period during which normal visual stimulation must be experienced. Adults blinded with cataracts from birth, who later have their vision restored, are able to perceive figure, ground, and colors but are severely limited in their ability to recognize objects that were familiar by touch. Kittens and monkeys who were outfitted with goggles since infancy had similar visual impairments when the goggles were removed.

3. Studies in which people and animals are given goggles that shift the world to the left, right, or even upside down demonstrate that vision is remarkably adaptable. After a relatively brief period of adjustment, most organisms are able to function normally in the distorted visual environment (chicks, however, cannot adapt). When the goggles are first removed, subjects experience a brief perceptual aftereffect, as their perceptual systems continue to compensate for the shifted visual input.

4. Experiences, assumptions, expectations, and contexts may give us a perceptual set, or mental predisposition, that influences what we perceive. Perceptual sets, which are based on the concepts, or schemas, that we form through our experiences, help us organize and interpret unfamiliar or ambiguous information.

   The immediate context of a stimulus also influences how it is perceived. For example, a person or object is more quickly recognized in an expected context than in a novel one. The effects of context and perceptual sets show how our experiences help us to construct meaningful perceptions from our sensory experiences.

5. Extrasensory perception refers to the controversial claim that perception can occur outside sensory input. Telepathy is the claimed ability of mind-to-mind communication between two people. Precognition refers to the claimed ability to perceive future events. Clairvoyance refers to the claimed ability to perceive remote events. Psychokinesis refers to the claimed ability to perform acts of "mind over matter."

   Despite the efforts of parapsychologists to document ESP, most research psychologists argue that many so-called psychic demonstrations are nothing more than deceptive illusions that any magician could perform and that no one has ever discovered a reproducible ESP phenomenon.

Stepping Through the Section

1. Kant
2. Locke
3. cannot
4. infancy; critical period; cataract
5. will; perceptual adaptation
6. perceptual set
7. context; stereotypes
8. extrasensory perception
9. parapsychologists
10. telepathy; clairvoyance; precognition; psychokinesis
11. chance-level; interpreted (retrofitted); reconstruct
12. reproducible
13. ganzfeld; beat; no effect

Progress Test 1

Multiple-Choice Questions

1. **c.** is the answer. According to Weber's law, the difference threshold is a constant proportion of the stimulus. There is a 10 percent difference between 10 and 11 pounds; since the difference threshold is a constant proportion, the weight closest to 100 pounds that can nonetheless be differentiated from it is 110 pounds (or 100 pounds plus 10 percent). (p. 144)

2. **d.** is the answer. (p. 145)
   a. "Sensory fatigue" is not a term in psychology.
   b. Accommodation refers to an adaptive change in shape by the lens of the eye.
   c. Sensory deprivation refers to lack of early sensory experience because of the loss of a sense such as lack of vision due to cataracts.
   e. Sensory interaction is the principle that one sense may influence another.

3. **d.** is the answer. (pp. 147–148)
   a. The lens lies behind the pupil and focuses light on the retina.
   b. The retina is the inner surface of the eyeball and contains the rods and cones.
   c. The cornea lies in front of the pupil and is the first structure that light passes through as it enters the eye.

4. **a.** is the answer. (p. 148)
   b. Sensory adaptation is our diminishing sensitivity to an unchanging stimulus.

   c. Focusing is the process through which light converges onto the retina as a sharp image. The image is focused because the lens accommodates its shape.
   d. Transduction refers to the conversion of an environmental stimulus, such as light, into a neural impulse by a receptor—a rod or a cone.

5. **e.** is the answer. (p. 148)
   a. The iris is not a receptor; it is the part of the eye that controls the size of the pupil.
   b. The ganglion cells' axons form the optic nerve.
   c. Cones have a higher threshold for brightness than rods and therefore do not function as well in dim light.
   d. Bipolar cells are not receptors; they are neurons in the retina that link rods and cones with ganglion cells, which make up the optic nerve.

6. **a.** is the answer. The Young-Helmholtz theory proposes that there are red-, green-, and blue-sensitive cones. (p. 153)
   b. This answer describes Hering's opponent-process theory.
   c. The Young-Helmholtz theory proposes that there are three types of cones, not four.
   d. The Young-Helmholtz theory concerns only color vision, not the detection of visual detail.

7. **b.** is the answer. Just as wave frequency determines pitch, so wave amplitude determines loudness. (p. 157)
   a. Amplitude is the physical basis of loudness; wavelength determines frequency and thereby pitch.
   c. & d. Wavelength, amplitude, and intensity are physical aspects of light and sound. Because the question is based on a relationship between a physical property (frequency) of a stimulus and its psychological attribute (pitch), these answers are incorrect.

8. **c.** is the answer. The receptors for hearing—those cells that transform sound energy into neural impulses—are the hair cells lining the basilar membrane of the cochlea. (p. 158)

9. **d.** is the answer. The small fibers conduct most pain signals; the large fibers conduct most other sensory signals from the skin. The gate either allows pain signals to pass on to the brain or blocks them from passing. When the large fibers are stimulated, the pain gate is closed and other sensations are felt in place of pain. (p. 160)

10. **b.** is the answer. (p. 151)
    a. Feature detection is the process by which nerve cells in the brain respond to specific visual features of a stimulus, such as movement, angle, or shape.

c. Accommodation is the process by which the lens changes its curvature to focus images on the retina.

d. The opponent-process theory suggests that color vision depends on the response of brain cells to red-green, yellow-blue, and black-white opposing colors.

11. **b.** is the answer. Kinesthesis, or the sense of the position and movement of body parts, is based on information from the muscles, tendons, and joints. (p. 164)

a. & c. The ear plays no role in kinesthesis.

d. The vestibular sense, which includes the sense of balance, is not involved in kinesthesis but is, rather, a companion sense.

12. **a.** is the answer. Wavelength determines hue, or color. (p. 146)

b. & d. The amplitude of light determines its brightness.

c. Opponent processes are neural systems involved in color vision, not properties of light.

13. **d.** is the answer. Color constancy is the perception that familiar objects have consistent color, even if changing illumination alters the wavelengths reflected by that object. (p. 155)

a. & b. These theories explain how the visual system detects color; they do not explain why colors do not seem to change when lighting does.

c. Feature detection explains how the brain recognizes visual images by analyzing their distinctive features of shape, movement, and angle.

14. **d.** is the answer. Gestalt psychology, which developed in Germany at the turn of the century, was interested in how clusters of sensations are organized into whole perceptions. (p. 165)

a. Parapsychology is the study of ESP and other paranormal phenomena.

b. & c. Behavioral and functional psychology developed later in the United States.

15. **e.** is the answer. (p. 166)

a. Connectedness refers to the tendency to see uniform and linked items as a unit.

b. Similarity refers to the tendency to group similar items.

c. Continuity refers to the tendency to group stimuli into smooth, continuous patterns.

d. Proximity refers to the tendency to group items that are close to each other.

16. **c.** is the answer. Although we always differentiate a stimulus into figure and ground, those elements of the stimulus we perceive as figure and those as ground may change. In this way, the same stimulus can trigger more than one perception. (p. 166)

a. The idea of a figure-ground relationship has no bearing on the issue of whether perception is innate.

b. Perception cannot be simply a point-for-point representation of sensation, since in figure-ground relationships a single stimulus can trigger more than one perception.

d. Figure-ground relationships demonstrate the existence of general, rather than individual, principles of perceptual organization. Significantly, even the same person can see different figure-ground relationships when viewing a scene.

17. **a.** is the answer. Perception of constant shape, like perception of constant size, is part of the phenomenon of perceptual constancy. (p. 173)

b. Relative motion is a monocular distance cue in which objects at different distances appear to move at different rates.

c. Linear perspective is a monocular distance cue in which lines we know to be parallel appear to converge in the distance, thus indicating depth.

d. Continuity is the perceptual tendency to group items into continuous patterns.

18. **d.** is the answer. (p. 156)

a., b., & c. Visual capture has nothing to do with forming impressions of people or whether we can attend to more than one stimulus at a time.

19. **b.** is the answer. (p. 175)

a. Locke argued that knowledge is not inborn but comes through learning.

c. & d. Gibson and Walk studied depth perception using the visual cliff; they made no claims about the source of knowledge.

20. **d.** is the answer. As discussed in the text, parapsychologists have conducted numerous experiments with both "psychic" and "normal" subjects. (pp. 180–181)

a., b., & c. These are all valid criticisms of parapsychology mentioned in the text.

21. **b.** is the answer. (p. 141)

a. Top-down processing refers to how our knowledge and expectations influence perception.

c. & d. Parapsychology is the study of perception outside normal sensory input, which is extrasensory.

22. **b.** is the answer. Because they have not had early visual experiences, these adults typically have difficulty learning to perceive objects. (p. 176)

a. Such patients typically could not visually recognize objects with which they were familiar by touch, and in some cases this inability persisted.

c. Being able to perceive figure-ground relationships, patients *are* able to follow moving objects with their eyes.

d. This answer is incorrect because eye-hand coordination is an acquired skill and requires much practice.

23. **a.** is the answer. The moon appears larger at the horizon than overhead in the sky because objects at the horizon provide distance cues that make the moon seem farther away and therefore larger. In the open sky, of course, there are no such cues. (pp. 173–174)

24. **c.** is the answer. We see a cloud as a figure against the background of sky. (p. 166)
    a., b., & d. The figure-ground relationship refers to the organization of the visual field into objects (figures) that stand out from their surroundings (ground).

25. **d.** is the answer. (pp. 180–181)

Matching Items

1. e (p. 148)	**6.** a (p. 158)	**11.** j (p. 164)
2. d (p. 148)	**7.** i (p. 158)	
3. g (p. 147)	**8.** b (p. 160)	
4. h (p. 148)	**9.** f (p. 160)	
5. k (p. 148)	**10.** c (p. 164)	

Progress Test 2

Multiple-Choice Questions

1. **c.** is the answer. The inner ear contains the receptors for audition (hearing) and the vestibular sense; those for kinesthesis are located in the muscles, tendons, and joints. (pp. 158, 164)

2. **c.** is the answer. After leaving the receptor cells, visual information is analyzed in terms of pairs of opponent colors; neurons stimulated by one member of a pair are inhibited by the other. (p. 155)
   a. The idea that there are three types of color-sensitive cones is the basis of the Young-Helmholtz three-color theory.
   b. According to the opponent-process theory, and all other theories of color vision, the process of color vision begins in the retina.

3. **b.** is the answer. Kinesthesis, the sense of movement of body parts, would enable you to feel your toes wiggling. (p. 164)
   a. The vestibular sense is concerned with movement and position, or balance, of the whole body, not of its parts.

c. The skin, or tactile, senses are pressure, pain, warmth, and cold; they have nothing to do with movement of body parts.
d. Sensory interaction, the principle that the senses influence each other, does not play a role in this example, which involves only the sense of kinesthesis.

4. **d.** is the answer. Feature detectors are cortical neurons and hence are located in the visual cortex. (p. 150)
   a. The lens focuses images on the retina.
   b. The optic nerve contains neurons that relay nerve impulses from the retina to higher centers in the visual system.
   c. The iris is simply a ring of muscle tissue, which controls the diameter of the pupil.
   e. The retina contains receptors that send information to the brain.

5. **d.** is the answer. Weber's law concerns difference thresholds (jnd's), not absolute thresholds, and states that these are constant proportions of the stimuli, not that they remain constant. (p. 144)

6. **d.** is the answer. (p. 162)
   a. Sensory restriction refers to situations in which the organism does not have use of a sense.
   b. Sensory adaptation is diminished sensitivity to unchanging stimulation.
   c. Weber's law states that the jnd is a constant proportion of a stimulus.

7. **e.** is the answer. (pp. 147–148)

8. **a.** is the answer. (p. 155)

9. **a.** is the answer. Wavelength determines hue, and intensity determines brightness. (pp. 146, 147)

10. **d.** is the answer. (p. 143)

11. **c.** is the answer. (p. 155)
    a. This is incorrect because separate red, green, and blue systems operate only in the retina.
    b. This answer is incorrect because opponent-process systems operate en route to the brain, after visual processing in the receptors is completed.
    d. This answer is incorrect because it reverses the correct order of the two stages of processing.

12. **c.** is the answer. The absolute threshold is the minimum stimulation needed to detect a stimulus. (p. 142)
    a. & b. The difference threshold, which is also known as the jnd, is the minimum difference between two stimuli that a person can detect. In this example, there is only one stimulus—the sound of the watch.
    d. Subliminal stimulation is the presentation of stimuli below the absolute threshold.

13. b. is the answer. (p. 166)
a. Closure refers to the tendency to perceptually fill in gaps in recognizable objects in the visual field.
c. Similarity refers to the tendency to group items that are similar.
d. Proximity refers to the tendency to group items that are near one another.
e. Connectedness refers to the tendency to group uniform and linked items.

14. a. is the answer. (p. 169)
b. & c. Convergence and retinal disparity are both binocular cues that depend on information from both eyes.

15. c. is the answer. (p. 165)
a. & b. The Gestalt psychologists did not deal with the origins of perception; they were more concerned with its form.
d. In fact, they argued just the opposite: Perception is more than mere sensory experience.

16. c. is the answer. Humans are able to adjust to upside-down worlds and other visual distortions, figuring out the relationship between the perceived and the actual reality; lower animals, such as chickens and fish, are typically unable to adapt. (p. 176)
a. Humans are able to adapt quite well to distorted visual environments (and then to readapt).
b. This answer is incorrect because humans are the most adaptable of creatures.
d. Humans are able to adapt at any age to distorted visual environments.

17. a. is the answer. (p. 177)
b. Retinal disparity is a binocular depth cue based on the fact that each eye receives a slightly different view of the world.
c. Convergence is a binocular depth cue based on the fact that the eyes swing inward to focus on near objects.
d. Visual capture refers to the tendency of vision to dominate the other senses.

18. c. is the answer. (p. 178)
a. This answer would be correct had Jack claimed to be able to read someone else's mind.
b. This answer would be correct had Jack claimed to be able to sense remote events, such as a friend in distress.
d. This answer would be correct had Jack claimed to be able to levitate objects or bend spoons without applying any physical force.

19. a. is the answer. (p. 175)
b. Kant claimed that knowledge is inborn.

c. & d. Gibson and Walk make no claims about the origins of perception.

20. b. is the answer. (p. 173)

21. c. is the answer. There appears to be a critical period for perceptual development, in that sensory deprivation has severe, even permanently, disruptive effects when it occurs in infancy but not when it occurs later in life. (p. 176)
a. & d. Sensory deprivation does not have the same effects at all ages, and it is more damaging to children than to adults. This is because there is a critical period for perceptual development; whether functional blindness will result depends in part on the nature of the sensory deprivation.
b. Research studies have not indicated that sensory deprivation is more damaging to humans than to animals.

22. c. is the answer. (p. 179)
a. Many ESP researchers are sincere, reputable researchers.
b. & d. There have been no reliable demonstrations of ESP.

23. c. is the answer. Because of perceptual constancy, we see the car's shape and size as always the same. (p. 173)
a. Perceptual set is a mental predisposition to perceive one thing and not another.
b. Retinal disparity means that our right and left eyes each receive slightly different images.
d. Convergence is a form of muscular feedback in which the eyes swing in, or out, as we view objects at different distances.

24. a. is the answer. Most infants refused to crawl out over the "cliff" even when coaxed, suggesting that much of depth perception is innate. Studies with the young of "lower" animals show the same thing. (p. 167)

25. d. is the answer. (p. 166)
a. Proximity is the tendency to group objects near to one another. The diagram is perceived as three distinct units, even though the points are evenly spaced.
b. Continuity is the tendency to group stimuli into smooth, uninterrupted patterns. There is no such continuity in the diagram.
c. Closure is the perceptual tendency to fill in gaps in a form. In the diagram, three disconnected units are perceived rather than a single whole.

Review and Reflect

Multiple-Choice Questions

1. **d.** is the answer. (p. 144)
   a. The absolute threshold refers to whether a single stimulus can be detected, not to whether two stimuli can be differentiated.
   b. Sensory adaptation refers to the decreased sensitivity that occurs with increased exposure to an unchanging stimulus.
   c. A receptor threshold is a minimum amount of energy that will elicit a neural impulse in a receptor cell.

2. **c.** is the answer. Since pain is felt in the limb that does not exist, the pain is simply the brain's (mis)interpretation of neural activity. (p. 160)
   a. If pain were a purely sensory phenomenon, phantom limb pain would not occur, since the receptors are no longer present.
   b. That pain is experienced when a limb is missing indicates that the central nervous system, especially the brain, is where pain is sensed.

3. **a.** is the answer. (pp. 160–161)
   b. Because endorphins relieve pain, a decrease in their production would have made Kirsten more likely to experience pain. Moreover, because endorphins are released in response to pain, their production probably would have increased.
   c. Neural activity in small fibers tends to open the pain gate.
   d. & e. An *increase* in large-fiber activity would tend to *close* the pain gate.

4. **d.** is the answer. Each of these is an example of the interaction of two senses—vision and taste in the case of a., taste and smell in the case of b., and hearing and the vestibular sense in the case of c. (p. 162)

5. **d.** is the answer. Just as light strikes the film of a camera, visual images entering the eye are projected onto the retina. (p. 148)
   a. The pupil would be analogous to the aperture of a camera, since both control the amount of light permitted to enter.
   b. The lens of the eye performs a focusing function similar to the lens of the camera.
   c. The cornea would be analogous to a camera's lens cap in that both protect delicate inner structures.

6. **b.** is the answer. (p. 141)
   a. Both recognition and interpretation are examples of perception.
   c. This answer would have been correct if the question had read, "Perception is to sensation as _____ is to _____."

   d. Sensation and perception are important processes in both hearing and seeing.

7. **d.** is the answer. (p. 155)
   a. Feature detectors are located in the visual cortex and respond to features such as movement, shape, and angle.
   b. & c. Cones and bipolar cells are located in the retina. Moreover, neither are excited by some colors and inhibited by others.

8. **a.** is the answer. (pp. 157–158)

9. **b.** is the answer. Rods and cones enable vision in dim and bright light, respectively. If an animal is active only at night, it is likely to have more rods than cones in its retinas. (p. 148)
   d. Bipolar cells link both cones and rods to ganglion cells. There is no reason to expect that a nocturnal mammal would have more bipolar cells than a mammal active both during the day and at night.

10. **b.** is the answer. (pp. 148–149)
    a. & c. It is the cones, rather than the rods, that enable color vision.
    d. If the cones' threshold were lower than the available light intensity, they would be able to function and therefore detect the colors of the players' uniforms.

11. **c.** is the answer. (p. 154)
    a. The trichromatic theory cannot account for the experience of afterimages.
    b. & d. Afterimages are experienced as the complementary color of a stimulus. Green, not blue, is red's complement.

12. **d.** is the answer. (pp. 160–161)

13. **c.** is the answer. Because of the powerful sensory interaction between taste and smell, eliminating the odor of the cough syrup should make its taste more pleasant. (p. 162)
    a. If anything, the contrasting tastes might make the bitter syrup even less palatable.
    b. If Tamiko keeps the syrup in her mouth for several seconds, it will ensure that her taste pores fully "catch" the stimulus, thus intensifying the bitter taste.
    d. It's impossible to miss the tongue completely.

14. **d.** is the answer. The two people interpreted a briefly perceived object in terms of their perceptual sets, or mental predispositions, in this case conditioned by their work experiences. (p. 177)
    a. Both Smith and Wesson had the same sensory experience of the object, so linear perspective cues would not cause their differing perceptions.
    b. Shape constancy refers to the perception that objects remain constant in shape even when our retinal images of them change.

c. & e. Retinal disparity and convergence are binocular depth cues; they have nothing to do with individual differences in perception.

15. **d.** is the answer. Although the amount of light reflected from a white object is less in dim light than in bright light—and may be less than the amount of light reflected from a brightly lit gray object—the brightness of the white object is perceived as remaining constant. Because a white object reflects a higher percentage of the light falling on it than does a gray object, and the brightness of objects is perceived as constant despite variations in illumination, white is perceived as brighter than gray even under dim illumination. (p. 174)

a. Relative luminance refers to the relative intensity of light falling on surfaces that are in close proximity. Lightness constancy is perceived despite variations in illumination.

b. Perceptual adaptation refers to the ability to adjust to an artificially modified perceptual environment, such as an inverted visual field.

c. Color contrast is not discussed in this text.

16. **b.** is the answer. The phenomenon described is the basis for the monocular cue of relative size. (p. 169)

a. The object casting the *larger* retinal image would be perceived as closer.

c. & d. Because of size constancy, the perceived size of familiar objects remains constant, despite changes in their retinal image size.

17. **e.** is the answer. As an object comes closer in our field of vision, the eyes swing inward (converge) and provide muscular cues as to the object's distance. (p. 169)

a. Retinal disparity refers to the slightly different images of an object received by the two eyes due to their different angles of viewing.

b. Interposition is a monocular cue to distance in which an object that partially blocks another is seen as closer.

c. & d. Continuity and proximity are Gestalt grouping principles, rather than distance cues.

18. **d.** is the answer. (p. 173)

19. **c.** is the answer. We perceive objects higher in our field of vision as farther away. Thus, the brain perceives a vertical line the same length as a horizontal line to be more distant and mentally adjusts its apparent length to make it seem longer. (p. 170)

a. & b. These monocular cues are irrelevant in this particular illusion.

d. Retinal disparity is a *binocular* cue to depth.

20. **b.** is the answer. This is an example of the principle of interposition in depth perception. (p. 170)

a. The partially *obscured* object is perceived as farther away.

c. The perceived size of an object is not altered when that object overlaps another.

21. **c.** is the answer. (p. 171)

a. Interposition is a monocular depth cue in which an object that partially covers another is perceived as closer.

b. Had we referred to the artist painting the trees so that the images of those at the top of the canvas were smaller, we would be describing relative size.

d. If the cue were light and shadow, the question would have referred to the dimmer trees in the distance.

22. **c.** is the answer. (p. 170)

b. & d. Linear perspective is the apparent convergence of parallel lines as a cue to distance.

23. **d.** is the answer. (p. 178)

a. Telepathy is the claimed ability to "read" minds.

b. Clairvoyance refers to the claimed ability to perceive remote events.

c. Precognition refers to the claimed ability to perceive future events.

24. **c.** is the answer. Although Leon's other senses would have told him his car was not moving, the visual images of the other cars moving forward "captured" his awareness and created the perception that he was rolling backward. (p. 156)

a. Relative motion is a distance cue that occurs when stationary objects appear to move as we move. Just the opposite is happening to Leon.

b. & d. Continuity and proximity are Gestalt principles of grouping, rather than distance cues.

25. **c.** is the answer. She perceives the line for the road as continuous, even though it is interrupted by lines indicating other roads. (p. 166)

a. Closure refers to the perceptual filling in of gaps in a stimulus to create a complete, whole object.

b. Similarity is the tendency to perceive similar objects as belonging together. On a road map, all of the lines representing roads appear similar. Thus, this cue could not be the basis for Colleen's ability to trace the route of a particular road.

d. Proximity is the tendency to group objects near to one another as a single unit.

e. Connectedness is the tendency to group linked items. In this case, the roads often are not clearly linked.

Essay Question

1. *Proximity.* We tend to perceive items that are near each other as belonging together. Thus, a small section of dancers or members of a marching band may separate themselves from the larger group in order to form part of a particular image.

2. *Similarity.* Because we perceive similar figures as belonging together, choreographers and band directors often create distinct visual groupings within the larger band or dance troupe by having the members of each group wear a distinctive costume or uniform.

3. *Continuity.* Because we perceive smooth, continuous patterns rather than discontinuous ones, dancers or marching musicians moving together (as in a column, for example) are perceived as a separate unit.

4. *Closure.* If a figure has gaps, we complete it, filling in the gaps to create a whole image. Thus, we perceptually fill in the relatively wide spacing between dancers or marching musicians in order to perceive the complete words or forms they are creating.

Summing Up

The Eye

1. Cornea. Light enters the eye through this transparent membrane, which protects the inner structures from the environment.
2. Iris. The colored part of the eye, the iris functions like the aperture of a camera, controlling the size of the pupil to optimize the amount of light that enters the eye.
3. Pupil. The adjustable opening in the iris, the pupil allows light to enter.
4. Lens. This transparent structure behind the pupil changes shape to focus images on the retina.
5. Retina. The light-sensitive inner surface of the eye, the retina contains the rods and cones, which transduce light energy into neural impulses.
6. Blind spot. The region of the retina where the optic nerve leaves the eye, the blind spot contains no rods or cones and so there is no vision here.
7. Optic nerve. This bundle of nerve fibers carries neural impulses from the retina to the brain.

The Ear

1. Outer ear. Hearing begins as sound waves enter the auditory canal of the outer ear.
2. Auditory canal. Sound waves passing through the auditory canal are brought to a point of focus at the eardrum.
3. Eardrum. Lying between the outer and middle ear, this membrane vibrates in response to sound waves.
4. Middle ear. Lying between the outer and inner ear, this air-filled chamber contains the hammer, anvil, and stirrup.
5. Hammer, anvil, and stirrup. These tiny bones of the middle ear concentrate the eardrum's vibrations on the cochlea's oval window.
6. Inner ear. This region of the ear contains the cochlea and the semicircular canals, which play an important role in balance.
7. Cochlea. This fluid-filled multichambered structure contains the hair cell receptors that transduce sound waves into neural impulses.
8. Auditory nerve. This bundle of fibers carries nerve impulses from the inner ear to the brain.

Key Terms

Writing Definitions

1. **Sensation** is the process by which we detect physical energy from the environment and encode it as neural signals. (p. 141)
2. **Perception** is the process by which the brain selects, organizes, and interprets sensory information. (p. 141)
3. **Bottom-up processing** is analysis that begins with the sense receptors and works up to the brain's integration of sensory information. (p. 141)
4. **Top-down processing** is information processing guided by higher-level mental processes. (p. 141)
5. **Psychophysics** is the study of relationships between the physical characteristics of stimuli and our psychological experience of them. (p. 142)
6. The **absolute threshold** is the minimum stimulation needed to detect a stimulus 50 percent of the time. (p. 142)
7. A stimulus that is **subliminal** is one that is below the absolute threshold for conscious awareness. (p. 143)

   Memory aid: Limen is the Latin word for "threshold." A stimulus that is **subliminal** is one that is *sub-* ("below") the *limen*, or threshold.
8. The **difference threshold**, or *just noticeable difference (jnd)*, is the minimum difference in two stimuli that a subject can detect 50 percent of the time. (p. 144)

9. **Weber's law** states that the just noticeable difference between two stimuli is a constant minimum proportion of the stimulus. (p. 144)

   Example: If a difference of 10 percent in weight is noticeable, **Weber's law** predicts that a person could discriminate 10- and 11-pound weights or 50- and 55-pound weights.

10. **Sensory adaptation** refers to the decreased sensitivity that occurs with continued exposure to an unchanging stimulus. (p. 145)

11. **Wavelength**, which refers to the distance from the peak of one light or sound wave to the next, gives rise to the perceptual experiences of **hue**, or color, in vision (and **pitch** in sound). (p. 146)

12. The **intensity** of light and sound is determined by the amplitude of the waves and is experienced as brightness and loudness, respectively. (p. 147)

    Example: Sounds that exceed 85 decibels in amplitude, or **intensity**, will damage the auditory system.

13. **Accommodation** is the process by which the lens of the eye changes shape to focus near objects on the retina. (p. 148)

14. The **retina** is the light-sensitive, multilayered inner surface of the eye that contains the rods and cones, as well as neurons that form the beginning of the optic nerve. (p. 148)

15. The **rods** and **cones** are visual receptors that transform light into neural impulses. The rods have poor sensitivity, detect black and white, and function well in dim light. The cones have excellent sensitivity, enable color vision, and function best in daylight or bright light. (p. 148)

16. Comprised of the axons of retinal ganglion cells, the **optic nerve** carries neural impulses from the eye to the brain. (p. 148)

17. The **blind spot** is the region of the retina where the optic nerve leaves the eye. Because there are no rods or cones in this area, there is no vision here. (p. 148)

18. **Feature detectors**, located in the visual cortex of the brain, are nerve cells that selectively respond to specific visual features, such as movement, shape, or angle. Feature detectors are evidently the basis of visual information processing. (p. 150)

19. **Parallel processing** is information processing in which several aspects of a stimulus, such as light or sound, are processed simultaneously. (p. 151)

20. The **Young-Helmholtz trichromatic (three-color) theory** maintains that the retina contains red-, green-, and blue-sensitive color receptors that in combination can produce the perception of any color. This theory explains the first stage of color processing. (p. 153)

21. The **opponent-process theory** maintains that color vision depends on pairs of opposing retinal processes (red-green, yellow-blue, and white-black). This theory explains the second stage of color processing. (p. 155)

22. **Color constancy** is the perception that familiar objects have consistent color despite changes in illumination that shift the wavelengths they reflect. (p. 155)

23. **Visual capture** is the tendency for vision to dominate the other senses. (p. 156)

24. **Audition** refers to the sense of hearing. (p. 156)

25. The **pitch** of a sound is determined by its **frequency**, that is, the number of complete wavelengths that can pass a point in a given time. Frequency, in turn, is directly related to wavelength: Longer waves produce lower pitch; shorter waves produce higher pitch. (p. 157)

26. The **middle ear** is the chamber between the eardrum and cochlea containing the three bones (hammer, anvil, and stirrup) that concentrate the eardrum's vibrations on the cochlea's oval window. (p. 158)

27. The **inner ear** contains the semicircular canals and the cochlea, which includes the receptors that transform sound energy into neural impulses. Because it also contains the vestibular sac, the inner ear plays an important role in balance, as well as in audition. (p. 158)

28. The **cochlea** is the coiled, bony, fluid-filled tube of the inner ear where the transformation of sound waves into neural impulses occurs. (p. 158)

29. Melzack and Wall's **gate-control theory** maintains that a "gate" in the spinal cord determines whether pain signals are permitted to reach the brain. Neural activity in small nerve fibers opens the gates; activity in large fibers or information from the brain closes the gate. (p. 160)

30. **Sensory interaction** is the principle that one sense may influence another. (p. 162)

31. **Kinesthesis** is the sense of the position and movement of the parts of the body. (p. 164)

32. The sense of body movement and position, including the sense of balance, is called the **vestibular sense.** (p. 164)

33. **Gestalt** means "organized whole." The Gestalt psychologists emphasized our tendency to integrate pieces of information into meaningful wholes. (p. 165)

34. The **figure-ground** relationship refers to the organization of the visual field into two parts: the figure, which stands out from its surroundings, and the surroundings, or background. (p. 166)

35. **Grouping** is the perceptual tendency to organize stimuli in order to arrive at meaningful forms. Gestalt psychologists identified various principles of grouping. (p. 166)

36. **Depth perception** is the ability to see objects in three dimensions although the images that strike the retina are two-dimensional. (p. 167)

37. The **visual cliff** is a laboratory device for testing depth perception, especially in infants and young animals. In their experiments with the visual cliff, Gibson and Walk found strong evidence that depth perception is at least in part innate. (p. 167)

38. **Binocular cues** are depth cues that depend on information from both eyes. (p. 168)

    Memory aid: *Bi-* indicates "two"; *ocular* means something pertaining to the eye. **Binocular cues** are cues for the "two eyes."

39. **Monocular cues** are depth cues that depend on information from either eye alone. (p. 168)

    Memory aid: *Mono-* means one; a monocle is an eyeglass for one eye. A **monocular cue** is one that is available to either the left or the right eye.

40. **Retinal disparity** refers to the differences between the images received by the left eye and the right eye as a result of viewing the world from slightly different angles. It is a binocular depth cue, since the greater the difference between the two images, the nearer the object. (p. 168)

41. **Convergence** is a binocular depth cue based on the extent to which the eyes converge, or turn inward, when looking at near or distant objects. The more the eyes converge, the nearer the objects. (p. 169)

42. **Perceptual constancy** is the perception that objects have consistent lightness, color, shape, and size, even as illumination and retinal images change. (p. 172)

43. **Perceptual adaptation** refers to our ability to adjust to an artificially displaced or even inverted visual field. Given distorting lenses, we perceive things accordingly, but soon adjust by learning the relationship between our distorted perceptions and the reality. (p. 176)

44. **Perceptual set** is a mental predisposition to perceive one thing and not another. (p. 177)

45. **Extrasensory perception (ESP)** refers to the controversial claim that perception can occur without sensory input. Supposed ESP powers include telepathy, clairvoyance, and precognition. (p. 178)

    Memory aid: *Extra-* means "beyond" or "in addition to"; **extrasensory perception** is perception outside or beyond the normal senses.

46. **Parapsychology** is the study of ESP, psychokinesis, and other paranormal forms of interaction between the individual and the environment. (p. 178)

    Memory aid: *Para-*, like *extra-*, indicates "beyond"; thus, paranormal is beyond the normal and **parapsychology** is the study of phenomena beyond the realm of psychology and known natural laws.

Cross-Check

ACROSS	DOWN
4. pitch	1. frequency
7. inner ear	2. retina
9. basilar	3. linear perspective
11. psychophysics	4. parapsychology
13. closure	5. interposition
14. hue	6. kinesthesis
15. cones	8. connectedness
16. parallel	10. figure-ground
17. absolute	12. convergence
19. jnd	18. rods
20. cochlea	
21. ESP	
22. disparity	

FOCUS ON VOCABULARY AND LANGUAGE

Page 141: Shown her own face in a mirror, she is again *stumped*. This person (E. H.) is suffering from *prosopagnosia* and cannot recognize faces and even fails (*she is stumped*) to recognize her own face in the mirror. What is interesting in this case is that she can process incoming sensory information (*bottom up*) but is unable to make any sense of it (*top down*). As Myers notes earlier, she has sensation (*bottom-up processing*), but her perception (*top-down processing*) is not working properly.

Sensing the World: Some Basic Principles

Page 142: A frog could starve to death *knee-deep* in motionless flies. But let one *zoom by* and the frog's *"bug detector"* cells *snap awake*. The frog's eyes and brain are organized in such a way that only fast-moving (*zooming*), small, dark objects will cause these specialized feature detector nerve cells (*"bug detectors"*) to become active (*snap awake*). If the frog is surrounded by flies that don't move (*knee-deep in motionless flies*), it will die of hunger, completely unaware of the food at its feet.

Page 142: The *shades* on our own senses are open just a *crack*, allowing us only a restricted awareness of this *vast sea* of energy. Just as sunblinds or curtains (*shades*) let only a little light in through any small opening (*a crack*), our sensory system is only able to detect a very small part of the large amount (*vast sea*) of the physical energy that exists in the world.

Page 143: . . . *"satanic messages"* . . . It has been suggested that some rock music recordings have hidden or subliminal messages, and that behavior can be influenced or manipulated by them (i.e., *hidden persuasion*). Claims have been made that some of these messages are antireligious and promote devil worship (*diabolical* or *satanic*). As Myers makes clear, there is not a shred of evidence to support these ideas.

Page 143: . . . *hucksters* . . . A *huckster* is someone who sells merchandise that may be of dubious value. Those who promote and sell subliminal tapes (*hucksters*) make claims that are not supported by scientific research. In fact, the available evidence suggests that subliminal tapes do not have the profound, enduring effects on behavior claimed by their marketers; rather, the effect is zero (*zilch*).

Page 144: . . . it might take a $5000 *price hike* in a $50,000 Mercedes to *raise the eyebrows* of its potential buyers. *Raised eyebrows* express surprise. So a $5000 increase in the cost (*price hike*) of a luxury car (Mercedes-Benz), which normally costs $50,000,

would be noticed by interested buyers (*would raise their eyebrows*). **Weber's law** states that a constant proportion of the original stimulus is needed in order for the difference to be detected, and the precise proportion will change depending on the stimulus. Thus, a $5 increase in the price of the car would not be a just noticeable difference, or jnd, but a $5 dollar increase (*price hike*) in the cost of a hamburger and fries would exceed a jnd.

Page 145: Thus, everywhere that Mary looks the scene is sure to go. In order to understand this sentence you need to be familiar with the old nursery rhyme: Mary had a little lamb, its fleece was white as snow, and *everywhere that Mary went the lamb was sure to go.* When a volunteer (Mary) is fitted with a special contact lens and miniature projector, she sees the same image no matter where her eyes "look" (*everywhere that Mary looks the scene is sure to go*). When an image is projected on the retina in this manner, the scene disappears bit by bit and then reappears and disappears again (in meaningful units). This happens because the image, which normally would be moving back and forth rapidly (*quivering*) due to tiny eye movements, is now stationary with respect to the retina and its receptors. As the receptors fatigue, the image fades away or disappears.

Vision

Page 148: This was *baffling*. Scientists were puzzled (*baffled*) by the fact that although the retina receives an upside-down image, we experience the world right side up. We now know that the retina doesn't analyze the image as a total unit; rather, it transforms (*transduces*) the light energy into neural impulses that are transmitted to the brain via the optic nerve, and there it is put together to form the impression of a right-side-up world.

Page 148: . . . **blind spot** . . . You can use the suggestion in Figure 5.7 of the text to demonstrate that there are two small parts of your visual field (one in the left and one in the right) where you have no sight. These tiny areas (*blind spots*) are where the optic nerve exits the eye.

Page 152 (caption): The answer to this question is the *Holy Grail* of vision research. This refers to the medieval legend that the cup (*grail*) Jesus Christ drank from at the Last Supper, and which was later used to catch his blood when he was crucified, survived and may have been brought to England. The quest, or search, for this sacred cup (*Holy Grail*) symbolized spiritual regeneration and enlightenment. Similarly, attempting to answer the question about how the brain deals with multiple aspects of a visual scene at the same time, automatically and without our awareness (**parallel processing**), is an important undertaking that, if successful, will enlighten us about brain functioning (*the Holy Grail of vision research*).

Page 152: . . . *blindsight* . . . *Blindsight* refers to the fact that some people with neurological damage have the ability to see, to some degree, without any conscious awareness of the visual experience. They are blind, yet they can see. This suggests that there are two parallel processing systems operating, one that unconsciously guides our actions (*the zombie within*) and one that gives us our conscious perceptions.

Page 153: Color, like all aspects of vision, resides not in the object but in the *theater of our brains.* Myers notes that when we view a colored object (for example, a blue balloon), it absorbs all the wavelengths except its own (blue) and reflects the wavelengths of blue back to us. The color we perceive is a product of our brain and exists only in the perceiver's mind (*theater of the brain*).

The Other Senses

Page 156: We also are remarkably sensitive to *faint sounds,* an obvious *boon* to our ancestors' survival when *hunting* or being *hunted* or to our need to detect a child's whimper. Humans are very good at detecting very quiet noises (*faint sounds*), which was clearly beneficial (*a boon*) to our predecessors' ability to survive when they were both predator (*hunter*) and prey (*being hunted*). Likewise, the ability to notice and respond to a youngster's quiet cry of distress (*a child's whimper*) would have had adaptive value. We are also very sensitive to changes in sounds, and we have the ability to differentiate among thousands of human voices.

Page 157: A *piccolo* produces much shorter, faster sound waves than does a *tuba.* Musical instruments produce stimulus energy called sound waves—molecules of air that bump and push each other along—and these may be long (low frequency) or short (high frequency). A *tuba* (a large, deep-toned, brass-wind instrument) produces low-frequency sound waves and thus has a lower pitch than a *piccolo* (a small flute), which produces high-frequency waves and has a higher pitch.

Page 158: If a car to the right *honks,* your right ear receives a more *intense* sound, and it receives sound slightly *sooner* than your left ear. We locate sounds because our ears are about 6 inches apart and there is a time difference, as well as a loudness difference, between auditory reception in each ear. If we hear the sound of a car horn (*it honks*) to our right, the left ear receives a less intense sound somewhat later than the right ear, and thus we locate the direction of the sound to the right.

Page 159: As lovers, we *yearn* to touch—to kiss, to stroke, *to snuggle.* Our sense of touch involves a mixture of at least four distinct senses, pressure, warmth, cold, and pain. Intimate relations often involve a desire or longing (*we yearn*) to caress, kiss, and closely embrace each other (*snuggle*).

Page 160: *Rubbing* the area around your *stubbed toe* will create competing stimulation that will *block* some of the pain messages. If you hit your toe against a solid object (*stub your toe*), it really hurts. If, however, you massage (*rub*) the part around the sore spot, it makes you feel better because stimulation interferes with (*blocks*) some of the pain messages. This supports the **gate-control** model, which suggests that this stimulation (*rubbing*) will activate "gate-closing" in large neural fibers and, thus, will reduce pain.

Page 161: A well-trained nurse may distract *needle-shy* patients by chatting with them and asking them to look away when inserting the needle. One method of pain control is through distraction. If you are nervous or anxious about being injected with a hypodermic needle (*a needle-shy patient*), the nurse may talk to you about unimportant matters (*she chats to you*) and request that you do not watch the procedure. This type of distraction can reduce the intensity of the pain.

Page 162: Taste buds are essential for taste, *but there's more to taste than meets the tongue.* The common expression *"there is more to this than meets the eye"* suggests that there is something extra going on over and above the obvious or apparent. Myers creates a variation of this expression using a different sense (taste). The flavors we experience are a function of more than just the taste buds in the tongue; they involve **sensory interaction** with the sense of smell (olfaction). Thus, the sense of taste involves more than simply responding to the chemicals that stimulate taste receptors in the tongue (*there is more to taste than meets the tongue*).

Page 162: Each day, as you inhale and exhale nearly 20,000 breaths of life-sustaining air, you *bathe* your nostrils in a *stream of scent-laden molecules.* Smell (olfaction) is a chemical sense and as substances (flowers, feet, fish, fertilizer, etc.) release molecules, they are carried by the air we breathe (*a stream of scent-laden molecules*) and wash over (*bathe*) receptors in our nasal cavities (nostrils).

Page 164: The biological *gyroscopes* for this sense of *equilibrium* are in the inner ear. A *gyroscope* is a mechanical device used as a stabilizer in navigation and scientific instruments. Likewise, we have biological stabilizers that monitor the movement and position of our bodies and provide us with a sense of balance (*equilibrium*). They are called the *semicircular canals* and the *vestibular sacs* and are located in the inner ear.

Perceptual Organization

Page 165 (Figure 5.20 caption): There is far more to perception than meets the senses. As noted earlier, *"there is more to this than meets the eye"* is a common expression, meaning something is going on beyond the obvious or the apparent. In this variation of the expression, Myers is noting that we create our own reality, not only from the incoming stimulation (sensations), but also by imposing organization and structure (perceptual processes) to create a greater reality (*there is far more to perception than meets the senses*).

Page 167: Usually, these grouping principles help us construct reality. Sometimes, however, they can *lead us astray . . .* Although we put together elements of sensation through active organization (the Gestalt grouping principles) and end up with a unitary experience, we sometimes make mistakes in the process (*we are led astray*).

Page 167: Their mothers then *coaxed* them to *crawl* out onto the glass. In the experiment with the **visual cliff**, 6- to 14-month-old children were gently encouraged (*coaxed*) by their mothers to move, on their hands and knees (*crawl*), onto the invisible glass top on the "deep" side of the apparatus. Most could not be persuaded to do so, leading to the conclusion that depth perception may be innate (inborn).

Page 168: The floating *finger sausage* (Figure 5.25). Try the demonstration (page 165) and you will experience the effect of **retinal disparity** and see a tubular shape (*finger sausage*) made by your brain from the two different images of your fingers.

Page 171: As we move, objects that are actually *stable* appear to move. Things that are stationary and do not move (*stable objects*) seem to move relative to us when we move.

Page 174: Take away these distance cues—by looking at the horizon moon (or each monster or each bar) through a *paper tube*—and it immediately shrinks. Observers have argued for centuries about why the moon near the horizon seems so much larger than the moon overhead in the sky. One explana-

tion involves the interaction of perceived size and perceived distance. Distance cues at the horizon make the moon appear further away than when it is overhead (where there are no distance cues). The moon casts the *same retinal image* in both situations, so the image that appears to be more distant (i.e., near the horizon) will therefore seem larger. We can eliminate the distance cues by looking at the moon through a rolled-up piece of paper (*paper tube*); the moon will appear much smaller (*it shrinks*).

Perceptual Interpretation

Page 176: Most had been born with cataracts—clouded lenses that allowed them to see only diffused light, rather as you or I might see a diffuse fog through a *Ping-Pong* ball sliced in half. People born with cataracts cannot see clearly because the normally transparent lenses in their eyes are opaque. To understand what their vision is like, imagine what you would see if you had your eyes covered with half of a small, white, plastic ball that is used in table tennis (*Ping-Pong*). When cataract patients have their vision restored, after being blind since birth, they can distinguish colors and figure from ground (innate capacities), but they cannot visually recognize things that were familiar by touch.

Page 176: Given a new pair of glasses, we may feel slightly disoriented, even dizzy. When we start wearing ordinary eyeglasses or when we are fitted with a new pair, our initial reaction is a little confusion and vertigo (*dizziness*). However, we quickly adapt within a few days. We can also adapt to lenses that distort what we are looking at by 40° to one side, and even to distortion lenses that invert reality (turn the visual image upside down—*a topsy-turvy world*). Young chickens cannot adapt in this way.

Page 177: As everyone knows, *to see is to believe.* As many people also know, but do not fully appreciate, *to believe is to see.* The expression *"seeing is believing"* means that we put much reliance on visual information when deciding (believing) what is true. Myers shows us that, on the contrary, what we believe may actually affect what we see. Our experiences, assumptions, expectations, and mental predispositions (**perceptual sets**) determine, to a large extent, our perceptions.

Page 180: In 1972, a British newspaper published genuine, unretouched photographs of *a "monster"* in Scotland's Loch Ness. . . . People who had heard about, or believed in, the Loch Ness Monster before seeing a very ambiguous picture of a log were more inclined to see what they expected to see (i.e., a monster) because of their **perceptual set**.

Page 181: Clearly, much of what we perceive comes not just from the world "out there" but also *from what's behind our eyes and between our ears.* Myers is reiterating the point that our mental predispositions, expectations, beliefs, etc. (*what's behind our eyes and between our ears*) influence much more of what we perceive than the sensory stimulation received from the outside world.

Page 182: Some gender differences, it seems, exist merely in the *eyes of their beholders.* The familiar saying "beauty is in the eye of the beholder" means that what is perceived as beautiful has more to do with what the perceiver subjectively believes than with the absolute qualities of the person or object being judged. Likewise, our stereotypes (rigid, conventional ideas or beliefs) about gender or culture can greatly influence (*color*) what is perceived.

Page 179: . . . uncanny . . . People who have dreams that coincide, by pure chance, with later events often have an eerie or strange (*uncanny*) feeling about the accuracy of their *apparent* precognitions.

Page 181: Or one more dashed hope? This means that an optimistic expectation (*hope*) does not materialize or prove to be real (*it gets dashed*). Other researchers in other labs have attempted to replicate Bem and Honorton (1994) ganzfeld tests of ESP that had initially shown positive results. Milton and Wiseman's (1999, 2001) statistical analysis of 30 follow-up ganzfeld experiments found no effect (*one more dashed hope*). Although the studies and the debate continue, no reproducible ESP phenomenon has ever been demonstrated.

chapter 6

States of Consciousness

Chapter Overview

Consciousness—our awareness of ourselves and our environment—can be experienced in various states. Chapter 6 examines not only waking consciousness, but also sleep and dreaming, daydreaming, fantasies, hypnotic states, drug-altered states, and near-death experiences.

Most of the terminology in this chapter is introduced in the sections on Sleep and Dreams and on Drugs and Consciousness. Among the issues discussed are why we sleep and dream, whether hypnosis is a unique state of consciousness, and possible psychological and social roots of drug use.

NOTE: Answer guidelines for all Chapter 6 questions begin on page 174.

Waking Consciousness (pp. 187–189)

> David Myers at times uses idioms that are unfamiliar to some readers. If you do not know the meaning of any of the following words, phrases, or expressions in the context in which they appear in the text, refer to page 184 for an explanation (note that one item appears in the chapter introduction): *a fundamental yet slippery concept; Psychology had nearly lost consciousness; your attentional spotlight shifts; you may draw a blank; consciousness is but the tip of the information-processing iceberg; Running on automatic pilot.*

Section Preview

First, skim the section, noting headings and boldface items. Then read the following objectives and, as you read the text, search for the information that will enable you to meet each objective. Answer guidelines begin on page 174.

1. Discuss the nature of consciousness and its significance in the history of psychology.

2. Explain what is meant by selective attention, and discuss the different levels of information processing.

Stepping Through the Section

After you have read the sections, complete the sentences and answer the questions. As you proceed, evaluate your performance by consulting the answers on page 175. Do not continue with the next section until you understand each answer. If you need to, review or reread the section in the textbook before continuing.

1. The study of _____ was central in the early years of psychology and in recent decades, but for quite some time it was displaced by the study of observable

_____ .

Define consciousness in a sentence.

2. Our tendency to focus at any moment on only a limited aspect of all that we are capable of experiencing is called _____ _____ . One example of this is the _____ _____ _____—the ability to attend selectively to only one voice among many.

3. In comparison with unconscious processing, conscious processing has a(n) _____ (limited/unlimited) capacity, is relatively _____ (fast/slow), and processes pieces of information _____ (simultaneously/successively).

4. Tasks that are less habitual _____ (require/do not require) conscious attention.

Sleep and Dreams (pp. 189–203)

If you do not know the meaning of any of the following words, phrases, or expressions in the context in which they appear in the text, refer to pages 184–186 for an explanation: *move in concert; with a depressed body; we may fret over concerns: Does a lovers' spat signal a split?; Pulling an all-nighter; jet lag; the machine went wild . . . deep zigzags; in deep slumber; you ascend from your initial sleep dive; As the night wears on; drowsy; sleep patterns that thwart . . .; Many fill this need by using their first class for an early siesta and after-lunch study hall for a slumber party; riddle of sleep; next-day blahs; snoozing is second only to boozing; a dream provides a psychic safety valve; it is time to wake up; buzz.*

Section Preview

Answer guidelines begin on page 175.

1. Describe the cyclical nature of sleep.

2. Discuss the effects of sleep deprivation and the possible functions of sleep.

3. Identify and describe the major sleep disorders.

4. Describe the normal content of dreams.

5. Discuss the possible functions of dreams as revealed in various theories.

Stepping Through the Section

Answers are provided on page 176.

1. The sleep-waking cycle follows a 24-hour clock called the _____ _____ .

2. When people are at their daily peak in circadian arousal, _____ is sharpest and _____ is most accurate. In contrast to university students, who often are at their peak in the _____ (morning/evening), older adults tend to peak in the _____ .

3. We may experience _____ _____ if our circadian rhythm is interrupted by travel across time zones.

4. Resetting of a disrupted biological clock is facilitated by exposure to _____ _____ , which triggers proteins in the _____ of the eyes to signal the brain's _____ gland to increase or decrease its production of _____ . We can also reset our biological clocks by adjusting our _____ _____ .

5. The sleep cycle consists of _____ distinct stages.

6. The rhythm of sleep cycles was discovered when Aserinsky noticed that, at periodic intervals during the night, the _____ of a sleeping child moved rapidly. This stage of sleep, during which _____ occur, is called _____ _____ .

7. The relatively slow brain waves of the awake but relaxed state are known as _____ waves.

8. During Stage 1 sleep, people often experience _____ sensations similar to _____ . These sensations may later be incorporated into _____ .

9. The bursts of brain-wave activity that occur during Stage 2 sleep are called _____ _____ .

10. Large, slow brain waves are called _____ waves. These begin during Stage _____ and predominate during Stage _____ sleep, which is therefore called _____- _____ sleep. A person in this stage of sleep generally will be _____ (easy/difficult) to awaken. It is during this stage that people may engage in sleep _____ .

Describe the bodily changes that accompany REM sleep.

11. During REM sleep, the motor cortex is _____ (active/relaxed), while the muscles are _____ (active/relaxed). For this reason, REM is often referred to as _____ sleep.

12. The rapid eye movements generally signal the beginning of a _____ .

13. The sleep cycle repeats itself about every _____ minutes. As the night progresses, Stage 4 sleep becomes _____ (longer/briefer) and REM periods become _____ (longer/briefer). Approximately _____ percent of a night's sleep is spent in REM sleep.

14. Newborns spend nearly _____ (how much?) of their day asleep, while adults spend no more than _____ .

15. Allowed to sleep unhindered, most people will sleep _____ hours a night. People who sleep less than that for several nights in a row often show signs of _____ _____ .

16. Teenagers typically need _____ hours of sleep but now average nearly _____ hours less sleep than teenagers of 80 years ago. To psychologist William _____ , this indicates that the vast majority of students are dangerously sleep-deprived. One indication of the hazards of this state is that the rate of _____ tends to increase immediately after the spring time change in Canada and the United States. Another is that sleep deprivation may suppress the functioning of the body's _____

system and alter metabolic and hormonal functioning in ways that mimic _____ and are conducive to _____ , _____ , and _____ _____ .

Describe the effects of sleep deprivation.

17. Two possible reasons for sleep are to keep us out of harm's way and to help restore body tissues, especially those of the _____ .

18. During sleep a growth hormone is released by the _____ gland. Adults spend _____ (more/less) time in deep sleep than children and so release _____ (more/less) growth hormone.

19. A persistent difficulty in falling or staying asleep is characteristic of _____ . People who report frequent stress average _____ (how much?) less sleep a night. Sleeping pills and alcohol may make the problem worse since they tend to _____ (increase/reduce) REM sleep.

20. The sleep disorder in which a person experiences uncontrollable sleep attacks is _____ . People with this disorder may collapse directly into _____ sleep and experience a loss of _____ _____ . The brains of people with this disorder lack a neural center in the _____ that produces the neurotransmitter _____ .

21. Individuals suffering from _____ _____ stop breathing while sleeping.

22. The sleep disorder characterized by extreme fright and rapid heartbeat and breathing is called _____ _____ . Unlike nightmares, these episodes usually happen early in the night, during Stage _____

sleep. The same is true of episodes of _____ and _____ , problems that _____ (run/do not run) in families. These sleep episodes are most likely to be experienced by _____ (young children/adolescents/older adults), in whom this stage tends to be the _____ and _____ .

23. During _____ dreams, the dreamer may be sufficiently aware to wonder whether he or she is, in fact, dreaming.

24. For both men and women, 8 in 10 dreams are marked by _____ (positive/negative) emotions, such as fears of being _____ .

25. People more commonly have dreams _____ (with sexual overtones/of events in their daily lives).

26. Freud referred to the actual content of a dream as its _____ content. Freud believed that this is a censored, symbolic version of the true meaning, or _____ _____ , of the dream.

27. According to Freud, most of the dreams of adults reflect _____ wishes and are the key to understanding inner _____ .

28. Freud's theory gave way to the theory that dreams serve an _____-processing function. Support for this theory is provided by the fact that REM sleep facilitates _____ .

29. Other theories propose that dreaming serves some _____ function, for example, that REM sleep provides the brain with needed _____ . Such an explanation is supported by the fact that _____ (infants/adults) spend the most time in REM sleep.

30. Still other theories propose that dreams are elicited by random bursts of _____ activity originating in lower regions of the brain, such as the _____ . According to the _____-_____ theory,

dreams are the brain's attempt to make sense of this activity. The bursts are believed to be given their emotional tone by the brain's _____ system. PET scans of sleeping people reveal increased activity in the brain's _____ system, especially the _____ .

31. After being deprived of REM sleep, a person spends more time in REM sleep; this is the _____ _____ effect.

32. REM sleep _____ (does/does not) occur in other mammals. Animals such as fish, whose behavior is less influenced by learning, _____ (do/do not) dream. This finding supports the _____-_____ theory of dreaming.

Hypnosis (pp. 203–208)

> If you do not know the meaning of any of the following words, phrases, or expressions in the context in which they appear in the text, refer to page 186 for an explanation: *psychological truth serum . . . considerable mischief; might the two views . . . be bridged?*

Section Preview

Answer guidelines begin on page 176.

1. Define hypnosis, and discuss several popular misconceptions about hypnosis.

2. Discuss the controversy over whether hypnosis is an altered state of consciousness.

Stepping Through the Section

Answers are provided on page 177.

1. The suggestion that a person forget things that occurred while he or she was under hypnosis may produce _____ _____ .

2. Most people are _____ (somewhat/not at all) hypnotically suggestible.

Describe people who are the most susceptible to hypnosis.

3. If people are led to expect that they are hypnotizable, their responsiveness under hypnosis _____ (will/will not) increase.

4. The hypnotic demonstration in which a subject supposedly relives earlier experiences is referred to as _____ _____ . Research studies show that the subjects in such demonstrations have memories that are _____ (more/no more) accurate than the memories of fully conscious persons.

5. The weight of research evidence suggests that hypnosis _____ (does/does not) allow a person to perform dangerous feats that are impossible in the normal waking state.

6. An _____ person in a legitimate _____ can induce people—hypnotized or not—to perform some unlikely acts.

7. Hypnotherapists have helped some people alleviate headaches through the use of _____ suggestions.

8. For _____ such as smoking, a subject's hypnotic responsiveness _____ (does/does not) make a difference in the effectiveness of hypnosis.

9. Hypnosis _____ (can/cannot) relieve pain. One theory of hypnotic pain relief is that hypnosis separates, or _____ , the sensory and emotional aspects of pain.

Another is that hypnotic pain relief is due to selective _____ , that is, to the person's focusing on stimuli other than pain.

10. PET scans show that hypnosis reduces brain activity in a region involved in _____ to painful stimuli, but not in the _____ cortex that receives the raw _____ input.

11. Hypnosis _____ (is/is not) a unique physiological state, which suggests that it reflects the workings of _____ _____ . These findings provide support for the _____ _____ theory of hypnosis. They believe that hypnotized people _____ (are/are not) faking it; that is, they _____ (are/are not) acting the role of "good hypnotized subjects."

12. Hilgard has advanced the idea that during hypnosis there is a _____ , or split, between different levels of consciousness.

13. The existence of a separate consciousness, which is aware of what takes place during hypnosis, is expressed in the concept of the _____ _____ .

Although this theory has provoked controversy, there is little doubt that _____ influences do play an important role in hypnosis.

Drugs and Consciousness (pp. 208–220)

> If you do not know the meaning of any of the following words, phrases, or expressions in the context in which they appear in the text, refer to page 186 for an explanation: *tipsy on one can of beer; tipsy restaurant patrons leave extravagant tips; quicker pick-her-upper; one pays a long-term price . . . gnawing craving for another fix; crack; "acid trip"; marijuana may spell relief; getting high.*

Section Preview

Answer guidelines are provided on page 177.

1. Discuss the physical and psychological effects common to all psychoactive drugs, and state three common misconceptions about addiction.

2. Describe the physiological and psychological effects of depressants, stimulants, and hallucinogens.

3. Discuss the biological, psychological, and social roots of drug use.

Stepping Through the Section

Answers begin on page 177.

1. Drugs that alter moods and perceptions are called _____ drugs.

2. Drug users who require increasing doses to experience a drug's effects have developed _____ for the drug. The user's brain counteracts the disruption to its normal functioning; thus, the user experiences _____ .

3. If a person begins experiencing withdrawal symptoms after ceasing to use a drug, the person has developed a physical _____ . Regular use of a drug to

relieve stress is an example of a
_____ dependence.

Briefly state three common misconceptions about addiction.

4. The three broad categories of drugs discussed in the text include _____ , which tend to slow body functions; _____ , which speed body functions; and _____ , which alter perception. These drugs all work by mimicking or affecting the activity of the brain's _____ .

5. Low doses of alcohol, which is classified as a _____ , slow the activity of the _____ nervous system.

6. Alcohol may make a person more _____ , more _____ , more _____ , or more _____ daring. Alcohol affects memory by interfering with the process of transferring experiences into _____-_____ memory. Also, blackouts after drinking result from alcohol's suppression of _____ _____ .

7. Excessive use of alcohol can also affect cognition by _____ the brain, especially in _____ (men/women). Alcohol also reduces _____ and focuses one's attention on the _____ _____ and away from _____ _____ .

Describe how a person's expectations can influence the behavioral effects of alcohol.

8. Tranquilizers, which are also known as _____ , have effects similar to those of alcohol.

9. Opium, morphine, and heroin all _____ (excite/depress) neural functioning. Together, these drugs are called the _____ . When they are present, the brain eventually stops producing _____ .

10. The most widely used stimulants are _____ , _____ , _____ , and _____ . Stimulants _____ (are/are not) addictive.

11. A lifelong smoker has a _____ percent chance of dying from the habit. Smoking also correlates with higher rates of _____ , _____ _____ , and _____ .

12. Because smoking usually begins during early adolescence, it is considered a _____ disease.

Identify several characteristics of teens who are especially likely to begin smoking.

13. As with other addictions, smokers become _____ , develop _____ , and experience _____ when they stop smoking.

14. Nicotine triggers the release of the neurotransmitters _____ and _____ , which in turn diminish _____ and

boost _____ . Nicotine also stimulates the release of _____ , which calms anxiety and reduces sensitivity to pain.

15. Cocaine and crack deplete the brain's supply of the neurotransmitters _____ , _____ , and _____ , and result in depression as the drugs' effects wear off. They do this by blocking the _____ of the neurotransmitters, which remain in the nerve cells' _____ .

16. Cocaine's psychological effects depend not only on dosage and form but also on _____ , _____ , and the _____ .

17. The drug _____ , or _____ , is both a _____ and a _____ _____ . This drug triggers the release of the neurotransmitters _____ and _____ . Among the adverse effects of this drug are disruption of the body's _____ clock, suppression of the _____ _____ , and impaired _____ .

18. Hallucinogens are also referred to as _____ . Two common synthetic hallucinogens are _____ and LSD, which is chemically similar to a subtype of the neurotransmitter _____ . The reports of people who have had near-death experiences are very similar to the _____ reported by drug users. These experiences may be the result of a deficient supply of _____ or other insults to the brain.

19. The active ingredient in marijuana is abbreviated _____ . Marijuana is being used therapeutically with those who suffer from _____ . However, these medical uses are complicated by marijuana's toxicity, which can cause _____ _____ .

Describe some of the physical and psychological effects of marijuana.

20. The negative aftereffects of drug use may be explained in part by the principle that emotions trigger _____ _____ .

21. Drug use by North American youth _____ (increased/declined) during the 1970s, then declined until the early 1990s due to increased _____ _____ and efforts by the media to deglamorize drug use.

22. In the twenty-first century, drug use by North American teens continues to _____ (decline/increase). At the same time, alcohol use is _____ (declining/on the rise).

23. Adopted individuals are more susceptible to alcoholism if they had a(n) _____ (adoptive/biological) parent with a history of alcoholism. Boys who at age 6 are _____ (more/less) excitable are more likely as teens to smoke, drink, and use other drugs. Children whose parents abuse alcohol have a _____ (higher/lower) tolerance for multiple drinks taken over an hour or two.

Identify some of the psychological and social roots of drug use.

24. Among teenagers, drug use _____ (varies/is about the same) across cultural groups.

25. African-American high school seniors report the _____ (highest/lowest) rates of drug use.

26. State three possible channels of influence for drug prevention and treatment programs.

    a. _____

    b. _____

    c. _____

Progress Test 1

Multiple-Choice Questions

Circle your answers to the following questions and check them with the answers beginning on page 178. If your answer is incorrect, read the explanation for why it is incorrect and then consult the appropriate pages of the text (in parentheses following the correct answer).

1. The cocktail party effect refers to the:
   a. effects of random noise on a person's mood.
   b. effects of random noise on a person's perception of low pitches.
   c. ability to attend selectively to one stimulus.
   d. cumulative effect of multiple uses of a depressant drug.

2. An important psychological contributor to drug use is:
   a. having overprotective parents.
   b. the feeling that life is meaningless.
   c. an overinflated ego.
   d. all of the above.

3. When our _____ is disrupted, we experience jet lag.
   a. daydreaming   d. Stage 4 sleep
   b. REM sleep   e. Stage 1 sleep
   c. circadian rhythm

4. Sleep spindles predominate during which stage of sleep?
   a. Stage 2   c. Stage 4
   b. Stage 3   d. REM sleep

5. During which stage of sleep does the body experience increased heart rate, rapid breathing, and genital arousal?
   a. Stage 2   c. Stage 4
   b. Stage 3   d. REM sleep

6. The sleep cycle is approximately _____ minutes.
   a. 30   c. 75
   b. 50   d. 90

7. The effects of chronic sleep deprivation include:
   a. suppression of the immune system.
   b. altered metabolic and hormonal functioning.
   c. impaired creativity.
   d. increased accident proneness.
   e. all of the above.

8. One effect of sleeping pills is to:
   a. decrease REM sleep.
   b. increase REM sleep.
   c. decrease Stage 2 sleep.
   d. increase Stage 2 sleep.

9. Alcohol may make a person more helpful, self-disclosing, and sexually daring because of the drug's tendency to:
   a. reduce inhibitions.
   b. suppress sleep.
   c. focus attention on the future.
   d. arouse the central nervous system.

10. Which of the following is classified as a depressant?
    a. amphetamines   d. alcohol
    b. LSD   e. MDMA
    c. marijuana

11. Cocaine and crack produce a euphoric rush by:
    a. blocking the actions of serotonin.
    b. depressing neural activity in the brain.
    c. blocking the reuptake of dopamine in brain cells.
    d. stimulating the brain's production of endorphins.
    e. preventing the body from producing endorphins.

12. Which of the following statements concerning hypnosis is true?
    a. People will do anything under hypnosis.
    b. Hypnosis is the same as sleeping.
    c. Hypnosis may reflect the workings of normal consciousness.
    d. Hypnosis improves memory recall.

13. People who heard unusual phrases prior to sleep were awakened each time they began REM sleep. The fact that they remembered less the next morning provides support for the _____ theory of dreaming.
    a. manifest content
    b. physiological
    c. information-processing
    d. activation-synthesis
    e. latent content

14. According to Freud, dreams are:
   a. a symbolic fulfillment of erotic wishes.
   b. the result of random neural activity in the brainstem.
   c. the brain's mechanism for self-stimulation.
   d. transparent representations of the individual's conflicts.

15. Psychoactive drugs affect behavior and perception through:
   a. the power of suggestion.
   b. the placebo effect.
   c. alteration of neural activity in the brain.
   d. psychological, not physiological, influences.

16. Which of the following is *not* a common *misconception* about addiction?
   a. To overcome an addiction a person almost always needs professional therapy.
   b. Psychoactive and medicinal drugs very quickly lead to addiction.
   c. Biological factors place some individuals at increased risk for addiction.
   d. Many other repetitive, pleasure-seeking behaviors fit the drug-addiction-as-disease-needing-treatment model.

17. At its beginning, psychology focused on the study of:
   a. observable behavior.
   b. consciousness.
   c. abnormal behavior.
   d. all of the above.

18. Which of the following is *not* a theory of dreaming mentioned in the text?
   a. Dreams facilitate information processing.
   b. Dreaming stimulates the developing brain.
   c. Dreams result from random neural activity originating in the brainstem.
   d. Dreaming is an attempt to escape from social stimulation.

19. The sleep-waking cycles of young people who stay up too late typically are _____ hours in duration.
   a. 23   **c.** 25
   b. 24   **d.** 26

20. The lowest rates of drug use among high school seniors is reported by:
   a. white males.
   b. white females.
   c. black males.
   d. Latinos.

Matching Items

Match each term with its appropriate definition or description.

Definitions or Descriptions

_____ **1.** surface meaning of dreams
_____ **2.** deeper meaning of dreams
_____ **3.** stage(s) of sleep associated with delta waves
_____ **4.** stage(s) of sleep associated with muscular relaxation
_____ **5.** sleep disorder in which breathing stops
_____ **6.** sleep disorder occurring in Stage 4 sleep
_____ **7.** depressant
_____ **8.** hallucinogen
_____ **9.** stimulant
_____ **10.** twilight stage of sleep associated with imagery resembling hallucinations
_____ **11.** disorder in which sleep attacks occur

Terms

   a. marijuana
   b. alcohol
   c. Stage 1 sleep
   d. night terrors
   e. manifest content
   f. cocaine
   g. narcolepsy
   h. sleep apnea
   i. Stages 3 and 4 sleep
   j. REM sleep
   k. latent content

Progress Test 2

Progress Test 2 should be completed during a final chapter review. Answer the following questions after you thoroughly understand the correct answers for the section reviews and Progress Test 1.

Multiple-Choice Questions

1. Which of the following statements regarding REM sleep is true?
   a. Adults spend more time than infants in REM sleep.
   b. REM sleep deprivation results in a REM rebound.
   c. People deprived of REM sleep adapt easily.
   d. Sleeping medications tend to increase REM sleep.
   e. REM sleep periods become shorter as the night progresses.

2. The hallucinatory sensations experienced by _____ users are similar to reports of _____ .
   a. amphetamine; near-death experiences
   b. LSD; near-death experiences
   c. barbiturate; divided consciousness
   d. cocaine; the phenomenon of dissociation

3. Alcohol has the most profound effect on:
   a. the transfer of experiences to long-term memory.
   b. immediate memory.
   c. previously established long-term memories.
   d. all of the above.

4. A person whose EEG shows a high proportion of alpha waves is most likely:
   a. dreaming.
   b. in Stage 2 sleep.
   c. in Stage 3 sleep.
   d. in Stage 4 sleep.
   e. awake and relaxed.

5. Circadian rhythms are the:
   a. brain waves that occur during Stage 4 sleep.
   b. muscular tremors that occur during opiate withdrawal.
   c. regular body cycles that occur on a 24-hour schedule.
   d. brain waves that are indicative of Stage 2 sleep.

6. A person who requires increasing amounts of a drug in order to feel its effect is said to have developed:
   a. tolerance.
   b. physical dependency.
   c. psychological dependency.
   d. resistance.
   e. withdrawal symptoms.

7. When a person suffers unpleasant withdrawal symptoms after discontinuing use of a drug, he or she is said to have developed:
   a. tolerance.
   b. physical dependency.
   c. psychological dependency.
   d. resistance.

8. Which of the following is characteristic of REM sleep?
   a. genital arousal
   b. increased muscular tension
   c. night terrors
   d. slow, regular breathing
   e. alpha waves

9. Which of the following is *not* a stimulant?
   a. amphetamines
   b. caffeine
   c. nicotine
   d. alcohol

10. Hypnotic responsiveness is:
    a. the same in all people.
    b. generally greater in women than men.
    c. generally greater in men than women.
    d. possible in nearly everyone.

11. According to Hilgard, hypnosis is:
    a. no different from a state of heightened motivation.
    b. a hoax perpetrated by frauds.
    c. the same as dreaming.
    d. a dissociation between different levels of consciousness.

12. Which of the following was *not* cited in the text as evidence that heredity influences alcohol use?
    a. Children whose parents abuse alcohol have a lower tolerance for multiple alcoholic drinks taken over a short period of time.
    b. Boys who are impulsive and fearless at age 6 are more likely to drink as teenagers.
    c. Laboratory mice have been selectively bred to prefer alcohol to water.
    d. Adopted children are more susceptible if one or both of their biological parents has a history of alcoholism.

13. As a form of therapy for relieving problems such as warts, hypnosis is:

a. ineffective.

b. no more effective than positive suggestions given without hypnosis.

c. highly effective.

d. more effective with adults than children.

14. Which of the following is usually the most powerful determinant of whether teenagers begin using drugs?

a. family strength   c. school adjustment

b. religiosity   d. peer influence

15. THC is the major active ingredient in:

a. nicotine.   d. cocaine.

b. MDMA.   e. amphetamine.

c. marijuana.

16. Those who believe that hypnosis is a social phenomenon argue that "hypnotized" individuals are:

a. consciously faking their behavior.

b. merely acting out a role.

c. underachievers striving to please the hypnotist.

d. all of the above.

17. "Consciousness" is defined in the text as:

a. mental life.

b. selective attention to ongoing perceptions, thoughts, and feelings.

c. information processing.

d. a vague concept no longer useful to contemporary psychologists.

e. our awareness of ourselves and our environment.

18. I am a synthetic stimulant and mild hallucinogen that produces euphoria and social intimacy by triggering the release of dopamine and serotonin. What am I?

a. LSD   c. THC

b. MDMA   d. cocaine

19. According to the activation-synthesis theory, dreaming represents:

a. the brain's efforts to integrate unrelated bursts of activity in brain areas that process visual images with emotional tone provided by activity in the limbic system.

b. a mechanism for coping with the stresses of daily life.

c. a symbolic depiction of a person's unfulfilled wishes.

d. an information-processing mechanism for converting the day's experiences into long-term memory.

20. How a particular psychoactive drug affects a person depends on:

a. the dosage and form in which the drug is taken.

b. the user's expectations and personality.

c. the situation in which the drug is taken.

d. all of the above.

Matching Items

Match each term with its appropriate definition or description.

Definitions or Descriptions

_____ **1.** drug that is both a stimulant and mild hallucinogen

_____ **2.** drugs that increase energy and stimulate neural activity

_____ **3.** brain wave of awake, relaxed person

_____ **4.** brain-wave activity during Stage 2 sleep

_____ **5.** sleep stage associated with dreaming

_____ **6.** drugs that reduce anxiety and depress central nervous system activity

_____ **7.** natural painkiller produced by the brain

_____ **8.** neurotransmitter that LSD resembles

_____ **9.** our awareness of ourselves and our environment

_____ **10.** theory that dreaming reflects our erotic drives

_____ **11.** a split between different levels of consciousness

Terms

a. Freud's theory

b. serotonin

c. Ecstasy

d. alpha

e. dissociation

f. amphetamines

g. consciousness

h. sleep spindle

i. endorphin

j. REM

k. barbiturates

Review and Reflect

Answer these questions the day before an exam as a final check on your understanding of the chapter's terms and concepts.

Multiple-Choice Questions

1. A person who falls asleep in the midst of a heated argument probably suffers from:
   a. sleep apnea.
   b. narcolepsy.
   c. night terrors.
   d. insomnia.

2. Which of the following was *not* suggested by the text as an important aspect of drug prevention and treatment programs?
   a. education about the long-term costs of a drug's temporary pleasures
   b. efforts to boost people's self-esteem and purpose in life
   c. attempts to modify peer associations
   d. "scare tactics" that frighten prepubescent children into avoiding drug experimentation

3. REM sleep is referred to as "paradoxical sleep" because:
   a. studies of people deprived of REM sleep indicate that REM sleep is unnecessary.
   b. the body's muscles remain relaxed while the brain and eyes are active.
   c. it is very easy to awaken a person from REM sleep.
   d. the body's muscles are very tense while the brain is in a nearly meditative state.
   e. erection during REM sleep indicates sexual arousal.

4. An attorney wants to know if the details and accuracy of an eyewitness's memory for a crime would be improved under hypnosis. Given the results of relevant research, what should you tell the attorney?
   a. Most hypnotically retrieved memories are either false or contaminated.
   b. Hypnotically retrieved memories are usually more accurate than conscious memories.
   c. Hypnotically retrieved memories are purely the product of the subject's imagination.
   d. Hypnosis only improves memory of anxiety-provoking childhood events.

5. Dan has recently begun using an addictive, euphoria-producing drug. Which of the following will probably occur if he repeatedly uses this drug?
   a. As tolerance to the drug develops, Dan will experience increasingly pleasurable "highs."
   b. The dosage needed to produce the desired effect will increase.
   c. After each use, he will become more and more depressed.
   d. Dependence will become less of a problem.
   e. Both b. and c. will occur.

6. Although her eyes are closed, Adele's brain is generating bursts of electrical activity. It is likely that Adele is:
   a. under the influence of a depressant.
   b. under the influence of an opiate.
   c. in NREM sleep.
   d. in REM sleep.
   e. having a near-death experience.

7. Concluding his presentation on levels of information processing, Miguel states that:
   a. humans process both conscious and subconscious information in parallel.
   b. conscious processing occurs in parallel, while subconscious processing is serial.
   c. conscious processing is serial, while subconscious processing is parallel.
   d. all information processing is serial in nature.

8. Roberto is moderately intoxicated by alcohol. Which of the following changes in his behavior is likely to occur?
   a. If angered, he is more likely to become aggressive than when he is sober.
   b. He will be less self-conscious about his behavior.
   c. If sexually aroused, he will be less inhibited about engaging in sexual activity.
   d. The next day he may be unable to remember what happened while he was drinking.
   e. All of the above are likely.

9. Jill dreams that her boyfriend pushes her in front of an oncoming car. Her psychoanalyst suggests that the dream might symbolize her fear that her boyfriend is rushing her into sexual activity prematurely. The analyst is evidently attempting to interpret the _____ content of Jill's dream.
   a. manifest
   b. latent
   c. dissociated
   d. overt

10. Barry has just spent four nights as a subject in a sleep study in which he was awakened each time he entered REM sleep. Now that the experiment is over, which of the following can be expected to occur?
    a. Barry will be extremely irritable until his body has made up the lost REM sleep.
    b. Barry will sleep so deeply for several nights that dreaming will be minimal.
    c. There will be an increase in sleep Stages 1–4.
    d. There will be an increase in Barry's REM sleep.

11. Of the following individuals, who is likely to be the most hypnotically suggestible?
    a. Bill, a reality-oriented stockbroker
    b. Janice, an actress with a rich imagination
    c. Megan, a sixth-grader who has trouble focusing her attention on a task
    d. Darren, who has never been able to really "get involved" in movies or novels

12. Which of the following statements concerning alcoholism is *not* true?
    a. Adopted individuals are more susceptible to alcoholism if they had an adoptive parent with alcoholism.
    b. Having an identical twin with alcoholism puts a person at increased risk for alcohol problems.
    c. Compared to children of parents who do not drink, children of parents with alcoholism have a higher tolerance for multiple alcoholic drinks.
    d. Researchers have bred rats that prefer alcohol to water.

13. Research studies of the effectiveness of hypnosis as a form of therapy have demonstrated that:
    a. for addictions, such as smoking, hypnosis is equally effective with subjects who can be deeply hypnotized and those who cannot.
    b. posthypnotic suggestions have helped alleviate headaches, asthma, warts, and stress-related skin disorders.
    c. positive suggestions given without hypnosis are often as effective as hypnosis as a form of therapy.
    d. all of the above are true.

14. I am the type of information that is processed slowly, serially, and for which the brain's processing capacity is limited. What type of information am I?
    a. subconscious   c. new
    b. conscious   d. old

15. I am a brain wave that predominates during Stage 4 slow-wave sleep. What am I?
    a. alpha wave   c. delta wave
    b. sleep spindle   d. beta wave

16. Which of the following statements concerning marijuana is *not* true?
    a. The by-products of marijuana are cleared from the body more quickly than are the by-products of alcohol.
    b. Regular users may achieve a high with smaller amounts of the drug than occasional users would need to get the same effect.
    c. Marijuana is not as addictive as nicotine or cocaine.
    d. Large doses of marijuana hasten the loss of brain cells.

17. For the past several days, Clay has felt irritable, unable to concentrate, and forgetful. Clay's symptoms are probably signs of:
    a. sleep loss.
    b. stimulant use.
    c. depressant use.
    d. hallucinogen use.

18. Those who consider hypnosis a social phenomenon contend that:
    a. hypnosis is an altered state of consciousness.
    b. hypnotic phenomena are unique to hypnosis.
    c. if a hypnotist eliminates the motivation for acting, hypnotized subjects become unresponsive.
    d. all of the above are true.

19. Which of the following statements concerning the roots of drug use is *not* true?
    a. Heavy users of alcohol, marijuana, and cocaine often are depressed.
    b. If an adolescent's friends use drugs, odds are that he or she will, too.
    c. Teenagers who come from happy families and do well in school seldom use drugs.
    d. It is nearly impossible to predict whether or not a particular adolescent will experiment with drugs.

20. A smoker friend states her intention to switch to low-nicotine cigarettes to minimize the hazards of smoking. You tell her that:

   a. low-nicotine cigarettes are as effective as regular cigarettes in stimulating the release of dopamine.

   b. smokers who switch to low-nicotine cigarettes often smoke more of them to maintain a constant level of nicotine in their blood.

   c. most smokers who switch to low-nicotine cigarettes eventually quit smoking altogether.

   d. most smokers who switch to low-nicotine cigarettes eventually resume smoking high-nicotine cigarettes.

Essay Question

You have just been assigned the task of writing an article tentatively titled "Alcohol and Alcoholism: Roots, Effects, and Prevention." What information should you include in your article? (Use the space below to list the points you want to make, and organize them. Then write the essay on a separate piece of paper.)

Key Terms

Writing Definitions

Using your own words, on a separate piece of paper write a brief definition or explanation of each of the following terms.

1. consciousness
2. selective attention
3. circadian rhythm
4. REM sleep
5. alpha waves
6. sleep
7. hallucinations
8. delta waves
9. insomnia
10. narcolepsy
11. sleep apnea
12. night terrors
13. dream
14. manifest content
15. latent content
16. REM rebound
17. hypnosis
18. posthypnotic amnesia
19. posthypnotic suggestion
20. dissociation
21. hidden observer
22. psychoactive drug
23. tolerance
24. withdrawal
25. physical dependence
26. psychological dependence
27. depressants
28. barbiturates
29. opiates
30. stimulants
31. amphetamines
32. Ecstacy (MDMA)
33. hallucinogens
34. LSD (lysergic acid diethylamide)
35. near-death experience
36. THC

Cross-Check

As you learned in Chapter 1, reviewing and overlearning of material are important to the learning process. After you have written the definitions of the key terms in this chapter, you should complete the crossword puzzle to ensure that you can reverse the process—recognize the term, given the definition.

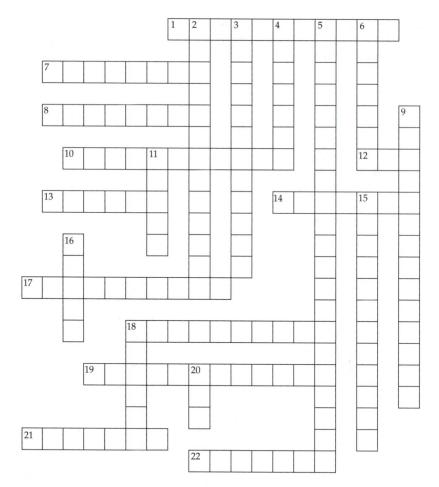

ACROSS

1. Term for REM sleep reflecting that the body is aroused but the muscles are relaxed.
7. Neurotransmitter whose reuptake is blocked by cocaine.
8. Widely used stimulant that is inhaled.
10. Dreams in which the dreamer is sufficiently aware to wonder if he or she is dreaming.
12. Powerful hallucinogen first used by Albert Hofmann.
13. Type of processing that describes how we deal with conscious information.
14. Type of brain wave that occurs during Stage 2 sleep.
17. Drug category that includes alcohol.
18. Stage 1 dream sensation similar to a hallucination.
19. Also known as tranquilizers.
21. Time of day at which the performance of older adults tend to be best.
22. Time of day at which the performance of college students tend to be best.

18. Depressant that causes a rush of euphoria.
20. Active ingredient in marijuana.

DOWN

2. In hypnosis, the supposed reliving of earlier experiences.
3. Drugs that "speed up" neural activity.
4. Drugs that depress neural activity, temporarily lessening pain.
5. Theory suggesting that dreams help fix daily experiences in our memories.
6. Drug that disrupts the processing of recent experiences into long-term memories.
9. Ernest Hilgard's term describing a hypnotized subject's awareness of unreported experiences.
11. Brain wave that predominates in Stage 4 sleep.
15. Divided consciousness (as during hypnosis).
16. Relatively slow brain waves of a relaxed, awake state.

Answers

Waking Consciousness

Section Preview

1. At its beginning, psychology focused on the description and explanation of states of consciousness. The difficulty of scientifically studying consciousness and the emergence of the school of behaviorism, however, caused psychology to shift to the study of overt behavior. By 1960, advances in neuroscience made it possible to relate brain activity to various mental states; as a result, mental concepts began to reenter psychology.

Contemporary psychologists define consciousness as "our awareness of ourselves and our environment" and conduct research on attention, sleeping, dreaming, and altered states of consciousness induced by hypnosis and drugs.

2. Selective attention refers to the focusing of conscious awareness on a particular stimulus—that is, we can focus on only one thing at a time. For example, as described by the cocktail party effect, we attend to only one voice among many.

Research reveals that information processing occurs at many levels, depending on the difficulty and familiarity of a task. Much information is processed without awareness. Less habitual tasks require conscious attention. Unlike the relatively slow, limited-capacity, serial processing of conscious information, subconscious information can be processed in parallel.

Stepping Through the Section

1. consciousness; behavior

Consciousness is our awareness of ourselves and our environment.

2. selective attention; cocktail party effect

3. limited; slow; successively

4. require

Sleep and Dreams

Section Preview

1. The sleep-waking cycle is a circadian (24-hour) rhythm. The cycle of sleep is a 90- or 100-minute rhythm that consists of five distinct stages. During Stage 1 sleep, which is brief, breathing rate slows, brain waves become slow and irregular, and people often experience hallucination-like and hypnogogic sensations. The approximately 20 minutes of Stage 2 sleep are characterized by bursts of brain-wave activity (sleep spindles). Starting in Stage 3 and increasingly in Stage 4, the sleeper's brain emits large, slow delta waves, which last about 30 minutes. During this period, it is difficult to awaken a sleeper. During REM sleep, brain waves, heart rate, and breathing become more rapid; genital arousal and rapid eye movements occur; and dreaming is common. Over the course of a night's sleep, REM sleep increases in duration, while Stages 3 and 4 become shorter.

2. The major effects of sleep deprivation are sleepiness and a general malaise. Other effects include impaired creativity, concentration, and communication; irritability; and slowed performance. Some researchers believe that sleep deprivation is widespread and contributes to traffic deaths and other accidents. Sleep deprivation may also suppress the functioning of the immune system, making people more susceptible to infections, and alter metabolic and hormonal functioning in ways that mimic aging and are conducive to obesity, hypertension, and memory impairment.

Why people need sleep is not fully understood. Sleep may have evolved for two reasons. First, sleep kept our ancestors out of harm's way during the dangerous hours of darkness. Second, sleep helps restore body tissues, especially those of the brain. That sleep plays a role in the growth process is indicated by evidence that during deep sleep, the pituitary gland releases a growth hormone.

3. Approximately 10 to 15 percent of adults suffer recurring problems in falling or staying asleep (insomnia). People with narcolepsy suffer overwhelming bouts of sleepiness and, in severe cases, collapse directly into a brief period of REM sleep. Those who suffer from sleep apnea intermittently stop breathing for a minute or so when they sleep. Unlike nightmares, which typically occur during early morning REM sleep, night terrors usually occur early in the night and during Stage 4 sleep; they are characterized by high arousal and an appearance of being terrified. Sleepwalking and sleeptalking are also Stage 4 phenomena, most often experienced by young children (who experience the lengthiest and deepest Stage 4 sleep).

4. REM dreams are vivid, emotional, and bizarre. Many dreams, however, are rather ordinary and deal with daily life events. People commonly dream of failure; of being attacked, pursued, or rejected; or of experiencing misfortune. Sexual imagery in dreams is less common than is popularly believed. Occasionally, people experience "lucid dreams," in which they are sufficiently aware during a dream to wonder whether they are, in fact, dreaming and are able to test their state of consciousness.

5. Freud argued that dreams are a psychic safety valve that discharges threatening feelings. According to this view, a dream's manifest content is a symbolic version of its true underlying meaning (latent content), which consists of unacceptable drives and erotic wishes.

According to the information-processing theory, dreams help with the processing and storage of daily experiences. In support of this theory is evidence that people who hear unusual phrases before bedtime remember more as long as they are not awakened during REM sleep.

Another theory holds that dreams provide the brain with needed stimulation that promotes development of neural pathways. In support of this theory is evidence that infants spend more time in REM sleep than adults.

According to the activation-synthesis theory, dreams are the brain's attempt to integrate unrelated bursts of activity in the visual cortex, imposing meaning on meaningless stimuli. The emotional "tone" of dreams is provided by activity in the limbic system.

Stepping Through the Section

1. circadian rhythm

2. thinking; memory; evening; morning

3. jet lag

4. bright light; retinas; pineal; melatonin; sleep schedules

5. five

6. eyes; dreams; REM sleep

7. alpha

8. hypnogogic; hallucinations; memories

9. sleep spindles

10. delta; 3; 4; slow-wave; difficult; walking

During REM sleep, brain waves become as rapid as those of Stage 1 sleep, heart rate and breathing become more rapid and irregular, and genital arousal and rapid eye movements occur.

11. active; relaxed; paradoxical

12. dream

13. 90; briefer; longer; 20 to 25

14. two-thirds; one-third

15. 9; sleep deprivation

16. 8 or 9; 2; Dement; accidents; immune; aging; obesity; hypertension; memory impairment

The major effect of sleep deprivation is sleepiness. Other effects include impaired creativity, concentration, and communication; slowed performance; and irritability.

17. brain

18. pituitary; less; less

19. insomnia; one hour; reduce

20. narcolepsy; REM; muscular tension; hypothalamus; hypocretin

21. sleep apnea

22. night terrors; 4; sleepwalking; sleeptalking; run; young children; lengthiest; deepest

23. lucid

24. negative; attacked, pursued, or rejected

25. of events in their daily lives

26. manifest; latent content

27. erotic; conflicts

28. information; memory

29. physiological; stimulation; infants

30. neural; brainstem; activation-synthesis; limbic; limbic; amygdala

31. REM rebound

32. does; do not; information-processing

Hypnosis

Section Preview

1. Hypnosis is a social interaction in which a hypnotist suggests to a subject that certain perceptions, feelings, thoughts, or behaviors will spontaneously occur. Approximately 20 percent of people are highly susceptible to hypnosis, although studies show that anyone can experience hypnotic responsiveness if led to expect it.

   Studies of hypnotic memory refreshment and age regression demonstrate that hypnosis does not boost memory. Age-regressed people merely act as they believe appropriate for a certain age.

   The belief that hypnosis can force people to act against their will, or perform acts that fully conscious people cannot, is also unsubstantiated.

   Posthypnotic suggestions have been used to help people alleviate headaches, asthma, warts, and stress-related skin disorders. But controlled studies demonstrate that giving patients positive suggestions without hypnosis is equally effective.

   Hypnosis can relieve pain, perhaps by allowing a person to dissociate the pain from conscious awareness or by focusing attention elsewhere. Several studies have shown that hypnosis relieves pain no better than relaxing and distracting people without hypnosis.

2. Most studies have found that hypnosis does not produce any unique physiological changes that would indicate it is an altered state of consciousness. Nor is the behavior of hypnotized people fundamentally different from that of fully conscious people. Therefore, hypnosis may be mainly a social phenomenon, with hypnotized subjects acting out the role of a "good hypnotic subject."

   The controversial divided-consciousness theory is based on Hilgard's idea that during hypnosis consciousness splits into a cooperating, suggestible component and a hidden observer that is passively aware of what is happening.

Stepping Through the Section

1. posthypnotic amnesia

2. somewhat

Those who are most susceptible frequently become deeply absorbed in imaginative activities. They also tend to have rich fantasy lives.

3. will

4. age regression; no more

5. does not

6. authoritative; context

7. posthypnotic

8. addictions; does not

9. can; dissociates; attention

10. attending; somatosensory; sensory

11. is not; normal consciousness; social influence; are not; are

12. dissociation

13. hidden observer; social

Drugs and Consciousness

Section Preview

1. All psychoactive drugs can produce tolerance and both physical and psychological dependence. This dependence is made clear by the fact that when a user stops taking a psychoactive drug, he or she experiences the undesirable side effects of withdrawal.

    There are several misconceptions about addiction, including the myth that psychoactive drugs automatically cause addiction, that addictions cannot be overcome without therapy, and that the addiction-as-disease-needing-treatment model can profitably be extended to many other pleasure-seeking behaviors.

2. Depressants such as alcohol, barbiturates, and opiates calm activity in the sympathetic nervous system and slow down body functions. Behaviorally, alcohol intake promotes aggressive, sexual, or helpful urges that the user's normal restraints might otherwise inhibit. Alcohol also disrupts the processing of recent experiences into long-term memories, reduces self-awareness, and suppresses REM sleep. The barbiturate drugs have effects similar to those of alcohol. With repeated use of artificial opiates, the brain stops producing endorphins, which leads to the agony of withdrawal when the drug is withdrawn.

    The stimulants, which include caffeine, nicotine, amphetamines, and cocaine, speed up body functions. When stimulants wear off, there is a compensatory slowdown of behavior that includes symptoms of tiredness, headaches, irritability, and depression. Cocaine produces its effects by blocking the reabsorption of excess dopamine, norepinephrine, and serotonin. Ecstasy (MDMA) is a synthetic stimulant and a mild hallucinogen. Its main effect is to block the reuptake of serotonin, thus prolonging that feel-good flood.

    Hallucinogens such as marijuana, LSD, and Ecstasy distort perceptions and evoke unpredictable psychological effects. Many hallucinogens produce their effects by blocking the actions of the neurotransmitter serotonin. Like alcohol, marijuana relaxes, disinhibits, and impairs memory and perceptual and motor skills.

3. Drug use by North American youth increased during the 1970s, then declined, indicating a changing national attitude toward drugs. Beginning in the early 1990s, however, drug use has rebounded.

    That some people may be biologically vulnerable to drug use is indicated by evidence that heredity influences alcoholic tendencies. Having an identical twin with alcoholism, for example, or adopted individuals who have a biological parent who has a history of alcoholism are at increased risk for problems.

    Several psychological factors may promote addiction, including feeling that one's life is meaningless, experiencing significant stress or failure, and depression.

    Especially for teenagers, social influences on drug use are strong. This is evident from differing rates of drug use across cultural groups. Peers influence attitudes about drugs, provide drugs, and establish the social context for their use. If an adolescent's friends use drugs, the odds are that he or she will, too.

Stepping Through the Section

1. psychoactive

2. tolerance; neuroadaptation

3. dependence; psychological

The following myths about addiction are false:

   a. Taking a psychoactive drug automatically leads to addiction.

   b. One cannot overcome an addiction without professional help.

   c. The addiction-as-disease-needing-treatment model is applicable to a broad spectrum of pleasure-seeking behaviors.

4. depressants; stimulants; hallucinogens; neuro-transmitters

5. depressant; sympathetic

6. aggressive; helpful; self-disclosing; sexually; long-term; REM sleep

7. shrinking; women; self-awareness; immediate situation; future consequences

Studies have found that if people believe that alcohol affects social behavior in certain ways, then, when they drink alcohol (or even mistakenly think that they have been drinking alcohol), they will behave according to their expectations. For example, if people believe alcohol promotes sexual feeling, on drinking they are likely to behave in a sexually aroused way.

8. barbiturates

9. depress; opiates; endorphins

10. caffeine; nicotine; amphetamines; cocaine; are

11. 50; depression, chronic disabilities, divorce

12. pediatric

Smoking is especially common among those who get low grades, who drop out of school, who feel less competent and in control of their futures and whose parents, friends, and siblings smoke.

13. dependent; tolerance; withdrawal

14. epinephrine; norepinephrine; appetite; alertness and mental efficiency; dopamine

15. dopamine; norepinephrine; serotonin; reuptake; synapses

16. expectations; personality; situation

17. Ecstacy; MDMA; stimulant; mild hallucinogen; dopamine; serotonin; circadian; immune system; memory

18. psychedelics; MDMA; serotonin; hallucinations; oxygen

19. THC; AIDS; cancer, lung damage, and pregnancy complications

Like alcohol, marijuana relaxes, disinhibits, and may produce a euphoric feeling. Also like alcohol, marijuana impairs perceptual and motor skills. Marijuana is a mild hallucinogen; it can amplify sensitivity to colors, sounds, tastes, and smells. Marijuana also interrupts memory formation.

20. opposing emotions

21. increased; drug education

22. increase; declining

23. biological; more; higher

A psychological factor in drug use is the feeling that one's life is meaningless and lacks direction. Regular users of psychoactive drugs often have experienced stress or failure and are somewhat depressed. Drug use often begins as a temporary way to relieve depression, anger, anxiety, or insomnia. A powerful social factor in drug use, especially among adolescents, is peer influence. Peers shape attitudes about drugs, provide drugs, and establish the social context for their use.

24. varies

25. lowest

26. a. education about the long-term costs of a drug's temporary pleasures
b. efforts to boost people's self-esteem and purpose in life
c. attempts to "inoculate" youth against peer pressures

Progress Test 1

Multiple-Choice Questions

1. c. is the answer. An example of selective attention, the cocktail party effect is the ability to attend to one voice among many. (p. 188)

2. b. is the answer. (p. 219)

3. c. is the answer. Jet lag is experienced because, having traveled across time zones, we are awake at a time when our biological clock says, "Sleep!" This biological clock is the circadian rhythm. (p. 190)

4. a. is the answer. (p. 192)
b. & c. Delta waves predominate during Stages 3 and 4. Stage 3 is the transition between Stages 2 and 4 and is associated with a pattern that has elements of both stages.
d. Faster, nearly waking brain waves occur during REM sleep.

5. d. is the answer. (p. 193)
a., b., & c. During non-REM Stages 1–4 heart rate and breathing are slow and regular and the genitals are not aroused.

6. d. is the answer. (p. 194)

7. e. is the answer. (pp. 195–196)

8. a. is the answer. Like alcohol, sleeping pills carry the undesirable consequence of reducing REM sleep and may make insomnia worse in the long run. (p. 198)
b., c., & d. Sleeping pills do not produce these effects.

9. **a.** is the answer. (p. 210)

   b. Alcohol does suppress REM sleep, but this effect doesn't explain the drug's impact on these behaviors.

   c. Alcohol focuses the drinker's attention on the immediate situation and *away* from future consequences.

   d. As a depressant, alcohol suppresses CNS activity.

10. **d.** is the answer. Alcohol, which slows body functions and neural activity, is a depressant. (p. 210)

    a. Amphetamines are stimulants.

    b., c., & e. LSD, MDMA, and marijuana are hallucinogens.

11. **c.** is the answer. They also block the reuptake of serotonin and norepinephrine. (p. 214)

    a. This answer describes the effect of LSD.

    b. Depressants such as alcohol have this effect. Cocaine and crack are classified as stimulants.

    d. None of the psychoactive drugs has this effect. Opiates, however, *suppress* the brain's production of endorphins.

    e. Use of opiates eventually does this.

12. **c.** is the answer. (p. 206)

    a. Hypnotized subjects usually perform only acts they might perform normally.

    b. The text does not suggest that sleeping and hypnosis are the same states.

    d. Hypnosis typically *disrupts*, or contaminates, memory.

13. **c.** is the answer. They remembered less than if they were awakened during other stages. (p. 202)

14. **a.** is the answer. Freud saw dreams as psychic safety valves that discharge unacceptable feelings that are often related to erotic wishes. (p. 201)

    b. & c. These physiological theories of dreaming are not associated with Freud.

    d. According to Freud, dreams represent the individual's conflicts and wishes but in disguised, rather than transparent, form.

15. **c.** is the answer. Such drugs work primarily at synapses, altering neural transmission. (p. 210)

    a. What people believe will happen after taking a drug will likely have some effect on their individual reactions, but psychoactive drugs actually work by altering neural transmission.

    b. Since a placebo is a substance without active properties, this answer is incorrect.

    d. This answer is incorrect because the effects of psychoactive drugs on behavior, perception, and so forth have a physiological basis.

16. **c.** is the answer. This is true. Heredity, for example, influences tendencies toward alcoholism. (p. 209)

17. **b.** is the answer. (p. 187)

    a. The behaviorists' emphasis on observable behavior occurred much later in the history of psychology.

    c. Psychology has never been primarily concerned with abnormal behavior.

18. **d.** is the answer. (pp. 201–203)

    a., b., & c. Each of these describes a valid theory of dreaming that was mentioned in the text.

19. **c.** is the answer. We can reset our biological clocks by adjusting our sleep schedules. Thus, young adults adopt something closer to a 25-hour day by staying up too late to get 8 hours of sleep. (p. 191)

20. **c.** is the answer. (p. 219)

Matching Items

1. e (p. 201)	**5.** h (p. 199)	**9.** f (p. 213)
2. k (p. 201)	**6.** d (p. 199)	**10.** c (p. 192)
3. i (p. 192)	**7.** b (p. 210)	**11.** g (p. 198)
4. j (p. 191)	**8.** a (p. 216)	

Progress Test 2

Multiple-Choice Questions

1. **b.** is the answer. Following REM deprivation, people temporarily increase their amount of REM sleep, in a phenomenon known as REM rebound. (p. 203)

   a. & e. Just the opposite is true: The amount of REM sleep is greatest in infancy, and the amount increases during the night.

   c. Deprived of REM sleep by repeated awakenings, people return more and more quickly to the REM stages after falling back to sleep. They by no means adapt easily to the deprivations.

   d. Just the opposite occurs: they tend to suppress REM sleep.

2. **b.** is the answer. (p. 215)

3. **a.** is the answer. Alcohol disrupts the processing of experiences into long-term memory but has little effect on either immediate or previously established memories. (p. 210)

4. **e.** is the answer. (p. 192)

   a. The brain waves of REM sleep (dream sleep) are more like those of Stage 1 sleep.

   b. Stage 2 is characterized by sleep spindles.

c. Stages 3 and 4 are characterized by slow, rolling delta waves.

5. **c.** is the answer. (p. 190)

6. **a.** is the answer. (p. 208)
b. Physical dependence may occur in the absence of tolerance. The hallmark of physical dependence is the presence of withdrawal symptoms when the person is off the drug.
c. Psychological dependence refers to a felt, or psychological, need to use a drug, for example, a drug that relieves stress.
d. There is no such thing as drug "resistance."
e. Withdrawal symptoms occur when the drug is no longer being taken.

7. **b.** is the answer. Physical dependence may occur in the absence of tolerance. The hallmark of physical dependence is the presence of withdrawal symptoms when the person is not taking the drug. (p. 209)
a. Tolerance involves requiring more and more of a drug before experiencing its effects.
c. Psychological dependence refers to a felt, or psychological, need to use a drug, for example, a drug that relieves stress.
d. There is no such thing as drug "resistance."

8. **a.** is the answer. (p. 193)
b. During REM sleep, muscular tension is low.
c. Night terrors are associated with Stage 4 sleep.
d. During REM sleep, respiration is rapid and irregular.
e. Alpha waves are characteristic of Stage 1 sleep.

9. **d.** is the answer. Alcohol is a depressant. (p. 212)

10. **d.** is the answer. (p. 204)
a. Hypnotic responsiveness varies greatly from person to person.
b. & c. There is no evidence of a gender difference in hypnotic responsiveness.

11. **d.** is the answer. Hilgard believes that hypnosis reflects a dissociation, or split, in consciousness, as occurs normally, only to a much greater extent. (p. 207)

12. **a.** is the answer. Compared with other children, children whose parents abuse alcohol have a *higher* tolerance for multiple drinks, making it more likely that they will, in fact, consume more alcohol. (p. 218)

13. **b.** is the answer. (p. 203)
a. & c. Hypnosis *can* be helpful in treating these problems, but it is no more effective than other forms of therapy.
d. Adults are not more responsive than children to hypnosis.

14. **d.** is the answer. If adolescents' friends use drugs, the odds are that they will, too. (p. 219)
a., b., & c. These are also predictors of drug use but seem to operate mainly through their effects on peer association.

15. **c.** is the answer. (p. 216)

16. **b.** is the answer. (p. 206)
a. & c. There is no evidence that hypnotically responsive individuals fake their behaviors or that they are underachievers.

17. **e.** is the answer. (p. 187)

18. **b.** is the answer. (p. 214)
a. & c. Unlike stimulants, LSD and THC do not speed up body functions.
d. Unlike hallucinogens, cocaine is a stimulant and does not generally distort perceptions.

19. **a.** is the answer. (p. 203)
b. & c. These essentially Freudian explanations of the purpose of dreaming are based on the idea that a dream is a psychic safety valve that harmlessly discharges otherwise inexpressible feelings.
d. This explanation of the function of dreaming is associated with the information-processing viewpoint.

20. **d.** is the answer. (p. 214)

Matching Items

1. c (p. 214)	**5.** j (p. 191)	**9.** g (p. 187)
2. f (p. 212)	**6.** k (p. 211)	**10.** a (p. 201)
3. d (p. 192)	**7.** i (p. 212)	**11.** e (p. 206)
4. h (p. 192)	**8.** b (p. 215)	

Review and Reflect

Multiple-Choice Questions

1. **b.** is the answer. Narcolepsy is characterized by uncontrollable sleep attacks. (p. 198)
a. Sleep apnea is characterized by the temporary cessation of breathing while asleep.
c. Night terrors are characterized by high arousal and terrified behavior, occurring during Stage 4 sleep.
d. Insomnia refers to chronic difficulty in falling or staying asleep.

2. **d.** is the answer. (p. 220)

3. **b.** is the answer. Although the body is aroused internally, the messages of the activated motor cortex do not reach the muscles. (p. 194)
a. Studies of REM-deprived subjects indicate just the opposite.

c. It is difficult to awaken a person from REM sleep.

d. Just the opposite occurs in REM sleep: The muscles are relaxed, yet the brain is aroused.

e. Arousal is usually not caused by sexual dreams.

4. **a.** is the answer. Although people recall more under hypnosis, they "recall" a lot of fiction along with fact and appear unable to distinguish between the two. (p. 205)

b. Hypnotically refreshed memories are usually no more accurate than conscious memories.

c. Although the hypnotized subject's imagination may influence the memories retrieved, some actual memory retrieval also occurs.

d. Hypnotically retrieved memories don't normally focus on anxiety-provoking events.

5. **e.** is the answer. Continued use of a drug produces a tolerance; to experience the same "high," Dan will have to use larger and larger doses. As the doses become larger, the negative aftereffects, or withdrawal symptoms, become worse. (pp. 208–209)

6. **d.** is the answer. The rapid eye movements of REM sleep coincide with bursts of activity in the visual cortex. (p. 193)

7. **c.** is the answer. (p. 189)

8. **e.** is the answer. Alcohol reduces self-consciousness and it loosens inhibitions, making people more likely to act on their feelings of anger or sexual arousal. It also disrupts the processing of experience into long-term memory. (pp. 210–211)

9. **b.** is the answer. The analyst is evidently trying to go beyond the events in the dream and understand the dream's hidden meaning, or the dream's latent content. (p. 201)

a. The manifest content of a dream is its actual story line.

c. Dissociation refers to a split in levels of consciousness.

d. There is no such term. In any case, "overt" would be the same as "manifest" content.

10. **d.** is the answer. Because of the phenomenon known as REM rebound, Barry, having been deprived of REM sleep, will now increase his REM sleep. (p. 203)

a. Increased irritability is an effect of sleep deprivation in general, not of REM deprivation specifically.

b. REM rebound will cause Barry to dream more than normal.

c. The increase in REM sleep is necessarily accompanied by decreases in Stages 1–4 sleep.

11. **b.** is the answer. People with rich fantasy lives and the ability to become imaginatively absorbed have essentially the characteristics associated with hypnotic suggestibility. The fact that Janice is an actress also suggests she possesses such traits. (p. 204)

a. Bill's reality orientation makes him an unlikely candidate for hypnosis.

c. The hypnotically suggestible are generally able to focus on tasks or on imaginative activities.

d. People who are hypnotically suggestible tend to become deeply engrossed in novels and movies.

12. **a.** is the answer. Adopted individuals are more susceptible to alcoholism if they had a *biological* parent with alcoholism. (p. 218)

b., c., & d. Each of these is true, which indicates that susceptibility to alcoholism is at least partially determined by heredity.

13. **d.** is the answer. (p. 205)

14. **b.** is the answer. (p. 189)

15. **c.** is the answer. (p. 192)

16. **a.** is the answer. THC, the active ingredient in marijuana, and its by-products linger in the body for a month or more. (p. 216)

17. **a.** is the answer. (pp. 195–196)

b., c., & d. The symptoms Clay is experiencing are not associated with any particular class of psychoactive drugs.

18. **c.** is the answer. (p. 207)

19. **d.** is the answer. As answers a., b., & c. (which are true) indicate, it *is* possible to predict whether or not an adolescent will experiment with drugs. (pp. 219–220)

20. **b.** is the answer. (p. 213)

Essay Question

As a depressant, alcohol slows neural activity and body functions. Although low doses of alcohol may produce relaxation, with larger doses reactions slow, speech slurs, skilled performance deteriorates, and the processing of recent experiences into long-term memories is disrupted. Alcohol also reduces self-awareness and may facilitate sexual and aggressive urges the individual might otherwise resist.

Some people may be biologically vulnerable to alcoholism. This is indicated by the fact that individuals who have a biological parent with alcoholism, or people who have an identical twin with alcoholism, are more susceptible to alcoholism.

Stress, depression, and the feeling that life is meaningless and without direction are common feelings among heavy users of alcohol and may create a psychological vulnerability to alcoholism.

Especially for teenagers, peer group influence is strong. If an adolescent's friends use alcohol, odds are that he or she will too.

Research suggests three important channels of influence for drug prevention and treatment programs: (1) education about the long-term consequences of alcohol use; (2) efforts to boost people's self-esteem and purpose in life; and (3) attempts to counteract peer pressure that leads to experimentation with drugs.

Key Terms

Writing Definitions

1. The text defines **consciousness** as our awareness of ourselves and our environment. (p. 187)

2. **Selective attention** refers to the fact that at any moment our conscious awareness is focused on only a small amount of what we could be experiencing. (p. 188)

3. A **circadian rhythm** is any regular biological rhythm, such as body temperature and sleep-wakefulness, that follows a 24-hour cycle. (p. 190)

   Memory aid: In Latin, *circa* means "about" and *dies* means "day." A **circadian rhythm** is one that is about a day, or 24 hours, in duration.

4. **REM sleep** is the sleep stage in which the brain and eyes are active, the muscles are relaxed, and vivid dreaming occurs; also known as paradoxical sleep. (p. 191)

   Memory aid: **REM** is an acronym for rapid eye movement, the distinguishing feature of this sleep stage that led to its discovery.

5. **Alpha waves** are the relatively slow brain waves characteristic of an awake, relaxed state. (p. 192)

6. **Sleep** is the natural, periodic, reversible loss of consciousness, on which the body and mind depend for healthy functioning. (p. 192)

7. **Hallucinations** are false sensory experiences that occur without any sensory stimulus. (p. 192)

8. **Delta waves** are the large, slow brain waves associated with deep sleep. (p. 192)

9. **Insomnia** is a sleep disorder in which the person regularly has difficulty in falling or staying asleep. (p. 198)

10. **Narcolepsy** is a sleep disorder in which the victim suffers sudden, uncontrollable sleep attacks, often characterized by entry directly into REM. (p. 198)

11. **Sleep apnea** is a sleep disorder in which the person ceases breathing while asleep, briefly arouses to gasp for air, falls back asleep, and repeats this cycle throughout the night. (p. 199)

    Example: One theory of the Sudden Infant Death Syndrome is that it is caused by **sleep apnea**.

12. A person suffering from **night terrors** experiences episodes of high arousal with apparent terror. Night terrors usually occur during Stage 4 sleep. (p. 199)

13. **Dreams** are vivid sequences of images, emotions, and thoughts, the most vivid of which occur during REM sleep. (p. 200)

14. In Freud's theory of dreaming, the **manifest content** is the remembered story line. (p. 201)

15. In Freud's theory of dreaming, the **latent content** is the underlying but censored meaning of a dream. (p. 201)

    Memory aids for 14 and 15: *Manifest* means "clearly apparent, obvious"; *latent* means "hidden, concealed." A dream's **manifest content** is that which is obvious; its **latent content** remains hidden until its symbolism is interpreted.

16. **REM rebound** is the tendency for REM sleep to increase following deprivation. (p. 203)

17. **Hypnosis** is a social interaction in which one person (the hypnotist) suggests to another (the subject) that certain perceptions, feelings, thoughts, or behaviors will spontaneously occur. (p. 204)

18. **Posthypnotic amnesia** is the condition in which, in response to the hypnotist's suggestion, subjects are unable to recall what happened while they were under hypnosis. (p. 204)

19. A **posthypnotic suggestion** is a suggestion made during a hypnosis session that is to be carried out when the subject is no longer hypnotized. (p. 205)

20. **Dissociation** is a split between different levels of consciousness, allowing a person to divide attention between two or more thoughts. (p. 206)

21. According to Hilgard, the **hidden observer** is a part of a hypnotized person's consciousness that remains aware of happenings even under hypnosis. Hilgard believes the hidden observer is an example of dissociation. (p. 207)

22. **Psychoactive drugs**—which include stimulants, depressants, and hallucinogens—are chemical substances that alter mood and perception. They work by affecting or mimicking the activity of neurotransmitters. (p. 208)

23. **Tolerance** is the diminishing of a psychoactive drug's effect that occurs with repeated use and the

need for progressively larger doses in order to produce the same effect. (p. 208)

24. **Withdrawal** refers to the discomfort and distress that follow the discontinued use of addictive drugs. (p. 209)

25. **Physical dependence** is a physiological need for a drug that is indicated by the presence of withdrawal symptoms when the drug is not taken. (p. 209)

26. The psychological need to use a drug is referred to as **psychological dependence**. (p. 209)

27. **Depressants** are psychoactive drugs, such as alcohol, opiates, and barbiturates, that reduce neural activity and slow body functions. (p. 210)

28. **Barbiturates** are depressants, sometimes used to induce sleep or reduce anxiety. (p. 211)

29. **Opiates** are depressants derived from the opium poppy, such as opium, morphine, and heroin; they reduce neural activity and relieve pain. (p. 212)

30. **Stimulants** are psychoactive drugs, such as caffeine, nicotine, amphetamines, and cocaine, that excite neural activity and speed up body functions. (p. 212)

31. **Amphetamines** are a type of stimulant and, as such, speed up body functions and neural activity. (p. 212)

32. A synthetic stimulant and a mild hallucinogen, **Ecstasy (MDMA)** produces euphoria by increasing serotonin levels in the brain. Repeated use may permanently damage serotonin neurons, suppress immunity, and disrupt cognition. (p. 214)

33. **Hallucinogens** are psychoactive drugs, such as LSD and marijuana, that distort perception and evoke sensory imagery in the absence of sensory input. (p. 215)

34. **LSD** (lysergic acid diethylamide) is a powerful hallucinogen capable of producing vivid false perceptions and disorganization of thought processes. LSD produces its unpredictable effects partially because it blocks the action of the neurotransmitter serotonin. (p. 215)

35. The **near-death experience** is an altered state of consciousness that has been reported by some people who have had a close brush with death. (p. 215)

36. The major active ingredient in marijuana, **THC** is classified as a mild hallucinogen. (p. 216)

Cross-Check

ACROSS	DOWN
1. paradoxical	2. age regression
7. dopamine	3. amphetamines
8. nicotine	4. opiates
10. lucid dreams	5. information processing
12. LSD	6. alcohol
13. serial	9. hidden observer
14. spindle	11. delta
17. depressant	15. dissociation
18. hypnogogic	16. alpha
19. barbiturates	18. heroin
21. morning	20. THC
22. evening	

FOCUS ON VOCABULARY AND LANGUAGE

Page 187: To psychologists, consciousness is similarly a *fundamental* yet *slippery* concept. In science many fundamental concepts are difficult to define (e.g., life, matter, energy). Consciousness is one of the most basic (*fundamental*) ideas in psychology, yet it is an elusive and difficult concept to grasp (*a slippery concept*).

Waking Consciousness

Page 187: Psychology had nearly *lost consciousness.* Myers is using a little humor here in order to illustrate the fact that changes (*swings*) have taken place during psychology's history. To *"lose consciousness"* can have two meanings in the above sentence: (1) to fall unconscious or pass out and (2) to fail to keep (lose) "consciousness" as the subject matter of psychology. Psychology started out as the study of conscious experience; then, because of problems in scientifically investigating the mind, overt behavior replaced consciousness in the 1920s. Finally, in the 1960s, psychology regained consciousness as a legitimate subject for psychologists to study.

Page 188: Now, suddenly, *your attentional spotlight shifts.* Your *feet feel encased, your nose stubbornly intrudes on the page* before you. **Selective attention** refers to our tendency to focus on only a small part of what is possible for us to experience. If you do attend to more aspects of your experience (*your attentional spotlight shifts*), you will be surprised at the amount of stimulation you process without awareness, such as the feel of the shoes on your feet (*your feet feel encased*) and the fact that your nose actually blocks your line of vision (*your nose stubbornly intrudes on the page*).

Page 188: . . . *you may draw a blank* . . . This means that you do not achieve the result you want; you don't succeed. When you attend to only one voice among many (*the cocktail party effect*), you may be unable to say what someone else, who was clearly within your hearing range, was saying (*you draw a blank*). Interestingly, you would very likely hear your own name if it were spoken by this person.

Page 189: Yet *consciousness* is but *the tip of the information-processing iceberg.* Just as most of the mass or volume of an iceberg is below the surface of the ocean and out of sight, most mental functioning goes on without conscious awareness. Consciousness is a small part (*the tip of the iceberg*) of total information processing.

Page 189: Running on automatic pilot allows consciousness—the mind's *CEO*—to monitor the whole system and deal with new challenges. Myers is pointing out that much of our information processing occurs outside of conscious awareness (*we run on automatic pilot*) and that conscious awareness is similar to the top manager of an organization (*CEO or chief executive officer*) whose many assistants take care of all the routine tasks, allowing him or her to pay attention to (*monitor*) the total system and tackle (*deal with*) new challenges.

Sleep and Dreams

Page 190: . . . limbs often *move in concert.* . . . To *"move in concert"* is to move simultaneously or in synchrony. When we dream of doing something, our arms and legs do *not* move in synchrony (*do not move in concert*) with the activity in the dream.

Page 190: Awake at 4:00 A.M., with a *depressed body,* we may *fret* over concerns: Does a *lovers' spat signal a split?* Our body temperature drops after we go to sleep and begins to rise again toward morning. So if we wake up in the middle of the night our temperature may be low (*depressed body*). We may start to worry (*fret*) over problems. For example, if we've had a minor disagreement or argument with a loved one (*lovers' spat*), we may think this means the relationship is going to end (*signals a split*).

Page 190: Pulling an all-nighter, we feel *groggiest* about 4:00 A.M., and then a *second wind* after our normal wake-up time arrives. If we decide to stay up all night (*pull an all-nighter*), say, to finish a term paper by the deadline, we feel most mentally confused and uncoordinated (*groggiest*) around the middle of the night, but as our usual time for getting up approaches, we begin to feel renewed energy (*a second wind*).

Page 190: . . . *jet lag* . . . When we travel by plane across several time zones we may experience mental and physical fatigue (*jet lag*). Because our biological clocks naturally tend toward a 25-hour day, we may find it easier to jet west, which gives us a longer day, than to travel east.

Page 191: Before long, the machine *went wild,* tracing *deep zigzags* on the graph paper. The discovery of REM (Rapid Eye Movement) occurred accidentally. To see if an EEG (electroencephalograph) was working properly Aserinsky placed the electrodes near his 8-year-old son's eyes. Periodically during the night the machine responded vigorously (*went wild*), producing a pattern of high-frequency waves (*deep zigzags*) on the printout. These patterns were produced by rapid, spasmodic (*jerky*) eye movements and accompanied by very frantic brain activity, and when awakened during one of these periods the boy said he was dreaming.

Page 193: Rather than continuing in deep *slumber,* you *ascend* from your initial *sleep dive.* During a typical night's sleep (*slumber*) you go through a number of distinct stages. If you are awake and relaxed, perhaps with your eyes closed, an EEG would show alpha waves. As you fall deeper and deeper into sleep (*sleep dive*), your brain waves continue to slow down. By Stage 4 your brain waves are long and slow (*delta waves*), but you don't stay here all night; instead, you go back up (*ascend*) through the stages into the most unique and interesting stage of all, REM (Rapid Eye Movement) sleep, where most dreams occur. Here, the brain waves resemble the fast, uneven Stage 1 waves (*sawtoothed*), but there is much more internal physiological arousal now, and, paradoxically, your muscles are almost paralyzed.

Page 194: As the night *wears on,* deep Stage 4 sleep gets progressively briefer and then disappears. As the night progresses (*wears on*), the time spent in Stage 4 deep sleep gets shorter (and eventually ceases altogether) and time spent in REM sleep gets longer.

Page 195: . . . *drowsy* . . . If you were deprived of sleep for a few nights, you would feel very tired and sleepy (*drowsy*).

Page 195: People today more than ever suffer from sleep patterns that *thwart* their having an energized feeling of well-being. Because of the pressures of work, school, social obligations, and so on, we often have sleep schedules that prevent (*thwart*) us from getting the amount of sleep we need. The consequence of this "sleep debt" (*accumulated insufficient sleep*) is a general lack of energy and discomfort (*malaise*) and a frequent feeling of sleepiness.

Page 195: Many fill this need [for sleep] by using their first class for an *early siesta* and after-lunch *study hall for a slumber party.* Today's young students often get much less sleep than they need and consequently many end up using the first class of the day for a short sleep or nap (*siesta*), and the quiet school period meant for study (*study hall*) may be occupied by whole groups of sleeping students (*slumber party*). Even so, 80 percent of students are still seriously sleep deprived (*they have a large sleep debt*), which results in diminished cognitive and intellectual functioning (*"a large sleep debt makes you stupid"*).

Page 197: These physiological discoveries are beginning to solve the ongoing *riddle* of sleep. Recent research has shown that sleep helps us repair and restore body tissue (*recuperate*) and plays a part in physical growth. These findings are starting to clear up the continuing puzzle (*riddle*) of sleep.

Page 198: Both [alcohol and sleeping pills] reduce REM sleep and can leave a person with *next-day blahs.* The most popular fast remedies (*quick fixes*) for insomnia are sleeping pills and alcohol. Unfortunately, they can make the problem worse (*aggravate it*) by suppressing REM sleep; the next day the person may have less energy and feel very tired (*next-day blahs*). When these "remedies" are discontinued, the insomnia may get worse.

Pages 199: As a traffic menace, *"snoozing is second only to boozing,"* says the American Sleep Disorders Association, and those with narcolepsy are especially at risk (Aldrich, 1989). Falling asleep (*snoozing*) while driving is almost as serious a problem as drinking (*boozing*) and driving. People with **narcolepsy** suffer from occasional periods of uncontrollable sleepiness often associated with emotional arousal, and are thus in danger, and dangerous, while driving.

Page 201: He [Freud] argued that by fulfilling wishes, a dream provides a *psychic safety valve* that discharges otherwise unacceptable feelings. The story line of the dream (**manifest content**) is a disguised version of the real, but hidden, meaning of the dream (**latent content**). According to Freud, by symbolically expressing our hidden desires and erotic wishes, dreams allow us to ventilate unconscious drives that might otherwise be harmful (*acts as a psychic safety valve*). (A *safety valve* allows a system to dissipate built-up pressure and thus may prevent an explosion.)

Page 202: However, his critics say *it is time to wake up* from Freud's dream theory, which actually is a scientific *nightmare.* Myers is having some fun with a play on words here. The expression "it is time to wake up from something" means one should start paying attention to reality and facts, rather than fantasy, and to say something is "a nightmare" means that it is unruly, difficult, or even frightening. Most contemporary psychologists believe that REM sleep and dreams are important aspects of our life but that Freud's theory of dream interpretation is erroneous, unscientific, and misguided (*a nightmare*); thus, we should not place much reliance on its explanations (*it is time to wake up from it*).

Page 202: The brain regions that *buzz* as rats learn to navigate a maze, or as people learn to perform a visual-spatial discrimination task, *buzz again* later during REM sleep. Studies demonstrate that sleeping helps memory and learning. The areas of the brain that are active (*that buzz*) when learning is taking place are also active once more (*they buzz again*) during REM sleep. This is important news for sleep-deprived students who tend to learn and remember less than their non-sleep-derived counterparts. Attempting to make up for the loss of sleep by sleeping longer and later on weekends (*a kind of sleep bulimia . . . binge sleeping*) will not compensate for the lower levels of learning and recall.

Hypnosis

Page 205 (margin): "Hypnosis is not a psychological *truth serum,* and to regard it as such has been a source of considerable *mischief.*" Research shows that hypnotists can subtly influence what people recall and they may inadvertently create false memories by making suggestions and asking leading questions. Thus, hypnosis is not like a so-called *truth serum* (a drug alleged to make people tell the truth) but rather has caused a great deal of annoying—and possibly harmful—effects (*considerable mischief*).

Page 208: So, might the two views—social influence and divided consciousness—*be bridged?* Although there are a number of different explanations about what hypnosis really is, Myers suggests that it may be possible to bring together some of these theories (*bridge the differences*). Thus, hypnosis may be both a part of normal aspects of social influence and our ability to have a divided (*or split*) consciousness.

Drugs and Consciousness

Page 209: A person who rarely drinks alcohol might get *tipsy* on one can of beer, but an experienced drinker may not get *tipsy* until the *second six-pack.* Prolonged use of a psychoactive drug produces an ability to take more and more of the substance (*tolerance*). Thus, an infrequent user of alcohol may get somewhat intoxicated (*tipsy*) from one beer, but for a regular drinker there might be little effect until six or more beers have been consumed (*until the second six-pack [of beer]*).

Page 210: . . . as when *tipsy* restaurant patrons leave extravagant tips. Alcohol can increase both harmful and helpful inclinations. Thus, it often happens that restaurant clientele give a larger gratuity (*extravagant tips*) when they are more intoxicated (*tipsy*). Whatever tendencies you have when sober will be more obvious when you are drunk.

Page 211: If, as commonly believed, liquor is the *quicker pick-her-upper,* the effect lies partly in that powerful sex organ, the mind. Alcohol (liquor) is thought by many to speed up the process of meeting members of the opposite sex and to lower sexual inhibitions. Thus, a male may believe that use of alcohol will facilitate his ability to initiate contact and get to know a female (a *quicker pick-her-upper*). Myers points out that not only alcohol is involved, but also our beliefs about its effects on sexual behavior (the effect lies partly in that *powerful sex organ, the mind*).

Page 212: But for short-term pleasure *one pays a long-term price,* which for the heroin user is the *gnawing craving* for another *fix . . . .* There is a cost (*one pays a long-term price*) for enjoying drug-induced pleasures, and for an addict this may be a persistent inner torment (*gnawing*) and an urgent, persistent desire (*craving*) for another dose of the drug (a *fix*).

Page 213 . . . crack . . . Crack is a very potent, synthetic form of cocaine which produces a feeling of euphoria (*a rush*) followed by deep depression, tiredness, and irritability (a "crash").

Page 215: . . . "acid trip" . . . Taking any psychoactive drug is called a *trip* or *tripping out.* When LSD (acid) is used, it is called an *acid trip;* regular users are sometimes called *acid-heads.*

Page 216: . . . marijuana may *spell* relief. Although there are many reasons for not taking marijuana, it does have some therapeutic applications, such as alleviating the sick feelings that result from taking the drugs used to treat cancer (chemotherapy) and the pain, nausea, and weight loss associated with AIDS. Thus, it may provide (*spell*) relief for some patients.

Page 216: Clearly, *getting high* is not conducive to learning. Marijuana use disrupts motor skills, perceptual abilities, memory formation, and short-term retention. Obviously, being under the influence of marijuana (*getting high*) does not help memory and learning.

chapter 7

Learning

Chapter Overview

"No topic is closer to the heart of psychology than learning, a relatively permanent change in an organism's behavior due to experience." Chapter 7 covers the basic principles of three forms of learning: classical, or respondent, conditioning, in which we learn associations between events; operant conditioning, in which we learn to engage in behaviors that are rewarded and to avoid behaviors that are punished; and observational learning, in which we learn by observing and imitating others.

The chapter also covers several important issues, including the generality of principles of learning, the role of cognitive processes in learning, and the ways in which learning is constrained by the biological predispositions of different species.

NOTE: Answer guidelines for all Chapter 7 questions begin on page 293.

Introducing Learning (pp. 225–227)

> David Myers at times uses idioms that are unfamiliar to some readers. If you do not know the meaning of any of the following words, phrases, or expressions in the context in which they appear in the text, refer to page 212 for an explanation: *. . . breeds hope; mugged; Japanese rancher reportedly herds cattle.*

Introduction Preview

First, skim the introduction. Then read the following objective and, as you read the text, search for the information that will enable you to meet that objective. Answer guidelines are provided on page 203.

1. Discuss the importance of experience in learning, and describe the role of association in learning.

Stepping Through the Introduction

After you have read the introduction, complete the sentences and answer the questions. As you proceed, evaluate your performance by consulting the answers on page 203. Do not continue with the next section until you understand each answer. If you need to, review or reread the section in the textbook before continuing.

1. A relatively permanent change in an organism's behavior due to experience is called

   _____ .

2. More than 200 years ago, philosophers such as John Locke and David Hume argued that an important factor in learning is our tendency to _____ events that occur in sequence. Even simple animals, such as the sea snail *Aplysia*, can learn simple _____ between stimuli. This type of learning is called _____

   _____ .

3. The type of learning in which the organism learns to associate two stimuli is _____ conditioning.

4. The tendency of organisms to associate a response and its consequence forms the basis of _____ conditioning.

5. Complex animals often learn behaviors merely by _____ others perform them.

Classical Conditioning (pp. 228–236)

> If you do not know the meaning of any of the following words, phrases, or expressions in the context in which they appear in the text, refer to pages 212–213 for an explanation: . . . *For many people, the name Ivan Pavlov . . . rings a bell; drooled; sets your mouth to watering; red-light district; breaking up . . . fire-breathing heartthrob; the thought that counts; we stand on his shoulders; crack cocaine users often feel a craving; legendary significance.*

Section Preview

Answer guidelines are provided on page 203.

1. Describe the nature of classical conditioning, and show how it demonstrates associative learning.

2. Explain the processes of acquisition, extinction, spontaneous recovery, generalization, and discrimination.

3. Discuss the importance of cognitive processes and biological constraints in classical conditioning.

4. Discuss the importance of Pavlov's work in classical conditioning, and explain how Pavlov paved the way for the behaviorist position.

Stepping Through the Section

Answers begin on page 203.

1. Classical conditioning was first explored by the Russian physiologist _____ . Early in the twentieth century, psychologist _____ urged psychologists to discard references to mental concepts in favor of studying observable behavior. This view, called _____ , influenced American psychology during the first half of that century.

2. In Pavlov's classic experiment, a tone, or _____ _____ , is sounded just before food, the _____ _____ , is placed in the animal's mouth.

3. An animal will salivate when food is placed in its mouth. This salivation is called the _____ _____ .

4. Eventually, the dogs in Pavlov's experiment would salivate on hearing the tone. This salivation is called the _____ _____ .

5. The initial learning of a conditioned response is called _____ . For many conditioning situations, the optimal interval between a

neutral stimulus and the UCS is

_____ _____ .

6. When the UCS is presented prior to a neutral stimulus, conditioning _____ (does/does not) occur.

Explain why learning theorists consider classically conditioned behaviors to be biologically adaptive.

7. Michael Domjan's sexual conditioning studies with quail demonstrate that classical conditioning is highly adaptive because it helps animals _____ and _____ . Associations that are not consciously noticed _____ (can/cannot) give rise to attitudes.

8. If a CS is repeatedly presented without the UCS, _____ soon occurs; that is, the CR diminishes.

9. Following a rest, however, the CR reappears in response to the CS; this phenomenon is called

_____ _____ .

10. Subjects often respond to a similar stimulus as they would to the original CS. This phenomenon is called _____ . Subjects can, however, also be trained not to respond to these similar stimuli. This learned ability is called

_____ .

11. Experiments by Rescorla and Wagner demonstrate that a CS must reliably _____ the UCS for an association to develop and, more generally, that _____ processes play a role in conditioning. It is as if the animal learns to _____ that the UCS will occur.

Describe two issues that have led to the recent reconsideration of behaviorism.

12. The importance of cognitive processes in human conditioning is demonstrated by the failure of classical conditioning as a treatment for

_____ .

13. Garcia discovered that rats would associate _____ with taste but not with other stimuli. Garcia found that taste-aversion conditioning _____ (would/would not) occur when the delay between the CS and the UCS was more than an hour.

14. Results such as these demonstrate that the principles of learning are constrained by the _____ predispositions of each animal species and that they help each species _____ to its environment.

Explain why the study of classical conditioning is important.

15. Research studies demonstrate that the body's immune system _____ (can/cannot) be classically conditioned.

Describe the Watson and Rayner experiment.

Operant Conditioning (pp. 236–248)

If you do not know the meaning of any of the following words, phrases, or expressions in the context in which they appear in the text, refer to pages 213–215 for an explanation: *to pull habits out of a rat; . . . between Bach's music and Stravinsky's; pastes gold stars; snooze button; goofing off; the kick that often comes within seconds; a sale with every pitch; paid on a piecework basis; a choppy stop-start pattern; loses a treat; drawbacks; hit with a couple of speeding tickets; backfire; piggy bank; stirred a hornet's nest.*

Section Preview

Answer guidelines begin on page 204.

1. Describe the process of operant conditioning, including the procedure of shaping.

2. Identify the different types of reinforcers, and describe the four major schedules of partial reinforcement.

3. Discuss the effects of punishment on behavior.

4. Discuss evidence of the importance of cognitive and biological processes in operant conditioning.

5. Describe some major applications of operant conditioning.

Stepping Through the Section

Answers are provided on page 205.

1. Classical conditioning associates _____ stimuli with stimuli that elicit responses that are _____ .

2. The reflexive responses of classical conditioning involve _____ behavior. In contrast, behavior that is more spontaneous and that is influenced by its consequences is called _____ behavior.

3. Using Thorndike's _____ _____ _____ as a starting point, Skinner developed a "behavioral technology." He designed an apparatus, called the _____ _____ , to investigate learning in animals.

4. The procedure in which a person teaches an animal to perform an intricate behavior by building up to it in small steps is called _____ . This method involves reinforcing successive _____ of the desired behavior.

5. An event that increases the frequency of a preceding response is a _____ .

6. A stimulus that strengthens a response by presenting a typically pleasurable stimulus after a response is a _____ _____ .

7. A stimulus that strengthens a response by reducing or removing an aversive (unpleasant) stimulus is a _____ _____ .

8. Reinforcers, such as food and shock, that are related to basic needs and therefore do not rely on learning are called _____ _____ . Reinforcers that must be conditioned and therefore derive their power through association are called _____ _____ .

9. Children who are able to delay gratification tend to become _____ (more/less) socially competent and high achieving as they mature.

10. Immediate reinforcement _____ (is/is not) more effective than its alternative, _____ reinforcement. This explains in part the difficulty that _____ users have in quitting their habits, as well as the tendency of some teens to engage in risky, _____ _____ .

11. The procedure involving reinforcement of each and every response is called

_____ _____ .

Under these conditions, learning is _____ (rapid/slow). When this type of reinforcement is discontinued, extinction is _____ (rapid/slow).

12. The procedure in which responses are reinforced only part of the time is called _____ reinforcement. Under these conditions, learning is generally _____ (faster/slower) than it is with continuous reinforcement. Behavior reinforced in this manner is _____ (very/not very) resistant to extinction.

13. When behavior is reinforced after a set number of responses, a _____-_____ schedule is in effect.

14. Three-year-old Yusef knows that if he cries when he wants a treat, his mother will sometimes give in. When, as in this case, reinforcement occurs after an unpredictable number of responses, a _____-_____ schedule is being used.

15. Reinforcement of the first response after a set interval of time defines the _____-_____ schedule. An example of this schedule is _____ .

16. When the first response after varying amounts of time is reinforced, a _____-_____ schedule is in effect.

Describe the typical patterns of response under fixed-interval, fixed-ratio, variable-interval, and variable-ratio schedules of reinforcement.

17. An aversive consequence that decreases the likelihood of the behavior that preceded it is called

_____ .

Describe some drawbacks to the use of physical punishment.

18. Skinner and other behaviorists resisted the growing belief that expectations, perceptions, and other _____ processes have a valid place in the science of psychology.

19. When a well-learned route in a maze is blocked, rats sometimes choose an alternative route, acting as if they were consulting a

_____ _____ .

20. Animals may learn from experience even when reinforcement is not available. When learning is not apparent until reinforcement has been provided, _____ _____ is said to have occurred.

21. Excessive rewards may undermine _____ _____ , which is the desire to perform a behavior for its own sake. The

motivation to seek external rewards and avoid punishment is called _____

_____ .

22. Operant conditioning _____
(is/is not) constrained by an animal's biological predispositions.

23. The use of teaching machines and programmed textbooks was an early application of the operant conditioning procedure of _____ to education. On-line _____ systems and software that is _____ are newer examples of this application of operant principles.

24. In boosting productivity in the workplace, positive reinforcement is _____
(more/less) effective when applied to specific behaviors than when given to reward general merit and when the desired performance is _____ . For such behaviors, immediate reinforcement is _____
(more/no more) effective than delayed reinforcement.

25. In using operant conditioning to change your own behavior, you would follow these four steps:
   a. _____
   b. _____
   c. _____
   d. _____

Learning by Observation (pp. 248–252)

> If you do not know the meaning of the following phrases in the context in which they appear in the text, refer to page 215 for an explanation: *those who observed the model's aggressive outburst were much more likely to lash out at the doll; Does the reel world affect the real world?*

Section Preview

Answer guidelines are provided on page 205.

1. Describe the process of observational learning.

2. Discuss the impact of viewing televised aggression on children.

Stepping Through the Section

Answers begin on page 205.

1. Learning by observing and imitating others is called _____ , or _____
_____ . This form of learning _____ (occurs/does not occur) in species other than our own.

2. Neuroscientists have found _____ neurons in the brain's _____ lobe that provide a neural basis for _____ learning. These neurons have been observed to fire when monkeys perform a simple task and when they _____ .
This type of neuron _____
(has/has not) been found in human brains.

3. By age _____ , infants will imitate acts modeled on television.

4. The psychologist best known for research on observational learning is _____ .
In one experiment, the child who viewed an adult punch an inflatable doll played _____ (more/less) aggressively than the child who had not observed the adult.

5. Children will also model positive, or _____ , behaviors.

6. Models are most effective when their words and actions are _____ and when they are perceived as _____ ,
_____ , or _____ .

7. Children in developed countries spend more time _____ _____ than they spend in school.

8. Compared to real-world crimes, television depicts a much higher percentage of crimes as being _____ in nature.

9. Correlational studies _____ (link/do not link) watching television violence with violent behavior.

10. The more hours children spend watching violent programs, the more at risk they are for _____ and _____ as teens and adults.

11. Correlation does not prove _____ . Most researchers believe that violence on television _____ (does/does not) lead to aggressive behavior.

12. The violence effect stems from several factors, including _____ of observed aggression and the tendency of prolonged exposure to violence to _____ viewers.

Progress Test 1

Multiple-Choice Questions

Circle your answers to the following questions and check them with the answers beginning on page 206. If your answer is incorrect, read the explanation for why it is incorrect and then consult the appropriate pages of the text (in parentheses following the correct answer).

1. Learning is best defined as:
   a. any behavior emitted by an organism without being elicited.
   b. a change in the behavior of an organism.
   c. a relatively permanent change in the behavior of an organism due to experience.
   d. behavior based on operant rather than respondent conditioning.

2. The type of learning associated with Skinner is:
   a. classical conditioning.
   b. operant conditioning.
   c. respondent conditioning.
   d. observational learning.

3. In Pavlov's original experiment with dogs, the meat served as a(n):
   a. CS.   c. UCS.
   b. CR.   d. UCR.

4. In Pavlov's original experiment with dogs, the tone was initially a(n) _____ stimulus; after it was paired with meat, it became a(n) _____ stimulus.
   a. conditioned; neutral
   b. neutral; conditioned
   c. conditioned; unconditioned
   d. unconditioned; conditioned

5. In order to obtain a reward a monkey learns to press a lever when a 1000-Hz tone is on but not when a 1200-Hz tone is on. What kind of training is this?
   a. extinction
   b. generalization
   c. classical conditioning
   d. spontaneous recovery
   e. discrimination

6. Which of the following statements concerning reinforcement is correct?
   a. Learning is most rapid with intermittent reinforcement, but continuous reinforcement produces the greatest resistance to extinction.
   b. Learning is most rapid with continuous reinforcement, but intermittent reinforcement produces the greatest resistance to extinction.
   c. Learning is fastest and resistance to extinction is greatest after continuous reinforcement.
   d. Learning is fastest and resistance to extinction is greatest following intermittent reinforcement.

7. Cognitive processes are:
   a. unimportant in classical and operant conditioning.
   b. important in both classical and operant conditioning.
   c. more important in classical than in operant conditioning.
   d. more important in operant than in classical conditioning.

8. The highest and most consistent rate of response is produced by a _____ schedule.
   a. fixed-ratio   c. fixed-interval
   b. variable-ratio   d. variable-interval

9. A response that leads to the removal of an unpleasant stimulus is one being:
   a. positively reinforced.
   b. negatively reinforced.
   c. punished.
   d. extinguished.

10. When a conditioned stimulus is presented without an accompanying unconditioned stimulus, _____ will soon take place.

    a. generalization
    d. aversion
    b. discrimination
    e. spontaneous recovery
    c. extinction

11. One difference between classical and operant conditioning is that:

    a. in classical conditioning the responses operate on the environment to produce rewarding or punishing stimuli.
    b. in operant conditioning the responses are triggered by preceding stimuli.
    c. in classical conditioning the responses are automatically elicited by stimuli.
    d. in operant conditioning the responses are reflexive.

12. In Garcia and Koelling's studies of taste-aversion learning, rats learned to associate:

    a. taste with electric shock.
    b. sights and sounds with sickness.
    c. taste with sickness.
    d. taste and sounds with electric shock.
    e. taste and sounds with electric shock, then sickness.

13. In Pavlov's original experiment with dogs, salivation to meat was the:

    a. CS.
    c. UCS.
    b. CR.
    d. UCR.

14. Learning by imitating others' behaviors is called _____ learning. The researcher best known for studying this type of learning is _____ .

    a. secondary; Skinner
    b. observational; Bandura
    c. secondary; Pavlov
    d. observational; Watson

15. Punishment is a controversial way of controlling behavior because:

    a. behavior is not forgotten and may return.
    b. punishing stimuli often create fear.
    c. punishment often increases aggressiveness.
    d. of all of the above reasons.

16. Classical conditioning experiments by Rescorla and Wagner demonstrate that an important factor in conditioning is:

    a. the subject's age.
    b. the strength of the stimuli.
    c. the predictability of an association.
    d. the similarity of stimuli.
    e. all of the above.

17. Which of the following is an example of reinforcement?

    a. presenting a positive stimulus after a response
    b. removing an unpleasant stimulus after a response
    c. being told that you have done a good job
    d. All of the above are examples.

18. Which of the following is a form of associative learning?

    a. classical conditioning
    b. operant conditioning
    c. observational learning
    d. all of the above

19. For the most rapid conditioning, a CS should be presented:

    a. about 1 second after the UCS.
    b. about one-half second before the UCS.
    c. about 15 seconds before the UCS.
    d. at the same time as the UCS.

20. Mirror neurons are found in the brain's _____ and are believed to be the neural basis for _____ .

    a. frontal lobe; observational learning
    b. frontal lobe; classical conditioning
    c. temporal lobe; operant conditioning
    d. temporal lobe; observational learning

Matching Items

Match each definition or description with the appropriate term.

Definitions or Descriptions

_____ 1. presentation of a desired stimulus
_____ 2. tendency for similar stimuli to evoke a CR
_____ 3. removal of an aversive stimulus
_____ 4. an innately reinforcing stimulus
_____ 5. an acquired reinforcer
_____ 6. responses are reinforced after an unpredictable amount of time
_____ 7. the motivation to perform a behavior for its own sake
_____ 8. reinforcing closer and closer approximations of a behavior
_____ 9. the reappearance of a weakened CR
_____ 10. presentation of an aversive stimulus
_____ 11. learning that becomes apparent only after reinforcement is provided
_____ 12. each and every response is reinforced
_____ 13. a desire to perform a behavior due to promised rewards

Terms

a. shaping
b. punishment
c. spontaneous recovery
d. latent learning
e. positive reinforcement
f. negative reinforcement
g. primary reinforcer
h. generalization
i. conditioned reinforcer
j. continuous reinforcement
k. variable-interval schedule
l. extrinsic motivation
m. intrinsic motivation

Progress Test 2

Progress Test 2 should be completed during a final chapter review. Answer the following questions after you thoroughly understand the correct answers for the section reviews and Progress Test 1.

Multiple-Choice Questions

1. During extinction, the _____ is omitted; as a result, the _____ seems to disappear.
   a. UCS; UCR
   b. CS; CR
   c. UCS; CR
   d. CS; UCR

2. In Watson and Rayner's experiment, the loud noise was the _____ and the white rat was the _____.
   a. CS; CR
   b. UCS; CS
   c. CS; UCS
   d. UCS; CR
   e. UCR; CR

3. In which of the following may classical conditioning play a role?
   a. emotional problems
   b. the body's immune response
   c. how animals adapt to the environment
   d. helping drug addicts
   e. all of the above

4. Shaping is a(n) _____ technique for _____ a behavior.
   a. operant; establishing
   b. operant; suppressing
   c. respondent; establishing
   d. respondent; suppressing

5. In Pavlov's studies of classical conditioning of a dog's salivary responses, spontaneous recovery occurred:
   a. during acquisition, when the CS was first paired with the UCS.
   b. during extinction, when the CS was first presented by itself.
   c. when the CS was reintroduced following extinction of the CR and a rest period.
   d. during discrimination training, when several conditioned stimuli were introduced.

6. For operant conditioning to be most effective, when should the reinforcers be presented in relation to the desired response?
   a. immediately before
   b. immediately after
   c. at the same time as
   d. at least a half hour before
   e. in any of the above sequences

7. In distinguishing between negative reinforcers and punishment, we note that:
   a. punishment, but not negative reinforcement, involves use of an aversive stimulus.
   b. in contrast to punishment, negative reinforcement decreases the likelihood of a response by the presentation of an aversive stimulus.
   c. in contrast to punishment, negative reinforcement increases the likelihood of a response by the presentation of an aversive stimulus.
   d. in contrast to punishment, negative reinforcement increases the likelihood of a response by the termination of an aversive stimulus.

8. The "piecework," or commission, method of payment is an example of which reinforcement schedule?
   a. fixed-interval   c. fixed-ratio
   b. variable-interval   d. variable-ratio

9. Putting on your coat when it is cold outside is a behavior that is maintained by:
   a. discrimination learning.
   b. punishment.
   c. negative reinforcement.
   d. classical conditioning.
   e. positive reinforcement.

10. On an intermittent reinforcement schedule, reinforcement is given:
    a. in very small amounts.
    b. randomly.
    c. for successive approximations of a desired behavior.
    d. only some of the time.

11. You teach your dog to fetch the paper by giving him a cookie each time he does so. This is an example of:
    a. operant conditioning.
    b. classical conditioning.
    c. conditioned reinforcement.
    d. partial reinforcement.

12. In promoting observational learning, the most effective models are those that we perceive as:
    a. similar to ourselves.
    b. respected and admired.
    c. successful.
    d. any of the above.

13. A cognitive map is a(n):
    a. mental representation of one's environment.
    b. sequence of thought processes leading from one idea to another.
    c. set of instructions detailing the most effective means of teaching a particular concept.
    d. biological predisposition to learn a particular skill.
    e. educational tool based on operant conditioning techniques.

14. After exploring a complicated maze for several days, a rat subsequently ran the maze with very few errors when food was placed in the goal box for the first time. This performance illustrates:
    a. classical conditioning.
    b. discrimination learning.
    c. observational learning.
    d. latent learning.

15. Leon's psychology instructor has scheduled an exam every third week of the term. Leon will probably study the most just before an exam and the least just after an exam. This is because the schedule of exams is reinforcing studying according to which schedule?
    a. fixed-ratio   c. fixed-interval
    b. variable-ratio   d. variable-interval

16. Operant conditioning is to _____ as classical conditioning is to _____ .
    a. Pavlov; Watson   c. Pavlov; Skinner
    b. Skinner; Bandura   d. Skinner; Pavlov

17. On-line testing systems and interactive software are applications of the operant conditioning principles of:
    a. shaping and immediate reinforcement.
    b. immediate reinforcement and punishment.
    c. shaping and primary reinforcement.
    d. continuous reinforcement and punishment.

18. Gambling is reinforced according to which schedule?
    a. fixed-interval   c. variable-interval
    b. fixed-ratio   d. variable-ratio

19. Which of the following is the best example of a conditioned reinforcer?
    a. putting on a coat on a cold day
    b. relief from pain after the dentist stops drilling your teeth
    c. receiving a cool drink after washing your mother's car on a hot day
    d. receiving an approving nod from the boss for a job well done
    e. having a big meal after going without food all day

20. Experiments on taste-aversion learning demonstrate that:
    a. for the conditioning of certain stimuli, the UCS need not immediately follow the CS.
    b. any perceivable stimulus can become a CS.
    c. all animals are biologically primed to associate illness with the taste of a tainted food.
    d. all of the above are true.

21. Regarding the impact of television violence on children, most researchers believe that:
    a. aggressive children simply prefer violent programs.
    b. television simply reflects, rather than contributes to, violent social trends.
    c. violence on television leads to aggressive behavior.
    d. there is only a weak correlation between exposure to violence and aggressive behavior.

True–False Items

Indicate whether each statement is true or false by placing *T* (*True*) or *F* (*False*) in the blank next to the item.

_____ 1. Operant conditioning involves behavior that is primarily reflexive.
_____ 2. The optimal interval between CS and UCS is about 15 seconds.
_____ 3. Negative reinforcement decreases the likelihood that a response will recur.
_____ 4. The learning of a new behavior proceeds most rapidly with continuous reinforcement.
_____ 5. As a rule, variable schedules of reinforcement produce more consistent rates of responding than fixed schedules.
_____ 6. Cognitive processes are of relatively little importance in learning.
_____ 7. Although punishment may be effective in suppressing behavior, it can have several undesirable side effects.
_____ 8. All animals, including rats and birds, are biologically predisposed to associate taste cues with sickness.
_____ 9. Whether the CS or UCS is presented first seems not to matter in terms of the ease of classical conditioning.
_____ 10. Spontaneous recovery refers to the tendency of extinguished behaviors to reappear suddenly.
_____ 11. Researchers have discovered brain neurons that fire when a person performs a task *or* when another person is observed performing the same task.

Review and Reflect

Answer these questions the day before an exam as a final check on your understanding of the chapter's terms and concepts.

Multiple-Choice Questions

1. You always rattle the box of dog biscuits before giving your dog a treat. As you do so, your dog salivates. Rattling the box is a(n) _____ ; your dog's salivation is a(n) _____ .
    a. CS; CR   c. UCS; CR
    b. CS; UCR   d. UCS; UCR

2. You are expecting an important letter in the mail. As the regular delivery time approaches you glance more and more frequently out the window, searching for the letter carrier. Your behavior in this situation typifies that associated with which schedule of reinforcement?
    a. fixed-ratio   c. fixed-interval
    b. variable-ratio   d. variable-interval

3. Jack finally takes out the garbage in order to get his father to stop pestering him. Jack's behavior is being influenced by:
    a. positive reinforcement.
    b. negative reinforcement.
    c. a primary reinforcer.
    d. punishment.

4. Mrs. Ramirez often tells her children that it is important to buckle their seat belts while riding in the car, but she rarely does so herself. Her children will probably learn to:
   a. use their seat belts and tell others it is important to do so.
   b. use their seat belts but not tell others it is important to do so.
   c. tell others it is important to use seat belts but rarely use them themselves.
   d. neither tell others that seat belts are important nor use them.

5. A pigeon can easily be taught to flap its wings in order to avoid shock but not for food reinforcement. According to the text, this is most likely so because:
   a. pigeons are biologically predisposed to flap their wings in order to escape aversive events and to use their beaks to obtain food.
   b. shock is a more motivating stimulus for birds than food is.
   c. hungry animals have difficulty delaying their eating long enough to learn *any* new skill.
   d. of all of the above reasons.

6. From a casino owner's viewpoint, which of the following jackpot-payout schedules would be the most desirable for reinforcing customer use of a slot machine?
   a. variable-ratio   c. variable-interval
   b. fixed-ratio   d. fixed-interval

7. After discovering that her usual route home was closed due to road repairs, Sharetta used her knowledge of the city and sense of direction to find an alternate route. This is an example of:
   a. latent learning.
   b. observational learning.
   c. shaping.
   d. using a cognitive map.
   e. discrimination.

For questions 8–11, use the following information.
As a child, you were playing in the yard one day when a neighbor's cat wandered over. Your mother (who has a terrible fear of animals) screamed and snatched you into her arms. Her behavior caused you to cry. You now have a fear of cats.

8. Identify the CS.
   a. your mother's behavior   c. the cat
   b. your crying   d. your fear today

9. Identify the UCS.
   a. your mother's behavior   c. the cat
   b. your crying   d. your fear today

10. Identify the CR.
    a. your mother's behavior   c. the cat
    b. your crying   d. your fear today

11. Identify the UCR.
    a. your mother's behavior   c. the cat
    b. your crying   d. your fear today

12. The manager of a manufacturing plant wishes to use positive reinforcement to increase the productivity of workers. Which of the following procedures would probably be the most effective?
    a. Deserving employees are given a general merit bonus at the end of each fiscal year.
    b. A productivity goal that seems attainable, yet is unrealistic, is set for each employee.
    c. Employees are given immediate bonuses for specific behaviors related to productivity.
    d. Employees who fail to meet standards of productivity receive pay cuts.

13. Bill once had a blue car that was in the shop more than it was out. Since then he will not even consider owning blue- or green-colored cars. Bill's aversion to green cars is an example of:
    a. discrimination.
    b. generalization.
    c. latent learning.
    d. extinction.

14. After watching coverage of the Olympics on television recently, Lynn and Susan have been staging their own "summer games." Which of the following best accounts for their behavior?
    a. classical conditioning   d. shaping
    b. observational learning   e. discrimination
    c. latent learning

15. Two groups of rats receive classical conditioning trials in which a tone and electric shock are presented. For Group 1 the electric shock always follows the tone. For Group 2 the tone and shock occur randomly. Which of the following is likely to result?
    a. The tone will become a CS for Group 1 but not for Group 2.
    b. The tone will become a CS for Group 2 but not for Group 1.
    c. The tone will become a CS for both groups.
    d. The tone will not become a CS for either group.

16. Last evening May-ling ate her first cheeseburger and French fries at an American fast-food restaurant. A few hours later she became ill. It can be expected that:
    a. May-ling will develop an aversion to the sight of a cheeseburger and French fries.
    b. May-ling will develop an aversion to the taste of a cheeseburger and French fries.
    c. May-ling will not associate her illness with the food she ate.
    d. May-ling will associate her sickness with something she experienced immediately before she became ill.

17. Reggie's mother tells him that he can watch TV after he cleans his room. Evidently, Reggie's mother is attempting to use _____ to increase room cleaning.
    a. operant conditioning
    b. secondary reinforcement
    c. positive reinforcement
    d. all of the above

18. Which of the following is an example of shaping?
    a. A dog learns to salivate at the sight of a box of dog biscuits.
    b. A new driver learns to stop at an intersection when the light changes to red.
    c. A parrot is rewarded first for making any sound, then for making a sound similar to "Laura," and then for "speaking" its owner's name.
    d. A psychology student reinforces a laboratory rat only occasionally, to make its behavior more resistant to extinction.

19. Lars, a shoe salesman, is paid every two weeks, whereas Tom receives a commission for each pair of shoes he sells. Evidently, Lars is paid on a _____ schedule of reinforcement, and Tom on a _____ schedule of reinforcement.
    a. fixed-ratio; fixed-interval
    b. continuous; intermittent
    c. fixed-interval; fixed-ratio
    d. variable-interval; variable-ratio
    e. variable-ratio; variable-interval

20. Nancy decided to take introductory psychology because she has always been interested in human behavior. Jack enrolled in the same course because he thought it would be easy. Nancy's behavior was motivated by _____ , Jack's by _____ .
    a. extrinsic motivation; intrinsic motivation
    b. intrinsic motivation; extrinsic motivation
    c. drives; incentives
    d. incentives; drives

Essay Question

Describe the best way for a pet owner to condition her dog to roll over. (Use the space below to list the points you want to make, and organize them. Then write the essay on a separate piece of paper.)

Key Terms

Using your own words, on a piece of paper write a brief definition or explanation of each of the following terms.

1. learning
2. associative learning
3. classical conditioning
4. behaviorism
5. unconditioned response (UCR)
6. unconditioned stimulus (UCS)
7. conditioned response (CR)
8. conditioned stimulus (CS)
9. acquisition
10. extinction
11. spontaneous recovery
12. generalization
13. discrimination
14. operant conditioning
15. respondent behavior
16. operant behavior
17. law of effect
18. operant chamber (Skinner box)
19. shaping
20. reinforcer
21. primary reinforcers
22. conditioned reinforcers
23. continuous reinforcement
24. partial (intermittent) reinforcement
25. fixed-ratio schedule
26. variable-ratio schedule
27. fixed-interval schedule
28. variable-interval schedule
29. punishment
30. cognitive map
31. latent learning
32. intrinsic motivation
33. extrinsic motivation
34. observational learning
35. modeling
36. mirror neurons
37. prosocial behavior

Summing Up

Complete the following flow charts.

CLASSICAL CONDITIONING

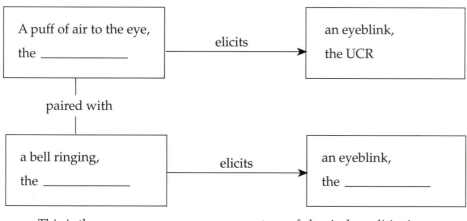

A puff of air to the eye, the _____   —elicits→   an eyeblink, the UCR

paired with

a bell ringing, the _____   —elicits→   an eyeblink, the _____

This is the _____ stage of classical conditioning.

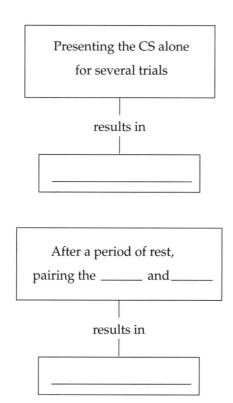

Presenting the CS alone for several trials

results in

_____

After a period of rest, pairing the _____ and _____

results in

_____

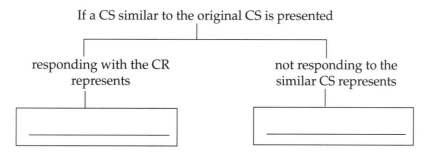

If a CS similar to the original CS is presented

responding with the CR represents

not responding to the similar CS represents

_____   _____

OPERANT CONDITIONING

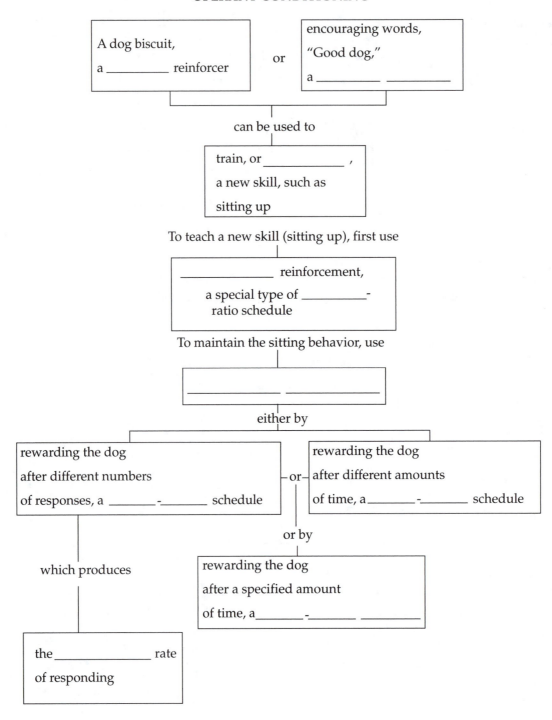

Answers

Introduction

Introduction Preview

1. Experience is the key to learning, which is defined as a relatively permanent change in an organism's behavior due to experience. This ability to learn from experience is the foundation for adaptability—the capacity to learn new behaviors that enable humans and animals to cope with ever-changing circumstances.

   As such philosophers as Aristotle, Locke, and Hume noted, our minds naturally link events that we have experienced together. This is the basis for associative learning, in which two stimuli (as in classical conditioning) or a response and a rewarding or punishing stimulus (as in operant conditioning) become linked because of their co-occurrence.

Stepping Through the Introduction

1. learning
2. associate; associations; associative learning
3. classical
4. operant
5. observing

Classical Conditioning

Section Preview

1. In associative learning, organisms learn that certain events occur together. Through classical conditioning, organisms learn to anticipate and prepare for significant events, such as the delivery of food or a painful stimulus. In other words, they learn to associate two events. Classical conditioning occurs when a neutral stimulus becomes associated with an unconditioned stimulus (UCS). By itself, the UCS will automatically trigger a reflexive, unconditioned response (UCR). If the association between the CS and UCS is predictable, conditioning will occur and the CS alone will eventually elicit a conditioned response (CR) similar to the UCR.

2. Acquisition refers to the initial stage of learning, during which the CR is established and gradually strengthened. Extinction refers to the diminishing of a CR when the CS is repeatedly presented without a UCS. Spontaneous recovery refers to the reappearance, after a period of rest, of a weakened CR. Generalization is the tendency for stimuli similar to the CS to evoke a CR.

Discrimination is the ability to distinguish between an actual CS and similar stimuli that have not been associated with the UCS.

3. Pavlov, Watson, and the early behaviorists underestimated the importance of cognitive processes and biological constraints on learning.

   Research by Rescorla and Wagner demonstrated that classical conditioning occurs best when the association between a CS and UCS is predictable. This indicates that subjects develop a cognitive expectancy, or an awareness of how likely it is that the UCS will follow the CS.

   Garcia and Koelling's studies of conditioned taste aversion demonstrated that animals are biologically primed to learn to associate certain CSs with certain UCSs. Rats, for example, develop aversions to the taste, but not the appearance, of tainted foods. In contrast, birds are biologically primed to develop aversions to the sight of tainted food. This violates the behaviorist tenet that any perceivable stimulus can become a CS.

4. Pavlov's work showed that virtually all organisms can learn to adapt to their environment. It also showed how a significant internal process, such as learning, could be studied objectively. Finally, Pavlov's findings also provided a basis for the behaviorist idea that human behavior consists, in part, of stimulus-response connections.

   The original behaviorist philosophy, as stated by John Watson, was that psychology should be an objective science that studied only observable behaviors and avoided references to all mental processes. Watson argued that by studying how organisms respond to stimuli in their environments, psychologists would eventually become able to understand, predict, and control behavior.

Stepping Through the Section

1. Ivan Pavlov; John Watson; behaviorism
2. conditioned stimulus; unconditioned stimulus
3. unconditioned response
4. conditioned response
5. acquisition; one-half second
6. does not

Learning theorists consider classical conditioning to be adaptive because conditioned responses help organisms to prepare for good or bad events (unconditioned stimuli) that are about to occur.

7. survive; reproduce; can
8. extinction
9. spontaneous recovery

10. generalization; discrimination

11. predict; cognitive; expect

The early behaviorists believed that all learned behavior could be reduced to stimulus-response mechanisms. This discounting of mental (cognitive) processes has been strongly challenged by experiments suggesting that even in animals cognition is important for learning. Second, the behaviorists' belief that learning principles would generalize from one response to another and from one species to another has been questioned by research indicating that conditioning principles are constrained by each organism's biological predispositions.

12. alcoholism

13. sickness; would

14. biological; adapt

Classical conditioning led to the discovery of general principles of learning that are the same for all species tested, including humans. Classical conditioning also provided an example to the young field of psychology of how complex, internal processes could be studied objectively. In addition, classical conditioning has proven to have many helpful applications to human health and well-being.

15. can

In Watson and Rayner's experiment, classical conditioning was used to condition fear of a rat in Albert, an 11-month-old infant. When Albert touched the white rat (neutral stimulus), a loud noise (unconditioned stimulus) was sounded. After several pairings of the rat with the noise, Albert began crying at the mere sight of the rat. The rat had become a conditioned stimulus, eliciting a conditioned response of fear.

Operant Conditioning

Section Preview

1. In contrast to classical conditioning, which works on automatic responses to stimuli, *operant* conditioning works on behaviors that *operate* on the environment to produce consequences that influence the future occurrence of those behaviors. Behaviors followed by favorable events (reinforcers) tend to be repeated. Behaviors followed by unpleasant stimuli (punishers) tend not to be repeated.

   Shaping is a systematic technique for establishing a new response in which successive approximations of a desired behavior are reinforced.

2. A positive reinforcer is a stimulus that strengthens a response that leads to its presentation. A negative reinforcer is an aversive stimulus that strengthens a response that leads to its removal. Primary reinforcers are innately reinforcing stimuli that satisfy biological needs. Conditioned reinforcers acquire their effectiveness by being associated with primary reinforcers.

   Fixed-ratio schedules deliver reinforcement after a set number of responses. Variable-ratio schedules deliver reinforcement after an unpredictable number of responses. Fixed-interval schedules deliver reinforcement for the first response that follows a specified amount of time. Variable-interval schedules deliver reinforcement for a response that follows an unpredictable time interval.

3. A punisher is any consequence that decreases the frequency of a behavior that it follows. Although punishment may be effective in the short run, it has its drawbacks. Because punished behavior is merely suppressed rather than forgotten, it may reappear in safe settings. Punishment may also promote aggressiveness as a way of coping with problems; fear of the person who administers it; fear of the situation in which it occurs; or, when it is unpredictable, a sense that events are beyond the person's control. Because punishment does not teach positive behaviors, it is usually more effective when used in combination with positive reinforcement.

4. Evidence of cognitive processes comes from studies of latent learning, which is learning that occurs without reinforcement. Rats allowed to explore a maze without reinforcement nevertheless learn a cognitive map of its layout. When they later are rewarded, they immediately perform as well as rats that have been reinforced with food all along.

   The importance of cognitive processes is further demonstrated in research on motivation. Intrinsic motivation is the desire to perform a behavior for its own sake. Extrinsic motivation is seeking external rewards and avoiding punishments. Intrinsic motivation promotes high achievement, as does the use of extrinsic rewards that inform people of their successes. Extrinsic rewards that are delivered to control people's behaviors, however, undermine intrinsic motivation.

   Evidence for biological processes in operant conditioning comes from studies demonstrating that animals have biologically predisposed response patterns that influence the effectiveness of operant procedures with certain behaviors.

5. Operant principles of shaping and immediate reinforcement have been applied in school settings through the use of on-line testing systems, interactive software, and Web-based learning. Operant principles have also helped business managers increase productivity among their employees. Operant principles also have helped people take charge of their own behavior by creating self-management programs to stop smoking, lose weight, study, or exercise.

Stepping Through the Section

1. neutral; automatic
2. respondent; operant
3. law of effect; operant chamber (Skinner box)
4. shaping; approximations
5. reinforcer
6. positive reinforcer
7. negative reinforcer
8. primary reinforcers; conditioned reinforcers
9. more
10. is; delayed; drug; unprotected sex
11. continuous reinforcement; rapid; rapid
12. partial (intermittent); slower; very
13. fixed-ratio
14. variable-ratio
15. fixed-interval; checking the mail as delivery time approaches
16. variable-interval

Following reinforcement on a fixed-interval schedule, there is a pause in responding and then an increasing rate of response as time for the next reinforcement draws near. On a fixed-ratio schedule there also is a post-reinforcement pause, followed, however, by a return to a consistent, high rate of response. Both kinds of variable schedules produce steadier rates of response, without the pauses associated with fixed schedules. In general, schedules linked to responses produce *higher* response rates and variable schedules produce more consistent responding than the related fixed schedules.

17. punishment

Because punished behavior is merely suppressed, it may reappear. Punishment can lead to fear and a sense of helplessness, as well as to the association of the aversive event with the person who administers it. Punishment also often increases aggressiveness. Finally, punishment alone does not guide the organism toward more desirable behavior.

18. cognitive
19. cognitive map
20. latent learning
21. intrinsic motivation; extrinsic motivation
22. is
23. shaping; testing; interactive
24. more; achievable; more
25. a. State your goal.
    b. Monitor the behavior (when and where it occurs).
    c. Reinforce the desired behavior.
    d. Reduce the incentives to perform the undesirable behavior.

Learning by Observation

Section Preview

1. Observational learning, in which people observe and imitate, or model, others' behaviors, explains how many social behaviors are acquired. Research studies have shown that children will imitate both antisocial and prosocial models. Models are most effective when their actions and words are consistent. We are most likely to imitate people we respect, those we perceive as similar to ourselves, and those we perceive as successful. Researchers have discovered mirror neurons in the brain's frontal lobe that generate nerve impulses when we perform certain tasks *and* when we observe other people performing those same tasks.

2. During the first 18 years, most children in developed countries spend more time watching television than they spend in school. Television depicts an unrealistic, and especially violent, society and typically does not show the harm done to victims. Correlational studies do link violence-viewing with violent behavior. The more hours children spend watching violent programs, the more at risk they are for aggression and crime later. This may be because children tend to imitate the violence they see and because prolonged exposure to violence desensitizes viewers.

Stepping Through the Section

1. modeling; observational learning; occurs
2. mirror; frontal; observational; observe other monkeys performing the same task; has
3. 14 months
4. Bandura; more

5. prosocial

6. consistent; similar; successful; admirable

7. watching television

8. violent

9. link

10. aggression; crime

11. causation; does

12. imitation; desensitize

Progress Test 1

Multiple-Choice Questions

1. **c.** is the answer. (p. 225)

   a. This answer is incorrect because it simply describes any behavior that is automatic rather than being triggered, or elicited, by a specific stimulus.

   b. This answer is too general, since behaviors can change for reasons other than learning.

   d. Respondently conditioned behavior also satisfies the criteria of our definition of learning.

2. **b.** is the answer. (p. 237)

   a. & c. Classical conditioning is associated with Pavlov; respondent conditioning is another name for classical conditioning.

   d. Observational learning is most closely associated with Bandura.

3. **c.** is the answer. Meat automatically triggers the response of salivation and is therefore an unconditioned stimulus. (p. 229)

   a. A conditioned stimulus acquires its response-eliciting powers through learning. A dog does not learn to salivate to meat.

   b. & d. Responses are behaviors elicited in the organism, in this case the dog's salivation. The meat is a stimulus.

4. **b.** is the answer. Prior to its pairing with meat (the UCS), the tone did not elicit salivation and was therefore a neutral stimulus. Afterward, the tone elicited salivation (the CR) and was therefore a conditioned stimulus (CS). (p. 229)

   c. & d. Unconditioned stimuli, such as meat, innately elicit responding. Pavlov's dogs had to learn to associate the tone with the food.

5. **e.** is the answer. In learning to distinguish between the conditioned stimulus and another, similar stimulus, the monkey has received training in discrimination. (p. 232)

   a. In extinction training, a stimulus and/or response is allowed to go unreinforced.

   b. Generalization training involves responding to stimuli similar to the conditioned stimulus; here

the monkey is being trained not to respond to a similar stimulus.

   c. This cannot be classical conditioning since the monkey is acting in order to obtain a reward. Thus, this is an example of operant conditioning.

   d. Spontaneous recovery refers to the reappearance, after a period of rest, of a weakened CR.

6. **b.** is the answer. A continuous association will naturally be easier to learn than one that occurs on only some occasions, so learning is most rapid with continuous reinforcement. Yet, once the continuous association is no longer there, as in extinction training, extinction will occur more rapidly than it would have had the organism not always experienced reinforcement. (p. 241)

7. **b.** is the answer. (pp. 233, 243)

   c. & d. The text does not present evidence regarding the relative importance of cognitive processes in classical and operant conditioning.

8. **b.** is the answer. (p. 242)

   a. With fixed-ratio schedules, there is a pause following each reinforcement.

   c. & d. Because reinforcement is not contingent on the rate of response, interval schedules, especially fixed-interval schedules, produce lower response rates than ratio schedules.

9. **b.** is the answer. (p. 239)

   a. Positive reinforcement involves presenting a favorable stimulus following a response.

   c. Punishment involves presenting an unpleasant stimulus following a response.

   d. In extinction, a previously reinforced response is no longer followed by reinforcement. In this situation, a response causes a stimulus to be terminated or removed.

10. **c.** is the answer. In this situation, the CR will decline, a phenomenon known as extinction. (p. 231)

    a. Generalization occurs when the subject makes a CR to stimuli similar to the original CS.

    b. Discrimination is when the subject does not make a CR to stimuli other than the original CS.

    d. An aversion is a CR to a CS that has been associated with an unpleasant UCS, such as shock or a nausea-producing drug.

    e. Spontaneous recovery is the reappearance, after a rest period, of a CR.

11. **c.** is the answer. (p. 237)

    a. In *operant* conditioning the responses operate on the environment.

    b. In *classical* conditioning responses are triggered, or elicited, by preceding stimuli.

    d. In *classical* conditioning responses are reflexive.

12. c. is the answer. (pp. 233–234)
a., d., & e. These studies also indicated that rats are biologically predisposed to associate visual and auditory stimuli, but not taste, with shock.
b. Rats are biologically predisposed to associate taste with sickness.

13. d. is the answer. A dog does not have to learn to salivate to food; therefore, this response is unconditioned. (p. 229)
a. & c. Salivation is a response, not a stimulus.

14. b. is the answer. (pp. 248, 249)
a. Skinner is best known for studies of *operant* learning. Moreover, there is no such thing as secondary learning.
c. Pavlov is best known for classical conditioning.
d. Watson is best known as an early proponent of behaviorism.

15. d. is the answer. (pp. 242–243)

16. c. is the answer. (p. 233)
a., b., & d. Rescorla and Wagner's research did not address the importance of these factors in classical conditioning.

17. d. is the answer. a. is an example of positive reinforcement, b. is an example of negative reinforcement, and c. is an example of conditioned reinforcement. (pp. 239–240)

18. d. is the answer. (p. 227)

19. b. is the answer. (p. 230)
a. Backward conditioning, in which the UCS precedes the CS, is ineffective.
c. This interval is longer than is optimum for the most rapid acquisition of a CS-UCS association.
d. Simultaneous presentation of CS and UCS is ineffective because it does not permit the subject to anticipate the UCS.

20. a. is the answer. (p. 248)

Matching Items

1. e (p. 239)	**6.** k (p. 244)	**11.** d (p. 244)
2. h (p. 232)	**7.** m (p. 244)	**12.** j (p. 241)
3. f (p. 239)	**8.** a (p. 238)	**13.** l (p. 244)
4. g (p. 240)	**9.** c (p. 231)	
5. i (p. 240)	**10.** b (p. 242)	

Progress Test 2

Multiple-Choice Questions

1. c. is the answer. (p. 231)

2. b. is the answer. The loud noise automatically elicited Albert's fear and therefore functioned as a UCS. After being associated with the UCS, the white rat acquired the power to elicit fear and thus became a CS. (p. 235)

3. e. is the answer. (p. 235)

4. a. is the answer. Shaping works on operant behaviors by reinforcing successive approximations to a desired goal. (p. 238)

5. c. is the answer. (p. 231)
a., b., & d. Spontaneous recovery occurs after a CR has been extinguished, and in the absence of the UCS. The situations described here all involve the continued presentation of the UCS and, therefore, the further strengthening of the CR.

6. b. is the answer. (pp. 240–241)
a., c., & d. Reinforcement that is delayed, presented before a response, or presented at the same time as a response does not always increase the response's frequency of occurrence.

7. d. is the answer. (pp. 239, 242)
a. Both involve an aversive stimulus.
b. All reinforcers, including negative reinforcers, increase the likelihood of a response.
c. In negative reinforcement, an aversive stimulus is withdrawn following a desirable response.

8. c. is the answer. Payment is given after a fixed number of pieces have been completed. (p. 242)
a. & b. Interval schedules reinforce according to the passage of time, not the amount of work accomplished.
d. Fortunately for those working on commission, the work ratio is fixed and therefore predictable.

9. c. is the answer. By learning to put on your coat before going outside, you have learned to reduce the aversive stimulus of the cold. (p. 239)
a. Discrimination learning involves learning to make a response in the presence of the appropriate stimulus and not other stimuli.
b. Punishment is the suppression of an undesirable response by the presentation of an aversive stimulus.
d. Putting on a coat is a response that is willfully emitted by the person. Therefore, this is an example of operant, not classical, conditioning.
e. Positive reinforcement involves the *presentation* of a stimulus.

10. d. is the answer. (p. 241)
a. Intermittent reinforcement refers to the ratio of responses to reinforcers, not the overall quantity of reinforcement delivered.
b. Unlike intermittent reinforcement, in which the delivery of reinforcement is contingent on responding, random reinforcement is delivered independently of the subject's behavior.

c. This defines the technique of shaping, not intermittent reinforcement.

11. **a.** is the answer. You are teaching your dog by rewarding him when he produces the desired behavior. (p. 237)
    b. This is not classical conditioning because the cookie is a primary reinforcer presented after the operant behavior of the dog fetching the paper.
    c. Food is a primary reinforcer; it satisfies an innate need.
    d. Rewarding your dog each time he fetches the paper is continuous reinforcement.

12. **d.** is the answer. (p. 249)

13. **a.** is the answer. (p. 244)

14. **d.** is the answer. The rat had learned the maze but did not display this learning until reinforcement became available. (p. 244)
    a. Negotiating a maze is clearly operant behavior.
    b. This example does not involve learning to distinguish between stimuli.
    c. This is not observational learning because the rat has no one to observe!

15. **c.** is the answer. Because reinforcement (earning a good grade on the exam) is available according to the passage of time, studying is reinforced on an interval schedule. Because the interval between exams is constant, this is an example of a fixed-interval schedule. (p. 242)

16. **d.** is the answer. (pp. 228, 237)
    a. Pavlov and Watson are both associated with classical conditioning.
    b. Skinner is associated with operant conditioning, and Bandura is associated with observational learning.

17. **a.** is the answer. On-line testing systems apply operant principles such as reinforcement, immediate feedback, and shaping to the teaching of new skills. (pp. 239, 246)
    b. & d. On-line testing systems provide immediate, and continuous, reinforcement for correct responses, but do not use aversive control procedures such as punishment.
    c. On-line testing systems are based on feedback for correct responses; this feedback constitutes conditioned, rather than primary, reinforcement.

18. **d.** is the answer. In gambling, the number of responses between wins is unpredictable. (p. 242)

19. **d.** is the answer. An approving nod from the boss is a conditioned reinforcer in that it doesn't satisfy an innate need but has become linked with desirable consequences. Cessation of cold, cessa-

tion of pain, and a drink are all primary reinforcers, which meet innate needs. (p. 240)

20. **a.** is the answer. Taste-aversion experiments demonstrate conditioning even with CS-UCS intervals as long as several hours. (pp. 233–234)
    b. Despite being perceivable, a visual or auditory stimulus cannot become a CS for illness in some animals, such as rats.
    c. Some animals, such as birds, are biologically primed to associate the *appearance* of food with illness.

21. **c.** is the answer. (p. 251)

True–False Items

1. F (p. 237)	5. T (p. 241)	9. F (p. 230)
2. F (p. 230)	6. F (pp. 233, 243)	10. T (p. 231)
3. F (p. 239)	7. T (pp. 242–243)	11. T (p. 248)
4. T (p. 241)	8. F (pp. 233–234)	

Review and Reflect

Multiple-Choice Questions

1. **a.** is the answer. Your dog had to learn to associate the rattling sound with the food. Rattling is therefore a conditioned, or learned, stimulus, and salivation in response to this rattling is a learned, or conditioned, response. (p. 229)

2. **c.** is the answer. Reinforcement (the letter) comes after a fixed interval, and as the likely end of the interval approaches, your behavior (glancing out the window) becomes more frequent. (p. 242)
    a. & b. These answers are incorrect because with ratio schedules, reinforcement is contingent upon the number of responses rather than on the passage of time.
    d. Assuming that the mail is delivered at about the same time each day, the interval is fixed rather than variable. Your behavior reflects this, since you glance out the window more often as the delivery time approaches.

3. **b.** is the answer. By taking out the garbage, Jack terminates an aversive stimulus—his father's nagging. (p. 237)
    a. Positive reinforcement would involve a desirable stimulus that increases the likelihood of the response that preceded it.
    c. This answer would have been correct if Jack's father had rewarded Jack for taking out the garbage by providing his favorite food.
    d. Punishment suppresses behavior; Jack is emitting a behavior in order to obtain reinforcement.

4. **c.** is the answer. Studies indicate that when a model says one thing but does another, partici-

pants do the same and learn not to practice what they preach. (p. 250)

5. **a.** is the answer. As in this example, conditioning must be consistent with the particular organism's biological predispositions. (p. 245)

b. Some behaviors, but certainly not all, are acquired more rapidly than others when shock is used as negative reinforcement.

c. Pigeons are able to acquire many new behaviors when food is used as reinforcement.

6. **a.** is the answer. Ratio schedules maintain higher rates of responding—gambling in this example—than do interval schedules. Furthermore, variable schedules are not associated with the pause in responding following reinforcement that is typical of fixed schedules. The slot machine would therefore be used more often, and more consistently, if jackpots were scheduled according to a variable-ratio schedule. (p. 242)

7. **d.** is the answer. Sharetta is guided by her mental representation of the city, or cognitive map. (p. 244)

a. & e. Latent learning, or learning in the absence of reinforcement that is demonstrated when reinforcement becomes available, has no direct relevance to the example. The same is true of discrimination.

b. Observational learning refers to learning from watching others.

c. Shaping is the technique of reinforcing successive approximations of a desired behavior.

8. **c.** is the answer. Because the cat was associated with your mother's scream, it elicited a fear response, and is thus the CS. (p. 229)

9. **a.** is the answer. Your mother's scream and evident fear, which naturally caused you to cry, was the UCS. (p. 229)

10. **d.** is the answer. Your fear of cats is the CR. An acquired fear is always a conditioned response. (p. 229)

11. **b.** is the answer. Your crying, automatically elicited by your mother's scream and fear, was the UCR. (p. 229)

12. **c.** is the answer. (p. 246)

a. Positive reinforcement is most effective in boosting productivity in the workplace when specific behavior, rather than vaguely defined general merit, is rewarded. Also, immediate reinforcement is much more effective than the delayed reinforcement described in a.

b. Positive reinforcement is most effective in boosting productivity when performance goals are achievable, rather than unrealistic.

d. The text does not specifically discuss the use of punishment in the workplace. However, it makes the general point that although punishment may temporarily suppress unwanted behavior, it does not guide one toward more desirable behavior. Therefore, workers who receive pay cuts for poor performance may learn nothing about how to improve their productivity.

13. **b.** is the answer. Not only is Bill extending a learned aversion to a specific blue car to all blue cars but also to cars that are green. (p. 232)

a. Whereas discrimination involves responding only to a particular stimulus, Bill is extending his aversive response to other stimuli (green cars) as well.

c. Latent learning is learning that becomes apparent only after reinforcement becomes available.

d. Extinction refers to the weakening of a CR when the CS is no longer followed by the UCS.

14. **b.** is the answer. The girls are imitating behavior they have observed and admired. (p. 248)

a. Because these behaviors are clearly willful rather than elicited, classical conditioning plays no role.

c. Latent learning plays no role in this example.

d. Shaping is a procedure for teaching the acquisition of a new response by reinforcing successive approximations of the behavior.

e. Discrimination involves responding to certain stimuli but not to others. In this example, only one stimulus (the televised Olympic games) is described.

15. **a.** is the answer. Classical conditioning proceeds most effectively when the CS and UCS are reliably paired and therefore appear predictably associated. Only for Group 1 is this likely to be true. (p. 230)

16. **b.** is the answer. (pp. 233–234)

a., c., & d. Taste-aversion research demonstrates that humans and some other animals, such as rats, are biologically primed to associate illness with the taste of tainted food, rather than with other cues, such as the food's appearance. Moreover, taste aversions can be acquired even when the interval between the CS and the illness is several hours.

17. **d.** is the answer. By making a more preferred activity (watching TV) contingent on a less preferred activity (room cleaning), Reggie's mother is employing the operant conditioning technique of positive reinforcement. (pp. 237, 240)

18. **c.** is the answer. The parrot is reinforced for making successive approximations of a goal behavior. This defines shaping. (p. 238)

a. Shaping is an operant conditioning procedure; salivation at the sight of dog biscuits is a classically conditioned response.

b. Shaping involves the systematic reinforcement of successive approximations of a more complex behavior. In this example there is no indication that the response of stopping at the intersection involved the gradual acquisition of simpler behaviors.

d. This is an example of the partial reinforcement of an established response, rather than the shaping of a new response.

19. **c.** is the answer. Whereas Lars is paid (reinforced) after a fixed period of time (fixed-interval), Tom is reinforced for each sale (fixed-ratio) he makes. (p. 242)

20. **b.** is the answer. Wanting to do something for its own sake is intrinsic motivation; wanting to do something for a reward (in this case, presumably, a high grade) is extrinsic motivation. (p. 244)

a. The opposite is true. Nancy was motivated to take the course for its own sake, whereas Jack was evidently motivated by the likelihood of a reward in the form of a good grade.

c. & d. A good grade, such as the one Jack is expecting, is an incentive. Drives, however, are aroused states that result from physical deprivation; they are not involved in this example.

Essay Question

The first step in shaping an operant response, such as rolling over, is to find an effective reinforcer. Some sort of biscuit or dog treat is favored by animal trainers. This primary reinforcement should be accompanied by effusive praise (secondary reinforcement) whenever the dog makes a successful response.

Rolling over (the goal response) should be divided into a series of simple approximations, the first of which is a response, such as lying down on command, that is already in the dog's repertoire. This response should be reinforced several times. The next step is to issue a command, such as "Roll over," and withhold reinforcement until the dog (usually out of frustration) makes a closer approximation (such as rotating slightly in one direction). Following this example, the trainer should gradually require closer and closer approximations until the goal response is attained. When the new response has been established, the trainer should switch from continuous to partial reinforcement, in order to strengthen the skill.

Key Terms

1. **Learning** is any relatively permanent change in an organism's behavior due to experience. (p. 225)

2. In **associative learning**, organisms learn that certain events occur together. Two variations of associative learning are classical conditioning and operant conditioning. (p. 225)

3. Also known as Pavlovian conditioning, **classical conditioning** is a type of learning in which an organism comes to associate stimuli; that is, a neutral stimulus becomes capable of eliciting a conditioned response after having become associated with an unconditioned stimulus. (p. 228)

4. **Behaviorism** is the view that psychology should be an objective science, study only observable behaviors, and avoid references to mental processes. (p. 228)

   Example: Because he was an early advocate of the study of observable behavior, John Watson is often called the father of **behaviorism.**

5. In classical conditioning, the **unconditioned response (UCR)** is the unlearned, involuntary response to the unconditioned stimulus. (p. 229)

6. In classical conditioning, the **unconditioned stimulus (UCS)** is the stimulus that naturally and automatically elicits the reflexive unconditioned response. (p. 229)

7. In classical conditioning, the **conditioned response (CR)** is the learned response to a previously neutral conditioned stimulus, which results from the acquired association between the CS and UCS. (p. 229)

8. In classical conditioning, the **conditioned stimulus (CS)** is an originally neutral stimulus that comes to elicit a CR after association with an unconditioned stimulus. (p. 229)

9. In a learning experiment, **acquisition** refers to the initial stage of conditioning in which the new response is established and gradually strengthened. In operant conditioning, it is the strengthening of a reinforced response. (p. 230)

10. **Extinction** refers to the weakening of a CR when the CS is no longer followed by the UCS; in operant conditioning extinction occurs when a response is no longer reinforced. (p. 231)

11. **Spontaneous recovery** is the reappearance of an extinguished CR after a rest period. (p. 231)

12. **Generalization** refers to the tendency, once a response has been conditioned, for stimuli similar to the original CS to evoke a CR. (p. 232)

13. **Discrimination** in classical conditioning refers to the ability to distinguish the CS from similar stimuli that do not signal a UCS. In operant conditioning, it refers to responding differently to stimuli that signal a behavior will be reinforced or will not be reinforced. (p. 232)

14. **Operant conditioning** is a type of learning in which behavior is strengthened if followed by reinforcement or diminished if followed by punishment. (p. 237)

    Example: Unlike classical conditioning, which works on automatic behaviors, **operant conditioning** works on behaviors that are willfully emitted by an organism.

15. **Respondent behavior** is that which occurs as an automatic response to some stimulus. (p. 237)

    Example: In classical conditioning, conditioned and unconditioned responses are examples of **respondent behavior** in that they are automatic responses elicited by specific stimuli.

16. **Operant behavior** is behavior the organism emits that operates on the environment to produce reinforcing or punishing stimuli. (p. 237)

17. E. L. Thorndike proposed the **law of effect**, which states that rewarded behavior is likely to recur. (p. 237)

18. An **operant chamber** (*Skinner box*) is an experimental chamber for the operant conditioning of an animal such as a pigeon or rat. The controlled environment enables the investigator to present visual or auditory stimuli, deliver reinforcement or punishment, and precisely measure simple responses such as bar presses or key pecking. (p. 237)

19. **Shaping** is the operant conditioning procedure for establishing a new response by reinforcing successive approximations of the desired behavior. (p. 238)

20. In operant conditioning, a **reinforcer** is any event that strengthens the behavior it follows. (p. 239)

21. The powers of **primary reinforcers** are inborn and do not depend on learning. (p. 240)

22. **Conditioned reinforcers** are stimuli that acquire their reinforcing power through their association with primary reinforcers. (p. 240)

23. **Continuous reinforcement** is the operant procedure of reinforcing the desired response every time it occurs. In promoting the acquisition of a new response it is best to use continuous reinforcement. (p. 241)

24. **Partial (intermittent) reinforcement** is the operant procedure of reinforcing a response intermittently. A response that has been partially reinforced is much more resistant to extinction than one that has been continuously reinforced. (p. 241)

25. In operant conditioning, a **fixed-ratio schedule** is one in which reinforcement is presented after a set number of responses. (p. 241)

    Example: Continuous reinforcement is a special kind of **fixed-ratio schedule**: Reinforcement is presented after *each* response, so the ratio of reinforcements to responses is one to one.

26. In operant conditioning, a **variable-ratio schedule** is one in which reinforcement is presented after a varying number of responses. (p. 242)

27. In operant conditioning, a **fixed-interval schedule** is one in which a response is reinforced after a specified time has elapsed. (p. 242)

28. In operant conditioning, a **variable-interval schedule** is one in which responses are reinforced after varying intervals of time. (p. 242)

29. In operant conditioning, **punishment** is the presentation of an aversive stimulus, such as shock, which decreases the behavior it follows. (p. 242)

    Memory aid: People often confuse negative reinforcement and **punishment**. The former strengthens behavior, while the latter weakens it.

30. A **cognitive map** is a mental picture of one's environment. (p. 244)

31. **Latent learning** is learning that occurs in the absence of reinforcement but only becomes apparent when there is an incentive to demonstrate it. (p. 244)

32. **Intrinsic motivation** is the desire to perform a behavior for its own sake, rather than for some external reason, and to be effective. (p. 244)

    Memory aid: Intrinsic means "internal": A person who is **intrinsically motivated** is motivated from within.

33. **Extrinsic motivation** is the desire to perform a behavior in order to obtain a reward or avoid a punishment. (p. 244)

    Memory aid: Extrinsic means "external": A person who is extrinsically motivated is motivated by some outside factor.

34. **Observational learning** is learning by watching and imitating the behavior of others. (p. 248)

35. **Modeling** is the process of watching and then imitating a specific behavior and is thus an important means through which observational learning occurs. (p. 248)

36. Found in the brain's frontal lobe, **mirror neurons** may be the neural basis for observational learning. These neurons generate impulses when certain actions are performed or when another individual who performs those actions is observed. (p. 248)

37. The opposite of antisocial behavior, **prosocial behavior** is positive, helpful, and constructive and is subject to the same principles of observational learning as is undesirable behavior, such as aggression. (p. 250)

Summing Up

Classical Conditioning

The flow chart reads as follows: A puff of air to the eye, the *UCS*, elicits an eye blink, the UCR. When the puff of air is paired with a bell ringing, a *CS*, the CS comes to elicit an eyeblink, a *CR*. This is the *acquisition* stage of classical conditioning. Presenting the CS alone for several trials results in *extinction*. After a period of rest, pairing the *CS* and *UCS* results in *spontaneous recovery*. If a CS similar to the original CS is presented, responding with the CR represents *generalization*, not responding to the similar CS represents *discrimination*.

Operant Conditioning

A dog biscuit, the *primary* reinforcer, or conditioned encouraging words such as "Good dog," the *conditioned reinforcer*, can be used to train, or *shape*, a new skill, such as sitting up. To teach a new skill (sitting up), first use *continuous* reinforcement, a special kind of *fixed-ratio* schedule. To maintain the skill, use *partial reinforcement* either by rewarding the dog after different numbers of responses (a *variable-ratio* schedule, which produces the *steadiest* rate of responding); rewarding the dog after different amounts of time (a *variable-interval* schedule); or rewarding the dog after a specified amount of time (a *fixed-interval* schedule).

FOCUS ON VOCABULARY AND LANGUAGE

Page 225: Learning in all such realms *breeds hope.* The fact that we can change and adapt as a result of experience (*learn*) in so many different areas (*realms*) gives rise to optimism (*breeds hope*) about our future prospects.

Page 225: . . . watching a TV character get *mugged* . . . This means to be attacked, (sometimes) beaten, and robbed. This example shows how associations are formed between events, such as between the sounds that precede an attack and the *mugging* itself. In movies and on TV, a certain type of music is often played before a frightening event or scene. After a few such associations, the music itself can elicit fear before you actually see the frightening or scary event. This is an example of classical conditioning.

Page 226: A clever Japanese *rancher* reportedly *herds* cattle by outfitting them with electronic *pagers*, which he calls from his cell phone. In this example of conditioning, the cattle farmer (*rancher*) has trained his animals (*steers*) to gather together and move (*he herds them*) to the feeding station (*food trough*). They have learned to associate the sound of the tone (*the beep*) made by the signaling device (*electronic pager*) with the delivery of food (classical conditioning), and they have learned that moving fast (*hustling*) to the trough is followed by the good feeling of satiating their hunger (operant conditioning).

Classical Conditioning

Page 228: For many people, the name Ivan Pavlov (1849–1936) *rings a bell.* Myers is making a little joke here. A common expression when hearing something familiar but vague is to say, *"That rings a bell."* Pavlov's name is familiar to many people, who may also be vaguely aware that his research involved dogs and ringing bells (classical conditioning).

Page 228: . . . what the dog was thinking and feeling as it *drooled.* . . . To *drool* means to salivate or produce spit. When food (UCS) is placed in a dog's mouth, the dog will automatically salivate or *drool* (UCR). If a tone (CS) is sounded before (or precedes) the UCS over a number of trials, then the CS alone (the tone) will be able to elicit salivation (CR). Pavlov decided that the dog's internal mental state (thinking and feeling) was not important in reaching an understanding of fundamental learning principles, and that focusing attention on cognitive processes only led to futile arguments (*fruitless debates*).

Page 230: (margin note): If the *aroma* of cake baking *sets your mouth to watering*, what is the UCS? The CS? The CR? When you bake a cake in the oven, there is a lovely smell (*aroma*) which makes you salivate or drool (*sets your mouth to watering*). This is an example of classical conditioning: The taste of the cake in your mouth is the UCS (this automatically produces saliva, the UCR), the aroma is the CS, and, because of its past associations with the UCS, it can now, by itself, elicit saliva (the CR).

Page 230: Moreover, the male quail developed a preference for their cage's *red-light district*. Traditionally, a red lamp hung in the window identified the house as a brothel, and the area of town populated by many brothels became known as the *red-light district*. In Domjan's experiments with male quail a red light (CS) was used to signal the arrival of a receptive female quail (UCS), which elicited sexual arousal (CR). Eventually, the red light (CS) alone elicited sexual arousal (CR), and the male quail appeared to develop a general liking (*preference*) for the cage with the red light (*the red-light district*).

Page 231: After *breaking up* with his *fire-breathing heartthrob*, Tirrell also experienced extinction and spontaneous recovery. He recalls that "the smell of onion breath (CS), no longer paired with the kissing (UCS), lost its ability to *shiver my timbers.*" This paragraph describes the end of the relationship (*breaking up*) with his girlfriend (*heartthrob*) who loved to eat onions and thus had hot, smelly breath (*fire-breathing*). The repeated smell of onions or onion breath (CS) without the UCS (kissing) resulted in extinction of his conditioned aroused state (CR), and, consequently, the CS lost its ability to get him excited (*shiver his timbers*). He later experienced spontaneous recovery (the extinguished CR returned briefly) when he smelled onion breath once more. [The idiom "shiver my timbers" has no simple explanation; it may be an old expression dating back to the days of wooden (*timbered*) sailing ships that would tremble or shiver in a storm, or alternatively, it may have been used in the game of cricket to describe what happens when the cricket ball shakes and scatters (*shivers*) the wooden wicket and stumps (*timbers*).]

Page 233: So, even in classical conditioning, it is not only the simple CS–UCS association but also *the thought that counts*. The expression "it's the thought that counts" recognizes that a person's intentions and motivations (*thoughts*) are just as important as the actual behavior. Myers is making the point that cognitions (*thoughts, perceptions, expectations*) are now viewed as being critically important in the process of learning through classical conditioning.

Page 235: But if we *see further* than Pavlov did, it is because we *stand on his shoulders*. This phrase is not to be taken literally; it simply means that we now know more than Pavlov did (*we see further*) because we can build and expand on his great work (*stand on his shoulders*).

Page 235: Former *crack* cocaine users often feel a *craving* when they again encounter cues (people, places) associated with previous *highs*. Crack cocaine users are drug addicts who use a drug that is a synthetic, but very potent, form of cocaine (*crack*). For those who are attempting abstinence, the strong desire (*craving*) for the drug may be a classically conditioned response (CR) to the sight or presence of people or places (CSs). These people or places (CSs) were associated with taking the drug (UCS) which produced the UCR (euphoric feelings or *highs*). Drug addicts are therefore advised to avoid (steer clear of) settings or people related to previous drug taking activity.

Page 236: . . . *legendary significance* . . . Watson and Rayner's work with Little Albert was the first investigation of how phobias or irrational fears might develop through the process of classical conditioning. Thus, the story was passed on to future generations of psychologists (it became a legend) and influenced their research.

Operant Conditioning

Page 238: . . . *to pull habits out of a rat.* David Myers is having fun playing with the English language here. The expression "to pull rabbits out of a hat" refers to stage magicians who are able to extract rabbits from a seemingly empty hat. Can you see the way Myers has twisted this expression? Both classical and operant conditioning involve teaching new habits to various organisms, including rats. Following classical conditioning the CS elicits a new response from the animal (i.e., the CS *"pulls a habit out of the rat"*), or the sight of the lever may elicit the habit of lever pressing (operant conditioning).

Page 238: With training, pigeons have even been taught to discriminate between *Bach's music and Stravinsky's.* Bach and Stravinsky were composers whose styles of musical composition were quite different. Through shaping (rewarding behaviors that are closer and closer to the target or desired response), psychologists have been able to train pigeons to discriminate (or choose) between the two musical sounds. For example, pigeons may be rewarded for pecking a disk when Bach is playing and for refraining from pecking when Stravinsky is playing. They can be trained to discriminate, or tell the difference, between the two.

Page 239: On a wall chart, the teacher pastes *gold stars* after the names of children scoring 100 percent on spelling tests. Teachers often use extrinsic rewards such as small, bright stickers (*gold stars*) for, say, the very best spellers in the class. Unfortunately, if only the top few students (*academic all-stars*) are recognized in this way, the rest of the students may lose motivation because, even if they improve their spelling and work very hard (but still don't get 100%), they don't get any reinforcers. Myers recommends a shaping procedure that rewards even small improvements and recognizes the child for making the effort to do better and better.

Page 240: Pushing the *snooze button*, silences the annoying alarm. When your radio alarm goes off in the morning, you may press the switch (*snooze button*) which turns off the irritating tone for a brief period of time. The ensuing quiet period, which may allow you to go back to sleep for a while (*snooze*), and the absence of the buzzer are negative reinforcers for pushing the snooze button. (Your button-pushing behavior has been strengthened because it removed an aversive event, the alarm.) Likewise, a regular smoker (*nicotine addict*) may be negatively reinforced for inhaling tobacco smoke (*dragging on a cigarette*) because doing so diminishes the pain (*pangs*) associated with going without the drug.

Page 240: . . . goofing off and getting a bad exam grade . . . Students may score poorly on an exam because they were doing something unproductive, such as watching TV, instead of studying (they were *goofing off*). As a consequence, they may decide to change their behavior and work hard to avoid further exam anxiety and the unpleasant possibility of getting a low grade. The new behavior may be strengthened if it avoids the aversive consequences of anxiety (negative reinforcement); in addition, getting a good score on the exam can positively reinforce good study habits. Remember, reinforcers of either kind (positive or negative) always strengthen behavior.

Page 240: . . . the *kick* that often comes within seconds [after taking drugs] . . . The term *kick* as used here refers to a jolt of pleasure (not as in "to kick the ball"). Myers is making the point that behaviors such as smoking, drinking, and drug taking, in general, are followed by some immediate pleasurable consequence, which controls the behavior more than does the delayed consequence (e.g., lung cancer, memory loss, cognitive impairment, etc.).

Page 241: A salesperson does not make a sale with every *pitch,* nor does an *angler* get a bite with every *cast.* The *pitch* referred to here is the sales talk (*pitch*) that the salesperson uses to promote the product or service. The bite the angler (fisherman) does not get refers to the fact that throwing out the line (*casting*)

does not always result in fish biting the bait. The idea is that much of our behavior is not continuously reinforced but persists, nevertheless, by being partially reinforced (you make a sale or catch a fish only once in a while despite many responses). Thus, intermittent rewards encourage the expectation of future reinforcement (*hope springs eternal*) and create greater resistance to extinction of the behavior compared to a continuous schedule.

Page 241: . . . paid on a piecework basis . . . This refers to situations in which someone is paid for the number of items produced (and not by the hour or the week). A worker gets paid only if he or she produces, so the number of responses (i.e., the number of items produced) is reinforced on a **fixed-ratio schedule**. An example would be factory worker sewing shirts who would be paid five dollars for each finished shirt (*piecework*). The more shirts she makes, the more money she earns, and thus the rate of responding is usually high.

Page 242: . . . a choppy stop-start pattern . . . When reinforcement is for the first response after a set time period (a **fixed-interval schedule**), responding is typically more frequent as the expected time for the reinforcer gets closer (*draws near*) and is much less frequent after the reward has been received. The pattern of responding is consequently uneven (*choppy*) because cycles of post-reinforcement pauses followed by higher levels of responding (a *stop-start pattern*) are characteristic of the fixed-interval schedule.

Page 242: . . . the child who *loses a treat* after running into the street . . . Here the phrase *"loses a treat"* refers to the withholding of some pleasant consequence such as a candy bar or piece of cake (appetitive stimulus) following some unwanted behavior. This is one type of punishment; it decreases the probability of the behavior being repeated. Another example is *time-out*, in which the child is put in a situation (such as in the corner) in which no reinforcement is available.

Page 242: . . . drawbacks . . . This means problems or bad consequences. One problem (*drawback*) with using punishment is that the behavior may be temporarily suppressed in the presence of the punisher but may reappear in other, safer settings. In addition, punishment may elicit aggression, create fear and apprehension, and generate avoidance behavior in those being punished. As Myers notes, punishment teaches what not to do, whereas reinforcement teaches what to do.

Page 242: The driver who is *hit with* a couple of speeding tickets. . . . The phrase *"hit with"* means issued with or given, but "hit" is also associated with punitive, aversive, or bad consequences. A driver who is issued (*hit with*) a speeding ticket may feel punished and, instead of changing the speeding behavior, may find ways to avoid getting tickets by using a radar detector. The point Myers is making is that punishment may not be the best way to change behavior.

Page 244: Actually, promising children a reward for a task they already enjoy can *backfire*. If children enjoy doing something because it is fun (intrinsic motivation), they may lose interest in the task if they are promised a reward for it (extrinsic motivation). Thus, in some circumstances offering material gains (a *payoff*) may have an effect opposite to the one expected (it can *backfire*).

Page 245: . . . *piggy bank* . . . This is a small container for saving money (usually coins) that is often in the shape of a pig. Children can learn to save their money by putting it in their *piggy bank*. However, as Myers points out, pigs who were trained to put big wooden coins in a large *piggy bank* soon reverted to their natural behavior of pushing the coins with their snouts (noses) despite the fact that they received no reward for doing this. This is an example of the biological constraints on learning.

Page 245: . . . *stirred a hornet's nest.* . . . A hornet is a large yellow and black stinging insect belonging to the wasp family. Up to 200 hornets live together in a sheltered home (*nest*); if disturbed or agitated (*stirred*), they will attack in an angry and aggressive manner. B. F. Skinner aroused a great deal of anger and hostility and was vehemently attacked by many people (*he stirred a hornet's nest*) for insisting that mental events and free will (internal events) were of little relevance as determinants of behavior compared to environmental factors such as rewards and punishments (external influences).

Learning by Observation

Page 249: Compared with children not exposed to the adult model, those who observed the model's *aggressive outburst* were much more likely to *lash out* at the doll. Bandura's experiments on observational learning demonstrated that children who saw an adult engage in (*model*) violent behavior (an *aggressive outburst*) were more inclined to attack and beat up (*lash out at*) a Bobo doll and copy (*imitate*) the words and gestures used by the role model.

Page 250: Does the *reel world affect the real world?* Traditionally motion pictures (*movies*) were projected on the screen from a large reel (*spool*) of film. Thus, the "reel" world referred to here is the fantasy world created by movie companies, TV networks, cable companies, etc. (*the media*). Myers notes that the actual (*real*) world is not accurately reflected in movies, TV shows, video games, cable programming, and so on (*the reel world*). Watching the excessive aggression and violence depicted in the media tends to be **correlated** with increased acceptance of aggressive attitudes, indifference to violent acts, and higher levels of antisocial behavior.

chapter 8

Memory

Chapter Overview

Chapter 8 explores human memory as a system that processes information in three steps. Encoding refers to the process of putting information into the memory system. Storage is the mechanism by which information is maintained in memory. Retrieval is the process by which information is accessed from memory through recall or recognition.

Chapter 8 also discusses the important role of meaning, imagery, and organization in encoding new memories, how memory is represented physically in the brain, and how forgetting may result from failure to encode or store information or to find appropriate retrieval cues. The final section of the chapter discusses the issue of memory construction. How "true" are our memories of events? A particularly controversial issue in this area involves suspicious claims of long-repressed memories of sexual abuse and other traumas that are "recovered" with the aid of hypnosis and other techniques. As you study this chapter, try applying some of the memory and studying tips discussed in the text.

NOTE: Answer guidelines for all Chapter 8 questions begin on page 232.

The Phenomenon of Memory (pp. 257–260)

> David Myers at times uses idioms that are unfamiliar to some readers. If you do not know the meaning of any of the following words, phrases, or expressions in the context in which they appear in the text, refer to page 241 for an explanation: . . . *mind's storehouse, the reservoir; the roots and fruits; medal winners in a memory Olympics; memory feats; shine the flashlight beam of our attention on.*

Section Preview

First, skim the section, noting headings and boldface items. Then read the following objective and, as you read the text, search for the information that will enable you to meet that objective. Answer guidelines are provided on page 232.

1. Explain memory in terms of information processing.

Stepping Through the Section

After you have read the section, complete the sentences and answer the questions. As you proceed, evaluate your performance by consulting the answers on page 232. Do not continue with the next section until you understand each answer. If you need to, review or reread the section in the textbook before continuing.

1. Learning that persists over time indicates the existence of _____ for that learning.

2. Memories for surprising, significant moments that are especially clear are called _____ memories.

3. Both human memory and computer memory can be viewed as _____-_____ systems that perform three tasks: _____ , _____ , and _____ .

4. The classic and influential model of memory is Atkinson and Shiffrin's _____-
_____ _____ model.
According to this model, we first record information as a fleeting _____
_____ , from which it is processed into a _____-_____
memory, where the information is _____ into a _____-
_____ memory for later retrieval.

5. The phenomenon of short-term memory has been clarified by the concept of _____
memory, which focuses more on the processing of briefly stored information. This type of memory is similar to a computer's _____ memory, which integrates incoming information with material retrieved from long-term storage.

Encoding: Getting Information In
(pp. 260–265)

> If you do not know the meaning of any of the following words, phrases, or expressions in the context in which they appear in the text, refer to pages 241–242 for an explanation: *boost; nonsense syllables; a raw script . . . finished stage production; mental snapshots; peg-word; talk until you are blue in the face.*

Section Preview

Answer guidelines are provided on page 232.

1. Explain the process of encoding, and distinguish between automatic and effortful processing.

2. Discuss the importance of rehearsal, spacing, and serial position in encoding.

3. Explain the importance of meaning, imagery, and organization in the encoding process.

Stepping Through the Section

Answers are provided on page 232.

1. A distinction is made between encoding that does not require conscious attention and is therefore _____ and that which is
_____ .

Give examples of material encoded by automatic processing and by effortful processing.

2. With novel information, conscious repetition, or _____ , boosts memory.

3. A pioneering researcher in verbal memory was _____ . In one experiment, he found that the longer he studied a list of nonsense syllables, the _____
(fewer/greater) the number of repetitions he required to relearn it later.

4. After material has been learned, additional repetition, or _____ , usually will increase retention.

5. When people go around a circle reading words, their poorest memories are for the _____ (least/most) recent information heard. This phenomenon is called the
_____-_____-
_____ effect.

6. Memory studies also reveal that distributed rehearsal is more effective for retention; this is called the _____ _____ .
A variation on this technique, in which we
_____ _____
_____ , involves gradually

increasing the length of time between periods in which new material is rehearsed.

7. The tendency to remember the first and last items in a list best is called the _____ _____ _____ .

Following a delay, first items are remembered _____ (better/less well) than last items.

8. We process information by encoding its _____ , its _____ , and by _____ _____ the information.

9. Memory that consists of mental pictures is based on the use of _____ .

10. Your earliest memories are most likely of events that occurred when you were about _____ years old.

11. Concrete, high-imagery words tend to be remembered _____ (better/less well) than abstract, low-imagery words. We remember the best or worst moments of our experiences; this is called _____ _____ .

12. Memory aids are known as _____ devices. One such device involves forming associations between a familiar series of locations and to-be-remembered words; this technique is called the "_____ _____ _____ ."

13. Using a jingle, such as the one that begins "one is a bun," is an example of the "_____-_____" system.

14. Memory may be aided by grouping information into meaningful units called _____ . An example of this technique involves forming words from the first letters of to-be-remembered words; the resulting word is called an _____ .

15. In addition, material may be processed into _____ , which are composed of a few broad concepts divided into lesser concepts, categories, and facts.

Storage: Retaining Information
(pp. 265–272)

> If you do not know the meaning of any of the following words, phrases, or expressions in the context in which they appear in the text, refer to page 242 for an explanation: *flashes of lightning; Sherlock Holmes; champion memorist; memory "software"; with tongue only partly in cheek; Arousal sears the events onto the brain; mirror-image writing . . . jigsaw puzzle; savoring.*

Section Preview

Answer guidelines begin on page 232.

1. Distinguish between iconic and echoic memory.

2. Describe memory capacity and duration.

3. Discuss research findings on the physical basis of memory.

4. Discuss what research with amnesia victims and animal conditioning studies reveals about the brain mechanisms involved in the dual explicit-implicit memory system.

Stepping Through the Section

Answers are provided on page 233.

1. If you are able to retrieve something from memory, you must have engaged in the process of
_____ .

2. Stimuli from the environment are first recorded in _____ memory.

3. George Sperling found that when people were briefly shown three rows of letters, they could recall _____ (virtually all/about half) of them. When Sperling sounded a tone immediately after a row of letters was flashed to indicate which letters were to be recalled, the subjects were much _____ (more/less) accurate. This suggests that people have a brief photographic, or _____ , memory lasting about a few tenths of a second.

4. Sensory memory for sounds is called _____ memory. This memory fades _____ (more/less) rapidly than photographic memory, lasting for as long as _____ .

5. Peterson and Peterson found that when _____ was prevented by asking subjects to count backward, memory for letters was gone after 12 seconds. Without _____ processing, short-term memories have a limited life.

6. Our short-term memory capacity is about _____ chunks of information.

7. Short-term memory for random _____ (digits/letters) is slightly better than for random _____ (digits/letters), and memory for information we hear is somewhat _____ (better/worse) than that for information we see.

8. Both children and adults have short-term recall for roughly as many words as they can speak in _____ (how many?) seconds.

9. In contrast to short-term memory—and contrary to popular belief—the capacity of permanent memory is essentially _____ .

10. Penfield's electrically stimulated patients _____ (do/do not) provide reliable evidence that our stored memories are precise and durable.

11. It is likely that forgetting occurs because new experiences _____ with our retrieval of old information and the physical memory trace _____ with the passage of time.

12. Lashley attempted to locate memory by cutting out pieces of rats' _____ after they had learned a maze. He found that no matter where he cut, the rats _____ (remembered/forgot) the maze.

13. Gerard found that a hamster's memory remained even after its body temperature was lowered to a point where the brain's _____ activity stopped.

14. Researchers believe that memory involves a strengthening of certain neural connections, which occurs at the _____ between neurons.

15. Kandel and Schwartz have found that when learning occurs in the sea snail *Aplysia*, the neurotransmitter _____ is released in greater amounts, making synapses more efficient.

16. After learning has occurred, a sending neuron needs _____ (more/less) prompting to fire, and the number of _____ _____ it stimulates may increase. This phenomenon, called _____-_____ _____ , may be the neural basis for learning and memory. Blocking this process with a specific _____ , or by genetic engineering that causes the absence of an _____ , interferes with learning. Rats given a drug that enhances _____ will learn a maze _____ (faster/more slowly).

17. A blow or an electric shock to the brain _____ (will/will not) disrupt old

memories and _____ (will/will not) wipe out recent experiences.

18. Hormones released when we are excited or under stress often _____ (facilitate/impair) learning and memory. Drugs that block the effects of stress hormones _____ (facilitate/disrupt) memories of emotional events.

19. The loss of memory is called _____ . Studies of people who have lost their memory suggest that there _____ (is/is not) a single unified system of memory.

20. Although amnesia victims typically _____ (have/have not) lost their capacity for learning, which is called _____ memory, they _____ (are/are not) able to declare their memory, suggesting a deficit in their _____ memory systems.

21. Amnesia patients typically have suffered damage to the _____ of their limbic system. This brain structure is important in the processing and storage of _____ memories. Damage on the left side of this structure impairs _____ memory; damage on the right side impairs memory for _____ designs and locations.

22. The hippocampus seems to function as a zone where the brain _____ (temporarily/permanently) stores the elements of a memory. However, memories _____ (do/do not) migrate for storage elsewhere. Recalling past experiences activates various parts of the _____ and _____ lobes.

23. The cerebellum is important in the processing of _____ memories. Humans and laboratory animals with a damaged cerebellum are incapable of simple _____-_____ conditioning. Those with damage to the _____ are incapable of _____ conditioning, indicating

that this brain region is important in the formation of _____ memories.

24. The dual explicit-implicit memory system helps explain _____ amnesia. We do not have explicit memories of our first three years because the _____ is one of the last brain structures to mature.

Retrieval: Getting Information Out
(pp. 272–275)

> If you do not know the meaning of any of the following words, phrases, or expressions in the context in which they appear in the text, refer to pages 242–243 for an explanation: *buoyant mood . . . rose-colored glasses; morph from devils into angels.*

Section Preview
Answer guidelines are provided on page 233.

1. Contrast recall, recognition, and relearning measures of memory.

2. Describe the importance of retrieval cues, noting the effects of priming, contexts, and moods on retrieval.

Stepping Through the Section
Answer guidelines begin on page 233.

1. The ability to retrieve information not in conscious awareness is called _____ .

2. Bahrick found that 25 years after graduation, people were not able to _____

(recall/recognize) the names of their classmates but were able to _____ (recall/recognize) 90 percent of their names and their yearbook pictures.

3. If you have learned something and then forgotten it, you will probably be able to _____ it _____ (more/less) quickly than you did originally.

4. The process by which associations can lead to retrieval is called _____ .The best retrieval cues come from the associations formed at the time we _____ a memory.

5. Studies have shown that retention is best when learning and testing are done in _____ (the same/different) contexts.

Summarize the text explanation of the déjà vu experience.

6. The type of memory in which emotions serve as retrieval cues is referred to as _____-_____ memory.

Describe the effects of mood on memory.

7. People who are currently depressed may recall their parents as _____ .

People who have recovered from depression typically recall their parents about the same as do people who _____ _____ .

Forgetting (pp. 275–281)

> If you do not know the meaning of any of the following words, phrases, or expressions in the context in which they appear in the text, refer to page 243 for an explanation: *applause for memory; may lie poised on the tip of the tongue; mental attic; sheepishly; The words relit a blown-out candle in the mind.*

Section Preview

Answer guidelines are provided on page 234.

1. Broadly describe Schacter's seven sins of memory as a categorization of the ways in which we forget.

2. Discuss forgetting as either a form of encoding failure or storage decay.

3. Discuss the roles of interference and motivated forgetting in the process of retrieval failure.

Stepping Through the Section

Answers are provided on page 234.

1. Memory researcher Daniel Schacter has identified the seven sins of memory, divided into three categories that identify the ways in which our memory can fail: the three sins of _____ , the three sins of _____ , and the one sin of _____ .

2. The first category of sins refers to forgetting caused by _____ failure, _____ _____ , and _____ _____ . The second category has to do with memory _____ , and the third category deals with _____ memories.

3. Encoding failure occurs because some of the information that we sense _____ _____ . One reason for age-related memory decline is that the brain areas responsible for _____ new information are _____ (more/less) responsive in older adults.

4. Studies by Ebbinghaus and by Bahrick indicate that most forgetting occurs _____ (soon/a long time) after the material is learned. This type of forgetting is known as _____ _____ .

5. When information that is stored in memory temporarily cannot be found, _____ failure has occurred.

6. Research suggests that memories are also lost as a result of _____ , which is especially possible if we simultaneously learn similar, new material.

7. The disruptive effect of previous learning on current learning is called _____ _____ . The disruptive effect of learning new material on efforts to recall material previously learned is called _____ _____ .

8. Jenkins and Dallenbach found that if subjects went to sleep after learning, their memory for a list of nonsense syllables was _____ (better/worse) than it was if they stayed awake.

9. In some cases, old information facilitates our learning of new information. This is called _____ _____ .

10. Freud proposed that motivated forgetting, or _____ , may protect a person from painful memories. Increasing numbers of memory researchers think that motivated forgetting is _____ (less/more) common than Freud believed.

Memory Construction (pp. 281–287)

> If you do not know the meaning of any of the following words, phrases, or expressions in the context in which they appear in the text, refer to page 243 for an explanation: *"hypnotically refreshed"; reconstruction as well as reproduction; sincerely wrong.*

Section Preview

Answer guidelines begin on page 234.

1. Discuss the evidence for memory's being constructive.

2. Discuss whether children are credible eyewitnesses.

3. Explain why memory researchers are suspicious of claims of long-repressed memories "recovered" with the aid of a therapist.

Stepping Through the Section

Answers are provided on page 235.

1. Research has shown that recall of an event is often influenced by past experiences and present assumptions. The workings of these influences illustrate the process of memory _____.

2. When witnesses to an event receive misleading information about it, they may experience a _____ _____ and misremember the event. A number of experiments have demonstrated that false memories _____ (can/cannot) be created when people are induced to imagine nonexistent events. People who believe they have recovered memories of alien abduction and child sex abuse tend to have _____ _____ and to score high on _____ _____ tests.

Describe what Loftus's studies have shown about the effects of misleading postevent information on eyewitness reports.

3. Memory construction explains why memories "refreshed" under _____ are often inaccurate.

4. At the heart of many false memories is _____ _____ , which occurs when we _____ an event to the wrong source.

5. Research studies of children's eyewitness recall reveal that preschoolers _____ (are/are not) more suggestible than older children or adults. For this reason, whether a child produces an accurate eyewitness memory depends heavily on how he or she is _____ .

6. Memories of events that happened before age _____ are unreliable. This phenomenon is called _____ _____ .

Improving Memory (pp. 287–288)

> If you do not know the meaning of the following word in the context in which it appears in the text, refer to page 243 for an explanation: *sprinkled*.

Section Preview

Answer guidelines are provided on page 235.

1. Discuss strategies for improving memory.

Progress Test 1

Multiple-Choice Questions

Circle your answers to the following questions and check them with the answers beginning on page 235. If your answer is incorrect, read the explanation for why it is incorrect and then consult the appropriate pages of the text (in parentheses following the correct answer).

1. The three steps in memory information processing are:
   a. input, processing, output.
   b. input, storage, output.
   c. input, storage, retrieval.
   d. encoding, storage, retrieval.
   e. encoding, retrieval, storage.

2. Visual sensory memory is referred to as:
   a. iconic memory.   c. photomemory.
   b. echoic memory.   d. implicit memory.

3. Echoic memories fade after approximately:
   a. 1 hour.   d. 1 second.
   b. 1 minute.   e. 3 to 4 seconds.
   c. 30 seconds.

4. Which of the following is *not* a measure of retention?
   a. recall
   b. recognition
   c. relearning
   d. retrieval

5. Our short-term memory span is approximately _____ items.
   a. 2
   b. 5
   c. 7
   d. 10

6. Memory techniques such as the method of loci, acronyms, and the peg-word system are called:
   a. consolidation techniques.
   b. imagery strategies.
   c. encoding strategies.
   d. mnemonic devices.

7. One way to increase the amount of information in memory is to group it into larger, familiar units. This process is referred to as:
   a. consolidating.
   b. organization.
   c. memory construction.
   d. encoding.
   e. chunking.

8. Kandel and Schwartz have found that when learning occurs, more of the neurotransmitter _____ is released into synapses.
   a. ACh
   b. dopamine
   c. serotonin
   d. noradrenaline

9. Research on memory construction reveals that memories:
   a. are stored as exact copies of experience.
   b. reflect a person's biases and assumptions.
   c. may be chemically transferred from one organism to another.
   d. even if long term, usually decay within about five years.

10. In a study on context cues, people learned words while on land or when they were underwater. In a later test of recall, those with the best retention had:
    a. learned the words on land, that is, in the more familiar context.
    b. learned the words underwater, that is, in the more exotic context.
    c. learned the words and been tested on them in different contexts.
    d. learned the words and been tested on them in the same context.

11. The spacing effect means that:
    a. distributed study yields better retention than cramming.
    b. retention is improved when encoding and retrieval are separated by no more than 1 hour.
    c. learning causes a reduction in the size of the synaptic gap between certain neurons.
    d. delaying retrieval until memory has consolidated improves recall.

12. Studies demonstrate that learning causes permanent neural changes in the _____ of animals' neurons.
    a. myelin
    b. cell bodies
    c. synapses
    d. all the above

13. In Sperling's memory experiment, research participants were shown three rows of three letters, followed immediately by a low-, medium-, or high-pitched tone. The participants were able to report:
    a. all three rows with perfect accuracy.
    b. only the top row of letters.
    c. only the middle row of letters.
    d. any one of the three rows of letters.

14. Studies of amnesia victims suggest that:
    a. memory is a single, unified system.
    b. there are two distinct types of memory.
    c. there are three distinct types of memory.
    d. memory losses following brain trauma are unpredictable.
    e. brain trauma eliminates the ability to learn.

15. Memory for skills is called:
    a. explicit memory.
    b. declarative memory.
    c. episodic memory.
    d. implicit memory.

16. The eerie feeling of having been somewhere before is an example of:
    a. state dependency.
    b. encoding failure.
    c. priming.
    d. déjà vu.

17. When Gordon Bower presented words grouped by category or in random order, recall was:
    a. the same for all words.
    b. better for the categorized words.
    c. better for the random words.
    d. improved when participants developed their own mnemonic devices.

18. Which of the following has been proposed as a neurophysiological explanation of infantile amnesia?

   a. The slow maturation of the hippocampus leaves the infant's brain unable to store images and events.

   b. The deficient supply of serotonin until about age 3 makes encoding very limited.

   c. The limited availability of association areas of the cortex until about age 3 impairs encoding and storage.

   d. All of the above explanations have been proposed.

19. Hypnotically "refreshed" memories may prove inaccurate—especially if the hypnotist asks leading questions—because of:

   a. encoding failure.

   b. state-dependent memory.

   c. proactive interference.

   d. memory construction.

20. Which area of the brain is most important in the processing of implicit memories?

   a. hippocampus

   b. cerebellum

   c. hypothalamus

   d. amygdala

21. Which of the following terms does *not* belong with the others?

   a. misattribution   **c.** suggestibility

   b. blocking   **d.** bias

Matching Items

Match each definition or description with the appropriate term.

Definitions or Descriptions

    1. sensory memory that decays more slowly than visual sensory memory

    2. the process by which information gets into the memory system

    3. mental pictures that aid memory

    4. the blocking of painful memories

    5. the phenomenon in which one's mood can influence retrieval

    6. memory for a list of words is affected by word order

    7. "one is a bun, two is a shoe" mnemonic device

    8. matching each of a series of locations with a visual representation of to-be-remembered items

    9. new learning interferes with previous knowledge

   10. a measure of memory

   11. old knowledge interferes with new learning

   12. misattributing the origin of an event

   13. the fading of unused information over time

   14. the lingering effects of misinformation

   15. a memory sin of intrusion

Terms

   a. repression

   b. relearning

   c. serial position effect

   d. persistence

   e. peg-word system

   f. method of loci

   g. proactive interference

   h. transience

   i. retroactive interference

   j. source amnesia

   k. suggestibility

   l. imagery

   m. mood-congruent memory

   n. echoic memory

   o. encoding

Progress Test 2

Progress Test 2 should be completed during a final chapter review. Answer the following questions after you thoroughly understand the correct answers for the section reviews and Progress Test 1.

Multiple-Choice Questions

1. Which of the following best describes the typical forgetting curve?
   a. a steady, slow decline in retention over time
   b. a steady, rapid decline in retention over time
   c. a rapid initial decline in retention becoming stable thereafter
   d. a slow initial decline in retention becoming rapid thereafter

2. Jenkins and Dallenbach found that memory was better in subjects who were _____ during the retention interval, presumably because _____ was reduced.
   a. awake; decay
   b. asleep; decay
   c. awake; interference
   d. asleep; interference

3. Which of the following measures of retention is the least sensitive in triggering retrieval?
   a. recall   c. relearning
   b. recognition   d. déjà vu

4. Amnesia victims typically have experienced damage to the _____ of the brain.
   a. frontal lobes   d. hippocampus
   b. cerebellum   e. cortex
   c. thalamus

5. According to the serial position effect, when recalling a list of words you should have the greatest difficulty with those:
   a. at the beginning of the list.
   b. at the end of the list.
   c. at the end and in the middle of the list.
   d. at the beginning and end of the list.
   e. in the middle of the list.

6. Experimenters gave people a list of words to be recalled. When the participants were tested after a delay, the items that were best recalled were those:
   a. at the beginning of the list.
   b. in the middle of the list.
   c. at the end of the list.
   d. at the beginning and the end of the list.

7. Lashley's studies, in which rats learned a maze and then had various parts of their brains surgically removed, showed that the memory:
   a. was lost when surgery took place within 1 hour of learning.
   b. was lost when surgery took place within 24 hours of learning.
   c. was lost when any region of the brain was removed.
   d. remained no matter which area of the brain was tampered with.

8. The disruption of memory that occurs when football players have been knocked out provides evidence for the importance of:
   a. consolidation in the formation of new memories.
   b. consolidation in the retrieval of long-term memories.
   c. nutrition in normal neural functioning.
   d. all of the above.

9. *Long-term potentiation* refers to:
   a. the disruptive influence of old memories on the formation of new memories.
   b. the disruptive influence of recent memories on the retrieval of old memories.
   c. our tendency to recall experiences that are consistent with our current mood.
   d. the increased efficiency of synaptic transmission between certain neurons following learning.
   e. our increased ability to recall long-ago events as we grow older.

10. Repression is an example of:
    a. encoding failure.   c. motivated forgetting.
    b. memory decay.   d. all of the above.

11. Studies by Loftus and Palmer, in which people were quizzed about a film of an accident, indicate that:
    a. when quizzed immediately, people can recall very little, due to the stress of witnessing an accident.
    b. when questioned as little as one day later, their memory was very inaccurate.
    c. most people had very accurate memories as much as 6 months later.
    d. people's recall may easily be affected by misleading information.

12. Which of the following was *not* recommended as a strategy for improving memory?

    a. active rehearsal
    b. distributed study
    c. speed reading
    d. encoding meaningful associations
    e. use of mnemonic devices

13. The process of getting information out of memory storage is called:

    a. encoding.   c. rehearsal.
    b. retrieval.   d. storage.

14. Amnesia patients typically experience disruption of:

    a. implicit memories.   c. iconic memories.
    b. explicit memories.   d. echoic memories.

15. Information is maintained in short-term memory only briefly unless it is:

    a. encoded.   c. iconic or echoic.
    b. rehearsed.   d. retrieved.

16. Textbook chapters are often organized into _____ in order to facilitate information processing.

    a. mnemonic devices   c. hierarchies
    b. chunks   d. recognizable units

17. Memory researchers are suspicious of long-repressed memories of traumatic events that are "recovered" with the aid of drugs or hypnosis because:

    a. such experiences usually are vividly remembered.
    b. such memories are unreliable and easily influenced by misinformation.
    c. memories of events happening before about age 3 are especially unreliable.
    d. of all of the above reasons.

18. It is easier to recall information that has just been presented when the information:

    a. consists of random letters rather than words.
    b. is seen rather than heard.
    c. is heard rather than seen.
    d. is experienced in an unusual context.

19. The misinformation effect provides evidence that memory:

    a. is constructed during encoding.
    b. is unchanging once established.
    c. may be reconstructed during recall according to how questions are framed.
    d. is highly resistant to misleading information.

20. According to memory researcher Daniel Schacter, blocking occurs when:

    a. our inattention to details produces encoding failure.
    b. we confuse the source of information.
    c. our beliefs influence our recollections.
    d. information is on the tip of our tongue, but we can't get it out.

21. The three-stage processing model of memory was proposed by:

    a. Atkinson and Shifrin.
    b. Herman Ebbinghaus.
    c. Loftus and Palmer.
    d. George Sperling.

True–False Items

Indicate whether each statement is true or false by placing *T* (*True*) or *F* (*False*) in the blank next to the item.

_____ 1. Studying that is distributed over time produces better retention than cramming.

_____ 2. Generally speaking, memory for pictures is better than memory for words.

_____ 3. Recall of childhood abuse through hypnosis indicates that memory is permanent, due to the reliability of such reports.

_____ 4. Most people do not have memories of events that occurred before the age of 3.

_____ 5. Studies by Ebbinghaus show that most forgetting takes place soon after learning.

_____ 6. Much of the material we think of as having been forgotten was never "remembered."

_____ 7. Recall of newly acquired knowledge is no better after sleeping than after being awake for the same period of time.

_____ 8. Time spent in developing imagery, chunking, and associating material with what you already know is more effective than time spent repeating information again and again.

_____ 9. Although repression has not been confirmed experimentally, therapists often believe that it happens.

_____ 10. Overlearning material by continuing to restudy it beyond mastery often disrupts recall.

Review and Reflect

Answer these questions the day before an exam as a final check on your understanding of the chapter's terms and concepts.

Multiple-Choice Questions

1. Complete this analogy: Fill-in-the-blank test questions are to multiple-choice questions as:
   a. encoding is to storage.
   b. storage is to encoding.
   c. recognition is to recall.
   d. recall is to recognition.
   e. encoding is to recall.

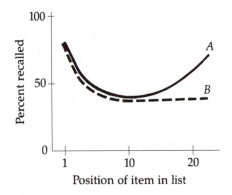

2. The above figure depicts the recall of a list of words under two conditions. Which of the following best describes the difference between the conditions?
   a. In *A*, the words were studied and retrieved in the same context; in *B*, the contexts were different.
   b. In *B*, the words were studied and retrieved in the same context; in *A*, the contexts were different.
   c. The delay between presentation of the last word and the test of recall was longer for *A* than for *B*.
   d. The delay between presentation of the last word and the test of recall was longer for *B* than for *A*.

3. After finding her old combination lock, Janice can't remember its combination because she keeps confusing it with the combination of her new lock. She is experiencing:
   a. proactive interference.
   b. retroactive interference.
   c. encoding failure.
   d. storage failure.
   e. repression.

4. Which of the following sequences would be best to follow if you wanted to minimize interference-induced forgetting in order to improve your recall on the psychology midterm?
   a. study, eat, test
   b. study, sleep, test
   c. study, listen to music, test
   d. study, exercise, test

5. Being in a bad mood after a hard day of work, Susan could think of nothing positive in her life. This is best explained as an example of:
   a. priming.
   b. memory construction.
   c. mood-congruent memory.
   d. retrieval failure.
   e. repression.

6. In an effort to remember the name of the classmate who sat behind her in fifth grade, Martina mentally recited the names of other classmates who sat near her. Martina's effort to refresh her memory by activating related associations is an example of:
   a. priming.   c. encoding.
   b. déjà vu.   d. relearning.

7. Walking through the halls of his high school 10 years after graduation, Tom experienced a flood of old memories. Tom's experience showed the role of:
   a. state-dependent memory.
   b. context effects.
   c. retroactive interference.
   d. echoic memory.
   e. iconic memory.

8. The first thing Karen did when she discovered that she had misplaced her keys was to re-create in her mind the day's events. That she had little difficulty in doing so illustrates:
   a. automatic processing.
   b. effortful processing.
   c. state-dependent memory.
   d. priming.

9. Which of the following is the best example of a flashbulb memory?
   a. suddenly remembering to buy bread while standing in the checkout line at the grocery store
   b. recalling the name of someone from high school while looking at his or her yearbook snapshot
   c. remembering to make an important phone call

d. remembering what you were doing on September 11, 2001, when terrorists crashed planes into the World Trade Center towers.

10. When Carlos was promoted, he moved into a new office with a new phone extension. Every time he is asked for his phone number, Carlos first thinks of his old extension, illustrating the effects of:

a. proactive interference.
b. retroactive interference.
c. encoding failure.
d. storage failure.

11. Your roommate mistakenly "remembers" your saying something at a recent party that you know to have actually been said by a mutual friend. Daniel Schachter would classify your roommate's misattribution as a "sin" of:

a. forgetting.
b. distortion.
c. intrusion.
d. none of the above.

12. At your high school reunion you cannot remember the last name of your homeroom teacher. Your failure to remember is most likely the result of:

a. encoding failure.
b. storage failure.
c. retrieval failure.
d. state-dependent memory.

13. Brenda has trouble remembering her new five-digit ZIP plus four-digit address code. What is the most likely explanation for the difficulty Brenda is having?

a. Nine digits are at or above the upper limit of most people's short-term memory capacity.
b. Nine digits are at or above the upper limit of most people's iconic memory capacity.
c. The extra four digits cannot be organized into easily remembered chunks.
d. Brenda evidently has an impaired implicit memory.

14. Lewis cannot remember the details of the torture he experienced as a prisoner of war. According to Freud, Lewis's failure to remember these painful memories is an example of:

a. repression.
b. retrieval failure.
c. state-dependent memory.
d. flashbulb memory.
e. implicit memory.

15. Which of the following illustrates the constructive nature of memory?

a. Janice keeps calling her new boyfriend by her old boyfriend's name.
b. After studying all afternoon and then getting drunk in the evening, Don can't remember the material he studied.
c. After getting some good news, elated Kareem has a flood of good memories from his younger years.
d. Although elderly Mrs. Harvey, who has Alzheimer's disease, has many gaps in her memory, she invents sensible accounts of her activities so that her family will not worry.

16. To help him remember the order of ingredients in difficult recipes, master chef Giulio often associates them with the route he walks to work each day. Giulio is using which mnemonic technique?

a. peg-word system   c. the method of loci
b. acronyms   d. chunking

17. During basketball practice Jan's head was painfully elbowed. If the trauma to her brain disrupts her memory, we would expect that Jan would be most likely to forget:

a. the name of her teammates.
b. her telephone number.
c. the name of the play during which she was elbowed.
d. the details of events that happened shortly after the incident.

18. After suffering damage to the hippocampus, a person would probably:

a. lose memory for skills such as bicycle riding.
b. be incapable of being classically conditioned.
c. lose the ability to store new facts.
d. experience all of the above changes.

19. When he was 8 years old, Frank was questioned by the police about a summer camp counselor suspected of molesting children. Even though he was not, in fact, molested by the counselor, today 19-year-old Frank "remembers" the counselor touching him inappropriately. Frank's false memory is an example of which "sin" of memory?

a. blocking   c. misattribution
b. transience   d. suggestibility

20. The concept of working memory is analogous to a computer's:

a. read-only memory (ROM).
b. random-access memory (RAM).
c. mouse.
d. keyboard.

Essay Question

Discuss the points of agreement among experts regarding the validity of recovered memories of child abuse. (Use the space below to list the points you want to make, and organize them. Then write the essay on a separate piece of paper.)

Key Terms

Using your own words, on a separate piece of paper write a brief definition or explanation of each of the following terms.

1. memory
2. flashbulb memory
3. encoding
4. storage
5. retrieval
6. sensory memory
7. short-term memory
8. long-term memory
9. automatic processing
10. effortful processing
11. rehearsal
12. spacing effect
13. serial position effect
14. imagery
15. mnemonics
16. chunking
17. iconic memory
18. echoic memory
19. long-term potentiation (LTP)
20. amnesia
21. implicit memory
22. explicit memory
23. hippocampus
24. recall
25. recognition
26. relearning
27. priming
28. déjà vu
29. mood-congruent memory
30. proactive interference
31. retroactive interference
32. repression
33. misinformation effect
34. source amnesia

Summing Up

Complete the following flow chart.

INFORMATION PROCESSING

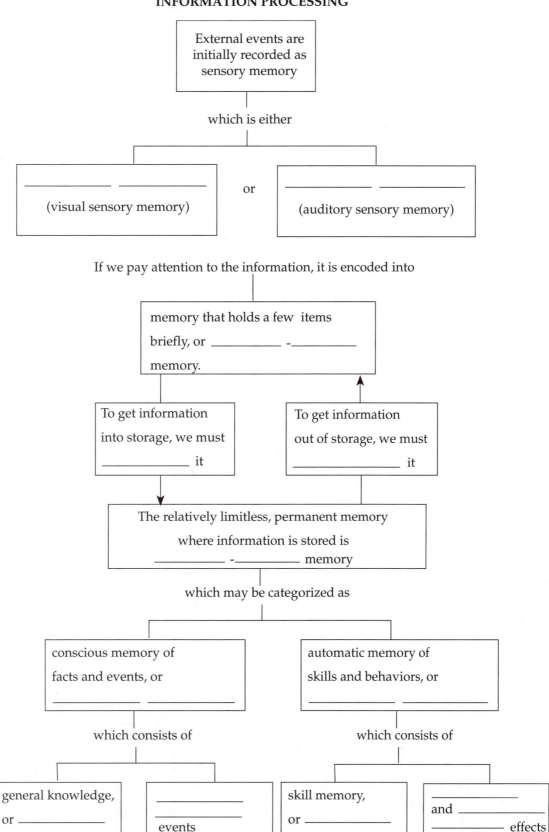

External events are
initially recorded as
sensory memory

which is either

_____ _____

(visual sensory memory)

or

_____ _____

(auditory sensory memory)

If we pay attention to the information, it is encoded into

memory that holds a few items

briefly, or _____ -_____

memory.

To get information
into storage, we must
_____ it

To get information
out of storage, we must
_____ it

The relatively limitless, permanent memory

where information is stored is

_____ -_____ memory

which may be categorized as

conscious memory of
facts and events, or
_____ _____

automatic memory of
skills and behaviors, or
_____ _____

which consists of

which consists of

general knowledge,

or _____

_____
_____
events

skill memory,

or _____

_____
and _____
_____ effects

Answers

The Phenomenon of Memory

Section Preview

1. To remember any event requires that we some-how get information into our brain (encoding), retain it (storage) as short- or long-term memory, and get it back out (retrieval). These three steps apply not only to human memory but also to other information-processing systems, such as computers. According to Atkinson and Shiffrin's three-stage processing model, we first record to-be-remembered information as a brief sensory memory, from which it is processed into a short-term memory and then encoded into a durable long-term memory.

Stepping Through the Section

1. memory
2. flashbulb
3. information-processing; encoding; storage; retrieval
4. three-stage processing; sensory memory; short-term; encoded; long-term
5. working; RAM

Encoding: Getting Information In

Section Preview

1. Encoding is the process by which sensory information is transferred into the memory system. Information about space, time, and frequency, as well as well-learned information, is encoded with little or no effort (automatic processing). Encoding of most other types of information requires attention and conscious rehearsal (effortful processing).

2. Ebbinghaus demonstrated that the amount of material remembered depends on the time spent rehearsing it. Even after material is learned, additional rehearsal (overlearning) increases retention.

   Experiments show that distributed study yields better long-term retention than cramming (spacing effect).

   The serial position effect refers to the finding that people often remember the first and last items in a list better than they do middle items.

3. When processing verbal information, we usually encode its meaning. Recall of information that is meaningful is particularly good.

   The imagery principle—that people have excellent memory for pictures and picture-evoking words—is at the heart of memory-enhancing mnemonic devices. In the method of loci and the "peg-word" system, we associate to-be-remembered items with visual codes.

   Organizing information into meaningful units, or chunks, also improves memory. The use of acronyms and hierarchies, for example, can facilitate both retention and retrieval.

Stepping Through the Section

1. automatic; effortful

Automatic processing includes the encoding of information about space, time, and frequency. It also includes the encoding of word meaning, a type of encoding that appears to be learned. Effortful processing, or encoding that requires attention and effort, is used to encode material like telephone numbers, word lists, textbook chapters, and so on.

2. rehearsal
3. Ebbinghaus; fewer
4. overlearning
5. most; next-in-line
6. spacing effect; expand spaced rehearsal
7. serial position effect; better
8. meaning; image; mentally organizing
9. imagery
10. 3 or 4
11. better; rosy retrospection
12. mnemonic; method of loci
13. peg-word
14. chunks; acronym
15. hierarchies

Storage: Retaining Information

Section Preview

1. Iconic memory is momentary photographic memory in which the eyes register an exact representation of a scene. George Sperling first demonstrated the existence of this type of sensory memory, which lasts for only about a few tenths of a second. Sensory memory for sound, called echoic memory, disappears after 3 or 4 seconds.

2. Studies by Peterson and Peterson demonstrate that without active processing, short-term memories have a limited life. Short-term memory stores approximately seven chunks of information. This type of memory is slightly better for random digits than for random letters and is slightly better for information we hear rather than see. Our capacity for storing long-term memories is essentially limitless. However, we do not store long-

term memories with the exactness of a tape recorder. Rather, forgetting occurs as new experiences interfere with retrieval and as the physical memory trace gradually decays.

3. Lashley's studies demonstrated that memories do not reside in single, specific parts of the cortex. Gerard demonstrated that lowering animals' body temperatures until their brains' electrical activity ceased did not disrupt long-term memories. Kandel and Schwartz found that when learning occurs in sea snails, more of the neurotransmitter serotonin is released at certain synapses, and neural transmission is more efficient. This increased efficiency, called long-term potentiation, may be the neural basis for learning and memory. Other studies have shown that when LTP is blocked by drugs, learning is disrupted. Conversely, learning and retention are boosted by emotion-triggered hormonal changes.

4. Although amnesia victims often can't recall new facts or recent experiences, most are capable of learning new skills. This suggests that there are two distinct types of memory: implicit (procedural) memory of skills and explicit (declarative) memory of facts and experiences that are consciously known.

The fact that most amnesia patients have suffered damage to the hippocampus suggests that this limbic structure plays a crucial role in the processing of explicit memories. Because older memories remain intact in amnesia victims, the hippocampus cannot be the permanent storehouse for such memories. It is likely that the hippocampus functions as a relay station that feeds new information to other brain circuits for permanent storage. In contrast, the cerebellum seems to be the site of implicit memories. Animal conditioning studies and studies of human patients with a damaged cerebellum demonstrate that when this area of the brain is not functioning, learning is disrupted.

Stepping Through the Section

1. storage
2. sensory
3. about half; more; iconic
4. echoic; less; 3 or 4 seconds
5. rehearsal; active
6. 7
7. digits; letters; better
8. 2
9. unlimited (limitless)

10. do not
11. interfere; decays
12. cortexes; remembered
13. electrical
14. synapses
15. serotonin
16. less; receptor sites; long-term potentiation; drug; enzyme; LTP; faster
17. will not; will
18. facilitate; disrupt
19. amnesia; is not
20. have not; implicit; are not; explicit
21. hippocampus; explicit; verbal; visual
22. temporarily; do; frontal; temporal
23. implicit; eye-blink; amygdala; fear; implicit
24. infantile; hippocampus

Retrieval: Getting Information Out

Section Preview

1. Recall is the ability to retrieve information not in conscious awareness. Recognition is a measure of memory in which one need only identify previously learned information. Relearning measures the amount of time saved when previously learned information is learned for a second time. Tests of recognition and relearning typically reveal that people remember more than they can recall. Recognition tests of memory are "easier" because they provide retrieval cues that serve as reminders of information that could not otherwise be recalled.

2. Priming and context effects indicate the importance of retrieval cues in memory. Emotions also trigger memories. State-dependent memory is the phenomenon that things learned in one emotional state are more easily recalled when we are again in the same state. Another aspect of this phenomenon is that our current mood influences our retrieval of past experiences. Mood also influences how we interpret other people's behavior and how attentive we are to new information.

Stepping Through the Section

1. recall
2. recall; recognize
3. relearn; more
4. priming; encode
5. the same

The déjà vu experience is most likely the result of being in a context similar to one that we *have* actually been in before. If we have previously been in a similar situation, though we cannot recall what it was, the current situation may present cues that unconsciously help us to retrieve the earlier experience.

   6. state-dependent

When happy, for example, we perceive things in a positive light and recall happy events; these perceptions and memories, in turn, prolong our good mood. Moods also influence how we interpret other people's behavior.

   7. rejecting, punitive, and guilt-promoting; have never suffered depression

Forgetting

Section Preview

   1. Daniel Schacter's seven sins of memory are grouped into three categories: sins of forgetting, sins of distortion, and a sin of intrusion. Broadly, these identify the different ways people forget. The first category can be applied to encoding failure, storage decay, and retrieval failure. The second refers to the ways in which our memory reconstructs reality. The final category deals with motivated forgetting of unwanted memories, for example.

   2. Much of the material we think of as having been forgotten was never "remembered." Although it was sensed, it never entered the memory system because it was not encoded; therefore, its "loss" can be attributed to encoding failure. The areas of the brain responsible for encoding become less responsive as we age, which is one reason that older people tend to recall less than younger adults do.

      Even when information has been encoded well, it may gradually fade with time. Ebbinghaus' famous "forgetting curve" and Bahrick's study of long-term retention of Spanish vocabulary showed that most forgetting occurs relatively soon after learning.

   3. Another explanation for the forgetting curve is that experiences interfere with retrieval. Proactive interference refers to the disruptive effect of previous learning on the recall of new information. Retroactive interference refers to the disruptive effect of new information on the recall of previous information. Jenkins and Dallenbach's classic study demonstrated that retroactive interference was reduced when subjects slept following a learning episode, presumably because the num-

ber of potentially interfering events was minimized.

Motivated forgetting refers to the irretrievability of memories that are embarrassing to remember. Similarly, with his concept of repression Freud proposed that memory is self-censoring. According to this viewpoint, repressed memories remain intact and may be retrieved at some later time.

Stepping Through the Section

   1. forgetting; distortion; intrusion
   2. encoding; storage decay; retrieval failure; construction; unwanted
   3. never actually enters the memory system; encoding; less
   4. soon; storage decay
   5. retrieval
   6. interference
   7. proactive interference; retroactive interference
   8. better
   9. positive transfer
   10. repression; less

Memory Construction

Section Preview

   1. Memory retrieval does not consist merely of a literal reporting of stored information. Instead, memories are constructed as we encode them, then alter them in the face of new experiences. Loftus and Palmer have shown that after exposure to subtle misinformation, eyewitnesses to an incident incorrectly recalled the actual incident (the misinformation effect). Another phenomenon, *source amnesia*, is at the heart of many false memories. This occurs whenever we misattribute an event that we experienced, read about, or imagined to the wrong source. Memory construction also explains why "hypnotically refreshed" memories often incorporate false information.

   2. Studies of eyewitness memory demonstrate that young children are more suggestible to memory plants than older children or adults. However, children are especially credible when questioned by a neutral person who asks nonleading questions.

   3. Researchers are skeptical of such claims because, although recovered memories are commonplace, memories of things happening before age 3 as

well as those "recovered" under hypnosis or the influence of drugs are unreliable. In addition, the "recovery" of painful memory rests on the assumption that the human mind commonly represses traumatic experiences—an assumption that increasingly is being challenged by contemporary researchers.

Stepping Through the Section

1. construction

2. misinformation effect; can; powerful (vivid) imaginations; false memory

When people viewed a film of a traffic accident and were quizzed a week later, misleading postevent information was found to influence recall of the event. Phrasing of questions affected answers; the word "smashed," for instance, made viewers mistakenly think they had seen broken glass.

3. hypnosis

4. source amnesia; misattribute

5. are; questioned

6. 3; infantile amnesia

Improving Memory

Section Preview

1. Suggestions for improving memory include rehearsing material over many separate and distributed study sessions with the objective of overlearning material. Studying should also involve active rehearsal, rather than mindless repetition of information. Organizing information, relating material to what is already known, developing numerous retrieval cues, and using mnemonic devices that incorporate vivid imagery are helpful too. Frequent activation of retrieval cues, such as the context and mood in which the original learning occurred, can also help strengthen memory, as can recalling events while they are fresh, before possible misinformation is encountered. Studying should also be arranged to minimize potential sources of interference. Finally, self-tests in the same format (recall or recognition) that will later be used on the actual test are useful. (The SQ3R technique described in Chapter 1 of the text incorporates several of these strategies.)

Progress Test 1

Multiple-Choice Questions

1. **d.** is the answer. Information must be encoded, or put into appropriate form; stored, or retained over time; and retrieved, or located and gotten out when needed. (p. 259)

2. **a.** is the answer. Iconic memory is our fleeting memory of visual stimuli. (p. 266)
   b. Echoic memory is auditory sensory memory.
   c. There is no such thing as photomemory.
   d. Implicit memory is memory for how to do something, not a form of sensory memory.

3. **e.** is the answer. Echoic memories last 3 to 4 seconds. (p. 266)

4. **d.** is the answer. Retrieval refers to the *process* of remembering. (p. 272)

5. **c.** is the answer. (p. 266)

6. **d.** is the answer. (p. 263)
   a. There is no such term as "consolidation techniques."
   b. & c. Imagery and encoding strategies are important in storing new memories, but mnemonic device is the general designation of techniques that facilitate memory, such as acronyms and the peg-word system.

7. **e.** is the answer. (p. 264)
   a. There is no such process of "consolidating."
   b. Organization *does* enhance memory, but it does so through hierarchies, not grouping.
   c. Memory construction refers to the ways in which memories are altered by the individual's basic assumptions and experiences.
   d. Encoding refers to the processing of information into the memory system.

8. **c.** is the answer. Kandel and Schwartz found that when learning occurred in the sea snail *Aplysia*, serotonin was released at certain synapses, which then became more efficient at signal transmission. (p. 268)

9. **b.** is the answer. In essence, we construct our memories, bringing them into line with our biases and assumptions, as well as with our subsequent experiences. (pp. 281–282)
   a. If this were true, it would mean that memory construction does not occur. Through memory construction, memories may deviate significantly from the original experiences.
   c. There is no evidence that such chemical transfers occur.
   d. Many long-term memories are apparently unlimited in duration.

10. **d.** is the answer. In general, being in a context similar to that in which you experienced something will tend to help you recall the experience. (p. 273)
   a. & b. The learning environment per se—and its familiarity or exoticness—did not affect retention.

11. a. is the answer. (p. 261)

b. & d. The text does not suggest that there is an optimal interval between encoding and retrieval.

c. Learning increases the efficiency of synaptic transmission in certain neurons, but not by altering the size of the synapse.

12. c. is the answer. (p. 268)

13. d. is the answer. When asked to recall all the letters, participants could recall only about half; however, if immediately after the presentation they were signaled to recall a particular row, their recall was near perfect. This showed that they had a brief photographic memory—so brief that it faded in less time than it would have taken to say all nine letters. (p. 265)

14. b. is the answer. Because amnesia victims lose their fact (explicit) memories but not their skill (implicit) memories or their capacity to learn, it appears that human memory can be divided into two distinct types. (p. 270)

d. As studies of amnesia victims show, memory losses following damage to the hippocampus are quite predictable.

15. d. is the answer. (p. 270)

a. & b. Explicit memory (also called declarative memory) is memory of facts and experiences that one can consciously know and declare.

c. Episodic memory is explicit memory for personally experienced events.

16. d. is the answer. (p. 274)

a. State-dependent memory is the phenomenon in which information is best retrieved when the person is in the same emotional or physiological state he or she was in when the material was learned.

b. Encoding failure occurs when a person has not processed information sufficiently for it to enter the memory system.

c. Priming is the process by which a memory is activated through retrieval of an associated memory.

17. b. is the answer. When the words were organized into categories, recall was two to three times better, indicating the benefits of hierarchical organization in memory. (pp. 264–265)

d. This study did not examine the use of mnemonic devices.

18. a. is the answer. We remember skills acquired in infancy, as such memories are recorded in earlier developing brain regions, but declarative memories involve the hippocampus. (p. 272)

b., c., & d. There is no evidence that serotonin levels or association areas are deficient until age 3. Moreover, such proposals are unlikely, as they

wouldn't explain why we remember skills learned in infancy while forgetting events experienced.

19. d. is the answer. It is in both encoding and retrieval that we construct our memories, and as Loftus's studies showed, leading questions affect people's memory construction. (p. 283)

a. The memory encoding occurred at the time of the event in question, not during questioning by the hypnotist.

b. State-dependent memory refers to the influence of one's own emotional or physiological state on encoding and retrieval, and would not apply here.

c. Proactive interference is the interfering effect of prior learning on the recall of new information.

20. b. is the answer. (p. 271)

a. The hippocampus is a temporary processing site for *explicit memories*.

c. & d. These areas of the brain are not directly involved in the memory system.

21. b. is the answer. Blocking is an example of retrieval failure. Each of the others is an example of a "sin of distortion," in which memories, although inaccurate, are retrieved. (p. 276)

Matching Items

1. n (p. 266)	**6.** c (p. 261)	**11.** g (p. 278)
2. o (p. 259)	**7.** e (p. 263)	**12.** j (p. 284)
3. l (p. 263)	**8.** f (p. 263)	**13.** h (p. 276)
4. a (p. 281)	**9.** i (p. 278)	**14.** k (p. 276)
5. m (p. 274)	**10.** b (p. 272)	**15.** d (p. 276)

Progress Test 2

Multiple-Choice Questions

1. c. is the answer. As Ebbinghaus and Bahrick both showed, most of the forgetting that is going to occur happens soon after learning. (p. 277)

2. d. is the answer. (p. 278)

a. & b. This study did not find evidence that memories fade (decay) with time.

c. When one is awake, there are many *more* potential sources of memory interference than when one is asleep.

3. a. is the answer. A test of recall presents the fewest retrieval cues and usually produces the most limited retrieval. (p. 272)

4. d. is the answer. (p. 271)

5. e. is the answer. According to the serial position effect, items at the beginning and end of a list tend to be remembered best. (p. 261)

6. a. is the answer. (p. 262)

b. In the serial position effect, the items in the middle of the list always show the *poorest* retention.

c. & d. Delayed recall erases the memory facilitation for items at the end of the list.

7. d. is the answer. Surprisingly, Lashley found that no matter where he cut, the rats had at least a partial memory of how to solve the maze. (p. 268)

a. & b. Lashley's studies did not investigate the significance of the interval between learning and cortical lesioning.

8. a. is the answer. A blow to the head wipes out recent experiences because information in STM did not have time to consolidate into LTM. (p. 269)

b. Such injuries disrupt the formation, rather than the retrieval, of memories.

c. Although nutrition plays an important role in neural functioning, the effects of such injuries are independent of nutrition.

9. d. is the answer. (p. 269)

10. c. is the answer. According to Freud, we repress painful memories to preserve our self-concepts. (pp. 281–282)

a. & b. The fact that repressed memories can sometimes be retrieved suggests that they were encoded and have not decayed with time.

11. d. is the answer. When misled by the phrasings of questions, subjects incorrectly recalled details of the film and even "remembered" objects that weren't there. (pp. 281–282)

12. c. is the answer. Speed reading, which entails little active rehearsal, yields poor retention. (p. 288)

13. b. is the answer. (p. 259)

a. Encoding is the process of getting information *into* memory.

c. Rehearsal is the conscious repetition of information in order to maintain it in memory.

d. Storage is the maintenance of encoded material over time.

14. b. is the answer. Amnesia patients typically have suffered damage to the hippocampus, a brain structure involved in processing explicit memories for facts. (p. 271)

a. Amnesia patients do retain implicit memories for how to do things; these are processed in the more ancient parts of the brain.

c. & d. Amnesia patients generally do not experience impairment in their iconic and echoic sensory memories.

15. b. is the answer. (pp. 260, 266)

a. Information in short-term memory has *already* been encoded.

c. Iconic and echoic are types of *sensory* memory.

d. Retrieval is the process of getting material out of storage and into conscious, short-term memory. Thus, all material in short-term memory has either already been retrieved or is about to be placed in storage.

16. c. is the answer. By breaking concepts down into subconcepts and yet smaller divisions and showing the relationships among these, hierarchies facilitate information processing. Use of main heads and subheads is an example of the organization of textbook chapters into hierarchies. (p. 264)

a. Mnemonic devices are the method of loci, acronyms, and other memory *techniques* that facilitate retention.

b. Chunks are organizations of knowledge into familiar, manageable units.

d. Recognition is a measure of retention.

17. d. is the answer. (pp. 285–286)

18. c. is the answer. Short-term recall is slightly better for information we hear rather than see, because echoic memory momentarily outlasts iconic memory. (p. 266)

a. Meaningful stimuli, such as words, are usually remembered more easily than meaningless stimuli, such as random letters.

b. Iconic memory does not last as long as echoic memory in short-term recall.

d. Although context is a powerful retrieval cue, there is no general facilitation of memory in an unusual context.

19. c. is the answer. Loftus and Palmer found that eyewitness testimony could easily be altered when questions were phrased to imply misleading information. (pp. 281–282)

a. Although memories *are* constructed during encoding, the misinformation effect is a retrieval, rather than an encoding, phenomenon.

b. & d. In fact, just the opposite is true.

20. d. is the answer. (p. 276)

a. This defines absent-mindedness.

b. This is misattribution.

c. This is bias.

21. a. is the answer. (p. 259)

b. Herman Ebbinghaus conducted pioneering studies of verbal learning and memory.

c. Loftus and Palmer conducted influential research studies of eyewitness memory.

d. George Sperling is known for his research studies of iconic memory.

True–False Items

1. T (p. 261)	**6.** T (p. 276)
2. T (p. 263)	**7.** F (p. 278)
3. F (p. 286)	**8.** T (p. 288)
4. T (p. 272)	**9.** F (p. 281)
5. T (p. 277)	**10.** F (p. 288)

Review and Reflect

Multiple-Choice Questions

1. **d.** is the answer. (p. 272)
   a., b., & e. In order to correctly answer either type of question, the knowledge must have been encoded and stored.
   c. With fill-in-the-blank questions, the answer must be recalled with no retrieval cues other than the question. With multiple-choice questions, the correct answer merely has to be recognized from among several alternatives.

2. **d.** is the answer. (p. 262)
   a. & b. A serial position effect would presumably occur whether the study and retrieval contexts were the same or different.
   c. As researchers found, when recall is delayed, only the first items in a list are recalled more accurately than the others. With immediate recall, both the first and last items are recalled more accurately.

3. **b.** is the answer. Retroactive interference is the disruption of something you once learned by new information. (p. 278)
   a. Proactive interference occurs when old information makes it difficult to correctly remember new information.
   c. & d. Interference produces forgetting even when the forgotten material was effectively encoded and stored. Janice's problem is at the level of retrieval.
   e. There is no reason to believe that Janice's old locker combination is a painful memory.

4. **b.** is the answer. (pp. 278, 279)
   a., c., & d. Involvement in other activities, even just eating or listening to music, is more disruptive than sleeping.

5. **c.** is the answer. Susan's memories are affected by her bad mood. (p. 274)
   a. Priming refers to the conscious or unconscious activation of particular associations in memory.
   b. Memory construction refers to changes in memory as new experiences occur.
   d. Although Susan's difficulty in recalling the good could be considered retrieval failure, it is

caused by the mood-congruent effect, which is therefore the best explanation.
   e. Repression involves the suppression of *painful* memories.

6. **a.** is the answer. Priming is the conscious or unconscious activation of particular associations in memory. (p. 273)
   b. Déjà vu is the false impression of having previously experienced a current situation.
   c. That Martina is able to retrieve her former classmates' names implies that they already have been encoded.
   d. Relearning is a measure of retention based on how long it takes to relearn something already mastered. Martina is recalling her former classmates' names, not relearning them.

7. **b.** is the answer. Being back in the context in which the original experiences occurred triggered memories of these experiences. (p. 273)
   a. The memories were triggered by similarity of place, not mood.
   c. Retroactive interference would involve difficulties in retrieving old memories.
   d. Echoic memory refers to momentary memory of auditory stimuli.
   e. Iconic memory refers to momentary memory of visual stimuli.

8. **a.** is the answer. Time and space—and therefore sequences of events—are often automatically processed. (p. 260)
   b. That she had *little difficulty* indicates that the processing was automatic, rather than effortful.
   c. & d. State-dependent memory and priming have nothing to do with the automatic processing of space and time.

9. **d.** is the answer. Flashbulb memories are unusually clear memories of emotionally significant moments in life. (p. 258)

10. **a.** is the answer. Proactive interference occurs when old information makes it difficult to recall new information. (p. 278)
    b. If Carlos were having trouble remembering the old extension, this answer would be correct.
    c. & d. Carlos has successfully encoded and stored the extension; he's just having problems retrieving it.

11. **b.** is the answer. (p. 276)

12. **c.** is the answer. (p. 278)
    a. & b. The name of your homeroom teacher, which you probably heard at least once each day of school, was surely processed into memory (encoded) and maintained there for some time (stored).

d. State-dependent memory is the tendency to recall information best in the same emotional or physiological state as when it was learned. It is unlikely that a single state was associated with learning your homeroom teacher's name.

13. **a.** is the answer. Short-term memory capacity is approximately seven digits. (p. 266)
    b. Because iconic memory lasts no more than a second or so, regardless of how much material is experienced, this cannot be the explanation for Brenda's difficulty.
    c. The final four digits should be no more difficult to organize into chunks than the first five digits of the address code.
    d. Memory for digits is an example of explicit, rather than implicit, memory.

14. **a.** is the answer. (p. 281)
    b. Although Lewis's difficulty in recalling these memories could be considered retrieval failure, it is caused by repression, which is therefore the *best* explanation.
    c. This answer is incorrect because it is clear that Lewis fails to remember these experiences because they are painful memories and not because he is in a different emotional or physiological state.
    d. Flashbulb memories are especially *vivid* memories for emotionally significant events. Lewis has no memory at all.
    e. Implicit memories are memories of skills.

15. **d.** is the answer. (p. 282)
    a. This is an example of proactive interference.
    b. This is an example of the disruptive effects of depressant drugs, such as alcohol, on the formation of new memories.
    c. This is mood-congruent memory.

16. **c.** is the answer. (p. 263)
    a. The peg-word system involves developing associations between rhyming words in a jingle and to-be-remembered items.
    b. Acronyms are words created from the first letters of to-be-remembered words.
    d. Chunking is the organization of information into meaningful units, such as acronyms.

17. **c.** is the answer. Blows to the head usually disrupt the most recent experiences, such as this one, rather than long-term memories like those in choices a. and b., or new learning such as that in choice d. (p. 269)

18. **c.** is the answer. The hippocampus is involved in processing new facts for storage. (p. 271)
    a., b., & d. Studies of amnesia victims with hippocampal damage show that neither classical conditioning nor skill memory are impaired, indicating that these aspects of memory are controlled by more primitive regions of the brain.

19. **d.** is the answer. In this example, the questions Frank was asked to answer created misinformation that later became part of his memory. (p. 276)
    a. This answer would have been correct if Frank had been molested by the counselor but had failed to encode it in his memory.
    b. This answer would have been correct if Frank had been molested but the memory trace had faded with time.
    c. Misattribution might have occurred if Frank had witnessed another camper being molested and later recalled himself as the actual victim.

20. **b.** is the answer. Like a computer's RAM, working memory integrates information coming in from a mouse (c.) or keyboard (d.) with that retrieved from long-term storage. (p. 260)

Essay Question

Experts agree that child abuse is a real problem that can have long-term adverse effects on individuals. They also acknowledge that forgetting of isolated events, both good and bad, is an ordinary part of life. Although experts all accept the fact that recovered memories are commonplace, they warn that memories "recovered" under hypnosis or with the use of drugs are unreliable, as are memories of events before age 3. Finally, they agree that memories can be traumatic, whether real or false.

Key Terms

1. **Memory** is the persistence of learning over time through the storage and retrieval of information. (p. 257)

2. A **flashbulb memory** is an unusually vivid memory of an emotionally important moment or event. (p. 258)

3. **Encoding** is the first step in memory; information is translated into some form that enables it to enter our memory system. (p. 259)

4. **Storage** is the process by which encoded information is maintained over time. (p. 259)

5. **Retrieval** is the process of bringing to consciousness information from memory storage. (p. 259)

6. **Sensory memory** is the immediate, initial recording of sensory information in the memory system. (p. 259)

7. **Short-term memory** is conscious memory, which can hold about seven items for a short time. (p. 259)

8. **Long-term memory** is the relatively permanent and unlimited capacity memory system into which information from short-term memory may pass. (p. 259)

9. **Automatic processing** refers to our unconscious encoding of incidental information such as space, time, and frequency and of well-learned information. (p. 260)

10. **Effortful processing** is encoding that requires attention and conscious effort. (p. 260)

11. **Rehearsal** is the conscious, effortful repetition of information that you are trying either to maintain in consciousness or to encode for storage. (p. 260)

12. The **spacing effect** is the tendency for distributed study or practice to yield better long-term retention than massed study or practice. (p. 261)

13. The **serial position effect** is the tendency for items at the beginning and end of a list to be more easily retained than those in the middle. (pp. 261–262)

14. **Imagery** refers to mental pictures and can be an important aid to effortful processing. (p. 263)

15. **Mnemonics** are memory aids (the method of loci, acronyms, peg-words, etc.), which often use visual imagery. (p. 263)

16. **Chunking** is the memory technique of organizing material into familiar, meaningful units. (p. 264)

17. **Iconic memory** is the visual sensory memory consisting of a perfect photographic memory, which lasts no more than a few tenths of a second. (p. 266)

    Memory aid: *Icon* means "image" or "representation." **Iconic memory** consists of brief visual images.

18. **Echoic memory** is the momentary sensory memory of auditory stimuli, lasting about 3 or 4 seconds. (p. 266)

19. **Long-term potentiation (LTP)** is an increase in a synapse's firing potential following brief, rapid stimulation. LTP is believed to be the neural basis for learning and memory. (pp. 268–269)

20. **Amnesia** is the loss of memory. (p. 269)

21. **Implicit memories** are memories of skills, preferences, and dispositions. These memories are evidently processed, not by the hippocampus, but by a more primitive part of the brain, the cerebellum. They are also called procedural or nondeclarative memories. (p. 270)

22. **Explicit memories** are memories of facts, including names, images, and events. They are also called declarative memories. (p. 270)

23. The **hippocampus** is a neural center located in the limbic system that is important in the processing of explicit memories for storage. (p. 271)

24. **Recall** is a measure of retention in which the person must remember, with few retrieval cues, information learned earlier. (p. 272)

25. **Recognition** is a measure of retention in which one need only identify, rather than recall, previously learned information. (p. 272)

26. **Relearning** is also a measure of retention in that the less time it takes to relearn information, the more that information has been retained. (p. 272)

27. **Priming** is the activation, often unconscious, of a web of associations in memory in order to retrieve a specific memory. (p. 273)

28. **Déjà vu** is the false sense that you have already experienced a current situation. (p. 274)

29. **Mood-congruent memory** is the tendency to recall experiences that are consistent with our current mood. (p. 274)

30. **Proactive interference** is the disruptive effect of something you already have learned on your efforts to learn or recall new information. (p. 278)

31. **Retroactive interference** is the disruptive effect of something recently learned on old knowledge. (p. 278)

    Memory aid: *Retro* means "backward." **Retroactive interference** is "backward-acting" interference.

32. **Repression** is an example of motivated forgetting in that painful and unacceptable memories are prevented from entering consciousness. In psychoanalytic theory, it is the basic defense mechanism. (p. 281)

33. The **misinformation effect** is the tendency of eyewitnesses to an event to incorporate misleading information into their memories of an event. (p. 281)

34. At the heart of many false memories, **source amnesia** refers to misattributing an event to the wrong source. (p. 284)

Summing Up

Information Processing

External events are initially recorded as sensory memory, which is either *iconic memory* (visual sensory memory) or *echoic memory* (auditory sensory memory). If we pay attention to the information, it is encoded into memory that holds a few items briefly, or *short-term* memory. To get information into storage, we must *encode* it. To get information out of storage, we must *retrieve* it. The relatively limitless, permanent memory where information is stored is *long-term* memory, which is categorized as *explicit memory* (conscious memory of facts and events) or *implicit memory* (automatic memory of skills and behaviors). Explicit memory consists of general knowledge (*facts*) and *personally experienced* events. Implicit memory includes skill memory (*motor and cognitive skills*) and *classical* and *operant conditioning* effects.

FOCUS ON VOCABULARY AND LANGUAGE

The Phenomenon of Memory

Page 257: Your memory is your mind's *storehouse,* the *reservoir* of your accumulated learning. Myers is using an analogy to help you understand the general concept of memory. Both *storehouses* and *reservoirs* are used to keep materials (water, food, etc.) until we need them. Likewise, your memory system retains most of the things you experienced (*accumulated learning*), and items can be recalled or retrieved as required.

Page 257: Some studies have explored *the roots and fruits* of memory loss. Some researchers have examined the origins and causes (*roots*) of memory loss, and others have noted the benefits (*fruits*) of not having a perfect memory for everything that happens.

Page 258: . . . *medal winners in a memory Olympics.* . . . People with exceptional memories are being likened or compared to the top athletes in the Olympic Games. S, for example, would clearly receive the top prize (*medal winner*) in any competition in which remembering vast amounts of information was being tested (*memory Olympics*).

Page 258: Do these memory *feats* make your own memory seem *feeble?* Myers is pointing out that although S may have demonstrated spectacular abilities in remembering all sorts of things (*memory feats*), normal memory in the average person is no less astounding in many ways (*pretty staggering*). Despite our occasional failures, our ordinary memory accomplishments, which we tend to take for granted, are quite remarkable (*they are far from being feeble*).

Page 259: Instead we *shine the flashlight beam of our attention on* certain incoming stimuli—often novel or important stimuli. One model of memory suggests that we only focus on (*shine the flashlight beam of our attention on*) and process one part or aspect of the total sensory input, particularly new (*novel*) or important stimuli. We can also locate and bring back stored information from long-term memory (**LTM**) into short-term memory (**STM**).

Encoding: Getting Information In

Page 260: . . . *boost* . . . One way to improve and increase the power of our memory is to use **rehearsal**. Thus, actively repeating some new information (such as a stranger's name or new terminology) will help strengthen (*boost*) our ability to remember this material. As Myers notes it is important for effective retention to space out or distribute rehearsals over time (the **spacing effect**) rather than doing the repetitions all at once (massed practice or cramming).

Page 261: His [Ebbinghaus's] solution was to form a list of all possible *nonsense syllables* created by *sandwiching* a vowel between two consonants. In order to avoid using meaningful words with prior associations, Hermann Ebbinghaus invented three-letter words that made no sense and had no meaning (*nonsense syllables*). He did this by putting a vowel (*sandwiching it*) between two consonants. His nonsense (*meaningless*) syllables were consonant (C), vowel (V), consonant (C), or CVCs.

Page 262: Gordon Bower and Daniel Morrow (1990) liken our minds to theater directors who, *given a raw script,* imagine a *finished stage production.* This suggests that what we remember is not an exact replica of reality. We construct some mental representation or model (*finished stage production*) from the basic sensory information (*raw script*) available to us, and so, when we recall something, it is our own version (*mental model*) that comes to mind and not the real thing.

Page 263: Thanks to the durability of our most vivid images, we recall our experiences with *mental snapshots* of their best or worst moments. The use of imagery or mental pictures (*snapshots*) is one way to enhance recall. We have exceptionally good memory for pictures and ideas that are encoded using visual imagery. As Myers notes, "imagery is at the heart of many memory aids" (e.g., method of loci, peg-word, etc.).

Page 263: For example, the *"peg-word"* system requires that you first memorize a *jingle.* A *jingle* is an easily remembered succession of words that ring or resound against each other due to alliteration or rhyme and are often used in radio or TV commercials. The mnemonic (memory aid) called the *"peg-word"* method is based on memorizing a short 10-item poem (*jingle*) that can be associated with a new list of 10 items through visual imagery. The new items are hung on, or pegged to, the familiar items.

Page 263 (caption) . . . *talk until you're blue in the face* . . . This refers to someone saying the same thing (e.g., a request, a plea, or a warning) over and over but not having any effect on the listener. You can warn people repeatedly about the dangers (*health hazards*) of sun tanning and smoking (*you can talk until you're blue in the face*) with little or no change in the target audience's behavior. Visual images of the consequences of tanning and smoking have a greater impact.

Storage: Retaining Information

Page 265: It was harder than reading by *flashes of lightning.* In his investigation of sensory storage, George Sperling showed his subjects an array of nine letters for a very brief period (for about the length of a *flash of lightning*). He demonstrated that this was sufficient time for them to briefly view (*glimpse*) all nine letters and that an image remained for less than half a second before fading away; he called this sensory image **iconic memory.**

Page 267: . . . *Sherlock Holmes* . . . Mystery writer Sir Arthur Conan Doyle's most popular character was a very intelligent and logical private detective named Sherlock Holmes. Holmes believed, as did many others, that our memory capacity was limited, much as a small empty room or attic can hold only so much furniture before it overflows. Contemporary psychologists now believe that our ability to store long-term memories is basically without any limit.

Page 267 (caption): Among animals, one contender for *champion memorist* would be a mere *birdbrain*—the Clark's nutcracker. . . . Clark's nutcracker is a small bird with a small brain (*birdbrain*) but a phenomenal memory (*champion memorist*) of where it buries its food. It can recall, after a period of more than six months, 6000 different locations of hidden food (*caches*).

Page 267: While cognitive psychologists study our memory *"software,"* neuroscientists are gaining new insights into our memory *"hardware."* . . . Throughout this chapter Myers uses the analogy of the computer as a model for how memory works. In attempting to understand memory, cognitive psychologists study the mind and how it works (*the computer "software"*) and neuroscientists study the physical aspect of the brain and the functioning of its neurons (*the computer "hardware"*).

Page 268: . . . with tongue only partly in cheek. When someone makes a statement that is not meant to be taken seriously, we note that it was said *with tongue in cheek.* When researchers stated that "memories are more of a spiritual than a physical reality," they were not totally serious (*tongue only partly in cheek*).

Page 269: Arousal sears the events onto the brain. When arousal level rises because of stress, so too do the levels of certain hormones. These in turn signal the brain that something important has happened and the events that triggered the arousal make an indelible impression on the brain much as a hot grill burns (*sears*) its shape on the surface of the meat placed on it.

Page 270: They [people with amnesia] can learn to read reversed *mirror-image writing* or do a *jigsaw puzzle and* . . . They can be classically conditioned. People who have lost the ability to remember new information (*amnesia victims*) may nevertheless be capable of learning through association (classical conditioning) and of learning to solve problems (e.g., *jigsaw puzzles*) even if they are not aware of having done so. Myers notes that these findings suggest that memory is not a single, unified system. Amnesics can learn how to *do* something (**implicit memory**) without any knowledge of this learning (**explicit**, or **declarative**, **memory**).

Page 271: Savoring that memory of your first kiss requires a *mental symphony conductor* that retrieves *snippets* from various cortical storage sites and integrates them with the emotional associations provided by your amygdala. Reliving and relishing (*savoring*) the memory of your first kiss needs the mind's equivalent of an orchestra's director and organizer (*a mental symphony's conductor*) to locate pieces (*snippets*) from different brain areas (*various cortical storage sites*) and integrate them with emotional associations provided by the amygdala.

Retrieval: Getting Information Out

Page 275: If put in a *buoyant mood* . . . people recall the world through *rose-colored glasses.* . . . Our memories are affected by our emotional states (*moods*). Thus, if we are in a good or happy (*buoyant*) mood, we are more likely to view the total situation in a more optimistic and hopeful way (*through rose-colored glasses*). Memory of events and people is influenced by the particular mood we are in, whether it is good or bad, and we tend to remember the events accordingly.

Page 275: When teenagers are *down,* their parents seem inhuman; as their mood *brightens,* their parents *morph from devils into angels.* Because our memories tend to be **mood-congruent,** we are likely to explain our present emotional state by remembering events and people as being consistent (*congruent*) with how we now feel. In one study when young adolescents were in a bad mood (*down*), they viewed their parents as cruel and uncaring (*inhuman*), but later when they were in a much better (*brighter*) mood their parents were described in much nicer terms. It seemed as though their parents had undergone an amazing change in character (*morphing from devils to angels*), but the change was simply in the teenagers' mood. As Myers notes, *"passions [or emotions] exaggerate."*

Forgetting

Page 275: Amid all the *applause for memory . . .* have any voices been heard in praise of forgetting? We tend to focus on the importance of remembering and recalling information (*there is much applause for memory*). However, if we could not forget, we would be like the Russian memory expert (*memory whiz*) S who was overwhelmed by the amount of useless information he had stored (*haunted by his junk heap of memories*). Thus, many people, from William James to contemporary cognitive psychologists, acknowledge the importance of forgetting.

Page 278: A name *may lie poised on the tip of the tongue,* waiting to be retrieved. The expression *"it's on the tip of my tongue"* refers to the feeling you get when you are trying to remember something (a name, place, etc.) but can't, even though you feel you know it and can *almost* say it (*it's on the tip of your tongue*). Given an appropriate retrieval cue (such as the first letter of the name or something it rhymes with, etc.) we can often remember the item.

Page 278: As you collect more and more information, your *mental attic* never fills, but it certainly gets *cluttered.* We may have an unlimited amount of space in our memory system or *mental attic* (a room at the top of a house), but with a constant flow of new information coming in, the storage can become disorganized (*cluttered*). The new information may get in the way of recalling old material (**retroactive interference**), or old material may block or disrupt recall of new information (**proactive interference**).

Page 280: We *sheepishly* accepted responsibility for 89 cookies. Still, we had not come close; there had been 160. The Myers family obviously loves chocolate chip cookies, and the story of how all 160 were devoured (*wolfed down, ate, scarfed, consumed*) within 24 hours (*not a crumb was left*) is quite funny but makes an important point. Embarrassed, guilty, and feeling a little foolish (*sheepish*), they could only account for and remember eating 89. This illustrates the self-serving nature of memory and how, unknowingly, we change and revise our own histories.

Page 281: The words *relit a blown-out candle* in the mind . . . Just as an extinguished (*blown-out*) candle can be reignited (*relit*) with a match, the presentation of a retrieval cue may help someone recall or retrieve a long forgotten memory. Although Freud proposed that we repress memories of painful experiences in the unconscious mind in order to protect our self-concepts and minimize anxiety, Myers notes that most contemporary memory researchers believe repression rarely, if ever, happens.

Memory Construction

Page 283: Memory construction helps explain why *"hypnotically refreshed"* memories of crimes so easily incorporate errors, some of which originate with the hypnotist's leading questions. Because of the tendency to manufacture events without being consciously aware of doing so (*memory construction*), people are likely to be influenced by suggestions and biased questions while under hypnosis. Their subsequent recollections (*"hypnotically refreshed"*) may therefore be a mixture of fact and fiction.

Page 284: Because memory is *reconstruction* as well as *reproduction,* we can't be sure whether a memory is real by how real it feels. It is difficult to determine if a memory is real simply by noting how real it feels or how confident we are about its accuracy. We not only recall and retrieve real memories (*reproduction*); we also manufacture false memories (*reconstruction*).

Page 284: If memories can be *sincere,* yet *sincerely wrong,* might children's recollections of sexual abuse be prone to err? The evidence suggests that under appropriate conditions children's memories can be reliable and accurate (*sincere*) but that they are also prone to the misinformation effect and can be misled by biased questions and suggestions; later, the children are not able to reliably separate real from false (*sincerely wrong*) memories.

Improving Memory

Page 288: Sprinkled throughout this chapter and summarized here for easy reference are *concrete* suggestions for improving memory. This chapter has many good ideas for memory improvement interspersed (*sprinkled*) throughout it. Myers has pulled them together in an easy-to-understand format—the **SQ3R** (**S**urvey, **Q**uestion, **R**ead, **R**ehearse, **R**eview) method. These real and tangible (*concrete*) methods will help you improve your memory. Use them!

chapter 9

Thinking, Language, and Intelligence

Chapter Overview

The beginning discussion of thinking emphasizes how people logically—or at times illogically—use tools such as algorithms and heuristics when making decisions and solving problems. Also explained are several common obstacles to problem solving, including fixations that prevent us from taking a fresh perspective on a problem and our bias to search for information that confirms rather than challenges existing hypotheses.

The chapter also explores language, including its development in children, relationship to thinking, and use by animals. Two theories of language acquisition are evaluated: Skinner's theory that language acquisition is based entirely on learning and Chomsky's theory that humans have a biological predisposition to acquire language.

The second part of the chapter describes the historical origins of intelligence tests and discusses several important issues concerning their use. These include the methods by which intelligence tests are constructed and whether such tests are valid, reliable, and free of bias. The chapter also discusses whether intelligence is a single general ability or several specific ones and its relationship to creativity and the extent of genetic and environmental influences on intelligence.

NOTE: Answer guidelines for all Chapter 9 questions begin on page 262.

Thinking (pp. 293–302)

> David Myers at times uses idioms that are unfamiliar to some readers. If you do not know the meaning of any of the following words, phrases, or expressions in the context in which they appear in the text, refer to pages 274–275 for an explanation: *kin to; birdier bird; stumbling upon one that worked; shoot the basketball; seat-of-the-pants; snap judgment; a broken promise; "mere statistics" on some world health ledger; plagues; flip-flop; fuels social conflict; filled with straw.*

Section Preview

First, skim the section, noting headings and boldface items. Then read the following objectives and, as you read the text, search for the information that will enable you to meet each objective. Answer guidelines begin on page 262.

1. Describe the nature, function, and formation of concepts.

2. Discuss the major problem-solving strategies, and describe the nature of insight.

3. Identify obstacles to problem solving.

4. Describe the heuristics that guide decision making, and explain how overconfidence, framing, and belief perseverance can affect judgment.

Stepping Through the Section

After you have read the section, complete the sentences and answer the questions. As you proceed, evaluate your performance by consulting the answers on page 263. Do not continue with the next section until you understand each answer. If you need to, review or reread the section in the textbook before continuing.

1. Thinking, or _____ , can be defined as _____

_____ .

Scientists who study these mental activities are called _____ _____ .

2. People tend to organize specific items into mental groupings called _____ , and many such groupings often are further organized into

_____ .

3. Concepts are typically formed through the development of a best example, or

_____ , of a category.

4. Humans are especially capable of using their reasoning powers for coping with new situations, and thus for _____

_____ .

5. Finding a problem's solution by trying each possibility is called _____

_____ _____ .

6. Logical, methodical, step-by-step procedures for solving problems are called

_____ .

7. Simple thinking strategies that provide us with problem-solving shortcuts are referred to as

_____ .

8. When you suddenly realize a problem's solution, _____ has occurred.

9. The tendency of people to look for information that verifies their preconceptions is called the

_____ _____ .

10. Not being able to take a new perspective when attempting to solve a problem is referred to as

_____ .

11. When a person is unable to envision using an object in an atypical way, _____

_____ is operating.

12. People judge how well something matches a particular prototype; this is the _____

_____ .

13. When we judge the likelihood of something occurring in terms of how readily it comes to mind, we are using the _____

_____ .

Explain how these two heuristics may lead us to make judgmental errors.

14. (Thinking Critically) Many people fear _____ more than

_____ and _____

more than _____ , despite the fact that these feats are not supported by death and injury statistics. This type of faulty thinking occurs because we fear

a. _____

b. _____

c. _____

d. _____

15. The tendency of people to overestimate the accuracy of their knowledge results in

_____ .

16. Overconfidence has _____ value because self-confident people tend to live _____ (more/less) happily and find it _____ (easier/harder) to make tough decisions. Furthermore, research has shown that when subjects are given feedback on the accuracy of their judgments, such feedback generally _____ (does/does not) help them become more realistic about how much they know.

17. Decision making can be significantly affected by the phrasing, or _____ , of an issue.

18. Research has shown that once we form a belief or a concept, it may take more convincing evidence for us to change the concept than it did to create it; this is because of _____

_____ .

Language (pp. 302–315)

> If you do not know the meaning of any of the following words, phrases, or expressions in the context in which they appear in the text, refer to pages 275–276 for an explanation: *catapulting our species forward; combine them on the fly; read lips; a Martian scientist; grammar switches are thrown; chicken-and-egg questions; rhapsodized; Spying the short stick; Were the chimps language champs or were the researchers chumps?*

Section Preview

Answer guidelines begin on page 263.

1. Trace the course of language acquisition, and discuss alternative theories of language development.

2. Discuss the impact of early experience on language development as revealed by cognitive scientists.

3. Discuss the relationship between thought and language.

4. Describe the research on animal communication, and discuss the controversy over whether animals have language.

Stepping Through the Section

Answers are provided on page 264.

1. The first stage of language development, in which children spontaneously utter different sounds, is the _____ stage. This stage typically begins at about _____ months of age. The sounds children make during this stage _____ (do/do not) include only the sounds of the language that they hear.

2. Deaf infants _____ (do/do not) babble.

3. By about _____ months of age, infant babbling begins to resemble the household language. By _____ months, the ability to perceive sound differences is _____ (lost/acquired).

4. During the second stage, called the

_____-_____ stage,

children convey complete thoughts using single
words. This stage begins at about

_____ year(s) of age.

5. During the _____-_____
stage, children speak in sentences containing
mostly nouns and verbs. This type of speech is
called _____ speech.

6. After this stage, children quickly begin to utter
longer phrases that _____ (do/do
not) follow the rules of syntax.

7. Skinner believed that language development follows the general principles of learning, including

_____ , _____ , and

_____ .

8. Other theorists believe that humans are biologically predisposed to learn language. One such
theorist is _____ , who believes that
we all are born with a _____

_____ _____ in

which _____ switches are thrown
as children experience their language.

Give several examples of linguistic behavior in children that support the argument that humans are biologically predisposed to acquire language.

9. Research by Jenny Saffran has demonstrated that
even before _____ year(s) of age,
infants are able to discern _____

_____ by analyzing which syllables
most often go together.

10. Those who learn a second language as adults
usually speak it with the _____ of
their first language. Moreover, they typically
show _____ (poorer/better) mas-
tery of the _____ of the second

language. Those who learn sign language later in
life show less brain activity in areas of the
_____ hemisphere that are active as
native signers read sign language.

11. According to the _____

_____ hypothesis, language shapes
our thinking. The linguist who proposed this
hypothesis is _____ .

12. Many people who are bilingual report feeling a
different sense of _____ , depend-
ing on which language they are using. There are
an estimated _____ languages in
the world today.

13. In several studies, researchers have found that
using the pronoun "he" (instead of "he or she")
_____ (does/does not) influence
people's thoughts concerning gender.

14. Bilingual children are better able to

_____ .

Bilingual education may also improve the
_____ of children who are in a
linguistic minority.

15. It appears that thinking _____
(can/cannot) occur without the use of language.
Athletes often supplement physical with
_____ practice.

16. In one study of psychology students preparing
for a midterm exam, the greatest benefits were
achieved by those who visualized themselves
_____ (receiving a high
grade/studying effectively).

Summarize the probable relationship between thinking and language.

17. Wolfgang Köhler demonstrated that chimpanzees
also exhibit the "aha" reaction that characterizes
reasoning by _____ .

18. Forest-dwelling chimpanzees learn to use branch-
es, stones, and other objects as _____ .

These behaviors, along with behaviors related to grooming and courtship, _____ (vary/do not vary) from one group to another, suggesting the transmission of _____ customs.

19. The Gardners attempted to communicate with the chimpanzee Washoe by teaching her

_____ _____ .

20. Human language appears to have evolved from _____ communications.

Summarize some of the arguments of skeptics of the "talking apes" research.

Intelligence (pp. 315–336)

> David Myers at times uses idioms that are unfamiliar to some readers. If you do not know the meaning of any of the following words, phrases, or expressions, in the context in which they appear in the text, refer to pages 276–277 for an explanation: *"dull" child; dumbfounded; island of brilliance; street-smart adolescent; how to read people; out of the blue; clustered; tape measure; the pendulum of opinion . . . complete swing; bludgeoning native intelligence; more newsworthy; sharpest at the extremes; computer camps.*

Section Preview

Answer guidelines begin on page 264.

1. Trace the origins of intelligence tests.

2. Describe the factor-analysis approach to understanding intelligence, and discuss evidence regarding intelligence as a general mental ability and/or as many specific abilities.

3. Discuss whether the ability to manage our emotions is a form of intelligence, and identify the factors associated with creativity.

4. Describe modern tests of mental abilities, and distinguish between aptitude and achievement tests.

5. Identify the major principles of good test construction, and illustrate their application to intelligence tests.

6. (Close-Up) Discuss the two extremes of intelligence.

7. Discuss evidence for genetic influences on intelligence.

8. Discuss evidence for environmental influences on intelligence.

9. Describe group differences in intelligence test scores, and show how they can be explained in terms of environmental factors.

10. Discuss whether intelligence tests are biased and/or discriminatory.

Stepping Through the Section

Answers begin on page 266.

1. Intelligence has been defined as the mental abilities needed to _____ , _____ to, and _____ environments.

2. The French psychologist who devised a test to predict the success of children in school was _____ . Predictions were made by

comparing children's chronological ages with their _____ ages, which were determined by the test.

3. Lewis Terman's revision of Binet's test is referred to as the _____-_____ . This test enables one to derive a(n) _____ _____ for an individual.

Give the original formula for computing IQ, and explain any items used in the formula.

4. Today's tests compute _____ (IQ/ a mental ability score) by comparing the individual's performance to the average performance of people of _____ (the same/different) age(s). These tests are designed so that a score of _____ is considered average.

5. One controversy regarding the nature of intelligence centers on whether intelligence is one _____ ability or several _____ abilities.

6. The statistical procedure used to identify groups of items that appear to measure a common ability is called _____ _____ . Charles Spearman, one of the developers of this technique, believed that a factor called *g*, or _____ _____ , runs through the more specific aspects of intelligence.

7. People with _____ _____ score at the low end of intelligence tests but possess extraordinary specific skills.

8. Howard Gardner proposes that there are _____ _____ , each independent of the others. However, critics point

out that the world is not so just: People with mental disadvantages often have lesser _____ abilities as well. General intelligence scores _____ (do/do not) predict performance on complex tasks and in various jobs.

9. Sternberg distinguishes three types of intelligence: _____ intelligence, _____ intelligence, and _____ intelligence.

10. A critical part of social intelligence is _____ _____ —the ability to _____ , _____ , _____ , and _____ emotions.

11. One research study found that 5-year-olds who could most accurately recognize and label _____ _____ later more easily made friends and effectively managed their emotions.

Briefly describe emotionally intelligent people.

12. Some scholars believe that the concept of _____ intelligence is stretching the idea of multiple intelligences too far.

13. Although general intelligence is most important in occupations that are mentally demanding, successful people usually have other traits as well, such as _____ and being well connected and extremely energetic.

14. The ability to produce ideas that are both novel and valuable is called _____ . The relationship between intelligence and creativity holds only up to a certain point—an intelligence score of about _____ .

Describe five components of creativity other than intelligence.

15. The most widely used intelligence test is the _____ _____ _____ _____ . Consisting of 11 subtests, it provides not only a general intelligence score but also _____ and _____ intelligence scores.

16. Tests designed to predict your ability to learn something new are called _____ tests. Tests designed to measure what you already have learned are called _____ tests.

17. Three requirements of a good test are _____ , _____ , and _____ .

18. The process of defining meaningful scores relative to a pretested comparison group is called _____ .

19. When scores on a test are compiled, they generally result in a bell-shaped pattern, or _____ distribution.

Describe the normal curve, and explain its significance in the standardization process.

20. If a test yields consistent results, it is said to be

_____ .

21. When a test is administered more than once to the same people, the psychologist is determining its _____-_____ reliability.

22. Alternatively, when a person's scores for the odd- and even-numbered questions on a test are compared, _____-_____ reliability is being assessed.

23. The degree to which a test measures or predicts what it is supposed to is referred to as the test's

_____ .

24. The degree to which a test measures the behavior it was designed to measure is referred to as the test's _____ _____ .

25. The degree to which a test predicts future performance of a particular behavior, called the test's _____ , is referred to as the test's

_____ _____ .

Choose a specific example and use it to illustrate and explain the concept of criterion and its relationship to predictive validity.

26. (Close-Up) Individuals whose intelligence scores fall below 70 and who have difficulty adapting to life may be labeled _____

_____ . This label applies to approximately _____ percent of the population.

27. (Close-Up) Severe retardation sometimes has a physical basis, such as _____

_____ , a genetic disorder caused by an extra chromosome.

28. The intelligence scores of identical twins reared together are _____ (more/no more) similar than those of fraternal twins. Brain scans also reveal that identical twins have similar volume to their brain's _____

_____ and those areas associated with _____ and

_____ intelligence.

29. A gene located on chromosome _____ (what number?) may occur more often in children with very high intelligence scores than those with average scores.

30. By inserting an extra gene that engineers a neural receptor involved in _____ into fertilized mouse eggs, researchers have created smarter mice.

31. The intelligence test scores of fraternal twins are _____ (more alike/no more alike) than the intelligence test scores of other siblings. This provides evidence of a(n) _____ (genetic/environmental) effect because fraternal twins, being the same _____ , are treated more alike.

32. Studies of adopted children and their adoptive and biological families demonstrate that with age, genetic influences on intelligence become _____ (more/less) apparent. Thus, children's intelligence scores are more like those of their _____ (biological/adoptive) parents than their _____ (biological/adoptive) parents.

33. The amount of variation in a trait within a group that is attributed to genetic factors is called its _____ . For intelligence, this has been estimated at _____ percent.

34. If we know a trait has perfect heritability, this knowledge _____ (does/does not) enable us to rule out environmental factors in explaining differences between groups.

35. Studies indicate that neglected children _____ (do/do not) show signs of recovery in intelligence and behavior when placed in more nurturing environments.

36. High-quality programs for disadvantaged children, such as the government-funded _____ _____ program, increase children's school readiness.

37. Intelligence scores _____ (rise/fall/remain stable) during the school year and _____ (rise/fall/remain stable) over the summer.

38. Research evidence suggests that group differences in intelligence may be entirely _____ (genetic/environmental).

Explain why heredity may contribute to individual differences in intelligence but not necessarily contribute to group differences.

39. Group differences in intelligence scores _____ (do/do not) provide an accurate basis for judging individuals. Individual differences within a race are _____ (greater than/less than) between-race differences.

40. Although Asian students on the average score _____ (higher/lower) than North American students on math tests, this difference may be due to the fact that _____ _____ .

41. On an infant intelligence measure (preference for looking at novel stimuli), black infants score _____ (lower than/higher than/about the same as) white infants.

42. Race _____ (is/is not) a neatly defined biological category.

43. Gender similarities in math and verbal ability are _____ (smaller/greater) than gender differences. Girls tend to outscore boys on _____ tests and are more

_____ fluent. Although girls have an edge in math _____ , boys score higher in math _____ . Boys tend to outscore girls on tests of _____ .

44. Working from an _____ perspective, some theorists speculate that these gender differences helped our ancestors survive.

45. There is evidence that spatial abilities are enhanced by high levels of _____ _____ during prenatal development.

46. Generally speaking, _____ (women/men) are better emotion detectors than _____ (women/men).

47. In the sense that they detect differences caused by cultural experiences, intelligence tests probably _____ (are/are not) biased.

48. Most psychologists agree that, in terms of predictive validity, the major aptitude tests _____ (are/are not) racially biased.

49. When women and members of ethnic minorities are led to expect that they won't do well on a test, a _____ _____ may result, and their scores may actually be lower.

Progress Test 1

Multiple-Choice Questions

Circle your answers to the following questions and check them with the answers beginning on page 267. If your answer is incorrect, read the explanation for why it is incorrect and then consult the appropriate pages of the text (in parentheses following the correct answer).

1. The text defines cognition as:
   a. silent speech.
   b. all mental activity.
   c. mental activity associated with processing, understanding, remembering, and communicating information.
   d. logical reasoning.
   e. problem solving.

2. When forming a concept, people often develop a best example, or _____ , of a category.
   a. denoter
   b. heuristic
   c. prototype
   d. algorithm

3. Confirmation bias refers to the tendency to:
   a. think of things only in terms of their usual functions.
   b. cling to one's initial conceptions after the basis on which they were formed has been discredited.
   c. search randomly through alternative solutions when problem solving.
   d. look for information that is consistent with one's beliefs.

4. Which of the following is *not* true of babbling?
   a. It is imitation of adult speech.
   b. It is the same in all cultures.
   c. It typically occurs from about age 4 months to 1 year.
   d. Babbling increasingly comes to resemble a particular language.
   e. Deaf babies babble with gestures.

5. Whorf's linguistic determinism hypothesis states that:
   a. language is primarily a learned ability.
   b. language is partially an innate ability.
   c. the size of a person's vocabulary reflects his or her intelligence.
   d. our language shapes our thinking.

6. Which of the following *best* describes Chomsky's view of language development?
   a. Language is an entirely learned ability.
   b. Language is an innate ability.
   c. Humans have a biological predisposition to acquire language.
   d. There are no cultural influences on the development of language.

7. Failing to solve a problem that requires using an object in an unusual way illustrates the phenomenon of:
   a. functional fixedness.
   b. framing.
   c. belief perseverance.
   d. overconfidence.

8. Which of the following is an example of the use of heuristics?
   a. trying every possible letter ordering when unscrambling a word
   b. considering each possible move when playing chess

c. using the formula "area = length × width" to find the area of a rectangle
   d. playing chess using a defensive strategy that has often been successful for you

9. The chimpanzee Sultan used a short stick to pull a longer stick that was out of reach into his cage. He then used the longer stick to reach a piece of fruit. Researchers hypothesized that Sultan's discovery of the solution to his problem was the result of:
   a. trial and error.
   b. heuristics.
   c. functional fixedness.
   d. insight.

10. You hear that one of the Smith children is an outstanding Little League player and immediately conclude it's their one son rather than any of their four daughters. You reached your quite possibly erroneous conclusion as the result of:
    a. the confirmation bias.
    b. the availability heuristic.
    c. the representativeness heuristic.
    d. belief perseverance.

11. According to the text, language acquisition is best described as:
    a. the result of conditioning and reinforcement.
    b. a biological process of maturation.
    c. an interaction between biology and experience.
    d. a mystery of which researchers have no real understanding.

12. The linguistic determinism hypothesis is challenged by the finding that:
    a. chimps can learn to communicate spontaneously by using sign language.
    b. people with no word for a certain color can still perceive that color accurately.
    c. the Eskimo language contains a number of words for snow, whereas English has only one.
    d. infants' babbling contains many sounds that do not occur in their own language and that they therefore cannot have heard.

13. Several studies have indicated that the generic pronoun "he":
    a. tends for children and adults alike to trigger images of both males and females.
    b. tends for adults to trigger images of both males and females, but for children to trigger images of males.
    c. tends for both children and adults to trigger images of males but not females.
    d. for both children and adults triggers images of females about one-fourth of the time it is used.

14. Studies of adopted children and their biological and adoptive families demonstrate that with age, genetic influences on intelligence:
    a. become more apparent.
    b. become less apparent.
    c. become more difficult to disentangle from environmental influences.
    d. become easier to disentangle from environmental influences.

15. A 6-year-old child has a mental age of 9. The child's IQ is:
    a. 96.   d. 150.
    b. 100.   e. 166.
    c. 125.

16. Which of the following is *not* true?
    a. In math grades, the average girl typically equals or surpasses the average boy.
    b. Boys are more capable of remembering the location of objects.
    c. Women are better than men at detecting emotions.
    d. Males score higher than females on tests of spatial abilities.

17. (Close-Up) Down syndrome is normally caused by:
    a. an extra chromosome in the person's genetic makeup.
    b. a missing chromosome in the person's genetic makeup.
    c. malnutrition during the first few months of life.
    d. prenatal exposure to an addictive drug.

18. Which of the following is *not* a requirement of a good test?
    a. reliability   d. validity
    b. standardization   e. criterion
    c. reification

19. Which of the following statements is true?
    a. The predictive validity of intelligence tests is not as high as their reliability.
    b. The reliability of intelligence tests is not as high as their predictive validity.
    c. Modern intelligence tests have extremely high predictive validity and reliability.
    d. The predictive validity and reliability of most intelligence tests is very low.

20. Which of the following best describes the relationship between creativity and intelligence?
    a. Creativity appears to depend on the ability to think imaginatively and has little if any relationship to intelligence.
    b. Creativity is best understood as a certain kind of intelligence.
    c. The more intelligent a person is, the greater his or her creativity.
    d. A certain level of intelligence is necessary but not sufficient for creativity.

21. The existence of _____ reinforces the generally accepted notion that intelligence is a multidimensional quality.
    a. adaptive skills   c. general intelligence
    b. mental retardation   d. savant syndrome

22. Which of the following provides the strongest evidence of the role of heredity in determining intelligence?
    a. The IQ scores of identical twins raised separately are very similar.
    b. The intelligence scores of fraternal twins are more similar than those of ordinary siblings.
    c. The intelligence scores of identical twins raised together are more similar than those of identical twins raised apart.
    d. The intelligence scores of adopted children show relatively weak correlations with scores of adoptive as well as biological parents.

23. Reported racial gaps in average intelligence scores are most likely attributable to:
    a. the use of biased tests of intelligence.
    b. the use of unreliable tests of intelligence.
    c. genetic factors.
    d. environmental factors.

24. The bell-shaped distribution of intelligence scores in the general population is called a:

    a. *g* distribution.
    b. standardization curve.
    c. bimodal distribution.
    d. normal distribution.

25. Research on the effectiveness of Head Start suggests that enrichment programs:

    a. produce permanent gains in intelligence scores.
    b. improve school readiness and may provide a small boost to emotional intelligence.
    c. improve intelligence scores but not school readiness.
    d. produce temporary gains in intelligence scores.

Matching Items

Match each definition or description with the appropriate term.

Definitions or Descriptions

_____ 1. the way an issue or question is posed

_____ 2. a test designed to predict a person's ability to learn something new

_____ 3. a test designed to measure current knowledge

_____ 4. the tendency to overestimate the accuracy of one's judgments

_____ 5. the consistency with which a test measures performance

_____ 6. the degree to which a test measures what it is designed to measure

_____ 7. Terman's revision of Binet's original intelligence test

_____ 8. the behavior that a test is designed to predict

_____ 9. an underlying, general intelligence factor

_____ 10. a person's score on an intelligence test based on performance relative to the average performance of people the same age

_____ 11. presuming that something is likely if it comes readily to mind

_____ 12. a very low intelligence score accompanied by one extraordinary skill

_____ 13. a statistical technique that identifies related items on a test

_____ 14. being unable to see a problem from a different angle

Terms

a. availability heuristic
b. mental ability score
c. *g*
d. savant syndrome
e. framing
f. overconfidence
g. factor analysis
h. aptitude test
i. fixation
j. achievement test
k. Stanford-Binet
l. criterion
m. content validity
n. reliability

Progress Test 2

Progress Test 2 should be completed during a final chapter review. Answer the following questions after you thoroughly understand the correct answers for the section reviews and Progress Test 1.

Multiple-Choice Questions

1. A common problem in everyday reasoning is our tendency to:
   a. accept as logical those conclusions that agree with our own opinions.
   b. accept as logical those conclusions that disagree with our own opinions.
   c. underestimate the accuracy of our knowledge.
   d. accept as logical conclusions that involve unfamiliar concepts.

2. Skinner and other behaviorists have argued that language development is the result of:
   a. imitation.   c. association.
   b. reinforcement.   d. all of the above.

3. Many psychologists are skeptical of claims that chimpanzees can acquire language because the chimps have not shown the ability to:
   a. use symbols meaningfully.
   b. acquire speech.
   c. acquire even a limited vocabulary.
   d. use syntax in communicating.

4. Representativeness and availability are examples of:
   a. belief perseverance.   c. fixation.
   b. algorithms.   d. heuristics.

5. Assume that Congress is considering revising its approach to welfare and to this end is hearing a range of testimony. A member of Congress who uses the availability heuristic would be most likely to:
   a. want to experiment with numerous possible approaches to see which of these seems to work best.
   b. be unable to see the welfare problem from a fresh perspective.
   c. refuse to be budged from his or her beliefs despite persuasive testimony to the contrary.
   d. base his or her ideas on the most vivid, memorable testimony given, even though many of the statistics presented run counter to this testimony.

6. If you want to be absolutely certain that you will find the solution to a problem you know *is* solvable, you should use:
   a. a heuristic.   c. insight.
   b. an algorithm.   d. trial and error.

7. Which of the following is *not* cited by Chomsky as evidence that language acquisition cannot be explained by learning alone?
   a. Children master the complicated rules of grammar with ease.
   b. Children create sentences they have never heard.
   c. Children make the kinds of mistakes that suggest they are attempting to apply rules of grammar.
   d. Children raised in isolation from language spontaneously begin speaking words.

8. Telegraphic speech is typical of the _____ stage.
   a. babbling   c. two-word
   b. one-word   d. three-word

9. Researchers taught the chimpanzee Washoe and the gorilla Koko to communicate by using:
   a. various sounds.
   b. plastic symbols of various shapes and colors.
   c. sign language.
   d. all of the above.

10. Which of the following is true regarding the relationship between thinking and language?
    a. "Real" thinking requires the use of language.
    b. People sometimes think in images rather than in words.
    c. A thought that cannot be expressed in a particular language cannot occur to speakers of that language.
    d. All of the above are true.

11. One reason an English-speaking adult may have difficulty pronouncing Russian words is that:
    a. the vocal tracts of English- and Russian-speaking people develop differently in response to the demands of the two languages.
    b. although English and Russian words have very similar meanings, their sound inventories are very different.
    c. although English and Russian words have very similar sounds, the words' meanings are very different.
    d. after the babbling stage, a child who hears only English stops uttering other sounds.

12. The test created by Alfred Binet was designed specifically to:
   a. measure inborn intelligence in adults.
   b. measure inborn intelligence in children.
   c. predict school performance in children.
   d. identify mentally retarded children so that they could be institutionalized.
   e. do all of the above.

13. Which of the following provides the strongest evidence of environment's role in intelligence?
   a. Adopted children's intelligence scores are more like their adoptive parents' scores than their biological parents'.
   b. Children's intelligence scores are more strongly related to their mothers' scores than to their fathers'.
   c. Children moved from a deprived environment into an intellectually enriched one show gains in intellectual development.
   d. The intelligence scores of identical twins raised separately are no more alike than those of siblings.

14. If a test designed to indicate which applicants are likely to perform the best on the job fails to do so, the test has:
   a. low reliability.
   b. low content validity.
   c. low predictive validity.
   d. not been standardized.

15. The formula for the intelligence quotient was devised by:
   a. Sternberg.   c. Terman.
   b. Binet.   d. Stern.

16. Current intelligence tests compute an individual's intelligence score as:
   a. the ratio of mental age to chronological age multiplied by 100.
   b. the ratio of chronological age to mental age multiplied by 100.
   c. the amount by which the test-taker's performance deviates from the average performance of others the same age.
   d. the ratio of the test-taker's verbal intelligence score to his or her nonverbal intelligence score.

17. J. McVicker Hunt found that institutionalized children given "tutored human enrichment":
   a. showed no change in intelligence test performance compared with institutionalized children who did not receive such enrichment.

   b. responded so negatively as a result of their impoverished early experiences that he felt it necessary to disband the program.
   c. thrived intellectually and socially on the benefits of positive caregiving.
   d. actually developed greater intelligence than control subjects who had lived in foster homes since birth.

18. The concept of a *g* factor implies that intelligence:
   a. is a single overall ability.
   b. is several specific abilities.
   c. cannot be defined or measured.
   d. is both a. and c.
   e. is a dynamic rather than stable phenomenon.

19. Gerardeen has superb social skills, manages conflicts well, and has great empathy for her friends and co-workers. Peter Salovey and John Mayer would probably say that Gerardeen possesses a high degree of:
   a. *g*.
   b. social intelligence.
   c. practical intelligence.
   d. emotional intelligence.

20. Most experts view intelligence as a person's:
   a. ability to perform well on intelligence tests.
   b. innate mental capacity.
   c. ability to learn from experience, solve problems, and adapt to new situations.
   d. diverse skills acquired throughout life.

21. High levels of male hormones during prenatal development may enhance:
   a. verbal reasoning.
   b. spatial abilities.
   c. overall intelligence.
   d. all of the above.

22. Which of the following is *not* cited as evidence of the reciprocal relationship between schooling and intelligence?
   a. Neither education level nor intelligence scores accurately predict income.
   b. Intelligence scores tend to rise during the school year.
   c. High school graduates have higher intelligence scores than do those who drop out early.
   d. High intelligence is conducive to prolonged schooling.

23. Originally, IQ was defined as:
    a. mental age divided by chronological age and multiplied by 100.
    b. chronological age divided by mental age and multiplied by 100.
    c. mental age subtracted from chronological age and multiplied by 100.
    d. chronological age subtracted from mental age and multiplied by 100.

24. Tests of _____ measure what an individual can do now, whereas tests of _____ predict what an individual will be able to do later.
    a. aptitude; achievement
    b. achievement; aptitude
    c. reliability; validity
    d. validity; reliability

25. Which of the following statements most accurately reflects the text's position regarding the relative contribution of genes and environment in determining intelligence?
    a. Except in cases of a neglectful early environment, each individual's basic intelligence is largely the product of heredity.
    b. With the exception of those with genetic disorders such as Down syndrome, intelligence is primarily the product of environmental experiences.
    c. Both genes and life experiences significantly influence performance on intelligence tests.
    d. Because intelligence tests have such low predictive validity, the question cannot be addressed until psychologists agree on a more valid test of intelligence.

True–False Items

Indicate whether each statement is true or false by placing *T* (*True*) or *F* (*False*) in the blank next to the item.

_____ 1. According to the confirmation bias, people often interpret ambiguous evidence as support for their beliefs.

_____ 2. Most human problem solving involves the use of heuristics rather than reasoning that systematically considers every possible solution.

_____ 3. When asked, most people underestimate the accuracy of their judgments.

_____ 4. Studies have shown that even animals may sometimes have insight reactions.

_____ 5. Thinking without using language is not possible.

_____ 6. In the current version of the Stanford-Binet intelligence test, one's performance is compared only with the performance of others the same age.

_____ 7. Most of the major aptitude tests have higher validity than reliability.

_____ 8. The gap in intelligence scores between black and white children is increasing.

_____ 9. The intelligence scores of adopted children are more similar to those of their adoptive parents than their biological parents.

_____ 10. The Stanford-Binet is the most widely used test today.

_____ 11. The variation in intelligence scores within a racial group is much larger than that between racial groups.

Review and Reflect

Answer these questions the day before an exam as a final check on your understanding of the chapter's terms and concepts.

Multiple-Choice Questions

1. A listener hearing a recording of Japanese, Spanish, and North American children babbling would:
   a. not be able to tell them apart.
   b. be able to tell them apart if they were older than 6 months.
   c. be able to tell them apart if they were older than 8 to 10 months.
   d. be able to tell them apart at any age.

2. Which of the following illustrates belief perseverance?
   a. Your belief remains intact even in the face of evidence to the contrary.
   b. You refuse to listen to arguments counter to your beliefs.
   c. You tend to become flustered and angered when your beliefs are refuted.
   d. You tend to search for information that supports your beliefs.

3. Complete the following analogy: Rose is to flower as:
   a. concept is to prototype.
   b. prototype is to concept.
   c. concept is to hierarchy.
   d. hierarchy is to concept.

4. Your stand on an issue such as the use of nuclear power for electricity involves personal judgment. In such a case, one memorable occurrence can weigh more heavily than a bookful of data, thus illustrating:
   a. belief perseverance.
   b. confirmation bias.
   c. the representativeness heuristic.
   d. the availability heuristic.

5. A dessert recipe that gives you the ingredients, their amounts, and the steps to follow is an example of a(n):
   a. prototype.   c. heuristic.
   b. algorithm.   d. concept.

6. Boris the chess master selects his next move by considering moves that would threaten his opponent's queen. His opponent, a chess-playing computer, selects its next move by considering *all* possible moves. Boris is using a(n) _____ and the computer is using a(n) _____ .
   a. algorithm; heuristic
   b. prototype; algorithm
   c. heuristic; prototype
   d. heuristic; algorithm

7. During a televised political debate, the Republican and Democratic candidates each argued that the results of a recent public opinion poll supported their party's platform regarding sexual harassment. Because both candidates saw the information as supporting their belief, it is clear that both were victims of:
   a. functional fixedness.   c. belief perseverance.
   b. overconfidence.   d. confirmation bias.

8. Experts in a field prefer heuristics to algorithms because heuristics:
   a. guarantee solutions to problems.
   b. often save time.
   c. prevent fixation.
   d. do all of the above.

9. Rudy is 6 feet 6 inches tall, weighs 210 pounds, and is very muscular. If you think that Rudy is more likely to be a basketball player than a computer programmer, you are a victim of:
   a. belief perseverance.
   b. the availability heuristic.
   c. functional fixedness.
   d. the representativeness heuristic.

10. Failing to see that an article of clothing can be inflated as a life preserver is an example of:
    a. belief perseverance.
    b. the availability heuristic.
    c. the representativeness heuristic.
    d. functional fixedness.

11. Airline reservations typically decline after a highly publicized airplane crash because people overestimate the incidence of such disasters. In such instances, people's decisions are being influenced by:
    a. belief perseverance.
    b. the availability heuristic.
    c. the representativeness heuristic.
    d. functional fixedness.

12. Most people tend to:
    a. accurately estimate the accuracy of their knowledge and judgments.
    b. underestimate the accuracy of their knowledge and judgments.
    c. overestimate the accuracy of their knowledge and judgments.
    d. lack confidence in their decision-making strategies.

13. In relation to ground beef, consumers respond more positively to an ad describing it as "75 percent lean" than to one referring to its "25 percent fat" content. This is an example of:
    a. the framing effect.   c. a prototype.
    b. confirmation bias.   d. overconfidence.

14. Regarding the relationship between thinking and language, which of the following most accurately reflects the position taken in the text?
    a. Language determines everything about our thinking.
    b. Language determines the way we think.
    c. Thinking without language is not possible.
    d. Thinking affects our language, which then affects our thought.

15. Vanessa is a very creative sculptress. We would expect that Vanessa also:
    a. has an exceptionally high intelligence score.
    b. is quite introverted.
    c. has a venturesome personality and is intrinsically motivated.
    d. lacks expertise in most other skills.
    e. is more successful than other sculptors.

16. To say that the heritability of a trait is approximately 50 percent means:
    a. that genes are responsible for 50 percent of the trait in an individual, and the environment is responsible for the rest.
    b. that the trait's appearance in a person will reflect approximately equal genetic contributions from both parents.
    c. that of the variation in the trait within a group of people, 50 percent can be attributed to heredity.
    d. all of the above.

17. (Close-Up) Twenty-two-year-old Dan has an intelligence score of 63 and the academic skills of a fourth-grader, and is unable to live independently. Dan *probably*:
    a. has Down syndrome.
    b. has savant syndrome.
    c. is mentally retarded.
    d. will eventually achieve self-supporting social and vocational skills.

18. A school psychologist found that 85 percent of those who scored above 115 on an aptitude test were "A" students and 75 percent of those who scored below 85 on the test were "D" students. The psychologist concluded that the test had high _____ validity because scores on it correlated highly with the _____ behavior.
    a. content; criterion
    b. predictive; criterion
    c. content; target
    d. predictive; target

19. Benito was born in 1937. In 1947, he scored 130 on an intelligence test. What was Benito's mental age when he took the test?
    a. 9   c. 11
    b. 10   d. 13
    e. It cannot be determined from the information provided.

20. Melvin has been diagnosed as having savant syndrome, which means that he:
    a. has an IQ of 120 or higher.
    b. would score high on a test of analytical intelligence.
    c. is mentally retarded but has one exceptional ability.
    d. was exposed to high levels of testosterone during prenatal development.

21. Hiroko's math achievement score is considerably higher than that of most American students her age. Which of the following is true regarding this difference between Asian and North American students:
    a. It is a recent phenomenon.
    b. It may be due to the fact that Asian students have a longer school year.
    c. It holds only for girls.
    d. Both a. and b. are true.
    e. a., b., and c. are true.

22. Jack takes the same test of mechanical reasoning on several different days and gets virtually identical scores. This suggests that the test has:
    a. high content validity.
    b. high reliability.
    c. high predictive validity.
    d. been standardized.
    e. all of the above qualities.

23. Before becoming attorneys, law students must pass a special licensing exam, which is an _____ test. Before entering college, high school students must take the SAT, which is an _____ test.
    a. achievement; aptitude
    b. aptitude; achievement
    c. achievement; achievement
    d. aptitude; aptitude

24. If you compare the same trait in people of similar heredity who live in very different environments, heritability for that trait will be _____ ; heritability for the trait is most likely to be _____ among people of very different heredities who live in similar environments.
    a. low; high
    b. high; low
    c. environmental; genetic
    d. genetic; environmental

25. Don's intelligence scores were only average, but he has been enormously successful as a corporate manager. Psychologists Sternberg and Wagner would probably suggest that Don's _____ intelligence exceeds his _____ intelligence.
    a. verbal; performance
    b. performance; verbal
    c. academic; practical
    d. practical; academic

Essay Question

You have been asked to devise a Psychology Achievement Test (PAT) that will be administered to freshmen who declare psychology as their major. What steps will you take to ensure that the PAT is a good intelligence test? (Use the space below to list the points you want to make, and organize them. Then write the essay on a separate sheet of paper.)

Key Terms

Writing Definitions

Using your own words, on a piece of paper write a brief definition or explanation of each of the following terms.

1. cognition
2. concept
3. prototype
4. algorithm
5. heuristic
6. insight
7. confirmation bias
8. fixation
9. functional fixedness
10. representativeness heuristic
11. availability heuristic
12. overconfidence
13. framing
14. belief perseverance
15. language
16. babbling stage
17. one-word stage
18. two-word stage
19. telegraphic speech
20. linguistic determinism
21. intelligence
22. mental age
23. Stanford-Binet
24. intelligence quotient (IQ)
25. factor analysis
26. general intelligence (*g*)
27. savant syndrome
28. emotional intelligence
29. creativity
30. Wechsler Adult Intelligence Scale—(WAIS)
31. aptitude tests
32. achievement tests
33. standardization
34. normal curve (normal distribution)
35. mental retardation
36. reliability
37. validity
38. Down syndrome
39. content validity
40. criterion
41. predictive validity
42. heritability
43. stereotype threat

Cross-Check

As you learned in Chapter 1, reviewing and overlearning of material are important to the learning process. After you have written the definitions of the key terms in this chapter, you should complete the crossword puzzle to ensure that you can reverse the process—recognize the term, given the definition.

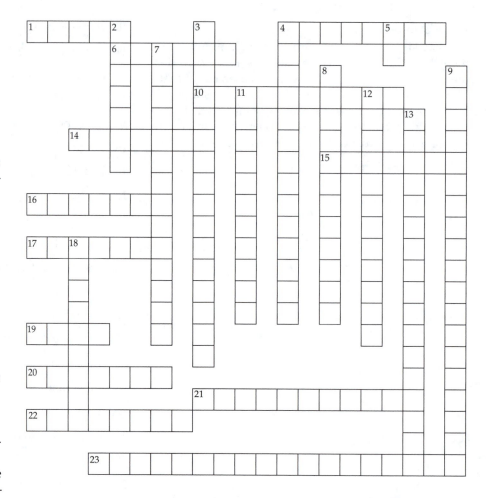

ACROSS

1. French educator who devised a test to predict children's learning potential.
4. An inability to approach a problem in a new way.
6. The chimpanzee taught by Allen and Beatrice Gardner to use sign language.
10. The type of fixedness in which a person can't envision a novel use for a familiar object.
14. Theorist who argues for the existence of multiple intelligences.
15. Behaviorist who explains language development with familiar learning principles.
16. Linguist who views language development as a process of maturation.
17. The stage of language development between 1 and 2 years of age.
19. The most widely used intelligence test (abbreviation).
20. A mental grouping of similar objects.
21. Type of test that measures a person's current knowledge.
22. Degree to which a test measures what it is supposed to measure.
23. An obstacle to rational thinking that may be eliminated by considering an opposing viewpoint.

DOWN

2. Stage of language development characterized by the use of telegraphic speech.
3. Tendency of people to search for information that confirms their preconceptions.
4. Statistical procedure that identifies clusters of items that seem to define a common ability.

5. Originally defined as the ratio of mental age to chronological age.
7. Condition in which a person of limited mental ability has one amazing skill.
8. Condition of mental retardation caused by an extra chromosome.
9. Charles Spearman's concept of *g*.
11. Bell-shaped distribution that reflects scores on aptitude tests.
12. Heuristic in which we estimate the likelihood of events based on how readily they come to mind.
13. Defined as an intelligence score below 70.
18. A critical part of social intelligence.

Answers

Thinking

Section Preview

1. Concepts are mental groupings of similar objects, events, and people. Because they provide a great deal of information with minimal cognitive effort, concepts are the basic units of thinking. Most concepts are formed around a best example, or prototype, of a particular category. Concepts are often

organized into hierarchies that further increase cognitive efficiency.

2. Trial and error is a haphazard strategy for solving problems, in which one solution after another is tried until success is achieved. Algorithms are step-by-step procedures that guarantee a solution; they often are laborious and inefficient. Heuristics are simple thinking strategies. Although formally not a problem-solving strategy, a sudden flash of inspiration (insight) often helps us to solve problems. Insight has been seen in chimpanzees given challenging problems to solve.

3. The confirmation bias is an obstacle to problem solving in which people search for information that confirms their preconceptions. Another common obstacle to problem solving is fixation, an inability to approach a familiar problem in a new way. One example of fixation is functional fixedness, whereby a person is unable to perceive unusual functions for familiar objects.

4. The representativeness heuristic is the tendency to judge the likelihood of things in terms of how well they represent particular prototypes. With the availability heuristic, we base our judgments on how readily information comes to mind.

   The overconfidence phenomenon is the tendency of people to overestimate the accuracy of their knowledge and judgments. Although overconfidence may blind us to our vulnerability to errors in reasoning, it has adaptive value in that it makes decision making somewhat easier.

   Framing refers to the way an issue or question is posed, which can greatly influence our perception of the issue or answer to the question.

   Belief perseverance is the tendency for people to cling to beliefs even when they have been discredited.

Stepping Through the Section

1. cognition; the mental activity associated with processing, understanding, remembering, and communicating; cognitive psychologists
2. concepts; hierarchies
3. prototype
4. problem solving
5. trial and error
6. algorithms
7. heuristics
8. insight
9. confirmation bias
10. fixation

11. functional fixedness
12. representativeness heuristic
13. availability heuristic

Using these heuristics often prevents us from processing other relevant information; because we overlook this information, we make judgmental errors. Thus, in the text example, the representativeness heuristic leads people to overlook the fact that there are many more truck drivers than Ivy League classics professors and, as a result, to wrongly conclude that the poetry reader is more likely to be an Ivy League classics professor. Also as noted in the text, the availability heuristic leads us to incorrectly think that words beginning with *k* are more common than words having *k* as their third letter.

14. flying; driving; terrorism; accidents
    a. what our ancestral history has prepared us to fear.
    b. what we cannot control.
    c. what is immediate.
    d. what is most readily available in memory.
15. overconfidence
16. adaptive; more; easier; does
17. framing
18. belief perseverance

Language

Section Preview

1. At about 4 months of age, babies enter a babbling stage in which they spontaneously utter sounds of all languages. By 1 year, children enter the one-word stage. In this stage, single-syllable words are used to name things and may even be inflected to convey the meaning of an entire sentence. By age 2, most children enter the two-word stage. At this time, their speech consists of telegraphic utterances containing mostly nouns and verbs, yet placed in a sensible syntactic order. Children then quickly begin uttering longer and more complex phrases and sentences.

   According to B. F. Skinner, language development can be explained according to the learning principles of association, imitation, and reinforcement. In contrast, Noam Chomsky believes that children are biologically prepared to learn language as they interact with their caregivers. Most theorists today believe that language development is the product of both hereditary and environmental influences.

2. Cognitive scientists emphasize the importance of grammatical learning that occurs during the first few years of life. Human infants display a

remarkable knack for soaking up language and discerning statistical aspects of human speech. The impact of early experiences is also evident in comparisons of children and adults who attempt to master a second language, whether spoken or gestured. Those who learn as adults typically speak with the accent of their first language and do not as easily (or accurately) master the grammar of the second language. This evidence for the importance of early learning challenges Chomsky's concept of an innate universal grammar.

3. According to Whorf's linguistic determinism hypothesis, language determines the way we think. Critics of this idea claim that our language *reflects* rather than creates the way we think. Studies of the ability of vocabulary enrichment to enhance thinking reveal that it is more accurate to say that language *influences*, rather than determines, thought. Some thoughts, such as the imagery involved in art, music, and athletics, do not depend on language.

4. Numerous studies demonstrate that animals have remarkable capacities for thinking. Studies with chimpanzees and other primates reveal reasoning by insight, tool use, and transmission of cultural traditions.

   Although animals communicate effectively among themselves, the question of whether these communications make up a language remains controversial.

   Several attempts have been made to teach sign language and other symbolic languages to chimpanzees. Although apes have a capacity to learn a relatively large vocabulary of sign words, critics contend that much of their signing is nothing more than imitation of their trainer's signs and shows little evidence of syntax.

Stepping Through the Section

1. babbling; 4; do not
2. do
3. 10; 12; lost
4. one-word; 1
5. two-word; telegraphic
6. do
7. association; imitation; reinforcement
8. Chomsky; language acquisition device; grammar

The rate at which children acquire vocabulary and grammar is too rapid to be explained solely by learning. Children create sentences that they have never heard and, therefore, could not be imitating. Children

learn grammatical rules in a predictable order. Children's linguistic errors are often overgeneralizations of logical grammatical rules.

9. 1; word breaks
10. accent; poorer; grammar; right
11. linguistic determinism; Whorf
12. self; 6000
13. does
14. inhibit their attention to irrelevant information; self-esteem
15. can; mental
16. studying effectively

The relationship is probably a two-way one: The linguistic determinism hypothesis suggests that language helps shape thought; that words come into the language to express new ideas indicates that thought also shapes language.

17. insight
18. tools; vary; cultural
19. sign language
20. gestured

Chimps have acquired only limited vocabularies and—in contrast to children—have acquired these vocabularies only with great difficulty. Also in contrast to children, it's unclear that chimps can use syntax to express meaning. Even simpler animals, such as birds, are capable of learning behavioral sequences that some chimp researchers consider language. The signing of chimps is often nothing more than imitation of the trainer's actions. People tend to interpret such ambiguous behavior in terms of what they want to see.

Intelligence

Section Preview

1. Modern intelligence testing began when Alfred Binet developed a test to predict children's future school performance. Binet's test was designed to compute a mental age for each child. Lewis Terman's revision of Binet's test, known as the Stanford-Binet, computed an IQ score as the ratio of mental age to chronological age. Modern intelligence tests no longer compute an intelligence quotient; instead, they produce a mental ability score based on the test-taker's performance relative to the average of others the same age.

2. Factor analysis is a statistical technique used to identify clusters of test items that measure a common ability, such as spatial or reasoning ability.

   Although psychologists agree that people have specific abilities, such as verbal or mathematical intelligence, they do not agree about the existence of an underlying general intelligence factor. People with savant syndrome, who score very low on intelligence tests but possess extraordinary specific abilities, provide support for the viewpoint that there are multiple intelligences, each independent of the others. Sternberg and Wagner, for example, distinguish among three intelligences—academic, practical, and creative—while Cantor and Kihlstrom distinguish between academic and social intelligence (including emotional intelligence) and Gardner among eight different intelligences.

3. Psychologists describe emotional intelligence, an aspect of social intelligence, as the ability to perceive, express, and regulate emotions. Emotionally intelligent people are especially self-aware, and their empathy enables them to read others' emotions.

Creativity is the ability to produce novel and valuable ideas. Although people with high intelligence scores do well on tests of creativity, beyond an intelligence score of about 120, the correlation between intelligence scores and creativity disappears.

Studies suggest five components to creativity other than intelligence: expertise, imaginative thinking skills, a venturesome personality, intrinsic motivation, and a creative environment.

4. The most widely used intelligence tests, the WAIS and the WISC, consist of 11 subtests and yield an overall intelligence score, as well as separate verbal and performance scores.

Aptitude tests, such as a college entrance exam, are intended to predict a person's ability to learn new skills. Achievement tests, such as a final exam in a college course, are intended to measure what already has been learned.

5. Good intelligence tests have been standardized and are reliable and valid. Standardization is the process of defining meaningful scores on the test relative to a pretested group. A random group of test results should form a normal distribution depicted on a normal curve.

Reliability is the extent to which a test yields consistent results. To check a test's reliability, people are tested twice using the same or a different form of the test. If the scores correlate, the test is reliable. The Stanford-Binet, WAIS, and WISC all have high reliabilities of about +.9.

Validity is the extent to which a test actually measures the behavior (content validity) it claims to, or predicts some criterion, such as future performance (predictive validity). The predictive

validity of general aptitude tests is not as high as their reliability.

6. Unlike the popular notion that gifted children are maladjusted, researchers have found that they are healthy, well adjusted, and unusually successful academically.

Approximately 1 percent of the population have very low intelligence scores, experience difficulty adapting to the normal demands of living independently, and are labeled as mentally retarded. Severe mental retardation sometimes results from physical causes, such as Down syndrome.

7. Studies of twins and adopted children point to the influence of heredity. For example, the most genetically similar people have the most similar intelligence scores, and adopted children's intelligence scores are more like their biological parents' scores than their adoptive parents' scores. Moreover, with age, genetic influences become even more apparent. Researchers have identified a gene located on chromosome 6 that is found more often in children with very high intelligence scores; they have also produced smarter mice by inserting an extra gene into fertilized mouse eggs. It is estimated that the *heritability* of intelligence is about 50 to 75 percent; that is, 50 to 75 percent of the variation in intelligence within a *group* of people can be attributed to heredity.

8. Research studies that compare children reared in neglectful environments—including those associated with poverty and malnutrition—with those who have been reared in normal environments point to the impact of environmental experiences on intelligence scores. However, there is no surefire environmental recipe for producing a child with superior intellect, beyond normal exposure to sights, sounds, and speech. Findings regarding Head Start and other preschool programs indicate that high-quality programs can increase school readiness. Studies also provide evidence that schooling and intelligence have a positive, reciprocal effect on each other.

9. Individual differences within a race are much greater than differences between races. However, on average, there *are* group differences in intelligence scores. For example, Asian students outperform North American students on math achievement and aptitude tests, females score higher than males in math computation, and white Americans tend to score higher than black Americans on IQ tests.

Although heredity contributes to individual

differences in intelligence, it does not necessarily contribute to group differences. Most experts believe that the intelligence score gaps between groups are the result of differences between privileged and disadvantaged groups around the world, as well as differences in educational enrichment.

10. In the sense that intelligence scores are sensitive to differences caused by cultural experience, aptitude tests are certainly biased. In terms of predictive validity, however, most experts agree that the major intelligence tests are not racially biased.

    Because intelligence tests are designed to distinguish different levels of aptitude, their purpose in this sense *is* to discriminate among individuals. In another sense, however, intelligence tests reduce discrimination by reducing the use of subjective criteria in school and job placement.

Stepping Through the Section

1. select; adapt; shape
2. Binet; mental
3. Stanford-Binet; intelligence quotient

In the original formula for IQ, measured mental age is divided by chronological age and multiplied by 100. "Mental age" refers to the chronological age that most typically corresponds to a given level of performance.

4. a mental ability score; the same; 100
5. overall (general); specific
6. factor analysis; general intelligence
7. savant syndrome
8. multiple intelligences; physical; do not
9. academic; practical; creative
10. emotional intelligence; perceive; express; understand; regulate
11. facial emotions

Emotionally intelligent people are self-aware. They can manage their emotions and they can delay gratification. They handle others' emotions skillfully.

12. emotional
13. conscientiousness
14. creativity; 120

Creative people tend to have *expertise*, or a solid base of knowledge; *imaginative thinking skills*, which allow them to see things in new ways, to recognize patterns, and to make connections; *intrinsic motivation*, or the tendency to focus on the pleasure and challenge of their work; and a *venturesome personality* that tolerates ambiguity and risk and seeks new experiences. Creative people also have generally benefited from living in *creative environments*.

15. Wechsler Adult Intelligence Scale; verbal; performance
16. aptitude; achievement
17. standardization; reliability; validity
18. standardization
19. normal

The normal curve describes the distribution of many physical phenomena and psychological attributes (including IQ scores), with most scores falling near the average and fewer and fewer near the extremes. When a test is standardized on a normal curve, individual scores are assigned according to how much they deviate above or below the distribution's average.

20. reliable
21. test-retest
22. split-half
23. validity
24. content validity
25. criterion; predictive validity

The criterion is the particular behavior that a predictive test, such as an aptitude test, is intended to predict. For example, performance in a relevant job situation would be the criterion for a test measuring managerial aptitude. The criterion determines whether a test has predictive validity. For example, the on-the-job success of those who do well on a job aptitude test would indicate the test has predictive validity.

26. mentally retarded; 1
27. Down syndrome
28. more; gray matter; verbal; spatial
29. 6
30. memory
31. more alike; environmental; age
32. more; biological; adoptive
33. heritability; 50 to 75
34. does not
35. do
36. Head Start
37. rise; fall
38. environmental

Because of the impact of environmental factors such as education and nutrition on intelligence test performance, even if the heritability of intelligence is high within a particular group, differences in intelligence *among* groups may be environmentally caused. One group may, for example, thrive in an enriched environment while another of the same genetic predisposition may falter in an impoverished one.

39. do not; greater than

40. higher; Asian students have a longer school year and spend more time studying math

41. about the same as

42. is not

43. greater; spelling; verbally; computation; problem solving; mental rotation

44. evolutionary

45. male sex hormones

46. women; men

47. are

48. are not

49. stereotype threat

Progress Test 1

Multiple-Choice Questions

1. **c.** is the answer. (p. 293)

2. **c.** is the answer. (p. 294)
    a. There is no such thing as a "denoter."
    b. & d. Heuristics and algorithms are problem-solving strategies.

3. **d.** is the answer. It is a major obstacle to problem solving. (p. 295)
    a. & b. These refer to functional fixedness and belief perseverance, respectively.
    c. This is trial-and-error problem solving.

4. **a.** is the answer. Babbling is not the imitation of adult speech since babbling infants produce sounds from languages they have not heard and could not be imitating. (p. 303)

5. **d.** is the answer. (p. 308)
    a. This is Skinner's position regarding language development.
    b. This is Chomsky's position regarding language development.
    c. The linguistic determinism hypothesis is concerned with the content of thought, not intelligence.

6. **c.** is the answer. (p. 305)
    a. This is Skinner's position.
    b. According to Chomsky, although the *ability* to acquire language is innate, the child can only acquire language in association with others.
    d. Cultural influences are an important example of the influence of learning on language development, an influence Chomsky fully accepts.

7. **a.** is the answer. Functional fixedness is the tendency to think of things only in terms of their usual functions. (p. 295)
    b. Framing refers to the way an issue is posed; this often influences our judgment.

    c. Belief perseverance is the tendency to cling to one's beliefs even after they have been refuted.
    d. Overconfidence is the tendency to think we know more than we do.

8. **d.** is the answer. Heuristics are simple thinking strategies—such as playing chess defensively—that are based on past successes in similar situations. (p. 294)
    a., b., & c. These are all algorithms.

9. **d.** is the answer. Sultan suddenly arrived at a novel solution to his problem, thus displaying apparent insight. (p. 312)
    a. Sultan did not randomly try various strategies of reaching the fruit; he demonstrated the "light bulb" reaction that is the hallmark of insight.
    b. Heuristics are simple thinking strategies.
    c. Functional fixedness is an impediment to problem solving. Sultan obviously solved his problem.

10. **c.** is the answer. Your conclusion is based on sex stereotypes, that is, athletic ability and participation are for you more *representative* of boys. Your conclusion is by no means necessarily right, however, especially since the Smiths have four daughters and only one son. (p. 296)
    a. The confirmation bias is the tendency to look for information that confirms one's preconceptions.
    b. The availability heuristic involves judging the probability of an event in terms of how readily it comes to mind.
    d. Belief perseverance is the tendency to cling to beliefs, even when the evidence has shown that they are wrong.

11. **c.** is the answer. Children are biologically prepared to learn language as they and their caregivers interact. (p. 308)
    a. This is Skinner's position.
    b. No psychologist, including Chomsky, believes that language is entirely a product of biological maturation.
    d. Although language acquisition is not completely understood, research has shed sufficient light on it to render it less than a complete mystery.

12. **b.** is the answer. The evidence that absence of a term for a color does not affect ability to perceive the color challenges the idea that language always shapes thought. (pp. 308–309)
    a. & d. These findings are not relevant to the linguistic relativity hypothesis, which addresses the relationship between language and thought.
    c. This finding is in keeping with the linguistic determinism hypothesis.

13. **c.** is the answer. The generic pronoun *he* evidently tends, for both adults and children, to conjure up images of males. (p. 309)

14. **a.** is the answer. (pp. 327–328)

c. & d. Separating genetic from environmental influences is difficult *at any age.*

15. **d.** is the answer. If we divide 9, the measured mental age, by 6, the chronological age, and multiply the result by 100, we obtain 150. (p. 316)

16. **b.** is the answer. Girls are better than boys at remembering locations. (p. 332)

17. **a.** is the answer. (p. 325)

b. Down syndrome is normally caused by an extra, rather than a missing, chromosome.

c. & d. Down syndrome is a genetic disorder that is manifest during the earliest stages of prenatal development, well before malnutrition and exposure to drugs would produce their harmful effects on the developing fetus.

18. **c.** is the answer. Reification is a reasoning error, in which an abstract concept such as IQ is regarded as though it were real. (pp. 323–324)

19. **a.** is the answer. (p. 325)

c. & d. Most modern tests have high reliabilities of about +.9; their validity scores are much lower.

20. **d.** is the answer. Up to an intelligence score of about 120, there is a positive correlation between intelligence and creativity. But beyond this point the correlation disappears, indicating that factors other than intelligence are also involved. (p. 321)

a. The ability to think imaginatively and intelligence are *both* components of creativity.

b. Creativity, the capacity to produce ideas that are novel and valuable, is related to and depends in part on intelligence but cannot be considered simply a kind of intelligence.

c. Beyond an intelligence score of about 120 there is no correlation between intelligence scores and creativity.

21. **d.** is the answer. That people with savant syndrome excel in one area but are intellectually retarded in others suggests that there are multiple intelligences. (p. 317)

a. The ability to adapt defines the capacity we call intelligence.

b. Mental retardation is an indicator of the range of human intelligence.

c. A general intelligence factor was hypothesized by Spearman to underlie each specific factor of intelligent behavior, but its existence is controversial and remains to be proved.

22. **a.** is the answer. Identical twins who live apart have the same genetic makeup but different environments; if their scores are similar, this is evidence for the role of heredity. (p. 326)

b. Since fraternal twins are no more genetically

alike than ordinary siblings, this could not provide evidence for the role of heredity.

c. That twins raised together have more similar scores than twins raised apart provides evidence for the role of the environment.

d. As both sets of correlations are weak, little evidence is provided either for or against the role of heredity.

23. **d.** is the answer. Findings from a range of studies—including adoption studies—have led experts to focus on the influence of environmental factors. (p. 332)

a. Most experts believe that in terms of predictive validity, the major tests are not racially biased.

b. The reliability of the major tests is actually very high.

c. The bulk of the evidence on which experts base their findings points to the influence of environmental factors.

24. **d.** is the answer. (p. 323)

a. *g* is Spearman's term for "general intelligence"; there is no such thing as a "*g* distribution."

b. There is no such thing.

c. A bimodal distribution is one having two (bi-) modes, or averages. The normal distribution has only one mode.

25. **b.** is the answer. Enrichment programs do improve school readiness, create better attitudes toward learning, and reduce school dropouts and criminality. (pp. 329–330)

Matching Items

1. e (p. 300)   6. m (p. 325)   11. a (p. 297)
2. h (p. 323)   7. k (p. 316)   12. d (p. 317)
3. j (p. 323)   8. l (p. 325)   13. g (p. 317)
4. f (p. 298)   9. c (p. 317)   14. i (p. 295)
5. n (p. 324)   10. b (p. 316)

Progress Test 2

Multiple-Choice Questions

1. **a.** is the answer. Reasoning in daily life is often distorted by our beliefs, which may lead us, for example, to accept conclusions that haven't been arrived at logically. (p. 295)

b., c., & d. These are just the opposite of what we tend to do.

2. **d.** is the answer. These are all basic principles of learning and, according to Skinner, explain language development. (p. 304)

3. **d.** is the answer. Syntax is one of the fundamental aspects of language, and chimps seem unable, for

example, to use word order to convey differences in meaning. (p. 314)

a. & c. Chimps' use of sign language demonstrates both the use of symbols and the acquisition of fairly sizable vocabularies.

b. No psychologist would require the use of speech as evidence of language; significantly, all the research and arguments focus on what chimps are and are not able to do in acquiring other facets of language.

4. **d.** is the answer. Both are simple thinking strategies that allow us to make quick judgments. (pp. 296–297)

a. Belief perseverance is the tendency to cling to one's beliefs even after they have ben refuted.

b. Algorithms are methodical strategies that guarantee a solution to a particular problem.

c. Fixation is an obstacle to problem solving, in which the person tends to repeat solutions that have worked in the past.

5. **d.** is the answer. If we use the availability heuristic, we base judgments on the availability of information in our memories, and more vivid information is often the most readily available. (p. 297)

a. This would exemplify use of the trial-and-error approach to problem solving.

b. This would exemplify a fixation.

c. This would exemplify belief perseverance.

6. **b.** is the answer. Because they involve the systematic examination of all possible solutions to a problem, algorithms guarantee that a solution will be found. (p. 294)

a., c., & d. None of these methods guarantees that a problem's solution will be found.

7. **d.** is the answer. Chomsky believes that the inborn capacity for language acquisition must be activated by exposure to language. And, in fact, children raised in isolation will *not* begin to speak spontaneously. (p. 305)

8. **c.** is the answer. (p. 304)

9. **c.** is the answer. (pp. 312–313)

10. **b.** is the answer. (p. 310)

a. Researchers do not make a distinction between "real" and other thinking, nor do they consider nonlinguistic thinking less valid than linguistic thinking.

c. As indicated by several studies cited in the text, this is not true.

11. **d.** is the answer. Following the babbling stage, the child's ability to produce all sounds becomes in a sense shaped and limited to the ability to produce those sounds he or she hears. (p. 303)

a. The vocal tract of *Homo sapiens* does not develop in specialized ways for different languages.

b. & c. English and Russian words differ significantly in both their sounds and their meanings. Nor is there any reason that differences in meanings would in and of themselves cause pronunciation difficulties.

12. **c.** is the answer. French compulsory education laws brought more children into the school system, and the government didn't want to rely on teachers' subjective judgments to determine which children would require special help. (p. 316)

a. & b. Binet's test was intended for children, and Binet specifically rejected the idea that his test measured inborn intelligence, which is an abstract capacity that cannot be quantified.

d. This was not a purpose of the test, which dealt with children in the school system.

13. **c.** is the answer. (p. 329)

a., b., & d. None of these is true.

14. **c.** is the answer. Predictive validity is the extent to which tests predict what they are intended to predict. (p. 325)

a. Reliability is the consistency with which a test samples the particular behavior of interest.

b. Content validity is the degree to which a test measures what it is designed to measure.

d. Standardization is the process of defining meaningful test scores based on the performance of a representative group.

15. **d.** is the answer. (p. 316)

16. **c.** is the answer. (p. 316)

a. This is William Stern's original formula for the intelligence quotient.

b. & d. Neither of these formulas is used to compute the score on current intelligence tests.

17. **c.** is the answer. Enrichment led to dramatic results and thereby testified to the importance of environmental factors. (p. 329)

a. & d. The study involved neither intelligence tests nor comparisons with control groups.

b. The children showed a dramatic positive response.

18. **a.** is the answer. (p. 317)

19. **d.** is the answer. (p. 319)

a. The concept of general intelligence pertains more to academic skills.

b. Although emotional intelligence *is* a key component of social intelligence, Salovey and Mayer coined the newer term "emotional intelligence" to refer to skills such as Gerardeen's.

c. Practical intelligence is that which is required for everyday tasks, not all of which involve emotions.

20. **c.** is the answer. (p. 315)
    a. Performance ability and intellectual ability are separate traits.
    b. This has been argued by some, but certainly not most, experts.
    d. Although many experts believe that there are multiple intelligences, this would not be the same thing as diverse acquired skills.

21. **b.** is the answer. (p. 333)

22. **a.** is the answer. Both schooling and intelligence enhance later income. (p. 330)
    b., c., & d. The issues of whether intelligence is innate and whether it is a single entity or multifaceted have relatively little bearing on the question of the potential for culture-free tests.

23. **a.** is the answer. (p. 316)

24. **b.** is the answer. (p. 323)
    c. & d. Reliability and validity are characteristics of good tests.

25. **c.** is the answer. (p. 329)
    a. & b. Studies of twins, family members, and adopted children point to a significant hereditary contribution to intelligence scores. These same studies, plus others comparing children reared in neglectful or enriched environments, indicate that life experiences also significantly influence test performance.

    d. Although the issue of how intelligence should be defined is controversial, intelligence tests generally have predictive validity, especially in the early years.

True–False Items

1. T (p. 295)
2. T (p. 294)
3. F (p. 298)
4. T (p. 312)
5. F (p. 310)
6. T (p. 316)
7. F (p. 325)
8. F (p. 331)
9. F (pp. 327–328)
10. F (p. 322)
11. T (p. 331)

Review and Reflect

Multiple-Choice Questions

1. **a.** is the answer. (p. 303)

2. **a.** is the answer. (p. 301)
    b. & c. These may very well occur, but they do not define belief perseverance.
    d. This is the confirmation bias.

3. **b.** is the answer. A rose is a prototypical example of the concept *flower*. (pp. 293–294)
    c. & d. Hierarchies are organized clusters of concepts. In this example, there is only the single concept *flower*.

4. **d.** is the answer. The availability heuristic is the judgmental strategy that estimates the likelihood of events in terms of how readily they come to mind, and the most vivid information is often the most readily available. (p. 297)

5. **b.** is the answer. Follow the directions precisely and you can't miss! (p. 294)
    a. A prototype is the best example of a concept.
    c. Heuristics are rules of thumb that help solve problems but, in contrast to a recipe that is followed precisely, do not guarantee success.
    d. A concept is a mental grouping of similar, objects, events, or people.

6. **d.** is the answer. (p. 294)
    b. & c. Prototypes have nothing to do with chess playing.

7. **d.** is the answer. The confirmation bias is the tendency to search for information that confirms one's preconceptions. In this example, the politicians' preconceptions are biasing their interpretation of the survey results. (p. 295)
    a. Functional fixedness is the inability to perceive an unusual use for a familiar object.
    b. Overconfidence is the tendency to overestimate the accuracy of one's beliefs and judgments.
    c. Belief perseverance is the tendency to cling to one's beliefs even after they have been refuted.

8. **b.** is the answer. (p. 294)
    a. & c. Heuristics do not guarantee solutions or prevent fixation.

9. **d.** is the answer. Your conclusion is based on the stereotype that muscular build is more *representative* of athletes than computer programmers. (p. 296)
    a. Belief perseverance is the tendency to cling to one's beliefs even after they have been refuted.
    b. The availability heuristic involves judging the probability of an event in terms of how readily it comes to mind.
    c. Functional fixedness is the tendency to think of things only in terms of their usual functions.

10. **d.** is the answer. (p. 295)

11. **b.** is the answer. The publicity surrounding disasters makes such events vivid and seemingly more probable than they actually are. (p. 297)
    a. The belief bias is the tendency for preexisting beliefs to distort logical thinking.

c. The representativeness heuristic operates when we judge the likelihood of things in terms of how well they represent particular prototypes. This example does not involve such a situation.

d. Functional fixedness operates in situations in which effective problem solving requires using an object in an unfamiliar manner.

12. **c.** is the answer. This is referred to as overconfidence. (p. 298)

13. **a.** is the answer. In this example, the way the issue is posed, or framed, has evidently influenced consumers' judgments. (p. 300)

   b. Confirmation bias is the tendency to search for information that confirms one's preconceptions.

   c. A prototype is the best example of a concept.

   d. Overconfidence is the tendency to be more confident than correct.

14. **d.** is the answer. (p. 308)

15. **c.** is the answer. (p. 321)

   a. Beyond an intelligence score of about 120, creativity and intelligence scores are not correlated.

   b. & d. There is no evidence that creative people are more likely to be introverted.

   e. This may be true, but it cannot be assumed to be a result of creativity.

16. **c.** is the answer. Heritability is a measure of the extent to which a trait's variation within a group of people can be attributed to heredity. (p. 328)

   a. & b. Heritability is *not* a measure of how much of an *individual's* behavior is inherited, nor of the relative contribution of genes from that person's mother and father. Further, the heritability of any trait depends on the context, or environment, in which that trait is being studied.

17. **c.** is the answer. To be labeled mentally retarded a person must have a test score below 70 and experience difficulty adapting to the normal demands of living independently. (p. 324)

   a. Down syndrome is a common cause of *severe* mental retardation; Dan's test score places him in the range of mild retardation.

   b. There is no indication that Dan possesses one extraordinary skill, as do people with savant syndrome.

   d. The text does not suggest that mentally retarded people eventually become self-supporting.

18. **b.** is the answer. (p. 325)

   a., c., & d. Content validity is the degree to which a test measures what it claims to measure. Furthermore, "target behavior" is not a term used by intelligence researchers.

19. **d.** is the answer. At the time he took the test, Benito's chronological age (CA) was 10. Knowing that IQ = 130 and CA = 10, solving the equation for mental age yields a value of 13. (p. 316)

20. **c.** is the answer. People with savant syndrome tend to score low on intelligence tests but have one exceptional ability. (p. 317)

21. **d.** is the answer. (p. 332)

   c. The racial gap is found in both girls and boys.

22. **b.** is the answer. (p. 324)

23. **a.** is the answer. An exam for a professional license is intended to measure whether you have gained the overall knowledge and skill to practice the profession. The SAT is designed to predict ability, or aptitude, for learning a new skill. (p. 323)

24. **a.** is the answer. If everyone has nearly the same heredity, then heritability—the variation in a trait attributed to heredity—must be low. If individuals within a group come from very similar environments, environmental differences cannot account for variation in a trait; heritability, therefore, must be high. (p. 328)

25. **d.** is the answer. Sternberg and Wagner distinguish among *academic* intelligence, as measured by intelligence tests; *practical* intelligence, which is involved in everyday life and tasks, such as managerial work; and *creative* intelligence. (p. 319)

   a. & b. Verbal and performance intelligence are both measured by standard intelligence tests such as the WAIS and would be included in Sternberg and Wagner's academic intelligence.

   c. Academic intelligence refers to skills assessed by intelligence tests; practical intelligence applies to skills required for everyday tasks and, often, for occupational success.

Essay Question

The first step in constructing the test is to create a valid set of questions that measure psychological knowledge and therefore give the test content validity. If your objective is to predict students' future achievement in psychology courses, the test questions should be selected to measure a criterion, such as information faculty members expect all psychology majors to master before they graduate.

   To enable meaningful comparisons, the test must be standardized. That is, the test should be administered to a representative sample of incoming freshmen at the time they declare psychology to be their major. From the scores of your pretested sample you will then be able to assign an average score and evaluate any individual score according to how much it deviates above or below the average.

To check your test's reliability you might retest a sample of people using the same test or another version of it. If the two scores are correlated, your test is reliable. Alternatively, you might split the test in half and determine whether scores on the two halves are correlated.

Key Terms

1. Thinking, or **cognition**, refers to the mental activity associated with processing, understanding, and communicating information. (p. 293)

2. A **concept** is a mental grouping of similar objects, events, or people. (p. 293)

3. A **prototype** is the best example of a particular category. (p. 294)

4. An **algorithm** is a methodical, logical procedure that, while sometimes slow, guarantees success. (p. 294)

5. A **heuristic** is a simple thinking strategy. Although heuristics are more efficient than algorithms, they do not guarantee success and sometimes even impede problem solving. (p. 294)

6. **Insight** is a sudden and often novel realization of the solution to a problem. Insight contrasts with strategy-based solutions. (p. 294)

7. The **confirmation bias** is an obstacle to problem solving in which people tend to search for information that validates their preconceptions. (p. 295)

8. **Fixation** is an inability to approach a problem in a new way. (p. 295)

9. **Functional fixedness** is a type of fixation in which a person can think of things only in terms of their usual functions. (p. 295)

10. The **representativeness heuristic** is the tendency to judge the likelihood of things in terms of how well they conform to one's prototypes. (p. 296)

11. The **availability heuristic** is based on estimating the probability of certain events in terms of how readily they come to mind. (p. 297)

12. Another obstacle to problem solving, **overconfidence** refers to the tendency to overestimate the accuracy of one's beliefs and judgments. (p. 298)

13. **Framing** refers to the way an issue or question is posed. It can affect people's perception of the issue or answer to the question. (p. 300)

14. **Belief perseverance** is the tendency for people to cling to a particular belief even after the informa-

tion that led to the formation of the belief is discredited. (p. 301)

15. **Language** refers to spoken, written, or signed words and how we combine them to communicate meaning. (p. 302)

16. The **babbling stage** of speech development, which begins by about 4 months, is characterized by the spontaneous utterance of speech sounds. During the babbling stage, children the world over sound alike. (p. 303)

17. Between 1 and 2 years of age children speak mostly in single words; they are therefore in the **one-word stage** of linguistic development. (p. 304)

18. Beginning about age 2, children are in the **two-word stage** and speak mostly in two-word sentences. (p. 304)

19. **Telegraphic speech** is the economical, telegram-like speech of children in the two-word stage. Utterances consist mostly of nouns and verbs; however, words occur in the correct order, showing that the child has learned some of the language's syntactic rules. (p. 304)

20. **Linguistic determinism** is Benjamin Whorf's hypothesis that language determines the way we think. (p. 308)

21. Most experts define **intelligence** as the mental abilities needed to select, adapt to, and shape environments. It reflects the ability to learn from experience, to solve problems, and to reason clearly. (p. 315)

22. A concept introduced by Binet, **mental age** is the chronological age that most typically corresponds to a given level of performance. (p. 316)

23. The **Stanford-Binet** is Lewis Terman's widely used revision of Binet's original intelligence test. (p. 316)

24. The **intelligence quotient**, or **IQ**, was defined originally as the ratio of mental age to chronological age multiplied by 100. Contemporary tests of intelligence assign a score of 100 to the average performance for a given age and define other scores as deviations from this average. (p. 316)

25. **Factor analysis** is a statistical procedure that identifies factors, or clusters of items, that seem to define a common ability. Using this procedure, psychologists have identified several clusters, including verbal intelligence, spatial ability, and reasoning ability factors. (p. 317)

26. **General intelligence**, or *g*, factor underlies each of the more specific intelligence clusters identified through factor analysis. (p. 317)

27. A person with **savant syndrome** has a very low intelligence score, yet possesses one exceptional ability, for example, in music or drawing. (p. 317)

28. **Emotional intelligence** is the ability to perceive, express, understand, and regulate emotions. (p. 319)

29. Most experts agree that **creativity** refers to an ability to generate novel and valuable ideas. People with high IQs may or may not be creative, which indicates that intelligence is only one component of creativity. (p. 321)

30. The **Wechsler Adult Intelligence Scale (WAIS)** is the most widely used intelligence test. It is individually administered, contains 11 subtests, and yields separate verbal and performance intelligence scores, as well as an overall intelligence score. (p. 322)

31. **Aptitude tests** are designed to predict future performance. They measure your capacity to learn new information, rather than measuring what you already know. (p. 323)

32. **Achievement tests** measure a person's current knowledge. (p. 323)

33. **Standardization** is the process of defining meaningful scores on a test by pretesting a large, representative sample of people. (p. 323)

34. The **normal curve** is a bell-shaped curve that represents the distribution (frequency of occurrence) of many physical and psychological attributes. The curve is symmetrical, with most scores near the average and fewer near the extremes. (p. 323)

35. The two criteria that designate **mental retardation** are an IQ below 70 and difficulty adapting to the normal demands of independent living. (p. 324)

36. **Reliability** is the extent to which a test produces consistent results. (p. 324)

37. **Validity** is the degree to which a test measures or predicts what it is supposed to. (p. 324)

38. A common cause of severe retardation and associated physical disorders, **Down syndrome** is usually the result of an extra chromosome in the person's genetic makeup. (p. 325)

39. The **content validity** of a test is the extent to which it samples the behavior that is of interest. (p. 325)

40. A test's **criterion** is the behavior the test is designed to predict. (p. 325)

41. **Predictive validity** is the extent to which a test predicts the behavior it is designed to predict. (p. 325)

42. **Heritability** is the proportion of variation in a trait among individuals that can be attributed to genes. (p. 328)

43. **Stereotype threat** is the phenomenon in which a person's concern that he or she will be evaluated based on a negative stereotype (as on an aptitude test, for example) is actually followed by lower performance. (p. 335)

Cross-Check

ACROSS	DOWN
1. Binet	2. two-word
4. fixation	3. confirmation bias
6. Washoe	4. factor analysis
10. functional	5. IQ
14. Gardner	7. savant syndrome
15. Skinner	8. Down syndrome
16. Chomsky	9. general intelligence
17. one-word	11. normal curve
19. WAIS	12. availability
20. concept	13. mental retardation
21. achievement	18. emotional
22. validity	
23. belief perseverance	

FOCUS ON VOCABULARY AND LANGUAGE

Page 293: . . . our species is *kin to* . . . Myers notes that we are biological creatures related to (*kin to*) other species of animals. We have exceptional abilities for innovation, learning, memory, and rational thinking; yet, at the same time we are prone to making mistakes and thinking and acting irrationally.

Thinking

Page 294: For most of us, the robin with its beak, size, and easy flying, is the *birdier bird* . . . We develop our ideas of how things go together (*concepts*) from definitions or by using **prototypes**. The best example (*prototype*) of a bird is a robin (*the birdier bird*) rather than a penguin, a kiwi, or an ostrich.

Page 294: Thomas Edison tried thousands of light-bulb filaments before *stumbling upon one that worked*. Edison was a famous inventor and he used a trial-and-error method in developing the metal filament that makes the light bulb glow brightly. Using trial and error, he came upon the solution by chance (*stumbled upon one that worked*). Myers contrasts this method with following an **algorithm** (a step-by-step method that always ends with the answer and is typical of computer programs).

Page 296: Should I *shoot* the basketball or pass to the player who's *hot*?—we seldom take the time and effort to reason systematically. (Don't take this sentence literally.) For example, in a game of basketball, the player holding the ball has to decide to throw it through the hoop (*shoot the basketball*) or pass it to a player who has scored frequently (*who's hot*). We usually follow our subjective feelings (*intuitions*) rather than taking the time to use logic and reason.

Page 296: . . . *seat-of-the-pants* decisions. When we make decisions based on subjective or intuitive reasons, rather than using logical, reflective problem-solving strategies, we are using *seat-of-the-pants* judgments. Thus, when we employ **heuristics** (simple thinking strategies), we may make decisions that are incorrect and not very smart (*dumb decisions*).

Page 296: The **representativeness heuristic** enabled you to make a *snap* judgment. We can make quick (*snap*) judgments using a strategy that allows us to determine the probability of things by how well they appear to be typical of some prototype (*representativeness heuristic*). For example, is person A, who is intelligent, unimaginative, compulsive, and generally lifeless, more likely to (a) play jazz for a hobby or (b) play jazz for a hobby and work as an accountant? The representativeness heuristic leads most people to incorrectly pick (b) as the answer.

Page 297: The faster people can remember an instance of some event (*"a broken promise"*), the more they expect it to recur. We tend to use whatever information is accessible in our memories when making decisions and judgments; similarly, events or mistakes that are easiest to access (i.e., those that most readily come to mind) will most likely be used. This is called the **availability heuristic.** So, if on one occasion, someone did not keep his or her word (*broke a promise*) about doing something, we tend to remember that event and use it in predicting future behavior. Sometimes the availability heuristic can cause errors in judgment.

Page 297: During those three days, more than 100,000 invisible children—*"mere statistics" on some world health ledger*—died of preventable starvation, diarrhea, and disease (Gore, 1992). There was worldwide media attention to the three-day rescue of a small child trapped in a deep hole (a well) in Texas. Due to the availability heuristic we tend to remember the vivid pictures associated with the danger to one child and ignore the statistics which showed that more than 100,000 children we did not observe (*invisible*) died during the same period. They were mere numbers (*statistics*) on some world health accounting book (*ledger*).

Page 298: Overconfidence *plagues* decisions outside the laboratory, too. Many factors combine to produce the tendency to overestimate the accuracy of our decisions, judgments, and knowledge (**overconfidence**). In everyday life, as well as in lab experiments, our judgments are greatly afflicted (*plagued*) by overconfidence.

Page 300: That our judgments can *flip-flop* so dramatically is startling. Presenting the same information in two different ways can cause people to react more negatively or positively depending on how the (logically equivalent) information was **framed**. The framing effect can cause alarming and dramatic reversals (*flip-flops*) in people's decisions and judgments. For example, a very fatty food product made by grinding meat (*ground beef*) will be seen more positively if described as "75% lean" as opposed to "25% fat," despite the fact that exactly the same information is conveyed in each case.

Page 301: Belief perseverance often *fuels social conflict*. Our irrationality also shows when we persist (*persevere*) in our views despite evidence to the contrary (**belief perseverance**). This can lead to an increase in strong feelings or passions over controversial issues (*fuels social conflict*). Myers suggests one solution for those who wish to restrain (*rein in*) the effect of belief perseverance, and that is to give serious consideration to beliefs *opposite* to your own.

Page 302: From this we might conclude that our heads are indeed *filled with straw*. The discussion about human irrationality might lead to the conclusion that we have ineffective and inefficient cognitions (*heads filled with straw*). Myers, however, is optimistic and suggests that we can learn about our irrational propensities (tendencies) and be alert to the dangers that can result in poor or foolish (*dumb*) decisions.

Language

Page 302: When the human vocal tract evolved the capacity to utter vowels, *our capacity for language exploded, catapulting our species forward*. When the physiological ability for complex vocalization evolved, the ability to communicate orally expanded exponentially (*exploded*). This new linguistic capacity propelled (*catapulted*) our species to new levels of accomplishments, enabling us to communicate from person to person and to transmit civilization's accumulated knowledge from generation to generation.

Page 303: With remarkable efficiency, you can selectively sample the tens of thousands of words in your memory, effortlessly *combine them on the fly* with near-perfect word order, and *spew them out three words a second*. Humans have an amazing facility for language. With little or no effort, we can select the appropriate words from the tens of thousands in memory, put them together hurriedly (*combine them on the fly*), and verbally produce them in rapid succession (*spew them out three words a second*).

Page 303: Yet by 4 months of age, babies can *read lips* and *discriminate* speech sounds. When people speak, their lips move in ways that correspond to the sounds they utter. Many deaf people can understand what is being said by watching how the lips move (*lip reading*). Very young children can not only tell the difference (*discriminate*) between sounds, but can also recognize lip movements that correspond with certain sounds (*read lips*).

Page 305: Surely, Chomsky has said, *a Martian scientist* observing children in a single-language community would conclude that language is almost entirely inborn. The famous linguist Chomsky believes that the behaviorist's views (as exemplified by Skinner) are simplistic (*naive*). He argues that language acquisition could not be simply a function of experience or learning. Instead, he contends that any unbiased observer (e.g., *an imaginary scientist from the planet Mars*) would have to arrive at the inescapable fact that our capacity for language is almost totally biologically inherited (*inborn*). The specific language you speak is a product of your environment, which builds on your innate capacity for language. As Myers puts it, *"we are born with the hardware and an operating system; experience writes the software."*

Page 307: Chomsky would say that once the *grammar switches are thrown* during a child's developing years, mastering another grammar becomes more difficult. Chomsky likens learning a particular grammar during early childhood to turning on (*throwing*) switches that influence language acquisition. When they have been turned on for one grammar, it becomes much harder to master a second grammar.

Page 308: Thinking and language intricately intertwine. Asking which comes first is one of psychology's *chicken-and-egg* questions. "Which came first: the chicken or the egg?" Clearly, you need an egg to produce a chicken, but you also need a chicken to lay the egg. So, like this age-old conundrum (*riddle*), psychologists have argued over which comes first, our ideas and thoughts or the words we use to name and verbalize them. Myers concludes that language influences (but does not determine) thought, and our thinking affects our language, which in turn affects thought (*the traffic runs both ways*).

Page 311: If in our use of language we humans are, as the psalmist long ago *rhapsodized*, "little lower than God," where do other animals fit in the scheme of things? The psalmist (an author of religious or sacred songs) spoke in an extravagantly enthusiastic manner (*rhapsodized*) about human nature, and Myers notes that it is our use of human language that elevates us above nonhumans. Nevertheless, we do share a capacity for language with other animals.

Page 312: *Spying* the short stick, Sultan [the chimp] grabbed it and tried to reach the fruit. Kohler's experiment with the chimpanzee Sultan showed that our closest relatives are capable of cognition. When the fruit was out of reach, Sultan noticed (*spied*) the short stick and used it to pull a longer stick into the cage, which he then used to get the fruit.

Page 313: Were the chimps *language champs* or were the researchers *chumps*? Critics of "ape language" argue that for animals, language acquisition is painfully slow, resembles conditioned responses, does not follow syntax, and is little more than imitation. In addition, demonstrations of animal language are always subjectively interpreted by their trainers. Myers asks: Were the chimps exceptionally talented (*language champs*) or were the researchers just easily duped (*were they chumps*) and acting foolishly (*mak-

ing monkeys out of themselves)? The answer is that the controversy has led to further research and progress, and a renewed appreciation of our own, as well as our closest relatives', capacity for communication and language.

Intelligence

Page 316: On tests, therefore, a *"dull"* child should perform as does a typical younger child, and a *"bright"* child as does a typical older child. Children develop intellectually at different rates and so Binet and Simon developed the concept of **mental age**. Children who performed below the average level of other children the same age (e.g., a 10-year-old who performed as the average 8-year-old did) would be considered retarded or slow in development (*"dull"*). Those who performed above the average (e.g., a 10-year-old who scored as the average 12-year-old did) would be considered developmentally advanced or precocious (*"bright"*).

Page 317: You may also know a talented artist who is *dumbfounded by* the simplest mathematical problems . . . . Researchers have used a statistical approach (factor analysis) to identify groups of test items that measure a common ability. So, someone who has a group, or cluster, of abilities in one area may be very puzzled by and completely unable to solve (*dumbfounded by*) a relatively simple problem in a different area. Spearman argued that there was a common factor (*general intelligence,* or *g*) underlying particular abilities.

Page 317: People with **savant syndrome**, for example, often score low on intelligence tests but have an *island of brilliance*—some incredible ability, as in computation, drawing, or musical memory. Some people are functionally retarded in almost every aspect except for one very specific ability (*island of brilliance*) in which they are exceptionally gifted **(savant syndrome)**. Despite having very poor language skills and other cognitive dysfunctions, they may be capable of outstanding performance in computation, memory for music heard only once, drawing, etc. Some psychologists argue that this is evidence for the notion of multiple intelligences.

Page 318: . . . *the street-smart* adolescent who becomes a *crafty* executive . . . Myers is attempting to simplify Howard Gardner's eight intelligences, referring to *word smarts, number smarts,* and so on. As an example of one of these intelligences, he uses the adolescent who has the ability to survive in urban environments (*street smart*) becoming a clever (*crafty*) executive.

Page 319: . . . *how to read people* . . . People who have good practical managerial intelligence may not score high on academic ability but will be good at motivating people; assigning work to others appropriately; and knowing and understanding peoples' needs, desires, and ambitions (*knowing how to read people*). They will also be alert, astute, and wise (*shrewd*) in their approach to life in general. Other people may demonstrate different types of intelligences (for example, academic, creative, or emotional intelligence).

Page 321: . . . *out of the blue* . . . The solution to a very complex problem can occur unexpectedly and suddenly (*out of the blue*). This happened to Andrew Wiles when he eventually solved Fermat's last theorem after working hard on the problem (*wrestling with it*) for over 30 years. This example illustrates the creative process, the ability to produce novel and valuable ideas.

Page 323: . . . scores often form a roughly symmetrical, bell-shaped distribution *clustered* around the average. Many variables that we measure (weight, height, intelligence, etc.) follow a bell-shaped curve when plotted on a frequency distribution. On intelligence tests, the average is 100; most scores (68%) are between 85 and 115, so they are gathered close together (*clustered*) near the mean (*average*).

Pages 324–325: If you use an inaccurate *tape measure* to measure people's heights, your height report would have high *reliability* (consistency) but low *validity*. In order for a test to be *reliable*, the instrument should have consistent results over numerous tests. So, if you use a tape measure that is inaccurate, it will meet the *reliability* criterion because it will always give you the same result; it will not, however, be valid. To be valid it should *accurately* measure what it is supposed to measure.

Page 325: During the last two centuries, *the pendulum of opinion* about how best to care for people with mental retardation has made a *complete swing*. Over time and in different ways we have taken care of the mentally retarded—first at home, then in small residential schools, then in massive institutions (*warehouses* for keeping people), and now back to a more normal situation in which they are integrated (mainstreamed) into regular classrooms. Our views about how people with mental retardation should be looked after have moved from one extreme to the other (*the pendulum of opinion . . . has made a complete swing*).

Page 329: Extreme deprivation was *bludgeoning native intelligence*. In this investigation of a destitute orphanage, Hunt (1982) found that the effect of extreme neglect was severe depression and a general mental and physical passivity (the children became *"glum lumps"*). Their inborn (*native*) intellectual capacity was taking a severe beating (*bludgeoning*) due to the physical and emotional neglect. Hunt's intervention program had dramatic results. This points to the strong influence of environment.

Page 332: Similarly, in the psychological domain, gender similarities vastly outnumber gender differences, but most people find those differences more *newsworthy*. Males and females are alike in many more ways than they are different. Although the similarities overwhelm (*vastly outnumber*) the dissimilarities, we are more intrigued by the dissimilarities (*we find them more newsworthy*).

Page 333: The score differences are *sharpest* at the *extremes*. Although the variability in ability is greater within the two groups, people tend to focus on the between-group male-female differences. The differences in scores between males and females on the SAT test are more noticeable (*sharpest*) at the high and low ends of the distribution (*extremes*) than in the middle. Thus, among the very highest scorers in math, the majority are likely to be male.

Page 334: . . . *computer camps* . . . Because math and science have historically been viewed as male subjects, boys have been encouraged to become involved in special science activities and computer workshops (*computer camps*), whereas girls have been urged to take an interest in English.

chapter 10

Motivation

Chapter Overview

Motivation is the study of forces that energize and direct our behavior. Chapter 10 discusses various motivational concepts and looks closely at four motives: hunger, sex, the need to belong, and the motivation to achieve. Research on hunger points to the interplay between physiological and psychological (internal and external) factors in motivation. Sexual motivation in men and women is triggered less by physiological factors and more by external incentives. Even so, research studies demonstrate that sexual orientation is neither willfully chosen nor easily changed. Achievement motivation demonstrates that a drive-reduction theory is of limited usefulness in explaining human behavior. Although this motivation serves no apparent physiological need, it may be extremely forceful nonetheless.

NOTE: Answer guidelines for all Chapter 10 questions begin on page 294.

Introducing Motivation (p. 341)

> David Myers at times uses idioms that are unfamiliar to some readers. If you do not know the meaning of the following phrase in the context in which it appears in the text, refer to page 303 for an explanation: *truant officer.*

Introduction Preview

First, skim the introduction. Then read the following objective and, as you read the text, search for the information that will enable you to meet that objective. An answer guideline is provided on page 294.

1. Define motivation.

Motivational Concepts (pp. 341–344)

> If you do not know the meaning of any of the following words, phrases, or expressions, in the context in which they appear in the text, refer to page 303 for an explanation: *this fad for naming instincts collapsed under its own weight; feedback loops; monkey around.*

Section Preview

First, skim the section, noting headings and boldface items. Then read the following objectives and, as you read the text, search for the information that will enable you to meet each objective. Answer guidelines begin on page 294.

1. Discuss the three perspectives that have influenced our understanding of motivation.

2. Discuss Maslow's hierarchy of needs.

Stepping Through the Section

After you have read the section, complete the sentences and answer the questions. As you proceed, evaluate your performance by consulting the answers on page 295. Do not continue with the next section until you understand each answer. If you need to, review or reread the section in the textbook before continuing.

1. As a result of Darwin's influence, many behaviors were classified as rigid, unlearned behavior patterns that are characteristic of a species, called _____.

Discuss why early instinct theory failed as an explanation of human behavior.

2. The idea underlying the theory that _____ predispose species-typical behavior remains popular.

3. According to another view of motivation, organisms may experience a physiological _____ , which creates a state of arousal that _____ the organism to reduce the need.

4. The aim of drive reduction is to maintain a constant internal state, called _____ . Behavior is often not so much pushed by our drives as it is pulled by _____ in the environment.

5. Rather than reduce a physiological need, some motivated behaviors actually _____ arousal. This demonstrates that human motives _____ (do/do not) always satisfy some biological need.

6. Starting from the idea that some needs take precedence over others, Maslow constructed a _____ of needs.

7. According to Maslow, the _____ needs are the most pressing, whereas the highest-order needs relate to _____ . A criticism of

Maslow's theory is that the sequence is _____ and not _____ experienced.

8. Surveys of life satisfaction reveal that _____ satisfaction is strongly predictive of subjective well-being in poorer nations, whereas _____ satisfaction matters more in wealthy nations and _____ in individualist nations.

Hunger (pp. 345–357)

> If you do not know the meaning of any of the following words, phrases, or expressions in the context in which they appear in the text, refer to pages 303–304 for an explanation: *feasted their eyes on delectable forbidden foods; keeping tabs; miser; win the battle of the bulge; binge-purge; thinner wallet; Couch potatoes beware.*

Section Preview

Answer guidelines begin on page 295.

1. Discuss the basis of hunger in terms of physiology.

2. Identify the various hormones involved in appetite regulation, and explain how taste preferences are determined.

3. (Close-Up) Describe the symptoms and possible causes of anorexia nervosa and bulimia nervosa.

4. Discuss the factors that contribute to obesity.

5. Explain whether genes play no role, some role, or an exclusive role in causing obesity.

Stepping Through the Section

Answers are provided on page 296.

1. Ancel Keys observed that men became preoccupied with thoughts of food when they underwent _____ .

2. Cannon and Washburn's experiment using a balloon indicated that there is an association between hunger and _____ _____ . When a portion of an obese person's stomach is surgically sealed off, the remaining stomach produces _____ (more/less) of the hunger-arousing hormone _____ .

3. When an animal has had its stomach removed, hunger _____ (does/does not) continue.

4. Increases in the hormone _____ diminish blood _____ , partly by converting it to stored fat, which causes hunger to _____ .

5. The brain area that plays a role in hunger and other bodily maintenance functions is the _____ . Animals will begin eating when the _____ _____ is electrically stimulated. When this region is destroyed, hunger _____ (increases/

decreases). Animals will stop eating when the _____ _____ is stimulated. When this area is destroyed, animals _____ (overeat/undereat).

6. When a rat is deprived of food and blood sugar levels wane, the _____ _____ churns out the hunger-triggering hormone _____ . Human patients with tumors in the _____ will eat excessively and become fat. Feedback from this area of the brain is sent to the

_____ _____ , which decide behavior.

For questions 7–10, identify the appetite hormone that is described.

7. Hunger-triggering hormone: _____ .

8. Hormone secreted by empty stomach: _____ .

9. Hormone secreted by pancreas: _____ .

10. Digestive tract hormone that signals fullness:

_____ .

11. The weight level at which an individual's body is programmed to stay is referred to as the body's

_____ _____ .

A person whose weight goes beyond this level will tend to feel _____ (more/less) hungry than usual and expend _____ (more/less) energy.

12. The rate of energy expenditure in maintaining basic functions when the body is at rest is the

_____ _____ rate. When food intake is reduced, the body compensates by _____ (raising/lowering) this rate.

13. The concept of a precise body set point that drives hunger _____ (is accepted/is not accepted) by all researchers. Some researchers believe that set point can be altered by _____ _____ .

In support of this idea is evidence that when people and other animals are given unlimited access to tasty foods, they tend to_____ and _____ _____ .

14. Research with amnesia patients indicates that part of knowing when to eat is our _____ of our last meal.

15. As a meal progresses and hunger and food tastiness decrease, people chew their food _____ (more/less).

16. Carbohydrates boost levels of the neurotransmitter _____ , which _____ (calms/arouses) the body.

17. Taste preferences for sweet and salty are _____ (genetic/learned). Other influences on taste include _____ and _____ . We have a natural dislike of many foods that are _____ ; this _____ was probably adaptive for our ancestors and protected them from toxic substances.

18. An estimated _____ (what percent?) of Americans are overweight. Government guidelines measure obesity as a _____ _____ of _____ or more; they encourage people to keep this number under _____ . Eating disorders are rare in cultures that do not have a _____-_____ for women.

Cite some of the ways in which significant obesity is a threat to physical and psychological health.

19. (Close-Up) The disorder in which a person becomes significantly underweight and yet feels fat is known as _____ _____ . In terms of sex and age, this disorder tends to develop in

_____ who are in their _____ .

20. (Close-Up) A more common disorder is _____ _____ , which is characterized by repeated _____-_____ episodes and by feelings of depression or anxiety.

21. (Close-Up) The families of bulimia patients have a high incidence of _____ , _____ , and _____ . The families of anorexia patients tend to be _____ , _____-_____ , and _____ . Eating disorders _____ (provide/do not provide) a telltale sign of childhood sexual abuse.

22. (Close-Up) Anorexia always begins as a _____-_____ _____ , and bulimia nearly always begins after _____ _____ .

23. (Close-Up) Genetic factors _____ (may/do not) influence susceptibility to eating disorders. Vulnerability to eating disorders _____ (increases/does not increase) with greater body dissatisfaction.

24. (Close-Up) Women students in _____ rate their actual shape as closer to the cultural ideal. In _____ cultures, however, the rise in eating disorders has coincided with an increasing number of women having a poor _____ _____ .

25. (Close-Up) Stice and Shaw found that when young women were shown pictures of unnaturally thin models, they felt more _____ , _____ , and _____ with their own bodies.

26. In one experiment, job applicants were rated as less worthy of hiring when they were made to appear _____ . Some studies suggest that weight discrimination is even greater than discrimination by _____ or

_____ .

27. The energy equivalent of a pound of fat is approximately _____ calories. The immediate determinant of body fat is the size and number of _____

_____ one has.

28. The size of fat cells _____ (can/cannot) be decreased by dieting; the number of fat cells _____ (can/cannot) be decreased by dieting.

29. Fat tissue has a _____ (higher/lower) metabolic rate than lean tissue. The result is that fat tissue requires _____ (more/less) food energy to be maintained.

30. The body weight "thermostat" of obese people _____ (is/is not) set to maintain a higher-than-average weight. When weight drops below this setting, _____ increases and _____ decreases.

Explain why, metabolically, many obese people find it so difficult to become and stay thin.

31. Studies of adoptees and twins _____ (do/do not) provide evidence of a genetic influence on obesity.

32. Obesity is _____ (more/less) common among lower-class than upper-class women and _____ (does/does not) vary from culture to culture.

Contrast the typical diets and life-styles of Americans today with their counterparts in the early 1900s.

33. The biggest factor in why one person is heavier than another is _____ ; the biggest factor in why people today are heavier than their counterparts 50 years ago is

_____ .

34. Most obese persons who lose weight _____ (gain/do not gain) it back.

(Close-Up) List several tips for losing weight.

Sexual Motivation (pp. 357–370)

> If you do not know the meaning of any of the following words, phrases, or expressions in the context in which they appear in the text, refer to pages 304–305 for an explanation: *rapid-fire questions; shift it into high gear; X-rated; the pendulum of sexual values has swung; fired; neither willfully chosen nor willfully changed; swung the pendulum toward; double-edged sword.*

Section Preview

Answer guidelines begin on page 296.

1. Discuss whether survey research has contributed to our understanding of sexual behavior, and describe the human sexual response cycle.

2. Identify some common sexual disorders and their possible type of treatment.

3. Discuss the basis of sexual motivation in terms of both internal physiology and external incentives.

4. Discuss cultural and historical variations in adolescent sexuality, identify several factors that contribute to the high rate of unprotected sex, and describe teens who most often delay sexual activity.

5. Describe research findings on the nature of sexual orientation.

6. Discuss the origins of homosexuality, including both myths and research findings.

7. Discuss the place of values in research and education about sexual behavior.

Stepping Through the Section

Answers are provided on page 298.

1. In the 1940s and 1950s, a biologist named _____ surveyed the sexual practices of thousands of men and women.

2. Many popular sexual surveys cannot be taken seriously because they are based on _____ samples of respondents.

3. The two researchers who identified a four-stage sexual response cycle are _____ and _____ . In order, the stages of the cycle are the _____ phase, the _____ phase, _____ , and the _____ phase.

4. During resolution, males experience a _____ _____ , during which they are incapable of another orgasm.

5. Problems that consistently impair sexual functioning are called _____ _____ . Examples of such problems include _____ _____ , _____ _____ , and _____ _____ . Personality disorders _____ (have/have not) been linked with most of the problems impairing sexual functioning. The most effective therapies for sexual problems are _____ oriented.

6. In most mammals, females are sexually receptive only during ovulation, when the hormone _____ has peaked.

7. The importance of the hormone _____ to male sexual arousal is

confirmed by the fact that sexual interest declines in animals if their _____ are removed. In women, low levels of the hormone _____ may cause a waning of sexual interest.

8. Normal hormonal fluctuations in humans have _____ (little/significant) effect on sexual motivation. In later life, frequency of intercourse _____ (increases/decreases) as sex hormone levels _____ (increase/decline).

9. Research has shown that erotic stimuli _____ (are/are not) as arousing for women as for men.

Explain some of the possible harmful consequences of sexually explicit material.

10. The importance of the brain in sexual motivation is indicated by the fact that people who, because of injury, have no genital sensation _____ (do/do not) feel sexual desire.

11. Most women and men _____ (have/do not have) sexual fantasies. Compared to women's fantasies, men' sexual fantasies are more _____

_____ .

Sexual fantasies do not indicate sexual _____ or _____ .

12. Attitudes toward premarital sex vary widely from one _____ to another and with the passage of _____ .
Rates of teen intercourse in the United States and

_____ _____

are much higher than those in _____ and _____ countries.

State five factors that contribute to the high rate of unprotected sex among teenagers.

13. Unprotected sex has led to an increase in adolescent _____ and rates of

_____ _____

_____ .

State several predictors of reduced teen sexuality and pregnancy.

14. A person's sexual attraction toward members of a particular gender is referred to as

_____ _____ .

15. Historically, _____ (all/a slight majority) of the world's cultures have been predominantly heterosexual. Most homosexuals begin thinking of themselves as gay or lesbian around age _____ .

16. Studies in Europe and the United States indicate that approximately _____ percent of men and _____ percent of women are exclusively homosexual. This finding suggests that popular estimates of the rate of homosexuality are _____ (high/low/accurate).

17. A person's sexual orientation _____ (does/does not) appear to be voluntarily chosen. Several recent research studies reveal that sexual orientation among _____ (women/men) tends to be less strongly felt and potentially more changeable than among the other gender.

18. Most gays and lesbians _____ (suffer/do not suffer) from some form of psychological disorder and _____ (accept/do not accept) their orientation.

19. Childhood events and family relationships _____ (are/are not) important factors in determining a person's sexual orientation.

20. Homosexuality _____ (does/does not) involve a fear of the other gender that leads people to direct their sexual desires toward members of their own gender.

21. Sex hormone levels _____ (do/do not) predict sexual orientation.

22. As children, most homosexuals _____ (were/were not) sexually victimized.

23. Homosexual people appear more often in certain populations, including men who live in _____ _____ ; _____ , _____ _____ , _____ , and _____ ; and men who have older _____ .

24. One theory proposes that people develop a homosexual orientation if they are segregated with _____ (their own/the other) gender at the time their sex drive matures. The fact that early homosexual behavior _____ (does/does not) make people homosexual _____ (supports/conflicts with) this theory.

25. Researcher Simon LeVay discovered a cluster of cells in the _____ that is larger in _____ men than in all others. Other studies have found a section of the brain's _____ _____ that is one-third larger in homosexual men than in heterosexual men.

26. Studies of twins suggest that genes probably _____ (do/do not) play a role in homosexuality.

27. In animals and some rare human cases, sexual orientation has been altered by abnormal _____ conditions during prenatal development. In humans, prenatal exposure to hormone levels typical of _____ , particularly between _____ and _____ months after conception, may predispose an attraction to males.

28. Gay males and lesbians may have certain physical traits more typical of those of the other gender, including _____ patterns, greater odds of being _____ (right/left)-handed, and anatomical traits of the _____ within the hearing system.

29. Most psychiatrists now believe that _____ (nature/nurture) plays the larger role in predisposing sexual orientation. Those who believe that sexual orientation is determined by _____ express more accepting attitudes toward homosexual persons.

30. Recent public opinion surveys reveal a _____ (more/less) accepting attitude toward homosexuality among Americans _____ (and/but not a liberalization of) all sex-related attitudes.

31. Teenagers who have had formal sex education are _____ (no more/more) likely to engage in premarital sex than those who have not.

The Need to Belong (pp. 370–373)

> If you do not know the meaning of any of the following words, phrases, or expressions in the context in which they appear in the text, refer to page 305 for an explanation: *colors our thoughts and emotions; Even to be shunned—given the cold shoulder . . . .*

Section Preview

Answer guidelines are provided on page 298.

1. Discuss the significance of the need to belong, including its origins and benefits.

Stepping Through the Section

Answers are provided on page 298.

1. From an evolutionary standpoint, social bonds in humans boosted our ancestors' _____ rates. If those who felt this need to

_____ survived and repro-
duced more successfully, their
_____ would in time
predominate.

2. When asked what makes life meaningful, most
people mention _____

_____ .

3. Feeling accepted and loved by others boosts our

_____ .

4. Much of our _____
behavior aims to increase our belonging. For
most people, familiarity leads to _____
(liking/disliking).

5. Researchers have found that people who are
rejected are more likely to engage in
_____ behaviors and may
exhibit more _____
behavior, such as _____ .

6. People who perceive strong social support from
others live with better _____
than those who lack social support. They also
have a lower risk of _____ dis-
order and premature _____ .

Achievement Motivation (pp. 373–374)

> If you do not know the meaning of any of the
> following word or expression in the context in
> which it appears in the text, refer to page 305
> for an explanation: _daredevils; ring-toss game._

Section Preview

Answer guidelines begin on page 298.

1. Describe the nature and origin of achievement
motivation.

Stepping Through the Section

Answers are provided on page 299.

1. The biological perspective on motivation is contradicted by the existence of many behaviors that
appear to satisfy no apparent biological
_____ . An example is the
desire for significant accomplishments, mastering
skills, and attaining a high standard—which psychologists refer to as _____

_____ .

2. Psychologists Murray, McClelland, and Atkinson
studied achievement motivation by having
people create _____ about
ambiguous pictures.

3. In experiments, individuals who chose extremely
difficult tasks tended to have a _____
(low/high) need for achievement.

4. The parents of highly motivated children tend to
encourage their _____ and
_____ and _____
them for the successes.

5. Achievement motivation has both
_____ roots and
_____ roots.

Progress Test 1

Multiple-Choice Questions

Circle your answers to the following questions and
check them with the answers beginning on page 369.
If your answer is incorrect, read the explanation for
why it is incorrect and then consult the appropriate
pages of the text (in parentheses following the correct
answer).

1. Motivation is best understood as a state that:
   a. reduces a drive.
   b. aims at satisfying a biological need.
   c. energizes an organism to act.
   d. energizes and directs behavior.

2. Which of the following is a difference between a
drive and a need?
   a. Needs are learned; drives are inherited.
   b. Needs are physiological states; drives are psychological states.
   c. Drives are generally stronger than needs.
   d. Needs are generally stronger than drives.

3. One problem with the idea of motivation as drive reduction is that:
   a. because some motivated behaviors do not seem to be based on physiological needs, they cannot be explained in terms of drive reduction.
   b. it fails to explain any human motivation.
   c. it cannot account for homeostasis.
   d. it does not explain the hunger drive.

4. Some scientific evidence makes a preliminary link between homosexuality and:
   a. late sexual maturation.
   b. the age of an individual's first erotic experience.
   c. atypical prenatal hormones.
   d. early problems in relationships with parents.
   e. all of the above.

5. Increases in insulin will:
   a. lower blood sugar and trigger hunger.
   b. raise blood sugar and trigger hunger.
   c. lower blood sugar and trigger satiety.
   d. raise blood sugar and trigger satiety.

6. Electrical stimulation of the lateral hypothalamus will cause an animal to:
   a. begin eating.
   b. stop eating.
   c. become obese.
   d. begin copulating.
   e. stop copulating.

7. The text suggests that a "neophobia" for unfamiliar tastes:
   a. is more common in children than in adults.
   b. protected our ancestors from potentially toxic substances.
   c. may be an early warning sign of an eating disorder.
   d. only grows stronger with repeated exposure to those tastes.
   e. does all of the above.

8. I am a protein secreted by the empty stomach that signals hunger to the brain. What am I?
   a. PYY
   b. ghrelin
   c. orexin
   d. insulin

9. Instinct theory and drive-reduction theory both emphasize _____ factors in motivation.
   a. environmental
   b. cognitive
   c. psychological
   d. social
   e. biological

10. The correct order of the stages of Masters and Johnson's sexual response cycle is:
    a. plateau; excitement; orgasm; resolution.
    b. excitement; plateau; orgasm; resolution.
    c. excitement; orgasm; resolution; refractory.
    d. plateau; excitement; orgasm; refractory.
    e. excitement; orgasm; plateau; resolution.

11. Few human behaviors are rigidly patterned enough to qualify as:
    a. needs.
    b. drives.
    c. instincts.
    d. incentives.

12. In his study of men on a semistarvation diet, Keys found that:
    a. the metabolic rate of the subjects increased.
    b. the subjects eventually lost interest in food.
    c. the subjects became obsessed with food.
    d. the subjects' behavior directly contradicted predictions made by Maslow's hierarchy of needs.

13. When asked what makes life meaningful, most people first mention:
    a. good health.
    b. challenging work.
    c. satisfying relationships.
    d. serving others.

14. Bulimia nervosa involves:
    a. binging.
    b. purging.
    c. dramatic weight loss.
    d. a. and b.
    e. a., b., and c.

15. Castration of male rats results in:
    a. reduced testosterone and sexual interest.
    b. reduced testosterone, but no change in sexual interest.
    c. reduced estrogen and sexual interest.
    d. reduced estrogen, but no change in sexual interest.

16. Which of the following has been found to be most effective in treating sexual disorders?
    a. psychoanalysis
    b. cognitive therapy
    c. drug therapy
    d. behavior therapy

17. It has been said that the body's major sex organ is the brain. With regard to sex education:
    a. transmission of value-free information about the wide range of sexual behaviors should be the primary focus of the educator.
    b. transmission of technical knowledge about the biological act should be the classroom focus, free from the personal values and attitudes of researchers, teachers, and students.
    c. the home, not the school, should be the focus of all instruction about reproductive behavior.
    d. people's attitudes, values, and morals cannot be separated from the biological aspects of sexuality.

18. Which of the following is *not* true regarding Alfred Kinsey's studies of sexual behavior?
    a. They were based on confidential interviews.
    b. The respondents were drawn from a large, random sample of Americans.
    c. The sample contained an overrepresentation of well-educated white people.
    d. Some of the questions encouraged admission of sexual activity.

19. Which of the following tends to foster a high need for achievement?
    a. frequent use of external controls on behavior
    b. encouraging young children to remain dependent
    c. using punishment for failures
    d. encouraging independence at an early age and praising children for their successes

20. Which of the following is *not* true regarding sexual orientation?
    a. Sexual orientation is neither willfully chosen nor willfully changed.
    b. Women's sexual orientation tends to be less strongly felt than men's.
    c. Men's sexual orientation is potentially more fluid and changeable than women's.
    d. Women, regardless of sexual orientation, respond to both female and male erotic stimuli.
    e. Homosexual behavior does not always indicate a homosexual orientation.

Matching Items

Match each term with its definition or description.

Terms

_____ 1. orgasmic disorder
_____ 2. set point
_____ 3. drive
_____ 4. achievement motivation
_____ 5. orexin
_____ 6. estrogen
_____ 7. homeostasis
_____ 8. sexual orientation
_____ 9. need
_____ 10. incentive
_____ 11. ghrelin

Definitions or Descriptions

a. hormone secreted more by females than by males
b. the body's tendency to maintain a balanced internal state
c. environmental stimulus that motivates behavior
d. a person's attraction to members of a particular sex
e. an inability to experience orgasm
f. a desire for significant accomplishment
g. an aroused state arising from some physiological need
h. a state of deprivation
i. the body's weight-maintenance setting
j. hormone secreted by an empty stomach
k. hunger-triggering hormone secreted by the hypothalamus

Progress Test 2

Progress Test 2 should be completed during a final chapter review. Answer the following questions after you thoroughly understand the correct answers for the section reviews and Progress Test 1.

Multiple-Choice Questions

1. I am a hunger-triggering hormone secreted by the hypothalamus. What am I?
   - **a.** PYY
   - **b.** ghrelin
   - **c.** orexin
   - **d.** insulin

2. Homeostasis refers to:
   - **a.** the tendency to maintain a steady internal state.
   - **b.** the tendency to choose either very easy or very difficult tasks.
   - **c.** the setting of the body's "weight thermostat."
   - **d.** a theory of the development of sexual orientation.

3. Research on obesity indicates that:
   - **a.** pound for pound, fat tissue requires more calories to maintain than lean tissue.
   - **b.** once fat cells are acquired, they are never lost, no matter how rigorously one diets.
   - **c.** one pound of weight is lost for every 3500-calorie reduction in diet.
   - **d.** when weight drops below the set point, hunger and metabolism also decrease.

4. Of the following parts of the world, teen intercourse rates are highest in:
   - **a.** Western Europe.
   - **b.** Canada.
   - **c.** The United States.
   - **d.** Asia.
   - **e.** Arab countries.

5. (Close-Up) Although the cause of eating disorders is still unknown, proposed explanations focus on all the following *except*:
   - **a.** metabolic factors.
   - **b.** genetic factors.
   - **c.** family background factors.
   - **d.** cultural factors.

6. The brain area that when stimulated suppresses eating is the:
   - **a.** lateral hypothalamus.
   - **b.** ventromedial hypothalamus.
   - **c.** lateral thalamus.
   - **d.** ventromedial thalamus.

7. Exposure of a fetus to the hormones typical of females between _____ and _____ months after conception may predispose the developing human to become attracted to males.
   - **a.** 1; 3
   - **b.** 2; 5
   - **c.** 4; 7
   - **d.** 6; 9
   - **e.** 9; 11

8. Which of the following statements concerning homosexuality is true?
   - **a.** Homosexuals have abnormal hormone levels.
   - **b.** As children, most homosexuals were molested by an adult homosexual.
   - **c.** Homosexuals had a domineering opposite-sex parent.
   - **d.** Research indicates that sexual orientation may be at least partly physiological.

9. (Close-Up) A turn-of-the-century survey of British bank and university staff found that:
   - **a.** men and women alike expressed significant self-dissatisfaction.
   - **b.** women were more accurate than men in their perception of their body weight.
   - **c.** men were more likely to be overweight and women were more likely to perceive themselves as overweight.
   - **d.** older women were more likely than younger women to perceive themselves as overweight.

10. According to Maslow's theory:
    - **a.** the most basic motives are based on physiological needs.
    - **b.** needs are satisfied in a specified order.
    - **c.** the highest motives relate to self-actualization.
    - **d.** all of the above are true.

11. Which of the following is *inconsistent* with the drive-reduction theory of motivation?
    - **a.** When body temperature drops below 98.6° Fahrenheit, blood vessels constrict to conserve warmth.
    - **b.** A person is driven to seek a drink when his or her cellular water level drops below its optimum point.
    - **c.** Monkeys will work puzzles even if not given a food reward.
    - **d.** A person becomes hungry when body weight falls below its biological set point.
    - **e.** None of the above is inconsistent.

12. (Close-Up) Which of the following is true concerning eating disorders?
    a. Genetic factors may influence susceptibility.
    b. Abnormal levels of certain neurotransmitters may play a role.
    c. People with eating disorders are at risk for anxiety or depression.
    d. Family background is a significant factor.
    e. All of the above are true.

13. Sexual orientation refers to:
    a. a person's tendency to display behaviors typical of males or females.
    b. a person's sense of identity as a male or female.
    c. a person's enduring sexual attraction toward members of a particular gender.
    d. all of the above.

14. Which of the following is *not* an aspect of Murray's definition of achievement motivation?
    a. the desire to master skills
    b. the desire for control
    c. the desire to gain approval
    d. the desire to attain a high standard

15. Which of the following is *not* true regarding condoms?
    a. They sometimes fail.
    b. They reduce the risk of contracting HIV.
    c. They prevent genital cancers caused by viruses.
    d. They are less likely to be used by those who feel excessive guilt related to sexual activity.

16. According to Masters and Johnson, the sexual response of males is most likely to differ from that of females during:
    a. the excitement phase.
    b. the plateau phase.
    c. orgasm.
    d. the resolution phase.

17. In animals, destruction of the lateral hypothalamus results in _____ , whereas destruction of the ventromedial hypothalamus results in _____ .
    a. overeating; loss of hunger
    b. loss of hunger; overeating
    c. an elevated set point; a lowered set point
    d. increased thirst; loss of thirst
    e. increased metabolic rate; weight loss

18. Beginning with the most basic needs, which of the following represents the correct sequence of needs in the hierarchy described by Maslow?
    a. safety; physiological; esteem; belongingness and love; self-fulfillment
    b. safety; physiological; belongingness and love; esteem; self-fulfillment
    c. physiological; safety; esteem; belongingness and love; self-fulfillment
    d. physiological; safety; belongingness and love; esteem; self-fulfillment
    e. physiological; safety; self-fulfillment; esteem; belongingness and love

19. Which of the following is currently true regarding first-year college students' opinions of casual sex?
    a. The majority feel that sex between persons who know each other for only a short time is acceptable.
    b. The majority feel that condom use is unnecessary, because they know when the safe times are.
    c. The majority feel that sex between persons who know each other for only a short time is unacceptable.
    d. The majority feel that they will be ostracized by their peers if they don't do "what everyone else is doing."

20. If your body weight rises above its set point, you will tend to feel:
    a. less hungry.
    b. more hungry.
    c. thirsty.
    d. angry.

True–False Items

Indicate whether each statement is true or false by placing *T* (*True*) or *F* (*False*) in the blank next to the item.

_____ 1. When body weight rises above set point, hunger increases.
_____ 2. According to Masters and Johnson, only males experience a plateau period in the cycle of sexual arousal.
_____ 3. Testosterone affects the sexual arousal of the male only.
_____ 4. Unlike men, women tend not to be aroused by sexually explicit material.
_____ 5. All taste preferences are conditioned.
_____ 6. Married people are less at risk for depression than are unattached people.

_____ 7. An increase in insulin increases blood glucose levels and triggers hunger.

_____ 8. Most types of sexual disorder are associated with personality disorders.

_____ 9. One's sexual orientation is not voluntarily chosen.

_____ 10. Public opinion surveys reveal that Americans today have more liberal attitudes related to homosexuality and all sex-related issues.

_____ 11. Adult women's sexual drive and interests are more flexible than adult men's.

Review and Reflect

Answer these questions the day before an exam as a final check on your understanding of the chapter's terms and concepts.

Multiple-Choice Questions

1. Which of the following is *not* necessarily a reason that obese people have trouble losing weight?
   a. Fat tissue has a lower metabolic rate than lean tissue.
   b. Once a person has lost weight, it takes fewer calories to maintain his or her current weight.
   c. The tendency toward obesity may be genetically based.
   d. Obese people don't try hard enough to lose weight.

2. After an initial rapid weight loss, a person on a diet loses weight much more slowly. This slowdown occurs because:
   a. most of the initial weight loss is simply water.
   b. when a person diets, metabolism decreases.
   c. people begin to "cheat" on their diets.
   d. insulin levels tend to increase with reduced food intake.

3. Mary loves hang-gliding. It would be most difficult to explain Mary's behavior according to:
   a. incentives.
   b. achievement motivation.
   c. drive-reduction theory.
   d. Maslow's hierarchy of needs.

4. For two weeks, Orlando has been on a hunger strike in order to protest his country's involvement in what he perceives as an immoral war. Orlando's willingness to starve himself in order to make a political statement conflicts with the theory of motivation advanced by:
   a. Kinsey.   d. Masters and Johnson.
   b. Murray.   e. Maslow.
   c. Keys.

5. (Close-Up) Kathy has been undergoing treatment for bulimia. There is an above-average probability that one or more members of Kathy's family have a problem with:
   a. high achievement.   c. alcoholism.
   b. overprotectiveness. d. all of the above.

6. Which of the following was *not* identified as a contributing factor in the high rate of unprotected sex among adolescents?
   a. alcohol use
   b. mass media sexual norms
   c. guilt related to sexual activity
   d. ignorance
   e. thrill-seeking

7. One shortcoming of the instinct theory of motivation is that it:
   a. places too much emphasis on environmental factors.
   b. focuses on cognitive aspects of motivation.
   c. applies only to animal behavior.
   d. does not explain human behaviors; it simply names them.

8. Which of the following is *not* typical of both anorexia and bulimia?
   a. far more frequent occurrence in women than in men
   b. preoccupation with food and fear of being overweight
   c. weight significantly and noticeably outside normal ranges
   d. low self-esteem and feelings of depression

9. Which of the following is *not* an example of homeostasis?
   a. perspiring in order to restore normal body temperature
   b. feeling hungry and eating to restore the level of blood glucose to normal
   c. feeling hungry at the sight of an appetizing food
   d. All of the above are examples of homeostasis.

10. Two rats have escaped from their cages in the neurophysiology lab. The technician needs your help in returning them to their proper cages. One rat is grossly overweight; the other is severely underweight. You confidently state that the overweight rat goes in the "_____-lesion" cage, while the underweight rat goes in the "_____-lesion" cage.
    a. hippocampus; amygdala
    b. amygdala; hippocampus
    c. lateral hypothalamus; ventromedial hypothalamus
    d. ventromedial hypothalamus; lateral hypothalamus

11. The fact that children who learn to attribute their accomplishments to their own competence have high self-expectations demonstrates that achievement:
    a. has emotional roots.
    b. has cognitive roots.
    c. can't be taught.
    d. is unpredictable.

12. Ali's parents have tried hard to minimize their son's exposure to sweet, fattening foods. If Ali has the occasion to taste sweet foods in the future, which of the following is likely?
    a. He will have a strong aversion to such foods.
    b. He will have a neutral reaction to sweet foods.
    c. He will display a preference for sweet tastes.
    d. It is impossible to predict Ali's reaction.

13. Children who are bribed to perform an activity such as writing:
    a. quickly lose their interest in it.
    b. remain interested as long as the reward system remains in place.
    c. remain interested if led to attribute their involvement internally.
    d. place less value on the activity than do children who are not bribed.

14. Summarizing her report on the need to belong, Rolanda states that:
    a. "Cooperation amongst our ancestors was uncommon."
    b. "Social bonding is not in our nature; it is a learned human trait."
    c. "Because bonding with others increased our ancestors' success at reproduction and survival, it became part of our biological nature."
    d. both a. and b. are true.

15. (Close-Up) Of the following individuals, who might be most prone to developing an eating disorder?
    a. Jason, an adolescent boy who is somewhat overweight and is unpopular with his peers
    b. Jennifer, a teenage girl who has a poor self-image and a fear of not being able to live up to her parents' high standards
    c. Susan, a 35-year-old woman who is a "workaholic" and devotes most of her energies to her high-pressured career
    d. Bill, a 40-year-old man who has had problems with alcoholism and is seriously depressed after losing his job of 20 years

16. Lucille has been sticking to a strict diet but can't seem to lose weight. What is the most likely explanation for her difficulty?
    a. Her body has a very low set point.
    b. Her prediet weight was near her body's set point.
    c. Her weight problem is actually caused by an underlying eating disorder.
    d. Lucille has no memory of her last meal.

17. Randy, who has been under a lot of stress lately, has intense cravings for sugary junk foods, which tend to make him feel more relaxed. Which of the following is the most likely explanation for his craving?
    a. Randy feels that he deserves to pamper himself with sweets because of the stress he is under.
    b. The extra sugar gives Randy the energy he needs to cope with the demands of daily life.
    c. Carbohydrates boost levels of serotonin, which has a calming effect.
    d. The extra sugar tends to lower blood insulin level, which promotes relaxation.

18. Which of the following teens is most likely to delay the initiation of sex?
    a. Jack, who has below-average intelligence
    b. Jason, who is not religiously active
    c. Ron, who regularly volunteers his time in community service
    d. It is impossible to predict

19. A course that Janice wants very much to take is being offered by three instructors. Janice chooses the instructor with a reputation for being moderately difficult over the one perceived as impossibly difficult and the other viewed as very easy. It is most likely that Janice's choice reflects her having a(n):

   a. optimum level of arousal.

   b. low need for achievement.

   c. high need for achievement.

   d. high level of arousal.

20. In order to predict excellence in a young scholar, athlete, or artist, for example, it would be best to examine the individual's:

   a. persistence.

   b. natural talent.

   c. peer group.

   d. home environment.

Essay Question

Differentiate the three major theories of motivation, discuss their origins, and explain why they cannot fully account for human behavior. (Use the space below to list the points you want to make, and organize them. Then write the essay on a separate sheet of paper.)

Key Terms

Writing Definitions

Using your own words, write on a separate piece of paper a brief definition or explanation of each of the following terms.

  1. motivation

  2. instinct

  3. drive-reduction theory

  4. homeostasis

  5. incentives

  6. hierarchy of needs

  7. glucose

  8. set point

  9. basal metabolic rate

10. anorexia nervosa

11. bulimia nervosa

12. sexual response cycle

13. refractory period

14. sexual disorder

15. estrogen

16. testosterone

17. sexual orientation

18. achievement motivation

Cross-Check

As you learned in Chapter 1, reviewing and overlearning of material are important to the learning process. After you have written the definitions of the key terms in this chapter, you should complete the crossword puzzle to ensure that you can reverse the process—recognize the term, given the definition.

ACROSS

3. Hormone secreted by an empty stomach

7. Region of the hypothalamus that, when electrically stimulated, causes an animal to eat.

13. In Maslow's theory, human needs are organized into a _____ .

14. In Maslow's theory, the needs that follow physiological needs in order of priority.

15. Major energy source for the body.

17. Final stage of the sexual response cycle.

19. Early researcher on sexual behavior patterns.

DOWN

1. Type of error that occurs when an employer's overall work evaluation of an employee is biased by a single trait.

2. Theory that explains behavior as arising from physiological needs and the states of tension they create.

4. Eating disorder characterized by repeated "binge-purge" episodes.

5. The body's rate of energy expenditure at rest.

6. Eating disorder in which a person restricts food intake to become significantly underweight and yet still feels fat.

8. Sex hormone secreted in greater amount by females than by males.

9. Type of motivation that reflects the degree to which a person is motivated by a desire for significant accomplishment.

10. Initial stage of the sexual response cycle.

11. In Maslow's theory, the most basic types of needs.

12. The resting period after orgasm, during which a male cannot be aroused to another orgasm.

16. A positive or negative stimulus that motivates behavior.

18. Digestive tract hormone

Answers

Introduction

Section Preview

1. Motivation is a need or desire that energizes behavior and directs it toward a goal.

Motivational Concepts

Section Preview

1. The earliest theory classified motivated behavior as instinctive and unlearned; more recently, the evolutionary perspective contends that genes predispose species-typical behavior. Drive-reduction theory argues that a physiological need—not necessarily an instinct—creates a psychological state.

People are not only pushed by the need to reduce drives but also pulled by incentives. Arousal theory emphasizes the urge for an optimum level of stimulation.

2. Maslow's hierarchy of needs expresses the idea that some needs are more fundamental than others. Maslow proposed that physiological needs, such as for food, water, and shelter, are the most basic and must be met before we are motivated to meet "higher" needs for safety, belongingness and love, self-esteem, and self-actualization. Critics of Maslow's theory contend that the proposed sequence of needs is arbitrary and not universally fixed.

Stepping Through the Section

1. instincts

According to instinct theory, any human behavior could be regarded as an instinct. The only evidence for each such "instinct" was the behavior used to identify it. Thus, instinct theory offered only circular explanations; it labeled behaviors but did not explain them.

2. genes

3. need; drives

4. homeostasis; incentives

5. increase; do not

6. hierarchy

7. physiological; self-actualization; arbitrary; universally

8. financial; home-life; self-esteem

Hunger

Section Preview

1. Although stomach pangs correlate with feelings of hunger, they are not the only source. Hunger also increases when increases in insulin diminish the secretion of glucose into the bloodstream. Blood chemistry is monitored by the lateral and ventromedial areas of the hypothalamus, which therefore control body weight. Animal research shows that when the LH is electrically stimulated, hunger increases; when the LH is destroyed, hunger decreases. Stimulation of the VMH depresses hunger, while its destruction will increase hunger and trigger rapid weight gain. Set point is the point at which each person's weight level is supposedly set. To maintain its set point, the body adjusts food intake, energy output, and the rate of energy expenditure in maintaining basic

functions when the body is resting (basal metabolic rate).

2. Several hormones are involved in regulating hunger and fullness. These include insulin, a hormone secreted by the pancreas that controls blood glucose; orexin, a hormone secreted by the hypothalamus that stimulates hunger; ghrelin, a hormone secreted by the empty stomach that sends a hunger signal to the brain; and PYY, a digestive tract hormone that signals fullness.

   Our preferences for sweet and salty tastes are genetic and universal. Culture and learning also affect taste, as when people given highly salted foods or foods common only in certain societies develop preferences for these tastes. Humans and some animals also have a natural dislike of many foods that are novel and unfamiliar. This "neophobia" was probably adaptive for our ancestors and protected them from toxic substances.

3. Anorexia nervosa is a disorder in which a person becomes significantly underweight yet feels fat. The disorder usually develops in adolescent females. Anorexia patients tend to come from competitive, high-achieving, and protective families.

   Bulimia nervosa is a more common disorder characterized by repeated episodes of overeating followed by vomiting, using a laxative, fasting, or excessive exercise ("binge-purge" episodes). The families of bulimia patients have a higher than usual incidence of alcoholism, obesity, and depression.

   Several factors may contribute to these eating disorders—for example, genetics or the presence of abnormal supplies of certain neurotransmitters may be implicated. Socially, a factor may be the increasingly stringent cultural standards of thinness for women. In addition, studies have demonstrated that, in Western societies such as the United States, women's self-reported ideal weights tend to be lighter than their current weights and that women tend to think that men prefer them to weigh less than the weight men actually prefer. Another indication of the impact of psychological factors is evidence that women with low self-esteem and those with greater body dissatisfaction are especially vulnerable to eating disorders.

4. Obesity is a threat to physical, social, and psychological well-being. The number of fat cells in our bodies is determined by genetic predisposition, early eating patterns, and adult overeating. Fat cells may shrink in size with dieting, but they will

never decrease in number. Because fat tissue has a low metabolic rate, it takes less food energy to maintain, and it is therefore difficult for dieters to lose weight. Because obese persons probably have a higher-than-average set-point weight, when they diet their hunger increases and metabolism decreases, making it even more difficult for them to lose weight.

5. Adoption and twin studies both provide evidence for a genetic influence on body weight. However, genes cannot explain why the percentage of overweight and obese people is increasing worldwide or why obesity is much more common in lower-class than in upper-class women and more common among Americans than Europeans. Genes mostly determine why one person today is heavier than another. Environment mostly determines why people today are heavier than their counterparts 50 years ago.

Stepping Through the Section

1. semistarvation

2. stomach contractions; less; ghrelin

3. does

4. insulin; glucose; increase

5. hypothalamus; lateral hypothalamus; decreases; ventromedial hypothalamus; overeat

6. lateral hypothalamus; orexin; hypothalamus; frontal lobes

7. orexin

8. ghrelin

9. insulin

10. PYY

11. set point; less; more

12. basal metabolic; lowering

13. is not accepted; slow, sustained changes in body weight; overeat; gain weight

14. memory

15. more

16. serotonin; calms

17. genetic; conditioning; culture; unfamiliar; neophobia

18. 65; body mass index; 30; 25; thin-ideal

Obesity increases one's risk of diabetes, high blood pressure and heart disease, gallstones, arthritis, sleep disorders, and certain types of cancer. It negatively affects self-image and the perceptions of others, particularly if the excess weight is seen as the fault of the individual.

19. anorexia nervosa; females; teens

20. bulimia nervosa; binge-purge

21. alcoholism; obesity; depression; competitive; high-achieving; protective; do not provide

22. weight-loss diet; a dieter has broken diet restrictions and gorged

23. may; increases

24. India; Western; body image

25. ashamed; depressed; dissatisfied

26. obese; race; gender

27. 3500; fat cells

28. can; cannot

29. lower; less

30. is; hunger; metabolism

Obese persons have higher set-point weights than nonobese persons. During a diet, metabolic rate drops to defend the set-point weight. The dieter therefore finds it hard to progress beyond an initial weight loss. When the diet is concluded, the lowered metabolic rate continues, so that relatively small amounts of food may prove fattening. Also, some people have lower metabolic rates than others.

31. do

32. more; does

As compared to their counterparts in the early 1900s, people are eating a higher-fat, higher-sugar diet, expending fewer calories, and suffering higher rates of diabetes at younger ages.

33. genes; environment

34. gain

Hints for losing weight include being motivated and self-disciplined, minimizing exposure to tempting food cues, taking steps to boost your metabolism, being realistic and moderate, eating healthy foods, not starving all day and eating one big meal at night, and avoiding binge eating.

Sexual Motivation

Section Preview

1. Biologist Alfred Kinsey interviewed 18,000 men and women in an effort to describe human sexual behavior. Although Kinsey's sample was not random, his statistics showed that sexual behavior is enormously varied. Other sex reports have been prepared, but because they were based on biased samples of people, they cannot be taken seriously.

Masters and Johnson outlined four stages in the sexual response cycle. During the initial excitement phase, the genital areas become engorged with blood, causing the penis and clitoris to swell and the vagina to expand and secrete lubricant. In the plateau phase, breathing, pulse, and blood pressure rates increase along with sexual excitement. During orgasm, rhythmic genital contractions create a pleasurable feeling of sexual release. During the resolution phase, the body gradually returns to its unaroused state, and males enter a refractory period during which they are incapable of another orgasm.

2. Sexual disorders are problems that consistently impair sexual arousal or functioning, such as premature ejaculation, the inability to have or maintain an erection, or infrequent orgasms (orgasmic disorder).

Sexual disorders do not appear to be linked to personality disorders. Researchers have found that sexual disorders can often be treated successfully with behaviorally oriented therapy.

3. Sex hormones direct the development of male and female sex characteristics and (especially in nonhuman animals) they activate sexual behavior. In most mammals, sexual activity coincides with ovulation and peak level of estrogen in the female. Sexual behavior in male animals is directly related to the level of testosterone in their bodies.

In humans, normal fluctuations in hormone levels have little effect on sex drive once the pubertal surge in sex hormones has occurred. A woman's sexual interest may wane if her testosterone level is low, but this can easily be restored by a replacement drug. In later life, however, for both women and men, the frequency of sexual fantasies and intercourse decreases as sex hormone levels decline.

External stimuli, such as touch and erotic material, can trigger sexual arousal in both men and women, although sexually explicit materials may lead people to devalue their partners. Our imagination—in dreams and fantasies—can also lead to arousal.

4. Sexual attitudes vary widely from one culture to another and across time within the same culture. For example, teen intercourse rates are higher in the United States and Western Europe than in Arab and Asian countries and much higher among American teens today than in the past.

Increased sexual activity has led to increases in teen pregnancies and sexually transmitted infections (STIs). Several factors contribute to the alarmingly high rate of unprotected sex among teens, including ignorance about the menstrual cycle, guilt, lack of communication about birth control, alcohol use, and mass media norms of unprotected promiscuity. Teens with high intelligence test scores, those who are actively religious, and those who participate in service learning programs more often delay sex.

5. Sexual orientation is an individual's enduring sexual attraction toward members of a particular sex. Although virtually all cultures in all times have been predominantly heterosexual, studies suggest that 3 or 4 percent of men and 1 or 2 percent of women are exclusively homosexual.

Most homosexuals report first being aware of same-gender sexual feelings around puberty, but they typically do not think of themselves as gay or lesbian until around age 20. The ostracism homosexuals often face may cause them to struggle with their sexual motivation. Because sexual orientation is neither willfully chosen nor willfully changed, however, homosexual feelings generally persist. Recent research, however, suggests that women's sexual orientation tends to be less strongly felt and potentially more fluid and changeable than men's.

6. There are many myths about the causes of homosexuality, including that it is linked with levels of sex hormones; as a child, being molested or seduced by an adult homosexual; having a domineering mother and an ineffectual father; or fearing or hating members of the opposite sex. Evidence suggests that genetic influence plays a role. In animals and some exceptional human cases, sexual orientation has been altered by abnormal prenatal hormone conditions, leading some researchers to suggest that exposure to hormone levels typical of females during a critical period of brain development may predispose the male to become attracted to males.

The consistency of genetic, prenatal, and brain research findings has caused most psychiatrists to now believe that nature more than nurture predisposes sexual orientation. Recent public opinion surveys reveal a more accepting attitude toward homosexuality among Americans.

7. Most sex educators and researchers aim for objectivity and strive to keep their writings on sexuality value-free. Critics contend that the study of sex cannot, and should not, be free of values. For example, the words we use to describe sexual behavior often reflect our personal values. Second, when sexual information is separated from the context of human values, young people are sent a message that sexual behavior is merely

recreational activity. Therefore, sex-related values should be discussed openly, rather than avoided.

Stepping Through the Section

1. Kinsey

2. biased

3. Masters; Johnson; excitement; plateau; orgasm; resolution

4. refractory period

5. sexual disorders; premature ejaculation; erectile disorder; orgasmic disorder; have not; behaviorally

6. estrogen

7. testosterone; testes; testosterone

8. little; decreases; decline

9. are

Erotic material may increase the viewer's acceptance of the false idea that women enjoy rape, may increase men's willingness to hurt women, may lead people to devalue their partners and relationships, and may diminish people's satisfaction with their own sexual partners.

10. do

11. have; frequent, physical, and less romantic; problems; dissatisfaction

12. culture; time; Western Europe; Asian; Arab

Among the factors that contribute to unprotected sex among adolescents are (1) ignorance about the safe and risky times of the menstrual cycle, (2) guilt related to sexual activity, (3) minimal communication about birth control, (4) alcohol use that influences judgment, and (5) mass media norms of unprotected promiscuity.

13. pregnancies; sexually transmitted infection (STI)

Teens with high intelligence test scores, those who are actively religious, and those who participate in service learning programs more often delay sex.

14. sexual orientation

15. all; 20

16. 3 or 4; 1 or 2; high

17. does not; women

18. do not suffer; accept

19. are not

20. does not

21. do not

22. were not

23. large cities; poets; fiction writers; artists; musicians; brothers

24. their own; does not; conflicts with

25. hypothalamus; heterosexual; anterior commissure

26. do

27. hormone; females; 2; 5

28. fingerprint; left; cochlea

29. nature; nature

30. more; but not a liberalization of

31. no more

The Need to Belong

Section Preview

1. Humans have a need to feel connected to others in enduring, close relationships. This need boosted our ancestors' success at survival and reproduction. Today, it influences our thoughts, emotions, and much of our social nature. By conforming to group standards and striving to make favorable impressions, we shape our social behavior to increase our social acceptance and inclusion.

   Children and adults who are denied others' acceptance and inclusion become withdrawn and may feel more depression, anxiety, jealousy, and loneliness. Those who have close friends and perceive strong social support live with better health and lower risk of psychological disorder and premature death.

Stepping Through the Section

1. survival; belong; genes

2. close, satisfying relationships with family, friends, or romantic partners

3. self-esteem

4. social; liking

5. self-defeating; antisocial; aggression

6. health; psychological; death

Achievement Motivation

Section Preview

1. As defined by Henry Murray, achievement motivation is the desire for significant accomplishment, for mastering skills or ideas, for control, and for rapidly attaining a high standard. People

with a low need for achievement prefer very easy or very difficult tasks, where failure is either unlikely or unembarrassing. People with a high need for achievement prefer moderately difficult tasks, where success is attainable and attributable to their own effort.

Children with a high need for achievement often have parents who encourage their independence from an early age and praise them for their successes. Achievement motivation has both emotional and cognitive roots, as children learn to associate achievement with positive emotions and to attribute their achievements to their own competence.

Stepping Through the Section

1. need; achievement motivation
2. stories
3. low
4. independence; praise; reward
5. emotional; cognitive

Progress Test 1

Multiple-Choice Questions

1. **d.** is the answer. (p. 341)
   a. & b. Although motivation is often aimed at reducing drives and satisfying biological needs, this is by no means always the case, as achievement motivation illustrates.
   c. Motivated behavior not only is energized but also is directed at a goal.

2. **b.** is the answer. A drive is the psychological consequence of a physiological need. (p. 342)
   a. Needs are unlearned states of deprivation.
   c. & d. Since needs are physical and drives psychological, their strengths cannot be compared directly.

3. **a.** is the answer. The curiosity of a child or a scientist is an example of behavior apparently motivated by something other than a physiological need. (p. 342)
   b. & d. Some behaviors, such as thirst and hunger, are partially explained by drive reduction.
   c. Drive reduction is directly based on the principle of homeostasis.

4. **c.** is the answer. (p. 367)
   a., b., & d. None of these is linked to homosexuality.

5. **a.** is the answer. Increases in insulin increase hunger indirectly by lowering blood sugar, or glucose. (p. 346)

6. **a.** is the answer. This area of the hypothalamus seems to elevate hunger. (p. 346)
   b. Stimulating the ventromedial hypothalamus has this effect.
   c. Lesioning the ventromedial hypothalamus has this effect.
   d. The hypothalamus is involved in sexual motivation, but not in this way.

7. **b.** is the answer. (pp. 348)
   a. Neophobia for taste is typical of all age groups.
   c. Neophobia for taste is *not* an indicator of an eating disorder.
   d. With repeated exposure, our appreciation for a new taste typically *increases.*

8. **b.** is the answer. (p. 346)
   a. PYY signals fullness, which is associated with decreased metabolism.
   c. Orexin is a hormone secreted by the hypothalamus.
   d. Insulin is produced in the pancreas.

9. **e.** is the answer. (pp. 341–342)

10. **b.** is the answer. (p. 358)

11. **c.** is the answer. (p. 342)
    a. & b. Needs and drives are biologically based states that stimulate behaviors but are not themselves behaviors.
    d. Incentives are the external stimuli that motivate behavior.

12. **c.** is the answer. The deprived subjects focused on food almost to the exclusion of anything else. (p. 345)
    a. In order to conserve energy, the men's metabolic rate actually *decreased.*
    b. & d. Far from losing interest in food, the subjects came to care only about food—a finding consistent with Maslow's hierarchy, in which physiological needs are at the base.

13. **c.** is the answer. (p. 371)

14. **d.** is the answer. (p. 350)

15. **a.** is the answer. (p. 359)
    c. & d. Castration of the testes, which produce testosterone, does not alter estrogen levels.

16. **d.** is the answer. (p. 359)
    a. Treating sexual disorder as though it were a personality disorder has not been successful.
    b. & c. Neither type of therapy is discussed in the text. However, it seems likely that they would be as unsuccessful as more traditional methods.

17. **d.** is the answer. Sex is much more than just a biological act, and its study therefore inherently involves values, attitudes, and morals, which should thus be discussed openly. (pp. 369–370)

18. **b.** is the answer. (p. 357)

19. **d.** is the answer. (p. 374)

    a., b., & c. Each of these has been shown to discourage the development of achievement motivation.

20. **c.** is the answer. Research studies suggest that women's sexual orientation is potentially more fluid and changeable than men's. (p. 365)

Matching Items

1. e (p. 359)
2. i (p. 347)
3. g (p. 342)
4. f (p. 373)
5. k (p. 346)
6. a (p. 359)
7. b (p. 342)
8. d (p. 364)
9. h (p. 342)
10. c (p. 342)
11. j (p. 346)

Progress Test 2

Multiple-Choice Questions

1. **c.** is the answer. (p. 346)

   a. PYY signals fullness, which is associated with decreased metabolism.

   b. Although it increases hunger, ghrelin is secreted by an empty stomach and sends its signals to the brain.

   d. Insulin is produced in the pancreas.

2. **a.** is the answer. (p. 342)

   b. This refers to people with low achievement motivation.

   c. This describes set point.

   d. Homeostasis has nothing to do with sexual orientation.

3. **b.** is the answer. Fat cells may change in size as a person gains or loses weight, but their number never decreases. (p. 353)

   a. In fact, because of its lower metabolic rate, fat tissue can be maintained on fewer calories.

   c. Because metabolism slows as food intake is restricted, a 3500-calorie reduction may not reduce weight by one pound.

   d. In fact, just the opposite is true for metabolism.

4. **a.** is the answer. (p. 361)

5. **a.** is the answer. The text does not indicate whether their metabolism is higher or lower than most. (pp. 350–351)

   b., c., & d. Genes, family background, and cultural influence have all been proposed as factors in eating disorders.

6. **b.** is the answer. (p. 346)

   a. Stimulation of the lateral hypothalamus triggers eating.

   c. & d. The thalamus is a sensory relay station; stimulation of it has no effect on eating.

7. **b.** is the answer. The time between the middle of the second and fifth months after conception may be a critical period for the brain's neurohormonal control system. Exposure to abnormal hormonal conditions at other times has no effect on sexual orientation. (p. 367)

8. **d.** is the answer. Researchers have not been able to find any clear differences, psychological or otherwise, between homosexuals and heterosexuals. Thus, the basis for sexual orientation remains unknown, although recent evidence points more to a physiological basis. (p. 368)

9. **c.** is the answer. (p. 351)

10. **d.** is the answer. (pp. 343–344)

11. **c.** is the answer. Such behavior, presumably motivated by curiosity rather than any biological need, is inconsistent with a drive-reduction theory of motivation. (p. 342)

    a., b., & d. Each of these examples is consistent with a drive-reduction theory of motivation.

12. **e.** is the answer. (pp. 350–351)

13. **c.** is the answer. (p. 364)

14. **c.** is the answer. (p. 373)

15. **c.** is the answer. (p. 363)

16. **d.** is the answer. During the resolution phase males experience a refractory period. (p. 358)

    a., b., & c. The male and female responses are very similar in each of these phases.

17. **b.** is the answer. (p. 346)

    a. & e. These effects are the reverse of what takes place.

    c. If anything, set point is lowered by destruction of the lateral hypothalamus and elevated by destruction of the ventromedial hypothalamus.

    d. These effects do not occur.

18. **d.** is the answer. (pp. 343, 344)

19. **c.** is the answer. (pp. 363–364)

20. **a.** is the answer. (p. 347)

True–False Items

1. F (p. 347)   **6.** T (p. 372)   **11.** T (p. 365)
2. F (p. 358)   **7.** F (p. 346)
3. F (p. 359)   **8.** F (p. 359)
4. F (p. 360)   **9.** T (p. 365)
5. F (p. 348)   **10.** F (pp. 368–369)

Review and Reflect

Multiple-Choice Questions

1. d. is the answer. (p. 355)

2. b. is the answer. Following the initial weight loss, metabolism drops as the body attempts to defend its set-point weight. This drop in metabolism means that eating an amount that once produced a loss in weight may now actually result in weight gain. (p. 355)

3. c. is the answer. Drive-reduction theory maintains that behavior is motivated when a biological need creates an aroused state, driving the individual to satisfy the need. It is difficult to believe that Mary's hang-gliding is satisfying a biological need. (p. 342)
a., b., & d. Mary may enjoy hang-gliding because it is a challenge that "is there" (incentive), because it satisfies a need to accomplish something challenging (achievement), or because it increases her self-esteem and sense of fulfillment in life (Maslow's hierarchy of needs).

4. e. is the answer. According to Maslow's theory, physiological needs, such as the need to satisfy hunger, must be satisfied before a person pursues loftier needs, such as making political statements. (p. 343)
a. Kinsey and Masters and Johnson were concerned with sexual behavior.
b. Murray was concerned with achievement motivation.
c. Keys was concerned with hunger.

5. c. is the answer. (p. 350)
a. & b. These are more typical of the families of anorexia patients.

6. e. is the answer. (p. 362)

7. d. is the answer. (p. 341)
a. & b. Instinct theory emphasizes biological factors rather than environmental or cognitive factors.
c. Instinct theory applies to both humans and other animals.

8. c. is the answer. Although people with anorexia are significantly underweight, those with bulimia often are not unusually thin or overweight. (p. 350)
a., b., & d. Both anorexia and bulimia victims are more likely to be women than men, preoccupied with food, fearful of becoming overweight, and suffer from depression or low self-esteem.

9. c. is the answer. This is an example of salivating in response to an incentive rather than to maintain a balanced internal state. (p. 342)
a. & b. Both of these are examples of behavior that maintains a balanced internal state (homeostasis).

10. d. is the answer. Lesions of the ventromedial hypothalamus produce overeating and rapid weight gains. Lesions of the lateral hypothalamus suppress hunger and produce weight loss. (p. 346)
a. & b. The hippocampus and amygdala are not involved in regulating eating behavior.

11. b. is the answer. (p. 354)

12. c. is the answer. Our preferences for sweet and salty tastes are genetic and universal. (p. 348)

13. c. is the answer. (p. 374)

14. c. is the answer. (p. 371)

15. b. is the answer. Adolescent females with low self-esteem and high-achieving families seem especially prone to eating disorders such as anorexia nervosa. (p. 350)
a. & d. Eating disorders occur much more frequently in women than in men.
c. Eating disorders usually develop during adolescence, rather than during adulthood.

16. b. is the answer. The body acts to defend its set point, or the weight to which it is predisposed. If Lucille was already near her set point, weight loss would prove difficult. (pp. 347, 353)
a. If the weight level to which her body is predisposed is low, weight loss upon dieting should not be difficult.
c. The eating disorders relate to eating behaviors and psychological factors and would not explain a difficulty with weight loss.
d. Nothing in the question indicates that this is true.

17. c. is the answer. Serotonin is a neurotransmitter that is elevated by the consumption of carbohydrates and has a calming effect. (p. 348)
a. & b. These answers do not explain the feelings of relaxation that Randy associates with eating junk food.
d. The consumption of sugar tends to elevate insulin level rather than lower it.

18. **c.** is the answer. (p. 363)
    a., b., & d. Teens with high rather than average intelligence (therefore, not a.) and those who are religiously active (therefore, not b.) are most likely to delay sex.

19. **c.** is the answer. Individuals with a high need for achievement tend to choose moderately difficult tasks at which they can succeed if they work at it. (p. 373)
    a. Janice may be at her optimum level of arousal but that is not the reason for her choosing the instructor.
    b. People with a low need for achievement are more likely to prefer the easy or the very difficult instructor.
    d. If anything, a high need for arousal would lead her to take the more difficult instructor.

20. **a.** is the answer. (p. 373)
    b. Natural talent is, of course, important, but persistence is generally more significant.
    c. & d. These were not identified as factors in outstanding achievement.

Essay Question

Under the influence of Darwin's evolutionary theory, it became fashionable to classify all sorts of behaviors as instincts. Instinct theory fell into disfavor for several reasons. First, instincts do not explain behaviors, they merely name them. Second, to qualify as an instinct, a behavior must have a fixed and automatic pattern and occur in all people, regardless of differing cultures and experiences. Apart from a few simple reflexes, however, human behavior is not sufficiently automatic and universal to meet these criteria. Although instinct theory failed to explain human motives, the underlying assumption that genes predispose many behaviors is as strongly believed as ever.

Instinct theory was replaced by drive-reduction theory and the idea that biological needs create aroused drive states that motivate the individual to satisfy these needs and preserve homeostasis. Drive-reduction theory failed as a complete account of human motivation because many human motives do not satisfy any obvious biological need. Instead, such behaviors are motivated by environmental incentives.

Arousal theory emerged in response to evidence that some motivated behaviors *increase*, rather than decrease, arousal.

Key Terms

Writing Definitions

1. **Motivation** is a need or desire that energizes and directs behavior. (p. 341)

2. An **instinct** is a complex behavior that is rigidly patterned throughout a species and is unlearned. (p. 342)

3. **Drive-reduction theory** attempts to explain behavior as arising from a physiological need that creates an aroused tension state (drive) that motivates an organism to satisfy the need. (p. 342)

4. **Homeostasis** refers to the body's tendency to maintain a balanced or constant internal state. (p. 342)

5. **Incentives** are positive or negative environmental stimuli that motivate behavior. (p. 342)

6. Maslow's **hierarchy of needs** proposes that human motives may be ranked from the basic, physiological level through higher-level needs for safety, love, esteem, and self-actualization; until they are satisfied, the more basic needs are more compelling than the higher-level ones. (p. 343)

7. **Glucose**, or blood sugar, is the major source of energy for the body's tissues. Elevating the level of glucose in the body will reduce hunger. (p. 346)

8. **Set point** is an individual's regulated weight level, which is maintained by adjusting food intake and energy output. (p. 347)

9. **Basal metabolic rate** is the body's base rate of energy expenditure when resting. (p. 347)

10. **Anorexia nervosa** is an eating disorder, most common in adolescent females, in which a person restricts food intake to become significantly underweight and yet still feels fat. (p. 350)

11. **Bulimia nervosa** is an eating disorder characterized by private "binge-purge" episodes of overeating followed by vomiting, laxative use, fasting, or excessive exercise. (p. 350)

12. The **sexual response cycle** described by Masters and Johnson consists of four stages of bodily reaction: excitement, plateau, orgasm, and resolution. (p. 358)

13. The **refractory period** is a resting period after orgasm, during which a male cannot be aroused to another orgasm. (p. 358)

14. A **sexual disorder** is a problem—such as erectile disorder, premature ejaculation, and orgasmic disorder—that consistently impairs sexual arousal or functioning. (p. 359)

15. **Estrogen** is a sex hormone secreted in greater amounts by females than by males. In mammals other than humans, estrogen levels peak during ovulation and trigger sexual receptivity. (p. 359)

16. **Testosterone** is the most important of the male sex hormones. Although females also have it, in males additional testosterone stimulates the growth of the male sex organs in the fetus and male sex characteristics during puberty. (p. 359)

17. **Sexual orientation** refers to a person's enduring attraction to members of either the same or the opposite gender. (p. 364)

18. **Achievement motivation** is a desire for significant accomplishment; mastery of things, people, or ideas; and attaining a high standard. (p. 373)

Cross-Check

ACROSS	DOWN
3. ghrelin	1. halo
7. lateral	2. drive-reduction
13. hierarchy	4. bulimia nervosa
14. safety	5. basal metabolic rate
15. glucose	6. anorexia nervosa
17. resolution	8. estrogen
19. Kinsey	9. achievement
	10. excitement
	11. physiological
	12. refractory
	16. incentive
	18. PYY

FOCUS ON VOCABULARY AND LANGUAGE

Page 341:. . . truant officer . . . A *truant* is a child who stays away from school without permission, and government officials who enforce compulsory education policy are called *truant officers*. Alfredo was forced to go to school and was spanked (*paddled*) for speaking Spanish. He decided to learn English and work hard to get good grades in school and college and he was successful. As a well-educated college administrator, Alfredo now tries to motivate others to become aware of (*wake up to*) their own potential and ability to do well.

Motivational Concepts

Page 341: Before long, *this fad for naming instincts collapsed under its own weight.* A good example of the misuse of a theory was when it became very popular (fashionable) to categorize a very broad range of behaviors as innately determined (a fad for naming instincts). In Darwinian theory, an instinct is an unlearned behavior that follows a fixed pattern in all members of the species. This fashion (fad) of naming thousands of behaviors as instincts, rather than explaining them, grew so large and cumbersome that it was finally abandoned as a useful explanatory system (it collapsed under its own weight).

Page 342: Both systems operate through *feedback loops.* A thermostat in a house and the body's temperature-regulation system are both examples of **homeostasis**. If temperature drops, the change is detected and the information is directed (*fed*) to the system so that necessary steps are taken to bring the temperature back up to its original position. This information is then transmitted back to the system, so that there is a continuous cycle of cooling down and heating up (*feedback loop*) in an attempt to maintain a steady state. This is the basis of **drive-reduction theory**.

Page 343: Curiosity drives monkeys to *monkey around* trying to figure out how to unlock a latch that opens nothing or how to open a window that allows them to see outside their room (Butler, 1954). The expression *"monkey around"* means to play or fool around with something. Monkeys and young children have a very great need to explore and find out about their surroundings. Arousal theory suggests that we are driven to seek stimulation and increase our level of arousal to some comfortable state which is neither too high nor too low (*optimum level*).

Hunger

Page 345: They talked food. They daydreamed food. They collected recipes, read cookbooks, and *feasted their eyes on delectable forbidden foods.* In this experiment, subjects were given only half their normal intake of food, and the men became lethargic (*listless*), focused all their thoughts on the topic of food, and looked longingly at (*feasted their eyes on*) pictures of delicious, but unobtainable, foods (*delectable forbidden foods*). This behavior is consistent with Maslow's theory that there is a hierarchy of needs.

Page 346: This suggests that the body is somehow, somewhere, *keeping tabs on* its available resources. People and other animals naturally and automatically tend to control food intake in order to keep a relatively constant body weight. This indicates that there is a mechanism, or mechanisms, which monitor (*keep tabs on*) energy fluctuations. Levels of the blood sugar glucose and certain brain chemicals may play a role in this process.

Page 347: . . . rather like a *miser* who runs every bit of extra money to the bank and resists taking any out (Pinel, 1993). One theory suggests that two parts of the hypothalamus, the lateral hypothalamus (LH) and ventromedial hypothalamus (VMH), regulate hunger. Stimulation of the LH increases hunger, while activity in the VMH depresses hunger. If the VMH is destroyed (*lesioned*), rats tend to create and store more fat, just as a person who loves money more than anything else (*a miser*) will keep banking money and use as little of it as possible.

Page 349: And why do so few overweight people *win the battle of the bulge?* Most overweight people who diet do not manage to permanently lose the many pounds of fat they want to (*they do not win the battle of the bulge*). Myers discusses a number of factors: (a) the number of fat cells in the body does not decrease when you diet; (b) the tissue in fat is easier to maintain and uses less energy than other tissue; and (c) when body weight drops below the set point, your overall metabolic rate slows down. For those wanting to diet, Myers lists some useful tips (see p. 638).

Page 350: . . . *binge-purge* . . . People who have an eating disorder called **bulimia nervosa** may have episodes of overeating (*binging*) similar to those who engage in drinking bouts (*spurts of drinking*). The bulimic person (typically females in their teens or twenties) usually follows the overeating episode (*gorging*) with self-induced vomiting and excessive laxative use (*purging*).

Page 355 (margin note): For most people, the only long-term result of participating in a commercial weight-loss program is a *thinner wallet*. Most commercial weight-loss programs cost a great deal of money but, at best, only help people lose weight temporarily. For those who lose and then regain weight over and over again, the end result is usually a greater weight gain each time and ultimately having less money (*thinner wallets*).

Page 356 (Close-Up caption): Couch potatoes beware . . . Myers admonishes those of us who sit around, watch TV, and eat junk food (*couch potatoes*) to get active.

Sexual Motivation

Page 357: . . . asked more than 350 *rapid-fire questions.* Kinsey and Pomeroy were the first sex researchers to systematically interview a large sample of the

American population. Their technique (*tactic*) involved starting with easy-to-answer questions (e.g., age, education, health, gender, etc.) and then moving on to questions that required subjects to divulge personal sexual information. These questions were asked in an aggressive interrogative style (*rapid-fire questions*) and that fact, along with a nonrepresentative sample, may have biased their results.

Page 360: The hormonal fuel is essential, but so are the psychological stimuli that *turn on the engine*, keep it running, and *shift it into high gear*. Myers makes an analogy between sex hormones and the fuel that propels a car. We need the hormones to be sexually motivated just as a car needs fuel to operate. In humans, however, there is a two-way interaction between the chemicals and sexuality. In addition to hormones, psychological factors are needed to initiate sexual desire (*turn on the engine*) and produce the associated behaviors (*shift it into high gear*).

Page 360: Viewing *X-rated sex films* similarly tends to diminish people's satisfaction with their own sexual partners (Zillmann, 1989). All films are rated by a censor, and those with an *X-rating* because of their sexually explicit content are restricted to adults only. There is much debate over the influence of such films on people, and some research suggests that there may be adverse effects. For example, they may create the false impression that females enjoy rape; they may increase men's willingness to hurt women; they tend to lead both males and females to devalue their partners and their relationships; and they may reduce people's feeling of fulfillment with their lovers.

Page 363: In recent history, the *pendulum* of sexual values has swung from the European eroticism of the early 1800s to the *conservative Victorian era* of the late 1800s, from the *libertine flapper era* of the 1920s to the family values period of the 1950s. The *pendulum* of a mechanical clock swings back and forth from one side, or extreme, to the other. Myers is pointing out that our views of sexuality tend to move from restrictive (*conservative Victorian*) at one extreme to those with fewer restraints (*libertine flapper*) at the other, during different periods of time (*eras*). Today's generation may be moving toward an era in which commitment and restraint are more important than sexual expression. (Note: A *flapper* was an emancipated young woman in the 1920s.)

Page 364: . . . *fired* . . . To be *fired* means to lose your job (*to be laid off, let go, or sacked*). Myers suggests that one way for heterosexual people to understand how a homosexual feels in a predominantly heterosexual society is to imagine what it would be like if the situation were reversed and homosexuality was the norm. How would it feel as a heterosexual to be ignored (*ostracized*), to lose one's job (*be fired*), to be confronted by media that showed or indicated homosexuality as the societal norm.

Page 365: Most of today's psychologists therefore view sexual orientation as neither *willfully chosen* nor *willfully changed.* Myers compares sexual orientation to handedness. You don't deliberately decide (*willfully choose*) to be right-handed or left-handed and you can't intentionally alter (*willfully change*) your inherent inclination to use one hand over the other. Like handedness, sexual orientation is not linked to criminality nor is it associated with personality or psychological disorder.

Page 368: Regardless of the process, the consistency of the genetic, prenatal, and brain findings has *swung the pendulum toward* a biological explanation. The debate over what causes different sexual orientations has continued for many years. Recent evidence from the research seems to favor (*has swung the pendulum toward*) a biologically based account.

Page 369: To gay and lesbian activists, the new biological research is a *double-edged sword* (Diamond, 1993). The research supporting a physiological explanation of sexual orientation has both positive and negative aspects (*a double-edged sword*). On the one hand, if sexual orientation is genetically influenced, there is a basis for claiming equal civil rights and there is no need to attribute blame. On the other hand, these findings create a nagging anxiety (*troubling possibility*) that sexual orientation may be controlled through genetic engineering or fetal abortions.

The Need to Belong

Page 371: The need to belong *colors our thoughts and emotions.* As humans, we have a desire to be connected to others and to develop close, long-lasting relationships, and this need to belong affects the way we think and feel (*colors our thoughts and emotions*).

Page 372: Even to be *shunned—given the cold shoulder or the silent treatment,* with others' eyes avoiding yours—is to have one's *need to belong threatened.* . . . For both adults and children, to be ignored (*shunned*), treated with disdain (*given the cold shoulder*), or to be deprived of verbal interactions with others (*given the silent treatment*) is very distressing and hurtful; this type of social ostracism makes us feel isolated and abandoned (*threatens our need to belong*) and can lead to depression and withdrawal.

Achievement Motivation

Page 373: Billionaire entrepreneurs may be motivated to make ever more money . . . *daredevils* to seek *greater thrills.* A person who tries very hard to be successful, by being better than others at whatever task is undertaken, has a high need for achievement (**achievement motivation**). For instance, some people are high risk-takers (*daredevils*) and they frequently look for activities that produce ever higher levels of stimulation or arousal (*greater thrills*).

Page 373: In a *ring-toss game* they often stand at an *intermediate distance* from the stake, enabling some successes while providing a suitable challenge. When faced with the task of throwing a small rubber ring onto a vertical post (*stake*) some distance away (*ring toss game*), those with a high need for achievement tend to stand neither too near nor too far away (*intermediate distance*). This makes the game somewhat difficult (*challenging*), yet ensures some correct responses which can then be attributed to skill and concentration. Those with low achievement motivation pick either a very close or a very far position from the stake.

chapter 11

Emotions, Stress, and Health

Chapter Overview

Emotions are responses of the whole individual, involving physiological arousal, expressive behaviors, and conscious experience. Chapter 11 first discusses several theoretical controversies concerning the relationship and sequence of the components of emotion, primarily regarding whether the body's response to a stimulus causes the emotion that is felt and whether thinking is necessary to and must precede the experience of emotion. After describing the physiology of emotion and emotional expressiveness, the chapter examines the components of emotion in detail, particularly as they relate to the emotions of fear, anger, and happiness.

Behavioral factors play a major role in maintaining health and causing illness. The effort to understand this role more fully has led to the emergence of the interdisciplinary field of behavioral medicine. This subfield of health psychology focuses on questions such as: How do our perceptions of a situation determine the stress we feel? How do our emotions and personality influence our risk of disease? How can psychology contribute to the prevention of illness?

Chapter 11 addresses key topics in health psychology. First and foremost is stress—its nature, its effects on the body, psychological factors that determine how it affects us, and how stress contributes to heart disease, infectious diseases, and cancer. The chapter concludes by looking at physical and psychological factors that promote good health.

NOTE: Answer guidelines for all Chapter 11 questions begin on page 329.

Introducing Emotion (p. 379)

> David Myers at times uses idioms that are unfamiliar to some readers. If you do not know the meaning of any of the following words, phrases, or expressions in the context in which they appear in the text, refer to page 341 for an explanation: *add color to your life; arousal of dread.*

Introduction Preview

First, skim the introduction. Then read the following objective and, as you read the text, search for the information that will enable you to meet that objective. Answer guidelines are provided on page 329.

1. Identify the three components of emotion.

Theories of Emotion (pp. 379–383)

> If you do not know the meaning of any of the following words, phrases, or expressions in the context in which they appear in the text, refer to page 341 for an explanation: *lash out; weeping, lumps in the throat . . .; Which is the chicken and which the egg?; testy; hijack; The heart is not always subject to the mind.*

Section Preview

First, skim the section, noting headings and boldface items. Then read the following objectives and, as you read the text, search for the information that will enable you to meet each objective. Answer guidelines are provided on page 329.

1. Contrast and critique the James-Lange and Cannon-Bard theories of emotion, and describe Schachter's two-factor theory of emotion.

2. Discuss evidence suggesting that some emotional reactions can precede cognition.

Stepping Through the Section

After you have read the section, complete the sentences and answer the questions. As you proceed, evaluate your performance by consulting the answers on page 329. Do not continue with the next section until you understand each answer. If you need to, review or reread the section in the textbook before continuing.

1. According to the James-Lange theory, emotional states _____ (precede/follow) body arousal.

Describe two problems that Walter Cannon identified with the James-Lange theory.

2. Cannon proposed that emotional stimuli in the environment are routed simultaneously to the _____ , which results in awareness of the emotion, and to the _____ nervous system, which causes the body's reaction. Because another scientist concurrently proposed similar ideas, this theory has come to be known as the _____-_____ theory.

3. For victims of spinal cord injuries who have lost all feeling below the neck, the intensity of emotions tends to _____ . This result supports the _____-_____ theory of emotion.

4. Most researchers _____ (agree/disagree) with Cannon and Bard's position that emotions involve _____ as well as arousal.

5. The two-factor theory of emotion proposes that emotion has two components: _____ arousal and a _____ label. This theory was proposed by _____ .

6. Schachter and Singer found that physically aroused subjects told that an injection would cause arousal _____ (did/did not) become emotional in response to an accomplice's aroused behavior. Physically aroused subjects not expecting arousal _____ (did/did not) become emotional in response to an accomplice's behavior.

7. Robert Zajonc believes that the feeling of emotion _____ (can/cannot) precede our cognitive labeling of that emotion.

Cite two pieces of evidence that support Zajonc's position.

8. A pathway from the _____ via the _____ to the _____ enables us to experience emotion before _____ .

9. The researcher who disagrees with Zajonc and argues that most emotions require cognitive processing is _____ . According to this view, emotions arise when we _____ an event as beneficial or harmful to our well-being.

Express some general conclusions that can be drawn about cognition and emotion.

Embodied Emotion (pp. 383–387)

> If you do not know the meaning of any of the following words, phrases, or expressions in the context in which they appear in the text, refer to pages 341–342 for an explanation: *your stomach develops butterflies; shooting free throws; clutching, sinking sensation; peppy left hemisphere . . . perky disposition; Pinocchio . . . telltale sign; a white lie.*

Section Preview

Answer guidelines begin on page 329.

1. Describe the physiological changes that occur during emotional arousal, noting the relationship between arousal and performance.

2. Discuss the research findings on the relationship between body states and specific emotions.

3. (Thinking Critically) Discuss the effectiveness of the polygraph in detecting lies.

Stepping Through the Section

Answers are provided on page 330.

1. Describe the major physiological changes that each of the following undergoes during emotional arousal:
   a. heart: _____
   b. muscles: _____
   c. liver: _____
   d. breathing: _____
   e. digestion: _____
   f. pupils: _____
   g. blood: _____
   h. skin: _____

2. The responses of arousal are activated by the _____ nervous system. In response to its signal, the _____ glands release the hormones _____ and _____ , which increase heart rate, blood pressure, and blood sugar levels.

3. When the need for arousal has passed, the body is calmed through activation of the _____ nervous system.

Explain the relationship between performance and arousal.

4. The various emotions are associated with _____ (similar/different) forms of physiological arousal.

5. The emotions _____ and _____ are accompanied by differing _____ temperatures and _____ secretions.

6. The brain circuits underlying different emotions _____ (are/are not) different. For example, seeing a fearful face elicits greater activity in the _____ than seeing a(n) _____ face. People who have generally negative personalities, and those who are prone to _____ , show more activity in the _____ _____ _____ of the brain.

7. Individuals with more active _____ (right/left) _____ lobes tend to be more cheerful than those in whom this pattern of brain activity is reversed. This may be due to the rich supply of _____ receptors in this area of the brain.

8. The physical accompaniments of emotion _____ (are/are not) innate and universal.

9. (Thinking Critically) The technical name for the "lie detector" is the _____ .

(Thinking Critically) Explain how lie detectors supposedly indicate whether a person is lying.

10. (Thinking Critically) How well the lie detector works depends on whether a person exhibits _____ while lying.

11. (Thinking Critically) Those who criticize lie detectors feel that the tests are particularly likely to err in the case of the _____ (innocent/guilty), because different _____ all register as _____ .

12. (Thinking Critically) By and large, experts _____ (agree/do not agree) that lie detector tests are highly accurate.

13. (Thinking Critically) A test that assesses a suspect's knowledge of details of a crime that only the guilty person should know is the _____ _____ _____ .

Expressed Emotion (pp. 387–393)

> If you do not know the meaning of any of the following words, phrases, or expressions in the context in which they appear in the text, refer to page 342 for an explanation: *good enough at reading; Fidgeting; Ditto; sneer; Fake a big grin.*

Section Preview

Answer guidelines are provided on page 330.

1. Discuss gender and personality differences in nonverbal communication.

2. Discuss whether nonverbal expressions of emotion are universally understood, and describe the effects of facial expressions on emotion.

Stepping Through the Section

Answers are provided on page 330.

1. Researchers have found that people who _____ (suppress/express) their emotions while watching a distressing film showed impaired _____ for details in the film. Emotions may be communicated in words and/or through body expressions, referred to as _____ communication.

2. Most people are especially good at interpreting nonverbal _____ . We read fear and _____ mostly from the _____ , and happiness from the _____ .

3. Introverts are _____ (better/worse) at reading others' emotions, whereas extraverts are themselves _____ (easier/harder) to read.

4. Experience can _____ people to particular emotions, as revealed by the fact that children who have been physically abused are quicker than others at perceiving _____ .

5. Women are generally _____ (better/worse) than men at detecting nonverbal signs of emotion and in spotting _____ . Women possess greater emotional _____ than men, as revealed by the tendency of men to describe their emotions in _____ terms. This gender difference may be a by-product of traditional _____ _____ and may contribute to women's greater emotional _____ .

6. Although women are _____ (more/less) likely than men to describe themselves as empathic, physiological measures reveal a much _____ (smaller/larger) gender difference. Women are _____ (more/less) likely than men to express empathy.

7. Various emotions may be linked with hard-to-control _____ _____ .

8. The absence of nonverbal cues to emotion is one reason that communications sent as _____ are easy to misread.

9. Gestures have _____ (the same/different) meanings in different cultures.

10. Studies of adults indicate that in different cultures facial expressions have _____ (the same/different) meanings. Studies of children indicate that the meaning of their facial expressions _____ (varies/does not vary) across cultures. The emotional facial expressions of blind children _____ (are/are not) the same as those of sighted children.

11. According to _____ , human emotional expressions evolved because they helped our ancestors communicate before language developed. It has also been adaptive for us to _____ faces in particular _____ .

12. In cultures that encourage _____ , emotional expressions are often intense and prolonged. In cultures that emphasize _____ , emotions such as _____ , _____ , and _____ are more common than in the _____ (East/West).

13. Darwin believed that when an emotion is accompanied by an outward facial expression, the emotion is _____ (intensified/diminished).

14. In one study, students who were induced to smile _____ (found/did not find) cartoons more humorous.

15. Studies have found that imitating another person's facial expressions _____ (leads/does not lead) to greater empathy with that person's feelings.

Experienced Emotion (pp. 393–402)

> If you do not know the meaning of any of the following words, phrases, or expressions in the context in which they appear in the text, refer to pages 342–343 for an explanation: *hostile outbursts; "blowing off steam"; rush of euphoria; lob a bombshell.*

Section Preview

Answer guidelines are provided on page 331.

1. Discuss the catharsis hypothesis, and identify some of the advantages and disadvantages of openly expressing anger.

2. Identify some potential causes and consequences of happiness, and discuss reasons for the relativity of happiness.

Stepping Through the Section

Answers are provided on page 331.

1. Izard believes that there are _____ basic emotions, most of which _____ (are/are not) present in infancy.

2. Averill has found that most people become angry several times per _____.

3. The belief that expressing pent-up emotion is adaptive is most commonly found in cultures that emphasize _____ . This is the _____ hypothesis. In cultures that emphasize _____ , such as those of _____ or _____ , expressions of anger are less common.

4. Psychologists have found that when anger has been provoked, retaliation may have a calming effect under certain circumstances. List the circumstances.

   a. _____
   b. _____
   c. _____

Identify some potential problems with expressing anger.

5. List two suggestions offered by experts for handling anger.

   a. _____
   b. _____

6. Researchers have found that students who mentally rehearsed times they _____ someone who had hurt them had lower bodily arousal than when they thought of times when they did not.

7. Happy people tend to perceive the world as _____ . They are also _____ (more/less) willing to help others. This is called the

   _____-_____ ,

   _____-_____ phenomenon. An individual's self-perceived happiness or satisfaction with life is called his or her

   _____ _____ .

8. Positive emotions _____ (rise/fall) early in the day and _____ (rise/fall) during the later hours.

9. Most people tend to _____ (underestimate/overestimate) the long-term emotional consequences of very bad news. After experiencing tragedy or dramatically positive events, people generally _____ (regain/do not regain) their previous degree of happiness.

10. Researchers have found that levels of happiness _____ (do/do not) mirror differences in standards of living. During the last four decades, spendable income in the United States has more than doubled; personal happiness has _____ (increased/decreased/remained almost unchanged).

11. Studies demonstrate that people generally experience a higher quality of life and greater well-being when they strive for _____

    _____

    _____ than

    when they strive for _____ .

12. The idea that happiness is relative to one's recent experience is stated by the _____-_____ phenomenon.

Explain how this principle accounts for the fact that, for some people, material desires can never be satisfied.

13. The principle that one feels worse off than others is known as _____

    _____ .

14. List six factors that have been shown to be positively correlated with feelings of happiness.

    _____

    _____

    _____

    _____

    _____

    _____

15. List five factors that are evidently unrelated to happiness.

    _____

    _____

    _____

    _____

    _____

16. Research studies of identical and fraternal twins have led to the estimate that _____ percent of the variation in people's happiness ratings is heritable.

17. (Close-Up) State several research-based suggestions for increasing your satisfaction with life.

Stress and Health (pp. 402–413)

> If you do not know the meaning of any of the following words, phrases, or expressions in the context in which they appear in the text, refer to pages 343–344 for an explanation: *tense . . . clenched teeth . . . churning stomach; slippery concept; heart rate zooms; uprooting; a cluster of crises; Daily Hassles; mellow and laid-back; after the honeymoon period; "combat ready"; headless horseman; hyping.*

Section Preview

Answer guidelines begin on page 331.

1. Define *stress* and describe the body's response to stress.

2. Discuss research findings on the health consequences of stressful life events, as well as the impact of perceived control and pessimism on health and our vulnerability to stress.

3. Discuss the role of stress in coronary heart disease, and contrast Type A and Type B personalities.

4. Describe how the immune system defends the body, and discuss the effect of stress on the immune system.

Stepping Through the Section

Answers begin on page 332.

1. Out of every 10 people, _____ (how many?) report experiencing frequent stress. Stress is not merely a _____ or a _____ . Rather, it is the _____ by which we perceive and respond to environmental threats and challenges. This definition highlights the fact that stressors can have _____ (only negative/both positive and negative) effects, depending on how they are perceived.

2. In the 1920s, physiologist Walter _____ began studying the effect of stress on the body. He discovered that the hormones _____ and _____ are released into the bloodstream in response to stress. This and other bodily changes due to stress are mediated by the _____ nervous system, thus preparing the body for "_____ _____ ." Another common response to stress among women has been called _____ _____ ,

which refers to the increased tendency to _____ .

3. Selye referred to this bodily response to stress as the _____ _____ _____ .

4. During the first phase of the GAS—the _____ reaction—the person is in a state of shock due to the sudden arousal of the _____ nervous system.

5. This is followed by the stage of _____ , in which the body's resources are mobilized to cope with the stressor.

6. If stress continues, the person enters the stage of _____ . During this stage, a person is _____ (more/less) vulnerable to disease.

7. The field that integrates behavioral and medical knowledge relevant to health and disease is _____ _____ . The subfield of psychology related to behavioral medicine is called _____ psychology.

8. In the wake of catastrophic events, such as floods, hurricanes, and fires, there often is an increase in the number of _____ _____ .

9. Research studies have found that people who have recently been widowed, fired, or divorced are _____ (more/no more) vulnerable to illness than other people.

10. For most people, the most significant sources of stress are _____ _____ . The stresses that accompany poverty and unemployment, for example, often compounded by _____ , may account for the higher rates of _____ among residents of urban ghettos.

11. Negative situations are especially stressful when they are appraised as _____ . Control may explain why poorer people are more at risk for premature _____ than those who are more affluent.

12. People at every income level tend to die younger in areas where there is greater income _____ . Among developed countries, for example, life expectancies in the _____ _____ and _____ are _____ (how much?) lower than those in _____ and _____ .

13. Recent studies in several countries indicate that _____ more than _____ predicts mortality.

14. People who have an _____ attitude are *less* likely than others to suffer ill health.

15. In animals and humans, sudden lack of control is followed by a drop in immune responses and a rise in the levels of _____ _____ .

16. The leading cause of death in North America is _____ _____ _____ . List several risk factors for developing this condition: _____ _____ _____ .

17. Friedman and Rosenman discovered that tax accountants experience an increase in blood _____ level and blood- _____ speed during tax season. This showed there was a link between coronary warning indicators and _____ .

Friedman and Rosenman, in a subsequent study, grouped people into Type A and Type B personalities. Characterize these types, and indicate the difference that emerged between them over the course of this nine-year study.

18. When a _____ (Type A/Type B) person is angered, blood flow is diverted away from the internal organs, including the liver, which is responsible for removing _____ and fat from the blood. Thus, such people have elevated levels of these substances in the blood.

19. The Type A characteristic that is most strongly linked with coronary heart disease is _____ _____ —especially _____ .

20. Another toxic emotion is _____ , which _____ (increases/ has no effect on) one's risk of having a heart attack or developing other heart problems.

21. In _____ illnesses, physical symptoms are produced by psychological causes. Examples of such illnesses are certain forms of _____ and some _____ . Such illnesses appear to be linked to _____ .

22. The body's system of fighting disease is the _____ system. This system includes two types of white blood cells, called _____ : the _____ _____ , which fight bacterial infections, and the _____ _____ , which form in the _____ and attack viruses, cancer cells, and foreign substances. Another immune agent, called the _____ , pursues and ingests foreign substances.

23. Responding too strongly, the immune system may attack the body's tissues and cause _____ or an _____ reaction. Or it may _____ , allowing a dormant virus to erupt or _____ cells to multiply.

24. _____ (Women/Men) are the immunologically stronger gender. This makes them less susceptible to _____ , but more susceptible to _____ diseases such as _____ and _____ _____ .

25. Stress can suppress the lymphocyte cells, resulting in a(n)_____ (increase/ decrease) in disease resistance. Stress diverts

energy from the _____

_____ to the

_____ and _____ ,

mobilizing the body for action.

26. Worldwide, the fourth leading cause of death is

_____ , caused by the

_____ _____

_____ , which is spread primari-

ly through the exchange of _____

and _____ . Stressful life circum-

stances _____ (have/have not)

been shown to accelerate the progression of this

chronic disease.

Characterize the link between stress and cancer.

27. Experiments by Ader and Cohen demonstrate
that the functioning of the body's immune system
_____ (can/cannot) be affected
by conditioning.

Promoting Health (pp. 414–424)

> If you do not know the meaning of any of the
> following words, phrases, or expressions in the
> context in which they appear in the text, refer
> to page 344 for an explanation: *run away from*
> *their troubles; The mood boost; overblown and over-*
> *sold; heartaches; cold fact . . . nothing to sneeze at;*
> *"open heart therapy."*

Section Preview

Answer guidelines are provided on page 333.

1. Identify and discuss different strategies for coping with stress.

2. Describe the relationship between health and
social support, and discuss whether there is a
"faith factor" in health and longevity.

3. (Thinking Critically) Discuss the growing popularity of complementary and alternative medicine.

Stepping Through the Section

Answers are provided on page 333.

1. Sustained exercise that increases heart and lung
fitness is known as _____ exer-
cise. Experiments _____
(have/have not) been able to demonstrate conclu-
sively that such exercise reduces anxiety and
depression and alleviates the effects of stress.

2. Exercise increases the body's production of
mood-boosting neurotransmitters such as

_____ , _____ ,

and the _____ . By one estimate,

moderate exercise adds _____

(how many?) years to one's life expectancy.

3. A system for recording a physiological response
and providing information concerning it is called
_____ . The instruments used in

this system _____ (provide/do

not provide) the individual with a means of con-

trolling physiological responses.

4. Lowered blood pressure, heart rate, and oxygen consumption have been found to be characteristic of people who regularly practice _____ . The _____ response accompanies sitting quietly, with closed eyes, while breathing deeply. Brain scans of experienced meditators reveal decreased activity in the _____lobe and increased activity in the _____lobe.

5. Meyer Friedman found that modifying Type A behavior in a group of heart attack survivors _____ (reduced/did not significantly reduce) the rate of recurrence of heart attacks.

6. Another buffer against the effects of stress is _____ support. Longitudinal research reveals that a _____ _____ at age 50 predicts healthy aging better than _____ _____ at the same age. James Pennebaker has found that emotional _____ can adversely affect our physical health, while _____ suppressed thoughts may promote well-being.

State several possible reasons for the link between health and social support.

7. Until fairly recently in history, the healing traditions of _____ and _____ have worked _____ (together/separately).

8. Polls reveal that most Americans _____ (believe/do not believe) that religion and spirituality are related to health and healing.

9. Several studies demonstrate that religious involvement _____ (predicts/ does not predict) health and longevity.

State two possible intervening variables that might account for the "faith factor" in health.

10. (Thinking Critically) Acupuncture, massage therapy, homeopathy, and similar treatments comprise the growing health care market called _____ _____ _____ _____ . In China, _____ therapies have flourished for centuries, as have acupuncture and acupressure therapies that claim to correct imbalances in the flow of the energy called _____ .

11. (Thinking Critically) Critics of alternative medicine point out that such treatments seem especially effective with _____ diseases such as arthritis and _____ _____ , as well as with diseases that disappear naturally—a phenomenon called _____ _____ .

Critics also argue that the seeming effectiveness of alternative medicine is due to a _____ effect.

Progress Test 1

Multiple-Choice Questions

Circle your answers to the following questions and check them with the answers beginning on page 333. If your answer is incorrect, read the explanation for why it is incorrect and then consult the appropriate pages of the text (in parentheses following the correct answer).

1. Which of the following is correct regarding the relationship between arousal and performance?
   a. Generally, performance is optimal when arousal is low.
   b. Generally, performance is optimal when arousal is high.
   c. On easy tasks, performance is optimal when arousal is low.
   d. On easy tasks, performance is optimal when arousal is high.

2. Which division of the nervous system is especially involved in bringing about emotional arousal?
   a. somatic nervous system
   b. peripheral nervous system
   c. sympathetic nervous system
   d. parasympathetic nervous system
   e. central nervous system

3. Concerning emotions and their accompanying body responses, which of the following appears to be true?
   a. Each emotion has its own body response and underlying brain circuit.
   b. All emotions involve the same body response as a result of the same underlying brain circuit.
   c. Many emotions involve similar body responses but have different underlying brain circuits.
   d. All emotions have the same underlying brain circuits but different body responses.

4. The Cannon-Bard theory of emotion states that:
   a. emotions have two ingredients: physical arousal and a cognitive label.
   b. the conscious experience of an emotion occurs at the same time as the body's physical reaction.
   c. emotional experiences are based on an awareness of the body's responses to an emotion-arousing stimulus.
   d. emotional ups and downs tend to balance in the long run.

5. Electrical stimulation of which brain region can produce terror or rage in cats?
   a. limbic system   c. cortex
   b. hypothalamus   d. cerebellum

6. The body's response to danger is triggered by the release of _____ by the _____ glands.
   a. acetylcholine; adrenal
   b. epinephrine and norepinephrine; adrenal
   c. acetylcholine; pituitary
   d. epinephrine and norepinephrine; pituitary

7. Which of the following was *not* raised as a criticism of the James-Lange theory of emotion?
   a. The body's responses are too similar to trigger the various emotions.
   b. Emotional reactions occur before the body's responses can take place.
   c. The cognitive activity of the cortex plays a role in the emotions we experience.
   d. People with spinal cord injuries at the neck typically experience less emotion.

8. (Thinking Critically) Current estimates are that the polygraph is inaccurate approximately _____ of the time.
   a. three-fourths   d. one-fourth
   b. one-half   e. one-tenth
   c. one-third

9. In the Schachter-Singer experiment, which subjects reported feeling an emotional change in the presence of the experimenter's highly emotional confederate?
   a. those receiving epinephrine and expecting to feel physical arousal
   b. those receiving a placebo and expecting to feel physical arousal
   c. those receiving epinephrine but not expecting to feel physical arousal
   d. those receiving a placebo and not expecting to feel physical arousal

10. Which of the following is true?
    a. People with more education tend to be happier.
    b. Beautiful people tend to be happier than plain people.
    c. Women tend to be happier than men.
    d. People with children tend to be happier.
    e. People who are socially outgoing or who exercise regularly tend to be happier.

11. Catharsis will be most effective in reducing anger toward another person if:
    a. you wait until you are no longer angry before confronting the person.
    b. the target of your anger is someone you feel has power over you.
    c. your anger is directed specifically toward the person who angered you.
    d. the other person is able to retaliate by also expressing anger.

12. Emotions are:
    a. physiological reactions.
    b. behavioral expressions.
    c. conscious feelings.
    d. all of the above.

13. Law enforcement officials sometimes use a lie detector to assess a suspect's responses to details of the crime believed to be known only to the perpetrator. This is known as the:
    a. inductive approach.
    b. deductive approach.
    c. guilty knowledge test.
    d. screening examination.
    e. prevarication probe.

14. Research on nonverbal communication has revealed that:
    a. it is easy to hide your emotions by controlling your facial expressions.
    b. facial expressions tend to be the same the world over, while gestures vary from culture to culture.
    c. most authentic expressions last between 7 and 10 seconds.
    d. most gestures have universal meanings; facial expressions vary from culture to culture.

15. Research suggests that people generally experience the greatest well-being when they strive for:
    a. wealth.
    b. modest income increases from year to year.
    c. slightly higher status than their friends, neighbors, and co-workers.
    d. intimacy and personal growth.

16. Research indicates that a person is most likely to be helpful to others if he or she:
    a. is feeling guilty about something.
    b. is happy.
    c. recently received help from another person.
    d. recently offered help to another person.

17. Darwin believed that:
    a. the expression of emotions helped our ancestors to survive.
    b. all humans express basic emotions using similar facial expressions.
    c. human facial expressions of emotion retain elements of animals' emotional displays.
    d. all of the above are true.

18. A graph depicting the course of positive emotions over the hours of the day since waking would:
    a. start low and rise steadily until bedtime.
    b. start high and decrease steadily until bedtime.
    c. remain at a stable, moderate level throughout the day.
    d. rise over the early hours and dissipate during the day's last several hours.
    e. vary too much from person to person to predict.

19. Evidence that changes in facial expression can directly affect people's feelings and body states has convinced Robert Zajonc that:
    a. the heart is always subject to the mind.
    b. emotional reactions involve deliberate rational thinking.
    c. cognition is not necessary for emotion.
    d. the interpretation of facial expressions is a learned skill.

20. Behavioral and medical knowledge about factors influencing health form the basis of the field of:
    a. health psychology.
    b. holistic medicine.
    c. behavioral medicine.
    d. osteopathic medicine.

21. The stress hormones epinephrine and norepinephrine are released by the _____ gland in response to stimulation by the _____ branch of the nervous system.
    a. pituitary; sympathetic
    b. pituitary; parasympathetic
    c. adrenal; sympathetic
    d. adrenal; parasympathetic

22. During which stage of the general adaptation syndrome is a person especially vulnerable to disease?
    a. alarm reaction   c. stage of exhaustion
    b. stage of resistance   d. stage of adaptation

23. The leading cause of death in North America is:
    a. lung cancer.
    b. AIDS.
    c. coronary heart disease.
    d. alcohol-related accidents.
    e. accidents.

24. Researchers Friedman and Rosenman refer to individuals who are very time-conscious, super-motivated, verbally aggressive, and easily angered as:
    a. ulcer-prone personalities.
    b. cancer-prone personalities.
    c. Type A.
    d. Type B.

25. One effect of stress hormones is to:
    a. lower the level of cholesterol in the blood.
    b. promote the buildup of fat deposits around the heart.
    c. divert blood away from the muscles of the body.
    d. reduce stress.
    e. decrease the amount of fat stored in the body.

26. Genuine illnesses that are caused by stress are called _____ illnesses.
    a. psychophysiological   c. psychogenic
    b. hypochondriacal   d. psychotropic

27. Stress has been demonstrated to place a person at increased risk of:
    a. cancer.
    b. progressing from HIV infection to AIDS.
    c. bacterial infections.
    d. viral infections.
    e. all of the above.

28. *Stress* is defined as:
    a. unpleasant or aversive events that cannot be controlled.
    b. situations that threaten health.
    c. the process by which we perceive and respond to challenging or threatening events.
    d. anything that decreases immune responses.

29. A study in which people were asked to confide troubling feelings to an experimenter found that participants typically:
    a. did not truthfully report feelings and events.
    b. experienced a sustained increase in blood pressure until the experiment was finished.
    c. became physiologically more relaxed after confiding their problem.
    d. denied having any problems.

30. Which of the following was *not* mentioned in the text as a potential health benefit of exercise?
    a. Exercise can increase ability to cope with stress.
    b. Exercise can lower blood pressure.
    c. Exercise can reduce stress, depression, and anxiety.
    d. Exercise improves functioning of the immune system.

31. Research studies demonstrate that after a catastrophe rates of _____ often increase.
    a. depression
    b. anxiety
    c. stress-related illnesses
    d. all of the above
    e. none of the above

32. In one study, laboratory rats drank sweetened water with a drug that causes immune suppression. After repeated pairings of the taste with the drug:
    a. the animals developed tolerance for the drug and immune responses returned to normal.
    b. sweet water alone triggered immune suppression.
    c. dependency on the drug developed and withdrawal symptoms appeared when the drug was withheld.
    d. many of the animals died.

33. Social support _____ our ability to cope with stressful events.
    a. has no effect on
    b. usually increases
    c. usually decreases
    d. has an unpredictable effect on

34. The AIDS virus is transmitted primarily by:
    a. airborne transmission of HIV.
    b. physical touching.
    c. an exchange of blood or semen.
    d. insect bites.

35. Research has demonstrated that as a predictor of health and longevity, religious involvement:
    a. has a small, insignificant effect.
    b. is more accurate for women than men.
    c. is more accurate for men than women.
    d. rivals nonsmoking and exercise.

Matching Items

Match each definition or description with the appropriate term.

Definitions or Descriptions

_____ 1. the tendency to react to changes on the basis of recent experience

_____ 2. an individual's self-perceived happiness

_____ 3. emotional release

_____ 4. the tendency to evaluate our situation negatively against that of other people

_____ 5. emotions consist of physical arousal *and* a cognitive label

_____ 6. an emotion-arousing stimulus triggers cognitive and body responses simultaneously

_____ 7. the division of the nervous system that calms the body following arousal

_____ 8. the division of the nervous system that activates arousal

_____ 9. a device that measures the physiological correlates of emotion

_____ 10. the tendency of people to be helpful when they are in a good mood

_____ 11. we are sad because we cry

Terms

a. adaptation-level phenomenon
b. two-factor theory
c. catharsis
d. sympathetic nervous system
e. James-Lange theory
f. polygraph
g. Cannon-Bard theory
h. parasympathetic nervous system
i. relative deprivation principle
j. feel-good, do-good phenomenon
k. subjective well-being

Progress Test 2

Progress Test 2 should be completed during a final chapter review. Answer the following questions after you thoroughly understand the correct answers for the section reviews and Progress Test 1.

Multiple-Choice Questions

1. Which of the following most accurately describes emotional arousal?
   a. Emotions prepare the body to fight or flee.
   b. Emotions are voluntary reactions to emotion-arousing stimuli.
   c. Because all emotions have the same physiological basis, emotions are primarily psychological events.
   d. Emotional arousal is always accompanied by cognition.
   e. All are accurate descriptions.

2. Schachter's two-factor theory emphasizes that emotion involves both:
   a. the sympathetic and parasympathetic divisions of the nervous system.
   b. verbal and nonverbal expression.
   c. physical arousal and a cognitive label.
   d. universal and culture-specific aspects.

3. Dermer found that students who had studied others who were worse off than themselves felt greater satisfaction with their own lives; this is the principle of:
   a. relative deprivation.
   b. adaptation level.
   c. behavioral contrast.
   d. opponent processes.

4. Which theory of emotion emphasizes the simultaneous experience of body response and emotional feeling?
   a. James-Lange theory
   b. Cannon-Bard theory
   c. two-factor theory
   d. relative deprivation theory

5. Izard believes that there are _____ basic emotions.
   a. 3   d. 10
   b. 5   e. 12
   c. 7

6. (Thinking Critically) The polygraph measures:
   a. lying.
   b. brain rhythms.
   c. chemical changes in the body.
   d. physiological indexes of arousal.

7. People who are exuberant and persistently cheerful show increased activity in the brain's _____ , which is rich in receptors for the neurotransmitter _____ .
   a. right frontal lobe; dopamine
   b. left frontal lobe; dopamine
   c. amygdala; serotonin
   d. thalamus; serotonin

8. Which of the following is true?
   a. Gestures are universal; facial expressions, culture-specific.
   b. Facial expressions are universal; gestures, culture-specific.
   c. Both gestures and facial expressions are universal.
   d. Both gestures and facial expressions are culture-specific.

9. Which theory of emotion implies that every emotion is associated with a unique physiological reaction?
   a. James-Lange theory
   b. Cannon-Bard theory
   c. two-factor theory
   d. catharsis theory

10. Which of the following was *not* presented in the text as evidence that some emotional reactions involve no deliberate, rational thinking?
    a. Some of the neural pathways involved in emotion are separate from those involved in thinking and memory.
    b. Emotional reactions are sometimes quicker than our interpretations of a situation.
    c. People can develop an emotional preference for visual stimuli to which they have been unknowingly exposed.
    d. Arousal of the sympathetic nervous system will trigger an emotional reaction even when artificially induced by an injection of epinephrine.

11. Concerning the catharsis hypothesis, which of the following is true?
    a. Expressing anger can be temporarily calming if it does not leave one feeling guilty or anxious.
    b. The arousal that accompanies unexpressed anger never dissipates.

    c. Expressing one's anger always calms one down.
    d. Psychologists agree that under no circumstances is catharsis beneficial.

12. In an emergency situation, emotional arousal will result in:
    a. increased rate of respiration.
    b. increased blood sugar.
    c. a slowing of digestion.
    d. pupil dilation.
    e. all of the above.

13. A relatively high level of arousal would be most likely to facilitate:
    a. remembering the lines of a play.
    b. shooting free throws in basketball.
    c. sprinting 100 meters.
    d. taking a final exam in introductory psychology.

14. Several studies have shown that physical arousal can intensify just about any emotion. For example, when people who have been physically aroused by exercise are insulted, they often misattribute their arousal to the insult. This finding illustrates the importance of:
    a. cognitive labels of arousal in the conscious experience of emotions.
    b. a minimum level of arousal in triggering emotional experiences.
    c. the simultaneous occurrence of physical arousal and cognitive labeling in emotional experience.
    d. all of the above.

15. (Thinking Critically) Psychologist David Lykken is opposed to the use of lie detectors because:
    a. they represent an invasion of a person's privacy and could easily be used for unethical purposes.
    b. there are often serious discrepancies among the various indicators such as perspiration and heart rate.
    c. polygraphs cannot distinguish the various possible causes of arousal.
    d. they are accurate only about 50 percent of the time.

16. Averill found that most people become angry:
    a. once a day.
    b. once a week.
    c. several times a week.
    d. several times a month.
    e. There is no common pattern to anger.

17. Which of these factors have researchers *not* found to correlate with happiness?
    a. a satisfying marriage or close friendship
    b. high self-esteem
    c. religious faith
    d. education

18. In cultures that emphasize social interdependence:
    a. emotional displays are typically intense.
    b. emotional displays are typically prolonged.
    c. negative emotions are rarely displayed.
    d. all of the above are true.

19. The field of health psychology is concerned with:
    a. the prevention of illness.
    b. the promotion of health.
    c. the treatment of illness.
    d. all of the above.

20. In order, the sequence of stages in the general adaptation syndrome is:
    a. alarm reaction, stage of resistance, stage of exhaustion.
    b. stage of resistance, alarm reaction, stage of exhaustion.
    c. stage of exhaustion, stage of resistance, alarm reaction.
    d. alarm reaction, stage of exhaustion, stage of resistance.

21. AIDS is a disorder that causes a breakdown in the body's:
    a. endocrine system.
    b. circulatory system.
    c. immune system.
    d. respiratory system.

22. "Tend and befriend" refers to:
    a. the final stage of the general adaptation syndrome.
    b. the health-promoting impact of having a strong system of social support.
    c. an alternative to the "fight-or-flight" response that may be more common in women.
    d. the fact that spiritual people typically are not socially isolated.

23. Which of the following statements concerning Type A and B persons is true?
    a. Even when relaxed, Type A persons have higher blood pressure than Type B persons.
    b. When stressed, Type A persons show greater output of stress hormones than Type B persons.

    c. Type B persons tend to suppress anger more than Type A persons.
    d. Type B persons tend to be more combat ready than Type A persons.

24. The disease- and infection-fighting cells of the immune system are:
    a. B lymphocytes.   c. both a. and b.
    b. T lymphocytes.   d. antigens.

25. One effect of stress on the body is to:
    a. suppress the immune system.
    b. facilitate the immune system response.
    c. increase disease resistance.
    d. increase the growth of B and T lymphocytes.

26. Compared to men, women:
    a. have stronger immune systems.
    b. are less susceptible to infections.
    c. are more susceptible to self-attacking diseases such as multiple sclerosis.
    d. have none of the above characteristics.
    e. have all the characteristics described in a., b., and c.

27. In response to uncontrollable shock, levels of stress hormones _____ and immune responses are _____ .
    a. decrease; suppressed   c. decrease; increased
    b. increase; suppressed   d. increase; increased

28. Allergic reactions and arthritis are caused by:
    a. an overreactive immune system.
    b. an underreactive immune system.
    c. the presence of B lymphocytes.
    d. the presence of T lymphocytes.

29. Research on cancer patients reveals that:
    a. stress affects the growth of cancer cells by weakening the body's natural resources.
    b. patients' attitudes can influence their rate of recovery.
    c. cancer occurs slightly more often than usual among those widowed, divorced, or separated.
    d. all of the above are true.

30. The component of Type A behavior that is the most predictive of coronary disease is:
    a. time urgency.   d. impatience.
    b. competitiveness.   e. anger.
    c. high motivation.

31. During biofeedback training:
   a. a person is given sensory feedback for a subtle body response.
   b. biological functions controlled by the autonomic nervous system may come under conscious control.
   c. the accompanying relaxation is much the same as that produced by other, simpler methods of relaxation.
   d. all of the above occur.

32. Which of the following was *not* suggested as a possible explanation of the "faith factor" in health?
   a. Having a coherent worldview is a buffer against stress.
   b. Religious people tend to have healthier lifestyles.
   c. Those who are religious have stronger networks of social support.
   d. Because they are more affluent, religiously active people receive better health care.

33. (Thinking Critically) Acupuncture, aromatherapy, and homeopathy are forms of:
   a. psychophysiological medicine.
   b. complementary and alternative medicine.
   c. Chi therapy.
   d. psychosomatic medicine.

True–False Items

Indicate whether each statement is true or false by placing *T* or *F* in the blank next to the item.

_____ 1. For easy tasks, the optimal level of arousal is higher than for difficult tasks.
_____ 2. Men are generally better than women at detecting nonverbal emotional expression.
_____ 3. The sympathetic nervous system triggers physiological arousal during an emotion.
_____ 4. The adrenal glands produce the hormones epinephrine and norepinephrine.
_____ 5. When one imitates an emotional facial expression, the body may experience physiological changes characteristic of that emotion.
_____ 6. People who have lost sensation only in their lower bodies experience a considerable decrease in the intensity of their emotions.
_____ 7. Wealthy people tend to be much happier than middle-income people.
_____ 8. Physical arousal can intensify emotion.

_____ 9. All emotions involve conscious thought.
_____ 10. The two-factor theory states that emotions are given a cognitive label before physical arousal occurs.
_____ 11. Stressors tend to increase activity in the immune system and in this way make people more vulnerable to illness.
_____ 12. Events are most stressful when perceived as both negative and controllable.
_____ 13. Optimists cope more successfully with stressful events than do pessimists.
_____ 14. Type A persons are more physiologically reactive to stress than are Type B persons.
_____ 15. The symptoms of psychophysiological illnesses are not real.
_____ 16. People with few social and community ties are more likely to die prematurely than are those who have many social ties.
_____ 17. People tend to die younger in areas where income inequality is greater.

Review and Reflect

Answer these questions the day before an exam as a final check on your understanding of the chapter's terms and concepts.

Multiple-Choice Questions

1. You are on your way to school to take a big exam. Suddenly, on noticing that your pulse is racing and that you are sweating, you feel nervous. With which theory of emotion is this experience most consistent?
   a. Cannon-Bard theory
   b. James-Lange theory
   c. relative deprivation theory
   d. adaptation-level theory

2. When Professor Simon acquired a spacious new office, he was overjoyed. Six months later, however, he was taking the office for granted. His behavior illustrates the:
   a. relative deprivation principle.
   b. adaptation-level phenomenon.
   c. catharsis hypothesis.
   d. optimum arousal principle.

3. After Brenda scolded her brother for forgetting to pick her up from school, the physical arousal that had accompanied her anger diminished. Which division of her nervous system mediated her physical *relaxation*?
   a. sympathetic division
   b. parasympathetic division
   c. somatic division
   d. peripheral nervous system

4. Two years ago Maria was in an automobile accident in which her spinal cord was severed, leaving her paralyzed from her neck down. Today, Maria finds that she experiences emotions less intensely than she did before her accident. This tends to support which theory of emotion?
   a. James-Lange theory
   b. Cannon-Bard theory
   c. adaptation-level theory
   d. relative deprivation theory

5. The candidate stepped before the hostile audience, panic written all over his face. It is likely that the candidate's facial expression caused him to experience:
   a. a lessening of his fear.
   b. an intensification of his fear.
   c. a surge of digestive enzymes in his body.
   d. increased body temperature.

6. Jane was so mad at her brother that she exploded at him when he entered her room. That she felt less angry afterward is best explained by the principle of:
   a. adaptation level.
   b. physiological arousal.
   c. relative deprivation.
   d. catharsis.

7. After hitting a grand-slam home run, Mike noticed that his heart was pounding. Later that evening, after nearly having a collision while driving on the freeway, Mike again noticed that his heart was pounding. That he interpreted this reaction as fear, rather than as ecstasy, can best be explained by the:
   a. James-Lange theory.
   b. Cannon-Bard theory.
   c. two-factor theory.
   d. adaptation-level theory.

8. As part of her job interview, Jan is asked to take a lie-detector test. Jan politely refuses and points out that:
   a. a guilty person can be found innocent by the polygraph.
   b. an innocent person can be found guilty.
   c. a liar can learn to fool a lie-detector test.
   d. these tests err one-third of the time.
   e. all of the above are true.

9. A student participating in an experiment concerned with physical responses that accompany emotions reports that her mouth is dry, her heart is racing, and she feels flushed. What emotion is the student experiencing?
   a. anger
   b. fear
   c. ecstasy
   d. It cannot be determined from the information given.

10. Who will probably be angrier after learning that he or she has received a parking ticket?
    a. Bob, who has just awakened from a nap
    b. Veronica, who has just finished eating a big lunch
    c. Dan, who has just completed a tennis match
    d. Alicia, who has been reading a romantic novel
    e. It cannot be determined from the information given.

11. Children in New York, Nigeria, and New Zealand smile when they are happy and frown when they are sad. This suggests that:
    a. the Cannon-Bard theory is correct.
    b. some emotional expressions are learned at a very early age.
    c. the two-factor theory is correct.
    d. facial expressions of emotion are universal and biologically determined.

12. Who is the *least* likely to display negative emotions openly?
    a. Paul, a game warden in Australia
    b. Niles, a stockbroker in Belgium
    c. Deborah, a physicist in Toronto
    d. Yoko, a dentist in Japan

13. Nine-month-old Nicole's left frontal lobe is more active than her right frontal lobe. We can expect that, all other things being equal, Nicole:
   a. may suffer from mild depression for most of her life.
   b. may have trouble "turning off" upsetting feelings later in her life.
   c. may be more cheerful than those with more active right frontal lobes.
   d. may have trouble expressing feelings later in her life.

14. Julio was extremely angry when he came in for a routine EEG of his brain activity. When he later told this to the doctor, she was no longer concerned about the:
   a. increased electrical activity in Julio's right prefrontal cortex.
   b. increased electrical activity in Julio's left prefrontal cortex.
   c. decreased electrical activity in Julio's amygdala.
   d. increased electrical activity in Julio's amygdala.

15. When the scientist electrically stimulated one area of a monkey's brain, the monkey became enraged. When another electrode was activated, the monkey cowered in fear. The electrodes were most likely implanted in the:
   a. pituitary gland.
   b. adrenal glands.
   c. limbic system.
   d. right hemisphere.

16. As elderly Mr. Hooper crosses the busy intersection, he stumbles and drops the packages he is carrying. Which passerby is most likely to help Mr. Hooper?
   a. Drew, who has been laid off from work for three months
   b. Leon, who is on his way to work
   c. Bonnie, who graduated from college the day before
   d. Nancy, whose father recently passed away

17. Expressing anger can be adaptive when you:
   a. retaliate immediately.
   b. have mentally rehearsed all the reasons for your anger.
   c. count to 10, then blow off steam.
   d. first wait until the anger subsides, then deal with the situation in a civil manner.

18. Cindy was happy with her promotion until she found out that Janice, who has the same amount of experience, receives a higher salary. Cindy's feelings are *best* explained according to the:
   a. adaptation-level phenomenon.
   b. theory of subjective well-being.
   c. catharsis hypothesis.
   d. principle of relative deprivation.

19. I am an emotionally literate person who is very accurate at reading others' nonverbal behavior, detecting lies, and describing my feelings. Who am I?
   a. an introvert
   b. an extrovert
   c. a woman
   d. a man

20. Concluding her presentation on spirituality and health, Maja notes that:
   a. historically, religion and medicine joined hands in caring for the sick.
   b. most Americans believe that spirituality and religion are related to health.
   c. people who attend religious services weekly have healthier life-styles.
   d. all of the above are true.

21. Each semester, Bob does not start studying until just before midterms. Then he is forced to work around the clock until after final exams, which makes him sick, probably because he is in the _____ phase of the _____ .
   a. alarm; post-traumatic stress syndrome
   b. resistance; general adaptation syndrome
   c. exhaustion; general adaptation syndrome
   d. depletion; post-traumatic stress syndrome

22. Connie complains to the campus psychologist that she has too much stress in her life. The psychologist tells her that the level of stress people experience depends primarily on:
   a. how many activities they are trying to do at the same time.
   b. how they appraise the events of life.
   c. their physical hardiness.
   d. how predictable stressful events are.

23. Karen and Kyumi are taking the same course with different instructors. Karen's instructor schedules quizzes every Friday, while Kyumi's instructor gives the same number of quizzes on an unpredictable schedule. Assuming that their instructors are equally difficult, and that the two students tend to perceive exam stress in the same way, which student is probably under more stress?
    a. Karen
    b. Kyumi
    c. There should be no difference in their levels of stress.
    d. It is impossible to predict stress levels in this situation.

24. Jill is an easygoing, noncompetitive person who is happy in her job and enjoys her leisure time. She would *probably* be classified as:
    a. Type A.   c. Type C.
    b. Type B.   d. Type D.

25. A white blood cell that is formed in the thymus and that attacks cancer cells is:
    a. a macrophage.   c. a T lymphocyte.
    b. a B lymphocyte. d. any of the above.

26. When would you expect that your immune responses would be *weakest*?
    a. during summer vacation
    b. during exam weeks
    c. just after receiving good news
    d. Immune activity would probably remain constant during these times.

27. Which of the following would be the *best* piece of advice to offer a person who is trying to minimize the adverse effects of stress on his or her health?
    a. "Avoid challenging situations that may prove stressful."
    b. "Learn to play as hard as you work."
    c. "Maintain a sense of control and a positive approach to life."
    d. "Keep your emotional responses in check by keeping your feelings to yourself."

28. Philip's physician prescribes a stress management program to help Philip control his headaches. The physician has apparently diagnosed Philip's condition as a _____ illness, rather than a physical disorder.
    a. psychogenic   c. psychophysiological
    b. hypochondriac   d. biofeedback

29. You have just transferred to a new campus and find yourself in a potentially stressful environment. According to the text, which of the following would help you cope with the stress?
    a. believing that you have some control over your environment
    b. being able to predict when stressful events will occur
    c. feeling optimistic that you will eventually adjust to your new surroundings
    d. All of the above would help.

30. (Thinking Critically) Andrew, who is convinced that an expensive herbal remedy "cured" his arthritis, has decided to turn to homeopathy and herbal medicine for all of his health care. You caution him by pointing out that:
    a. arthritis is a cyclical disease that often improves on its own.
    b. botanical herbs have never been proven effective in controlled experiments.
    c. alternative medicine is a recent fad in this country that has few proponents in other parts of the world.
    d. all of the above are true.

Essay Questions

1. Discuss biological and cultural influences on emotions. (Use the space below to list the points you want to make, and organize them. Then write the essay on a separate sheet of paper.)

2. Discuss several factors that enhance a person's ability to cope with stress. (Use the space below to list the points you want to make, and organize them. Then write the essay on a separate sheet of paper.)

Key Terms

Writing Definitions

Using your own words, on a separate piece of paper write a brief definition or explanation of each of the following terms.

1. emotion
2. James-Lange theory
3. Cannon-Bard theory
4. two-factor theory
5. polygraph
6. catharsis
7. feel-good, do-good phenomenon
8. subjective well-being
9. adaptation-level phenomenon
10. relative deprivation
11. stress
12. general adaptation syndrome (GAS)
13. health psychology
14. coronary heart disease
15. Type A
16. Type B
17. psychophysiological illness
18. lymphocytes
19. aerobic exercise
20. biofeedback
21. complementary and alternative medicine

Summing Up

Complete the following flow chart.

THEORIES OF EMOTION

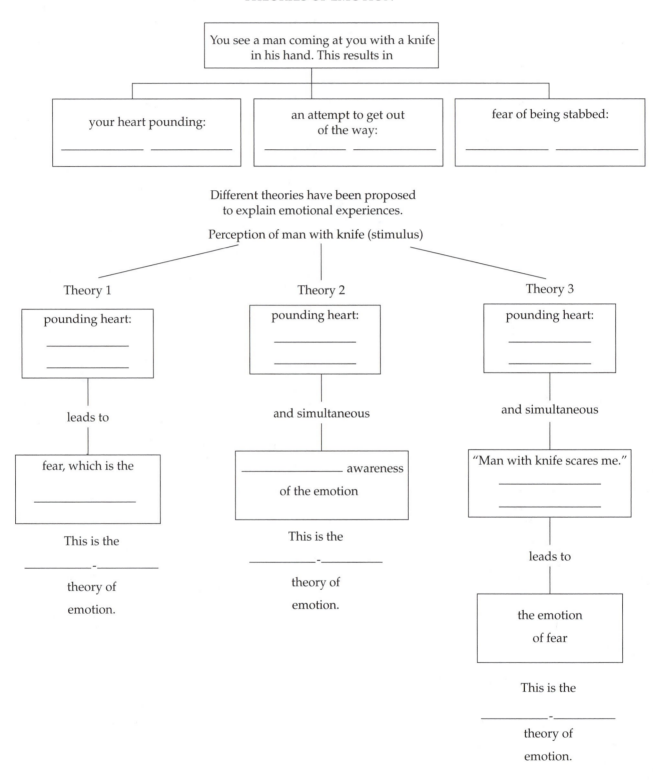

You see a man coming at you with a knife in his hand. This results in

your heart pounding:
_____ _____

an attempt to get out of the way:
_____ _____

fear of being stabbed:
_____ _____

Different theories have been proposed to explain emotional experiences.

Perception of man with knife (stimulus)

Theory 1

pounding heart:
_____
_____

leads to

fear, which is the
_____

This is the

_____-_____

theory of

emotion.

Theory 2

pounding heart:
_____
_____

and simultaneous

_____ awareness

of the emotion

This is the

_____-_____

theory of

emotion.

Theory 3

pounding heart:
_____
_____

and simultaneous

"Man with knife scares me."
_____
_____

leads to

the emotion
of fear

This is the

_____-_____

theory of

emotion.

Answers

Introducing Emotion

Introduction Preview

1. Emotions involve a mixture of physiological arousal, expressive behaviors, and conscious experience.

Theories of Emotion

Section Preview

1. According to the James-Lange theory, the experience of emotion results from awareness of the physiological responses to emotion-arousing stimuli. According to the Cannon-Bard theory, an emotion-arousing stimulus is simultaneously routed to the cortex, which causes the subjective experience of emotion, and to the sympathetic nervous system, which causes the body's physiological arousal.

   In criticizing the James-Lange theory, Walter Cannon argued that the body's responses were not sufficiently distinct to trigger the different emotions. The James-Lange theory has recently received support from evidence showing that there are physiological distinctions among the emotions and that emotions are diminished when the brain's awareness of the body's reactions is reduced. However, many researchers continue to agree with Cannon and Bard that the experience of emotion also involves cognitive activity.

   Schachter's two-factor theory of emotion proposes that emotions have two components: physical arousal and a cognitive label. Like the James-Lange theory, the two-factor theory presumes that our experience of emotion stems from our awareness of physical arousal. Like the Cannon-Bard theory, the two-factor theory presumes that emotions are physiologically similar and require a conscious interpretation of the arousal.

2. Although complex emotions, such as hatred and love, clearly arise from conscious thought, there is evidence that we can experience some emotions before we have time to think about the situation. When people view subliminal stimuli, for example, they are primed to feel better or worse about follow-up stimuli. Furthermore, some neural pathways involved in emotion, such as the one that links the eye to the amygdala, bypass cortical areas involved in thinking and enable an automatic emotional response.

Stepping Through the Section

1. follow

   Cannon argued that the body's responses were not sufficiently distinct to trigger the different emotions and, furthermore, that physiological changes occur too slowly to trigger sudden emotion.

2. cortex; sympathetic; Cannon-Bard

3. diminish; James-Lange

4. agree; cognition

5. physiological; cognitive; Schachter

6. did not; did

7. can

First, experiments on subliminal perception indicate that although stimuli are not consciously perceived, subjects later feel better or worse about a follow-up stimulus. Second, there is some separation of the neural pathways involved in emotion and cognition.

8. eye or ear; thalamus; amygdala; cognition

9. Lazarus; appraise

It seems that some emotional responses—especially simple likes, dislikes, and fears—involve no conscious thinking. Other emotions are greatly affected by our interpretations and expectations.

Embodied Emotion

Section Preview

1. Physiological arousal occurs when the sympathetic nervous system directs the adrenal glands to release epinephrine and norepinephrine. These hormones trigger increased heart rate, blood pressure, and blood sugar levels.

   Our performance on a task is usually best when arousal is moderate. However, the difficulty of the task affects optimum arousal level. A relatively high level of arousal is best on easy or well-learned tasks; a relatively low level of arousal is best on difficult or unrehearsed tasks.

2. Although the autonomic arousal that accompanies the different emotions often is similar, there are real, if subtle, physiological differences. For example, different brain circuits underlie different emotions. Limbic stimulation will trigger rage or terror in an animal. Fear and rage are accompanied by different finger temperatures and hormone secretions. Negative emotions and positive emotions tend to be accompanied by greater activity in the right and left prefrontal cortexes, respectively. People with greater activity in their left frontal lobes tend to be more cheerful than those with more active right frontal lobes.

3. The polygraph, or lie detector, measures the physiological responses that accompany emotions. How well the polygraph works depends on whether liars become anxious and exhibit detectable physiological arousal. Critics of the use of lie detectors argue that the tests are inaccurate about one-third of the time because they can't distinguish among anxiety, irritation, and guilt. Thus, they may label the innocent guilty when a question is upsetting. The polygraph may be somewhat more effective in criminal investigations that use the guilty knowledge test, which assesses a subject's response to details of the crime known only to the police and the guilty person.

Stepping Through the Section

1. **a.** Heart rate increases.

   b. Muscles become tense.

   c. The liver pours extra sugar into the bloodstream.

   d. Breathing rate increases.

   e. Digestion slows.

   f. Pupils dilate.

   g. Blood tends to clot more rapidly.

   h. Skin perspires.

2. sympathetic; adrenal; epinephrine (adrenaline); norepinephrine (noradrenaline)

3. parasympathetic

Performance on a task is usually best when arousal is moderate. However, the difficulty of the task affects optimum arousal level. A relatively high level of arousal is best on easy and well-learned tasks; a relatively low level of arousal is best on difficult tasks.

4. similar

5. fear; rage; finger; hormone

6. are; amygdala; angry; depression; right prefrontal cortex

7. left; frontal; dopamine

8. are

9. polygraph

The polygraph measures several of the physiological responses that accompany emotion, such as changes in breathing, pulse rate, blood pressure, and perspiration. The assumption is that lying is stressful, so a person who is lying will become physiologically aroused.

10. anxiety

11. innocent; emotions; arousal

12. do not agree

13. guilty knowledge test

Expressed Emotion

Section Preview

1. People differ in their abilities to detect nonverbal expressions of emotion; introverts and women are better at reading others' emotions, and extraverts are easier to read. Women are also more likely to express empathy when observing someone in distress.

2. Although there are many cultural variations in the meaning of gestures, facial expressions have universal meaning. Cultures differ in how and how much they use nonverbal expressions, however. In cultures that encourage individuality, emotional displays often are more intense and prolonged than in communal cultures that value interdependence.

   Research demonstrates that facial expressions intensify emotions and also trigger physiological changes in the autonomic nervous system. Imitating others' expressions also promotes empathy with others' feelings.

Stepping Through the Section

1. suppress; memory; nonverbal

2. threats; anger; eyes; mouth

3. better; easier

4. sensitize; anger

5. better; lies; literacy; simpler; gender roles; responsiveness

6. more; smaller; more

7. facial muscles

8. e-mail

9. different

10. the same; does not vary; are

11. Darwin; interpret; contexts

12. individuality; interdependence; sympathy; respect; shame; West

13. intensified

14. found

15. leads

Experienced Emotion

Section Preview

1. The catharsis hypothesis maintains that expressing emotion results in emotional release. Research shows that the cathartic expression of anger is most likely to reduce anger *temporarily* when it is specifically directed against the provoker, when it is justifiable, and when the provoker is not intimidating. Other studies show that openly expressing anger can have the opposite effect and amplify underlying hostility. Angry outbursts may also be habit-forming if they temporarily calm the individual.

   Anger experts recommend that the best way to handle anger is to first bring down the level of physiological arousal by waiting, then deal with the anger in a way that involves neither being chronically angry nor passively sulking.

2. People who are happy perceive the world as safer, make decisions more easily, rate job applicants more favorably, are more cooperative, live healthier and more energized and satisfied lives, and are more willing to help others. Factors that predict happiness include having high self-esteem, a close friendship or a satisfying marriage, or a meaningful religious faith; being optimistic and outgoing; sleeping well; exercising; and engaging in challenging work and leisure activities.

   The effect of dramatically positive or negative events on happiness is typically temporary. Happiness is also relative to our recent experiences (adaptation-level phenomenon) and to how we compare ourselves with others (relative deprivation principle). These principles help explain why middle- and upper-income people in a given country tend to be slightly more satisfied with life than the relatively poor, even though happiness does not directly increase with affluence.

Stepping Through the Section

1. 10; are
2. week
3. individuality; catharsis; interdependence; Tahiti; Japan
4. a. Retaliation must be directed against the person who provoked the anger.
   b. Retaliation must be justifiable.
   c. The target of the retaliation must not be someone who is intimidating.

One problem with expressing anger is that it breeds more anger, in part because it may trigger retaliation.

Expressing anger can also magnify anger and reinforce its occurrence.

5. a. Wait to calm down.
   b. Deal with anger in a civil way that promotes reconciliation rather than retaliation.
6. forgave
7. safer; more; feel-good, do-good; subjective well-being
8. rise; fall
9. overestimate; regain
10. do not; remained almost unchanged
11. intimacy, personal growth, and contribution to the community; wealth
12. adaptation-level

If we acquire new possessions, we feel an initial surge of pleasure. But we then adapt to having these new possessions, come to see them as normal, and require other things to give us another surge of happiness.

13. relative deprivation
14. high self-esteem; satisfying marriage or close friendships; meaningful religious faith; optimistic outgoing personality; good sleeping habits; regular exercise
15. age; gender; education; parenthood; physical attractiveness
16. 50
17. Realize that happiness doesn't come from financial success. Take control of your time. Act happy. Seek work and leisure that engage your skills. Engage in regular aerobic exercise. Get plenty of sleep. Give priority to close relationships. Focus beyond self. Be grateful. Nurture your spiritual self.

Stress and Health

Section Preview

1. Stress is the process by which we appraise and respond to events that threaten or challenge us. Stress triggers an outpouring of epinephrine and norepinephrine from nerve endings in the adrenal glands of the sympathetic nervous system. These stress hormones increase heart rate and respiration, divert blood from digestion to skeletal muscles, dull pain, and release sugar and fat from the body's stores to prepare the body for "fight or flight." Hans Selye saw the body's reaction to stress as having three phases (general adaptation syndrome): the alarm reaction, in which the body's resources are mobilized; resistance, in which stress hormones flow freely to help cope with the stressor; and exhaustion,

when reserves are depleted and illness is more likely.

2. Some studies have shown that stressful events, such as catastrophes, are closely followed by an increase in psychological disorders. The level of stress we experience depends on how we appraise such events. Catastrophes, significant life changes, and daily hassles are especially stressful when they are appraised as uncontrollable and negative and when we have a pessimistic outlook. Pessimism and a perceived loss of control, for example, trigger an outpouring of stress hormones. In such circumstances, vulnerability to disease may increase. Lack of control may help explain the fact that poor people are at increased risk for poor health and premature death. Regardless of their income, people also tend to die younger in areas where there is greater income inequality.

3. Friedman and Rosenman discovered that stress triggers a variety of physical changes, such as increased blood cholesterol and clotting speed, that may promote coronary heart disease. According to their designation, Type A people are competitive, hard-driving, impatient, time-conscious, verbally aggressive, and easily angered, and thus more prone to coronary disease. The most significant factor is the tendency toward the negative emotions of anger, pessimism, and depression. In contrast, Type B people are more relaxed and easygoing.

4. The immune system includes two types of white blood cells (lymphocytes) that defend the body by destroying foreign substances. The B lymphocytes form in the bone marrow and release antibodies that combat bacterial infections. The T lymphocytes form in the thymus and other lymphatic tissue and attack cancer cells, viruses, and foreign substances. Another immune agent, the macrophage, identifies and ingests harmful invaders.

Stress lowers the body's resistance to disease by suppressing the disease-fighting lymphocytes of the immune system. This may explain the link between stress and AIDS and between stress and cancer. Stress and negative emotions are positively correlated with the progression from HIV infection to AIDS and a more rapid decline in the health of those who are already infected. Animal research has shown that when the immune system is weakened by stress, tumor cells develop sooner and grow larger. Research has also shown that immune suppression can be classically con-

ditioned. Conversely, studies of cancer patients demonstrate that reducing stress and creating a hopeful, relaxed state may improve chances of survival.

Stepping Through the Section

1. 4; stimulus; response; process; both positive and negative

2. Cannon; epinephrine (adrenaline); norepinephrine (noradrenaline); sympathetic; fight or flight; tend and befriend; seek and give support

3. general adaptation syndrome

4. alarm; sympathetic

5. resistance

6. exhaustion; more

7. behavioral medicine; health

8. psychological disorders

9. more

10. daily hassles; racism; hypertension

11. uncontrollable; death

12. inequality; United States; Britain; two to four years; Japan; Sweden

13. income; inequality

14. optimistic

15. stress hormones

16. coronary heart disease; smoking, obesity, high-fat diet, physical inactivity, elevated blood pressure and cholesterol levels

17. cholesterol; clotting; stress

Type A people were competitive, hard-driving, supermotivated, impatient, time-conscious, verbally aggressive, and easily angered. Type B people were more relaxed and easygoing. Heart attack victims over the course of the study came overwhelmingly from the Type A group.

18. Type A; cholesterol

19. negative emotions; the anger associated with an aggressively reactive temperament

20. depression; increases

21. psychophysiological; hypertension; headaches; stress

22. immune; lymphocytes; B lymphocytes; T lymphocytes; thymus; macrophage

23. arthritis; allergic; underreact; cancer

24. Women; infections; self-attacking; lupus; multiple sclerosis

25. decrease; immune system; brain; muscles

26. AIDS; human immunodeficiency virus (HIV); blood; semen; have

Stress can affect the spread of cancer by weakening the body's defenses against malignant cells. When rodents were inoculated with tumor cells, tumors developed sooner in those that were also exposed to uncontrollable stress. Stress does not cause cancer, however, nor can relaxation prevent it.

27. can

Promoting Health

Section Preview

1. Stress management includes aerobic exercise, biofeedback, relaxation, social support, and spirituality. Aerobic exercise can reduce stress, depression, and anxiety. Research has also shown that those who exercise regularly tend to live longer and suffer from fewer illnesses than those who don't. Exercise may produce its benefits by increasing the production of mood-boosting neurotransmitters, by strengthening the heart, by lowering both blood pressure and the blood pressure reaction to stress, and by modestly enhancing cognition.

   Biofeedback systems allow people to monitor their subtle physiological responses and enjoy a calm, tranquil experience. Simple relaxation produces the same effects, however, including lowered blood pressure and strengthened immune defenses.

2. People with strong social support systems eat better, exercise more, smoke and drink less, receive medical treatment more quickly, and have more opportunities to confide painful feelings. Research shows that such people report fewer illnesses and are less likely to die prematurely than people who lack close supportive relationships. Until fairly recently in history, the healing traditions of religion and medicine worked together. As medicine matured, however, the two traditions separated. There is mounting evidence, however, of a "faith factor" in health and healing. The correlation between religious involvement and health may be due to the fact that religiously active people tend to have healthier life-styles, have stronger networks of social support, and be married.

3. The growing popularity of acupuncture, massage therapy, homeopathy, spiritual healing, and other forms of complementary and alternative medicine in the United States indicates that many people believe such therapies are effective. However, critics point out that alternative medicine seems most effective with cyclical diseases that improve anyway and with conditions that naturally disappear (spontaneous remission). They also suggest that much of the apparent effectiveness of such treatments is due to a placebo effect. Unfortunately, controlled research studies simply haven't been conducted for many alternative therapies.

Stepping Through the Section

1. aerobic; have
2. norepinephrine; serotonin; endorphins; two
3. biofeedback; do not provide
4. meditation (relaxation); relaxation; parietal; frontal
5. reduced
6. social; good marriage; low cholesterol; suppression; disclosing

People with strong social ties may be healthier because they eat better, exercise more, smoke and drink less, and are helped to receive medical treatment quicker. Close relationships also provide the opportunity to bolster self-esteem and to confide painful feelings, which may mitigate physical reactions to stressful events.

7. religion; medicine; together
8. believe
9. predicts

Religiously active people have healthier life-styles. They also tend to have stronger networks of social support and are more likely to be married.

10. complementary and alternative medicine; herbal; Qi or Chi
11. cyclical; allergic reactions; spontaneous remission; placebo

Progress Test 1

Multiple-Choice Questions

1. **d.** is the answer. Generally speaking, performance is optimal when arousal is moderate; for easy tasks, however, performance is optimal when arousal is high. For difficult tasks, performance is optimal when arousal is low. (p. 384)

2. **c.** is the answer. (p. 384)
   a. The somatic division of the peripheral nervous system carries sensory and motor signals to and from the central nervous system.
   b. The peripheral nervous system is too general an answer, since it includes the sympathetic and

parasympathetic divisions, as well as the somatic division.

d. The parasympathetic nervous system restores the body to its unaroused state.

e. The central nervous system is involved in the labeling of emotional arousal.

3. **c.** is the answer. Although many emotions have the same general body arousal, resulting from activation of the sympathetic nervous system, they appear to be associated with different brain circuits. (p. 385)

4. **b.** is the answer. (p. 380)
   a. This expresses the two-factor theory.
   c. This expresses the James-Lange theory.
   d. This theory was not discussed.

5. **a.** is the answer. (p. 385)
   b. The hypothalamus is involved in eating, thirst, and sexual motivation.
   c. The cortex is the center of higher cognitive functions, such as memory and thinking.
   d. The cerebellum is involved in motor coordination.

6. **b.** is the answer. (p. 384)
   a. & c. Acetylcholine, a neurotransmitter involved in motor responses, is not a hormone and therefore is not secreted by a gland.

7. **d.** is the answer. The finding that people whose brains can't sense the body's responses experience considerably less emotion in fact supports the James-Lange theory, which claims that experienced emotion follows from body responses. (p. 380)
   a., b., & c. All these statements go counter to the theory's claim that experienced emotion is essentially just an awareness of the body's response.

8. **c.** is the answer. (p. 386)

9. **c.** is the answer. The men who received epinephrine without an explanation felt arousal and experienced this arousal as whatever emotion the experimental confederate in the room with them was displaying. (p. 382)
   a. Epinephrine recipients who expected arousal attributed their arousal to the drug and reported no emotional change in reaction to the confederate's behavior.
   b. & d. In addition to the two groups discussed in the text, the experiment involved placebo recipients; these subjects were not physically aroused and did not experience an emotional change.

10. **e.** is the answer. Education level, parenthood, gender, and physical attractiveness seem unrelated to happiness. (p. 400)

11. **c.** is the answer. (p. 395)

a. This would not be an example of catharsis, since catharsis involves releasing, rather than suppressing, aggressive energy.
b. Expressions of anger in such a situation tend to cause the person anxiety and thus tend not to be effective.
d. One danger of expressing anger is that it will lead to retaliation and an escalation of anger.

12. **d.** is the answer. These are the three components of emotions identified in the text. (p. 379)

13. **c.** is the answer. If the suspect becomes physically aroused while answering questions about details only the perpetrator of the crime could know, it is presumed that he or she committed the crime. (p. 386)

14. **b.** is the answer. (p. 390)
   a. The opposite is true; relevant facial muscles are hard to control voluntarily.
   c. Authentic facial expressions tend to fade within 4 or 5 seconds.
   d. Facial expressions are generally universal; many gestures vary from culture to culture.

15. **d.** is the answer. (p. 398)

16. **b.** is the answer. (p. 396)
   a., c., & d. Research studies have not found these factors to be related to altruistic behavior.

17. **d.** is the answer. (p. 391)

18. **d.** is the answer. (p. 396)

19. **c.** is the answer. (p. 382)
   a. & b. These answers imply that cognition *always* precedes emotion.
   d. That changes in facial expression can directly affect people's feelings and body states does not imply a learned ability to interpret facial expressions. In fact, facial expressions apparently speak a universal language, which implies that the ability to interpret them is inborn.

20. **c.** is the answer. (p. 404)
   a. Health psychology is a subfield within behavioral medicine.
   b. Holistic medicine is an older term that refers to medical practitioners who take more of an interdisciplinary approach to treating disorders.
   d. Osteopathy is a medical therapy that emphasizes manipulative techniques for correcting physical problems.

21. **c.** is the answer. (p. 403)
   a., b., & d. The pituitary does not produce stress hormones nor is the parasympathetic division involved in arousal.

22. **c.** is the answer. (p. 403)

a. & b. During these stages the body's defensive mechanisms are at peak function.
d. This is not a stage of the GAS.

23. **c.** is the answer. Coronary heart disease is followed by cancer, stroke, and chronic lung disease. AIDS has not yet become one of the four leading causes of death in North America among the general population. (p. 408)

24. **c.** is the answer. (p. 408)
a. & b. Researchers have not identified such personality types.
d. Individuals who are more easygoing are labeled Type B.

25. **b.** is the answer. Stress hormones accelerate the buildup of cholesterol deposits around the heart. This likely occurs because during arousal, blood is diverted from internal organs such as the liver, which removes cholesterol from the blood, to the muscles of the body. These hormones are released in response to stress; they do not reduce stress. (p. 408)

26. **a.** is the answer. (p. 409)
b. Hypochondriacs think something is wrong with them, but nothing physical can be detected.
c. *Psychogenic* means "originating in the mind." One's reaction to stress is partially psychological, but this term is not used to refer to stress-related illness.
d. There is no such term in psychology.

27. **e.** is the answer. Because stress depresses the immune system, stressed individuals are prone to all of these conditions. (pp. 410–411)

28. **c.** is the answer. (p. 402)
a., b., & d. Whether an event is stressful or not depends on how it is appraised.

29. **c.** is the answer. The finding that talking about grief leads to better health makes a lot of sense in light of this physiological finding. (p. 418)
a., b., & d. The study by Pennebaker did not find these to be true.

30. **d.** is the answer. Regular aerobic exercise has been shown to increase ability to cope with stress, lower blood pressure, and reduce depression and anxiety. The text does not cite evidence that exercise enhances immune function. (pp. 414–415)

31. **d.** is the answer. (pp. 404–405)

32. **b.** is the answer. (p. 412)

33. **b.** is the answer. (p. 418)

34. **c.** is the answer. (pp. 410–411)

35. **d.** is the answer. (pp. 422–423)
b. & c. The text does not indicate that a gender difference exists in the "faith factor" in health.

Matching Items

1. a (p. 399)	**5.** b (p. 381)	**9.** f (p. 386)
2. k (p. 396)	**6.** g (p. 380)	**10.** j (p. 396)
3. c (p. 394)	**7.** h (p. 384)	**11.** e (p. 380)
4. i (p. 400)	**8.** d (p. 384)	

Progress Test 2

Multiple-Choice Questions

1. **a.** is the answer. Emotional arousal activates the sympathetic nervous system, causing the release of sugar into the blood for energy, pupil dilation, and the diverting of blood from the internal organs to the muscles, all of which help prepare the body to meet an emergency. (p. 384)
b. Being autonomic responses, most emotions are *involuntary* reactions.
c. All emotions do *not* have the same physiological basis.
d. Some emotions occur without cognitive awareness.

2. **c.** is the answer. According to Schachter, the two factors in emotion are (1) physical arousal and (2) conscious interpretation of the arousal. (p. 381)

3. **a.** is the answer. The principle of relative deprivation states that happiness is relative to others' attainments. This helps explain why those who are relatively well off tend to be slightly more satisfied than the relatively poor, with whom the better-off can compare themselves. (p. 400)
b. Adaptation level is the tendency for our judgments to be relative to our prior experience.
c. This phenomenon has nothing to do with the interpretation of emotion.
d. Opponent processes are not discussed in the text.

4. **b.** is the answer. (p. 380)
a. The James-Lange theory states that the experience of an emotion is an awareness of one's physical response to an emotion-arousing stimulus.
c. The two-factor theory states that to experience emotion one must be physically aroused and attribute the arousal to an emotional cause.
d. There is no such theory.

5. **d.** is the answer. (p. 393)

6. **d.** is the answer. No device can literally measure lying. The polygraph measures breathing, pulse rate, blood pressure, and perspiration for changes indicative of physiological arousal. (p. 386)

7. **b.** is the answer. (p. 385)

8. **b.** is the answer. Whereas the meanings of gestures vary from culture to culture, facial expressions seem to have the same meanings around the world. (p. 390)

9. **a.** is the answer. If, as the theory claims, emotions are triggered by physiological reactions, then each emotion must be associated with a unique physiological reaction. (p. 380)
   b. According to the Cannon-Bard theory, the same general body response accompanies many emotions.
   c. The two-factor theory states that the cognitive interpretation of a general state of physical arousal determines different emotions.
   d. Catharsis is the release of emotions.

10. **d.** is the answer. As the Schachter-Singer study indicated, physical arousal is not always accompanied by an emotional reaction. Only when arousal was attributed to an emotion was it experienced as such. The results of this experiment, therefore, support the viewpoint that conscious interpretation of arousal must precede emotion. (p. 382)
    a., b., & c. Each of these was presented as a supporting argument in the text.

11. **a.** is the answer. (p. 394)
    b. The opposite is true. Any emotional arousal will simmer down if you wait long enough.
    c. Catharsis often magnifies anger, escalates arguments, and leads to retaliation.
    d. When counterattack is justified and can be directed at the offender, catharsis may be helpful.

12. **e.** is the answer. (p. 384)

13. **c.** is the answer. Easy or well-rehearsed tasks, such as sprinting, are best performed when arousal is high; more difficult tasks are best performed when arousal is lower. (p. 384)

14. **a.** is the answer. That physical arousal can be misattributed demonstrates that it is the cognitive interpretation of arousal, rather than the intensity or specific nature of the body's arousal, that determines the conscious experience of emotions. (p. 382)
    b. & c. The findings of these studies do not indicate that a minimum level of arousal is necessary for an emotional experience nor that applying a cognitive label must be simultaneous with the arousal.

15. **c.** is the answer. As heightened arousal may reflect feelings of anxiety or irritation rather than of guilt, the polygraph, which simply measures arousal, may easily err. (p. 386)

a. Misuse and invasion of privacy are valid issues, but Lykken primarily objects to the use of lie detectors because of their inaccuracy.
b. Although there are discrepancies among the various measures of arousal, this was not what Lykken objected to.
d. The lie detector errs about one-third of the time.

16. **c.** is the answer. (p. 394)

17. **d.** is the answer. (p. 400)

18. **c.** is the answer. (p. 391)
    a. & b. These are true of cultures that emphasize individuality rather than interdependence.

19. **d.** is the answer. (p. 404)

20. **a.** is the answer. (p. 403)

21. **c.** is the answer. (pp. 410–411)

22. **c.** is the answer. (p. 403)
    a. The final stage of the general adaptation syndrome is exhaustion.
    b. & d. Although both of these are true, neither has anything to do with "tend and befriend."

23. **b.** is the answer. The greater reactivity of Type A people includes much higher levels of stress hormones in stress situations. (p. 408)
    a. Under relaxed situations, there is no difference in blood pressure.
    c. Anger, both expressed and suppressed, is more characteristic of Type A people.
    d. Type A persons tend to be combat ready.

24. **c.** is the answer. B lymphocytes fight bacterial infections; T lymphocytes attack cancer cells, viruses, and foreign substances. (p. 409)
    d. Antigens cause the production of antibodies when they are introduced into the body.

25. **a.** is the answer. A variety of studies have shown that stress depresses the immune system, increasing the risk and potential severity of many diseases. (p. 410)

26. **e.** is the answer. (p. 410)

27. **b.** is the answer. Both human and animal studies indicate that uncontrollable negative events trigger an outpouring of stress hormones and a drop in immune responses. (pp. 405–406)

28. **a.** is the answer. (p. 410)
    b. An *under*reactive immune system would make an individual more susceptible to infectious diseases or the proliferation of cancer cells.
    c. & d. Lymphocytes are disease- and infection-fighting white blood cells in the immune system.

29. **d.** is the answer. (p. 411)

30. e. is the answer. The crucial characteristic of Type A behavior seems to be a tendency to react with negative emotions, especially anger; other aspects of Type A behavior appear not to predict heart disease, and some appear to be helpful to the individual. (p. 408)

31. d. is the answer. In biofeedback training, people are given sensory feedback about autonomic responses. Although biofeedback may promote relaxation, its benefits may be no greater than those produced by simpler, and less expensive, methods. (pp. 415–416)

32. d. is the answer. As a group, religiously active people are no more affluent than other people. (pp. 422–423)

33. b. is the answer. (p. 420)
a. There is no such subfield of medicine.
c. Chi is an alleged form of energy, imbalances of which Chinese herbal therapies and acupuncture are intended to treat.
d. The term psychosomatic was once used to describe psychologically caused symptoms. Many forms of alternative medicine, including acupuncture, are intended to treat a full range of symptoms and diseases.

True–False Items

1. T (p. 384)		**10.** F (p. 381)	
2. F (p. 388)		**11.** F (p. 410)	
3. T (p. 384)		**12.** F (p. 405)	
4. T (p. 384)		**13.** T (p. 407)	
5. T (pp. 392–393)		**14.** T (p. 408)	
6. F (p. 380)		**15.** F (p. 409)	
7. F (p. 398)		**16.** T (p. 417)	
8. T (p. 382)		**17.** T (p. 406)	
9. F (p. 382)			

Review and Reflect

Multiple-Choice Questions

1. b. is the answer. The James-Lange theory proposes that the experienced emotion is an awareness of a prior body response: Your pulse races, and so you feel nervous. (p. 380)
a. According to the Cannon-Bard theory, your body's reaction would occur simultaneously with, rather than before, your experience of the emotion.
c. Relative deprivation refers to our sense that we are worse off than others with whom we compare ourselves.
d. The adaptation-level phenomenon concerns our tendency to judge stimuli on the basis of recent experience.

2. b. is the answer. Professor Simon's judgment of his office is affected by his recent experience: When that experience was of a smaller office, his new office seemed terrific; now, however, it is commonplace. (p. 399)
a. Relative deprivation is the sense that one is worse off than those with whom one compares oneself.
c. Catharsis refers to emotional release.
d. This is the principle that there is an inverse relationship between the difficulty of a task and the optimum level of arousal.

3. b. is the answer. The parasympathetic division is involved in calming arousal. (p. 384)
a. The sympathetic division is active during states of arousal and hence would not be active in the situation described.
c. The somatic division is involved in transmitting sensory information and controlling skeletal muscles; it is not involved in arousing and calming the body.
d. This answer is too general, since the peripheral nervous system includes not only the parasympathetic division but also the sympathetic division and the somatic division.

4. a. is the answer. According to the James-Lange theory, Maria's emotions should be greatly diminished since her brain is unable to sense physical arousal. (p. 380)
b. Cannon and Bard would have expected Maria to experience emotions normally because they believed that the experiencing of emotions occurs separately from the body's responses.
c. & d. These theories and principles make no particular prediction regarding the importance of physical arousal in the conscious experience of emotion.

5. b. is the answer. Expressions may amplify the associated emotions. (p. 392)
a. Laboratory studies have shown that facial expressions *intensify* emotions.
c. Arousal of the sympathetic nervous system, such as occurs when one is afraid, slows digestive function.
d. Increased body temperature accompanies anger but not fear.

6. d. is the answer. In keeping with the catharsis hypothesis, Jane feels less angry after releasing her aggression. (p. 394)

a. Adaptation level is our tendency to judge things relative to our experiences.

b. This is not a specific theory.

c. Relative deprivation is the sense that one is worse off relative to those with whom one compares oneself.

7. **c.** is the answer. According to the two-factor theory, it is cognitive interpretation of the same general physiological arousal that distinguishes the two emotions. (p. 381)

a. According to the James-Lange theory, if the same physical arousal occurred in the two instances, the same emotions should result.

b. The Cannon-Bard theory argues that conscious awareness of an emotion and body reaction occur at the same time.

d. Adaptation level concerns our tendency to judge things relative to our experiences.

8. **e.** is the answer. (p. 386)

9. **d.** is the answer. (p. 385)

10. **c.** is the answer. Because physical arousal tends to intensify emotions, Dan (who is likely to be physically aroused after playing tennis) will probably be angrier than Bob or Veronica, who are in more relaxed states. (p. 382)

11. **d.** is the answer. (p. 390–391)

a. & c. The Cannon-Bard and two-factor theories of emotion do not address the universality of emotional expressions.

b. Even if it is true that emotional expressions are acquired at an early age, this would not necessarily account for the common facial expressions of children from around the world. If anything, the different cultural experiences of the children might lead them to express their feelings in very *different* ways.

12. **d.** is the answer. In Asian and other cultures that emphasize human connections and interdependence, negative emotional displays are rare and typically brief. (p. 391)

a., b., & c. In cultures that encourage individuality, as in Western Europe, Australia, and North America, emotional displays often are intense and prolonged.

13. **c.** is the answer. (p. 385)

a. Individuals with more active right frontal lobes tend to be less cheerful and are more likely to be depressed.

b. In fact, just the opposite is true: People with greater left frontal activity tend to be better able to turn off upsetting feelings.

d. The text does not suggest that greater left or right frontal activity influences a person's ability to express his or her feelings.

14. **a.** is the answer. As people experience negative emotions, such as anger, the right hemisphere becomes more electrically active. (p. 385)

c. & d. The EEG measures electrical activity on the surface of the cortex, not at the level of structures deep within the brain, such as the amygdala.

15. **c.** is the answer. (p. 385)

a., b., & d. Direct stimulation of these brain areas will not trigger fear or rage.

16. **c.** is the answer. People who are in a good mood are more likely to help others. Bonnie, who is probably pleased with herself following her graduation from college, is likely to be in a better mood than Drew, Leon, or Nancy. (p. 395)

17. **d.** is the answer. (p. 394)

a. Venting anger immediately may lead you to say things you later regret and/or may lead to retaliation by the other person.

b. Going over the reasons for your anger merely prolongs the emotion.

c. Counting to 10 may give you a chance to calm down, but "blowing off steam" may rekindle your anger.

18. **d.** is the answer. Cindy is unhappy with her promotion because she feels deprived relative to Janice. (p. 400)

a. The adaptation-level phenomenon would predict that Cindy's raise would cause an increase in her happiness, since her most recent experience was to earn a lower salary.

b. Subjective well-being is not measured in relation to any other person.

c. The catharsis hypothesis maintains that venting one's anger may relieve aggressive urges.

19. **c.** is the answer. (p. 389)

20. **d.** is the answer. (pp. 422–423)

21. **c.** is the answer. According to Selye's general adaptation syndrome, diseases are most likely to occur in this final stage. (p. 403)

a. & b. Resistance to disease is greater during the alarm and resistance phases because the body's mobilized resources are not yet depleted.

d. There is no such thing as the "depletion phase." Moreover, the post-traumatic stress syndrome refers to the haunting nightmares and anxiety of those who have suffered extreme stress, such as that associated with combat.

22. **b.** is the answer. (p. 402)

a., c., & d. Each of these is a factor in coping with stress, but it is how an event is *perceived* that determines whether it is stressful or not.

23. **b.** is the answer. Unpredictable events are more stressful than predictable events. (p. 404)

24. **b.** is the answer. (p. 408)

    a. Type A persons are hard-driving and competitive.

    c. There is no such thing as a "Type C" person.

    d. Type D people, who are not discussed in the text, tend to have negative emotions.

25. **c.** is the answer. (p. 409)

    a. Macrophages are immune agents that search for and ingest harmful invaders.

    b. B lymphocytes form in the bone marrow and release antibodies that fight bacterial infections.

26. **b.** is the answer. Stressful situations, such as exam weeks, decrease immune responses. (p. 410)

27. **c.** is the answer. (pp. 405–407)

    a. This is not realistic.

    b. & d. These might actually *increase* the health consequences of potential stressors.

28. **c.** is the answer. (p. 409)

    a. The text does not discuss any such thing as a "psychogenic" illness.

    b. Hypochondriasis is the misinterpreting of normal physical sensations as symptoms of a disease.

    d. Biofeedback is a system for recording information regarding a subtle physiological state, such as blood pressure.

29. **d.** is the answer. (pp. 405–407)

30. **a.** is the answer. (p. 420)

    b. In fact, botanical herbs have given us many widely used drugs, including morphine and penicillin, each of which was proven to be useful in controlled research studies.

    c. Herbal remedies and acupuncture—to name two forms of complementary and alternative medicine—have a long tradition in other parts of the world, and remain enormously popular today.

Essay Questions

1. All emotions involve some degree of physiological arousal of the sympathetic nervous system. Although the arousal that occurs with different emotions is in most ways undifferentiated, there may be subtle differences in the brain pathways and hormones associated with different emotions. Another example of the influence of biological factors on emotion is the universality of facial expressions of emotion.

   Unlike facial expressions of emotion, the meaning of many gestures is culturally determined. Culture also influences how people express their feelings. In cultures that encourage individuality, for example, emotional displays often are intense and prolonged. In cultures that emphasize human interdependence, negative emotions that might disrupt group harmony are rarely expressed, while displays of "other-sensitive" emotions such as sympathy, respect, and shame are more common than in the West.

2. When potentially stressful events occur, a person's appraisal is a major determinant of their impact. Catastrophes, significant life events, and daily hassles are especially stressful when appraised as negative, unpredictable, and uncontrollable, and when the person has a pessimistic outlook on life. Under these circumstances, stressful events may suppress immune responses and make the person more vulnerable to disease. If stressors cannot be eliminated, aerobic exercise, biofeedback, relaxation, and social support can help the person cope. Aerobic exercise can reduce stress, depression, and anxiety, perhaps by increasing production of mood-boosting neurotransmitters. During biofeedback training, people enjoy a calm, relaxing experience that can be helpful in reducing stress. Research demonstrates that people who regularly practice relaxation techniques enjoy a greater sense of tranquility and have lower blood pressure and stronger immune responses. People with strong social ties eat better, exercise more, and smoke and drink less. Social support may also help people evaluate and overcome stressful events. In addition, confiding painful feelings to others has been demonstrated to reduce the physiological responses linked to stress.

Key Terms

1. **Emotion** is a response of the whole organism, involving three components: (1) physical arousal, (2) expressive behaviors, and (3) conscious experience. (p. 379)

2. The **James-Lange theory** states that emotional experiences are based on an awareness of the body's responses to emotion-arousing stimuli: a stimulus triggers the body's responses that in turn trigger the experienced emotion. (p. 380)

3. The **Cannon-Bard theory** states that the conscious, subjective experience of an emotion occurs at the same time as the body's physical reaction. (p. 380)

4. The **two-factor theory** of emotion proposes that emotions have two ingredients: physical arousal and a cognitive label. Thus, physical arousal is a

necessary, but not a sufficient, component of emotional change. For an emotion to be experienced, arousal must be attributed to an emotional cause. (p. 381)

5. The **polygraph**, or lie detector, is a device that measures several of the physiological responses accompanying emotion. (p. 386)

6. **Catharsis** is emotional release; according to the catharsis hypothesis, by expressing our anger, we can reduce it. (p. 394)

7. The **feel-good, do-good phenomenon** is the tendency of people to be helpful when they are in a good mood. (p. 396)

8. **Subjective well-being** refers to a person's sense of satisfaction with his or her life. (p. 396)

9. The **adaptation-level phenomenon** refers to our tendency to judge things relative to our prior experience. (p. 399)

10. The principle of **relative deprivation** is the sense that we are worse off relative to those with whom we compare ourselves. (p. 400)

11. **Stress** refers to the process by which people perceive and react to stressors or to events they perceive as threatening or challenging. (p. 402)

12. The **general adaptation syndrome (GAS)** is the three-stage sequence of bodily reaction to stress outlined by Hans Selye. (p. 403)

13. **Health psychology** is a subfield of psychology that studies how health and illness are influenced by emotions, stress, personality, life-style, and other psychological factors. (p. 404)

14. The leading cause of death in the United States today, **coronary heart disease** results from the clogging of the coronary arteries and the subsequent reduction in blood and oxygen supply to the heart muscle. (p. 408)

15. **Type A** personality is Friedman and Rosenman's term for the coronary-prone behavior pattern of competitive, hard-driving, impatient, verbally aggressive, and anger-prone people. (p. 408)

16. **Type B** personality is Friedman and Rosenman's term for the coronary-resistant behavior pattern of easygoing people. (p. 408)

17. A **psychophysiological illness** is any genuine illness such as hypertension and headaches that is apparently linked to stress rather than caused by a physical disorder. (p. 409)

Memory aid: Psycho- refers to mind; physio- refers to body; a **psychophysiological illness** is a mind-body disorder.

18. **Lymphocytes** are the two types of white blood cells of the immune system that fight bacterial infections (B lymphocytes) and viruses, cancer cells, and foreign substances in the body (T lymphocytes). (p. 409)

19. **Aerobic exercise** is any sustained activity such as running, swimming, or cycling that promotes heart and lung fitness and may help alleviate depression and anxiety. (p. 414)

20. **Biofeedback** refers to a system for electronically recording, amplifying, and feeding back information regarding a subtle physiological state. (p. 415)

Memory aid: A **biofeedback** device, such as a brain-wave trainer, provides auditory or visual feedback about biological responses.

21. **Complementary and alternative medicine** is a collection of health care remedies and treatments that have not been accepted by medical science nor verified by controlled research trials. (p. 420)

Summing Up

Theories of Emotion

You see a man coming at you with a knife in his hand. This results in your heart pounding (*physiological arousal*), an attempt to get out of the way (*expressive behaviors*), and fear of being stabbed (*conscious experience*).

Different theories have been proposed to explain emotional experiences.

Perception of man with knife (stimulus): Theory 1: pounding heart (*physiological arousal*) leads to fear: the *emotion*. This is the *James-Lange* theory of emotion. Theory 2: pounding heart (*physiological arousal*) and simultaneous *subjective* awareness of emotion. This is the *Cannon-Bard* theory of emotion. Theory 3: pounding heart (*physiological arousal*) and simultaneous thought that "Man with knife scares me" (*conscious experience*) lead to the emotion of fear. This is the *two-factor* theory of emotion.

FOCUS ON VOCABULARY AND LANGUAGE

Page 379: No one needs to tell you that feelings add *color* to your life. . . . Without emotions we would experience a very dull and uninteresting existence; we would have no feelings of intense happiness or excitement nor would we experience depression and sadness. Thus, emotions add a variety of interesting qualities (*color*) to our lives.

Page 379: . . . In an instant, the *arousal of dread* spilled into the *elation of ecstasy*. When Dr. Myers finally located his lost child (*toddler*) in the store, his apprehension and fear (*the arousal of dread*) transformed into a heightened and intense feeling of happiness (*the elation of ecstasy*) and he was overcome with positive emotions (*awash in joy*). This story illustrates the various components of emotion—physiological arousal, expressive behavior, and conscious experience.

Theories of Emotion

Page 379: Common sense tells most of us that we cry because we are sad, *lash out* because we are angry, *tremble* because we are afraid. The James-Lange theory states that physiological arousal precedes the experience of emotion. Thus, we cry first, then feel sad; we strike someone (*lash out*), then experience the anger; we shiver and shake (*tremble*), then feel fear. The Cannon-Bard theory proposes that physiological arousal and the experience of emotion occur at the same time but separately. One does not cause the other.

Page 380: Virtually all the men Hohmann interviewed reported increases in *weeping, lumps in the throat*, and getting *choked up* when saying *good-bye, worshipping, or watching a touching movie*. For emotions expressed mostly in body areas above the neck, people with high spinal cord injuries reported more intense reactions, such as crying (*weeping*), becoming inarticulate (*lumps in the throat*), and being overcome emotionally (*choked up*) when parting company (*saying good-bye*), participating in religious ceremonies (*worshipping*), or viewing a sentimental film (*watching a touching movie*). On the other hand, emotional intensity for most other feelings decreased substantially, especially if they involved body areas below the neck. This provides partial support for the James-Lange theory, which proposes that physical reactions are important in the experience of emotions.

Page 381: Which is the chicken and which the egg? The old riddle asks, "Which came first, the chicken or the egg?" Myers asks which comes first, our cognitions or our emotions? The two-factor theory suggests that physiological arousal has to be cognitively interpreted in order for one to experience different emotions. Stanley Schachter's research showed that the same arousal (*stirred-up state*) can be experienced as two very different emotional states (e.g., euphoria or irritation) depending on how we interpret and label it. Thus, thinking comes before feeling.

Page 382: . . . *testy* . . . This means to be ill-tempered or irritable. Those subjects who were physiologically aroused but did not know why were affected by (*"caught"*) the apparent emotional state of the person they were with. They made different attributions about their aroused (*stirred-up*) state ("I'm happy" or "I'm feeling testy") on the basis of whether the accomplice acted in a euphoric or irritated way.

Page 382: This makes it easier for our feelings to *hijack* our thinking than for our thinking to *rule* our feelings . . . Some neural pathways go from the ear or eye via the thalamus to the amygdala, an emotional control center, and detour around (*bypass*) the cortical areas involved in thinking. This makes it possible to have extremely rapid (*greased-lightning*) emotional responses before cognitive factors become involved. Thus, our feelings can take over (*hijack*) our thinking, instead of our thinking controlling (*ruling*) our emotions.

Page 382: The *heart* is not always subject to the *mind*. Robert Zajonc proposed that some emotional states are not preceded by cognitions. The emotions (*heart*) are not determined by our thoughts (*mind*). We can have *some* feelings, at least, without thinking first.

Embodied Emotion

Page 383: . . . *your stomach develops butterflies* . . . When you are apprehensive, fearful, and nervous, you have visceral (internal) sensations that may feel as though small flying insects (*butterflies*) are fluttering around in your stomach (*it develops butterflies*).

Page 384: Basketball players *shooting free throws*—a less automatic skill—may not perform quite as well if a *packed fieldhouse* makes them *hyperaroused* (Sokoll & Mynatt, 1984). When a basketball player is allowed (without interference) to throw the ball through the hoop (*shooting free throws*), it requires a lot of concentration because it is not a usual part of the game. If the player gets anxious and is overaroused (*hyperaroused*) because of the attention of a large crowd (*packed fieldhouse*), he is more likely to make a mistake. A high level of arousal is beneficial for the performance of easy, routine tasks.

Page 385: If afraid, you may feel a *clutching, sinking sensation* in your chest and a *knot in your stomach.* Different emotions (anger, fear, sadness) feel different. Someone who is extremely afraid may have certain internal reactions such as tightness in the upper abdomen (*a clutching, sinking sensation*) and a feeling of a lump (*knot*) in the stomach.

Page 385: The left frontal lobe's rich supply of dopamine receptors may help explain why a *peppy left hemisphere* correlates with a *perky* disposition. For some people, the left frontal lobe has more lively electrical activity (*it is peppy*), compared to the right, and these particular individuals tend to have more cheerful and happier personalities (*perky dispositions*).

Page 386 (Box): Given the physical indicators of emotion, might we, like *Pinocchio,* give some *telltale sign* whenever we lie? Pinocchio is a fictional character in a children's story whose nose grows longer every time he tells a lie. The polygraph, or lie detector, does not detect lies; rather, it measures a number of physiological reactions (heart rate, blood pressure, and perspiration) (*telltale signs*) which indicate a change in emotional state. Unlike Pinocchio, people display no reliable or valid indicators of whether they are lying or telling the truth.

Page 386 (Box) . . . a white lie . . . When we tell a rather harmless or benign falsehood (*a white lie*), we are failing to reveal the truth about something relatively trivial. The polygraph can detect the physiological arousal that results from falsely answering control questions; this level of arousal is compared to reactions to the critical questions. Myers makes it clear that inferring guilt or innocence on the basis of these comparisons is fraught with problems. The innocent are more often labeled guilty than the guilty innocent; as Myers suggests, you should "never take a lie detector test if you are innocent."

Expressed Emotion

Page 387: Most of us are good enough at *reading* nonverbal cues to decipher the emotions in an old *silent film.* We communicate our feelings with words (verbally) and through body language (nonverbally). Without hearing a single word, as in a movie with no soundtrack (*silent film*), we can discern much about someone's emotional state by observing (*reading*) his or her bodily actions and facial expressions. As Myers notes, when we look at a large group of faces, a single angry one will be extremely noticeable (*it will "pop out"*) and will be detected more quickly than a single happy one.

Page 390: Fidgeting, for example, may reveal *anxiety* or *boredom.* Many popular books and articles suggest what to look for in body language during interviews, business meetings, and so on. However, specific interpretations of gestures or posture cannot be made accurately or reliably. For example, restlessness, accompanied by frequent small movements (*fidgeting*), may be indicative of either disinterest (*boredom*) or extreme nervousness (*anxiety*).

Page 390: Ditto for anger, and to a lesser extent the other basic expressions . . . There is a great deal of consistency across cultures in the interpretation of different emotional expressions. In tests, people the world over could reliably tell which face expressed happiness; this result was found over and over again (*ditto*), and similar results were found for other fundamental expressions (e.g., anger and fear).

Page 391: A *sneer,* for example, retains elements of an animal's baring its teeth in *a snarl.* Darwin believed that all humans have inherited the ability to express emotions through very similar facial expressions. Thus, a person's scornful or contemptuous grimace (*sneer*) has many aspects of the fierce growl with teeth showing (*a snarl*) typical of dogs and other animals. Emotional expressions are one form of social communication.

Page 392: Fake a big grin. Now scowl. Can you feel the *"smile therapy"* difference? Clearly, our moods affect how we look, but Myers is inviting you to test the idea that your facial expression can affect your mood. Make a large, false smile (*fake a grin*). Next, wrinkle or furrow your brow, frown, and look sullen (*scowl*). Subjects in numerous experiments felt different emotions under these conditions. Smile and inside you feel happy, scowl and you may see the world as more miserable than it is. Myers jokingly refers to the beneficial effects of "putting on a happy face" (*faking a big grin*) as "smile therapy."

Experienced Emotion

Page 394: Popular books and articles on aggression at times advise that even releasing angry feelings as *hostile outbursts* can be better than internalizing them. The idea is that expressing your anger openly (*hostile outbursts* or *"venting your anger"*) provides some form of emotional release (**catharsis**) and that this is better than not expressing your feelings and holding your anger inside (*internalizing it*). Under certain circumstances, this may provide temporary relief, but the evidence also suggests that expressing anger can increase or magnify (*breed more*) anger.

Page 395: . . . *"blowing off steam"* . . . This means to openly express your anger and rage. Myers notes that doing this can increase or amplify your hostile emotions, but it may also be reinforcing because it releases some of the frustration. Consequently, the next time these feelings arise, the more likely it is that the anger-driven behavior (*hostile outbursts*) will be repeated.

Page 397: Once their *rush of euphoria* wears off, state lottery winners typically find their overall happiness unchanged. . . . We probably all dream of winning large amounts of money through gambling (*state lottery winners*) and then living happily ever after. However, once the initial feelings of excitement (*rush of euphoria*) diminish, most winners discover that they are no happier. Myers puts it succinctly: "Wealth is like health. Its utter absence breeds misery, yet having it is no guarantee of happiness."

Page 398: Such findings *lob a bombshell* at modern materialism. . . . The contemporary tendency to accumulate wealth and possessions (*modern materialism*) in industrialized and affluent countries has not resulted in greater happiness. This finding challenges and destroys (*lobs a bombshell at*) the myth that riches (*affluence*) bring happiness and social well-being.

Stress and Health

Page 402: Afterward, she notices her *tense* muscles, *clenched teeth*, and *churning stomach*. Our response to stress can be beneficial (e.g., Karl's escape from the snake) or destructive (e.g., Karen's reaction to relatively minor routine problems or *daily hassles*). Following a number of stressful events (missing her train, rush-hour pedestrian traffic, late for an appointment, etc.), she becomes aware of her physiological reaction. Her muscles feel strained and taut (*tense*), her jaws are clamped shut (*clenched teeth*), and her stomach feels upset (*churning stomach*).

Page 402: Stress is a *slippery concept*. The term *stress* is often used to describe a stimulus (a threatening or challenging event) or a response (fear or anxiety). Most psychologists refer to the former as a *stressor*, the latter as a *stress reaction*, and use the word *stress* to refer to the entire process of evaluating and dealing with threatening events. Thus, stress is not a simple or easily grasped (understood) construct (*it is a slippery concept*).

Page 403: Your heart rate *zooms*. According to Selye's general adaptation syndrome (GAS), there are three phases in our response to stress: *alarm reaction, resistance,* and *exhaustion.* During the first phase, the sympathetic nervous system responds rapidly; your heart rate quickly increases (*zooms*), blood is directed to the muscles, and you experience the weakness associated with being startled. You are now ready to fight or cope with the stressor (*resistance phase*); if the situation is not resolved soon, you will experience *exhaustion* (the third phase).

Page 405: . . . *uprooting* . . . Refugees and others who are forcibly made to leave their homes (*they are uprooted*) have increased rates of depression, anxiety, psychological disorders, and other stress symptoms. In most instances, the health impairments come from long-term exposure to stress.

Page 405: Experiencing *a cluster of crises* puts one even more at risk. Important and significant changes in our lives are other types of life-event stressors that increase the probability of health problems. If a number of these events occur close together (*a cluster of crises*), people become more vulnerable to disease.

Page 405: Daily Hassles Small, routine, annoying events and the little things that go wrong day by day (*daily hassles*) can have an accumulative effect on health and well-being. Some people can handle these daily hassles (*they shrug them off*) while others are severely distressed (*"driven up the wall"*) by these inconveniences. Continual work-related hassles can lead to mental, physical, and emotional exhaustion.

Page 408: Moreover, not one of the *"pure"* Type Bs —the most *mellow* and *laid-back* of their group—had suffered a *heart attack*. Researchers have identified two personality types: Type As are reactive (*easily angered*), competitive, verbally aggressive, highly motivated, always rushed, and lacking in patience; Type Bs are less easily angered (*mellow*) and are easy-going (*laid-back*), patient, understanding, and noncompetitive. The most prototypical (*"pure"*) Type Bs were the least likely to be afflicted by coronary heart disease (*heart attacks*).

Page 408: But *after the honeymoon period,* in which the finding seemed definitive and revolutionary, other researchers began asking, Is the finding reliable? The discovery of the relationship between personality type (A or B) and health and well-being aroused much interest. However, once the initial excitement abated (*after the honeymoon period*), other investigators started more detailed research and asked questions about the specific mechanisms involved in personality type and risk of disease.

Page 408: Further research found that reactive Type A individuals are more often *"combat ready."* Research has shown that Type As are physiologically more reactive and ready to fight (*combat ready*) than

Type Bs. When stressed, their sympathetic nervous systems operate to increase the levels of cholesterol and fat in the blood; in addition, their negative (*toxic*) emotions, especially anger and depression, make them more coronary-prone.

Page 410: Your immune system is not *a headless horseman.* The immune system does not operate as an autonomous system independent of other systems (*a headless horseman*). Instead, it works in close harmony with various brain systems and with the endocrine system, which secretes hormones. All these interact and affect each other in a very complex way.

Page 411: One danger in *hyping* reports on attitudes and cancer is that some patients may be led to blame themselves for their illness . . . One problem with overstating (*hyping*) the relationship between attitudes and cancer is that some cancer victims may feel that they have somehow caused their sickness. The biological factors involved in the disease cannot easily be mitigated (*derailed*) by believing good health is due to a healthy character (the *wellness macho*). Nor is it appropriate to blame (*lay a guilt trip on*) those who develop the illness. As Myers notes, we should be aware of the fine distinction (*thin line*) that separates science from desperately hopeful beliefs (*wishful thinking*).

Promoting Health

Page 414: Many of them had, quite literally, *run away from their troubles.* Many research studies have shown the beneficial effect of aerobic exercise on depression and anxiety. In one study, women who took up jogging (*running*) showed a substantial reduction in depression. As Myers humorously puts it, they had, in reality, *run away from their problems.*

Page 415 (caption): The mood boost Regular exercise increases longevity and cardiovascular fitness, reduces anxiety and depression, and enhances positive emotional states (*boosts our moods*). So the popular trend toward being more physically active has many benefits.

Page 415: After a decade of study, however, researchers decided the initial claims for biofeedback were *overblown and oversold* (Miller, 1985). Biofeedback became very popular in the 1970s, and the reports of its effectiveness for all kinds of problems led to much excitement. By the mid-1980s, however, it became clear that these assertions were exaggerated (*overblown*) and falsely promoted (*oversold*). Simple relaxation without the use of costly equipment is just as beneficial.

Page 417: . . . heartaches . . . Heartaches is a term that refers to persistent mental anguish or suffering, usually resulting from the loss of a loved one or from disappointment in love. Myers points out that while close relationships and family tend to contribute to our well-being and contentment, they also can be the cause of much misery, strain, and strife (*heartaches*).

Page 418: The *cold fact* is that the effect of social ties is *nothing to sneeze at.* Myers is being humorous here. The expression "that is nothing to sneeze at" indicates that something (the object, event, accomplishment, etc.) is not minor or insignificant, and, of course, people with colds tend to sneeze a lot. In research on resistance to cold viruses, the finding that healthy volunteers who had the most social ties were less likely to catch a cold and produced less mucus (the *cold fact*) is not an insignificant result (*nothing to sneeze at*). In addition, research shows that social support calms the cardiovascular system, lowering blood pressure and stress hormones.

Page 418: Talking about our troubles can be *"open heart therapy."* Research has shown that those with close, supportive friends and family tend to have fewer health problems and live longer. One reason for this may be that trusting relationships provide the opportunity to talk about our problems and feelings and, just as "open heart surgery" can save lives, having someone to talk to can be a form of *"open heart therapy."*

chapter 12
Personality

Chapter Overview

Personality refers to each individual's characteristic pattern of thinking, feeling, and acting. Chapter 12 examines four perspectives on personality. Psychoanalytic theory emphasizes the unconscious and irrational aspects of personality. Trait theory led to advances in techniques for evaluating and describing personality. Humanistic theory draws attention to the concept of self and to human potential for healthy growth. The social-cognitive perspective emphasizes the effects of our interactions with the environment. The text first describes and then evaluates the contributions, shortcomings, and historical significance of the psychoanalytic and humanistic perspectives. Next, the text turns to contemporary research on personality, focusing on how the trait and social-cognitive perspectives explore and assess traits and the focus of many of today's researchers on the concept of self. A final section explores the status of the concept of the unconscious mind in psychology today.

NOTE: Answer guidelines for all Chapter 12 questions begin on page 363.

Introducing Personality (p. 429)

Introduction Preview

First, skim the introduction. Then read the following objective and, as you read the text, search for the information that will enable you to meet that objective. Answer guidelines are provided on page 363.

1. Define personality, and explain how its study differs from that of other psychological research interests.

Historic Perspectives on Personality
(pp. 429–442)

> David Myers at times uses idioms that are unfamiliar to some readers. If you do not know the meaning of any of the following words, phrases, or expressions in the context in which they appear in the text, refer to pages 374–375 for an explanation: *mind running; glimpse; virtuous . . . wantonly; utter biting sarcasm; twig of personality is bent; icebreaker; linguistic-flip-flops; seared; scientific shortcomings; bumbling; crippled spirits; thwarted . . . acorn, primed for growth; rugged individual.*

Section Preview

First, skim the section, noting headings and boldface items. Then read the following objectives and, as you read the text, search for the information that will enable you to meet each objective. Answer guidelines begin on page 364.

1. Describe how Freud's search for the psychological roots of nervous disorders led to his study of the unconscious, and explain psychoanalysis.

2. Describe Freud's views of personality structure.

3. Outline and describe Freud's psychosexual stages of personality development.

4. Explain Freud's view of maladaptive behavior, and describe how defense mechanisms operate.

5. Explain how projective tests are used to assess personality, and describe research findings regarding their validity and reliability.

6. Discuss the major ideas of the neo-Freudians and today's psychodynamic theorists.

7. Evaluate the psychoanalytic perspective.

8. Describe the humanistic perspective on personality, and discuss the basic ideas of Maslow and Rogers.

9. Evaluate the humanistic perspective.

Stepping Through the Section

After you have read the section, complete the sentences and answer the questions. As you proceed, evaluate your performance by consulting the answers beginning on page 365. Do not continue with the next section until you understand each answer. If you need to, review or reread the section in the textbook before continuing.

1. The psychoanalytic perspective on personality was proposed by _____ _____ . A second, historically significant perspective was the _____ approach, which focused on people's capacities for _____ and _____ .

2. At first, Freud thought _____ would unlock the door to the unconscious. The technique later used by Freud, in which the patient relaxes and says whatever comes to mind, is called _____ _____ .

3. Freud called his theory and associated techniques, whereby painful unconscious memories are exposed, _____ .

4. According to this theory, the mind is like an iceberg in that many of a person's thoughts, wishes, and feelings are hidden in a large _____ region. Some of the thoughts in this region can be retrieved at will into consciousness; these thoughts are said to be _____ . Many of the memories of this region, however, are blocked, or _____ , from consciousness.

5. Freud believed that a person's _____ wishes are often reflected in his or her dreams and _____ of the tongue or pen. Freud called the remembered content of dreams the _____ _____ , which he believed to be a censored version of the dream's true _____ _____ .

6. Freud believed that all facets of personality arise from conflict between our _____ impulses and the _____ restraints against them.

7. According to Freud, personality consists of three interacting structures: the _____ , the _____ , and the _____ .

8. The id is a reservoir of energy that is primarily _____ (conscious/unconscious) and operates according to the _____ principle.

9. The ego develops _____ (before/after) the id and consists of perceptions, thoughts, and memories that are mostly _____ (conscious/unconscious). The ego operates according to the _____ principle.

Explain why the ego is considered the "executive" of personality.

10. The personality structure that reflects moral values is the _____ , which Freud believed began emerging at about age _____ .

11. A person with a _____ (strong/weak) superego may be self-indulgent; one with an unusually _____ (strong/weak) superego may be continually guilt-ridden.

12. According to Freud, personality is formed as the child passes through a series of _____ stages.

13. The first stage is the _____ stage, which takes place during the first 18 months of life. During this stage, the id's energies are focused on behaviors such as _____ .

14. The second stage is the _____ stage, which lasts from about age _____ months to _____ months.

15. The third stage is the _____ stage, which lasts roughly from ages _____ to _____ . During this stage the id's energies are focused on the _____ . Freud also believed that during this stage children develop sexual desires for the_____ (same/opposite)-sex parent. Freud referred to these feelings as the _____ _____ in boys. Some psychoanalysts believe that girls experience a parallel _____ _____ .

16. Freud believed that _____ with the same-sex parent is the basis for _____ _____ .

Explain how this complex of feelings is resolved through the process of identification.

17. During the next stage, sexual feelings are repressed: this phase is called the _____ stage and lasts until adolescence.

18. The final stage of development is called the _____ stage.

19. According to Freud, it is possible for a person's development to become blocked in any of the stages; in such an instance, the person is said to be _____ .

20. The ego attempts to protect itself against anxiety through the use of _____ _____ . The process underlying

each of these mechanisms is

_____ .

21. Dealing with anxiety by returning to an earlier stage of development is called

_____ .

22. When a person reacts in a manner opposite that of his or her true feelings, _____ _____ is said to have occurred.

23. When a person attributes his or her own feelings to another person, _____ has occurred.

24. When a person offers a false, self-justifying explanation for his or her actions, _____ has occurred.

25. When impulses are directed toward an object other than the one that caused arousal, _____ has occurred.

Matching Items

Match each defense mechanism in the following list with the proper example of its manifestation.

Defense Mechanisms

_____ 1. displacement
_____ 2. projection
_____ 3. reaction formation
_____ 4. rationalization
_____ 5. regression

Manifestations

a. nail biting or thumb sucking in an anxiety-producing situation
b. overzealous crusaders against "immoral behaviors" who don't want to acknowledge their own sexual desires
c. saying you drink "just to be sociable" when in reality you have a drinking problem
d. thinking someone hates you when in reality you hate that person
e. a child who is angry at his parents and vents this anger on the family pet, a less threatening target

26. Defense mechanisms are _____ (conscious/unconscious) processes.

27. Tests that provide subjects with ambiguous stimuli for interpretation are called _____ tests.

28. The most widely used projective test is the _____ , in which subjects are shown a series of _____ . Generally, these tests appear to have _____ (little/significant) validity and reliability.

29. The theorists who established their own, modified versions of psychoanalytic theory are called _____-_____ .

These theorists typically place _____ (more/less) emphasis on the conscious mind than Freud did and _____ (more/less) emphasis on sex and aggression.

Briefly summarize how each of the following theorists departed from Freud.

a. Adler _____

_____

b. Horney _____

_____

_____

c. Jung _____

_____

30. Today's psychologists _____ (accept/reject) the idea that people inherit a common reservoir of experiences, which _____ (which theorist?) called a _____ _____ .

31. More recently, some of Freud's ideas have been incorporated into _____ theory. Unlike Freud, the theorists advocating this perspective do not believe that _____ is the basis of personality. They do agree, however, that much of mental life is _____ , that _____ shapes personality, and that we often struggle with _____ _____ .

32. Contrary to Freud's theory, research indicates that human development is _____ (fixed in childhood/lifelong), children gain their gender identity at a(n) _____ (earlier/later) age, and the presence of a same-sex parent _____ (is/is not) necessary for the child to become strongly masculine or feminine.

33. Research also disputes Freud's belief that dreams disguise _____ and that defense mechanisms disguise _____ and _____ impulses. Another Freudian idea that is no longer widely accepted is that psychological disorders are caused by _____ _____ .

34. Psychoanalytic theory rests on the assumption that the human mind often _____ painful experiences. Many of today's researchers think that this process is much _____ (more common/rarer) than Freud believed. They also believe that when it does occur, it is a reaction to terrible _____ .

35. Criticism of psychoanalysis as a scientific theory centers on the fact that it provides _____-_____-_____ explanations and does not offer _____ _____ .

State several of Freud's ideas that have endured.

36. Two influential theories of humanistic psychology were proposed by _____ and _____ .

37. According to Maslow, humans are motivated by needs that are organized into a _____ . Maslow refers to the

process of fulfilling one's potential as

_____ .

List some of the characteristics Maslow associated with those who fulfilled their potential.

38. According to Rogers, a person nurtures growth in a relationship by being _____ , _____ , and _____ .
People who are accepting of others offer them

_____ _____

_____ .

39. For both Maslow and Rogers, an important feature of personality is how an individual perceives himself or herself; this is the person's _____ . Humanistic psychologists have influenced such diverse areas as

_____ , _____ ,

_____ , and _____ .
They have also had a major impact on today's _____ psychology, perhaps because the emphasis on the individual self strongly reflects _____ cultural values.

State three criticisms of humanistic psychology.

Contemporary Research on Personality
(pp. 442–464)

If you do not know the meaning of any of the following words, phrases, or expressions in the context in which they appear in the text, refer to pages 375–377 for an explanation: *Flabbergasted; spoofing; scoff; suckering methods; "stock spiel"; dubbed the Big Five; blind date; labeling and pigeonholing; cold shoulder; leaping a hurdle; put an optimistic spin on their setbacks; bombing the upcoming exam; dumbfounded; negative about themselves; prowess; Lake Wobegon; pride does often go before a fall; swelled head; put-downs; lose face.*

Section Preview

Answer guidelines begin on page 366.

1. Discuss trait theories of personality, and describe how they identify traits.

2. Describe the assessment techniques associated with the trait perspective.

3. Identify the Big Five personality factors, and discuss recent research findings regarding them.

4. Evaluate the trait perspective on personality, and describe research findings regarding the consistency of behavior over time and across situations.

5. Describe the social-cognitive perspective, and define reciprocal determinism, giving three examples.

6. Discuss research findings on personal control.

7. Describe how social-cognitive researchers study behavior, and evaluate this perspective on personality.

8. Describe recent research on the way people view themselves, including research on stigmatized people.

9. Discuss how culture affects one's sense of self, including research findings on differences between individualist and collectivist cultures.

10. Explain the modern concept of the unconscious mind.

Stepping Through the Section

Answers begin on page 367.

1. Today's personality researchers are less interested in _____ theories than in focused analyses of the _____ _____ of personality, on the _____ roots of these dimensions and the interaction of _____ and _____ .

2. Gordon Allport developed trait theory, which defines personality in terms of people's characteristic _____ and conscious _____ . He was generally less interested in _____ individual traits than in _____ them.

3. The _____-_____ _____ _____ classifies people according to Carl Jung's personality types. Although recently criticized for its lack of predictive value, this test has been widely used in _____ and _____ counseling.

4. To reduce the number of traits to a few basic ones, psychologists use the statistical procedure of _____ _____ . The Eysencks think that two or three genetically influenced personality dimensions are sufficient;

these include _____ –
_____ and emotional
_____ – _____ .

5. Some researchers believe that extraverts seek stimulation because their level of _____ _____ is relatively low.

6. PET scans reveal an area of the brain's _____ lobe that is less active in _____ (extraverts/introverts) than in _____ (extraverts/ introverts).

7. Jerome Kagan attributes differences in children's _____ and _____ to autonomic nervous system reactivity.

8. Research increasingly reveals that our _____ play an important role in defining our _____ and _____ style.

9. Questionnaires that categorize personality traits are called _____ _____ . The most widely used of all such personality tests is the _____ _____ _____ _____ . This test was developed by testing a large pool of items and selecting those that differentiated particular individuals; in other words, the test was _____ derived.

10. In contrast to the projective tests, personality inventories are scored _____ , but that does not guarantee _____ .

(Thinking Critically) Explain several techniques used by astrologers to persuade people to accept their advice.

11. Researchers have arrived at a cluster of five factors that seem to describe the major features of personality. List and briefly describe the Big Five.
    a. _____
    b. _____
    c. _____
    d. _____
    e. _____

12. In adulthood, the Big Five are quite _____ (stable/variable), with heritability estimated at _____ percent or more for each dimension. Moreover, these traits _____ (describe/do not describe) personality in other cultures.

13. Human behavior is influenced both by our inner _____ and by the external _____ . The issue of which of these is the more important influence on personality is called the _____ - _____ controversy.

14. To be considered a personality trait, a characteristic must persist over _____ and across _____ . Research studies reveal that personality trait scores _____ (correlate/do not correlate) with scores obtained seven years later. The consistency of specific behaviors from one situation to the next is _____ (predictably consistent/not predictably consistent).

15. An individual's score on a personality test _____ (is/is not) very predictive of his or her behavior in any given situation.

16. People's expressive styles, which include their _____ , manner of _____ , and _____ , are quite _____ (consistent/inconsistent).

Defend trait theory against the criticism that people seem not to have clear, consistent personalities.

17. Social-cognitive theory, which focuses on how the individual and the _____ interact, was proposed by _____ .

18. Social-cognitive theorists propose that personality is shaped by the mutual influence of our

_____ , _____

_____ factors, and

_____ factors. This is the principle of _____ _____ .

Describe three different ways in which the environment and personality interact.

19. In studying how we interact with our environment, social-cognitive theorists point to the importance of our sense of _____

_____ . Individuals who believe that they control their own destinies are said to perceive an _____

_____ _____

_____ . Individuals who believe that their fate is determined by outside forces are said to perceive an _____

_____ _____

_____ . Self-control predicts good _____ , better _____ , and _____ success.

20. Seligman found that exposure to inescapable punishment produced a passive resignation in behavior, which he called _____

_____ .

21. People become happier when they are given _____ (more/less) control over what happens to them.

22. One measure of a person's feelings of effectiveness is his or her degree of _____ . Our characteristic manner of explaining negative and positive events is called our

_____ _____ .

23. One factor that may help explain Asian-American students' academic achievements is their some-

what greater _____ . Success requires enough _____ to provide hope and enough _____ to prevent complacency.

24. (Close-Up) During its first century, psychology focused primarily on understanding and alleviating _____ _____ . Today, however, thriving Western cultures have an opportunity to create a more _____ psychology, focused on three pillars:

a. _____

b. _____

c. _____

25. People tend to be most overconfident of their abilities in areas where they are, in fact, most _____ (competent/incompetent).

26. It follows from the social-cognitive perspective that the best means of predicting people's future behavior is their _____

_____ .

Describe a criticism of the social-cognitive perspective.

27. One of Western psychology's most vigorously researched topics today is the _____ . Hazel Markus and colleagues introduced the concept of an individual's _____

_____ to emphasize how our aspirations motivate us through specific goals.

28. Our tendency to overestimate the the extent to which others are noticing and evaluating us is called the _____ _____ .

29. According to self theorists, personality development hinges on our feelings of self-worth, or _____ . People who feel good about themselves are relatively _____ (dependent on/independent of) outside pressures, while people who fall

short of their ideals are more prone to

_____ and _____ .

30. People who are vulnerable to depression often feel they are falling short of their

_____ . Those vulnerable to anxiety often feel they are falling short of what they

_____ .

31. In a series of experiments, researchers found that people who were made to feel insecure were

_____ (more/less) critical of other persons or tended to express heightened

_____ _____ .

32. Research studies demonstrate that ethnic minorities, people with disabilities, and women generally _____ (have/do not have) lower self-esteem.

33. Members of stigmatized groups maintain self-esteem in three ways:

    a. _____

    b. _____

    c. _____

34. Research has shown that most people tend to have _____ (low/high) self-esteem.

35. The tendency of people to judge themselves favorably is called the _____ bias.

36. Responsibility for success is generally accepted _____ (more/less) readily than responsibility for failure.

37. Most people perceive their own behavior and traits as being _____ (above/below) average.

38. Bushman and Baumeister found that students with unrealistically _____ (low/high) self-esteem were most likely to become exceptionally aggressive after criticism.

39. A number of psychologists have suggested that humans function best with modest self-enhancing

_____ .

40. People who give priority to personal goals and define their identity in terms of personal attributes are members of _____ cultures. People who give priority to the goals of their groups belong to _____ cultures.

Contrast the influences of individualism and collectivism on personal identity.

41. Direct confrontation and blunt honesty are rare in _____ cultures. People in _____ cultures have more personal _____ , but they also experience more _____ , more _____ , more _____ , and more _____-_____ disease. Within individualist cultures, people with the strongest _____ _____ express the greatest satisfaction with their lives.

42. In recent decades, Western individualism has _____ (increased/decreased).

43. Cognitive science reveals that the unconscious is not the site of instinctual urges, as _____ thought, but rather the site where _____ is processed without awareness.

44. Recent research provides some support for the Freudian defense mechanism _____ , which today's researchers call the _____ _____ _____ .

More supportive evidence exists for defenses that defend _____ than for defenses tied to _____ _____ such as _____ .

Progress Test 1

Multiple-Choice Questions

Circle your answers to the following questions and check them with the answers beginning on page 368. If your answer is incorrect, read the explanation for why it is incorrect and then consult the appropriate pages of the text (in parentheses following the correct answer).

1. The text defines *personality* as:
   a. the set of personal attitudes that characterizes a person.
   b. an individual's characteristic pattern of thinking, feeling, and acting.
   c. a predictable set of responses to environmental stimuli.
   d. an unpredictable set of responses to environmental stimuli.

2. Which of the following places the greatest emphasis on the unconscious mind?
   a. the humanistic perspective
   b. the social-cognitive perspective
   c. the trait perspective
   d. the psychoanalytic perspective

3. Which of the following is the correct order of psychosexual stages proposed by Freud?
   a. oral; anal; phallic; latency; genital
   b. anal; oral; phallic; latency; genital
   c. oral; anal; genital; latency; phallic
   d. anal; oral; genital; latency; phallic
   e. oral; phallic; anal; genital; latency

4. According to Freud, defense mechanisms are methods of reducing:
   a. anger.   c. anxiety.
   b. fear.   d. lust.

5. Collectivist cultures:
   a. give priority to the goals of their groups.
   b. value the maintenance of social harmony.
   c. foster social interdependence.
   d. are characterized by none of the above.
   e. are characterized by a., b., and c.

6. Neo-Freudians such as Adler and Horney believed that:
   a. Freud placed too great an emphasis on the conscious mind.
   b. Freud placed too great an emphasis on sexual and aggressive instincts.
   c. the years of childhood were more important in the formation of personality than Freud had indicated.
   d. Freud's ideas about the id, ego, and superego as personality structures were incorrect.

7. Research on locus of control indicates that internals are _____ than externals.
   a. more dependent
   b. more intelligent
   c. better able to cope with stress
   d. more sociable
   e. more depressed

8. Which two dimensions of personality have the Eysencks emphasized?
   a. extraversion–introversion and emotional stability–instability
   b. internal–external locus of control and extraversion–introversion
   c. internal–external locus of control and emotional stability–instability
   d. melancholic–phlegmatic and choleric–sanguine

9. With regard to personality, it appears that:
   a. there is little consistency of behavior from one situation to the next and little consistency of traits over the life span.
   b. there is little consistency of behavior from one situation to the next but significant consistency of traits over the life span.
   c. there is significant consistency of behavior from one situation to the next but little consistency of traits over the life span.
   d. there is significant consistency of behavior from one situation to the next and significant consistency of traits over the life span.

10. The humanistic perspective on personality:
   a. emphasizes the driving force of unconscious motivations in personality.
   b. emphasizes the growth potential of "healthy" individuals.
   c. emphasizes the importance of interaction with the environment in shaping personality.
   d. describes personality in terms of scores on various personality scales.

11. According to Rogers, three conditions are necessary to promote growth in personality. These are:
    a. honesty, sincerity, and empathy.
    b. high self-esteem, honesty, and empathy.
    c. high self-esteem, genuineness, and acceptance.
    d. high self-esteem, acceptance, and honesty.
    e. genuineness, acceptance, and empathy.

12. Regarding the self-serving bias, psychologists who study the self have found that self-affirming thinking:
    a. is generally maladaptive to the individual because it distorts reality by overinflating self-esteem.
    b. is generally adaptive to the individual because it maintains self-confidence and minimizes depression.
    c. tends to prevent the individual from viewing others with compassion and understanding.
    d. tends *not* to characterize people who have experienced unconditional positive regard.

13. Which of Freud's ideas would *not* be accepted by most contemporary psychologists?
    a. Development is essentially fixed in childhood.
    b. Sexuality is a potent drive in humans.
    c. The mind is an iceberg with consciousness being only the tip.
    d. Repression can be the cause of forgetting.

14. Individualist cultures:
    a. value communal solidarity.
    b. emphasize personal achievement and identity.
    c. are less competitive than collectivist cultures.
    d. are characterized by none of the above.
    e. are characterized by a., b., and c.

15. Projective tests such as the Rorschach inkblot test have been criticized because:
    a. their scoring system is too rigid and leads to unfair labeling.
    b. they were standardized with unrepresentative samples.
    c. they have low reliability and low validity.
    d. it is easy for people to fake answers in order to appear healthy.

16. A major criticism of trait theory is that it:
    a. places too great an emphasis on early childhood experiences.
    b. overestimates the consistency of behavior in different situations.
    c. underestimates the importance of heredity in personality development.
    d. places too great an emphasis on positive traits.

17. For humanistic psychologists, many of our behaviors and perceptions are ultimately shaped by whether our _____ is _____ or _____ .
    a. ego; strong; weak
    b. locus of control; internal; external
    c. personality structure; introverted; extraverted
    d. self-concept; positive; negative

18. In studying personality, a trait theorist would *most likely*:
    a. use a projective test.
    b. observe a person in a variety of situations.
    c. use a personality inventory.
    d. use the method of free association.

19. Id is to ego as _____ is to _____ .
    a. reality principle; pleasure principle
    b. pleasure principle; reality principle
    c. conscious forces; unconscious forces
    d. conscience; "personality executive"

20. Which of the following is a major criticism of the social-cognitive perspective?
    a. It focuses too much on early childhood experiences.
    b. It focuses too little on the inner traits of a person.
    c. It provides descriptions but not explanations.
    d. It lacks appropriate assessment techniques.

21. Recent research has provided more support for defense mechanisms such as _____ than for defense mechanisms such as _____ .
    a. displacement; reaction formation
    b. reaction formation; displacement
    c. displacement; regression
    d. displacement; projection

22. Today's personality researchers focus their work on:
    a. basic dimensions of personality.
    b. the interaction of persons and environments.
    c. grand theories of behavior.
    d. a. and b.
    e. a., b., and c.

Matching Items

Match each definition or description with the appropriate term.

Definitions or Descriptions

_____ 1. redirecting impulses to a less threatening object

_____ 2. test consisting of a series of inkblots

_____ 3. the conscious executive of personality

_____ 4. personality inventory

_____ 5. disguising an impulse by imputing it to another person

_____ 6. switching an unacceptable impulse into its opposite

_____ 7. the unconscious repository of instinctual drives

_____ 8. a statistical technique that identifies clusters of personality traits

_____ 9. personality structure that corresponds to a person's conscience

_____ 10. providing self-justifying explanations for an action

Terms

a. id
b. ego
c. superego
d. reaction formation
e. rationalization
f. displacement
g. factor analysis
h. projection
i. Rorschach
j. MMPI

Progress Test 2

Progress Test 2 should be completed during a final chapter review. Answer the following questions after you thoroughly understand the correct answers for the section reviews and Progress Test 1.

Multiple-Choice Questions

1. Which perspective on personality emphasizes the interaction between the individual and the environment in shaping personality?
   a. psychoanalytic
   b. trait
   c. humanistic
   d. social-cognitive

2. According to Freud's theory, personality arises in response to conflicts between:
   a. our unacceptable urges and our tendency to become self-actualized.
   b. the process of identification and the ego's defense mechanisms.
   c. the collective unconscious and our individual desires.
   d. our biological impulses and the social restraints against them.

3. The _____ classifies people according to Carl Jung's personality types.
   a. Myers-Briggs Type Indicator
   b. MMPI
   c. Locus of Control Scale
   d. Kagan Temperament Scale
   e. TAT

4. Seligman has found that humans and animals who are exposed to aversive events they cannot escape may develop:
   a. an internal locus of control.
   b. a reaction formation.
   c. learned helplessness.
   d. neurotic anxiety.
   e. displacement.

5. Research has shown that individuals who are made to feel insecure are subsequently:
   a. more critical of others.
   b. less critical of others.
   c. more likely to display a self-serving bias.
   d. less likely to display a self-serving bias.

6. An example of the self-serving bias described in the text is the tendency of people to:
   a. see themselves as better than average on nearly any desirable dimension.
   b. accept more responsibility for successes than failures.
   c. be overly critical of other people.
   d. be overly sensitive to criticism.
   e. do both a. and b.

7. The Minnesota Multiphasic Personality Inventory (MMPI) is a(n):
   a. projective personality test.
   b. empirically derived and objective personality test.
   c. personality test developed mainly to assess job applicants.
   d. personality test used primarily to assess locus of control.

8. Trait theory attempts to:
   a. show how development of personality is a lifelong process.
   b. describe and classify people in terms of their predispositions to behave in certain ways.
   c. determine which traits are most conducive to individual self-actualization.
   d. explain how behavior is shaped by the interaction between traits, behavior, and the environment.

9. With which of the following statements would a social-cognitive psychologist agree?
   a. People with an internal locus of control achieve more in school.
   b. "Externals" are better able to cope with stress than "internals."
   c. "Internals" are less independent than "externals."
   d. All of the above are true.

10. Which of the following statements about self-esteem is *not* correct?
    a. People with low self-esteem tend to be negative about others.
    b. People with high self-esteem are less prone to drug addiction.
    c. People with low self-esteem tend to be nonconformists.
    d. People with high self-esteem suffer less from insomnia.
    e. People with high self-esteem are more persistent at difficult tasks.

11. The Oedipus and Electra complexes have their roots in the:
    a. anal stage.   d. phallic stage.
    b. oral stage.   e. genital stage.
    c. latency stage.

12. Which of the following is a common criticism of the humanistic perspective?
    a. Its concepts are vague and subjective.
    b. The emphasis on the self encourages selfishness in individuals.
    c. Humanism fails to appreciate the reality of evil in human behavior.
    d. All of the above are common criticisms.

13. In studying personality, a social-cognitive theorist would *most likely* make use of:
    a. personality inventories.
    b. projective tests.
    c. observing behavior in different situations.
    d. factor analyses.

14. A major difference between the psychoanalytic and trait perspectives is that:
    a. trait theory defines personality in terms of behavior; psychoanalytic theory, in terms of its underlying dynamics.
    b. trait theory describes behavior but does not attempt to explain it.
    c. psychoanalytic theory emphasizes the origins of personality in childhood sexuality.
    d. all of the above are differences.

15. Compared to those in collectivist cultures, people in individualist cultures:
    a. are less geographically bound to elderly parents.
    b. tend to be lonelier.
    c. are more vulnerable to stress-related disease.
    d. have all of the above characteristics.

16. The Big Five personality factors are:
    a. emotional stability, openness, introversion, sociability, locus of control.
    b. neuroticism, extraversion, openness, emotional stability, sensitivity.
    c. neuroticism, gregariousness, extraversion, impulsiveness, conscientiousness.
    d. emotional stability, extraversion, openness, agreeableness, conscientiousness.
    e. emotional stability, extraversion, openness, locus of control, sensitivity.

17. Which of the following was *not* mentioned in the text as a criticism of Freud's theory?
    a. The theory is sexist.
    b. It offers few testable hypotheses.
    c. There is no evidence of anything like an "unconscious."
    d. The theory ignores the fact that human development is lifelong.

18. According to Freud, _____ is the process by which children incorporate their parents' values into their _____ .
    a. reaction formation; superegos
    b. reaction formation; egos
    c. identification; superegos
    d. identification; egos

19. Which of the following groups tend to suffer from relatively low self-esteem?
    a. women
    b. ethnic minorities
    c. disabled persons
    d. all of the above
    e. none of the above

20. In promoting personality growth, the person-centered perspective emphasizes all but:
    a. empathy.   c. genuineness.
    b. acceptance.   d. altruism.

21. Recent research on the Big Five personality factors provides evidence that:
    a. some tendencies decrease during adulthood, while others increase.
    b. these traits only describe personality in Western, individualist cultures.
    c. the heritability of individual differences in these traits generally runs about 25 percent or less.
    d. all of the above are true.

22. The behavior of many people has been described in terms of a "spotlight effect." This means that they
    a. tend to see themselves as being above average in ability.
    b. perceive that their fate is determined by forces not under their personal control.
    c. overestimate the extent to which other people are noticing them.
    d. do all of the above.

Matching Items

Match each term with the appropriate definition or description.

Terms

_____ 1. projective test
_____ 2. identification
_____ 3. collective unconscious
_____ 4. reality principle
_____ 5. psychosexual stages
_____ 6. pleasure principle
_____ 7. empirically derived test
_____ 8. reciprocal determinism
_____ 9. personality inventory
_____ 10. Oedipus complex
_____ 11. preconscious

Definitions or Descriptions

a. the id's demand for immediate gratification
b. a boy's sexual desires toward the opposite-sex parent
c. information that is retrievable but currently not in conscious awareness
d. stages of development proposed by Freud
e. questionnaire used to assess personality traits
f. the two-way interactions of behavior with personal and environmental factors
g. personality test that provides ambiguous stimuli
h. the repository of universal memories proposed by Jung
i. the process by which children incorporate their parents' values into their developing superegos
j. the process by which the ego seeks to gratify impulses of the id in nondestructive ways
k. developed by testing a pool of items and then selecting those that discriminate the group of interest

Review and Reflect

Answer these questions the day before an exam as a final check on your understanding of the chapter's terms and concepts.

Multiple-Choice Questions

1. A psychoanalyst would characterize a person who is impulsive and self-indulgent as possessing a strong _____ and a weak _____ .
   a. id and ego; superego
   b. id; ego and superego
   c. ego; superego
   d. id; superego
   e. superego; ego

2. Because Ramona identifies with her politically conservative parents, she chose to enroll in a conservative college. After four years in this environment Ramona's politics have become even more conservative. Which perspective best accounts for the mutual influences of Ramona's upbringing, choice of school, and political viewpoint?
   a. psychoanalytic
   b. trait
   c. humanistic
   d. social-cognitive

3. Jill has a biting, sarcastic manner. According to Freud, she is:
   a. projecting her anxiety onto others.
   b. fixated in the oral stage of development.
   c. fixated in the anal stage of development.
   d. displacing her anxiety onto others.

4. James attributes his failing grade in chemistry to an unfair final exam. His attitude exemplifies:
   a. internal locus of control.
   b. unconditional positive regard.
   c. the self-serving bias.
   d. reciprocal determinism.

5. Being fed up with your cultural background, you decide to move to a culture that places greater value on maintaining social harmony and family identity. To which of the following countries should you move?
   a. the United States
   b. Canada
   c. Australia
   d. Japan
   e. Great Britain

6. Because you have a relatively low level of brain arousal, a trait theorist would suggest that you are a(n) _____ who would naturally seek _____ .
   a. introvert; stimulation
   b. introvert; isolation
   c. extravert; stimulation
   d. extravert; isolation

7. A psychologist at the campus mental health center administered an empirically derived personality test to diagnose an emotionally troubled student. Which test did the psychologist *most likely* administer?
   a. the MMPI
   b. the False Consensus Test
   c. the Rorschach
   d. the Locus of Control Scale

8. The personality test Teresa is taking involves her describing random patterns of dots. What type of test is she taking?
   a. an empirically derived test
   b. the MMPI
   c. a personality inventory
   d. the Myers-Briggs Type Indicator
   e. a projective test

9. Dr. Gonzalez believes that most students can be classified as "Type A" or "Type B" according to the intensities of their personalities and competitiveness. Evidently, Dr. Gonzalez is working within the _____ perspective.
   a. psychoanalytic
   b. trait
   c. humanistic
   d. social-cognitive

10. According to the psychoanalytic perspective, a child who frequently "slips" and calls her teacher "mom" *probably*:
   a. has some unresolved conflicts concerning her mother.
   b. is fixated in the oral stage of development.
   c. did not receive unconditional positive regard from her mother.
   d. can be classified as having a weak sense of personal control.

11. Isaiah is sober and reserved; Rashid is fun-loving and affectionate. The Eysencks would say that Isaiah _____ and Rashid _____ .

    a. has an internal locus of control; has an external locus of control

    b. has an external locus of control; has an internal locus of control

    c. is an extravert; is an introvert

    d. is an introvert; is an extravert

12. In high school, Britta and Debbie were best friends. They thought they were a lot alike, as did everyone else who knew them. After high school, they went on to very different colleges, careers, and life courses. Now, at their twenty-fifth reunion, they are shocked at how little they have in common. Bandura would suggest that their differences reflect the interactive effects of environment, personality, and behavior, which he refers to as:

    a. reciprocal determinism.

    b. personal control.

    c. identification.

    d. the self-serving bias.

13. For his class presentation, Bruce plans to discuss the Big Five personality factors used by people throughout the world to describe others or themselves. Which of the following is *not* a factor that Bruce will discuss?

    a. extraversion   d. conscientiousness

    b. openness   e. agreeableness

    c. independence

14. Dayna is not very consistent in showing up for class and turning in assignments when they are due. Research studies would suggest that Dayna's inconsistent behavior:

    a. indicates that she is emotionally troubled and may need professional counseling.

    b. is a sign of learned helplessness.

    c. is not necessarily unusual.

    d. probably reflects a temporary problem in another area of her life.

15. Andrew's grandfather, who has lived a rich and productive life, is a spontaneous, loving, and self-accepting person. Maslow might say that he:

    a. has an internal locus of control.

    b. is an extravert.

    c. has resolved all the conflicts of the psychosexual stages.

    d. is a self-actualizing person.

16. The school psychologist believes that having a positive self-concept is necessary before students can achieve their potential. Evidently, the school psychologist is working within the _____ perspective.

    a. psychoanalytic   c. humanistic

    b. trait   d. social-cognitive

17. Wanda wishes to instill in her children an accepting attitude toward other people. Maslow and Rogers would probably recommend that she:

    a. teach her children first to accept themselves.

    b. use discipline sparingly.

    c. be affectionate with her children only when they behave as she wishes.

    d. do all of the above.

18. Suzy bought a used, high-mileage automobile because it was all she could afford. Attempting to justify her purchase, she raves to her friends about the car's attractiveness, good acceleration, and stereo. According to Freud, Suzy is using the defense mechanism of:

    a. displacement.   c. rationalization.

    b. reaction formation. d. projection.

19. Nadine has a relatively high level of brain arousal. Trait theorists would probably predict that she is:

    a. an extravert.   c. an unstable person.

    b. an introvert.   d. both a. and c.

20. (Close-Up) During a class discussion, Trevor argues that "positive psychology" is sure to wane in popularity, since it suffers from the same criticisms as humanistic psychology. You counter his argument by pointing out that, unlike humanistic psychology, positive psychology:

    a. focuses on advancing human fulfillment.

    b. is rooted in science.

    c. is not based on the study of individual characteristics.

    d. has all of the above characteristics.

Essay Question

You are an honest, open, and responsible person. Discuss how these characteristics would be explained according to the major perspectives on personality. (Use the space below to list points you want to make, and organize them. Then write the essay on a separate piece of paper.)

Key Terms

Writing Definitions

Using your own words, on a separate piece of paper write a brief definition or explanation of each of the following terms.

1. personality
2. free association
3. psychoanalysis
4. unconscious
5. id
6. ego
7. superego
8. psychosexual stages
9. Oedipus complex
10. identification
11. fixation
12. defense mechanisms
13. repression
14. regression
15. reaction formation
16. projection
17. rationalization
18. displacement
19. projective tests
20. Rorschach inkblot test
21. collective unconscious
22. self-actualization
23. unconditional positive regard
24. self-concept
25. traits
26. personality inventory
27. Minnesota Multiphasic Personality Inventory (MMPI)
28. empirically derived test
29. social-cognitive perspective
30. reciprocal determinism
31. personal control
32. external locus of control
33. internal locus of control
34. learned helplessness
35. positive psychology
36. spotlight effect
37. self-esteem
38. self-serving bias
39. individualism
40. collectivism

Cross-Check

As you learned in Chapter 1, reviewing and overlearning of material are important to the learning process. After you have written the definitions of the key terms in this chapter, you should complete the crossword puzzle to ensure that you can reverse the process—recognize the term, given the definition.

ACROSS

5. Defense mechanism in which an impulse is shifted to an object other than the one that originally aroused the impulse.
7. A cultural emphasis on personal goals over group goals.
13. In Freud's theory, the personality system consisting of basic sexual and aggressive drives.
16. Locus of control that reflects the belief that one's fate is determined by forces not under personal control.
17. In Freud's theory, the conscious division of personality.
18. Defense mechanism in which a person reverts to a less mature pattern of behavior.

DOWN

1. In Freud's theory, the complex developed by boys in which they are sexually attracted to their mother and resent their father.
2. A person's characteristic pattern of behavior.
3. Type of test developed by testing many items to see which best distinguish between groups of interest.
4. A person's sense of being male or female.
6. The passive resignation a person or animal develops from repeated exposure to inescapable aversive events.
8. The ego's methods of unconsciously protecting itself against anxiety.
9. In Freud's theory, the process by which the child's superego develops and incorporates the parents' values.

10. The most widely used personality inventory.
11. In Freud's theory, the area of the unconscious containing material that is retrievable into conscious awareness.
12. The Rorschach is an example of a _____.
14. An individual's characteristic pattern of thinking, feeling, and acting.
15. A widely used test in which people are asked to interpret 10 inkblots.

Answers

Introducing Personality

Introduction Preview

1. Personality is your characteristic pattern of thinking, feeling, and acting. Unlike other areas of study in psychology, which focus on similarities among people, personality emphasizes the uniqueness of the individual.

Historic Perspectives on Personality

Section Preview

1. Freud discovered that, under hypnosis, his patients were sometimes able to talk freely about their neurological symptoms, which led to their improvement. He later began using free association instead of hypnosis, believing that this technique triggered a chain of thoughts leading into a patient's unconscious, thereby retrieving and releasing painful unconscious memories.

   Psychoanalysis is based on Freud's belief that below our surface consciousness is a much larger, unconscious region that contains thoughts, feelings, wishes, and memories of which we are unaware. Although some of these thoughts are held in a preconscious area and can be retrieved at will into consciousness, some unacceptable thoughts and wishes are forcibly blocked, or repressed, from consciousness. These unconscious thoughts and urges often are expressed in troubling symptoms.

2. To Freud, personality is composed of three interacting, and often conflicting, systems: the id, ego, and superego. Operating on the pleasure principle, the unconscious id strives to satisfy basic drives to survive, reproduce, and aggress. Operating on the reality principle, the ego seeks to gratify the id's impulses in realistic and nondestructive ways. The superego, which represents the individual's internalization of the morals and values of parents and culture, forces the ego to consider not only the real but also the ideal. Because the ego must intervene among the impulsive demands of the id, the restraining demands of the superego, and those of the external world, it is the personality "executive."

3. Freud believed that children pass through a series of psychosexual stages during which the id's pleasure-seeking energies focus on particular erogenous zones. Between birth and 18 months (oral stage), pleasure centers on the mouth. Between 18 and 36 months (anal stage), pleasure focuses on bowel and bladder retention and elimination. Between 3 and 6 years (phallic stage), the pleasure zone shifts to the genitals, and boys develop unconscious sexual desires for their mothers and the fear that their fathers will punish them (Oedipus complex). Children eventually cope with these threatening feelings by repressing them and identifying with their same-sex parent.

   Between 6 years of age and puberty (latency stage), sexual feelings are repressed and redirected. At puberty, sexual interests mature as youths begin to experience sexual feelings toward others (genital stage).

4. According to Freud, maladaptive adult behavior results from unresolved conflicts during earlier psychosexual stages. Such unresolved conflicts may cause the person's pleasure-seeking energies to become fixated in one psychosexual stage, leading to later problem behaviors or distinctive personality characteristics.

   Defense mechanisms are the ego's attempt to reduce or redirect anxiety by distorting reality. Examples of defense mechanisms include the banishing of thoughts from consciousness (repression), retreating to behavior characteristic of an earlier stage (regression), turning threatening impulses into their opposites (reaction formation) or attributing them to others (projection), self-justification of unacceptable actions (rationalization), and diverting sexual or aggressive impulses to a more acceptable object (displacement).

5. Projective tests, such as the Rorschach inkblot test, ask people to describe or tell a story about an ambiguous stimulus that has no inherent meaning. In doing so, people presumably project their own interests and conflicts and provide a sort of psychological "x-ray" of their personalities. Despite their widespread use, projective tests are considered by most researchers to be lacking in validity and reliability. For example, there is no single accepted scoring system for interpreting the Rorschach, so two raters may not interpret a person's responses similarly (although a new computer-aided scoring and interpretation tool is improving agreement among raters and enhancing validity). Furthermore, the test is not very successful at predicting future behavior or discriminating between groups.

6. The neo-Freudians placed more emphasis than Freud on the role of the conscious mind in determining personality, and less emphasis on sex and aggression as all-consuming motivations. Alfred Adler and Karen Horney emphasized the importance of social rather than sexual tensions in the formation of the child's personality. Horney also countered the male bias inherent in Freud's theory. Carl Jung expanded Freud's view of the unconscious into the idea of a collective unconscious, a common reservoir of thoughts derived from the experiences of our ancestors.

   Psychodynamic theorists downplay the importance of sex in personality formation. They do agree with Freud, however, that much of mental life is unconscious, that childhood shapes personality and attachment, and that we often struggle with inner conflicts.

7. Freud's idea that development is fixed in childhood has been contradicted by research showing that development is lifelong. It is also clear that children gain their gender identity earlier than Freud believed and become strongly feminine or masculine even without a same-sex parent present. Freud's theory of dreams, memory losses, and defense mechanisms as disguising unfulfilled or repressed urges also has been disputed. Today's researchers contend that repression is actually quite rare and, contrary to Freud's views, occurs as a mental response to terrible trauma. In addition, Freud's theory has been criticized for offering after-the-fact explanations of behavior, yet failing to generate testable predictions of those behaviors. Freud's ideas concerning our limited access to all that goes on in the mind, the importance of sexuality, our attempts to defend ourselves against anxiety, and the tension between our biological impulses and our social well-being have endured, however. Recent evidence has provided some support for defense mechanisms that defend self-esteem such as reaction formation.

8. The humanistic perspective emerged as a reaction against several other perspectives on personality. In contrast to Freud's study of the negative motives of "sick" people, the humanistic psychologists have focused on the strivings of "healthy" people.

   Maslow proposed that people are motivated by a hierarchy of needs and that if basic needs are fulfilled, people will strive to reach their highest potential (self-actualization). Carl Rogers agreed with much of Maslow's thinking, adding that people nurture others' actualizing tendencies by being genuine, accepting, and empathic. For both theorists a central feature of personality is a person's self-concept.

9. The ideas of humanistic psychologists have influenced counseling, education, child-rearing, and management. Critics contend, however, that the concepts of humanistic psychology are vague, subjective, and so focused on the individual that they promote self-indulgence, selfishness, and an erosion of moral restraints. Furthermore, the humanistic psychologists have been accused of being naively optimistic and unrealistic and failing to appreciate the human capacity for evil.

Stepping Through the Section

1. Sigmund Freud; humanistic; growth; self-fulfillment
2. hypnosis; free association
3. psychoanalysis
4. unconscious; preconscious; repressed
5. unconscious; slips; manifest content; latent content
6. biological; social
7. id; ego; superego
8. unconscious; pleasure
9. after; conscious; reality

The ego is considered the executive of personality because it directs our actions as it intervenes among the impulsive demands of the id, the reality of the external world, and the ideals of the superego.

10. superego; 4 or 5
11. weak; strong
12. psychosexual
13. oral; sucking (also biting, chewing)
14. anal; 18; 36
15. phallic; 3; 6; genitals; opposite; Oedipus complex; Electra complex
16. identification; gender identity

Children eventually cope with their feelings for the opposite-sex parent by repressing them and by identifying with the rival (same-sex) parent. Through this process children incorporate many of their parents' values, thereby strengthening the superego.

17. latency
18. genital
19. fixated
20. defense mechanisms; repression
21. regression
22. reaction formation
23. projection
24. rationalization
25. displacement

Matching Items

1. e   4. c
2. d   5. a
3. b

26. unconscious

27. projective

28. Rorschach; inkblots; little

29. neo-Freudians; more; less

    a. Adler emphasized the social, rather than the sexual, tensions of childhood and said that much of behavior is driven by the need to overcome feelings of inferiority.

    b. Horney questioned the male bias in Freud's theory, such as the assumptions that women have weak egos and suffer "penis envy." Like Adler, she emphasized social tensions.

    c. Jung emphasized an inherited collective unconscious.

30. reject; Jung; collective unconscious

31. psychodynamic; sex; unconscious; childhood; inner conflicts

32. lifelong; earlier; is not

33. wishes; sexual; aggressive; sexual suppression

34. represses; rarer; trauma

35. after-the-fact; testable predictions

Freud drew attention to the unconscious and the irrational, to human defenses against anxiety, to the importance of human sexuality, to the tension between our biological impulses and our social well-being, and to our potential for evil.

36. Maslow; Rogers

37. hierarchy; self-actualization

For Maslow, such people were self-aware, self-accepting, open, spontaneous, loving, caring, not paralyzed by others' opinions; secure, and problem-centered rather than self-centered.

38. genuine; accepting; empathic; unconditional positive regard

39. self-concept; counseling; education; child-rearing; management; popular; Western

Humanistic psychology is criticized for being vague and subjective, for encouraging self-indulgence and selfishness, and for failing to appreciate the capacity of humans for evil.

Contemporary Research on Personality

Section Preview

1. Trait theories define personality in terms of identifiable behavior patterns and conscious motives. As compared with psychoanalytic theories, they are less concerned with explaining personality and more concerned with its description.

    A popular procedure today, especially in business and career counseling, is to classify peo-ple according to Carl Jung's personality types using the Myers-Briggs Type Indicator.

    The statistical technique called factor analysis is used to identify clusters of personality test items that make up basic traits. Hans and Sybil Eysenck believe that many of the personality traits researchers have identified using factor analysis can be reduced to two genetically influenced dimensions: extraversion–introversion and emotional stability–instability. Extraverts, for example, seek stimulation because their level of arousal in an area of the frontal lobe is lower than in introverts, while emotionally stable people have less active autonomic nervous systems than do unstable people.

2. To assess traits, psychologists use trait scales that measure single traits or personality inventories that assess several traits at once. In contrast to the subjectivity of projective tests, personality inventories are scored objectively. The most widely used personality inventory is the Minnesota Multiphasic Personality Inventory (MMPI) for assessing psychological disorders. The MMPI is an empirically derived test that contains 10 clinical scales, several validity scales, and 15 content scales.

3. Across the world, people describe others in terms roughly consistent with these five trait dimensions: emotional stability, extraversion, openness, agreeableness, and conscientiousness. Recent research provides evidence that these traits are quite stable in adulthood, apply to various cultures, predict other personal attributes, and have heritability values of approximately 50 percent. Most personality traits are subject to genetic influences.

4. To be a genuine personality trait, a characteristic must persist over time and across situations. Critics of this perspective question the consistency of traits. Although people's traits do seem to persist over time, research has revealed much less consistency of specific behaviors from one situation to another. However, although people do not act with perfect consistency, their *average* behavior over *many* situations is predictable. Although in unfamiliar situations, where we pay attention to social cues, we may hide our traits, we cannot so easily change our characteristic style of expressiveness.

5. The social-cognitive perspective applies principles of learning, cognition, and social behavior to personality and emphasizes the ways in which our personalities shape and are shaped by external events. Reciprocal determinism refers to the

ways in which our personalities are influenced by the interaction of our situations, our thoughts and feelings, and our behaviors. There are many examples of reciprocal determinism. For one, different people choose different environments. For another, our personalities shape how we interpret and react to events. Finally, our personalities help create situations to which we react.

6. Whether people see themselves as controlling, or as controlled by, their environments is an important aspect of their personalities. Research reveals that people who perceive an internal locus of control achieve more in school and are more independent, less depressed, better able to delay gratification, and better able to cope with various life stresses than people who perceive an external locus of control. Seligman found that animals and people who experience uncontrollable negative events may perceive a lack of control in their lives and develop the passive resignation of learned helplessness. One measure of how helpless or effective people feel is whether they generally are optimistic or pessimistic.

7. Social-cognitive researchers study personality by exploring the effect of differing situations on people's behavior patterns and attitudes. This perspective has increased our awareness of how social situations influence, and are influenced by, individuals. Critics contend, however, that the theory explains behavior after the fact and that it focuses so much on the situation that it ignores the importance of people's inner traits, unconscious motives, and emotions in the formation of personality.

8. Research on the self documents the concept of possible selves, including people's visions of the self or selves they would like to become in motivating their behavior. Another finding is that people with high self-esteem have fewer sleepless nights, succumb less easily to pressures to conform, are less likely to use drugs, strive more at difficult tasks, and are happier than people with low self-esteem. Contrary to popular belief, and despite discrimination and lower social status, ethnic minorities, people with disabilities, and women do not suffer lower self-esteem. One of the most firmly established findings is people's readiness to perceive themselves favorably through the self-serving bias. This bias is revealed in the willingness of people to accept responsibility for good deeds and successes more readily than for bad deeds and failures and in the tendency of people to see themselves as better than average on nearly any desirable dimension.

9. Individualist cultures nurture the development of personal goals and define identity in terms of individual attributes. Collectivist cultures give priority to the goals of their groups—often the family, clan, or work group. While individualists easily move in and out of social groups, collectivists have fewer but deeper, more stable attachments to their groups and friends. Collectivist cultures also place a premium on maintaining harmony and allowing others to save face. People in individualist cultures have greater personal freedom and more privacy. But compared to collectivists, individualists also tend to be lonelier, more likely to divorce, more homicidal, and more vulnerable to stress-related diseases.

10. Cognitive science has revealed that we are not consciously aware of all that goes on in our minds and that our capacity for unconscious learning is actually quite sophisticated. This is not the same as Freud's view, however. The contemporary view of the unconscious is that it consists of schemas that control our perceptions, parallel processing of information, implicit memories that operate without conscious recall, and self-concepts and stereotypes that can instantly be activated.

Stepping Through the Section

1. grand; basic dimensions; biological; persons; environments

2. behaviors; motives; explaining; describing

3. Myers-Briggs Type Indicator; business; career

4. factor analysis; extraversion–introversion; stability–instability

5. brain arousal

6. frontal; extraverts; introverts

7. shyness; inhibition

8. genes; temperament; behavioral

9. personality inventories; Minnesota Multiphasic Personality Inventory; empirically

10. objectively; validity

Astrologers use a "stock spiel" that includes information that is generally true of almost everyone. The willingness of people to accept this type of phony information is called the *Barnum effect*. A second technique used by astrologers is to "read" a person's clothing, features, reactions, etc. and build their advice from these observations.

11. **a.** Emotional stability: on a continuum from calm to anxious; secure to insecure

    b. Extraversion: from sociable to retiring

    c. Openness: from preference for variety to routine

d. Agreeableness: from soft-hearted to ruthless
e. Conscientiousness: from disciplined to impulsive

12. stable; 50; describe

13. traits (or dispositions); situation (or environment); person-situation

14. time; situations; correlate; not predictably consistent

15. is not

16. animation; speaking; gestures; consistent

At any given moment a person's behavior is powerfully influenced by the immediate situation, so that it may appear that the person does not have a consistent personality. But averaged over many situations a person's outgoingness, happiness, and carelessness, for instance, are more predictable.

17. environment; Bandura

18. behaviors; internal personal; environmental; reciprocal determinism

Different people choose different environments partly on the basis of their dispositions. Our personality shapes how we interpret and react to events. It also helps create the situations to which we react.

19. personal control; internal locus of control; external locus of control; adjustment; grades; social

20. learned helplessness

21. more

22. optimism; attributional style

23. pessimism; optimism; pessimism

24. negative states; positive
    a. positive subjective well-being
    b. positive character
    c. positive groups, communities, and cultures

25. incompetent

26. past behavior in similar situations

One criticism is that the theory has overemphasized situational influences to the neglect of inner traits.

27. self; possible selves

28. spotlight effect

29. self-esteem; independent of; anxiety; depression

30. hopes; think they ought to be

31. more; racial prejudice

32. do not have

33. **a.** They value the things at which they excel.
    b. They attribute problems to prejudice.
    c. They compare themselves to those in their own group.

34. high

35. self-serving

36. more

37. above

38. high

39. illusions

40. individualist; collectivist

Individualists identify themselves in terms of their personal convictions and values. They strive for personal control and individual achievement. Collectivists give priority to their groups and define their identity accordingly. They place a premium on maintaining harmony and allowing others to save face.

41. collectivist; individualist; freedom; loneliness; divorce; homicide; stress-related; social ties

42. increased

43. Freud; information

44. projection; false consensus effect; self-esteem; instinctual energy; displacement

Progress Test 1

Multiple-Choice Questions

1. **b.** is the answer. Personality is defined as patterns of response—of thinking, feeling, and acting—that are relatively consistent across a variety of situations. (p. 429)

2. **d.** is the answer. (p. 430)
   a. & b. Conscious processes are the focus of these perspectives.
   c. The trait perspective focuses on the description of behaviors.

3. **a.** is the answer. (p. 432)

4. **c.** is the answer. According to Freud, defense mechanisms reduce anxiety unconsciously, by disguising one's threatening impulses. (p. 433)
   a., b., & d. Unlike these specific emotions, anxiety need not be focused. Defense mechanisms help us cope when we are unsettled but are not sure why.

5. **e.** is the answer. (pp. 461–462)

6. **b.** is the answer. (p. 435)
   a. According to most neo-Freudians, Freud placed too great an emphasis on the *unconscious* mind.
   c. Freud placed great emphasis on early childhood, and the neo-Freudians basically agreed with him.
   d. The neo-Freudians accepted Freud's ideas about the basic personality structures.

7. **c.** is the answer. (p. 452)
   a., d., & e. In fact, just the opposite is true.
   b. Locus of control is not related to intelligence.

8. **a.** is the answer. (p. 444)
b. & c. Locus of control is emphasized by the social-cognitive perspective.
d. This is how the ancient Greeks described personality.

9. **b.** is the answer. Studies have shown that people do not act with predictable consistency from one situation to the next. But, over a number of situations, consistent patterns emerge, and this basic consistency of traits persists over the life span. (p. 449)

10. **b.** is the answer. (p. 439)
a. This is true of the psychoanalytic perspective.
c. This is true of the social-cognitive perspective.
d. This is true of the trait perspective.

11. **e.** is the answer. (p. 440)

12. **b.** is the answer. Psychologists who study the self emphasize that for the individual, self-affirming thinking is generally adaptive (therefore, not a.); such thinking maintains self-confidence, minimizes depression, and enables us to view others with compassion and understanding (therefore, not c.); unconditional positive regard tends to promote self-esteem and thus self-affirming thinking (therefore, not d.). (p. 460)

13. **a.** is the answer. Developmental research indicates that development is lifelong. (p. 436)
b., c., & d. To varying degrees, research has partially supported these Freudian ideas.

14. **b.** is the answer. (pp. 461–462)
a. & c. These are characteristics of collectivist cultures.

15. **c.** is the answer. As scoring is largely subjective and the tests have not been very successful in predicting behavior, their reliability and validity have been called into question. (p. 435)
a. This is untrue.
b. Unlike empirically derived personality tests, projective tests are not standardized.
d. Although this may be true, it was not mentioned as a criticism of projective tests.

16. **b.** is the answer. In doing so, it underestimates the influence of the environment. (p. 449)
a. The trait perspective does not emphasize early childhood experiences.
c. This criticism is unlikely since trait theory does not seek to explain personality development.
d. Trait theory does not look on traits as being "positive" or "negative."

17. **d.** is the answer. (p. 440)
a. & c. Personality structure is a concern of the psychoanalytic perspective.

b. Locus of control is a major focus of the social-cognitive perspective.

18. **c.** is the answer. (pp. 444–445)
a. & d. A psychoanalytic theorist would be most likely to use a projective test or free association.
b. This would most likely be the approach taken by a social-cognitive theorist.

19. **b.** is the answer. In Freud's theory, the id operates according to the pleasure principle; the ego operates according to the reality principle. (p. 431)
c. The id is presumed to be unconscious.
d. The superego is, according to Freud, the equivalent of a conscience; the ego is the "personality executive."

20. **b.** is the answer. The social-cognitive theory has been accused of putting so much emphasis on the situation that inner traits are neglected. (p. 456)
a. Such a criticism has been made of the psychoanalytic perspective but is not relevant to the social-cognitive perspective.
c. Such a criticism might be more relevant to the trait perspective; the social-cognitive perspective offers an explanation in the form of reciprocal determinism.
d. There are assessment techniques appropriate to the theory, namely, questionnaires and observations of behavior in situations.

21. **b.** is the answer. (p. 464)
a., c., & d. The evidence supports defenses that defend self-esteem, rather than those that are tied to instinctual energy.

22. **d.** is the answer. (pp. 450–451)

Matching Items

1. f (p. 434)
2. i (p. 434)
3. b (p. 431)
4. j (p. 444)
5. h (p. 434)
6. d (p. 433)
7. a (p. 431)
8. g (p. 444)
9. c (p. 431)
10. e (p. 434)

Progress Test 2

Multiple-Choice Questions

1. **d.** is the answer. (p. 450)
a. This perspective emphasizes unconscious dynamics in personality.
b. This perspective is more concerned with *describing* than *explaining* personality.
c. This perspective emphasizes the healthy, self-actualizing tendencies of personality.

2. **d.** is the answer. (p. 431)
a. Self-actualization is a concept of the humanistic perspective.

b. Through identification, children *reduce* conflicting feelings as they incorporate their parents' values.

c. Jung, rather than Freud, proposed the concept of the collective unconscious.

3. **a.** is the answer. (p. 443)

4. **c.** is the answer. In such situations, passive resignation, called learned helplessness, develops. (p. 452)

a. This refers to the belief that one controls one's fate; the circumstances described lead to precisely the opposite belief.

b. Reaction formation is a defense mechanism in which unacceptable impulses are channeled into their opposites.

d. Seligman did not specify that neurotic anxiety occurs.

5. **a.** is the answer. Feelings of insecurity reduce self-esteem, and those who feel negative about themselves tend to feel negative about others as well. (p. 460)

6. **e.** is the answer. (pp. 458–459)

7. **b.** is the answer. The MMPI was developed by selecting from many items those that differentiated between the groups of interest; hence, it was empirically derived. That it is an objective test is shown by the fact that it can be scored by computer. (pp. 444–445)

a. Projective tests present ambiguous stimuli for people to interpret; the MMPI is a questionnaire.

c. Although sometimes used to assess job applicants, the MMPI was developed to assess emotionally troubled people.

d. The MMPI does not focus on control but, rather, measures various aspects of personality.

8. **b.** is the answer. Trait theory attempts to describe behavior and not to develop explanations or applications. The emphasis is more on consistency than on change. (p. 443)

9. **a.** is the answer. "Internals," or those who have a sense of personal control, have been shown to achieve more in school. Relative to externals, they also cope better with stress and are more independent. (p. 452)

10. **c.** is the answer. In actuality, people with *high* self-esteem are generally more independent of pressures to conform. (p. 457)

11. **d.** is the answer. (p. 432)

12. **d.** is the answer. (pp. 441–442)

13. **c.** is the answer. In keeping with their emphasis on interactions between people and situations, social-cognitive theorists would most likely make use of observations of behavior in relevant situations. (p. 455)

a. & d. Personality inventories and factor analyses would more likely be used by a trait theorist.

b. Projective tests would more likely be used by a psychologist working within the psychoanalytic perspective.

14. **d.** is the answer. Trait theory defines personality in terms of behavior and is therefore interested in describing behavior; psychoanalytic theory defines personality as dynamics underlying behavior and therefore is interested in explaining behavior in terms of these dynamics. (pp. 430, 432, 443)

15. **d.** is the answer. (pp. 461–462)

16. **d.** is the answer. (p. 448)

17. **c.** is the answer. Although many researchers think of the unconscious as information processing without awareness rather than as a reservoir of repressed information, they agree with Freud that we do indeed have limited access to all that goes on in our minds. (pp. 438, 463)

18. **c.** is the answer. (p. 432)

a. & b. Reaction formation is the defense mechanism by which people transform unacceptable impulses into their opposites.

d. It is the superego, rather than the ego, that represents parental values.

19. **e.** is the answer. (p. 458)

20. **d.** is the answer. (p. 440)

21. **a.** is the answer. Neuroticism, extraversion, and openness tend to decrease, while agreeableness and conscientiousness tend to increase. (p. 448)

b. The Big Five dimensions describe personality in various cultures reasonably well.

c. Heritability generally runs 50 percent or more for each dimension.

22. **c.** is the answer. (p. 457)

a. This describes the self-serving bias.

b. This describes external locus of control.

Matching Items

1. g (p. 434)   5. d (p. 432)   9. e (p. 444)
2. i (p. 432)   6. a (p. 431)   10. b (p. 432)
3. h (p. 436)   7. k (p. 445)   11. c (p. 430)
4. j (p. 431)   8. f (p. 451)

Review and Reflect

Multiple-Choice Questions

1. **d.** is the answer. Impulsiveness is the mark of a strong id; self-indulgence is the mark of a weak superego. Because the ego serves to mediate the demands of the id, the superego, and the outside world, its strength or weakness is judged by its decision-making ability, not by the character of the decision—so the ego is not relevant to the question asked. (p. 431)

2. **d.** is the answer. The social-cognitive perspective emphasizes the reciprocal influences between people and their situations. In this example, Ramona's parents (situational factor) helped shape her political beliefs (internal factor), which influenced her choice of colleges (situational factor), and created an environment that fostered her predisposed political attitudes. (p. 450)

3. **b.** is the answer. Sarcasm is said to be an attempt to deny the passive dependence characteristic of the oral stage. (p. 432)
   a. A person who is projecting attributes his or her own feelings to others.
   c. Such a person might be either messy and disorganized or highly controlled and compulsively neat.
   d. Displacement involves diverting aggressive or sexual impulses onto a more acceptable object than that which aroused them.

4. **c.** is the answer. (p. 458)
   a. A person with an internal locus of control would be likely to *accept* responsibility for a failing grade.
   b. Unconditional positive regard is an attitude of total acceptance directed toward others.
   d. Reciprocal determinism refers to the mutual influences among personality, environment, and behavior.

5. **d.** is the answer. Of the countries listed, only Japan has a collectivist culture that emphasizes family identity and social harmony. (pp. 461–462)

6. **c.** is the answer. (p. 444)
   a. & b. According to this theory, introverts have relatively *high* levels of arousal, causing them to crave solitude.
   d. Isolation might lower arousal level even further.

7. **a.** is the answer. (p. 444)
   b. There is no such test.
   c. The Rorschach is a projective test that was not empirically derived.

d. A personality test that measures locus of control would not be helpful in identifying troubled behaviors.

8. **e.** is the answer. Projective tests provide ambiguous stimuli, such as random dot patterns, in an attempt to trigger in the test-taker projection of his or her personality. (p. 434)

9. **b.** is the answer. (p. 443)
   a. The psychoanalytic perspective emphasizes unconscious processes in personality dynamics.
   c. The humanistic perspective emphasizes each person's potential for healthy growth and self-actualization.
   d. The social-cognitive perspective emphasizes the reciprocal influences of personality and environment.

10. **a.** is the answer. Freud believed that dreams and such slips of the tongue reveal unconscious conflicts. (pp. 430–431)
    b. A person fixated in the oral stage might have a sarcastic personality; this child's slip of the tongue reveals nothing about her psychosexual development.
    c. & d. Unconditional positive regard and personal control are not psychoanalytic concepts.

11. **d.** is the answer. (p. 444)
    a. & b. The traits of Isaiah and Rashid reveal nothing about their sense of personal control.

12. **a.** is the answer. Reciprocal determinism refers to the mutual influences among personal factors, environmental factors, and behavior. (p. 451)
    b. Personal control is one's sense of controlling, or being controlled by, the environment.
    c. In Freud's theory, identification is the process by which children incorporate parental values into their developing superegos.
    d. The self-serving bias describes our readiness to perceive ourselves favorably.

13. **c.** is the answer. (p. 448)

14. **c.** is the answer. (p. 449)

15. **d.** is the answer. (p. 439)
    a. & b. These are concepts used by social-cognitive and trait theorists rather than humanistic theorists such as Maslow.
    c. This reflects Freud's viewpoint.

16. **c.** is the answer. (p. 440)
    a., b., & d. The self-concept is not relevant to the psychoanalytic, trait, or social-cognitive perspectives.

17. **a.** is the answer. (p. 440)
    b. The text does not discuss the impact of discipline on personality.

c. This would constitute *conditional*, rather than unconditional, positive regard and would likely cause the children to be *less* accepting of themselves and others.

18. **c.** is the answer. Suzy is trying to justify her purchase by generating (inaccurate) explanations for her behavior. (p. 434)

    a. Displacement is the redirecting of impulses toward an object other than the one responsible for them.

    b. Reaction formation is the transformation of unacceptable impulses into their opposites.

    d. Projection is the attribution of one's own unacceptable thoughts and feelings to others.

19. **b.** is the answer. Introverts do not need to seek stimulation because their normal level of brain arousal is already high. (p. 444)

    c. Nadine's high level of brain arousal might imply instability but not necessarily so.

20. **b.** is the answer. (p. 454)

    a. Both positive psychology and humanistic psychology focus on advancing human fulfillment.

    c. Both perspectives focus, at least partly, on individual characteristics.

Essay Question

Since you are apparently in good psychological health, according to the psychoanalytic perspective you must have experienced a healthy childhood and successfully passed Freud's stages of psychosexual development. Freud would also say that your ego is functioning well in balancing the demands of your id with the restraining demands of your superego and reality. Freud might also say that your honest nature reflects a well-developed superego, while Jung might say it derives from a universal value found in our collective unconscious.

According to the humanistic perspective, your open and honest nature indicates that your basic needs have been met and you are in the process of self-actualization (Maslow). Furthermore, your openness indicates that you have a healthy self-concept and were likely nurtured by genuine, accepting, and empathic caregivers (Rogers). More recently, researchers who emphasize the self would also focus on the importance of a positive self-concept.

Trait theorists would be less concerned with explaining these specific characteristics than with describing them, determining their consistency, and classifying your personality type. Some trait theorists, such as Allport, Eysenck, and Kagan, attribute certain trait differences to biological factors such as autonomic reactivity and heredity.

According to the social-cognitive perspective, your internal personal factors, behavior, and environmental influences interacted in shaping your personality and behaviors. The fact that you are a responsible person indicates that you perceive yourself as controlling, rather than as controlled by, your environment.

Key Terms

Writing Definitions

1. **Personality** is an individual's characteristic pattern of thinking, feeling, and acting. (p. 429)

2. **Free association** is the Freudian technique in which the person is encouraged to say whatever comes to mind as a means of exploring the unconscious. (p. 430)

3. In Freud's theory, **psychoanalysis** refers to the treatment of psychological disorders by seeking to expose and interpret the tensions within a patient's unconscious, using methods such as free association. (p. 430)

4. In Freud's theory, the **unconscious** is the repository of mostly unacceptable thoughts, wishes, feelings, and memories. According to contemporary psychologists, it is a level of information processing of which we are unaware. (p. 430)

5. In Freud's theory, the **id** is the unconscious system of personality, consisting of basic sexual and aggressive drives, that supplies psychic energy to personality. (p. 431)

6. In psychoanalytic theory, the **ego** is the conscious division of personality that attempts to mediate between the demands of the id, the superego, and reality. (p. 431)

7. In Freud's theory, the **superego** is the division of personality that contains the conscience and develops by incorporating the perceived moral standards of society. (p. 431)

8. Freud's **psychosexual stages** are developmental periods children pass through during which the id's pleasure-seeking energies are focused on different erogenous zones. (p. 432)

9. According to Freud, boys in the phallic stage develop a collection of feelings, known as the **Oedipus complex**, that center on sexual attraction to the mother and resentment of the father. Some psychologists believe girls have a parallel Electra complex. (p. 432)

10. In Freud's theory, **identification** is the process by which the child's superego develops and incorporates the parents' values. Freud saw identification as crucial, not only to resolution of the Oedipus complex, but also to the development of gender identity. (p. 432)

11. In Freud's theory, **fixation** occurs when development becomes arrested, due to unresolved conflicts, in an immature psychosexual stage. (p. 432)

12. In Freud's theory, **defense mechanisms** are the ego's methods of unconsciously protecting itself against anxiety by distorting reality. (p. 433)

13. The basis of all defense mechanisms, **repression** is the unconscious exclusion of anxiety-arousing thoughts, feelings, and memories from the conscious mind. Repression is an example of motivated forgetting: One "forgets" what one really does not wish to remember. (p. 433)

14. **Regression** is the defense mechanism in which a person faced with anxiety reverts to a less mature pattern of behavior. (p. 433)

15. **Reaction formation** is the defense mechanism in which the ego converts unacceptable impulses into their opposites. (p. 433)

16. In psychoanalytic theory, **projection** is the unconscious attribution of one's own unacceptable feelings, attitudes, or desires to others. (p. 434)

   Memory aid: To project is to thrust outward. **Projection** is an example of thrusting one's own feelings outward to another person.

17. **Rationalization** is the defense mechanism in which one devises self-justifying but incorrect reasons for one's behavior. (p. 434)

18. **Displacement** is the defense mechanism in which a sexual or aggressive impulse is shifted to a more acceptable object other than the one that originally aroused the impulse. (p. 434)

19. **Projective tests**, such as the TAT and Rorschach, present ambiguous stimuli onto which people supposedly *project* their own inner feelings. (p. 434)

20. The **Rorschach inkblot test**, the most widely used projective test, consists of ten inkblots that people are asked to interpret. (p. 434)

21. The **collective unconscious** is Jung's concept of an inherited unconscious shared by all people and deriving from our early ancestors' universal experiences. (p. 436)

22. In Maslow's theory, **self-actualization** describes the process of fulfilling one's potential and becoming spontaneous, loving, creative, and self-accepting. Self-actualization is at the very top of Maslow's need hierarchy and therefore becomes active only after the more basic physical and psychological needs have been met. (p. 439)

23. **Unconditional positive regard** is, according to Rogers, an attitude of total acceptance and one of the three conditions essential to a "growth-promoting" climate. (p. 440)

24. **Self-concept** refers to one's personal awareness of "who I am." In the humanistic perspective, the self-concept is a central feature of personality; life happiness is significantly affected by whether the self-concept is positive or negative. (p. 440)

25. **Traits** are people's characteristic patterns of behavior. (p. 443)

26. **Personality inventories**, associated with the trait perspective, are questionnaires used to assess personality traits. (p. 444)

27. Consisting of 10 clinical scales, the **Minnesota Multiphasic Personality Inventory (MMPI)** is the most widely used personality inventory. (p. 444)

28. An **empirically derived test** is one developed by testing many items to see which best distinguish between groups of interest. (p. 445)

29. According to the **social-cognitive perspective,** behavior is the result of interactions between people and their situations. (p. 450)

30. According to the social-cognitive perspective, personality is shaped through **reciprocal determinism,** or the interaction between personality and environmental factors. (p. 451)

31. **Personal control** refers to a person's sense of controlling the environment. (p. 452)

32. **External locus of control** is the perception that one's fate is determined by forces not under personal control. (p. 452)

33. **Internal locus of control** is the perception that, to a great extent, one controls one's own destiny. (p. 452)

34. **Learned helplessness** is the passive resignation and perceived lack of control that a person or animal develops from repeated exposure to inescapable aversive events. (p. 452)

35. Focusing on subjective well-being, character virtues such as creativity and compassion, and healthy families and neighborhoods, **positive psychology** is the scientific study of optimal human functioning. (p. 454)

36. The **spotlight effect** is the tendency of people to overestimate the extent to which other people are noticing and evaluating them. (p. 457)

37. Self-esteem refers to an individual's sense of self-worth. (p. 457)

38. The **self-serving bias** is the tendency to perceive oneself favorably. (p. 458)

39. Individualism is a cultural emphasis on personal goals over group goals, and defining one's identity in terms of personal attributes rather than group identifications. (p. 460)

40. Collectivism is a cultural emphasis on the goals of one's group, and defining one's identity accordingly. (p. 460)

Cross-Check

ACROSS	**DOWN**
5. displacement	1. Oedipus
7. individualism	2. trait
13. id	3. empirically derived
16. external	4. gender identity
17. ego	6. learned helplessness
18. regression	8. defense mechanisms
	9. identification
	10. MMPI
	11. preconscious
	12. projective test
	14. personality
	15. Rorschach

FOCUS ON VOCABULARY AND LANGUAGE

Historic Perspectives on Personality

Page 430: Freud's search for a cause for such disorders set his *mind running* . . . Patients came to Freud with strange neurological (*nervous*) disorders which had no obvious physiological explanation. Freud suspected that the problems were psychological in nature, and the questions raised by this theorizing caused him to think (*set his mind running*) in a way that changed the way we view human nature.

Page 430: He [Freud] believed he could *glimpse* the unconscious seeping not only into people's free associations, beliefs, habits, and symptoms but also into their dreams and *slips of the tongue and pen*. Freud used the technique of free association to gain access to the unconscious. He also thought he got a fleeting look at (*glimpse of*) the unconscious in the content of people's dreams and in the inadvertent verbal mistakes we make in speech and writing (*slips of the tongue and pen*).

Page 431: Someone with an exceptionally strong superego may be *virtuous* yet, ironically, guilt-ridden; another with a weak superego may be *wantonly* self-indulgent and remorseless. In Freud's theory, the superego (our conscience) develops when the 4-to-5-year-old child incorporates society's values through identification with the parent of the opposite sex. A person with a well-developed superego may behave in an appropriately moral way (*virtuous*) yet still feel ashamed and anxious (*guilt-ridden*); someone with a poorly developed superego may be excessively and willfully (*wantonly*) selfish and aggressive.

Pages 432–433: . . . *uttering biting sarcasm.* If there are unresolved conflicts at any of the psychosexual stages, the person may become stuck (**fixated**) at that stage, which will directly affect the development of a psychologically healthy personality. People fixated at the oral stage may become very dependent or may pretend to be the opposite by acting strong and independent and by using cruel and destructive humor (*biting sarcasm*) to attack the self-respect of others. In addition, this personality type may have an excessive need for oral gratification (smoking, nail biting, eating, chewing on pens, etc.).

Page 433: In such ways, Freud suggested, the *twig of personality* is *bent* at an early age. Freud believed that adult personality was formed during the first 4 or 5 years of life and was a function of the way the conflicts of the first three psychosexual stages (oral, anal, and phallic) were handled. Just as the shape of the grown tree is the result of how the young tree (*twig*) was twisted (*bent*), adult personality is a function of early childhood experiences.

Page 435: Other clinicians view it [the Rorschach inkblot test] . . . as an *icebreaker* and a revealing interview technique. Because of problems in scoring and interpreting the Rorschach inkblot test, most researchers question its validity and reliability. Some clinicians use the test to help generate hypotheses about the client's problems, and others use it as a point of departure to help get the interview under way (*as an icebreaker*).

Page 437 (margin note): . . . linguistic flip-flops ("spoonerisms"). Professor Spooner became well known because of his habit of inadvertently twisting and distorting his sentences (*linguistic flip-flops*). For example, instead of saying "lighting a fire in the quadrangle," he said "fighting a liar in the quadrangle"; "you missed my history lecture" came out as "you hissed my mystery lecture," and "you have wasted two hours" appeared as "you have tasted two worms." Psychoanalysts call these "slips of the tongue" (Freudian slips) and believe that they represent unconscious motives and desires seeping through.

Page 438: They are *seared onto the soul.* Traumatic events are likely to be remembered very well; they can occur as unwanted, persistent, and intrusive memories (*flashbacks*) that appear often (*they haunt the survivors*). In a sense, they are indelibly impressed in memory (*seared onto the soul*).

Page 438: Psychologists also criticize Freud's theory for its *scientific shortcomings.* In order for a theory to be considered scientifically acceptable, it must be able to explain observations and provide testable hypotheses. Freud's theory fails on this account. In addition, his theory offers explanations only after the events or behaviors have occurred (*after-the-fact explanations*). Freud's theory does not meet acceptable or desired scientific standards (*it has scientific shortcomings*).

Page 438: Freud's most *searing* critic, Frederick Crews (1998) likens Freud to Peter Sellers' *bumbling* Inspector Clouseau, albeit with a unique talent for *bamboozling* an entire century. One very caustic (*searing*) critic compares Freud to the self-important, blundering (*bumbling*) Inspector Clouseau (played by Peter Sellers in the *Pink Panther* movies) but with one difference. In contrast to the incompetent detective, Freud had a remarkable ability (*a unique talent*) for tricking and duping (*bamboozling*) people with his ideas. Others, however, note that it is unfair to criticize Freudian theory for failing to do things it never claimed to be able to do in the first place.

Page 439 (caption): . . . *crippled spirits.* Abraham Maslow, a humanistic psychologist, studied healthy, motivated, creative people and came to the conclusion that once our basic needs are met, we all seek **self-actualization.** He believed that any theory of personality and motivation must be based on more than the study of psychologically impaired individuals (*crippled spirits*); rather, it should also include those who have achieved or fulfilled their innate potential (*self-actualized people*).

Page 440: Unless *thwarted* by an environment that inhibits growth, each of us is like an *acorn, primed* for growth and fulfillment. Carl Rogers was another pioneer in humanistic psychology. We are born with an innate striving (*we are primed*) for achieving our potential and like the seed of the oak tree (*an acorn*) we will grow and develop unless we are blocked (*thwarted*) by an uncaring and unaccepting environment. As Rogers puts it, genuineness, acceptance, and empathy are the water, sun, and nutrients that enable people to grow like vigorous oak trees.

Page 441: Movie plots feature *rugged* individualists . . . Humanistic psychology has been popular because it is consistent with Western cultural values, which emphasize strong, capable (*rugged*) individuals who follow their own beliefs (*are true to themselves*) and actively oppose social norms and restrictions (*buck social conventions or take the law into their own hands*). This popular acceptance of the humanistic movement has elicited a strongly adverse and disapproving reaction (*set off a backlash of criticism*).

Contemporary Research on Personality

Page 443: Flabbergasted . . . This means to be shocked with overwhelming surprise. When Allport interviewed Freud in Vienna, he was astounded and confused (*flabbergasted*) by Freud's mistaken suggestion about the trivial story he told him. In fact, he was simply telling Freud about the events on the bus in order to start the conversation (*conversational gambit*). Nevertheless, it aroused Allport's interest in personality (*started a deep train of thought*), which finally led to his development of a trait theory.

Page 445: Nevertheless, people have had fun *spoofing* the MMPI with their own *mock* items . . . Some items on the MMPI may appear nonsensical (*sound silly*), but they differentiated, say, depressed from nondepressed people, and so were retained in the form. Some authorities have created some humorous but false (*mock*) items for a personality test that is a parody (*spoof*) of the MMPI.

Page 446 (Thinking Critically): . . . *scoff* . . . This means to have a contemptuously mocking attitude toward something. Astronomers who study the universe scientifically *scoff* at astrologers who believe that the planets and stars determine human affairs.

Page 446 (Thinking Critically): . . . *suckering methods* . . . To get suckered means to be easily fooled and exploited. Psychologists, such as Ray Hyman, show us how astrologers, palm (hand) readers, graphologists (who allegedly analyze handwriting to reveal personality), and others fool and exploit people by use of a few simple techniques (*suckering methods*).

Page 446 (Thinking Critically): . . . "*stock spiel*" . . . A "stock spiel" is a well-rehearsed and glib story. Astrologers, horoscope writers, and such often use statements that are generally true of almost everybody (their "stock spiel"), and most people find it hard to resist believing the flattering descriptions of themselves; consequently, many view astrology as an authentic art.

Page 448: A slightly expanded set of factors—*dubbed the Big Five*—does a better job. . . . The Eysencks use two prime personality dimensions, or factors—extraversion–introversion and emotional stability–instability. Other researchers offer another three dimensions (openness, agreeableness, and conscientiousness), bringing the total to five factors, which they named (*dubbed*) the Big Five.

Page 448: . . . *blind date* . . . If a social outing (*a date*) is arranged with a person you have never seen before, this is called a *blind date*. Having the person ranked on the Big Five dimensions would tell you a lot about the person's character and personality.

Page 449: If we remember such results, says Mischel, we will be more cautious about *labeling* and *pigeonholing* individuals. Research has shown that some behavior can be context specific (i.e., determined by the situation and not by the personality) and that personality test scores are poorly correlated with people's actual behavior on any particular occasion. Mischel warns that we should be careful about classifying individuals (*labeling*) and concluding that they belong in one particular slot (*pigeonholing*).

Page 451: If we expect someone to be angry with us, we may give the person a *cold shoulder, touching off* the very anger we expect. The way we are (our personalities) may influence how we are treated by others. If we believe that someone has hostile intentions toward us, we may ignore and treat the person with indifference (*give the person a cold shoulder*), and this in turn may cause (*touch off*) the angry behavior we predicted or expected from that person. As Myers notes, we are both the results (*products*) and the creators (*architects*) of our environments.

Page 452: Later placed in another situation where they *could* escape the punishment by simply *leaping a hurdle,* the dogs cowered as if without hope. In Seligman's experiments, dogs learned that nothing they did had any effect on what happened to them (**learned helplessness**), so they would not make even a minimal effort, such as jumping over a small barrier (*leaping a hurdle*), to escape being shocked. People, too, who feel they have no control over what happens to them may become depressed and feel hopeless and helpless.

Page 453: Those who *put an optimistic spin on their setbacks*—seeing them as *flukes* or as a means to learning a new approach, rather than viewing them as signs of incompetence—. . . . People who view unwelcome reversals of fortune (*setbacks*) as just pure chance (*flukes*) or see them as challenges and as an opportunity to try something different (*put an optimistic spin on them*) are more likely to be successful and content. As Myers points out, positive thinking when confronted by problems (*in the face of adversity*) has many benefits (*pays dividends*).

Page 453: . . . *bombing* the upcoming exam . . . Students who are excessively optimistic and overconfident may not do as well as those who are concerned about failing (*bombing*) the exam and therefore study extremely hard. Extreme optimism may prevent us from becoming aware of potential hazards (*blind us to real risks*).

Page 455: . . . so many low-scoring students are *dumbfounded* after doing badly on an exam. People often are most overconfident when most incompetent, mainly because it is difficult for them to recognize incompetence without having competence in the first place. Consequently, many students who do not recognize that they are having problems are often astounded (*dumbfounded*) when they find they are not in the top half of the class. (As Myers notes, like pride, illusory or blind optimism may precede a negative outcome or fall.)

Page 458: Those who are *negative about themselves* also tend to be *thin-skinned* and *judgmental*. . . . People who have low self-esteem (*are negative about themselves*) are more likely to be anxious, depressed, insecure, and very sensitive to criticism (*thin-skinned*). In addition, they are also more likely to disparage and be critical (*judgmental*) of others.

Page 458: Athletes often privately credit their victories to their own *prowess* and their losses to *bad breaks, lousy officiating,* or the other team's exceptional performance. Athletes, like the rest of us, want to feel that desirable outcomes are due to their own abilities (*prowess*) and that failures are due to factors beyond their control such as poor luck (*bad breaks*), unfair refereeing (*lousy officiating*), or their opponents' unexpectedly outstanding efforts. This is called the **self-serving bias**.

Page 459: The world, it seems, is Garrison Keillor's *Lake Wobegon* writ large—a place where "all the women are strong, all the men are good-looking, and all the children are above average." Lake Wobegon is a fictional but ideal community satirized by comedian Garrison Keillor. Most abilities follow a bell-shaped distribution (the normal curve), so approximately half the population will be below average and half above on any given trait, such as strength, looks, or intelligence. The self-serving bias, which prompts most of us to rate ourselves as above average, appears to be almost universal, and the world is a magnified reflection of the Lake Wobegon community.

Page 459: Moreover, *pride does often go before a fall.* Our conceit and self-important attitudes (*pride*) often precede a harsh lesson from reality (*a fall*). Myers notes that it was national self-righteousness that led both sides in the cold war (Americans and Soviets) to perceive their own stockpiling of weapons of mass destruction (the arms race) as defensive, but to perceive the other side's accumulation of the same types of weapons as aggressive and threatening. Thus, excessive national pride on both sides could have led to the destruction of the planet.

Page 460: Someone with a *swelled head* that gets deflated by insult or rejection is potentially dangerous. Overly self-confident people with high self-esteem (*swelled heads or large egos*) do more than retaliate in kind (*put others down*) when criticized, insulted, or rejected. Instead, they are more likely to react violently and aggressively (they are potentially dangerous). Researchers suggest that this negative aspect (*dark side*) of self-esteem is the result of threatened egotism and not low self-esteem.

Page 460: Sometimes self-directed *put-downs* are subtly strategic: They *elicit* reassuring *strokes*. When people disparage themselves with criticisms aimed at themselves (*self-directed put-downs*), they sometimes have an insidious or hidden purpose (*are subtly strategic*). They may want to have people reassure them that the opposite is true (*they want strokes*), or they may want to prepare for the worst possible outcome and have a rationalization for failure ready, just in case.

Page 462: . . . *lose face.* This means public disgrace or injury to one's pride or self-esteem. In collectivist cultures, people observe the rules (*norms*) that emphasize pleasant and nonconfrontational relationships. In order to maintain group cohesion, they avoid publicly embarrassing others (they make sure others never *lose face*), do not bring up sensitive issues, give way to others' opinions, and show proper respect to those who are older and those who are in charge. Happiness is being concerned with and sensitive (*attuned*) to others.

chapter 13

Psychological Disorders

Chapter Overview

Although there is no clear-cut line between normal and abnormal behavior, we can characterize as abnormal those behaviors that are atypical, disturbing, maladaptive, and unjustifiable. Chapter 13 discusses types of anxiety, dissociative disorders, personality disorders, mood disorders, and schizophrenia, as classified by the *Diagnostic and Statistical Manual of Mental Disorders* (DSM-IV). Although this classification system follows a medical model, in which disorders are viewed as illnesses, the chapter discusses psychological as well as physiological factors, as advocated by the current bio-psycho-social perspective. Thus, psychoanalytic theory, learning theory, social-cognitive theory, and other psychological perspectives are drawn on when relevant. The chapter concludes with a discussion of the incidence of serious psychological disorders in society today.

Your major task in this chapter is to learn about psychological disorders, their various subtypes and characteristics, and their possible causes. Since the material to be learned is extensive, it may be helpful to rehearse it by mentally completing the fill-in questions several times.

NOTE: Answer guidelines for all Chapter 13 questions begin on page 393.

Perspectives on Psychological Disorders
(pp. 470–476)

> David Myers at times uses idioms that are unfamiliar to some readers. If you do not know the meaning of any of the following words, phrases, or expressions in the context in which they appear in the text, refer to page 402 for an explanation: *eerie sense of self-recognition; draw the line; "The devil made him do it"; handy shorthand; fault the manual; "Hinckley Insane, Public Mad"; self-fulfilling prophecies.*

Section Preview

First, skim the section, noting headings and boldface items. Then read the following objectives and, as you read the text, search for the information that will enable you to meet each objective. Answer guidelines begin on page 393.

1. List the criteria for judging whether behavior is disordered.

2. Explain and contrast two perspectives on psychological disorders.

3. Describe the system used to classify psychological disorders, and explain the reasons for its development.

4. Discuss the controversy surrounding the use of diagnostic labels.

Stepping Through the Section

After you have read the section, complete the sentences and answer the questions. As you proceed, evaluate your performance by consulting the answers on page 394. Do not continue with the next section until you understand each answer. If you need to, review or reread the section in the textbook before continuing.

1. Psychological disorders are _____ _____ that must be judged to be _____ , _____ , _____ , and _____ . This definition emphasizes that standards of acceptability for behavior are _____ (constant/variable).

2. The view that psychological disorders are sicknesses is the basis of the _____ model. According to this view, psychological disorders are viewed as mental _____ , or _____ .

3. One of the first reformers to advocate this position and call for providing more humane living conditions for the mentally ill was _____ .

4. Today's psychologists recognize that all behavior arises from the interaction of _____ and _____ . To presume that a person is "mentally ill" attributes the condition solely to an _____ problem.

5. Major psychological disorders such as _____ and _____ are universal; others, such as _____ _____ and _____ , are culture-bound. These culture-bound disorders may share an underlying _____ , such as _____ , yet differ in their _____ .

6. Most mental health workers today work from the _____-_____-_____ perspective, which assumes that disorders are influenced by _____ _____ and _____ _____ , inner _____ _____ , and _____ and _____ circumstances.

7. The most widely used system for classifying psychological disorders is the American Psychiatric Association manual, commonly known by its abbreviation, _____ . This manual defines _____ (how many?) disorder categories.

8. Independent diagnoses made with the current manual generally _____ (show/do not show) agreement.

9. One criticism of DSM-IV is that as the number of disorder categories has _____ (increased/decreased), the number of adults who meet the criteria for at least one psychiatric ailment has _____ (increased/decreased).

(Close-Up) Briefly describe the "unDSM."

10. Studies have shown that labeling has
_____ (little/a significant) effect
on our interpretation of individuals and their
behavior.

Outline the pros and cons of labeling psychological
disorders.

Anxiety Disorders (pp. 476–482)

> If you do not know the meaning of any of the
> following words, phrases, or expressions in the
> context in which they appear in the text, refer
> to page 402 for an explanation: *heart palpita-*
> *tions . . . ringing in the ears . . . fidgeting; flash-*
> *backs and nightmares; Grooming gone wild.*

Section Preview

Answer guidelines are provided on page 394.

1. Describe the various anxiety disorders.

2. Discuss anxiety disorders from the psychoanalytic, learning, and biological perspectives.

Stepping Through the Section

Answers are provided on page 394.

1. When a person tends to feel anxious for no apparent reason, he or she is diagnosed as suffering
   from a _____
   _____ disorder.

2. In generalized anxiety disorder, the body reacts
   physiologically with the arousal of the
   _____ nervous system. In some
   instances, anxiety may intensify dramatically and
   be accompanied by trembling or dizziness; people with these symptoms are said to have

   _____ _____ .

3. People who fear situations in which escape or
   help might not be possible when panic strikes
   suffer from _____ .

4. When a person has an irrational fear of a specific
   object, activity, or situation, the diagnosis is a
   _____ . Although in many situa-
   tions, the person can live with the problem, some

   _____ _____ ,

   such as a fear of thunderstorms, are
   incapacitating.

5. When a person has an intense fear of being scrutinized by others, the diagnosis is a

   _____ _____ .

6. When a person cannot control repetitive thoughts
   and actions, an _____-
   _____ disorder is diagnosed.
   Older people are _____
   (more/less) likely than teens and young adults to
   suffer from this disorder.

7. Freud assumed that anxiety disorders are symptoms of submerged mental energy that derives
   from intolerable impulses that were
   _____ during childhood.

8. Learning theorists, drawing on research in which
   rats are given unpredictable shocks, link general
   anxiety with _____ conditioning
   of _____ .

9. Some fears arise from _____ _____ , such as when a person who fears heights after a fall also comes to fear airplanes.

10. Phobias and compulsive behaviors reduce anxiety and thereby are _____ . Through _____ learning, someone might also learn fear by seeing others display their own fears.

11. Humans probably _____ (are/are not) biologically prepared to develop certain fears. Compulsive acts typically are exaggerations of behaviors that contributed to our species' _____ .

12. The anxiety response probably _____ (is/is not) genetically influenced.

13. PET scans of persons with obsessive-compulsive disorder reveal excessive activity in a region of the _____ lobes. Some antidepressant drugs dampen fear-circuit activity in the _____ , thus reducing this behavior.

14. (Close-Up)) Traumatic stress, such as that associated with witnessing atrocities or combat, can produce _____-_____ _____ disorder, symptoms of which include _____ _____ .

   Despite such symptoms, some psychologists believe this disorder is _____ .

Dissociative and Personality Disorders
(pp. 482–486)

> If you do not know the meaning of any of the following words, phrases, or expressions in the context in which they appear in the text, refer to page 403 for an explanation: *a ruse; go fishing for multiple personalities; con artist; woven of biological as well as psychological strands.*

Section Preview

Answer guidelines begin on page 394.

1. Describe the nature and possible causes of dissociative disorders.

2. Describe the nature and causes of personality disorders and the specific characteristics of the antisocial personality disorder.

Stepping Through the Section

Answers are provided on page 395.

1. In _____ disorders, a person's _____ _____ becomes separated from painful memories, thoughts, and feelings.

2. A person who develops two or more distinct personalities is suffering from _____ _____ disorder.

3. Nicholas Spanos has argued that such people may merely be playing different _____ .

4. Those who accept this as a genuine disorder point to evidence that differing personalities may be associated with distinct _____ and _____ states.

Identify two pieces of evidence brought forth by those who do not accept dissociative identity disorder as a genuine disorder.

5. The psychoanalytic and learning perspectives view dissociative disorders as ways of dealing with _____ . Others view them as a protective response to histories of

_____ _____ .

Skeptics claim these disorders are sometimes contrived by _____-_____ people, and sometimes constructed out of the _____-_____ interaction.

6. Personality disorders exist when an individual has character traits that are enduring and impair

_____ _____ .

7. An individual who seems to have no conscience; lies, steals, is generally irresponsible; and may be criminal is said to have an _____ personality. Previously, this person was labeled a

_____ .

8. When awaiting electric shocks, antisocial persons show _____ (little/some/much) arousal of the autonomic nervous system.

9. Some studies have detected early signs of antisocial behavior in children as young as

_____ . Antisocial adolescents tended to have been _____ , _____ , unconcerned with

_____ _____ , and low in _____ .

10. PET scans of murderers' brains reveal reduced activity in the _____

_____ .

11. As in other disorders, in antisocial personality, genetics _____ (is/is not) the whole story.

Mood Disorders (pp. 486–496)

If you do not know the meaning of any of the following words, phrases, or expressions in the context in which they appear in the text, refer to page 403 for an explanation: *To grind temporarily to a halt; blue mood; slow motion . . . fast forward; view life through dark glasses; two-way traffic.*

Section Preview

Answer guidelines are provided on page 395.

1. Describe two principal mood disorders.

2. Discuss the alternative explanations of mood disorders.

Stepping Through the Section

Answers begin on page 395.

1. The leading cause of disability worldwide is _____ . The experience of prolonged depression with no discernible cause is called _____ _____ disorder.

2. When a person's mood alternates between depression and the hyperactive state of
_____ , a
_____ disorder is diagnosed.

3. Although _____ are more common, _____ is the number one reason that people seek mental health services.

4. The possible signs of depression include
_____
_____ .

5. Major depression occurs when its signs last
_____ _____ or
more with no apparent cause.

6. Depressed persons usually _____
(can/cannot) recover without therapy.

7. Symptoms of mania include _____
_____ .
The bipolar disorder occurs in approximately
_____ percent of men and
women.

8. Compared with men, women are _____
(more/less) vulnerable to major depression. In general, women are most vulnerable to
_____ (active/passive) disorders, such as _____
_____ .
Men's disorders tend to be _____
(active/passive) and include _____
_____ .

9. It usually _____ (is/is not) the case that a depressive episode has been triggered by a stressful event. An individual's vulnerability to depression also increases following the early
_____ .

10. With each new generation, the rate of depression is _____ (increasing/decreasing) and the disorder is striking _____
(earlier/later).

11. In North America today, young adults are
_____ times (how many?) as
likely as their grandparents to suffer depression.

State the psychoanalytic explanation of depression.

12. Mood disorders _____
(tend/do not tend) to run in families. Studies of
_____ also reveal that genetic influences on mood disorders are
_____ (weak/strong).

13. To determine which genes are involved in depression, researchers use
_____ _____ , in
which they examine the _____
of both affected and unaffected family members.

14. Depression may also be caused by
_____ (high/low) levels of two neurotransmitters, _____ and
_____ .

15. Drugs that alleviate mania reduce
_____ ; drugs that relieve depression increase _____ or
_____ supplies by blocking either their _____ or their
chemical _____ .

16. The brains of depressed people tend to be
_____ (more/less) active, especially in an area of the _____
_____ lobe of the brain. In severely depressed patients, this brain area may also be _____ (smaller/larger) in size. The brain's _____ , which is important in processing _____ , is vulnerable to stress-related damage. Antidepressant drugs that boost
_____ may promote recovery by stimulating neurons in this area of the brain.

(Close-Up) Identify several group differences in suicide rates.

17. According to the social-cognitive perspective, depression may be linked with beliefs that are _____ . Such beliefs may arise from _____ _____ , the feeling that can arise when the individual repeatedly experiences uncontrollable, painful events.

18. Gender differences in _____ _____ help explain why women have been twice as vulnerable to depression.

Describe how depressed people differ from others in their explanations of failure and how such explanations tend to feed depression.

19. Research studies suggest that depressing thoughts usually _____ (precede/follow/coincide with) a depressed mood.

20. Depression-prone people respond to bad events in an especially _____ , _____ way.

21. Research studies with college students reveal that _____ thinkers are vulnerable to depression. Students who exhibit _____ develop more _____ _____ , which lowers their risk of depression.

22. Being withdrawn, self-focused, and complaining tends to elicit social _____ (empathy/rejection).

23. (Close-Up) People commonly experience one of four types of loneliness: feeling _____ from a group, feeling _____ and uncared about by those around you, feeling _____ and unable to share your private concerns, or feeling _____ , or different.

Outline the vicious cycle of depression.

Schizophrenia (pp. 496–501)

> If you do not know the meaning of any of the following words, phrases, or expressions in the context in which they appear in the text, refer to pages 403–404 for an explanation: *hodge-podge; flat affect; traffic . . . runs both ways.*

Section Preview

Answer guidelines are provided on page 396.

1. Describe the symptoms and types of schizophrenia.

2. Discuss research on the causes of schizophrenia.

Stepping Through the Section

Answers are provided on page 396.

1. Schizophrenia, or "split mind," refers not to a split personality but rather to a split from

   _____ .

2. Three manifestations of schizophrenia are disorganized _____ , disturbed _____ , and inappropriate _____ and _____ .

3. The distorted, false beliefs of schizophrenia patients are called _____ .

4. Many psychologists attribute the disorganized thinking of schizophrenia to a breakdown in the capacity for _____

   _____ .

5. The disturbed perceptions of people suffering from schizophrenia may take the form of _____ , which usually are _____ (visual/auditory).

6. Some victims of schizophrenia lapse into a zombielike state of apparent apathy, or

   _____ _____ ; others, who exhibit _____ , may remain motionless for hours.

7. The term *schizophrenia* describes a _____ (single disorder/cluster of disorders).

8. Positive symptoms of schizophrenia include

   _____

   _____ .

   Negative symptoms include

   _____

   _____ .

9. When schizophrenia develops slowly (called _____ schizophrenia), recovery is _____ (more/less) likely than when it develops rapidly in reaction to particular life stresses (called _____ schizophrenia).

10. The brain tissue of schizophrenia patients has been found to have an excess of receptors for the neurotransmitter _____ . Drugs that block these receptors have been found to

_____ (increase/decrease) schizophrenia symptoms.

11. Brain scans have shown that many people suffering from schizophrenia have abnormal patterns of brain _____ in the frontal lobes.

12. Enlarged, _____-filled areas and a corresponding _____ of cerebral tissue are also characteristic of schizophrenia. Schizophrenia patients also have a smaller-than-normal _____ , which may account for their difficulty in filtering

   _____ _____

   and focusing _____ .

13. Some scientists contend that the brain abnormalities of schizophrenia may be caused by a prenatal problem, such as _____

   _____ _____ ,

   birth complications such as _____

   _____ , or a

   _____ _____

   contracted by the mother.

List several pieces of evidence for this theory.

14. Twin and adoptive studies _____ (support/do not support) the contention that heredity plays a role in schizophrenia.

15. The role of the prenatal environment in schizophrenia is demonstrated by the fact that identical twins who share the same _____ , and are therefore more likely to experience the same prenatal _____ , are more likely to share the disorder.

16. Although adoption studies _____ (do/do not) confirm the genetic link, other factors such as prenatal viral infections and deprivation of _____ or _____ at birth may also be factors in the disease.

17. It appears that for schizophrenia to develop there must be both a _____ predisposition and some _____ trigger.

Rates of Psychological Disorders
(pp. 501–502)

Section Preview

Answer guidelines begin on page 396.

1. Briefly discuss the prevalence of psychological disorders.

Stepping Through the Section

Answers are provided on page 397.

1. Research reveals that approximately 1 in every _____ (how many?) Americans suffers clinically significant mental disorders.

2. The incidence of serious psychological disorders is _____ (higher/lower) among those below the poverty line.

3. In terms of age of onset, most psychological disorders appear by _____ (early/middle/late) adulthood. Some, such as the _____ _____ and _____ , appear during childhood.

Progress Test 1

Multiple-Choice Questions

Circle your answers to the following questions and check them with the answers beginning on page 397. If your answer is incorrect, read the explanation for why it is incorrect and then consult the appropriate pages of the text (in parentheses following the correct answer).

1. Gender differences in the prevalence of depression may be partly due to the fact that when stressful experiences occur, women tend to _____ while men tend to _____ .
   a. act; think
   b. think; act

   c. distract themselves by drinking; delve into their work
   d. delve into their work; distract themselves by drinking

2. The criteria for classifying behavior as psychologically disordered:
   a. vary from culture to culture.
   b. vary from time to time.
   c. are characterized by both a. and b.
   d. have remained largely unchanged over the course of history.

3. Most mental health workers today take the view that disordered behaviors:
   a. are usually genetically triggered.
   b. are organic diseases.
   c. arise from the interaction of nature and nurture.
   d. are the product of learning.

4. The French reformer who insisted that madness was not demon possession and who called for humane treatment of patients was:
   a. Nadel.   d. Spanos.
   b. Freud.   e. Pinel.
   c. Szasz.

5. Which of the following is the most pervasive of the psychological disorders?
   a. depression
   b. schizophrenia
   c. bipolar disorder
   d. generalized anxiety disorder

6. Which of the following is *not* true concerning depression?
   a. Depression is more common in females than in males.
   b. Most depressive episodes appear not to be preceded by any particular factor or event.
   c. Most depressive episodes last less than three months.
   d. Most people recover from depression without professional therapy.

7. Which of the following is *not* true regarding schizophrenia?
   a. It occurs more frequently in people born in winter and spring months.
   b. It occurs less frequently as infectious disease rates have declined.
   c. It occurs more frequently in lightly populated areas.
   d. It usually appears during adolescence or early adulthood.

8. Evidence of environmental effects on psychological disorders is seen in the fact that certain disorders, such as _____ , are universal, whereas others, such as _____ , are culture-bound.
   a. schizophrenia; depression
   b. depression; schizophrenia
   c. antisocial personality; neurosis
   d. depression; anorexia nervosa

9. The effect of drugs that block receptors for dopamine is to:
   a. alleviate schizophrenia symptoms.
   b. alleviate depression.
   c. increase schizophrenia symptoms.
   d. increase depression.

10. The diagnostic reliability of DSM-IV:
    a. is unknown.
    b. depends on the age of the patient.
    c. is very low.
    d. is relatively high.

11. What have researchers concluded regarding the question of whether stress can trigger schizophrenia?
    a. Schizophrenia is caused by genes, not stress.
    b. Schizophrenia can definitely be triggered by extreme stress alone.
    c. Stress may trigger schizophrenia in people who are genetically predisposed to develop the disorder.
    d. Researchers have been unable to predict the development of schizophrenia.

12. (Thinking Critically) The term *insanity* refers to:
    a. legal definitions.
    b. psychotic disorders only.
    c. personality disorders only.
    d. both psychotic disorders and personality disorders.

13. Phobias and obsessive-compulsive behaviors are classified as:
    a. anxiety disorders.
    b. mood disorders.
    c. dissociative disorders.
    d. personality disorders.

14. According to the social-cognitive perspective, a person who experiences unexpected aversive events may develop helplessness and manifest a(n):
    a. obsessive-compulsive disorder.
    b. dissociative disorder.
    c. personality disorder.
    d. mood disorder.

15. Which of the following was presented in the text as evidence of biological influences on anxiety disorders?
    a. Identical twins often develop similar phobias.
    b. PET scans of persons with obsessive-compulsive disorder reveal unusually high activity in an area of the frontal lobes.
    c. Drugs that dampen fear-circuit activity in the amygdala also alleviate OCD.
    d. All of the above were presented.
    e. None of the above was presented.

16. Most of the hallucinations of schizophrenia patients involve the sense of:
    a. smell.   c. hearing.
    b. vision.   d. touch.

17. When expecting to be electrically shocked, people with an antisocial disorder, as compared to normal people, show:
    a. less fear and greater arousal of the autonomic nervous system.
    b. less fear and less autonomic arousal.
    c. greater fear and greater autonomic arousal.
    d. greater fear and less autonomic arousal.

18. Hearing voices would be a(n) _____ ; believing that you are Napoleon would be a(n) _____ .
    a. obsession; compulsion
    b. compulsion; obsession
    c. delusion; hallucination
    d. hallucination; delusion

19. In treating depression, a psychiatrist would probably prescribe a drug that would:
    a. increase levels of acetylcholine.
    b. decrease levels of dopamine.
    c. increase levels of norepinephrine.
    d. decrease levels of serotonin.

20. When schizophrenia is slow to develop, called _____ schizophrenia, recovery is _____ .
    a. reactive; unlikely   c. process; unlikely
    b. process; likely   d. reactive; likely

Matching Items

Match each term with the appropriate definition or description.

Terms

_____ **1.** dissociative disorder
_____ **2.** paranoid
_____ **3.** mood disorders
_____ **4.** social phobia
_____ **5.** catatonic
_____ **6.** mania
_____ **7.** obsessive-compulsive disorder
_____ **8.** schizophrenia
_____ **9.** hallucination
_____ **10.** panic attack

Definitions or Descriptions

a. psychological disorders marked by emotional extremes
b. an extremely elevated mood
c. a false sensory experience
d. subtype of schizophrenia associated with a preoccupation with delusions or hallucinations
e. a sudden escalation of anxiety often accompanied by a sensation of choking or other physical symptoms
f. a disorder in which conscious awareness becomes separated from previous memories, feelings, and thoughts
g. subtype of schizophrenia associated with immobility or excessive, purposeless movement
h. intense fear of being scrutinized by others
i. a group of disorders marked by disorganized thinking, disturbed perceptions, and inappropriate emotions and actions
j. a disorder characterized by repetitive thoughts and actions

Progress Test 2

Progress Test 2 should be completed during a final chapter review. Answer the following questions after you thoroughly understand the correct answers for the Chapter Review and Progress Test 1.

Multiple-Choice Questions

1. Which of the following is true concerning abnormal behavior?
   a. Definitions of abnormal behavior are culture-dependent.
   b. A behavior cannot be defined as abnormal unless it is considered harmful to society.
   c. Abnormal behavior can be defined as any behavior that is atypical.
   d. Definitions of abnormal behavior are based on physiological factors.

2. The psychoanalytic perspective would most likely view phobias as:
   a. conditioned fears.
   b. displaced responses to incompletely repressed impulses.
   c. biological predispositions.
   d. manifestations of self-defeating thoughts.

3. Many psychologists believe the disorganized thoughts of people with schizophrenia result from a breakdown in:
   a. selective attention.   **d.** memory retrieval.
   b. memory storage.   **e.** memory encoding.
   c. motivation.

4. Research evidence links the brain abnormalities of schizophrenia to _____ during prenatal development.
   a. maternal stress
   b. a viral infection contracted
   c. abnormal levels of certain hormones
   d. the weight of the unborn child
   e. alcohol use

5. The fact that disorders such as schizophrenia are universal and influenced by heredity, whereas other disorders such as anorexia nervosa are culture-bound provides evidence for the _____ model of psychological disorders.
   a. medical   **c.** social-cultural
   b. bio-psycho-social   **d.** psychoanalytic

6. Our early ancestors commonly attributed disordered behavior to:
   a. "bad blood."   **c.** brain injury.
   b. evil spirits.   **d.** laziness.

7. In general, women are more vulnerable than men to _____ disorders such as _____ .
   a. active; anxiety
   b. passive; depression
   c. active; antisocial conduct
   d. passive; alcohol abuse

8. Which of the following statements concerning the labeling of disordered behaviors is *not* true?
   a. Labels interfere with effective treatment of psychological disorders.
   b. Labels promote research studies of psychological disorders.
   c. Labels may create preconceptions that bias people's perceptions.
   d. Labels may influence behavior by creating self-fulfilling prophecies.

9. Nicholas Spanos considers dissociative identity disorder to be:
   a. a genuine disorder.
   b. merely role playing.
   c. a disorder that cannot be explained according to the learning perspective.
   d. both a. and c.

10. Which neurotransmitter is present in overabundant amounts during the manic phase of bipolar disorder?
    a. dopamine   c. epinephrine
    b. serotonin   d. norepinephrine

11. After falling from a ladder, Joseph is afraid of airplanes, although he has never flown. This demonstrates that some fears arise from:
    a. observational learning.
    b. reinforcement.
    c. stimulus generalization.
    d. stimulus discrimination.

12. Which of the following provides evidence that human fears have been subjected to the evolutionary process?
    a. Compulsive acts typically exaggerate behaviors that contributed to our species' survival.
    b. Most phobias focus on objects that our ancestors also feared.
    c. It is easier to condition some fears than others.
    d. All of the above provide evidence.

13. Which of the following is true of the medical model?
    a. In recent years, it has been in large part discredited.
    b. It views psychological disorders as sicknesses that are diagnosable and treatable.

    c. It emphasizes the role of psychological factors in disorders over that of physiological factors.
    d. It focuses on cognitive factors.

14. Psychoanalytic and learning theorists both agree that dissociative and anxiety disorders are symptoms that represent the person's attempt to deal with:
    a. unconscious conflicts.
    b. anxiety.
    c. unfulfilled wishes.
    d. unpleasant responsibilities.

15. Behavior is classified as disordered when it is:
    a. atypical.   d. disturbing.
    b. maladaptive.   e. all of the above.
    c. unjustifiable.

16. Many psychologists dislike using DSM-IV because of its:
    a. failure to emphasize observable behaviors in the diagnostic process.
    b. learning theory bias.
    c. medical model bias.
    d. psychoanalytic bias.
    e. social-cultural bias.

17. Which of the following is *not* a symptom of schizophrenia?
    a. inappropriate emotions
    b. disturbed perceptions
    c. panic attacks
    d. disorganized thinking

18. Social-cognitive theorists contend that depression is linked with:
    a. negative moods.
    b. maladaptive explanations of failure.
    c. self-defeating beliefs.
    d. all of the above.

19. According to psychoanalytic theory, memory of losses, especially in combination with internalized anger, is likely to result in:
    a. learned helplessness.
    b. the self-serving bias.
    c. weak ego defense mechanisms.
    d. depression.

20. Among the following, which is generally accepted as a possible cause of schizophrenia?
    a. an excess of endorphins in the brain
    b. being a twin
    c. extensive learned helplessness
    d. a genetic predisposition

Matching Items

Match each term with the appropriate definition or description.

Terms

_____ 1. dissociative identity disorder
_____ 2. phobia
_____ 3. dopamine
_____ 4. post-traumatic stress disorder
_____ 5. antisocial personality
_____ 6. norepinephrine
_____ 7. serotonin
_____ 8. bipolar disorder
_____ 9. delusions
_____ 10. agoraphobia

Definitions or Descriptions

a. a neurotransmitter for which there are excess receptors in some schizophrenia patients
b. a neurotransmitter that is overabundant during mania and scarce during depression
c. an individual who seems to have no conscience
d. false beliefs that may accompany psychological disorders
e. an anxiety disorder marked by a persistent, irrational fear of a specific object or situation
f. a disorder formerly called multiple personality disorder
g. a neurotransmitter possibly linked to obsessive-compulsive behavior
h. a type of mood disorder
i. a disorder marked by haunting memories and numbed social withdrawal
j. a fear of situations in which help might not be available during a panic attack

Review and Reflect

Answer these questions the day before an exam as a final check on your understanding of the chapter's terms and concepts.

Multiple-Choice Questions

1. Joe has an intense, irrational fear of snakes. He is suffering from a(n):
   a. generalized anxiety disorder.
   b. obsessive-compulsive disorder.
   c. phobia.
   d. mood disorder.
   e. bipolar disorder.

2. As a child, Monica was criticized severely by her mother for not living up to her expectations. This criticism was always followed by a beating with a whip. As an adult, Monica is generally introverted and extremely shy. Sometimes, however, she acts more like a young child, throwing tantrums if she doesn't get her way. At other times, she is a flirting, happy-go-lucky young lady. Most likely, Monica is suffering from:
   a. a phobia.
   b. dissociative schizophrenia.
   c. dissociative identity disorder.
   d. bipolar disorder.

3. Bob has never been able to keep a job. He's been in and out of jail for charges such as theft, sexual assault, and spousal abuse. Bob would most likely be diagnosed as having:
   a. a dissociative identity disorder.
   b. major depressive disorder.
   c. schizophrenia.
   d. an antisocial personality.

4. Julia's psychologist believes that Julia's fear of heights can be traced to a conditioned fear she developed after falling from a ladder. This explanation reflects a _____ perspective.
   a. medical   c. social-cognitive
   b. psychoanalytic   d. learning

5. Before he can study, Rashid must arrange his books, pencils, paper, and other items on his desk so that they are "just so." The campus counselor suggests that Rashid's compulsive behavior may help alleviate his anxiety about failing in school, which reinforces the compulsive actions. This explanation of obsessive-compulsive behavior is most consistent with which perspective?
   a. learning   c. humanistic
   b. psychoanalytic   d. social-cognitive

6. Sharon is continually tense, jittery, and apprehensive for no specific reason. She would probably be diagnosed as suffering a(n):

   a. phobia.
   b. major depressive disorder.
   c. obsessive-compulsive disorder.
   d. generalized anxiety disorder.

7. Jason is so preoccupied with staying clean that he showers as many as 10 times each day. Jason would be diagnosed as suffering from a(n):

   a. dissociative disorder.
   b. generalized anxiety disorder.
   c. personality disorder.
   d. obsessive-compulsive disorder.

8. (Close-Up) Although she escaped from war-torn Bosnia two years ago, Zheina still has haunting memories and nightmares. Because she is also severely depressed, her therapist diagnoses her condition as:

   a. dissociative identity disorder.
   b. bipolar disorder.
   c. schizophrenia.
   d. post-traumatic stress disorder.

9. Claiming that she heard a voice commanding her to warn other people that eating is harmful, Sandy attempts to convince others in a restaurant not to eat. The psychiatrist to whom she is referred finds that Sandy's thinking and speech are often fragmented and incoherent. In addition, Sandy has an unreasonable fear that someone is "out to get her" and consequently trusts no one. Her condition is most indicative of:

   a. schizophrenia.
   b. generalized anxiety disorder.
   c. a phobia.
   d. obsessive-compulsive disorder.
   e. personality disorder.

10. Irene occasionally experiences unpredictable episodes of intense dread accompanied by chest pains and a sensation of smothering. Since her symptoms have no apparent cause, they would probably be classified as indicative of:

    a. schizophrenia.
    b. bipolar disorder.
    c. post-traumatic stress disorder.
    d. panic attack.

11. To which of the following is a person *most* likely to acquire a phobia?

    a. heights
    b. being in public
    c. being dirty
    d. All of the above are equally likely.

12. Dr. Jekyll, whose second personality was Mr. Hyde, had a(n) _____ disorder.

    a. anxiety   c. mood
    b. dissociative   d. personality

13. For the past six months, a woman has complained of feeling isolated from others, dissatisfied with life, and discouraged about the future. This woman could be diagnosed as suffering from:

    a. bipolar disorder.
    b. major depressive disorder.
    c. generalized anxiety disorder.
    d. dissociative disorder.

14. On Monday, Matt felt optimistic, energetic, and on top of the world. On Tuesday, he felt hopeless and lethargic, and thought that the future looked very grim. Matt would *most* likely be diagnosed as having:

    a. bipolar disorder.
    b. major depressive disorder.
    c. schizophrenia.
    d. panic disorder.

15. Connie's therapist has suggested that her depression stems from unresolved anger toward her parents. Evidently, Connie's therapist is working within the _____ perspective.

    a. learning   c. biological
    b. social-cognitive d. psychoanalytic

16. Ken's therapist suggested that his depression is a result of his self-defeating thoughts and negative assumptions about himself, his situation, and his future. Evidently, Ken's therapist is working within the _____ perspective.

    a. learning   c. biological
    b. social-cognitive d. psychoanalytic

17. Alicia's doctor, who thinks that Alicia's depression has a biochemical cause, prescribes a drug that:

    a. reduces norepinephrine.
    b. increases norepinephrine.
    c. reduces serotonin.
    d. increases acetylcholine.

18. Wayne's doctor attempts to help Wayne by prescribing a drug that blocks receptors for dopamine. Wayne has apparently been diagnosed with:

    a. a mood disorder.
    b. an anxiety disorder.
    c. a personality disorder.
    d. schizophrenia.

19. (Close-up) Hussein, who suffers from chronic loneliness, probably attributes his unsatisfactory social relationships to:
    a. an inherited trait.
    b. his own inadequacies.
    c. a cultural norm.
    d. the social incompetence of other people.

20. Janet, whose class presentation is titled "Current Views on the Causes of Schizophrenia," concludes her talk with the statement:
    a. "Schizophrenia is caused by intolerable stress."
    b. "Schizophrenia is inherited."
    c. "Genes may predispose some people to react to particular experiences by developing schizophrenia."
    d. "As of this date, schizophrenia is completely unpredictable and its causes are unknown."

Essay Question

Clinical psychologists label people disordered if their behavior is (1) atypical, (2) disturbing, (3) maladaptive, and (4) unjustifiable. Demonstrate your understanding of the classification process by giving examples of behaviors that might be considered atypical, disturbing, maladaptive, or unjustifiable but, because they do not fit all four criteria, would not necessarily be labeled disordered. (Use the space below to list the points you want to make, and organize them. Then write the essay on a separate piece of paper.)

Key Terms

Writing Definitions

Using your own words, on a separate piece of paper write a brief definition or explanation of each of the following terms.

1. psychological disorder

2. medical model

3. bio-psycho-social perspective

4. DSM-IV

5. anxiety disorders

6. generalized anxiety disorder

7. panic disorder

8. phobia

9. obsessive-compulsive disorder

10. dissociative disorders

11. dissociative identity disorder

12. personality disorders

13. antisocial personality disorder

14. mood disorders

15. major depressive disorder

16. manic episode

17. bipolar disorder

18. schizophrenia

19. delusions

Cross-Check

As you learned in Chapter 1, review-ing and overlearning of material are important to the learning process. After you have written the defini-tions of the key terms in this chapter, you should complete the crossword puzzle to ensure that you can reverse the process—recognize the term, given the definition.

ACROSS

1. Category of schizophrenia symptoms that includes halluci-nations, delusions, and disorga-nized talk.
6. Category of disorders that includes phobias and obsessive-compulsive disorder.
8. A widely used system of classi-fying psychological disorders.
10. Category of schizophrenia symptoms that includes having a toneless voice, expressionless face, and a mute or rigid body.
11. False beliefs that often are symp-toms of schizophrenia.
12. Subtype of schizophrenia in which there is immobility or excessive, purposeless movement.
15. Mood disorder in which a person alternates between depression and mania.

DOWN

1. A persistent, irrational fear of a specific object or situation.
2. Neurotransmitter that is scarce in depression.
3. The "common cold" of psychological disorders.
4. Neurotransmitter for which there are excess receptors in the brains of schizophrenia patients.
5. Biomedical research technique used to determine which genes are involved in a specific psycholog-ical disorder.
7. Perspective that assumes that genes, psychologi-cal factors, and social and cultural circumstances combine and interact to produce psychological disorders.
9. False sensory experiences.
11. Subtype of schizophrenia in which emotion is flat or inappropriate.
13. Category of disorders that includes major depres-sion and bipolar disorder.
14. A euphoric, hyperactive state.

Answers

Perspectives on Psychological Disorders

Section Preview

1. Psychological disorders are harmful dysfunctions that are judged to be atypical, disturbing to oth-ers, maladaptive, and unjustifiable.
2. According to the medical perspective, psycholog-ical disorders are sicknesses that can be diag-nosed on the basis of their symptoms and cured through therapy. Psychologists who work from the bio-psycho-social perspective assume that biological, sociocultural, and psychological fac-tors combine and interact to produce psychologi-cal disorders.
3. DSM-IV-TR lists 400 disorder categories. Diagnostic classification is intended to describe a disorder, predict its future course, imply its appropriate treatment, and stimulate research into its causes.
4. Most clinicians believe that diagnostic labels help in describing, treating, and researching the causes

of psychological disorders. Critics contend that these labels are arbitrary value judgments that create preconceptions that can bias our perceptions and interpretations. Labels can also affect people's self-images and stigmatize them in others' eyes. Finally, labels can change reality by serving as self-fulfilling prophecies.

Stepping Through the Section

1. harmful dysfunctions; atypical; disturbing; maladaptive; unjustifiable; variable

2. medical; illness; psychopathology

3. Pinel

4. nature; nurture; internal

5. depression; schizophrenia; anorexia nervosa; bulimia; dynamic; anxiety; symptoms

6. bio-psycho-social; genetic predispositions; physiological states; psychological dynamics; social; cultural

7. DSM-IV; 400

8. show

9. increased; increased

The "unDSM" is a new classification system that identifies 24 human strengths and virtues grouped into six clusters: wisdom and knowledge, courage, love, justice, temperance, and transcendance.

10. a significant

Psychological labels may be arbitrary. They can create preconceptions that bias our perceptions and interpretations and they can affect people's self-images. Moreover, labels can change reality, by serving as self-fulfilling prophecies. Despite these drawbacks, labels are useful in describing, treating, and researching the causes of psychological disorders.

Anxiety Disorders

Section Preview

1. There are four types of anxiety disorder: generalized anxiety disorder, in which a person feels inexplicably tense and apprehensive; phobia, in which a person has an irrational fear of a specific object or situation; obsessive-compulsive disorder, in which a person is troubled by repetitive thoughts or actions; and panic disorder, an extreme form of anxiety in which a person experiences sudden episodes of intense dread.

2. Freud viewed an anxiety disorder as a manifestation of repressed impulses, ideas, and feelings that influence the sufferer's actions and emotions. Learning theorists link anxiety disorders with classical conditioning of fear, which may arise

from stimulus generalization. Phobic and compulsive behaviors reduce anxiety by allowing the person to avoid or escape the feared situation; this reinforces the behavior. According to this perspective, fear may also be learned through observational learning. Biologically oriented researchers see these disorders as evolutionary adaptations or as genetic predispositions to particular fears and high anxiety. The anxiety of persons with obsessive-compulsive disorder, for example, is measurable as unusually high activity in a particular region of the frontal lobes.

Stepping Through the Section

1. generalized anxiety

2. autonomic; panic disorder

3. agoraphobia

4. phobia; specific phobias

5. social phobia

6. obsessive-compulsive; less

7. repressed

8. classical; fears

9. stimulus generalization

10. reinforced; observational

11. are; survival

12. is

13. frontal; amygdala

14. post-traumatic stress; haunting memories, nightmares, social withdrawal, jumpy anxiety, and insomnia; overdiagnosed

Dissociative and Personality Disorders

Section Preview

1. In dissociative disorders, a person's conscious awareness becomes separated from previous memories, thoughts, and feelings. Most mysterious is the dissociative identity disorder, in which people have two or more distinct personalities; however, some skeptics believe that such persons are merely enacting a role for strategic reasons.

    Psychoanalysts view the symptoms of these disorders as defenses against anxiety. Learning theorists see them as behaviors reinforced by anxiety reduction. Some theorists see dissociative behaviors as states that serve as protective escape responses to traumatic childhood experiences. The recent explosion of diagnosis of dissociative disorders in North America has led skeptics to argue that the disorder is a cultural phenomenon, rather than a genuine disorder. However, supporters point to evidence of distinct brain and body states associated with differing personalities.

2. Personality disorders are inflexible and enduring behavior patterns, such as attention-getting emotionality or exaggerated self-importance, that impair a person's social functioning. Those with the antisocial personality disorder display a lack of conscience at an early age, as they begin to lie, steal, fight, or evidence unrestrained sexual behavior. As adults, they exhibit antisocial behavior that may manifest itself in an inability to hold down a job, in marital and parental irresponsibility, or in criminal behavior. Twin and adoption studies suggest that some individuals may possess a genetic vulnerability to the antisocial personality disorder, but the manifestation of the disorder also depends on environmental factors.

Stepping Through the Section

1. dissociative; conscious awareness

2. dissociative identity

3. roles

4. brain; body

Skeptics point out that the recent increase in the number of reported cases of dissociative identity disorder indicates that it has become a fad. The fact that the disorder is almost nonexistent outside North America also causes skeptics to doubt the disorder's genuineness.

5. anxiety; childhood trauma; fantasy-prone; therapist-patient

6. social functioning

7. antisocial; psychopath or sociopath

8. little

9. 3 to 6; impulsive; uninhibited; social rewards; anxiety

10. frontal lobe

11. is not

Mood Disorders

Section Preview

1. There are two principal mood disorders: major depressive disorder and the bipolar disorder. Major depressive disorder, the "common cold" of psychological disorders, occurs when signs of depression last two weeks or more without any discernible cause. Alternating between depressive episodes and the hyperactive, wildly opti-

mistic state of mania is characteristic of the bipolar disorder.

2. According to the psychoanalytic perspective, depression occurs when significant losses evoke feelings associated with losses experienced in childhood and when unresolved anger toward one's parents is directed inward against the self.

   According to the biological perspective, mood disorders involve genetic predispositions and biochemical imbalances in which norepinephrine is overabundant during mania and scarce during depression. A second neurotransmitter, serotonin, is also scarce during depression. The brains of depressed people also tend to be less active and even have somewhat smaller frontal lobes.

   According to the social-cognitive perspective, depression is a vicious cycle in which stressful experiences trigger self-focused negative thinking and a self-blaming style of explaining events that hamper the way the person thinks and acts. This negative thinking and self-blaming style leads to further negative experiences.

Stepping Through the Section

1. depression; major depressive

2. mania; bipolar

3. phobias; depression

4. lethargy, feelings of worthlessness, and loss of interest in family, friends, and activities

5. two weeks

6. can

7. euphoria, hyperactivity, and a wildly optimistic state; 1

8. more; passive; depression, anxiety, and inhibited sexual desire; active; alcohol abuse, antisocial conduct, and lack of impulse control

9. is; loss of a parent

10. increasing; earlier

11. three

The psychoanalytic perspective suggests that adulthood depression can be triggered by losses that evoke feelings associated with earlier childhood losses. Alternatively, unresolved anger toward one's parents is turned inward and takes the form of depression.

12. tend; twins; strong

13. linkage analysis; DNA

14. low; norepinephrine; serotonin

15. norepinephrine; norepinephrine; serotonin; reuptake; breakdown

16. less; left frontal; smaller; hippocampus; memories; serotonin

Suicide rates are higher among white Americans, the rich, older men, the nonreligious, and those who are single, widowed, or divorced. Although women more often attempt suicide, men are more likely to succeed. Suicide rates also vary widely around the world.

17. self-defeating; learned helplessness

18. uncontrollable stress

Depressed people are more likely than others to explain failures or bad events in terms that are *stable* (it's going to last forever), *global* (it will affect everything), and *internal* (it's my fault). Such explanations lead to feelings of hopelessness, which in turn feed depression.

19. coincide with

20. self-focused; self-blaming

21. negative; optimism; social support

22. rejection

23. excluded; unloved; constricted; alienated

Depression is often brought on by stressful experiences. Depressed people brood over such experiences with maladaptive explanations that produce self-blame and amplify their depression, which in turn triggers other symptoms of depression. In addition, being withdrawn and complaining tends to elicit social rejection and other negative experiences.

Schizophrenia

Section Preview

1. Schizophrenia is a cluster of disorders in which there is a split from reality that shows itself in disorganized and delusional thinking, disturbed perceptions, and inappropriate emotions and actions. *Positive symptoms* of schizophrenia include disorganized or deluded thinking and speech as well as inappropriate emotions. *Negative symptoms* include toneless voices, expressionless faces, or mute and rigid bodies. Schizophrenia may develop gradually (chronic, or process, schizophrenia), in which case recovery is doubtful, or rapidly (acute, or reactive, schizophrenia) in response to stress, in which case recovery is much more likely.

2. Some schizophrenia patients have an excess of brain receptors for dopamine. Others have abnormally low brain activity in the frontal lobes or enlarged fluid-filled areas and a corresponding shrinkage of cerebral tissue. Evidence suggests that the brain abnormalities of schizophrenia might be caused by a problem during prenatal development, such as a prenatal viral infection, nutritional deprivation, or oxygen deprivation at birth. In addition, studies of identical twins and adopted children reveal a strong genetic link to schizophrenia. Genes may predispose some people to react to particular experiences by developing a form of schizophrenia. Psychological causes of schizophrenia are difficult to pinpoint due to the variety of forms of the disorder.

Stepping Through the Section

1. reality

2. thinking; perceptions; emotions; actions

3. delusions

4. selective attention

5. hallucinations; auditory

6. flat affect; catatonia

7. cluster of disorders

8. disorganized and deluded thinking, inappropriate emotions; expressionless faces, toneless voices, mute or rigid bodies

9. chronic (or process); less; acute (or reactive)

10. dopamine; decrease

11. activity

12. fluid; shrinkage; thalamus; sensory input; attention

13. low birth weight; oxygen deprivation; viral infection

Risk of schizophrenia increases for those who undergo fetal development during a flu epidemic, or simply during the flu season. People born in densely populated areas and those born during winter and spring months are at increased risk. The months of excess schizophrenia births are reversed in the southern hemisphere, where the seasons are the reverse of the northern hemisphere's. Mothers who were sick with influenza during their pregnancy may be more likely to have children who develop schizophrenia. Blood drawn from pregnant women whose children develop schizophrenia have higher-than-normal levels of viral infection antibodies.

14. support

15. placenta; viruses

16. do; nutrition; oxygen

17. genetic; psychological

Rates of Psychological Disorders

Section Preview

1. Research reveals that approximately 1 in 6 American adults have experienced a psychologi-

cal disorder at some time in their lives and that a similar 1 in 6 have an active disorder. Those who experience a psychological disorder usually do so by early adulthood. Some disorders, such as the antisocial personality and phobic disorders, often appear earlier, during childhood.

Stepping Through the Section

1. 6
2. higher
3. early; antisocial personality; phobias

Progress Test 1

Multiple-Choice Questions

1. **b.** is the answer. (p. 488)
   c. & d. Men are more likely than women to cope with stress in these ways.
2. **c.** is the answer. (p. 470)
3. **c.** is the answer. Most clinicians agree that psychological disorders may be caused by both psychological (d.) and physical factors (a. and b.) (p. 471)
4. **e.** is the answer. (p. 471)
5. **a.** is the answer. (p. 486)
6. **b.** is the answer. Usually, depression is preceded by a stressful event related to work, marriage, or a close relationship. (p. 489)
7. **c.** is the answer. (p. 499)
8. **d.** is the answer. Although depression is universal, anorexia nervosa and bulimia are rare outside of Western culture. (p. 471)
   a. & b. Schizophrenia and depression are both universal.
   c. The text mentions only schizophrenia and depression as universal disorders. Furthermore, neurosis is no longer utilized as a category of diagnosis.
9. **a.** is the answer. (p. 498)
   b. & d. Thus far, only norepinephrine and serotonin have been implicated in depression and bipolar disorder.
   c. Schizophrenia has been associated with an excess of dopamine receptors. Blocking them alleviates, rather than increases, schizophrenia symptoms.
10. **d.** is the answer. (p. 472)
    b. The text does not mention DSM-IV's reliability in terms of a person's age.
11. **c.** is the answer. (p. 500)

12. **a.** is the answer. (p. 474)
13. **a.** is the answer. (p. 476)
    b. The mood disorders include major depressive disorder and bipolar disorder.
    c. The dissociative disorders include dissociative amnesia, dissociative fugue, and dissociative identity disorder.
    d. The personality disorders include the antisocial and histrionic personalities.
14. **d.** is the answer. Learned helplessness may lead to self-defeating beliefs, which in turn are linked with depression, a mood disorder. (p. 492)
15. **d.** is the answer. (p. 482)
16. **c.** is the answer. (p. 497)
17. **b.** is the answer. Those with antisocial personality disorders show less autonomic arousal in such situations, and emotions, such as fear, are tied to arousal. (p. 485)
18. **d.** is the answer. Hallucinations are false sensory experiences; delusions are false beliefs. (pp. 496, 497)
    a. & b. Obsessions are repetitive and unwanted thoughts. Compulsions are repetitive behaviors.
19. **c.** is the answer. Drugs that relieve depression tend to increase levels of norepinephrine. (p. 491)
    a. Acetylcholine is a neurotransmitter involved in muscle contractions.
    b. It is in certain types of schizophrenia that decreasing dopamine levels is known to be helpful.
    d. On the contrary, it appears that a particular type of depression may be related to *low* levels of serotonin.
20. **c.** is the answer. (p. 498)

Matching Items

1. f (p. 482)	**5.** g (p. 497)	**9.** c (p. 497)
2. d (p. 496)	**6.** b (p. 487)	**10.** e (p. 477)
3. a (p. 486)	**7.** j (p. 478)	
4. h (p. 478)	**8.** i (p. 496)	

Progress Test 2

Multiple-Choice Questions

1. **a.** is the answer. Different cultures have different standards for behaviors that are considered acceptable and normal. (p. 471)
   b. Some abnormal behaviors are simply maladaptive for the individual.
   c. Many individuals who are atypical, such as Olympic gold medalists, are not considered abnormal. There are other criteria that must be met in order for behavior to be considered abnormal.

d. Although physiological factors play a role in the various disorders, they do not define abnormal behavior. Rather, behavior is said to be abnormal if it is atypical, disturbing, maladaptive, and unjustifiable.

2. **b.** is the answer. (p. 479)

   a. This answer reflects the learning perspective.

   c. Although certain phobias are biologically predisposed, this could not fully explain phobias, nor is it the explanation offered by psychoanalytic theory.

   d. Social-cognitive theorists propose self-defeating thoughts as a cause of depression.

3. **a.** is the answer. Schizophrenia sufferers are easily distracted by irrelevant stimuli, evidently because of a breakdown in the capacity for selective attention. (p. 496)

4. **b.** is the answer. (p. 499)

5. **b.** is the answer. The fact that some disorders are universal and at least partly genetic in origin implicates biological factors in their origin. The fact that other disorders appear only in certain parts of the world implicates sociocultural and psychological factors in their origin. (pp. 471–472)

6. **b.** is the answer. (p. 471)

7. **b.** is the answer. (p. 488)

   a. Anxiety is a passive disorder.

   d. Alcohol abuse is an active disorder.

8. **a.** is the answer. In fact, just the opposite is true. Labels are useful in promoting effective treatment of psychological disorders. (pp. 473–475)

9. **b.** is the answer. (p. 483)

   c. Playing a role is most definitely a learned skill.

10. **d.** is the answer. In bipolar disorder, norepinephrine appears to be overabundant during mania and in short supply during depression. (p. 491)

    a. There is an overabundance of dopamine receptors in some schizophrenia patients.

    b. Serotonin sometimes appears to be scarce during depression.

    c. Epinephrine has not been implicated in psychological disorders.

11. **c.** is the answer. Joseph's fear has generalized from ladders to airplanes. (p. 479)

    a. Had Joseph acquired his fear after seeing someone *else* fall, observational learning would be implicated. This process would not, however, explain how his fear was transferred to airplanes.

    b. There is no indication that Joseph's phobia was acquired through reinforcement.

    d. Through stimulus discrimination, Joseph's fear would *not* generalize from ladders to airplanes.

12. **d.** is the answer. (pp. 480–481)

13. **b.** is the answer. (p. 471)

    a. This isn't the case; in fact, the medical model has gained credibility from recent discoveries of genetic and biochemical links to some disorders.

    c. & d. The medical perspective tends to place more emphasis on physiological factors.

14. **b.** is the answer. The psychoanalytic explanation is that these disorders are a manifestation of incompletely repressed impulses over which the person is anxious. According to the learning perspective, the troubled behaviors that result from these disorders have been reinforced by anxiety reduction. (p. 484)

    a. & c. These are true of the psychoanalytic, but not the learning, perspective.

15. **e.** is the answer. (p. 470)

16. **c.** is the answer. DSM-IV was shaped by the medical model. (p. 472)

    a. In fact, just the opposite is true. DSM-IV was revised in order to improve reliability by basing diagnoses on observable behaviors.

    b., d., & e. DSM-IV does not reflect a learning, a psychoanalytic, or a social-cultural bias.

17. **c.** is the answer. Panic attacks are characteristic of certain anxiety disorders, not of schizophrenia. (pp. 496–497)

18. **d.** is the answer. (pp. 492–493)

19. **d.** is the answer. A loss may evoke feelings of anger associated with an earlier loss. Such anger is turned against the self. This internalized anger results in depression. (p. 489)

    a. Learned helplessness would be an explanation offered by the social-cognitive perspective.

    b. The self-serving bias is not discussed in terms of its relationship to depression.

    c. This is the psychoanalytic explanation of anxiety.

20. **d.** is the answer. Risk for schizophrenia increases for individuals who are related to a schizophrenia victim, and the greater the genetic relatedness, the greater the risk. (p. 499)

    a. Schizophrenia victims have an overabundance of the neurotransmitter dopamine, not endorphins.

    b. Being a twin is, in itself, irrelevant to developing schizophrenia.

    c. Although learned helplessness has been suggested by social-cognitive theorists as a cause of self-defeating depressive behaviors, it has not been suggested as a cause of schizophrenia.

Matching Items

1. f (p. 483)   5. c (p. 485)   9. d (p. 496)
2. e (p. 477)   6. b (p. 491)   10. j (p. 477)
3. a (p. 498)   7. g (p. 491)
4. i (p. 480)   8. h (p. 487)

Review and Reflect

Multiple-Choice Questions

1. **c.** is the answer. An intense fear of a specific object is a phobia. (p. 477)
   a. His fear is focused on a specific object, not generalized.
   b. In this disorder a person is troubled by repetitive thoughts and actions.
   d. & e. Conditioned fears form the basis for anxiety rather than mood disorders.

2. **c.** is the answer. (p. 483)
   a. Phobias focus anxiety on a specific object, activity, or situation.
   b. There is no such disorder.
   d. In this mood disorder, a person alternates between feelings of hopeless depression and overexcited mania.

3. **d.** is the answer. Repeated wrongdoing and aggressive behavior are part of the pattern associated with the antisocial personality disorder, which may also include marital problems and an inability to keep a job. (p. 485)
   a. Although dissociative identity disorder may involve an aggressive personality, there is nothing in the example to indicate a dissociation.
   b. Nothing in the question indicates that Bob is passive and resigned and having the self-defeating thoughts characteristic of depression.
   c. Bob's behavior does not include the disorganized thinking and disturbed perceptions typical of schizophrenia.

4. **d.** is the answer. In the learning perspective, a phobia, such as Julia's, is seen as a conditioned fear. (p. 479)
   a. Because the fear is focused on a specific stimulus, the medical model does not easily account for the phobia. In any event, it would presumably offer an internal, biological explanation.
   b. The psychoanalytic view of phobias would be that they represent incompletely repressed anxieties that are displaced onto the feared object.
   c. The social-cognitive perspective would emphasize a person's conscious, cognitive processes, not reflexive conditioned responses.

5. **a.** is the answer. According to the learning view, compulsive behaviors are reinforced because they reduce the anxiety created by obsessive thoughts. Rashid's obsession concerns failing, and his desk-arranging compulsive behaviors apparently help him control these thoughts. (p. 479)
   b. The psychoanalytic perspective would view obsessive thoughts as a symbolic representation of forbidden impulses. These thoughts may prompt the person to perform compulsive acts that counter these impulses.
   c. & d. The text does not offer explanations of obsessive-compulsive behavior based on the humanistic or social-cognitive perspectives. Presumably, however, these explanations would emphasize growth-blocking difficulties in the person's environment (humanistic perspective) and the reciprocal influences of personality and environment (social-cognitive perspective), rather than symbolic expressions of forbidden impulses.

6. **d.** is the answer. (p. 476)
   a. In phobias, anxiety is focused on a specific object.
   b. Major depressive disorder does not manifest these symptoms.
   c. The obsessive-compulsive disorder is characterized by repetitive and unwanted thoughts and/or actions.

7. **d.** is the answer. Jason is obsessed with cleanliness; as a result, he has developed a compulsion to shower. (p. 478)
   a. Dissociative disorders involve a separation of conscious awareness from previous memories and thoughts.
   b. Generalized anxiety disorder does not have a specific focus.
   c. This disorder is characterized by maladaptive character traits.

8. **d.** is the answer. (p. 480)
   a. There is no evidence that Zheina has *lost* either her memory or her identity, as would occur in dissociative disorders.
   b. Although she has symptoms of depression, Zheina does not show signs of mania, which occurs in bipolar disorder.
   c. Zheina shows no signs of disorganized thinking or disturbed perceptions.

9. **a.** is the answer. Because Sandy experiences hallucinations (hearing voices), delusions (fearing someone is "out to get her"), and incoherence, she would most likely be diagnosed as suffering from schizophrenia. (pp. 496–497)

b., c., d., & e. These disorders are not characterized by disorganized thoughts and perceptions.

10. **d.** is the answer. (p. 477)
    a. Baseless physical symptoms rarely play a role in schizophrenia.
    b. There is no indication that she is exhibiting euphoric behavior.
    c. There is no indication that she has suffered a trauma.

11. **a.** is the answer. Humans seem biologically prepared to develop a fear of heights and other dangers that our ancestors faced. (p. 480)

12. **b.** is the answer. (p. 482)

13. **b.** is the answer. The fact that this woman has had these symptoms for more than two weeks indicates that she is suffering from major depressive disorder. (pp. 486–487)

14. **a.** is the answer. Matt's alternating states of the hopelessness and lethargy of depression and the energetic, optimistic state of mania are characteristic of bipolar disorder. (p. 487)
    b. Although he was depressed on Tuesday, Matt's manic state on Monday indicates that he is not suffering from major depressive disorder.
    c. Matt was depressed, not detached from reality.
    d. That Matt is not exhibiting episodes of intense dread indicates that he is not suffering from panic disorder.

15. **d.** is the answer. Freud believed that the anger once felt toward parents was internalized and would produce depression. (p. 489)
    a. & b. The learning and social-cognitive perspectives focus on environmental experiences, conditioning, and self-defeating attitudes in explaining depression.
    c. The biological perspective focuses on genetic predispositions and biochemical imbalances in explaining depression.

16. **b.** is the answer. (pp. 492–495)

17. **b.** is the answer. Norepinephrine, which increases arousal and boosts mood, is scarce during depression. Drugs that relieve depression tend to increase norepinephrine. (p. 491)
    c. Increasing serotonin, which is sometimes scarce during depression, might relieve depression.
    d. This neurotransmitter is involved in motor responses but has not been linked to psychological disorders.

18. **d.** is the answer. Schizophrenia patients sometimes have an excess of receptors for dopamine. Drugs that block these receptors can therefore reduce symptoms of schizophrenia. (p. 498)

a., b., & c. Dopamine receptors have not been implicated in these psychological disorders.

19. **b.** is the answer. (p. 494)

20. **c.** is the answer. (p. 500)

Essay Question

There is more to a psychological disorder than being different from other people. Gifted artists, athletes, and scientists have atypical capabilities, yet are not considered psychologically disordered. To be considered disordered, other people must find the atypical behavior disturbing. But what is disturbing in one culture may not be in another, or at another time. Homosexuality, for example, was once classified as a psychological disorder, but it is no longer. Similarly, nudity is common in some cultures and disturbing in others. Atypical and disturbing behaviors are more likely to be considered disordered when judged as maladaptive to the individual. Prolonged feelings of depression or the use of drugs to avoid dealing with problems are examples of maladaptive behaviors that may signal a psychological disorder if they become disabling. Finally, abnormal behavior is most likely to be considered disordered when others find it unjustifiable. A student loudly reciting the Greek alphabet in public, for example, who can justify his or her unusual behavior as being part of a fraternity or sorority ritual, would not be considered psychologically disordered.

Key Terms

Writing Definitions

1. In order to be classified as a **psychological disorder**, behavior must be atypical, disturbing, maladaptive, and unjustifiable. (p. 470)

2. The **medical model** holds that psychological disorders are illnesses that can be diagnosed, treated, and cured through therapy. (p. 471)

3. The **bio-psycho-social perspective** assumes that *bio*logical, *psycho*logical, and *socio*cultural factors combine and interact to produce psychological disorders. (p. 472)

4. **DSM-IV** is a short name for the American Psychiatric Association's *Diagnostic and Statistical Manual of Mental Disorders* (*Fourth Edition*), which provides a widely used system of classifying psychological disorders. (p. 472)

5. **Anxiety disorders** involve distressing, persistent anxiety or maladaptive behaviors that reduce anxiety. (p. 476)

6. In the **generalized anxiety disorder**, the person is continually tense, apprehensive, and in a state of autonomic nervous system arousal for no apparent reason. (p. 476)

7. A **panic disorder** is an episode of intense dread accompanied by chest pain, dizziness, or choking. It is essentially an escalation of the anxiety associated with generalized anxiety disorder. (p. 477)

8. A **phobia** is an anxiety disorder in which a person has a persistent, irrational fear and avoidance of a specific object or situation. (p. 477)

9. The **obsessive-compulsive disorder** is an anxiety disorder in which the person experiences uncontrollable and repetitive thoughts (obsessions) and actions (compulsions). (p. 478)

10. **Dissociative disorders** involve a separation of conscious awareness from one's previous memories, thoughts, and feelings. (p. 482)

    Memory aid: To *dissociate* is to separate or pull apart. In the **dissociative disorder** a person becomes dissociated from his or her memories and identity.

11. The **dissociative identity disorder** is a dissociative disorder in which a person exhibits two or more distinct and alternating personalities. (p. 483)

12. **Personality disorders** are characterized by inflexible and enduring maladaptive character traits that impair social functioning. (p. 484)

13. The **antisocial personality disorder** is a personality disorder in which the person is aggressive, ruthless, and shows no sign of a conscience that would inhibit wrongdoing. (p. 485)

14. **Mood disorders** are characterized by emotional extremes. (p. 486)

15. **Major depressive disorder** is the mood disorder that occurs when a person exhibits the lethargy, feelings of worthlessness, or loss of interest in family, friends, and activities characteristic of depression for more than a two-week period and for no discernible reason. Because of its relative frequency, depression has been called the "common cold" of psychological disorders. (p. 487)

16. A **manic episode** is the wildly optimistic, euphoric, hyperactive state that alternates with depression in the bipolar disorder. (p. 487)

17. The **bipolar disorder** is the mood disorder in which a person alternates between depression and the euphoria of a manic state. (p. 487)

    Memory aid: *Bipolar* means having two poles, that is, two opposite qualities. In the **bipolar disorder,** the opposing states are mania and depression.

18. **Schizophrenia** refers to the group of severe psychotic disorders whose symptoms may include disorganized and delusional thinking, inappropriate emotions and actions, and disturbed perceptions. (p. 496)

19. **Delusions** are false beliefs that often are symptoms of psychotic disorders. (p. 496)

Cross-Check

ACROSS	DOWN
1. positive	**1.** phobia
6. anxiety	**2.** serotonin
8. DSM-IV	**3.** major depressive
10. negative	**4.** dopamine
11. delusions	**5.** linkage analysis
12. catatonia	**7.** bio-psycho-social
15. bipolar	**9.** hallucinations
	11. disorganized
	13. mood
	14. mania

FOCUS ON VOCABULARY AND LANGUAGE

Page 469: It's no wonder then that studying psychological disorders may at times evoke an *eerie sense* of self-recognition, one that *illuminates* the dynamics of our own personality. When reading this chapter, you may sometimes experience the strange, uncanny feeling (*eerie sense*) that Myers is writing about you. On occasion, we all feel, think, and behave in ways similar to disturbed people, and becoming aware of how alike we sometimes are may help shed some light on (*illuminate*) the processes underlying personality.

Perspectives on Psychological Disorders

Page 470: Where should we *draw the line* between normality and disorder? Myers is addressing the problem of how exactly to define psychological disorders. How do we distinguish (*draw the line*) between someone who is "abnormal" (*disordered*) and someone who is not? For psychologists and other mental-health workers, a behavior will be labeled harmful and dysfunctional if it is judged to be atypical, disturbing, maladaptive, and unjustifiable.

Page 470: "*The devil made him do it.*" Our ancestors explained strange and puzzling behavior by appealing to what they knew and believed about the nature of the world (e.g., gods, stars, demons, spirits, etc.). A person, who today would be classified as psychologically disturbed because of his or her bizarre behavior, in the past would have been considered to be possessed by evil spirits or demons (*the devil made him do it*). These types of nonscientific explanations persisted up until the nineteenth century.

Page 472: Thus, "schizophrenia" provides *a handy shorthand* for describing a complex disorder. Psychology uses a classification system (DSM-IV) to describe and impose order on complicated psychological problems. When a descriptive label (diagnostic classification) is used to identify a disorder, it does not explain the problem, but it does provide a quick and useful means of communicating a great deal of information in abbreviated form (*it is a handy shorthand*).

Page 473: Some critics *fault* the manual for *casting too wide a net* and bringing "almost any kind of behavior within the *compass* of psychiatry." . . . The DSM-IV classification system has been received with a less-than-enthusiastic response by some practitioners (*they were not enthralled*). Many criticize (*fault*) the

inclusion of a large number of behaviors as psychologically disordered (*it casts too wide a net*) and suggest that just about any behavior is now within the purview (*compass*) of psychiatry. Nevertheless, many other clinicians find DSM-IV a useful and practical tool or device.

Page 474 (Thinking Critically): "Hinckley *Insane,* Public *Mad.*" The word *mad* has a number of meanings: (a) angry, (b) insane, (c) foolish and irrational, (d) rash, (e) enthusiastic about something, (f) frantic. John Hinckley, who shot President Reagan, was not sent to prison; instead, he was confined to a mental hospital. The public was angry and upset (*mad*) because Hinckley was judged to be mad (*insane*). Myers notes that others in similar circumstances have been sent to jail or even executed, mainly because of public outrage over their crimes.

Page 475: *Labels* can serve as *self-fulfilling prophecies.* A prophecy is a prediction about the future. When we characterize or classify (*label*) someone as a certain type of person, the very act of labeling may help bring about or create the actions described by the label (*self-fulfilling prophesy*).

Anxiety Disorders

Pages 476–477: heart palpitations . . . ringing in the ears . . . edgy . . . jittery . . . sleeplessness . . . furrowed brows . . . twitching eyelids . . . fidgeting. These are all descriptions of the symptoms of generalized anxiety disorder. The person may have increased heart rate (*heart palpitations*); may hear high-pitched sounds (*ringing in the ears*); may be nervous and jumpy (*edgy*); and may start trembling (*jittery*). The sufferer may worry all the time, be unable to sleep (*sleeplessness or insomnia*), and feel apprehensive, which may show in frowning (*furrowed brows*), rapidly blinking eyes (*twitching eyelids*), and restless movements (*fidgeting*).

Page 480 (Close-Up): Years later, images of these events intrude on him as *flashbacks* and *nightmares.* Many war veterans (*vets*) and others who experienced traumatic stressful events develop post-traumatic stress disorder. Symptoms include terrifying images of the event (*flashbacks*), very frightening dreams (*nightmares*), extreme nervousness, anxiety or depression, and a tendency to become socially isolated.

Page 481: Grooming gone wild becomes hair pulling. The biological perspective explains our tendency to be anxious (*anxiety-prone*) in evolutionary or genetic terms. A normal behavior that once had survival value in our evolutionary past may now be distorted into compulsive action. Thus, compulsive hair pulling may be an exaggerated version of normal grooming behavior (*grooming gone wild*).

Dissociative and Personality Disorders

Page 483: . . . a ruse . . . Kenneth Bianchi is a convicted psychopathic murderer who pretended to be a multiple personality in order to avoid jail or the death penalty, and his cunning ploy (*ruse*) fooled many psychologists and psychiatrists. It also raised the question of the reality of dissociative identity as a genuine disorder.

Page 484: Rather, note skeptics, therapists *go fishing for multiple personalities . . .* Those who doubt the existence of dissociative identity disorder (*skeptics*) find it strange that the number of diagnosed cases in North America has increased dramatically (*exploded*) in the last decade. (In the rest of the world it is rare or nonexistent.) In addition, the average number of personalities has multiplied (*mushroomed*) from 3 to 12 per patient. One explanation for the disorder's popularity is that many therapists expect it to be there, so they actively solicit (*go fishing for*) symptoms of dissociative identity disorder from their patients.

Page 485: . . . con artist . . . A person who has an antisocial personality is usually a male who has no conscience, who lies, steals, cheats, and is unable to keep a job or take on the normal responsibilities of family and society. When combined with high intelligence and no moral sense, the result may be a clever, smooth talking, and deceitful trickster or confidence man (*con artist*).

Page 485: . . . the antisocial personality disorder is *woven* of biological and psychological *strands*. The analogy here is between the antisocial personality and how cloth is made (*woven*). Both psychological and biological factors (*strands*) combine to produce the disorder. If the biological predispositions are fostered (*channeled*) in more positive ways, the result may be a fearless hero; alternatively, the same disposition may produce a killer or a confidence trickster (*con artist*). Research confirms that with antisocial behavior, as with many other things, nature and nurture interact.

Mood Disorders

Page 487: To grind temporarily to a halt and *ruminate,* as depressed people do, is to reassess one's life when feeling threatened and to *redirect energy in more promising ways.* From a biological point of view,

depression is a natural reaction to stress and painful events. It is like a warning signal that brings us to a complete stop (*we grind to a halt*) and allows us time to reflect on life and contemplate (*ruminate on*) the meaning of our existence and to focus more optimistically on the future.

Page 487: The difference between a *blue mood* after bad news and a mood disorder is like the difference between gasping for breath after a hard run and being chronically short of breath. We all feel depressed and sad (*we have blue moods*) in response to painful events and sometimes just to life in general. These feelings are points on a continuum; at the extreme end, and very distinct from ordinary depression, are the serious mood disorders (e.g., major depressive disorder) in which the signs of chronic depression (loss of appetite, sleeplessness, tiredness, low self-esteem, and a disinterest in family, friends and social activities) last two weeks or more.

Page 487: If depression is living in *slow motion*, mania is *fast forward.* Bipolar disorder is characterized by mood swings. While depression slows the person down (*like living in slow motion*), the hyperactivity and heightened exuberant state (*mania*) at the other emotional extreme seems to speed the person up, similar to the images you get when you press the fast forward button on the VCR or see a "speeded-up" film.

Page 492: Depressed people *view life through dark glasses.* Social-cognitive theorists point out that biological factors do not operate independently of environmental influences. People who are depressed often have negative beliefs about themselves and about their present and future situations (*they view life through dark glasses*). These self-defeating beliefs can accentuate or amplify a nasty (*vicious*) cycle of interactions between chemistry, cognition, and mood.

Page 495: Knowing that there is *two-way traffic* between depressed mood and negative thinking . . . The latest research shows that there is an interaction (*two-way traffic*) between depression and negative thinking. Depression tends to make people prone to self-blaming and self-focused negative thinking, and in response to painful events this style of thinking puts people at risk for becoming depressed.

Schizophrenia

Page 497: . . . hodge-podge . . . The symptoms of schizophrenia include fragmented and distorted thinking, disturbed perception, and inappropriate feelings and behaviors. Schizophrenia victims, when talking, may move rapidly from topic to topic and idea to idea so that their speech is incomprehensible (*a word salad*). This may be the result of a breakdown in selective attention, whereby an assorted mixture (*hodge-podge*) of stimuli continually distracts the person.

Page 497: Other victims of schizophrenia sometimes lapse into *flat affect,* a zombielike state of apparent apathy. The emotions of schizophrenia are frequently not appropriate for the situation. There may be laughter at a funeral, anger and tears for no appar-ent reason, or no expression of emotion whatsoever (*flat affect*), which resembles a half-dead, trancelike (*zombielike*) state of indifference (*apathy*).

Page 501: But as the bio-psycho-social perspective emphasizes, the *traffic* between brain biochemistry and psychological experiences *runs both ways.* Neither genetic predispositions nor stressful psycho-logical events alone cause schizophrenia. Rather, there seems to be some interaction (*the traffic runs both ways*) between the two.

chapter 14

Therapy

Chapter Overview

Chapter 14 discusses the major psychotherapies and biomedical therapies for maladaptive behaviors. The various psychotherapies all derive from the personality theories discussed earlier, namely, the psychoanalytic, humanistic, behavioral, and cognitive theories. The chapter groups the therapies by perspective but also emphasizes the common threads that run through them. In evaluating the therapies, the chapter points out that, although people who are untreated often improve, those receiving psychotherapy tend to improve somewhat more, regardless of the type of therapy they receive. This section includes a discussion of several popular alternative therapies.

The biomedical therapies discussed are drug therapies; electroconvulsive therapy; and psychosurgery, which is seldom used. By far the most important of the biomedical therapies, drug therapies are being used in the treatment of psychotic, anxiety, and mood disorders.

Because the origins of problems often lie beyond the individual, the chapter concludes with approaches that aim at preventing psychological disorders by focusing on the family or on the larger social environment as possible contributors to psychological disorders.

NOTE: Answer guidelines for all Chapter 14 questions begin on page 419.

The Psychological Therapies
(pp. 507–518)

David Myers at times uses idioms that are unfamiliar to some readers. If you do not know the meaning of any of the following words, phrases, or expressions in the context in which they appear in the introduction and this section, refer to pages 427–428 for an explanation: *bewildering variety of harsh and gentle methods; gawk; common threads; fueled . . . residue; aim to boost; knocks the props out from under you; lore; drinks laced with a drug; aggressive and self-abusive behaviors; colors our feelings; catastrophizing.*

Section Preview

First, skim the section, noting headings and boldface items. Then read the following objectives and, as you read the text, search for the information that will enable you to meet each objective. Answer guidelines begin on page 419.

1. Briefly explain the current approach to therapy.

2. Discuss the aims and methods of psychoanalysis and psychodynamic therapy, and explain the critics' concerns with these forms of therapy.

3. Identify the basic themes of humanistic therapies and describe Rogers' client-centered approach.

4. Identify the basic assumptions of behavior therapy, and discuss the classical conditioning therapies.

5. Describe the premise behind operant conditioning techniques, and explain the critics' concerns with these techniques.

6. Identify the basic assumptions of the cognitive therapies.

Stepping Through the Section

After you have read the section, complete the sentences and answer the questions. As you proceed, evaluate your performance by consulting the answers on page 420. Do not continue with the next section until you understand each answer. If you need to, review or reread the section in the textbook before continuing.

1. Psychological therapy is more commonly called _____.

2. Therapists who blend several psychotherapy techniques are said to take an _____ approach.

3. The major psychotherapies are based on four perspectives: the _____ , _____ , _____ , and _____ perspectives.

4. Freud's technique in which a patient says whatever comes to mind is called _____ _____ .

5. When, in the course of therapy, a person omits shameful or embarrassing material, _____ is occurring. Insight is facilitated by the analyst's _____ of the meaning of such omissions, of dreams, and of other information revealed during therapy sessions.

6. Freud referred to the hidden meaning of a dream as its _____ _____ .

7. When strong feelings, similar to those experienced in other important relationships, are developed toward the therapist, _____ has occurred.

8. Therapists who are influenced by Freud's psychoanalysis but who talk to the patient face to face are _____ therapists. In addition, they work with patients only _____ (how often?) and for only a few weeks or months.

9. A brief alternative to psychodynamic therapy that has proven effective with _____ patients is _____ _____ . While this approach aims to help people gain _____ into their difficulties, it focuses on

_____ _____

rather than on past hurts.

10. Humanistic therapies attempt to help people meet their potential for _____ .

List several ways that humanistic therapy differs from psychoanalysis.

11. The humanistic therapy based on Rogers' theory is called _____-_____ therapy, which is described as _____ therapy because the therapist _____ (interprets/does not interpret) the person's problems.

12. In order to promote growth in clients, Rogerian therapists exhibit _____ , _____ , and _____ .

13. Rogers' technique of restating and clarifying what a person is saying is called

_____ _____ .

Given a nonjudgmental environment that provides _____ _____ _____ , patients are better able to accept themselves as they are and to feel valued and whole.

14. Three tips for listening more actively in your own relationships are to _____ , _____ _____ , and _____ _____ .

Contrast the assumptions of the behavior therapies with those of psychoanalysis and humanistic therapy.

15. One cluster of behavior therapies is based on the principles of _____ _____ , as developed in Pavlov's experiments. This technique, in which a new, incompatible response is substituted for a maladaptive one, is called _____ . Two examples of this technique are

_____ _____ and _____ _____ .

16. The most widely used techniques of behavior therapy are the _____ _____ . The technique of systematic desensitization has been most fully developed by the therapist _____ . The assumption behind this technique is that one cannot simultaneously be _____ and relaxed.

17. The first step in systematic desensitization is the construction of a _____ of anxiety-arousing stimuli. The second step involves training in _____ _____ . In the final step, the person is trained to associate the _____ state with the _____-arousing stimuli.

18. For those who are unable to _____ _____ an anxiety-arousing situation, or too afraid or embarrassed to do so, _____ _____ _____ therapy offers a promising alternative.

19. In helping people to overcome fears of snakes and spiders, for example, therapists sometimes combine systematic desensitization with

_____ _____ and other techniques.

20. In aversive conditioning, the therapist attempts to substitute a _____ (positive/negative) response for one that is currently _____ (positive/negative). In this technique, a person's unwanted behaviors

become associated with _____ feelings.

21. Therapies that influence behavior by controlling its consequences are based on principles of _____ conditioning. One application of this form of therapy to institutional settings is the _____ _____ , in which desired behaviors are rewarded.

State two criticisms of *behavior modification.*

22. Therapists who teach people new, more constructive ways of thinking are using _____ therapy.

23. One variety of cognitive therapy attempts to reverse the _____ beliefs often associated with _____ by helping clients see their irrationalities. This therapy was developed by _____ .

24. Treatment that combines an attack on negative thinking with efforts to modify behavior is known as _____- _____ therapy.

25. Training people to restructure their thinking in stressful situations is the goal of _____ _____ training. Students trained to _____ their negative thoughts are less likely to experience future depression.

Group and Family Therapies
(pp. 518–519)

Section Preview

Answer guidelines are provided on page 420.

1. Describe group therapies.

Stepping Through the Section

Answers are provided on page 420s.

List several advantages of group therapy.

1. The most common types of group therapy are _____ and _____ groups for the addicted, the divorced, and those simply looking for fellowship and growth, for example. Most support groups focus on _____ , _____ , and _____ - _____ - _____ illnesses.

2. The type of group interaction that focuses on the social context in which the individual exists is _____ _____ .

3. In this type of group, therapists focus on improving _____ within the family and helping family members to discover new ways of preventing or resolving _____ .

Evaluating Psychotherapies
(pp. 519–529)

If you do not know the meaning of any of the following words, phrases, or expressions in the context in which they appear in the text, refer to pages 428–429 for an explanation: *Hang in there; testimonials; ebb and flow of events; clear-cut; fertile soil for pseudotherapies; harness; empathy are hallmarks.*

Section Preview

Answer guidelines are provided on page 421.

1. Identify five reasons clients' and therapists' perceptions of therapy's effectiveness may be inflated.

2. Discuss the findings regarding the effectiveness of the psychotherapies.

3. Discuss the relative effectiveness of different psychotherapies.

4. Evaluate the effectiveness of three popular alternative therapies.

5. Discuss the commonalities among the psychotherapies.

6. Discuss the roles of culture and values in psychotherapy.

Stepping Through the Section

Answers are provided on page 421.

1. In contrast to earlier times, most therapy today _____ (is/is not) provided by psychiatrists.

2. A majority of psychotherapy clients express _____ (satisfaction/dissatisfaction) with their therapy.

3. Client testimonials _____ (are/are not) persuasive evidence of psychotherapy's effectiveness. One reason is that people often enter therapy when they are in

_____ .

4. Clients' and therapists' perceptions of therapy's effectiveness may be inflated by their belief that a treatment works. This phenomenon is called the

_____ _____ .

Discuss other factors that may inflate clients' and therapists' perceptions of therapy's effectiveness.

5. The debate over the effectiveness of psychotherapy began with a study by _____ ; it showed that the rate of improvement for those who received therapy _____ (was/was not) higher than the rate for those who did not.

6. Overall, studies that combine the results of many different psychotherapy outcome studies indicate that psychotherapy is _____ (somewhat effective/ineffective).

7. As a rule, psychotherapy is most effective with problems that are _____ (specific/nonspecific).

8. Comparisons of the effectiveness of different forms of therapy reveal _____ (clear/no clear) differences.

9. Controlled treatment studies have demonstrated that depression may be effectively treated with

_____ , _____ , and _____ _____ therapies. Cognitive-behavior therapy has proven effective in treating _____ , and behavioral conditioning therapies in treating _____

_____ .

10. Today, many forms of _____

_____ are touted as effective treatments for a variety of complaints. Among the most popular is _____

_____ , in which practitioners move their hands over a patient's body. Empirical support for this form of therapy is _____ (strong/nonexistent).

11. In another popular alternative therapy, a therapist triggers eye movements in patients while they imagine _____

_____ . This therapy, called

_____ _____

_____ _____

_____ , has proven

_____ (completely ineffective/somewhat effective) as a treatment for nonmilitary _____-

_____ _____

_____ . However, skeptics point to evidence that _____

_____ is just as effective as triggered eye movements in producing beneficial results.

12. For people who suffer from the wintertime form of depression called _____

_____ _____ ,

timed _____-_____ therapy may be beneficial in shifting secretion of the hormone _____ .

13. Several studies found that treatment for mild problems offered by paraprofessionals _____ (is/is not) as effective as that offered by professional therapists.

14. Generally speaking, psychotherapists' personal values _____ (do/do not) influence their therapy.

The Biomedical Therapies (pp. 529–534)

> If you do not know the meaning of any of the following words, phrases, or expressions in the context in which they appear in the text, refer to pages 429–430 for an explanation: *sluggishness, tremors, and twitches; "popping a Xanax"; lift people up; barbaric image; jump-starting the brain.*

Section Preview

Answer guidelines are provided on page 422.

1. Identify the common forms of drug therapy.

2. Describe the use of electroconvulsive therapy and psychosurgery in the treatment of psychological disorders.

Stepping Through the Section

Answers are provided on page 422.

1. The most widely used biomedical treatments are the _____ therapies. Thanks to these therapies, the number of residents in mental hospitals has _____ (increased/decreased) sharply.

2. The field that studies the effects of drugs on the mind and behavior is _____ .

3. When neither the patients nor the staff are aware of which condition a given individual is in, a _____-_____ study is being conducted.

4. One effect of _____ drugs such as _____ is to help those experiencing _____ (positive/negative) symptoms of schizophrenia by decreasing their responsiveness to irrelevant stimuli; schizophrenia patients who are apathetic and withdrawn may be more effectively treated with the drug _____ . These drugs work by blocking the receptor sites for the neurotransmitters _____ and _____ .

5. Xanax and Valium are classified as _____ drugs. These drugs depress activity in the _____ _____ _____ .

6. Drugs that are prescribed to alleviate depression are called _____ drugs. These drugs also work by increasing levels of the neurotransmitters _____ and _____ . One example of this type of drug is _____ , which works by blocking the reabsorption of _____ from synapses and is therefore called a _____-_____-_____ drug.

7. Equally effective in calming anxious people and energizing depressed people is _____ _____ , which has positive side effects.

8. Although people with depression often improve after one month on antidepressants, a large percentage of the effectiveness is due to a _____ _____ .

9. In order to stabilize the mood swings of a bipolar disorder, the chemical _____ is often prescribed.

10. The therapeutic technique in which the patient receives an electric shock to the brain is referred to as _____ therapy, abbreviated as _____ .

11. ECT is most often used with patients suffering from severe _____ . Research evidence _____ (confirms/does not confirm) ECT's effectiveness with such patients.

12. One theory of how ECT works suggests that it increases release of the neurotransmitter _____ .

13. A gentler procedure called _____ _____ _____ _____ aims to treat depression by presenting pulses through a magnetic coil held close to a person's skull above the right eyebrow. This procedure may work by energizing the brain's left _____ _____ , which is relatively inactive in depressed patients.

14. The biomedical therapy in which a portion of brain tissue is removed or destroyed is called _____ .

15. In the 1930s, Moniz developed an operation called the _____ . In this procedure, the _____ lobe of the brain is disconnected from the rest of the brain.

16. Today, most psychosurgery has been replaced by the use of _____ or some other form of treatment.

Preventing Psychological Disorders
(pp. 534–535)

> If you do not know the meaning of the following expression in the context in which it appears in the text, refer to page 430 for an explanation: *upstream work.*

Section Preview

Answer guidelines are provided on page 422.

1. Explain the rationale and goals of preventive mental health programs.

Progress Test 1

Multiple-Choice Questions

Circle your answers to the following questions and check them with the answers beginning on page 422. If your answer is incorrect, read the explanation for why it is incorrect and then consult the appropriate pages of the text (in parentheses following the correct answer).

1. Electroconvulsive therapy is most useful in the treatment of:
   a. schizophrenia.
   b. depression.
   c. personality disorders.
   d. anxiety disorders.
   e. bipolar disorder.

2. The technique in which a person is asked to report everything that comes to his or her mind is called _____ _____ ; this technique is favored by _____ therapists.
   a. active listening; cognitive
   b. spontaneous remission; humanistic
   c. free association; psychoanalytic
   d. systematic desensitization; behavior

3. Of the following categories of psychotherapy, which is known for its nondirective nature?
   a. psychoanalysis   c. behavior therapy
   b. humanistic therapy   d. cognitive therapy

4. Which of the following is *not* a common criticism of psychoanalysis?
   a. It emphasizes the existence of repressed memories.
   b. It provides interpretations that are hard to disprove.
   c. It is generally a very expensive process.
   d. It gives therapists too much control over patients.

5. Which of the following types of therapy does *not* belong with the others?
   a. cognitive therapy
   b. family therapy
   c. self-help group
   d. support group

6. Which of the following is *not* necessarily an advantage of group therapies over individual therapies?
   a. They tend to take less time for the therapist.
   b. They tend to cost less money for the client.
   c. They are more effective.
   d. They allow the client to test new behaviors in a social context.

7. Which biomedical therapy is *most* likely to be practiced today?
   a. psychosurgery
   b. electroconvulsive therapy
   c. drug therapy
   d. counterconditioning
   e. aversive conditioning

8. The effectiveness of psychotherapy has been assessed both through clients' perspectives and through controlled research studies. What have such assessments found?
   a. Clients' perceptions and controlled studies alike strongly affirm the effectiveness of psychotherapy.
   b. Whereas clients' perceptions strongly affirm the effectiveness of psychotherapy, studies point to more modest results.
   c. Whereas studies strongly affirm the effectiveness of psychotherapy, many clients feel dissatisfied with their progress.
   d. Clients' perceptions and controlled studies alike paint a very mixed picture of the effectiveness of psychotherapy.

9. The results of studies assessing the effectiveness of different psychotherapies reveal that:
   a. no single type of therapy is consistently superior.
   b. behavior therapies are most effective in treating specific problems, such as phobias.
   c. cognitive therapies are effective in treating depressed emotions.
   d. all of the above are true.

10. The antipsychotic drugs appear to produce their effects by blocking the receptor sites for:
    a. dopamine.   c. norepinephrine.
    b. epinephrine.   d. serotonin.

11. Psychologists who advocate a _____ approach to mental health contend that many psychological disorders could be prevented by changing the disturbed individual's _____ .
    a. biomedical; diet
    b. family; behavior
    c. humanistic; feelings
    d. psychoanalytic; behavior
    e. preventive; environment

12. An eclectic psychotherapist is one who:
    a. takes a nondirective approach in helping clients solve their problems.
    b. views psychological disorders as usually stemming from one cause, such as a biological abnormality.
    c. uses one particular technique, such as psychoanalysis or counterconditioning, in treating disorders.
    d. uses a variety of techniques, depending on the client and the problem.

13. The technique in which a therapist echoes and restates what a person says in a nondirective manner is called:
    a. active listening.
    b. free association.
    c. systematic desensitization.
    d. interpretation.

14. Unlike traditional psychoanalytic therapy, interpersonal psychotherapy:
    a. helps people gain insight into the roots of their problems.
    b. offers interpretations of patients' feelings.
    c. focuses on current relationships.
    d. does all of the above.

15. The technique of systematic desensitization is based on the premise that maladaptive symptoms are:
    a. a reflection of irrational thinking.
    b. conditioned responses.
    c. expressions of unfulfilled wishes.
    d. all of the above.

16. The operant conditioning technique in which desired behaviors are rewarded with points or poker chips that can later be exchanged for various rewards is called:
    a. counterconditioning.
    b. systematic desensitization.
    c. a token economy.
    d. exposure therapy.

17. One variety of _____ therapy is based on the finding that depressed people often attribute their failures to _____ .
    a. humanistic; themselves
    b. behavior; external circumstances
    c. cognitive; external circumstances
    d. cognitive; themselves

18. A person can derive benefits from psychotherapy simply by believing in it. This illustrates the importance of:
    a. spontaneous remission.
    b. the placebo effect.
    c. the transference effect.
    d. interpretation.

19. Before 1950, the main mental health providers were:
    a. psychologists.   d. the clergy.
    b. paraprofessionals.   e. social workers.
    c. psychiatrists.

20. In one research study of therapeutic touch, the experimenter placed a hand over one of the practitioner's unseen hands to see if the practitioner could detect the hovering hand's purported energy field. The results demonstrated that the practitioners were able to do so:
    a. 100 percent of the time.
    b. about 75 percent of the time.
    c. less than 50 percent of the time.
    d. only if the experimenter mentally concentrated on which hand was being "stimulated."

Matching Items

Match each term with the appropriate definition or description.

Terms

_____ 1. cognitive therapy
_____ 2. behavior therapy
_____ 3. systematic desensitization
_____ 4. cognitive-behavior therapy
_____ 5. client-centered therapy
_____ 6. exposure therapies
_____ 7. aversive conditioning
_____ 8. psychoanalysis
_____ 9. preventive mental health
_____ 10. biomedical therapy
_____ 11. counterconditioning

Definitions or Descriptions

a. associates unwanted behavior with unpleasant experiences
b. associates a relaxed state with anxiety-arousing stimuli
c. emphasizes the social context of psychological disorders
d. integrated therapy that focuses on changing self-defeating thinking and unwanted behavior
e. category of therapies that teach people more adaptive ways of thinking and acting
f. therapies to treat anxiety in which people confront things they fear and avoid
g. therapy developed by Carl Rogers
h. therapy based on Freud's theory of personality
i. treatment with psychosurgery, electroconvulsive therapy, or drugs
j. classical conditioning procedure in which new responses are conditioned to stimuli that trigger unwanted behaviors
k. category of therapies based on learning principles derived from classical and operant conditioning

Progress Test 2

Progress Test 2 should be completed during a final chapter review. Answer the following questions after you thoroughly understand the correct answers for the section reviews and Progress Test 1.

Multiple-Choice Questions

1. Carl Rogers was a _____ therapist who was the creator of _____ .
   a. behavior; systematic desensitization
   b. psychoanalytic; insight therapy
   c. humanistic; client-centered therapy
   d. cognitive; cognitive therapy for depression

2. Using techniques of classical conditioning to develop an association between unwanted behavior and an unpleasant experience is known as:
   a. aversive conditioning.
   b. systematic desensitization.
   c. transference.
   d. electroconvulsive therapy.
   e. a token economy.

3. Which type of psychotherapy emphasizes the individual's inherent potential for self-fulfillment?
   a. behavior therapy   c. humanistic therapy
   b. psychoanalysis   d. biomedical therapy

4. Light-exposure therapy has proven useful as a form of treatment for people suffering from:
   a. bulimia.
   b. seasonal affective disorder.
   c. schizophrenia.
   d. dissociative identity disorder.

5. Which type of psychotherapy focuses on changing unwanted behaviors rather than on discovering their underlying causes?
   a. behavior therapy
   b. cognitive therapy
   c. humanistic therapy
   d. psychoanalysis
   e. family therapy

6. The techniques of counterconditioning are based on principles of:
   a. observational learning.
   b. classical conditioning.
   c. operant conditioning.
   d. behavior modification.

7. In which of the following does the client learn to associate a relaxed state with a hierarchy of anxiety-arousing situations?
   a. cognitive therapy
   b. aversive conditioning
   c. counterconditioning
   d. systematic desensitization

8. Principles of operant conditioning underlie which of the following techniques?
   a. counterconditioning
   b. systematic desensitization
   c. stress inoculation training
   d. aversive conditioning
   e. the token economy

9. Which of the following is *not* a common criticism of behavior therapy?
   a. Clients may not develop intrinsic motivation for their new behaviors.
   b. Behavior control is unethical.
   c. Although one symptom may be eliminated, another may replace it unless the underlying problem is treated.
   d. All of the above are criticisms of behavior therapy.

10. Which type of therapy focuses on eliminating irrational thinking?
    a. EMDR
    b. client-centered therapy
    c. cognitive therapy
    d. behavior therapy

11. Antidepressant drugs are believed to work by affecting serotonin or:
    a. dopamine.   c. norepinephrine.
    b. lithium.   d. acetylcholine.

12. Which of the following is the drug most commonly used to treat bipolar disorder?
    a. Valium   c. Xanax
    b. chlorpromazine   d. lithium

13. The type of drugs criticized for reducing symptoms without resolving underlying problems are the:
    a. antianxiety drugs.
    b. antipsychotic drugs.
    c. antidepressant drugs.
    d. amphetamines.

14. Which form of therapy is *most* likely to be successful in treating depression?
    a. behavior therapy   c. cognitive therapy
    b. psychoanalysis   d. humanistic therapy

15. Although Moniz won the Nobel prize for developing the lobotomy procedure, the technique is not widely used today because:
    a. it produces a lethargic, immature personality.
    b. it is irreversible.
    c. calming drugs became available in the 1950s.
    d. of all of the above reasons.

16. Research studies comparing the effectiveness of professional therapists with paraprofessionals have generally found that:
    a. the professionals were much more effective than the paraprofessionals.
    b. the paraprofessionals were much more effective than the professionals.
    c. except in treating depression, the paraprofessionals were about as effective as the professionals.
    d. the paraprofessionals were about as effective as the professionals.

17. Among the common ingredients of the psychotherapies is:
    a. the offer of a therapeutic relationship.
    b. the expectation among clients that the therapy will prove helpful.
    c. the chance to develop a fresh perspective on oneself and the world.
    d. all of the above.

18. Family therapy differs from other forms of psychotherapy because it focuses on:
    a. using a variety of treatment techniques.
    b. conscious rather than unconscious processes.
    c. the present instead of the past.
    d. how family tensions may cause individual problems.

19. One reason that aversive conditioning may only be temporarily effective is that:
    a. for ethical reasons, therapists cannot use sufficiently intense unconditioned stimuli to sustain classical conditioning.
    b. patients are often unable to become sufficiently relaxed for conditioning to take place.
    c. patients know that outside the therapist's office they can engage in the undesirable behavior without fear of aversive consequences.
    d. most conditioned responses are elicited by many nonspecific stimuli and it is impossible to countercondition them all.

20. Cognitive-behavior therapy aims to:
    a. alter the way people act.
    b. Make people more aware of their irrational negative thinking.
    c. Alter the way people think and act.
    d. Countercondition anxiety-provoking stimuli.

Matching Items

Match each term with the appropriate definition or description.

Terms

_____ 1. active listening
_____ 2. token economy
_____ 3. placebo effect
_____ 4. lobotomy
_____ 5. lithium
_____ 6. eclectic
_____ 7. psychopharmacology
_____ 8. double-blind technique
_____ 9. Valium
_____ 10. free association
_____ 11. stress inoculation training

Definitions or Descriptions

a. type of psychosurgery
b. therapy that draws on a combination of techniques
c. mood-stabilizing drug
d. empathic technique used in person-centered therapy
e. the beneficial effect of a person's expecting that treatment will be effective
f. antianxiety drug
g. technique of psychoanalytic therapy
h. an operant conditioning procedure
i. the study of the effects of drugs on the mind and behavior
j. experimental procedure in which both the patient and staff are unaware of a patient's treatment condition
k. cognitive-behavior therapy in which people are trained to restructure their thinking in stressful situations

Review and Reflect

Answer these questions the day before an exam as a final check on your understanding of the chapter's terms and concepts.

Multiple-Choice Questions

1. During a session with his psychoanalyst, Jamal hesitates while describing a highly embarrassing thought. In the psychoanalytic framework, this is an example of:
   a. transference.
   b. insight.
   c. mental repression.
   d. resistance.

2. During psychoanalysis, Jane has developed strong feelings of hatred for her therapist. The analyst interprets Jane's behavior in terms of a _____ of her feelings toward her father.
   a. projection
   b. resistance
   c. regression
   d. transference

3. Given that Jim's therapist attempts to help him by offering genuineness, acceptance, and empathy, she is probably practicing:
   a. psychoanalysis.
   b. behavior therapy.
   c. cognitive therapy.
   d. client-centered therapy.

4. To help Sam quit smoking, his therapist blew a blast of smoke into Sam's face each time Sam inhaled. Which technique is the therapist using?
   a. exposure therapy
   b. behavior modification
   c. systematic desensitization
   d. aversive conditioning

5. After Darnel dropped a pass in an important football game, he became depressed and vowed to quit the team because of his athletic incompetence. The campus psychologist challenged his illogical reasoning and pointed out that Darnel's "incompetence" had earned him an athletic scholarship. The psychologist's response was most typical of a _____ therapist.
   a. behavior
   b. psychoanalytic
   c. client-centered
   d. cognitive

6. Seth enters therapy to talk about some issues that have been upsetting him. The therapist prescribes some medication to help him. The therapist is most likely a:
   a. clinical psychologist.
   b. psychiatrist.
   c. psychiatric social worker.
   d. clinical social worker.

7. In an experiment testing the effects of a new antipsychotic drug, neither Dr. Cunningham nor her patients know whether the patients are in the experimental or the control group. This is an example of the _____ technique.
   a. eclectic
   b. within-subjects
   c. double-blind
   d. single-blind

8. A close friend who for years has suffered from wintertime depression is seeking your advice regarding the effectiveness of light-exposure therapy. What should you tell your friend?
   a. "Don't waste your time and money. It doesn't work."
   b. "A more effective treatment for seasonal affective disorder is eye movement desensitization and reprocessing."
   c. "You'd be better off with a prescription for lithium."
   d. "It might be worth a try. There is some evidence that morning light exposure affects the secretion of melatonin, which helps regulate the body's circadian rhythm."

9. A relative wants to know which type of therapy works best. You should tell your relative that:
   a. psychotherapy does not work.
   b. behavior therapy is the most effective.
   c. cognitive therapy is the most effective.
   d. group therapy is best for his problem.
   e. no one type of therapy is consistently the most successful.

10. Leota is startled when her therapist says that she needs to focus on eliminating her problem behavior rather than gaining insight into its underlying cause. Most likely, Leota has consulted a _____ therapist.
    a. behavior
    b. humanistic
    c. cognitive
    d. psychoanalytic

11. In order to help him overcome his fear of flying, Duane's therapist has him construct a hierarchy of anxiety-triggering stimuli and then learn to associate each with a state of deep relaxation. Duane's therapist is using the technique called:
    a. systematic desensitization.
    b. aversive conditioning.
    c. shaping.
    d. free association.

12. A patient in a hospital receives poker chips for making her bed, being punctual at meal times, and maintaining her physical appearance. The poker chips can be exchanged for privileges, such as television viewing, snacks, and magazines. This is an example of the _____ therapy technique called _____ .
    a. psychodynamic; systematic desensitization
    b. behavior; token economy
    c. cognitive; token economy
    d. humanistic; systematic desensitization

13. Ben is a cognitive-behavior therapist. Compared to Rachel, who is a behavior therapist, Ben is more likely to:
    a. base his therapy on principles of operant conditioning.
    b. base his therapy on principles of classical conditioning.
    c. address clients' attitudes as well as behaviors.
    d. focus on clients' unconscious urges.

14. A psychotherapist who believes that the best way to treat psychological disorders is to prevent them from developing would be *most* likely to view disordered behavior as:
    a. maladaptive thoughts and actions.
    b. expressions of unconscious conflicts.
    c. conditioned responses.
    d. an understandable response to stressful social conditions.

15. Linda's doctor prescribes medication that blocks the activity of dopamine in her nervous system. Evidently, Linda is being treated with an _____ drug.
    a. antipsychotic   c. antidepressant
    b. antianxiety   d. anticonvulsive

16. Abraham's doctor prescribes medication that increases the availability of norepinephrine or serotonin in his nervous system. Evidently, Abraham is being treated with an _____ drug.
    a. antipsychotic
    b. antianxiety
    c. antidepressant
    d. anticonvulsive

17. In concluding her talk entitled "Psychosurgery Today," Ashley states that:
    a. "Psychosurgery is still widely used throughout the world."
    b. "Electroconvulsive therapy is the only remaining psychosurgical technique that is widely practiced."

    c. "With advances in psychopharmacology, psychosurgery has largely been abandoned."
    d. "Although lobotomies remain popular, other psychosurgical techniques have been abandoned."

18. A psychiatrist has diagnosed a patient as having bipolar disorder. It is likely that she will prescribe:
    a. an antipsychotic drug.
    b. lithium.
    c. an antianxiety drug.
    d. a drug that blocks receptor sites for serotonin.

19. Which type(s) of psychotherapy would be most likely to use the interpretation of dreams as a technique for bringing unconscious feelings into awareness?
    a. psychoanalysis
    b. psychodynamic therapy
    c. cognitive therapy
    d. all of the above
    e. both a. and b.

20. Of the following therapists, who would be most likely to interpret a person's psychological problems in terms of repressed impulses?
    a. a behavior therapist
    b. a cognitive therapist
    c. a humanistic therapist
    d. a psychoanalyst

Essay Question

Willie has been diagnosed as suffering from major depressive disorder. Describe the treatment he might receive from a psychoanalyst, a cognitive therapist, and a biomedical therapist. (Use the space below to list points you want to make, and organize them. Then write the essay on a separate sheet of paper.)

Key Terms

Using your own words, on a separate piece of paper write a brief definition or explanation of each of the following terms.

1. psychotherapy

2. eclectic approach

3. psychoanalysis

4. resistance

5. interpretation

6. transference

7. client-centered therapy

8. active listening

9. behavior therapy

10. counterconditioning

11. exposure therapies

12. systematic desensitization

13. aversive conditioning

14. token economy

15. cognitive therapy

16. cognitive-behavior therapy

17. family therapy

18. psychopharmacology

19. lithium

20. electroconvulsive therapy (ECT)

21. psychosurgery

22. lobotomy

Answers

The Psychological Therapies

Section Preview

1. Psychotherapy is "a planned, emotionally charged, confiding interaction between a socially sanctioned healer and a sufferer." The various types of psychotherapy derive from psychology's major personality theories: psychoanalytic, humanistic, behavioral, and cognitive. Half of all contemporary psychotherapists take an eclectic approach, using a blend of therapies tailored to meet their clients' particular problems.

2. Psychoanalysis assumes that psychological problems are caused by repressed unconscious impulses and conflicts that develop during childhood, and so its goal is to bring these feelings into conscious awareness and help the person work through them.

   Psychoanalysts may ask their patients to report everything that comes to mind (free association). Blocks in the flow of retrieval (resistance) are believed to indicate the repression of sensitive material. The analyst's interpretations of resistances aim to provide the patients with insight into their underlying meaning. Psychoanalysts interpret dreams for their latent content and the transference of feelings from early relationships in order to expose repressed feelings.

   Psychodynamic therapists also try to understand a patient's symptoms by exploring childhood experiences, but may talk face to face, with therapy lasting for only a few weeks or months. A new form of this therapy, interpersonal psychotherapy, focuses on current relationships (rather than on past hurts) and symptom relief in the here and now.

   Psychoanalysis has been criticized for offering interpretations that are impossible to prove or disprove and for being a lengthy and expensive process that only the relatively well-off can afford.

3. Humanistic therapists aim to boost self-fulfillment by helping people grow in self-awareness and self-acceptance. Unlike psychoanalysis, humanistic therapies focus on conscious thoughts as they occur in the present. Carl Rogers' nondirective client-centered therapy (which is also called person-centered therapy), which is based on the assumption that most people have within themselves the resources for growth, aims to provide an environment in which therapists exhibit genuineness, acceptance, and empathy. Humanistic therapists often use *active listening* to provide a psychological mirror that helps clients see themselves more clearly.

4. Behavior therapy applies learning principles to eliminate unwanted behavior. Counterconditioning describes classical-conditioning procedures that condition new responses to stimuli that trigger unwanted behaviors. One type of counterconditioning, systematic desensitization, is used to treat phobias, for example, by conditioning people to associate a pleasant, relaxed state with gradually increasing anxiety-provoking stimuli. It is a prime example of exposure therapy. Aversive conditioning is a type of counterconditioning that

associates unwanted behavior (such as drinking alcohol) with unpleasant feelings (such as nausea).

5. Operant conditioning procedures are used to treat specific behavioral problems by reinforcing desired behaviors and withholding reinforcement for undesired behaviors. In institutional settings, for example, a token economy is employed to shape desired behaviors. With this procedure, patients earn tokens for exhibiting desired behavior, then exchange the accumulated tokens for various privileges.

Critics note that because "behavior modification" depends on extrinsic rewards, the appropriate behaviors may disappear when the person leaves the conditioning environment. Second, critics question whether it is ethical for a therapist to exercise so much control over a person's behavior.

6. The cognitive therapies assume that our thinking influences our feelings and that maladaptive thinking patterns can be replaced with new, more constructive ones. Aaron Beck's form of cognitive therapy helps patients with depression to discover and reform their habitually negative patterns of thinking. Cognitive-behavior therapy expands upon standard cognitive therapy to include helping people to practice their newly learned positive approach in everyday settings.

Stepping Through the Section

1. psychotherapy
2. eclectic
3. psychoanalytic; humanistic; behavioral; cognitive
4. free association
5. resistance; interpretation
6. latent content
7. transference
8. psychodynamic; once a week
9. depressed; interpersonal psychotherapy; insight; current relationships
10. self-fulfillment

Unlike psychoanalysis, humanistic therapy is focused on the present instead of the past, on awareness of feelings as they occur rather than on achieving insights into the childhood origins of the feelings, on conscious rather than unconscious processes, on promoting growth and fulfillment instead of curing illness, and on helping clients take immediate responsibility for their feelings and actions rather than on uncovering the obstacles to doing so.

11. client-centered; nondirective; does not interpret
12. genuineness; acceptance; empathy
13. active listening; unconditional positive regard
14. paraphrase; invite clarification; reflect feelings

Whereas psychoanalysis and humanistic therapies assume that problems diminish as self-awareness grows, behavior therapists doubt that self-awareness is the key. Instead of looking for the inner cause of unwanted behavior, behavior therapy applies learning principles to directly attack the unwanted behavior itself.

15. classical conditioning; counterconditioning; systematic desensitization; aversive conditioning
16. exposure therapies; Wolpe; anxious
17. hierarchy; progressive relaxation; relaxed; anxiety
18. vividly imagine; virtual reality exposure
19. observational learning
20. negative; positive; unpleasant
21. operant; token economy

Behavior modification is criticized because the desired behavior may stop when the rewards are stopped. Also, critics contend that one person should not be allowed to control another.

22. cognitive
23. catastrophizing; depression; Beck
24. cognitive-behavior
25. stress inoculation; dispute

Group and Family Therapies

Section Preview

1. Group therapies provide a social context, which allows people to discover that others have similar problems and to try out new ways of behaving. Self-help and support groups are examples of the group approach to psychotherapy. Another is family therapy, which treats individuals within their family system.

Stepping Through the Section

Group therapy saves therapists time and clients money. The social context of group therapy allows people to discover that others have similar problems and to try out new ways of behaving.

1. self-help; support; stigmatized, embarrassing, hard-to-discuss
2. family therapy
3. communication; conflict

Evaluating Psychotherapies

Section Preview

1. One reason clients' and therapists' perceptions of therapy's effectiveness are vulnerable to inflation is that people often enter therapy in crisis; when they improve, they attribute their improvement to therapy. Another is the placebo effect, or the power of belief in a treatment. A third reason is the tendency for unusual events (such as undesirable emotions or other psychological problems) to return ("regress") toward their average state. A fourth is self-justification of the time and money involved in therapy. Finally, clients tend to speak kindly of their therapists.

2. The effectiveness of psychotherapy depends on how it is measured. Although clients' testimonials and clinicians' perceptions strongly affirm the effectiveness of psychotherapy, controlled research studies, such as those originated by Hans Eysenck, report a similar improvement rate among treated and untreated people. Research combining the results of many different studies reveals that psychotherapy is somewhat effective and that it is cost-effective compared with the greater costs of physician care for underlying psychological ailments. More recent research confirms these findings.

3. Research studies have revealed that although no particular type of therapy proved consistently superior, certain therapies work best with certain disorders. In general, therapy is most effective when problems are clear-cut. For example, bulimia and bed-wetting have been successfully treated with cognitive-behavior therapy and behavioral conditioning therapies, respectively.

4. There have been very few controlled research studies of most forms of alternative therapy. Therapeutic touch is the popular therapy in which practitioners move their hands a few inches over a patient's body, allegedly in order to restore balance to "energy fields." The limited evidence that is available is that therapeutic touch does not work. In eye movement desensitization and reprocessing (EMDR) therapy, a practitioner triggers eye movements in patients, who are imagining traumatic events, by waving a finger in front of their eyes. While EMDR has proven to be beneficial in treating nonmilitary post-traumatic stress disorder, it is probably the combination of exposure therapy and a placebo effect (rather than eye movements) that accounts for this success. Light-exposure therapy may help combat

seasonal affective disorder by affecting secretion of the hormone melatonin.

5. First, because they enable people to believe that things can and will get better, psychotherapies provide hope for demoralized people. This placebo effect explains why all sorts of treatments may produce cures. Second, therapy offers people a plausible explanation of problems and alternative ways of responding. Third, therapy establishes an empathic, trusting, caring relationship between client and therapist.

6. All therapists have their own values, which may differ radically, as illustrated by Albert Ellis and Allen Bergin's widely divergent views. Because these values influence their therapy, they should be divulged to patients. Value differences may become particularly significant when a therapist from one culture meets a client from another.

Stepping Through the Section

1. is not

2. satisfaction

3. are not; crisis

4. placebo effect

Clients' and therapists' perceptions of the effectiveness of therapy may be inflated by the tendency of unusual events and emotions to return (regress) toward their average state, by the client's need to believe that the therapy was worth the time and money, and by the fact that clients generally like their therapists and speak kindly of them.

5. Eysenck; was not

6. somewhat effective

7. specific

8. no clear

9. cognitive; interpersonal; standard drug; bulimia; bed-wetting, phobias, compulsions, or sexual disorders

10. alternative therapy; therapeutic touch; nonexistent

11. traumatic events; eye movement desensitization and reprocessing (EMDR); somewhat effective; post-traumatic stress disorder; finger tapping

12. seasonal affective disorder; light-exposure; melatonin

13. is

14. do

The Biomedical Therapies

Section Preview

1. Discoveries in psychopharmacology revolutionized the treatment of disordered people and greatly reduced the need for psychosurgery or hospitalization. Antipsychotic drugs such as Thorazine and Clozaril are used to reduce positive and negative symptoms of schizophrenia, respectively. These drugs work by blocking receptor sites for the neurotransmitter dopamine. Antianxiety drugs, such as Xanax and Valium, reduce tension and anxiety by depressing central nervous system activity. Antidepressant drugs elevate mood by increasing the availability of the neurotransmitters norepinephrine and serotonin; fluoxetine (Prozac) blocks the reabsorption and removal of serotonin from synapses. The drug lithium is used to stabilize the manic-depressive mood swings of the bipolar disorder.

2. Electroconvulsive therapy (ECT), which is used by psychiatrists to treat severe depression, produces marked improvement in at least 80 percent of patients without discernible brain damage. ECT may work by increasing the release of norepinephrine or by inducing seizures that calm neural centers in which overactivity produces depression. A gentler treatment called repetitive transcranial magnetic stimulation (rTMS) shows promise in reducing depression without the seizures, memory loss, or other side effects associated with ECT.

   Because its effects are irreversible, psychosurgery, which removes or destroys brain tissue to change behavior, is the most drastic biomedical intervention. The best-known form, the lobotomy, was developed by Moniz in the 1930s to calm emotional and violent patients. During the 1950s, with advances in psychopharmacology, psychosurgery was largely abandoned.

Stepping Through the Section

1. drug; decreased
2. psychopharmacology
3. double-blind
4. antipsychotic; chlorpromazine (Thorazine); positive; clozapine (Clozaril); dopamine; serotonin
5. antianxiety; central nervous system
6. antidepressant; norepinephrine; serotonin; fluoxetine (Prozac); serotonin; selective-serotonin-reuptake-inhibitor
7. aerobic exercise
8. placebo effect
9. lithium
10. electroconvulsive; ECT
11. depression; confirms
12. norepinephrine
13. repetitive transcranial magnetic stimulation (rTMS); frontal lobe
14. psychosurgery
15. lobotomy; frontal
16. drugs

Preventing Psychological Disorders

Section Preview

1. Psychotherapists who view psychological disorders as responses to a disturbed and stressful society contend that the best approach is to prevent problems from developing by treating not only the person but also the person's social context. Accordingly, programs that help alleviate poverty, discrimination, constant criticism, unemployment, sexism, and other demoralizing situations that undermine people's sense of competence, personal control, and self-esteem are thought to be effective in reducing people's risk of psychological disorders.

Progress Test 1

Multiple-Choice Questions

1. **b.** is the answer. Although no one is sure how ECT works, one possible explanation is that it increases release of norepinephrine, the neurotransmitter that elevates mood. (p. 533)

2. **c.** is the answer. (p. 508)
   a. Active listening is a Rogerian technique in which the therapist echoes, restates, and seeks clarification of the client's statements.
   b. Spontaneous remission, which is not mentioned in the text, refers to improvement without treatment.
   d. Systematic desensitization is a process in which a person is conditioned to associate a relaxed state with anxiety-triggering stimuli.

3. **b.** is the answer. (p. 510)

4. d. is the answer. This is not among the criticisms commonly made of psychoanalysis. (It would more likely be made of behavior therapies.) (pp. 508–509)

5. a. is the answer. (p. 518)
b., c., & d. Each of these is a type of group therapy.

6. c. is the answer. (p. 518)

7. c. is the answer. (p. 529)
a. The fact that its effects are irreversible makes psychosurgery a drastic procedure, and with advances in psychopharmacology, psychosurgery was largely abandoned.
b. ECT is still widely used as a treatment of severe depression, but in general it is not used as frequently as drug therapy.
d. & e. Counterconditioning and aversive conditioning are not biomedical therapies.

8. b. is the answer. Clients' testimonials regarding psychotherapy are generally very positive. The research, in contrast, seems to show that therapy is only *somewhat* effective. (pp. 520–522)

9. d. is the answer. (pp. 522–523)

10. a. is the answer. By occupying receptor sites for dopamine, these drugs block its activity and reduce its production. (p. 530)

11. e. is the answer. (p. 535)

12. d. is the answer. Today, half of psychotherapists describe themselves as eclectic—as using a blend of therapies. (p. 507)
a. An eclectic therapist may use a nondirective approach with certain behaviors; however, a more directive approach might be chosen for other clients and problems.
b. In fact, just the opposite is true. Eclectic therapists generally view disorders as stemming from many influences.
c. Eclectic therapists, in contrast to this example, use a combination of treatments.

13. a. is the answer. (p. 510)

14. c. is the answer. (p. 509)

15. b. is the answer. (p. 513)
a. This reflects a cognitive perspective.
c. This reflects a psychoanalytic perspective.

16. c. is the answer. (p. 515)
a. & b. Counterconditioning is the replacement of an undesired response with a desired one by means of aversive conditioning or systematic desensitization.
d. Exposure therapy exposes a person, in imagination or in actuality, to a feared situation.

17. d. is the answer. (p. 517)

18. b. is the answer. (p. 520)
a. Spontaneous remission refers to improvement without any treatment.
c. Transference is the psychoanalytic phenomenon in which a client transfers feelings from other relationships onto his or her analyst.
d. Interpretation is the psychoanalytic procedure through which the analyst helps the client become aware of resistances and understand their meaning.

19. c. is the answer. (p. 520)

20. c. is the answer. (pp. 524–525)

Matching Items

1. e (p. 516)	**5.** g (p. 510)	**9.** c (p. 535)
2. k (p. 512)	**6.** f (p. 512)	**10.** i (p. 529)
3. b (p. 513)	**7.** a (p. 514)	**11.** j (p. 512)
4. d (p. 517)	**8.** h (p. 508)	

Progress Test 2

Multiple-Choice Questions

1. c. is the answer. (p. 510)
a. This answer would be a correct description of Joseph Wolpe.
b. There is no such thing as insight therapy.
d. This answer would be a correct description of Aaron Beck.

2. a. is the answer. (p. 514)
b. In systematic desensitization, a hierarchy of anxiety-provoking stimuli is gradually associated with a relaxed state.
c. Transference refers to a patient's transferring of feelings from other relationships onto his or her psychoanalyst.
d. Electroconvulsive therapy is a biomedical shock treatment.
e. A token economy is based on operant conditioning techniques.

3. c. is the answer. (p. 510)
a. Behavior therapy focuses on behavior, not self-awareness.
b. Psychoanalysis focuses on bringing repressed feelings into awareness.
d. Biomedical therapy focuses on physical treatment through drugs, ECT, or psychosurgery.

4. b. is the answer. (pp. 525–526)

5. a. is the answer. For behavior therapy, the problem behaviors *are* the problems. (p. 512)

b. Cognitive therapy teaches people to think and act in more adaptive ways.

c. Humanistic therapy promotes growth and self-fulfillment by providing an empathic, genuine, and accepting environment.

d. Psychoanalytic therapy focuses on uncovering and interpreting repressed feelings.

e. Family therapy focuses on the individual's relation to others.

6. **b.** is the answer. Counterconditioning techniques involve conditioning new responses to stimuli that trigger unwanted behaviors. (p. 512)

a. As indicated by the name, counterconditioning techniques are a form of conditioning; they do not involve learning by observation.

c. & d. The principles of operant conditioning are the basis of behavior modification, which, in contrast to counterconditioning techniques, involves use of reinforcement.

7. **d.** is the answer. (p. 513)

a. This is a confrontational therapy, which is aimed at teaching people to think and act in more adaptive ways.

b. Aversive conditioning is a form of counterconditioning in which unwanted behavior is associated with unpleasant feelings.

c. Counterconditioning is a general term, including not only systematic desensitization, in which a hierarchy of fears is desensitized, but also other techniques, such as aversive conditioning.

8. **e.** is the answer. (p. 515)

a., b., & d. These techniques are based on classical conditioning.

c. This is a type of cognitive therapy.

9. **d.** is the answer. (p. 516)

10. **c.** is the answer. (p. 516)

a. This is an alternative therapy in which the practitioner triggers eye movements in patients who are imagining traumatic events.

b. In this humanistic therapy, the therapist facilitates the client's growth by offering a genuine, accepting, and empathic environment.

d. Behavior therapy concentrates on modifying the actual symptoms of psychological problems.

11. **c.** is the answer. (p. 531)

12. **d.** is the answer. Lithium works as a mood stabilizer. (p. 532)

a. & c. Valium and Xanax are antianxiety drugs.

b. Chlorpromazine is an antipsychotic drug.

13. **a.** is the answer. (p. 531)

14. **c.** is the answer. (p. 522)

a. Behavior therapy is most likely to be successful in treating specific behavior problems, such as phobias.

b. & d. The text does not single out particular disorders for which these therapies tend to be most effective.

15. **d.** is the answer. (p. 534)

16. **d.** is the answer. Even when dealing with seriously depressed adults, the paraprofessionals were as effective as the professionals. (p. 527)

17. **d.** is the answer. (pp. 526–527)

18. **d.** is the answer. (p. 519)

a. This is true of most forms of psychotherapy.

b. & c. This is true of humanistic, cognitive, and behavior therapies.

19. **c.** is the answer. Although aversive conditioning may work in the short run, the person's ability to discriminate between the situation in which the aversive conditioning occurs and other situations can limit the treatment's effectiveness. (p. 514)

a., b., & d. These were not offered in the text as limitations of the effectiveness of aversive conditioning.

20. **c.** is the answer. (p. 517)

Matching Items

1. d (p. 510)   5. c (p. 532)   9. f (p. 531)
2. h (p. 515)   6. b (p. 507)   10. g (p. 508)
3. e (p. 520)   7. i (p. 529)   11. k (p. 518)
4. a (p. 534)   8. j (p. 530)

Review and Reflect

Multiple-Choice Questions

1. **d.** is the answer. Resistances are blocks in the flow of free association that hint at underlying anxiety. (p. 508)

a. In transference, a patient redirects feelings from other relationships to his or her analyst.

b. The goal of psychoanalysis is for patients to gain insight into their feelings.

c. Although such hesitation may well involve material that has been repressed, the hesitation itself is a resistance.

2. **d.** is the answer. In transference, the patient develops feelings toward the therapist that were experienced in important early relationships but were repressed. (p. 508)

a. Projection is a defense mechanism in which a person imputes his or her own feelings to someone else.

b. Resistances are blocks in the flow of free association that indicate repressed material.

c. Regression is a defense mechanism in which a person retreats to an earlier form of behavior.

3. **d.** is the answer. According to Rogers' client-centered therapy, the therapist must exhibit genuineness, acceptance, and empathy if the client is to move toward self-fulfillment. (p. 510)

   a. Psychoanalysts are much more directive in providing interpretations of clients' problems than are humanistic therapists.

   b. Behavior therapists focus on modifying the behavioral symptoms of psychological problems.

   c. Cognitive therapists teach people to think and act in new, more adaptive ways.

4. **d.** is the answer. Aversive conditioning is the classical conditioning technique in which a positive response is replaced by a negative response. (In this example, the unpleasant state is the blast of smoke, the harmful stimulus is the taste of the cigarette as it is inhaled, and the intended negative response is aversion to cigarettes.) (p. 514)

   a. Exposure therapy exposes someone, in imagination (virtual reality exposure therapy) or actuality, to a feared situation.

   b. Behavior modification applies the principles of operant conditioning and thus, in contrast to the example, uses reinforcement.

   c. Systematic desensitization is used to help people overcome specific anxieties.

5. **d.** is the answer. Because the psychologist is challenging Darnel's illogical, self-defeating attitude, this response is most typical of rational-emotive therapy. (p. 516)

   a. Behavior therapists treat behaviors rather than thoughts.

   b. Psychoanalysts focus on helping patients gain insight into previously repressed feelings.

   c. Client-centered therapists attempt to facilitate clients' growth by offering a genuine, accepting, empathic environment.

6. **b.** is the answer. Psychiatrists are physicians who specialize in treating psychological disorders. As doctors they can prescribe medications. (p. 528)

   a., c., & d. These professionals cannot prescribe drugs.

7. **c.** is the answer. (p. 530)

   a. This refers to the use of techniques from various forms of therapy.

   b. In this design, which is not mentioned in the text, there is only a single research group.

   d. This answer would be correct if the experimenter, but not the subjects, knew which condition was in effect.

8. **d.** is the answer. (p. 526)

   a. In fact, there is evidence that light-exposure therapy can be effective in treating SAD.

b. There is no evidence that EMDR is effective as a treatment for SAD.

c. Lithium is an antidepressant drug that is often used to treat bipolar disorder.

9. **e.** is the answer. (p. 523)

   a. Psychotherapy has proven "somewhat effective" and more cost-effective than physician care for psychological disorders.

   b. & c. Behavior and cognitive therapies are effective in treating specific behavior problems and depression, respectively, but not necessarily in treating other problems.

   d. The text does not specify which problems are best treated with group therapy.

10. **a.** is the answer. (p. 512)

    b. & c. These types of therapists are more concerned with promoting self-fulfillment (humanistic) and healthy patterns of thinking (cognitive) than with correcting specific problem behaviors.

    d. Psychoanalysts see the behavior merely as a symptom and focus their treatment on its presumed underlying cause.

11. **a.** is the answer. (pp. 512–513)

    b. Aversive conditioning associates unpleasant states with unwanted behaviors.

    c. Shaping is an operant conditioning technique in which successive approximations of a desired behavior are reinforced.

    d. Free association is a psychoanalytic technique in which a patient says whatever comes to mind.

12. **b.** is the answer. (p. 515)

13. **c.** is the answer. (p. 517)

    a. & b. Behavior therapists make extensive use of techniques based on both operant and classical conditioning.

    d. Neither behavior therapists nor cognitive behavior therapists focus on clients' unconscious urges.

14. **d.** is the answer. (p. 535)

    a. This would be the perspective of a cognitive behavior therapist.

    b. This would be the perspective of a psychoanalyst.

    c. This would be the perspective of a behavior therapist.

15. **a.** is the answer. (p. 530)

16. **c.** is the answer. (p. 531)

17. **c.** is the answer. (p. 534)

    b. Although still practiced, electroconvulsive therapy is not a form of psychosurgery.

18. **b.** is the answer. (p. 532)

19. **e.** is the answer. Both psychoanalysis and psychodynamic therapy seek insight into a patient's unconscious feelings. The analysis of dreams, slips of the tongue, and resistances are considered a window into these feelings. (pp. 508, 509)

   c. Cognitive therapists avoid reference to unconscious feelings and would therefore be uninterested in interpreting dreams.

20. **d.** is the answer. A key aim of psychoanalysis is to unearth and understand repressed impulses. (p. 508)

   a., b., & c. Behavior and cognitive therapists avoid concepts such as "repression" and "unconscious"; behavior and humanistic therapists focus on the present rather than the past.

Essay Question

Psychoanalysts assume that psychological problems such as depression are caused by unresolved, repressed, and unconscious impulses and conflicts from childhood. A psychoanalyst would probably attempt to bring these repressed feelings into Willie's conscious awareness and help him gain insight into them. He or she would likely try to interpret Willie's resistance during free association, the latent content of his dreams, and any emotional feelings he might transfer to the analyst.

Cognitive therapists assume that a person's emotional reactions are influenced by the person's thoughts in response to the event in question. A cognitive therapist would probably try to teach Willie new and more constructive ways of thinking in order to reverse his catastrophizing beliefs about himself, his situation, and his future.

Biomedical therapists attempt to treat disorders by altering the functioning of the patient's brain. A biomedical therapist would probably prescribe an antidepressant drug such as fluoxetine to increase the availability of norepinephrine and serotonin in Willie's nervous system. If Willie's depression is especially severe, a *psychiatrist* might treat it with several sessions of electroconvulsive therapy.

Key Terms

1. **Psychotherapy** is an emotionally charged, confiding interaction between a trained therapist and someone who suffers from psychological difficulties. (p. 507)

2. With an **eclectic approach**, therapists are not locked into one form of psychotherapy, but draw on whatever combination seems best suited to a client's needs. (p. 507)

3. **Psychoanalysis**, the therapy developed by Freud, attempts to give clients self-insight by bringing into awareness and interpreting previously repressed feelings. (p. 508)

   Example: The tools of the **psychoanalyst** include free association, the analysis of dreams and transferences, and the interpretation of repressed impulses.

4. **Resistance** is the psychoanalytic term for the blocking from consciousness of anxiety-provoking memories. Hesitation during free association may reflect resistance. (p. 508)

5. **Interpretation** is the psychoanalytic term for the analyst's helping the client to understand resistances and other aspects of behavior, so that the client may gain deeper insights. (p. 508)

6. **Transference** is the psychoanalytic term for a patient's redirecting to the analyst emotions from other relationships. (p. 508)

7. **Client-centered therapy** is a humanistic therapy developed by Rogers, in which growth and self-awareness are facilitated in an environment that offers genuineness, acceptance, and empathy. (p. 510)

8. **Active listening** is a nondirective technique of client-centered therapy, in which the listener echoes, restates, and seeks clarification of, but does not interpret, clients' remarks. (p. 510)

9. **Behavior therapy** is therapy that applies principles of operant or classical conditioning to the elimination of problem behaviors. (p. 512)

10. **Counterconditioning** is a category of behavior therapy in which new responses are classically conditioned to stimuli that trigger unwanted behaviors. (p. 512)

11. **Exposure therapies** treat anxiety by exposing people to things they normally fear and avoid. Among these therapies are systematic desensitization and virtual reality exposure therapy. (pp. 512–513)

12. **Systematic desensitization** is a type of counterconditioning in which a state of relaxation is classically conditioned to a hierarchy of gradually increasing anxiety-provoking stimuli. (p. 513)

    Memory aid: This is a form of **counterconditioning** in which sensitive, anxiety-triggering stimuli are *desensitized* in a progressive, or **systematic**, fashion.

13. **Aversive conditioning** is a form of counterconditioning in which an unpleasant state becomes associated with an unwanted behavior. (p. 514)

14. A **token economy** is an operant conditioning procedure in which desirable behaviors are promoted in people by rewarding them with tokens, or positive reinforcers, which can be exchanged for privileges or treats. Token economies have been used successfully in hospitals, schools, and other institutional settings. (p. 515)

15. **Cognitive therapy** focuses on teaching people new and more adaptive ways of thinking and acting. The therapy is based on the idea that our feelings and responses to events are strongly influenced by our thinking, or cognition. (p. 516)

16. **Cognitive-behavior therapy** is an integrated therapy that focuses on changing self-defeating thinking (cognitive therapy) and unwanted behaviors (behavior therapy). (p. 517)

17. **Family therapy** views problem behavior as partially engendered by the client's family system and environment. Therapy therefore focuses on relationships and problems among the various members of the family. (p. 518)

18. **Psychopharmacology** is the study of the effects of drugs on mind and behavior. (p. 529)

Memory aid: Pharmacology is the science of the uses and effects of drugs. *Psycho***pharmacology** is the science that studies the psychological effects of drugs.

19. **Lithium** is a chemical that is commonly used as a drug therapy to stabilize the manic-depressive mood swings of the bipolar disorder. (p. 532)

20. In **electroconvulsive therapy (ECT)**, a biomedical therapy often used to treat severe depression, a brief electric current is passed through the brain of an anesthetized patient. (p. 533)

21. **Psychosurgery** is a biomedical therapy that attempts to change behavior by removing or destroying brain tissue. Since drug therapy became widely available in the 1950s, psychosurgery has been infrequently used. (p. 534)

22. Once used to control violent patients, the **lobotomy** is a form of psychosurgery in which the nerves linking the emotion centers of the brain to the frontal lobes are severed. (p. 534)

FOCUS ON VOCABULARY AND LANGUAGE

Page 507: . . . . bewildering variety of harsh and gentle methods . . . Myers is referring to the many odd and strange techniques (*bewildering variety of harsh and gentle methods*) that have been used in the past to deal with people suffering from psychological disorders, such as cutting holes in the skull, piercing veins or attaching leeches to remove blood from the body (*bleeding*), whipping or striking people in order to force demons out of the body ("*beating the devil out of people*"), and so on. Today's less harsh (*gentle*) therapies are classified into two main categories, psychological and biomedical.

Page 507 (caption): Visitors paid to *gawk* at the *patients* as if they were viewing zoo animals. In the past, mentally disordered people (*patients*) were confined to hospitals (*insane asylums*) and were often treated badly. For instance, some hospitals raised money by selling tickets to the public who could come and stare (*gawk*) at the inmates (*patients*), much as we do today when we visit the zoo and look at the captive animals.

The Psychological Therapies

Page 507: Although each technique is distinctive, there are *common threads*. The most common forms of psychological therapy (**psychotherapy**) are based on the four major perspectives in psychology: psychoanalytic, humanistic, behavioral, and cognitive. While each type of therapy is unique (*distinctive*), their effectiveness may derive from similar underlying factors (*common threads*). About fifty percent of psychotherapists claim that they use a combination (*blend*) of techniques (an **eclectic approach**).

Page 508: Freud assumed that many psychological problems are *fueled* by childhood's *residue* of *repressed impulses and conflicts*. Freud's psychoanalytic techniques are used by many therapists; their fundamental tenet (*assumption*) is that mental disorders are created and kept in existence (*fueled*) by hidden (*repressed*) childhood urges and opposing psychic forces (*conflicts*). Psychoanalysis attempts to restore the patient to mental health by bringing these submerged (*buried*) feelings into conscious awareness where they can be examined and dealt with (*worked through*). As Myers puts it, psychoanalysis digs up (*unearths*) the past in the hopes of uncovering (*unmasking*) the present.

Page 510: Not surprisingly, then, humanistic therapists *aim to boost* self-fulfillment by helping people grow in self-awareness and self-acceptance. The most popular humanistic technique is Carl Rogers' nondirective person-centered therapy. The goal is to increase (*the aim is to boost*) the client's feelings of accomplishment and achievement (self-actualization) by providing nonthreatening opportunities for living in the present, for becoming less critical of one's self, and for becoming more self-aware.

Page 511: "And that just really knocks the props out from under you." In Carl Rogers' therapy sessions, he attempts to be genuine, accepting, and empathic; he also mirrors (*reflects*) back to the client in different words the feelings that were expressed. The client said he had been told that he was no good, and Rogers reflects the feelings he detects by saying that it must seem that the client's self-worth had been undermined (*knocked the props out from under you*).

Page 512: . . . Jones' story of Peter and the rabbit did not immediately become part of psychology's *lore.* Mary Cover Jones was the first to demonstrate **counterconditioning** (replacing a fear response with an incompatible response, such as relaxation through classical conditioning). This technique, however, did not become part of psychology's tradition and store of knowledge (*lore*) until Wolpe developed systematic desensitization more than 30 years later.

Page 514: To treat alcoholism, an aversion therapist offers the client appealing drinks *laced* with a drug that produces *severe nausea.* Behavior therapists, focusing on observable behaviors, use a number of techniques based on well-established learning principles. Two counterconditioning techniques based on classical conditioning are **systematic desensitization** and **aversive conditioning.** In aversive therapy, people who regularly drink too much are given enticing alcoholic beverages which are infused (*laced*) with a substance that induces sickness (*severe nausea*). Alcohol should now be a potent conditioned stimulus that elicits unpleasant feelings; as a result, the person with alcoholism should want to avoid these drinks. Research shows some limited success with this approach.

Page 515: The combination of positively reinforcing desired behaviors and ignoring or punishing *aggressive and self-abusive* behaviors *worked wonders.* Another type of behavior therapy is based on operant conditioning principles and involves voluntary behavior followed by pleasant or unpleasant consequences. Socially withdrawn autistic children, treated to an intensive two-year program of positive reinforcement for desired behaviors and punishment for violent and self-injurious (*aggressive and self-abusive*) behaviors, responded extremely well (*it worked wonders for them*).

Page 516: The **cognitive therapies** assume that our thinking *colors* our feelings. . . . The underlying assumption of the cognitive approach to therapy is that thoughts precede and influence (*color*) our feelings. If certain destructive patterns of thinking are learned, then it must be possible to unlearn them and replace them with more constructive ways of viewing what happens to us.

Page 517: . . . *catastrophizing* . . . Aaron Beck, a cognitive therapist, believes that the way to help depressed people feel better is to turn around (*reverse*) their negative, distorted thinking, which tends to transform ordinary events into disasters (*catastrophizing*). The goal is to get them to think about their lives in more positive terms (*convince them to take off the dark glasses*).

Evaluating Psychotherapies

Page 519: "Hang in there until you find [a psychotherapist] who fills the bill." Each year in the United States about 15 percent of the population seek help for psychological and addictive disorders. Many people, including the late advice columnist Ann Landers, recommend that troubled people get professional help and that they persevere (*hang in there*) in finding the right therapist to meet their needs (*who fills the bill*).

Page 520: If clients' *testimonials* were the only yardstick, we could strongly affirm the effectiveness of psychotherapy. The question of whether or not psychotherapy is effective is a very complex issue. If the only measure (*yardstick*) was what clients said about their therapy (*testimonials*), then the conclusion would have to be that psychotherapy works. (Three-quarters, or more, of those surveyed were satisfied.) Myers points out that such testimonials can be misleading and invalid.

Page 520: When, with the normal *ebb and flow* of events, the crisis passes, people may attribute their improvement to the therapy. Because of some serious traumatic events (*crises*) in their lives, people may end up seeing a therapist; after many sessions they may feel much better. During the ordinary course (*ebb and flow*) of events, however, the crisis is likely to have passed; thus, their present feelings of well-being may have little to do with the psychotherapy.

Page 523: Indeed, therapy is most effective when the problem is *clear-cut* (Singer, 1981; Westin & Morrison, 2001). Psychotherapy tends to work best when the disturbances are well-defined (*clear-cut*) and explicitly stated or understood. For example, those who suffer from irrational fears (*phobias*), are timid or shy (*unassertive*), or have a psychologically caused sexual disorder respond better to therapy than those who suffer from *schizophrenia* or who want a total personality change.

Page 523: The tendency of abnormal states of mind to "regress" to normal, combined with the placebo effect, creates *fertile soil* for *pseudotherapies*. So called alternative therapies may appear to be effective for a couple of reasons: worse-than-normal mental states tend to diminish and move back to more normal mental states (*regression to the average*) over time, and if people expect that a particular therapy will help them, they may get better as a result of their belief alone (*the placebo effect*). These factors provide a basis (*fertile soil*) for the growth and popularity of therapies that have not been empirically validated (*pseudotherapies*). Indeed, supported (*bolstered*) by anecdotes, exuberantly reported (*heralded*) by the media, given accolades (*praised*) on the Internet, alternative therapies can thrive and flourish (*can spread like wildfire*).

Page 526: Each therapy, in its individual way, may *harness* the person's own healing powers. Research has shown that actual therapy is better than no treatment, but that placebo-treated people improve significantly. This suggests that therapies work in part because they offer hope; each different type of therapy may be effective to the extent that it capitalizes on and uses (*harnesses*) the clients' ability for self-healing.

Page 527: Indeed, some believe warmth and *empathy* are *hallmarks* of healers everywhere, whether psychiatrists, witch doctors, or shamans (Torrey, 1986). In general, therapies are approximately the same in effectiveness, but that does not mean that all therapists are equal in this respect. Fundamental qualities (*hallmarks*) of effective therapists are an ability to understand other people's experiences (*empathy*) and a capacity to show genuine concern and care (*warmth*). In addition, good listening skills, a reassuring manner, and concern for gaining (*earning*) the client's respect and trust help in the therapeutic process.

The Biomedical Therapies

Pages 530–531: Antipsychotics such as Thorazine are powerful drugs. They can produce *sluggishness, tremors, and twitches* similar to those of Parkinson's disease, which is marked by too little dopamine (Kaplan & Saddock, 1989). Because of the serious side effects of some antipsychotic drugs—tiredness and apathy (*sluggishness*), shaking limbs (*tremors*), and sudden involuntary spasms (*twitches*)—therapists have to be very careful (*they have to tread a fine line*) in selecting the dose that will relieve the symptoms but will not produce the side effects.

Page 531: However, *"popping a Xanax"* at the first sign of tension can produce psychological dependence on the drug. The most popular antianxiety drugs (Xanax and Valium) are central nervous system depressants, and they reduce tension without causing too much drowsiness. As a consequence, they are prescribed for a variety of problems, including minor emotional stresses. If a person regularly takes an antianxiety drug (*routinely "pops a Xanax"*) whenever there is the slightest feeling of anxiety, the result can be psychological dependence on the drug. Withdrawal symptoms for heavy users include increased anxiety and an inability to sleep (*insomnia*).

Page 531: As the antianxiety drugs can calm people down from a state of anxiety, the antidepressants sometimes *lift people up from* a state of depression. Antidepressants work by either increasing the availability of the neurotransmitters norepinephrine or serotonin, blocking their reabsorption, or by inhibiting an enzyme that breaks them down. Thus, they tend to make depressed people feel more alive and aroused (*they lift them up*).

Page 533: ECT therefore gained a *barbaric* image, one that lingers still. **Electroconvulsive therapy (ECT)** has proven quite effective and is used mainly for chronically depressed people who have not responded to drug therapy. In 1938, when ECT was first introduced, wide-awake patients were strapped to a table to prevent them from hurting themselves during the convulsions and were shocked (*jolted*) with 100 volts of electricity to the brain. Although the procedure is different today, these inhumane (*barbaric*) images tend to remain in people's minds. As Myers notes, ECT is credited with saving many from suicide, but its Frankensteinlike image continues. (Dr. Frankenstein is a fictional character who created a living monster from the body parts of dead people.)

Page 533: Hopes are now rising for gentler alternative for *jump-starting* the depressed brain. (Using power from another car's battery to start a car with a flat or dead battery is called *jump-starting*.) Depressed moods appear to improve when a painless procedure called repetitive transcranial magnetic stimulation (rTMS) is used on wide-awake patients. Thus, optimism is increasing (*hopes are rising*) for a better way to activate (*jump-start*) the depressed brain.

Preventing Psychological Disorders

Page 535: Preventive mental health is *upstream work.* Some psychologists believe that prevention is better than cure and they support programs that help relieve and stop poverty, racism, discrimination, and other disempowering or demoralizing situations. The attempt to prevent psychological disorders by getting rid of conditions that may cause them is extremely difficult (*upstream work*).

chapter 15

Social Psychology

Chapter Overview

Chapter 15 demonstrates the powerful influences of social situations on the behavior of individuals. Central to this topic are research studies on attitudes and actions, conformity, compliance, and group and cultural influences. The social principles that emerge help us to understand how individuals are influenced by advertising, political candidates, and the various groups to which they belong. Although social influences are powerful, it is important to remember the significant role of individuals in choosing and creating the social situations that influence them.

The chapter also discusses how people relate to one another, from the negative—developing prejudice, behaving aggressively, and provoking conflict—to the positive—being attracted to people who are nearby and/or similar and behaving altruistically.

The chapter concludes with a discussion of techniques that have been shown to promote conflict resolution.

Although there is some terminology for you to learn in this chapter, your primary task is to absorb the findings of the many research studies discussed. The chapter headings, which organize the findings, should prove especially useful to you here. In addition, you might, for each main topic (conformity, group influence, aggression, etc.), ask yourself the question, "What situational factors promote this phenomenon?" The research findings can then form the basis for your answers.

NOTE: Answer guidelines for all Chapter 15 questions begin on page 448.

Social Thinking (pp. 539–544)

> David Myers at times uses idioms that are unfamiliar to some readers. If you do not know the meaning of any of the following words, phrases, or expressions in the context in which they appear in the text, refer to page 458 for an explanation: *tart-tongued remark; freeloaders; people often brainwashed; chicken-and-egg spiral; heartening implications.*

Section Preview

First, skim the section, noting headings and boldface items. Then read the following objectives and, as you read the text, search for the information that will enable you to meet each objective. Answer guidelines begin on page 448.

1. Discuss attribution theory, focusing on the fundamental attribution error, and describe some possible effects of attribution.

2. Define *attitude*, and identify the conditions under which attitudes predict behavior.

3. Describe how actions influence attitudes, and explain how cognitive dissonance theory accounts for this phenomenon.

4. Beliefs and feelings that predispose our responses are called _____ .

List three conditions under which our attitudes do predict our actions. Give examples.

Stepping Through the Section

After you have read the section, complete the sentences and answer the questions. As you proceed, evaluate your performance by consulting the answers on page 448. Do not continue with the next section until you understand each answer. If you need to, review or reread the section in the textbook before continuing.

1. Psychologists who study how we think about, influence, and relate to one another are called

   _____ _____ .

2. Heider's theory of how we explain others' behavior is the _____ theory. According to this theory, we attribute behavior either to an internal cause, which is called a

   _____ _____ ,

   or to an external cause, which is called a

   _____ _____ .

3. Most people tend to_____ (overestimate/underestimate) the extent to which people's actions are influenced by social situations because their _____ is focused on the person. This tendency is called the

   _____ _____

   _____ . When explaining our own behavior, or that of someone we know well, this tendency is _____ (stronger/weaker). When observers view the world from others' perspectives, attributions are _____ (the same/reversed).

Give an example of the practical consequences of attributions.

5. Our attitudes predict our _____ imperfectly. One example of this relationship is the tendency for people who agree to a small request to comply later with a larger one. This is the _____-_____-

   _____-_____

   phenomenon.

6. When you follow the social prescriptions for how you should act as, say, a college student, you are adopting a _____ .

7. Taking on a set of behaviors, or acting in a certain way, generally _____ (changes/does not change) people's attitudes.

8. According to _____

   _____ theory, thoughts and feelings change because people are motivated to justify actions that would otherwise seem hypocritical. This theory was proposed by

   _____ .

9. Dissonance theory predicts that people induced (without coercion) to behave contrary to their true attitudes will be motivated to reduce the resulting _____ by changing their _____ .

Social Influence (pp. 545–554)

> If you do not know the meaning of any of the following words, phrases, or expressions in the context in which they appear in the text, refer to pages 458–459 for an explanation: *canned laughter; open-minded; draw slips from a hat; draw back; kindness and obedience on a collision course; zap; devilish villains; tug-of-war; nerds become nerdier; waffles.*

Section Preview

Answer guidelines begin on page 448.

1. Describe the results of Asch's experiments on conformity, and distinguish between normative and informational social influence.

2. Summarize the findings from Milgram's obedience studies.

3. Discuss how the presence of others may produce social facilitation, social loafing, or deindividuation.

4. Describe group polarization, and show how it can be a source of groupthink.

5. Discuss how personal control and social control interact in guiding behavior, and explain how a minority can influence the majority.

Stepping Through the Section

Answers are provided on page 449.

1. The "chameleon effect" refers to our natural tendency to unconsciously _____ others' expressions, postures, and voice tones.

2. Copycat violence is a serious example of the effects of _____ on behavior.

3. The term that refers to the tendency to adjust one's behavior to coincide with an assumed group standard is _____ .

4. The psychologist who first studied the effects of group pressure on conformity is

   _____ .

5. In this study, when the opinion of other group members was contradicted by objective evidence, subjects _____ (were/were not) willing to conform to the group opinion.

6. One reason that people comply with social pressure is to gain approval or avoid rejection; this is called _____

   _____ _____ .

   Understood rules for accepted and expected behavior are called social _____ .

7. Another reason people comply is that they have genuinely been influenced by what they have learned from others; this type of influence is called _____

   _____ _____ .

8. Conformity rates tend to be lower in _____ (individualistic/ collectivistic) cultures.

9. The classic social psychology studies of obedience were conducted by _____ .
When ordered by the experimenter to electrically shock the "learner," the majority of participants (the "teachers") in these studies _____ (complied/refused). Later studies found that women's compliance rates in similar situations were _____ (higher than/lower than/similar to) men's.

List the conditions under which obedience was highest in Milgram's studies.

10. In getting people to administer increasingly larger shocks, Milgram was in effect applying the _____-_____-_____-_____ technique.

11. The tendency to perform a task better when other people are present is called _____ _____ . In general, people become aroused in the presence of others, and arousal enhances the correct response on a(n) _____ (easy/difficult) task. Later research revealed that arousal strengthens the response that is most _____ in a given situation.

12. Researchers have found that the reactions of people in crowded situations are often _____ (lessened/amplified).

13. Ingham found that people worked _____ (harder/less hard) in a team tug-of-war than they had in an individual contest. This phenomenon has been called _____ _____ .

14. The feeling of anonymity and loss of restraint that an individual may develop when in a group is called _____ .

15. Over time, the initial differences between groups usually _____ (increase/decrease). The enhancement of each group's prevailing tendency is called _____ _____ .

Future research studies will reveal whether electronic discussions on the _____ also demonstrate this tendency.

16. When the desire for group harmony overrides realistic thinking in individuals, the phenomenon known as _____ has occurred.

17. In considering the power of social influence, we cannot overlook the interaction of _____ _____ (the power of the situation) and _____ _____ (the power of the individual).

18. The power of one or two individuals to sway the opinion of the majority is called _____ _____ .

19. A minority opinion will have the most success in swaying the majority if it takes a stance that is _____ (unswerving/flexible).

Social Relations (pp. 555–578)

> If you do not know the meaning of any of the following words, phrases, or expressions in the context in which they appear in the text, refer to pages 459–461 for an explanation: *"horsing around"; with the toss of a coin; boost ingroup members' self-esteem; Ferdinand; she melts; an outlet for bottled-up impulses; diabolical images; familiarity breeds fondness; "beauty is only skin deep"; E.T. was uglier than Darth Vader; opposites retract; revved up; bystanders turns people away from the path that leads to helping; blasé; "sneaky," "smart-alecky stinkers"; down the tension ladder to a safer rung.*

Section Preview

Answer guidelines begin on page 449.

1. Describe the roles of social inequalities, ingroup bias, and scapegoating in prejudice.

2. Discuss the cognitive roots of prejudice.

7. Describe and explain the bystander effect.

3. Describe the impact of biology, aversive events, and learning experiences on aggressive behavior.

8. Discuss how social exchange theory and social norms explain altruism.

4. Discuss the media effect on sexual violence.

Stepping Through the Section

Answers begin on page 450.

1. Prejudice is an _____ and usually _____ attitude toward a group that involves overgeneralized beliefs known as _____ . Negative behavior directed toward a group or its members defines _____ .

2. Americans today express _____ (less/the same/more) racial and gender prejudice than they did in the previous three decades.

3. Blatant forms of prejudice _____ (have/have not) diminished. However, _____ and _____ prejudice lingers.

4. Worldwide, _____ (women/men) are more likely to live in poverty, and two-thirds of children without basic schooling are _____ (girls/boys). However, people tend to perceive women as being more _____ and _____ , and less _____ than men.

5. For those with money, power, and prestige, prejudice often serves as a means of _____ social inequalities.

5. Identify factors that fuel conflict, and discuss effective ways of resolving such conflict.

6. Identify the determinants of social attraction, and distinguish between passionate and companionate love.

6. Discrimination increases prejudice through the tendency of people to _____ victims for their plight.

7. Through our _____ _____ , we associated ourselves with certain groups.

8. Prejudice is also fostered by the _____ _____ , a tendency to favor groups to which one belongs—called the _____—while excluding others, or the _____ .

9. That prejudice derives from attempts to blame others for one's frustration is proposed by the _____ theory. People who feel loved and supported become more _____ to and _____ of those who differ from them.

10. Research suggests that prejudice may also derive from _____ , the process by which we attempt to simplify our world by classifying people into groups. One by-product of this process is that people tend to _____ the similarity of those within a group.

11. Another factor that fosters the formation of group stereotypes and prejudice is the tendency to _____ from vivid or memorable cases.

12. The belief that people get what they deserve—that the good are rewarded and the bad punished—is expressed in the _____-_____ phenomenon. This phenomenon is based in part on _____ _____ , the tendency to believe that one would have foreseen how something turned out.

13. Aggressive behavior is defined by the text as _____ _____ .

14. Freud believed that people have a self-destructive _____ _____ that is manifested as aggression when it is _____ toward others. Today,

most psychologists _____ (do/do not) consider human aggression to be instinctive.

15. In humans, aggressiveness _____ (varies/does not vary) greatly from culture to culture and person to person.

16. That there are genetic influences on aggression can be shown by the fact that many species of animals have been _____ for aggressiveness.

17. Twin studies suggest that genes _____ (do/do not) influence human aggression. One genetic marker of those who commit the most violence is the _____ chromosome. Studies of violent criminals reveal diminished activity in the brain's _____ _____ , which play an important role in controlling _____ .

18. In humans and animals, aggression is activated and inhibited by _____ systems, such as those in the _____ _____ , which are in turn influenced by _____ and other substances in the blood.

19. The aggressive behavior of animals can be manipulated by altering the levels of the hormone _____ . When this level is _____ (increased/decreased), aggressive tendencies are reduced.

20. High levels of testosterone correlate with _____ , low tolerance for _____ , _____ , and _____ . Among teenage boys and adult men, high testosterone also correlates with _____ , hard _____ _____ , and aggressive responses to _____ . With age, testosterone levels—and aggressiveness—_____ (increase/decrease).

21. One drug that unleashes aggressive responses to provocation is _____ .

22. According to the _____-_____ principle, inability to achieve a goal leads to anger, which may generate aggression.

23. Aggressive behavior can be learned through _____ , as shown by the fact that people use aggression where they've found it pays, and through _____ of others.

24. Crime rates are higher in countries in which there is a large disparity between those who are _____ and those who are _____ . High violence rates also are typical of cultures and families in which there is minimal _____

    _____ .

25. Violence on television tends to _____ people to cruelty and _____ them to respond aggressively when they are provoked.

26. A woman's risk of rape is generally _____ (greater/less) today than it was half a century ago.

27. Studies of R-rated "slasher" films and X-rated films and aggression _____ (generally/do not generally) show a relationship between availability of these films and the incidence of sexual aggression.

Comment on the impression of women that pornography frequently conveys and the effects this impression has on attitudes and behavior.

Summarize the findings of the Zillmann and Bryant study on the effects of pornography on attitudes toward rape.

28. Experiments have shown that it is not eroticism but depictions of _____ _____ that most directly affect men's acceptance and performance of aggression against women. Such depictions may create

    _____ _____

    to which people respond when they are in new situations or are uncertain how to act.

29. (Thinking Critically) Research studies of the impact of violent video games _____ (confirm/disconfirm) the idea that we feel better if we "blow of steam" by venting our emotions. This idea is the _____

    _____ . Playing violent video games increases _____

    _____ , _____ ,

    and _____ .

30. A perceived incompatibility of actions, goals, or ideas is called _____ . This perception can take place between individuals,

    _____ , or _____ .

31. Two destructive social processes that contribute to conflict are _____

    _____ and _____ perceptions.

32. When the "non-zero-sum game" is played, most people fall into the social trap by mistrusting the other player and pursuing their own

    _____ .

33. The diabolical images people in conflict form of each other are called _____-

    _____ perceptions.

34. Several psychological tendencies foster biased perceptions. First, people tend to accept credit for good deeds but not blame for bad deeds, a phenomenon called the _____

    _____ . Second, conflicting parties tend to attribute the other's actions to a negative disposition, an example of the

    _____ _____

    _____ . Preconceived attitudes, or _____ , also contribute to the problem, as does the _____ that often emerges within a group as the members' attitudes become _____ .

35. A prerequisite for, and perhaps the most powerful predictor of, attraction is _____ .

36. When people are repeatedly exposed to unfamiliar stimuli, their liking of the stimuli _____ (increases/decreases). This phenomenon is the _____ _____ effect. One implication of this is that _____ against those who are culturally different may be a primitive, _____ , emotional response.

37. Our first impression of another person is most influenced by the person's _____ .

38. In a sentence, list several of the characteristics that physically attractive people are judged to possess: _____ _____ .

39. A person's attractiveness _____ (is/is not) strongly related to his or her self-esteem or happiness. Since 1970, the number of women unhappy with their appearance has _____ (increased/decreased/ remained stable).

40. Cross-cultural research reveals that men judge women as more attractive if they have a _____ appearance, whereas women judge men who appear _____ , _____ , and _____ as more attractive.

41. Relationships in which the partners are very similar are _____ (more/less) likely to last.

42. Compared with strangers, friends and couples are more likely to be similar in terms of _____ _____ .

Explain what a reward theory of attraction is and how it can account for the three predictors of liking—proximity, attractiveness, and similarity.

43. Hatfield has distinguished two types of love: _____ love and _____ love.

44. According to the two-factor theory, emotions have two components: physical _____ and a _____ label.

45. When college men were placed in an aroused state, their feelings toward an attractive woman _____ (were/were not) more positive than those of men who had not been aroused.

46. Non-Western cultures, where people rate love _____ (less/more) important for marriage, have _____ (lower/ higher) divorce rates.

47. Companionate love is promoted by _____—mutual sharing and giving by both partners. Another key ingredient of loving relationships is the revealing of intimate aspects of ourselves through _____ .

48. An unselfish regard for the welfare of others is called _____ .

49. According to Darley and Latané, people will help only if a three-stage decision-making process is completed: Bystanders must first _____ the incident, then _____ it as an emergency, and finally _____ for helping.

50. When people who overheard a seizure victim calling for help thought others were hearing the same plea, they were _____ (more/less) likely to go to his aid than when they thought no one else was aware of the emergency.

51. In a series of staged accidents, Latané and Darley found that a bystander was _____ (more/less) likely to help if other bystanders were present. This phenomenon has been called the _____ _____ .

Identify the circumstances in which a person is most likely to offer help during an emergency.

52. The idea that social behavior aims to maximize rewards and minimize costs is proposed by _____ _____ theory.

53. One rule of social behavior tells us to return help to those who have helped us; this is the _____ norm. Another tells us to help those who need our help; this is the _____ _____ norm.

54. Conflict resolution is most likely in situations characterized by _____ , _____ , and _____ .

55. In most situations, establishing contact between two conflicting groups _____ (is/is not) sufficient to resolve conflict.

56. In Sherif's study, two conflicting groups of campers were able to resolve their conflicts by working together on projects in which they shared _____ goals. Shared _____ breed solidarity, as demonstrated by a surge in use of the word _____ in the weeks after 9/11.

57. When conflicts arise, a third-party _____ may facilitate communication and promote understanding.

58. Osgood has advanced a strategy of conciliation called GRIT, which stands for _____ and _____ _____ in _____ - _____ . The key to this method is each side's offering of a small _____ gesture in order to increase mutual trust and cooperation.

Progress Test 1

Multiple-Choice Questions

Circle your answers to the following questions and check them with the answers beginning on page 451. If your answer is incorrect, read the explanation for why it is incorrect and then consult the appropriate pages of the text (in parentheses following the correct answer).

1. In his study of obedience, Stanley Milgram found that the majority of subjects:
   a. refused to shock the learner even once.
   b. complied with the experiment until the "learner" first indicated pain.
   c. complied with the experiment until the "learner" began screaming in agony.
   d. complied with all the demands of the experiment.

2. According to cognitive dissonance theory, dissonance is most likely to occur when:
   a. a person's behavior is not based on strongly held attitudes.
   b. two people have conflicting attitudes and find themselves in disagreement.
   c. an individual does something that is personally disagreeable.
   d. an individual is coerced into doing something that he or she does not want to do.

3. Which of the following statements is true?
   a. Groups are almost never swayed by minority opinions.
   b. Group polarization is most likely to occur when group members frequently disagree with one another.
   c. Groupthink provides the consensus needed for effective decision making.
   d. A group that is like-minded will probably not change its opinions through discussion.

4. Conformity increased under which of the following conditions in Asch's studies of conformity?
   a. The group had three or more people.
   b. The group had high status.
   c. Individuals were made to feel insecure.
   d. The group was unanimous.
   e. All of the above increased conformity.

5. Social traps are situations in which:
   a. conflicting parties realize that they have shared goals, the attainment of which requires their mutual cooperation.
   b. conflicting parties have similar, and generally negative, views of one another.
   c. conflicting parties each pursue their self-interests and become caught in mutually destructive behavior.
   d. two conflicting groups meet face-to-face in an effort to resolve their differences.

6. The phenomenon in which individuals lose their identity and relinquish normal restraints when they are part of a group is called:
   a. groupthink.   c. empathy.
   b. cognitive dissonance.   d. deindividuation.

7. Subjects in Asch's line-judgment experiment conformed to the group standard when their judgments were observed by others but not when they were made in private. This tendency to conform in public demonstrates:
   a. social facilitation.
   b. overjustification.
   c. informational social influence.
   d. normative social influence.

8. In Milgram's obedience studies, subjects were *less* likely to follow the experimenter's orders when:
   a. they heard the "learner" cry out in pain.
   b. they merely administered the test while someone else delivered the shocks.
   c. the "learner" was an older person or mentioned having some physical problem.
   d. they saw another subject disobey instructions.

9. *Aggression* is defined as behavior that:
   a. hurts another person.
   b. is intended to hurt another person.
   c. is hostile, passionate, and produces physical injury.
   d. has all of the above characteristics.

10. Which of the following is true about aggression?
    a. It varies too much to be instinctive in humans.
    b. It is just one instinct among many.
    c. It is instinctive but shaped by learning.
    d. It is the most important human instinct.

11. Research studies have found a positive correlation between aggressive tendencies in animals and levels of the hormone:
    a. estrogen.   d. testosterone.
    b. adrenaline.   e. epinephrine.
    c. noradrenaline.

12. Research studies have indicated that the tendency of viewers to misperceive normal sexuality, devalue their partners, and trivialize rape is:
    a. increased by exposure to pornography.
    b. not changed after exposure to pornography.
    c. decreased in men by exposure to pornography.
    d. decreased in both men and women by exposure to pornography.

13. Increasing the number of people that are present during an emergency tends to:
    a. increase the likelihood that people will cooperate in rendering assistance.
    b. decrease the empathy that people feel for the victim.
    c. increase the role that social norms governing helping will play.
    d. decrease the likelihood that anyone will help.

14. Which of the following was *not* mentioned in the text discussion of the roots of prejudice?
    a. people's tendency to overestimate the similarity of people within groups
    b. people's tendency to assume that exceptional, or especially memorable, individuals are unlike the majority of members of a group
    c. people's tendency to assume that the world is just and that people get what they deserve
    d. people's tendency to discriminate against those they view as "outsiders"

15. The mere exposure effect demonstrates that:
    a. familiarity breeds contempt.
    b. opposites attract.
    c. birds of a feather flock together.
    d. familiarity breeds fondness.

16. In one experiment, college men were physically aroused and then introduced to an attractive woman. Compared to men who had not been aroused, these men:
    a. reported more positive feelings toward the woman.
    b. reported more negative feelings toward the woman.
    c. were ambiguous about their feelings toward the woman.

d. were more likely to feel that the woman was "out of their league" in terms of attractiveness.

e. focused more on the woman's attractiveness and less on her intelligence and personality.

17. The deep affection that is felt in long-lasting relationships is called _____ love; this feeling is fostered in relationships in which _____ .

a. passionate; there is equity between the partners

b. passionate; traditional roles are maintained

c. companionate; there is equity between the partners

d. companionate; traditional roles are maintained

18. Which of the following is associated with an increased tendency on the part of a bystander to offer help in an emergency situation?

a. being in a good mood

b. having recently needed help and not received it

c. observing someone as he or she refuses to offer help

d. being a female

19. The belief that those who suffer deserve their fate is expressed in the:

a. just-world phenomenon.

b. phenomenon of ingroup bias.

c. fundamental attribution error.

d. mirror-image perception principle.

20. According to social exchange theory, a person's tendency toward altruistic behavior is based on:

a. a determination of the relatedness of those who will be affected.

b. a cost-benefit analysis of any action.

c. social norms.

d. all of the above.

Matching Items

Match each term with the appropriate definition or description.

Terms

_____ 1. social facilitation
_____ 2. social loafing
_____ 3. bystander effect
_____ 4. conformity
_____ 5. ingroup bias
_____ 6. normative social influence
_____ 7. informational social influence
_____ 8. group polarization
_____ 9. stereotype
_____ 10. attribution
_____ 11. altruism
_____ 12. mere exposure effect

Definitions or Descriptions

a. a causal explanation for someone's behavior

b. a generalized belief about a group of people

c. people work less hard in a group

d. performance is improved by an audience

e. the tendency to favor one's own group

f. the effect of social approval or disapproval

g. adjusting one's behavior to coincide with a group standard

h. group discussion enhances prevailing tendencies

i. the effect of accepting others' opinions about something

j. unselfish regard for others

k. the tendency that a person is less likely to help someone in need when others are present

l. the increased liking of a stimulus that results from repeated exposure to it

Progress Test 2

Progress Test 2 should be completed during a final chapter review. Answer the following questions after you thoroughly understand the correct answers for the section reviews and Progress Test 1.

Multiple-Choice Questions

1. Which theorist argued that aggression was a manifestation of a person's "death instinct" redirected toward another person?
   a. Milgram   **d.** Janis
   b. Freud   **e.** Asch
   c. Lorenz

2. We tend to perceive the members of an ingroup as _____ and the members of an outgroup as _____ .
   a. similar to one another; different from one another
   b. different from one another; similar to one another
   c. above average in ability; below average in ability
   d. below average in ability; above average in ability

3. Regarding the influence of alcohol and testosterone on aggressive behavior, which of the following is true?
   a. Consumption of alcohol increases aggressive behavior; injections of testosterone reduce aggressive behavior.
   b. Consumption of alcohol reduces aggressive behavior; injections of testosterone increase aggressive behavior.
   c. Consumption of alcohol and injections of testosterone both promote aggressive behavior.
   d. Consumption of alcohol and injections of testosterone both reduce aggressive behavior.

4. Most people prefer mirror-image photographs of their faces. This is best explained by:
   a. the principle of equity.
   b. the principle of self-disclosure.
   c. the mere exposure effect.
   d. mirror-image perceptions.
   e. deindividuation.

5. Research studies have shown that frequent exposure to sexually explicit films:
   a. may promote increased acceptance of promiscuity.
   b. diminishes the attitude that rape is a serious crime.

   c. may lead individuals to devalue their partners.
   d. may produce all of the above effects.

6. Research studies indicate that in an emergency situation, the presence of others often:
   a. prevents people from even noticing the situation.
   b. prevents people from interpreting an unusual event as an emergency.
   c. prevents people from assuming responsibility for assisting.
   d. leads to all of the above.

7. Two neighboring nations are each stockpiling weapons. Each sees its neighbor's actions as an act of aggression and its own actions as self-defense. Evidently, these nations are victims of:
   a. prejudice.
   b. groupthink.
   c. the self-serving bias.
   d. the fundamental attribution error.

8. Which of the following factors is the *most* powerful predictor of friendship?
   a. similarity in age
   b. common racial and religious background
   c. similarity in physical attractiveness
   d. physical proximity

9. Most researchers agree that:
   a. media violence is a factor in aggressive behavior.
   b. there is a negative correlation between media violence and aggressiveness.
   c. paradoxically, watching excessive pornography ultimately diminishes an individual's aggressive tendencies.
   d. media violence is too unreal to promote aggression in viewers.

10. When male students in an experiment were told that a woman to whom they would be speaking had been instructed to act in a friendly or unfriendly way, most of them subsequently attributed her behavior to:
    a. the situation.
    b. the situation *and* her personal disposition.
    c. her personal disposition.
    d. their own skill or lack of skill in a social situation.

11. Which of the following is true?
    a. Attitudes and actions rarely correspond.
    b. Attitudes predict behavior about half the time.
    c. Attitudes are excellent predictors of behavior.
    d. Attitudes predict behavior under certain conditions.

12. People with power and status may become prejudiced because:
    a. they tend to justify the social inequalities between themselves and others.
    b. those with less status and power tend to resent them.
    c. those with less status and power appear less capable.
    d. they feel proud and are boastful of their achievements.

13. Which of the following most accurately states the effects of crowding on behavior?
    a. Crowding makes people irritable.
    b. Crowding sometimes intensifies people's reactions.
    c. Crowding promotes altruistic behavior.
    d. Crowding usually weakens the intensity of people's reactions.

14. Research has found that for a minority to succeed in swaying a majority, the minority must:
    a. make up a sizable portion of the group.
    b. express its position as consistently as possible.
    c. express its position in the most extreme terms possible.
    d. be able to convince a key leader of the majority.

15. Which of the following conclusions did Milgram derive from his studies of obedience?
    a. Even ordinary people, without any particular hostility, can become agents in a destructive process.
    b. Most people are able, under the proper circumstances, to suppress their natural aggressiveness.
    c. The need to be accepted by others is a powerful motivating force.
    d. All of the above conclusions were reached.

16. Which of the following best summarizes the relative importance of personal control and social control of our behavior?
    a. Situational influences on behavior generally are much greater than personal influences.
    b. Situational influences on behavior generally are slightly greater than personal influences.
    c. Personal influences on behavior generally are much greater than situational influences.
    d. Situational and personal influences interact in determining our behavior.

17. Which of the following best describes how GRIT works?
    a. The fact that two sides in a conflict have great respect for the other's strengths prevents further escalation of the problem.
    b. The two sides engage in a series of reciprocated conciliatory acts.
    c. The two sides agree to have their differences settled by a neutral, third-party mediator.
    d. The two sides engage in cooperation in those areas in which shared goals are possible.

18. Which of the following is important in promoting conformity in individuals?
    a. whether an individual's behavior will be observed by others in the group
    b. whether the individual is male or female
    c. the size of the room in which a group is meeting
    d. the age of the members in a group
    e. whether the individual is of a higher status than other group members

19. Which theory describes how we explain others' behavior as being due to internal dispositions or external situations?
    a. social exchange theory
    b. reward theory
    c. two-factor theory
    d. attribution theory

20. Which of the following is most likely to promote groupthink?
    a. The group's leader fails to take a firm stance on an issue.
    b. A minority faction holds to its position.
    c. The group consults with various experts.
    d. Group polarization is evident.

True–False Items

Indicate whether each statement is true or false by placing *T* (*True*) or *F* (*False*) in the blank next to the item.

_____ 1. When explaining another's behavior, we tend to underestimate situational influences.

_____ 2. When explaining our own behavior, we tend to underestimate situational influences.

_____ 3. An individual is more likely to conform when the rest of the group is unanimous.

_____ 4. The tendency of people to conform is influenced by the culture in which they were socialized.

_____ 5. A bystander is more likely to offer help in an emergency if other bystanders are present.

_____ 6. Counter-attitudinal behavior (acting contrary to our beliefs) often leads to attitude change.

_____ 7. Human aggression is instinctual.

_____ 8. Group polarization tends to prevent groupthink from occurring.

_____ 9. Crowded conditions usually subdue people's reactions.

_____ 10. When individuals lose their sense of identity in a group, they often become more uninhibited.

Review and Reflect

Answer these questions the day before an exam as a final check on your understanding of the chapter's terms and concepts.

Multiple-Choice Questions

1. After waiting in line for an hour to buy concert tickets, Teresa is told that the concert is sold out. In her anger she pounds her fist on the ticket counter, frightening the clerk. Teresa's behavior is best explained by:
   a. evolutionary psychology.
   b. the reciprocity norm.
   c. social exchange theory.
   d. the frustration-aggression principle.

2. Before she gave a class presentation favoring gun control legislation, Wanda opposed it. Her present attitude favoring such legislation can best be explained by:
   a. attribution theory.
   b. cognitive dissonance theory.
   c. social exchange theory.
   d. evolutionary psychology.
   e. two-factor theory.

3. Which of the following would most likely be subject to social facilitation?
   a. proofreading a page for spelling errors
   b. typing a letter with accuracy
   c. playing a difficult piece on a musical instrument
   d. giving a speech
   e. running quickly around a track

4. Jane and Sandy were best friends as freshmen. Jane joined a sorority; Sandy didn't. By the end of their senior year, they found that they had less in common with each other than with the other members of their respective circles of friends. Which of the following phenomena most likely explains their feelings?
   a. group polarization   c. deindividuation
   b. groupthink   d. social facilitation

5. Which of the following strategies would be *most* likely to foster positive feelings between two conflicting groups?
   a. Take steps to reduce the likelihood of social traps.
   b. Separate the groups so that tensions diminish.
   c. Have one representative from each group visit the other and field questions.
   d. Increase the amount of contact between the two conflicting groups.
   e. Have the groups work on a superordinate goal.

6. José is the one student member on the college board of trustees. At the board's first meeting, José wants to disagree with the others on several issues but in each case decides to say nothing. Studies on conformity suggest all except one of the following are factors in José's not speaking up. Which one is *not* a factor?
   a. The board is a large group.
   b. The board is prestigious and most of its members are well known.
   c. The board members are already aware that José and the student body disagree with them on these issues.

d. Because this is the first meeting José has attended, he feels insecure and not fully competent.

7. Given the tendency of people to categorize information according to preformed schemas, which of the following stereotypes would Juan, a 65-year-old political liberal and fitness enthusiast, be most likely to have?
   a. "People who exercise regularly are very extraverted."
   b. "All political liberals are advocates of a reduced defense budget."
   c. "Young people today have no sense of responsibility."
   d. "Older people are lazy."

8. Ever since their cabin lost the camp softball competition, the campers have become increasingly hostile toward one camper in their cabin, blaming her for every problem in the cabin. This behavior is best explained in terms of:
   a. the ingroup bias.
   b. prejudice.
   c. the scapegoat theory.
   d. the reciprocity norm.
   e. mirror-image perceptions.

9. Maria recently heard a speech calling for a ban on aerosol sprays that endanger the earth's ozone layer. Maria's subsequent decision to stop using aerosol sprays is an example of:
   a. informational social influence.
   b. normative social influence.
   c. deindividuation.
   d. social facilitation.

10. Mr. and Mrs. Samuels are constantly fighting, and each perceives the other as hard-headed and insensitive. Their conflict is being fueled by:
    a. self-disclosure.
    b. stereotypes.
    c. a social trap.
    d. mirror-image perceptions.

11. Which of the following situations should produce the *greatest* cognitive dissonance?
    a. A soldier is forced to carry out orders he finds disagreeable.
    b. A student who loves animals has to dissect a cat in order to pass biology.
    c. As part of an experiment, a subject is directed to deliver electric shocks to another person.
    d. A student volunteers to debate an issue, taking the side he personally disagrees with.

12. Professor Washington's students did very poorly on the last exam. The tendency to make the fundamental attribution error might lead her to conclude that the class did poorly because:
    a. the test was unfair.
    b. not enough time was given for students to complete the test.
    c. students were distracted by some social function on campus.
    d. students were unmotivated.

13. Students at State University are convinced that their school is better than any other; this most directly illustrates:
    a. an ingroup bias.
    b. prejudice and discrimination.
    c. the scapegoat effect.
    d. the just-world phenomenon.
    e. mirror-image perceptions.

14. After Sandy helped Jack move into his new apartment, Jack felt obligated to help Sandy when she moved. Jack's sense of responsibility can best be explained by:
    a. evolutionary psychology.
    b. two-factor theory.
    c. the social responsibility norm.
    d. the reciprocity norm.

15. Ahmed and Monique are on a blind date. Which of the following will probably be *most* influential in determining whether they like each other?
    a. their personalities
    b. their beliefs
    c. their social skills
    d. their physical attractiveness

16. Opening her mail, Joan discovers a romantic greeting card from her boyfriend. According to the two-factor theory, she is likely to feel the most intense romantic feelings if, prior to reading the card, she has just:
    a. completed her daily run.
    b. finished reading a chapter in her psychology textbook.
    c. awakened from a nap.
    d. finished eating lunch.
    e. been listening to a tape of love songs.

17. Driving home from work, Althea saw a car run off the road and burst into flames. Althea stopped her car, ran to the burning vehicle, and managed to pull the elderly driver to safety before the car exploded. Althea's behavior can best be explained by:
    a. the social responsibility norm.
    b. the reciprocity norm.
    c. two-factor theory.
    d. reward theory.

18. Having read the chapter, which of the following is best borne out by research on attraction?
    a. Birds of a feather flock together.
    b. Opposites attract.
    c. Familiarity breeds contempt.
    d. Absence makes the heart grow fonder.

19. Alexis believes that all male athletes are self-centered and sexist. Her beliefs are an example of:
    a. in-group bias.
    b. groupthink.
    c. stereotypes.
    d. the fundamental attribution error.

20. Which of the following is an example of the foot-in-the-door phenomenon?
    a. To persuade a customer to buy a product a store owner offers a small gift.
    b. After agreeing to wear a small "Enforce Recycling" lapel pin, a woman agrees to collect signatures on a petition to make recycling required by law.
    c. After offering to sell a car at a ridiculously low price, a car salesperson is forced to tell the customer the car will cost $1000 more.
    d. All of the above are examples.

Essay Question

The Panhellenic Council on your campus has asked you to make a presentation on the topic "Social Psychology" to all freshmen who have signed up to "rush" a fraternity or sorority. In a fit of cynicism following your rejection last year by a prestigious fraternity or sorority, you decide to speak on the negative influences of groups on the behavior of individuals. What will you discuss? (Use the space below to list the points you want to make, and organize them. Then write the essay on a separate sheet of paper.)

Key Terms

Writing Definitions

Using your own words, on a separate piece of paper write a brief definition or explanation of each of the following terms.

1. social psychology
2. attribution theory
3. fundamental attribution error
4. attitudes
5. foot-in-the-door phenomenon
6. role
7. cognitive dissonance theory
8. conformity
9. normative social influence
10. informational social influence
11. social facilitation
12. social loafing
13. deindividuation
14. group polarization
15. groupthink
16. prejudice

17. stereotype
18. discrimination
19. ingroup
20. outgroup
21. ingroup bias
22. scapegoat theory
23. just-world phenomenon
24. aggression
25. frustration-aggression principle
26. conflict
27. social trap

28. mere exposure effect
29. passionate love
30. companionate love
31. equity
32. self-disclosure
33. altruism
34. bystander effect
35. social exchange theory
36. superordinate goals
37. GRIT

Cross-Check

As you learned in Chapter 1, reviewing and overlearning of material are important to the learning process. After you have written the definitions of the key terms in this chapter, you should complete the cross-word puzzle to ensure that you can reverse the process—recognize the term, given the definition.

ACROSS
4. A generalized belief about a group of people.
5. A strategy of conflict resolution in which both groups make conciliatory gestures. (abbrev.)
6. Theory that proposes that prejudice provides an outlet for anger by finding someone to blame.
8. The tendency to change one's attitudes to coincide with those held by a group.
9. An unselfish regard for the welfare of others.
12. Mutual giving and receiving in a relationship.
13. Type of love that refers to an aroused state of intense positive absorption in another person.
14. Perceived incompatibility between individuals or groups.
15. Personal beliefs and feelings that influence our behavior.

DOWN
1. A person's tendency not to offer help to someone if others are present.
2. Type of social influence that results when one goes along with a group when one is unsure of what to do.
3. Psychological discomfort we experience when two of our thoughts conflict.
7. Phenomenon whereby people who agree to a small request are more likely to comply later with a larger request.
8. Type of love in which there is a deep, enduring attachment.
10. Our tendency to underestimate situational influences and overestimate dispositional influences upon the behavior of others is the _____ attribution error.
11. A causal explanation of a given behavior.

Answers

Social Thinking

Section Preview

1. According to attribution theory, people explain others' behavior as being due either to their dispositions or to their situations. Because people have enduring personality traits, we tend to overestimate the influence of personality and underestimate the impact of situational influences, particularly when explaining others' behavior. This is called the *fundamental attribution error*. When explaining our own behavior, or when we take another's perspective, we are less likely to make this type of error. Our attributions, of course, have important practical consequences. For example, there are political implications to the question of whether people's behavior is attributed to social conditions or to their own choices, abilities, and shortcomings.

2. An attitude is a belief and feeling that predisposes our reactions to objects, people, and events. Our attitudes are most likely to guide our actions when outside influences on what we say and do are minimal, when the attitude is specifically relevant to the behavior, and when we are aware of our attitudes.

3. Studies of the foot-in-the-door phenomenon and role playing demonstrate that our actions can influence our attitudes. The foot-in-the-door phenomenon is the tendency for people who agree to a small request to comply later with a larger one. Similarly, people who play a role tend to adjust their attitudes to coincide with behavior enacted while playing the role. The theory of cognitive dissonance maintains that when our thoughts and behaviors don't coincide, we experience tension. To relieve this tension, we bring our attitudes into line with our actions.

Stepping Through the Section

1. social psychologists
2. attribution; dispositional attribution; situational attribution
3. underestimate; attention; fundamental attribution error; weaker; reversed

Our attributions—to individuals' dispositions or to situations—have important practical consequences. A hurtful remark from an acquaintance, for example, is more likely to be forgiven if it is attributed to a temporary situation than to a mean disposition.

4. attitudes

Attitudes predict actions when other influences on the attitudes and actions are minimized, when the attitude is specifically relevant to the behavior, and when we are especially aware of our attitudes. Thus, our attitudes are more likely to predict behavior when we are not attempting to adjust our behavior to please others, when we are in familiar situations in which we don't have to stop and think about our attitudes, and when the attitude pertains to a specific behavior, such as purchasing a product or casting a vote.

5. actions or behavior; foot-in-the-door
6. role
7. changes
8. cognitive dissonance; Festinger
9. dissonance; attitudes

Social Influence

Section Preview

1. Suggestibility studies conducted by Solomon Asch demonstrate that a unanimous group makes us unsure about our behavior or thinking, and so we are more likely to conform to the group standard, even if it is incorrect. Conformity is promoted when people feel incompetent or insecure, when they are in groups of three or more, when the group is unanimous and of high status and attractiveness, when no prior commitment has been made, when behavior will be observed, and when people have been socialized in a culture that encourages respect for social standards. We conform to gain social approval (normative social influence) or because the group provides valuable information (informational social influence).

2. Participants in Milgram's experiments were ordered to teach a list of word pairs to another person by punishing the learner's wrong answers with electric shocks. Obedience was highest when the experimenter was nearby and was perceived as a legitimate authority supported by a prestigious institution, when the victim was depersonalized or at a distance, and when there was no role model for defiance.

3. Social facilitation occurs when tasks are simple or well-learned but not when they are difficult or unfamiliar. When observed by others, people become aroused. Arousal *facilitates* the most likely response—the correct one on an easy task, an incorrect one on a difficult task. Social loafing occurs when people who work anonymously as

part of a group exert less effort than those individually accountable for performance. Deindividuation occurs when group participation makes individuals feel aroused, anonymous, and less self-conscious. The uninhibited and impulsive behavior of mobs may occur as a result of this phenomenon.

4. Group polarization refers to the enhancement of a group's prevailing tendencies that occurs when like-minded members discuss issues and attitudes. The unrealistic group decision making called groupthink occurs when the desire for group harmony outweighs the desire for realistic thinking. It is fed by overconfidence, conformity, self-justification, and group polarization. Groupthink can be prevented when the leader welcomes dissenting opinions and invites criticism.

5. The power of the situation (social control) and of the individual (personal control) interact. When feeling pressured, people may react by doing the opposite. The impact of a minority in swaying the majority opinion illustrates the power of personal control. Research reveals that a minority that unswervingly holds to its position is more likely to be successful in swaying the majority than a minority that waffles.

Stepping Through the Section

1. mimic

2. suggestibility

3. conformity

4. Asch

5. were

6. normative social influence; norms

7. informational social influence

8. individualistic

9. Milgram; complied; similar to

Obedience was highest when the person giving the orders was close at hand and perceived to be a legitimate authority figure, the authority figure was supported by a prestigious institution, the victim was depersonalized, and when there were no role models for defiance.

10. foot-in-the-door

11. social facilitation; easy; likely

12. amplified

13. less hard; social loafing

14. deindividuation

15. increase; group polarization; Internet

16. groupthink

17. social control; personal control

18. minority influence

19. unswerving

Social Relations

Section Preview

1. Prejudice is an unjustifiable (and usually negative) attitude toward a group that may also entail the unjustifiable behavior of discrimination. People who have money, power, and prestige may become prejudiced toward those less fortunate in order to rationalize social inequalities. The reactions provoked in victims of discrimination may further increase prejudice. The tendencies to favor one's own group (ingroup bias) and to blame victims for their plight may also lead to prejudice. According to the scapegoat theory of prejudice, when people are frustrated or angry, blaming another individual or group may provide an outlet for their anger.

2. Stereotyped beliefs emerge as a result of our tendency to cognitively simplify the world. One way to do this is by categorizing people into groups and then overestimating the similarity of people within groups other than our own. Group stereotypes are also influenced by vivid but exceptional cases involving individuals from other groups, because they are more readily available to memory. Another cognitive root of prejudice is the just-world phenomenon, or the idea that good is rewarded and evil is punished, so those who are successful are good and those who suffer are bad. Hindsight bias also fosters prejudice, as people blame victims after the fact for "getting what they deserved."

3. Biology influences aggression at three levels—the genetic, the neural, and the biochemical. Studies of human twins and selective breeding in animals reveal that genes influence aggression. Electrical stimulation and injuries to certain regions of the limbic system, such as the amygdala, suggest that animal and human brains have neural systems that control aggressive behavior (although no one spot in the brain actually controls aggression). Studies of animal aggression and violent criminals demonstrate that aggressive tendencies increase with blood levels of the hormone testosterone (although the reverse is also true).

A variety of psychological factors influence aggression. The frustration-aggression principle indicates that pain, insults, foul odors, excessive heat, and other aversive stimuli can evoke hostility. Learning also plays a role in aggression. Aggressive reactions are more likely in situations in which experience has taught the individual that aggression will be rewarded. Furthermore, children who observe aggressive models often imitate their behavior.

4. Research indicates that depictions of sexual violence portray women as enjoying being the victims of sexual aggression, and this perception increases the acceptance of coercion in sexual relationships. Repeated viewing of pornography can also lead viewers to trivialize rape and devalue their partners. Although other factors—dominance motives, disinhibition by alcohol, and a history of child abuse—can create a disposition to sexual violence, media influence is not a minor issue.

5. Conflict is a seeming incompatibility of actions, goals, or ideas among individuals, groups, or nations. Conflict is fostered by social traps in which conflicting parties get caught up in mutually destructive behavior by pursuing their own self-interests. Another factor that fuels conflict is the tendency for those in conflict to form diabolical images of each other (mirror-image perceptions). The psychological roots of distorted perceptions include the self-serving bias, the fundamental attribution error, stereotyping, group polarization, and groupthink.

   Conflict resolution is most likely in situations characterized by cooperation, communication, and conciliation. Studies by Sherif and others demonstrate that cooperation between groups in the pursuit of superordinate goals is more effective than mere contact between conflicting groups in reducing differences. Communication between conflicting groups can be facilitated by a third-party mediator when conflicts are so intense that civil discussion between the groups is not possible. When cooperation and communication are impossible between conflicting groups, Osgood's "Graduated and Reciprocated Initiatives in Tension-Reduction" (GRIT) may help reduce hostilities. GRIT promotes trust and cooperation between groups by having each group initiate one or more small, conciliatory acts.

6. Studies of attraction indicate that proximity is the most powerful predictor of friendship, in part because being repeatedly exposed to any person or thing tends to increase our liking for it (mere exposure effect). Experiments also reveal that physical appearance is the most powerful factor in the first impression a person triggers. Al-

though many aspects of attractiveness vary with place and time, some may be universal. Once relationships are formed, similarity of attitudes, beliefs, interests, and other characteristics increases attraction between people.

   Passionate love is an intense state of physical arousal triggered by another person, usually at the beginning of a relationship, that is cognitively labeled as love. Companionate love is the steadier, deeply felt attachment that emerges as love matures. Companionate love is fostered by feelings of equity between the partners in a relationship and the acceptability of self-disclosures.

7. The bystander effect states that a bystander is less likely to give aid if other bystanders are present. Darley and Latané maintain that bystanders will help only if they notice the incident, interpret it as an emergency, and assume responsibility for helping. At each step in this decision-making process the presence of other bystanders makes it less likely a helping decision will be made. Further research reveals that bystanders are most likely to help when they have seen someone else being helpful, when they are not in a hurry, when the victim appears similar to them and deserving of assistance, when they are in a small town or rural area, when they feel guilty, when they are focused on others and not preoccupied, and when they are in a good mood.

8. The social exchange theory maintains that self-interest underlies all human interactions, including altruism, so that our constant goal is to maximize rewards and minimize costs. This theory helps explain why people often help those whose approval they seek or who can reciprocate favors in the future.

   People are also sensitive to social norms that promote helping. The reciprocity norm, for example, dictates that we should help those who have helped us. The social responsibility norm is the expectation that we should help those who need our help.

Stepping Through the Section

1. unjustifiable; negative; stereotypes; discrimination
2. less
3. have; subtle; unconscious
4. women; girls; nurturant; sensitive; aggressive
5. justifying
6. blame
7. social identities

8. ingroup bias; ingroup; outgroup

9. scapegoat; open; accepting

10. categorization; overestimate

11. overgeneralize

12. just-world; hindsight bias

13. any physical or verbal behavior intended to hurt or destroy

14. death instinct; displaced; do not

15. varies

16. bred

17. do; Y; frontal lobes; impulses

18. neural; limbic system (or the amygdala); hormones

19. testosterone; decreased

20. irritability; frustration; assertiveness; impulsiveness; delinquency; drug use; frustration; decrease

21. alcohol

22. frustration-aggression

23. rewards; observation (or imitation)

24. rich; poor; father care

25. desensitize; prime

26. greater

27. generally

Pornography tends to portray women as enjoying being the victims of sexual aggression, and this perception increases the acceptance of coercion in sexual relationships.

The Zillmann and Bryant study found that after viewing sexually explicit films for several weeks, undergraduates were more likely to recommend a lighter prison sentence for a convicted rapist than were subjects who viewed nonerotic films.

28. sexual violence; social scripts

29. disconfirm; catharsis hypothesis; aggressive thoughts; emotions; behaviors

30. conflict; groups; nations

31. social traps; distorted

32. self-interests

33. mirror-image

34. self-serving bias; fundamental attribution error; stereotypes; groupthink; polarized

35. proximity

36. increases; mere exposure; prejudice; automatic

37. appearance

38. Attractive people are perceived as happier, more sensitive, more successful, and more socially skilled.

39. is not; increased

40. youthful; mature; dominant; affluent

41. more

42. attitudes, beliefs, interests, religion, race, education, intelligence, smoking behavior, economic status, age

Reward theories of attraction say that we are attracted to, and continue relationships with, those people whose behavior provides us with more benefits than costs. Proximity makes it easy to enjoy the benefits of friendship at little cost, attractiveness is pleasing, and similarity is reinforcing to us.

43. passionate; companionate

44. arousal; cognitive

45. were

46. less; lower

47. equity; self-disclosure

48. altruism

49. notice; interpret; assume responsibility

50. less

51. less; bystander effect

People are most likely to help someone when they have just observed someone else being helpful; when they are not in a hurry; when the victim appears to need and deserve help; when they are in some way similar to the victim; when in a small town; when feeling guilty; when not preoccupied; and when in a good mood.

52. social exchange

53. reciprocity; social responsibility

54. cooperation; communication; conciliation

55. is not

56. superordinate; predicaments; "we"

57. mediator

58. Graduated; Reciprocated Initiatives; Tension-Reduction; conciliatory

Progress Test 1

Multiple-Choice Questions

1. **d.** is the answer. In Milgram's initial experiments, 65 percent of the subjects fully complied with the experiment. (p. 548)

2. **c.** is the answer. Cognitive dissonance is the tension we feel when we are aware of a discrepancy between our thoughts and actions, as would occur when we do something we find distasteful. (pp. 543–544)
   a. Dissonance requires strongly held attitudes, which must be perceived as not fitting behavior.
   b. Dissonance is a personal cognitive process.
   d. In such a situation the person is less likely to experience dissonance, since the action can be attributed to "having no choice."

3. **d.** is the answer. In such groups, discussion usually strengthens prevailing opinion; this phenomenon is known as group polarization. (p. 552)
   a. Minority opinions, especially if consistently and firmly stated, can sway the majority in a group.
   b. Group polarization, or the strengthening of a group's prevailing tendencies, is most likely in groups where members agree.
   c. When groupthink occurs, there is so much consensus that decision making becomes less effective.

4. **e.** is the answer. (p. 547)

5. **c.** is the answer. Social traps foster conflict in that two parties, by pursuing their self-interests, create a result that neither group wants. (p. 566)
   a. As Sherif's studies demonstrated, the possession of shared or superordinate goals tends to reduce conflict between groups.
   b. This is an example of mirror-image perceptions, which, along with social traps, foster conflict.
   d. Face-to-face confrontations between conflicting parties generally do not reduce conflict, nor are they social traps.

6. **d.** is the answer. (p. 552)
   a. Groupthink refers to the mode of thinking that occurs when the desire for group harmony overrides realistic and critical thinking.
   b. Cognitive dissonance refers to the discomfort we feel when two thoughts (which include the knowledge of our *behavior*) are inconsistent.
   c. Empathy is feeling what another person feels.

7. **d.** is the answer. Normative social influence refers to influence on behavior that comes from a desire to look good to others. Subjects who were observed conformed because they didn't want to look like oddballs. (p. 547)
   a. Social facilitation involves performing tasks better or faster in the presence of others.
   b. Overjustification occurs when a person is rewarded for doing something that is already enjoyable.

c. Informational social influence is the tendency of individuals to accept the opinions of others, especially in situations where they themselves are unsure.

8. **d.** is the answer. Role models for defiance reduce levels of obedience. (p. 549)
   a. & c. These did not result in diminished obedience.
   b. This "depersonalization" of the victim resulted in increased obedience.

9. **b.** is the answer. Aggression is any behavior, physical or verbal, that is intended to hurt or destroy. (p. 559)
   a. A person may accidentally be hurt in a nonaggressive incident; aggression does not necessarily prove hurtful.
   c. Verbal behavior, which does not result in physical injury, may also be aggressive. Moreover, acts of aggression may be cool and calculated, rather than hostile and passionate.

10. **a.** is the answer. The very wide variations in aggressiveness from culture to culture indicate that aggression cannot be considered an instinct, or unlearned, universal characteristic of the species. (p. 560)

11. **d.** is the answer. (p. 561)

12. **a.** is the answer. (p. 564)

13. **d.** is the answer. This phenomenon is known as the bystander effect. (pp. 574–575)
   a. This answer is incorrect because individuals are less likely to render assistance at all if others are present.
   b. Although people are less likely to assume responsibility for helping, this does not mean that they are less empathic.
   c. This answer is incorrect because norms such as the social responsibility norm encourage helping others, yet people are less likely to help with others around.

14. **b.** is the answer. In fact, people tend to overgeneralize from vivid cases, rather than assume that they are unusual. (pp. 558–559)
   a., c., & d. Each of these is an example of a cognitive (a. & c.) or a social (d.) root of prejudice.

15. **d.** is the answer. Being repeatedly exposed to novel stimuli increases our liking for them. (p. 568)
   a. For the most part, the opposite is true.
   b. & c. The mere exposure effect concerns our tendency to develop likings on the basis, not of similarities or differences, but simply of familiarity, or repeated exposure.

16. **a.** is the answer. This result supports the two-factor theory of emotion and passionate attraction, according to which arousal from any source can facilitate an emotion, depending on how we label the arousal. (p. 572)

17. **c.** is the answer. Deep affection is typical of companionate love, rather than passionate love, and is promoted by equity, whereas traditional roles may be characterized by the dominance of one sex. (pp. 572–573)

18. **a.** is the answer. (p. 575)
    b. & c. These factors would most likely decrease a person's altruistic tendencies.
    d. There is no evidence that one sex is more altruistic than the other.

19. **a.** is the answer. (p. 559)
    b. Ingroup bias is the tendency of people to favor their own group.
    c. The fundamental attribution error is the tendency of people to underestimate situational influences when observing the behavior of other people.
    d. The mirror-image perception principle is the tendency of conflicting parties to form similar, diabolical images of each other.

20. **b.** is the answer. (p. 575)
    a. This is a tenet of evolutionary psychology.
    c. Social exchange theory focuses on costs and benefits, rather than on norms.

Matching Items

1. d (p. 551)	**5.** e (p. 558)	**9.** b (p. 555)
2. c (p. 551)	**6.** f (p. 547)	**10.** a (p. 537)
3. k (p. 575)	**7.** i (p. 547)	**11.** j (p. 573)
4. g (p. 546)	**8.** h (p. 552)	**12.** l (p. 568)

Progress Test 2

Multiple-Choice Questions

1. **b.** is the answer. (p. 560)
   a. Milgram conducted studies of obedience.
   c. Lorenz, too, was an instinct theorist, but only Freud argued the existence of a "death instinct."
   d. Janis studied the process that led to groupthink.
   e. Asch studied conformity.

2. **b.** is the answer. (p. 558)
   a. We are keenly sensitive to differences within our group, less so to differences within other groups.

c. & d. Although we tend to look more favorably on members of the ingroup, the text does not suggest that ingroup bias extends to evaluations of abilities.

3. **c.** is the answer. (p. 561)

4. **c.** is the answer. The mere exposure effect refers to our tendency to like what we're used to, and we're used to seeing mirror images of ourselves. (pp. 568–569)
   a. Equity refers to equality in giving and taking between the partners in a relationship.
   b. Self-disclosure is the sharing of intimate feelings with a partner in a loving relationship.
   d. Although people prefer mirror images of their faces, mirror-image perceptions are often held by parties in conflict. Each party views itself favorably and the other negatively.
   e. Deindividuation involves a loss of self-awareness.

5. **d.** is the answer. (pp. 563–564)

6. **d.** is the answer. (p. 574)

7. **d.** is the answer. In this case, each nation has mistakenly attributed the other's action to a *dispositional* trait, whereas its own action is viewed as a *situational* response. (p. 540)

8. **d.** is the answer. Because it provides people with an opportunity to meet, proximity is the most powerful predictor of friendship, even though, once a friendship is established, the other factors mentioned become more important. (p. 568)

9. **a.** is the answer. (p. 563)

10. **c.** is the answer. In this example of the fundamental attribution error, even when given the situational explanation for the woman's behavior, students ignored it and attributed her behavior to her personal disposition. (p. 540)

11. **d.** is the answer. Our attitudes are more likely to guide our actions when other influences are minimal, when there's a specific connection between the two, and when we're keenly aware of our beliefs. The presence of other people would more likely be an outside factor that would lessen the likelihood of actions being guided by attitude. (pp. 541–542)

12. **a.** is the answer. Such justifications arise as a way to preserve inequalities. The just-world phenomenon presumes that people get what they deserve. According to this view, someone who has less must deserve less. (p. 557)

13. **b.** is the answer. (p. 551)
    a. & c. Crowding may amplify irritability or altruistic tendencies that are already present.

Crowding does not, however, produce these reactions as a general effect.

d. In fact, just the opposite is true. Crowding often intensifies people's reactions.

14. **b.** is the answer. (p. 554)

a. Even if they made up a sizable portion of the group, although still a minority, their numbers would not be as important as their consistency.

c. & d. These aspects of minority influence were not discussed in the text; however, they are not likely to help a minority sway a majority.

15. **a.** is the answer. (p. 550)

16. **d.** is the answer. The text emphasizes the ways in which personal and social controls interact in influencing behavior. It does not suggest that one factor is more influential than the other. (p. 554)

17. **b.** is the answer. (p. 578)

a. GRIT is a technique for reducing conflict through a series of conciliatory gestures, not for maintaining the status quo.

c. & d. These measures may help reduce conflict but they are not aspects of GRIT.

18. **a.** is the answer. As Solomon Asch's experiments demonstrated, individuals are more likely to conform when they are being observed by others in the group. The other factors were not discussed in the text and probably would not promote conformity. (p. 547)

19. **d.** is the answer. (p. 539)

20. **d.** is the answer. Group polarization, or the enhancement of a group's prevailing attitudes, promotes groupthink, which leads to the disintegration of critical thinking. (p. 553)

a. Groupthink is more likely when a leader highly favors an idea, which may make members reluctant to disagree.

b. A strong minority faction would probably have the opposite effect: It would diminish group harmony while promoting critical thinking.

c. Consulting experts would discourage groupthink by exposing the group to other opinions.

True–False Items

1. T (p. 540)	**6.** T (pp. 543–544)
2. F (p. 540)	**7.** F (p. 560)
3. T (p. 547)	**8.** F (p. 553)
4. T (p. 547)	**9.** F (p. 551)
5. F (p. 574)	**10.** T (p. 552)

Review and Reflect

1. **d.** is the answer. According to the frustration-aggression principle, the blocking of an attempt

to achieve some goal—in Teresa's case, buying concert tickets—creates anger and can generate aggression. (p. 561)

a. Evolutionary psychology maintains that aggressive behavior is a genetically based drive. Teresa's behavior clearly was a reaction to a specific situation.

b. The reciprocity norm—that we should return help to those who have helped us—would not engender Teresa's angry reaction.

c. Social exchange theory views behavior as an exchange process in which people try to maximize the benefits of their behavior by minimizing the costs. Teresa's behavior likely brought her few benefits while exacting some costs, including potential injury, embarrassment, and retaliation by the clerk.

2. **b.** is the answer. Dissonance theory focuses on what happens when our actions contradict our attitudes. (pp. 543–544)

a. Attribution theory holds that we give causal explanations for others' behavior, often by crediting either the situation or people's dispositions.

c. Social exchange theory maintains that social behaviors maximize benefits and minimize costs. It is not clear in this example whether Wanda perceives such costs and benefits.

d. & e. These are not theories of social influence.

3. **e.** is the answer. Social facilitation, or better performance in the presence of others, occurs for easy tasks but not for more difficult ones. For tasks such as proofreading, typing, playing an instrument, or giving a speech, the arousal resulting from the presence of others can lead to mistakes. (p. 551)

4. **a.** is the answer. Group polarization means that the tendencies within a group—and therefore the differences among groups—grow stronger over time. Thus, because the differences between the sorority and nonsorority students have increased, Jane and Sandy are likely to have little in common. (p. 552)

b. Groupthink is the tendency for realistic decision making to disintegrate when the desire for group harmony is strong.

c. Deindividuation is the loss of self-consciousness and restraint that sometimes occurs when one is part of a group.

d. Social facilitation refers to improved performance of a task in the presence of others.

5. **e.** is the answer. Sherif found that hostility between two groups could be dispelled by giving the groups superordinate, or shared, goals. (p. 576)

a. Although reducing the likelihood of social traps might reduce mutually destructive behavior, it would not lead to positive feelings between the groups.

b. Such segregation would likely increase ingroup bias and group polarization, resulting in further group conflict.

c. This might help, or it might increase hostilities; it would not be as helpful a strategy as communication through an outside mediator or, as in e., cooperation toward a superordinate goal.

d. Contact by itself is not likely to reduce conflict.

6. **c.** is the answer. Prior commitment to an opposing view generally tends to work against conformity. In contrast, large group size, prestigiousness of a group, and an individual's feelings of incompetence and insecurity all strengthen the tendency to conform. (p. 547)

7. **c.** is the answer. People tend to overestimate the similarity of people within groups other than their own. Thus, Juan is not likely to form stereotypes of fitness enthusiasts (a.), political liberals (b.), or older adults (d.), because these are groups to which he belongs. (p. 557)

8. **c.** is the answer. According to the scapegoat theory, when things go wrong, people look for someone on whom to take out their anger and frustration. (p. 558)

a. These campers are venting their frustration on a member of their *own* cabin group (although this is not always the case with scapegoats).

b. Prejudice refers to an unjustifiable and usually negative attitude toward another group.

d. The reciprocity norm, which refers to our tendency to help those who have helped us, was not discussed as a root of prejudice.

e. Mirror-image perceptions involve our perceptions of groups other than our own, not of members of our ingroup.

9. **a.** is the answer. As illustrated by Maria's decision to stop buying aerosol products, informational social influence occurs when people have genuinely been influenced by what they have learned from others. (p. 547)

b. Had Maria's behavior been motivated by the desire to avoid rejection or to gain social approval (which we have no reason to suspect is the case), it would have been an example of normative social influence.

c. Deindividuation refers to the sense of anonymity a person may feel as part of a group.

d. Social facilitation is the improvement in performance of well-learned tasks that may result when one is observed by others.

10. **d.** is the answer. The couple's similar, and presumably distorted, feelings toward each other fuel their conflict. (p. 567)

a. Self-disclosure, or the sharing of intimate feelings, fosters love.

b. Stereotypes are overgeneralized ideas about groups.

c. Social traps are situations in which conflicting parties engage in mutually destructive behavior while pursuing their own self-interests.

11. **d.** is the answer. In this situation, the counter-attitudinal behavior is performed voluntarily and cannot be attributed to the demands of the situation. (pp. 543–544)

a., b., & c. In all of these situations, the counter-attitudinal behaviors should not arouse much dissonance because they can be attributed to the demands of the situation.

12. **d.** is the answer. The fundamental attribution error refers to the tendency to underestimate situational influences in favor of this type of dispositional attribution when explaining the behavior of other people. (p. 540)

a., b., & c. These are situational attributions.

13. **a.** is the answer. (p. 558)

b. Prejudices are unjustifiable and usually negative attitudes toward other groups. They may result from an ingroup bias, but they are probably not why students favor their own university.

c. Scapegoats are individuals or groups toward which prejudice is directed as an outlet for the anger of frustrated individuals or groups.

d. The just-world phenomenon is the tendency for people to believe others "get what they deserve."

e. Mirror-image perception refers to the tendency of conflicting parties to form similar, diabolical images of each other.

14. **d.** is the answer. (p. 575)

a. Evolutionary psychology is not discussed in terms of altruism, but it would maintain that altruistic actions are predisposed by our genes.

b. The two-factor theory holds that emotions consist of physical arousal and an appropriate cognitive label.

c. The social responsibility norm refers to the social attitude that we should help those who need our help.

15. **d.** is the answer. Hundreds of experiments indicate that first impressions are most influenced by physical appearance. (p. 569)

16. **a.** is the answer. According to the two-factor theory, physical arousal can intensify whatever

emotion is currently felt. Only in the situation described in a. is Joan likely to be physically aroused. (p. 572)

17. **a.** is the answer. (p. 576)

    b. The reciprocity norm mandates that we help those who have helped us.

    c. The two-factor theory of emotion, which assumes that emotions are based on physical arousal and a cognitive label, makes no predictions regarding altruism.

    d. The reward theory, which states that social behavior is maintained by rewards, would explain Althea's altruism as being due to her having previously been rewarded for similar altruistic actions.

18. **a.** is the answer. Friends and couples are much more likely than randomly paired people to be similar in views, interests, and a range of other factors. (p. 571)

    b. The opposite is true.

    c. The mere exposure effect demonstrates that familiarity tends to breed fondness.

    d. This is unlikely, given the positive effects of proximity and intimacy.

19. **c.** is the answer. (p. 555)

    a. The ingroup bias is the tendency to favor one's own group.

    b. Groupthink refers to the unrealistic thought processes and decision making that occur within groups when the desire for group harmony becomes paramount.

    d. The fundamental attribution error is our tendency to underestimate the impact of situations and to overestimate the impact of personal dispositions on the behavior of others.

20. **b.** is the answer. In the foot-in-the-door phenomenon, compliance with a small initial request, such as wearing a lapel pin, later is followed by compliance with a much larger request, such as collecting petition signatures. (p. 542)

Essay Question

Your discussion might focus on some of the following topics: normative social influence; conformity, which includes suggestibility; obedience; group polarization; and groupthink.

    As a member of any group with established social norms, individuals will often act in ways that enable them to avoid rejection or gain social approval. Thus, a fraternity or sorority pledge would probably be very suggestible and likely to eventually conform to the attitudes and norms projected by the group—or be rejected socially. In extreme cases of pledge hazing, acute social pressures may lead to atypical and antisocial individual behaviors—for example, on the part of pledges complying with the demands of senior members of the fraternity or sorority. Over time, meetings and discussions will probably enhance the group's prevailing attitudes (group polarization). This may lead to the unrealistic and irrational decision making that is groupthink. The potentially negative consequences of groupthink depend on the issues being discussed, but may include a variety of socially destructive behaviors.

Key Terms

Writing Definitions

1. **Social psychology** is the scientific study of how we think about, influence, and relate to one another. (p. 539)

2. **Attribution theory** deals with our causal explanations of behavior. We attribute behavior to the individual's disposition or to the situation. (p. 539)

3. The **fundamental attribution error** is our tendency to underestimate the impact of situations and to overestimate the impact of personal dispositions on the behavior of others. (p. 540)

4. **Attitudes** are beliefs and feelings that predispose a person to respond in particular ways to objects, people, and events. (p. 541)

5. The **foot-in-the-door phenomenon** is the tendency for people who agree to a small request to comply later with a larger request. (p. 542)

6. A **role** is a set of expectations, or norms, about a social position. (p. 543)

7. **Cognitive dissonance theory** refers to the theory that we act to reduce the psychological discomfort we experience when our behavior conflicts with what we think and feel, or more generally, when two of our thoughts conflict. This is frequently accomplished by changing our attitude rather than our behavior. (p. 543)

    Memory aid: *Dissonance* means "lack of harmony." **Cognitive dissonance** occurs when two thoughts, or cognitions, are at variance with one another.

8. **Conformity** is the tendency to change one's thinking or behavior to coincide with a group standard. (p. 546)

9. **Normative social influence** refers to the pressure on individuals to conform in order to avoid rejection or gain social approval. (p. 547)

    Memory aid: *Normative* means "based on a norm, or pattern, regarded as typical for a specific group." **Normative social influence** is the pressure groups exert on the individual to behave in ways acceptable to the group standard.

10. **Informational social influence** results when one goes along with a group when one is unsure or lacks information. (p. 547)

11. **Social facilitation** is the improvement in performance of simple or well-learned tasks that occurs when other people are present. (p. 551)

12. **Social loafing** is the tendency for individual effort to be diminished when one is part of a group working toward a common goal. (p. 551)

13. **Deindividuation** refers to the loss of self-awareness and self-restraint that sometimes occurs in group situations that foster arousal and anonymity. (p. 552)

    Memory aid: As a prefix, *de-* indicates reversal or undoing. To **deindividuate** is to undo one's individuality.

14. **Group polarization** refers to the enhancement of a group's prevailing tendencies through discussion, which often has the effect of accentuating the group's differences from other groups. (p. 552)

    Memory aid: To *polarize* is to "cause thinking to concentrate about two poles, or contrasting positions."

15. **Groupthink** refers to the unrealistic thought processes and decision making that occur within groups when the desire for group harmony becomes paramount. (p. 553)

    Example: The psychological tendencies of self-justification, conformity, and group polarization foster the development of the "team spirit" mentality known as **groupthink**.

16. **Prejudice** is an unjustifiable and usually negative attitude toward a group and its members. (p. 555)

17. A **stereotype** is a generalized (often overgeneralized) belief about a group of people. (p. 555)

18. **Discrimination** refers to unjustifiable negative behavior toward a group or its members. (p. 555)

19. The **ingroup** refers to the people and groups with whom we share a common identity. (p. 557)

20. The **outgroup** refers to the people and groups that are excluded from our ingroup. (p. 557)

21. The **ingroup bias** is the tendency to favor one's own group. (p. 558)

22. The **scapegoat theory** proposes that prejudice provides an outlet for anger by finding someone to blame. (p. 558)

23. The **just-world phenomenon** is a manifestation of the commonly held belief that good is rewarded and evil is punished. The logic is indisputable: "If I am rewarded, I must be good." (p. 559)

24. **Aggression** is any physical or verbal behavior intended to hurt or destroy. (p. 559)

25. The **frustration-aggression principle** states that aggression is triggered when people become angry because their efforts to achieve a goal have been blocked. (p. 561)

26. **Conflict** is a perceived incompatibility of actions, goals, or ideas between individuals or groups. (p. 566)

27. A **social trap** is a situation in which conflicting parties become caught up in mutually harmful behavior as they pursue their perceived best interests. (p. 566)

28. The **mere exposure effect** refers to the fact that repeated exposure to an unfamiliar stimulus increases our liking of it. (p. 568)

29. **Passionate love** refers to an aroused state of intense positive absorption in another person, especially at the beginning of a relationship. (p. 572)

30. **Companionate love** refers to a deep, enduring, affectionate attachment. (p. 572)

31. **Equity** refers to the condition in which there is mutual giving and receiving between the partners in a relationship. (p. 573)

32. **Self-disclosure** refers to a person's sharing intimate feelings with another. (p. 573)

33. **Altruism** is unselfish regard for the welfare of others. (p. 573)

34. The **bystander effect** is the tendency of a person to be less likely to offer help to someone if there are other people present. (pp. 574–575)

35. **Social exchange theory** states that our social behavior revolves around exchanges, in which we try to minimize our costs and maximize our benefits. (p. 575)

36. **Superordinate goals** are mutual goals that require the cooperation of individuals or groups otherwise in conflict. (p. 576)

37. **GRIT** (Graduated and Reciprocated Initiatives in Tension-Reduction) is a strategy of conflict resolution based on the defusing effect that conciliatory gestures can have on parties in conflict. (p. 578)

Cross-Check

ACROSS	DOWN
4. stereotype	**1.** bystander effect
5. GRIT	**2.** informational
6. scapegoat	**3.** cognitive dissonance
8. conformity	**7.** foot-in-the-door
9. altruism	**8.** companionate
12. equity	**10.** fundamental
13. passionate	**11.** attribution
14. conflict	
15. attitudes	

FOCUS ON VOCABULARY AND LANGUAGE

Social Thinking

Page 541: Happily married couples attribute *their spouse's tart-tongued remark* to a temporary situation ("She must have had a bad day at work"). How we make attributions can have serious consequences. Couples who think that their partner's sarcastic or unkind comment (*tart-tongued remark*) was due to a cruel personality (*mean disposition*) are more likely to be dissatisfied with their marriages than couples who believe that the same remark was simply a result of some situational influence, such as a stressful day at work.

Page 541: . . . *freeloaders.* This refers to people who voluntarily live off other people. Those who believe that people are poor and/or unemployed because of personal dispositions tend to underestimate the influence of situational variables. Thus, they might call someone on welfare a *freeloader* rather than simply a victim of circumstances.

Page 542: . . . "*brainwashed*" . . . This refers to a person's beliefs, values, and attitudes being changed by relentless indoctrination and mental torture. One component of this mind-changing process ("*thought-control*") involves use of the **foot-in-the-door phenomenon**, whereby a person is first coerced into agreeing to a small request, then to complying with much greater requests. Frequently, people's attitudes change to be consistent with their new behavior.

Page 542: This *chicken-and-egg spiral* of actions feeding attitudes feeding actions enables behavior to escalate. Whether used for good or for bad, the foot-in-the-door strategy involves starting with small requests, then slowly increasing the level of demand. The new behavior will be followed by a change in attitude which, in turn, will make the behavior more

likely and that will then lead to more change in belief, etc. (*the chicken-and-egg spiral*).

Page 544: The attitudes-follow-behavior principle has some *heartening implications*. When our attitudes and behaviors are inconsistent, we feel a certain amount of tension (**cognitive dissonance**), which makes us want to do something to reduce this uncomfortable state. Thus, if we are feeling depressed (*down in the dumps*) and we behave in a more outgoing manner, talk in a more positive way, and *act* as though we are happy, we may, in fact, start feeling much better. As Myers notes, the feelings-follow-actions notion has positive ramifications (*heartening implications*).

Social Influence

Page 545: Laughter, even *canned laughter*, can be *infectious*. Many TV and radio comedy shows do not have live audiences. Instead, they play recorded soundtracks of people laughing (*canned laughter*) at the appropriate moments; the laughter can be very contagious (*infectious*) for listeners, making them laugh heartily, too. This is a form of suggestibility.

Page 547: When influence supports what we approve, we applaud those who are "*open-minded*" and "*sensitive*" enough to be "*responsive*." We can be influenced by others because they provide useful knowledge (**informational influence**) or because we want them to view us favorably and not ignore us (**normative influence**). Conformity that is consistent with what we believe is true will be seen in a positive light (the conformists are "*open-minded*," etc.), and conformity that is not will be viewed negatively ("*submissive conformity*").

Page 547: You and another person *draw slips from a hat* to see who will be the "teacher" (which your slip says) and who will be the "learner." In Milgram's famous obedience experiments participants were deceived into believing they were randomly assigned to one of two conditions ("teacher" or "learner") by picking a piece of paper out of a container (*drawing slips from a hat*). All the subjects were actually "teachers" and were asked to "shock" the "learners" whenever they made mistakes on a memory task. A majority of the participants complied with the experimenter's request.

Page 548: When you hear these pleas, you *draw back*. But the experimenter *prods* you: "Please continue—the experiment requires that you continue." If you were a participant ("teacher") in Milgram's experiment, you would be pressured (*prodded*) by the research assistant to carry on with the experiment even though you may show great reluctance (*you draw back*) after hearing the "learner's" cries of distress at being "shocked."

Page 550: With *kindness and obedience on a collision course*, obedience usually won. Milgram's research on obedience showed that social factors that foster conformity are powerful enough to make almost any one of us behave in ways inconsistent with our beliefs. When subjects were in a conflict over (*torn between*) whether to refuse to harm an individual or to follow orders (*kindness and obedience were on a collision course*), they usually did what they were asked to do.

Page 550: Milgram did not entrap his "teachers" by asking them first to *zap* "learners" with enough electricity to make their hair stand on end. Milgram used the foot-in-the-door tactic to get his subjects to comply with his requests to shock (*zap*) the "learners" with larger and larger voltages. He started with a small amount (*a little tickle*) of electricity; after obtaining compliance (*obedience*), he asked them to increase the level, and so on. Subjects tended to rationalize their behavior; for some, their attitudes became consistent with their behavior over the course of the experiment.

Page 550: Contrary to images of *devilish villains*, evil does not require *monstrous characters*; all it takes is ordinary people corrupted by an evil situation. . . . We tend to think that pain and suffering (*evil*) are always caused by inhumane and cruel people (*devilish villains* or *monstrous characters*), but the research in social psychology shows that almost anyone can be led to behave badly given the right (or wrong) circumstances.

Page 551: In a team *tug-of-war*, for example, do you suppose the effort that a person puts forth would be more than, less than, or the same as the effort he or she would exert in a *one-on-one tug-of-war*? In a game in which opponents pull on each end of a rope (*tug-of-war*), when two individuals compete (*one-on-one*), they work much harder (*exert more effort*) than if they were members of a group competing on the same task. This lowering of individual effort when part of a team is called **social loafing**. (Note: The term *to loaf* means *to work less hard, to slack off, to take it easy*, or *to free ride*.)

Page 553: With their views echoing one another's, will *nerds become nerdier, goths gothier, conspiracy wacos wackier*? **Group polarization** occurs when people within a group discuss issues and opinions that most of them either favor or oppose. Myers wonders if the Internet will provide a medium for electronic discussion that parallels (*mirrors*) in-person dialogue (*face-to-face discussions*). With their expressed views being repeated and reinforced (*echoing one another's*) will the socially inept but intelligent (*nerds*) become more so (*nerdier*), will the aggressive and belligerent (*goths*) become more warlike (*gothier*), and will those who believe that unlawful and secretive groups are plotting evil deeds (*conspiracy wacos*) become more extreme in their views (*wackier*).

Page 554: They repeatedly found that a minority that unswervingly holds to its position is far more successful in swaying the majority than is a minority that *waffles*. Committed individuals and small groups of individuals can convince (*sway*) the majority to their point of view if they adhere strictly to their agenda and do not appear to be uncertain or unsure (*to waffle*).

Social Relations

Page 555: In one study, most white participants perceived a white man shoving a black man as *"horsing around."* Prejudices involve beliefs, emotions, and tendencies to behave in certain ways. They are a form of prejudgment that influences (*colors*) how we interpret what we see. Thus, in an experiment in which white people saw a white man pushing a black person, most interpreted the behavior as playful activity (*horsing around*); when the roles were reversed, the behavior was more likely to be described as aggressive or hostile (*"violent"*).

Page 558: Even arbitrarily creating an us–them distinction—by grouping people *with the toss of a coin*—leads people to show favoritism to their own group when dividing any rewards (Tajfel, 1982; Wilder, 1981). One of the factors affecting prejudice is our propensity to define ourselves through identification with a particular group (**ingroup bias**); this in turn creates an outgroup consisting of those who do not belong to our group. Even if the groups are artificially created by random assignment (*with the toss of a coin*), we will tend to see our own group as more deserving, superior, and so on.

Page 558: In addition to providing a convenient emotional outlet for anger, despised outgroups can also *boost ingroup members' self-esteem*. When we have a problem, we frequently look for someone, who is usually innocent, to blame (*scapegoating*); these target people or groups are then a convenient source for venting our anger and frustration. In addition, having someone else to disparage can increase our own status and sense of self-worth (*boost our self-esteem*).

Page 561: A raging bull will become a gentle *Ferdinand* when its testosterone level is reduced by castration. Biological explanations of aggression examine the influences of genes, clusters of neurons in the brain, and biochemical agents in the blood, such as hormones and alcohol. Levels of the male sex hormone can be reduced by castration; thus, an aggressive, ferocious bull can be reduced to a playful, friendly animal similar to the fictional character (*Ferdinand*) of children's stories.

Page 563: In less graphic form, the same unrealistic script—she resists, he persists, *she melts*—is commonplace on TV and in romance novels. A common theme in certain types of films and books is the idea that if the main male character overcomes the lovely female's reluctance to be romantically or sexually involved (*she resists, he persists*), then she will be totally devoted to him (*she melts*). This depiction of male-female relationships, in both pornographic and non-pornographic media, has little to do with reality and may, in fact, promote sexual aggression.

Page 564: Contrary to much popular opinion, viewing such *depictions* does not provide *an outlet* for *bottled-up impulses*. Laboratory studies have demonstrated that watching media that show sexual violence against women does not decrease the acceptance and performance of aggression against females. In contrast to what many believe, such portrayals (*depictions*) do not allow vicarious expression (*an outlet*) for pent-up hostile urges (*bottled-up impulses*) and may have the opposite effect.

Page 567: Psychologists have noted that those in conflict have a curious tendency to form *diabolical images* of one another. We have a propensity to perceive our enemies in a very distorted manner, often cate-

gorizing them as evil, cruel, untrustworthy, and devilish (*diabolical*). They, of course, view us in the same way (*each demonizes the other*); the biased pictures we form of each other are called *mirror-image perceptions*.

Page 568: Within certain limits . . . *familiarity breeds fondness*. Under some circumstances, the more often we see (*become familiar with*) someone, the more likely it is that we will grow to like (*become fond of*) that person. This is called the **mere exposure effect.**

Page 569: . . . *"beauty is only skin deep"* . . . This saying suggests that physical attractiveness (*beauty*) is only a superficial quality (*skin deep*). Research, however, has shown that how we look influences social interactions, how frequently we date, our popularity, how we are perceived by others, etc.

Page 571: Until you got to know him, *E.T. was uglier than Darth Vader*. E.T. was a small, unattractive, extraterrestrial creature (and just as repulsive looking as Darth Vader, another movie character), but as we came to know and like his cute little personality, he no longer appeared so ugly. Studies have shown that with increased exposure to people, we come to like them and are less likely to notice their physical blemishes (*imperfections*) and more likely to become aware of their endearing characteristics.

Page 571: In real life, *opposites retract*. The old saying *"opposites attract"* has not been supported by research in social psychology. In fact, we tend to dislike those we do not perceive as similar to ourselves (*opposites retract*). Rather than fostering *contempt*, Myers humorously suggests that similarity breeds *content*.

Page 572: To be *revved up* and to associate some of that arousal with a desirable person is to feel the pull of passion. Research has shown that one component of romantic or passionate love is physiological arousal; a second aspect is some cognitive interpretation and labeling of that feeling. So, if a person is in an aroused state (*revved up*) and this is easily linked to the presence of an attractive person, then attributions of romantic love may be made. As Myers cheerfully notes, rather than *absence, adrenaline makes the heart grow fonder* (intensifies love).

Page 574: At each step, the presence of other *bystanders turns people away from the path that leads to helping*. Darley and Latané displayed their findings in a flow diagram (See Figure 15.12, p. 574). At each decision point (i.e., noticing the event, interpreting it as an emergency, and assuming responsibility), the presence of others who appear to have observed the event (*bystanders*) causes people to be less likely to give assistance to someone in need (*they are turned away from the path that leads to helping*).

Page 574: . . . *blasé* . . . This means to be indifferent or uncaring. We arrive at the decision (especially in ambiguous situations) to help or not to help by watching the reactions of others. If they appear to be unconcerned (*blasé*), we may conclude that there is no emergency and thus may not intervene or help. This **bystander effect** means that the presence of others decreases the probability that any particular observer will provide help.

Page 576: Before long, each group became intensely proud of itself and hostile to the other group's "*sneaky*," "*smart-alecky stinkers.*" In Sherif's experiment, competitive conditions were created in order to foster the formation of two antagonistic groups. Each group soon saw itself as superior to the other group's "dishonest and sly" (*sneaky*) "rotten know-it-alls" (*smart-alecky stinkers*). Sherif then used shared objectives and common problems (**superordinate goals**) to create reconciliation and cooperation.

Page 578: Conciliations allow both parties to begin edging *down the tension ladder to a safer rung* where communication and mutual understanding can begin. Social psychologist Charles Osgood has developed a tactic called **GRIT** (Graduated and Reciprocated Initiatives in Tension-Reduction) for increasing cooperation and trust between parties in conflict. When one side makes a small gesture or offer of goodwill (*a conciliatory act*), the other side has an opportunity to reciprocate and thus move the conflict toward some resolution (*down the tension ladder to a safer rung*) and start the process of mutual respect and understanding.

appendixA

Statistical Reasoning in Everyday Life

Appendix Overview

A basic understanding of statistical reasoning has become a necessity in everyday life. Statistics are tools that help the psychologist and layperson to interpret the vast quantities of information they are confronted with on a daily basis. Appendix A discusses how statistics are used to describe data and to generalize from instances.

In studying this chapter you must concentrate on learning a number of procedures and understanding some underlying principles in the science of statistics. The graphic and computational procedures in the section called "Describing Data" include how data are distributed in a sample; measures of central tendency such as the mean, median, and mode; variation measures such as the range and standard deviation; and correlation, or the degree to which two variables are related. Most of the conceptual material is then covered in the section entitled "Making Inferences." You should be able to discuss three important principles concerning populations and samples, as well as the concept of significance in testing differences. The ultimate goal is to make yourself a better consumer of statistical research by improving your critical thinking skills.

NOTE: Answer guidelines for all questions in the Appendix begin on page 470.

Describing Data (pp. A-1–A-6)

> David Myers at times uses idioms that are unfamiliar to some readers. If you do not know the meaning of any of the following words, phrases, or expressions in the context in which they appear in the text, refer to page 476 for an explanation: *top-of-the head estimates often misread reality and mislead the public; national income pie; gauges; naked eye.*

Section Preview

First, skim the section, noting headings and boldface items. Then read the following objectives and, as you read the text, search for the information that will enable you to meet each objective. Answer guidelines begin on page 470.

1. Explain how bar graphs are used to describe data, and discuss a potential hazard in interpreting such graphs.

2. Define the three measures of central tendency, and explain how they describe data differently.

3. Describe measures of variation and the normal curve.

4. Describe the correlation coefficient and explain its importance in assessing relationships between variables.

5. Identify factors that may contribute to illusory correlation and an illusion of control.

Stepping Through the Section

After you have read the section, complete the sentences and answer the questions. As you proceed, evaluate your performance by consulting the answers on page 471. Do not continue with the next section until you understand each answer. If you need to, review or reread the section in the textbook before continuing.

1. The first step in describing data is to _____ it, such as by displaying it as a _____ _____ .

2. The three measures of central tendency are the _____ , the _____ , and the _____ .

3. The most frequently occurring score in a distribution is called the _____ .

4. The mean is computed as the _____ of all the scores divided by the _____ of scores.

5. The median is the score at the _____ percentile.

6. When a distribution is lopsided, or _____ , the _____ (mean/median/mode) can be biased by a few extreme scores.

7. Averages derived from scores with _____ (high/low) variability are more reliable than those with _____ (high/low) variability.

8. The measures of variation include the _____ and the _____ _____ .

9. The range is computed as the _____ _____ .

10. The range provides a(n) _____ (crude/accurate) estimate of variation because it _____ (is/is not) influenced by extreme scores.

11. The standard deviation is a _____ (more accurate/less accurate) measure of variation than the range. Unlike the range, the standard deviation _____ (takes/does not take) into consideration information from each score in the distribution.

12. List the four steps in computing the standard deviation.

    a. _____

    b. _____

    c. _____

    d. _____

13. The bell-shaped distribution that often describes large amounts of data is called the _____ _____ .

14. In this distribution, approximately _____ percent of the individual scores fall within 1 standard deviation on either side of the mean. Within 2 standard deviations on either side of the mean fall _____ percent of the individual scores.

Calculate what a score of 116 on the normally distributed Wechsler IQ test would mean with regard to percentile rank. (Recall that the mean is 100; the standard deviation is ±15 points. Hint: You might find it helpful to draw the normal curve first.)

15. A measure of the direction and extent of relationship between two sets of scores is called the

_____ _____ .
Numerically, this measure can range from

_____ to _____ .

16. When there is no relationship at all between two sets of scores, the correlation coefficient is

_____ . The strongest possible correlation between two sets of scores is either

_____ or _____ .
When the correlation between two sets of scores is negative, as one increases, the other

_____ .

Cite an example of a positive correlation and a negative correlation. Your examples can be drawn from previous chapters of the text or can be based on observations from daily life.
An example of positive correlation is

An example of negative correlation is

17. The correlation coefficient _____ (gives/does not give) information about cause-and-effect relationships.

18. A correlation that is perceived but doesn't really exist is called an _____

_____ .

19. When we believe that a relationship exists between two things, we are most likely to recall instances that _____ (confirm/disconfirm) our belief.

20. This type of correlation feeds the illusion of _____—that we can control events that actually are due to _____ .
It is also fed by a statistical phenomenon called

_____ _____

_____ _____ , the

idea that average results are more typical than extreme results.

Making Inferences (pp. A-6–A-8)

If you do not know the meaning of the following expression in the context in which it appears in the text, refer to page 476 for an explanation: *Data are "noisy."*

Section Preview

Answer guidelines are provided on page 472.

1. Discuss three important principles in making generalizations about populations on the basis of samples.

2. Describe how psychologists make statistical inferences about differences between groups.

Stepping Through the Section

Answer guidelines are provided on page 472.

1. The best basis for generalizing is not from
   _____ cases but from a
   _____ sample of cases.

2. Averages are more reliable when they are based
   on scores with _____ (high/low)
   variability.

3. Averages based on a large number of cases are
   _____ (more/less) reliable than
   those based on a few cases.

4. Tests of statistical _____ are used
   to estimate whether observed differences are real,
   that is, to make sure they are not simply the
   result of _____ variation. The differences are probably real if the sample averages
   are _____ and the difference
   between them is _____ .

Progress Test 1

Multiple-Choice Questions

Circle your answers to the following questions and
check them with the answers beginning on page 472.
If your answer is incorrect, read the explanation for
why it is incorrect and then consult the appropriate
pages of the text (in parentheses following the correct
answer). Use the page margins if you need extra
space for your computations.

1. What is the mean of the following distribution of
   scores: 2, 3, 7, 6, 1, 4, 9, 5, 8, 2?
   a. 5   c. 4.7
   b. 4   d. 3.7

2. What is the median of the following distribution
   of scores: 1, 3, 7, 7, 2, 8, 4?
   a. 1   c. 3
   b. 2   d. 4

3. What is the mode of the following distribution: 8,
   2, 1, 1, 3, 7, 6, 2, 0, 2?
   a. 1   c. 3
   b. 2   d. 7

4. Compute the range of the following distribution:
   9, 14, 2, 8, 1, 6, 8, 9, 1, 3.
   a. 10   c. 8
   b. 9   d. 13

5. Squaring the difference between each score in a
   distribution and the mean is the first step in computing the:
   a. median.   c. range.
   b. mode.   d. standard deviation.

6. If two sets of scores are negatively correlated, it
   means that:
   a. as one set of scores increases, the other
      decreases.
   b. as one set of scores increases, the other
      increases.
   c. there is only a weak relationship between the
      sets of scores.
   d. there is no relationship at all between the sets
      of scores.

7. Regression toward the mean is the:
   a. tendency for unusual scores to fall back
      toward a distribution's average.
   b. basis for all tests of statistical significance.
   c. reason the range is a more accurate measure
      of variation than the standard deviation.
   d. reason the standard deviation is a more accu-
      rate measure of variation than the range.

8. In a normal distribution, what percentage of
   scores fall between +2 and −2 standard deviations
   of the mean?
   a. 50 percent   c. 95 percent
   b. 68 percent   d. 99.7 percent

9. Which of the following statistics must fall on or
   between −1.00 and +1.00?
   a. the mean
   b. the standard deviation
   c. the correlation coefficient
   d. none of the above

10. In generalizing from a sample to the population,
    it is important that:
    a. the sample is representative of the population.
    b. the sample is large.
    c. the scores in the sample have low variability.
    d. all of the above are observed.

11. When a difference between two groups is "statistically significant," this means that:
    a. the difference is statistically real but of little practical significance.
    b. the difference is probably the result of sampling variation.
    c. the difference is not likely to be due to chance variation.
    d. all of the above are true.

12. A lopsided set of scores that includes a number of extreme or unusual values is said to be:
    a. symmetrical.   c. skewed.
    b. normal.   d. dispersed.

13. Which of the following is *not* a measure of central tendency?
    a. mean   c. median
    b. range   d. mode

14. Which of the following is the measure of central tendency that would be most affected by a few extreme scores?
    a. mean   c. median
    b. range   d. mode

15. The symmetrical, bell-shaped distribution in which most scores are near the mean and fewer near the extremes forms a:
    a. skewed curve.   c. normal curve.
    b. bimodal curve.   d. bar graph.

16. A homogeneous sample with little variation in scores will have a(n) _____ standard deviation.
    a. small
    b. moderate
    c. large
    d. unknown (It is impossible to determine.)

17. If there is no relationship between two sets of scores, the coefficient of correlation equals:
    a. 0.00   c. +1.00
    b. −1.00   d. 0.50

18. Illusory correlation refers to:
    a. the perception that two negatively correlated variables are positively correlated.
    b. the perception of a relationship between two unrelated variables.
    c. an insignificant correlation coefficient.
    d. a correlation coefficient that equals −1.00.

19. Gamblers who blow on their dice "for luck" are victims of:
    a. regression toward the mean.
    b. the illusion of control.
    c. hindsight bias.
    d. the fundamental attribution error.

Matching Items

Match each term with the appropriate definition or description.

Terms

_____   1. bar graph
_____   2. median
_____   3. normal curve
_____   4. regression toward the mean
_____   5. mode
_____   6. range
_____   7. standard deviation
_____   8. skewed
_____   9. mean
_____ 10. measures of central tendency
_____ 11. measures of variation

Definitions or Descriptions

a. the mean, median, and mode
b. the difference between the highest and lowest scores
c. the arithmetic average of a distribution
d. the range and standard deviation
e. a symmetrical, bell-shaped distribution
f. the most frequently occurring score
g. the tendency for extremes of unusual scores to fall back toward the average
h. a graph depicting a table of data
i. the middle score in a distribution
j. an asymmetrical distribution
k. the square root of the average squared deviation of scores from the mean

Progress Test 2

Progress Test 2 should be completed during a final chapter review. Answer the following questions after you thoroughly understand the correct answers for the Chapter Review and Progress Test 1.

Multiple-Choice Questions

1. What is the mode of the following distribution of scores: 2, 2, 4, 4, 4, 14?
   - a. 2
   - b. 4
   - c. 5
   - d. 6

2. What is the mean of the following distribution of scores: 2, 5, 8, 10, 11, 4, 6, 9, 1, 4?
   - a. 2
   - b. 10
   - c. 6
   - d. 15

3. What is the median of the following distribution: 10, 7, 5, 11, 8, 6, 9?
   - a. 6
   - b. 7
   - c. 8
   - d. 9

4. Which statistic is the average amount by which the scores in a distribution vary from the average?
   - a. standard deviation
   - b. range
   - c. median
   - d. mode

5. The most frequently occurring score in a distribution is the:
   - a. mean.
   - b. median.
   - c. mode.
   - d. range.

6. In the following distribution, the mean is _____ the mode and _____ the median: 4, 6, 1, 4, 5.
   - a. less than; less than
   - b. less than; greater than
   - c. equal to; equal to
   - d. greater than; equal to

7. Which of the following is the measure of variation that is most affected by extreme scores?
   - a. mean
   - b. standard deviation
   - c. mode
   - d. range

8. What is the standard deviation of the following distribution: 3, 1, 4, 10, 12?
   - a. 10
   - b. 15
   - c. $\sqrt{18}$
   - d. 4

9. Which of the following sets of scores would likely be most representative of the population from which it was drawn?
   - a. a sample with a relatively large standard deviation
   - b. a sample with a relatively small standard deviation
   - c. a sample with a relatively large range
   - d. a sample with a relatively small range

10. The *value* of the correlation coefficient indicates the _____ of relationship between two variables, and the *sign* (positive or negative) indicates the _____ of the relationship.
    - a. direction; strength
    - b. strength; direction
    - c. direction; reliability
    - d. reliability; strength

11. If a difference between two samples is *not* statistically significant, which of the following can be concluded?
    - a. The difference is probably not a true one.
    - b. The difference is probably not reliable.
    - c. The difference could be due to sampling variation.
    - d. All of the above are true.

12. The first step in constructing a bar graph is to:
    - a. measure the standard deviation.
    - b. organize the data.
    - c. calculate a correlation coefficient.
    - d. determine the range.

13. Why is the median at times a better measure of central tendency than the mean?
    - a. It is more sensitive to extreme scores.
    - b. It is less sensitive to extreme scores.
    - c. It is based on more of the scores in the distribution than the mean.
    - d. Both a. and c. explain why.

14. Standard deviation is to mode as _____ is to _____ .
    - a. mean; median
    - b. variation; central tendency
    - c. median; mean
    - d. central tendency; variation

15. In a normal distribution, what percentage of scores fall between –1 and +1 standard deviation units of the mean?
    - a. 50 percent
    - b. 68 percent
    - c. 95 percent
    - d. 99.7 percent

16. The precision with which sample statistics reflect population parameters is greater when the sample is:
    a. large.
    b. characterized by high variability.
    c. small in number but consists of vivid cases.
    d. statistically significant.

17. The following plot depicts a correlation coefficient that would be close to:

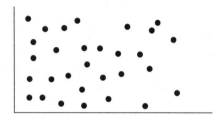

    a. +1.0.   c. 0.00.
    b. −1.0.   d. 0.50.

18. Which of the following correlation coefficients indicates the strongest relationship between two variables?
    a. −.73   c. 0.00
    b. +.66   d. −.50

19. A correlation coefficient:
    a. indicates the direction of relationship between two variables.
    b. indicates the strength of relationship between two variables.
    c. does *not* indicate whether there is a cause-and-effect relationship between two variables.
    d. does all of the above.

True–False Items

Indicate whether each statement is true or false by placing a *T* (*True*) or *F* (*False*) in the blank next to the item.

_____ 1. The first step in describing raw data is to organize it.
_____ 2. In almost all distributions, the mean, the median, and the mode will be the same.
_____ 3. When a distribution has a few extreme scores, the range is more misleading than the standard deviation.
_____ 4. If increases in the value of variable *x* are accompanied by decreases in the value of variable *y*, the two variables are negatively correlated.
_____ 5. Over time, extreme results tend to fall back toward the average.

_____ 6. If a sample has low variability, it cannot be representative of the population from which it was drawn.
_____ 7. The mean is always the most precise measure of central tendency.
_____ 8. Averages that have been derived from scores with low variability are more reliable than those derived from scores that are more variable.
_____ 9. If a difference between two groups is due to sampling variation, it cannot be statistically significant.
_____ 10. Small samples are less reliable than large samples for generalizing to the population.

Review and Reflect

Answer these questions the day before an exam as a final check on your understanding of the chapter's terms and concepts.

Multiple-Choice Questions

1. Compute the standard deviation of the following distribution: 3, 5, 6, 2, 4.
   a. 1   c. $\sqrt{10}$
   b. $\sqrt{2}$ d. 4

2. Jane usually averages 175 in bowling. One night her three-game average is 215. What will probably happen to her bowling average over the next several weeks of bowling?
   a. It will return to about the level of her average.
   b. It will continue to increase.
   c. It will dip down to about 155.
   d. There is no way to predict her average scores.

3. If height and body weight are positively correlated, which of the following is true?
   a. There is a cause-and-effect relationship between height and weight.
   b. As height increases, weight decreases.
   c. Knowing a person's height, one can predict his or her weight.
   d. All of the above are true.

4. The football team's punter wants to determine how consistent his punting distances have been during the past season. He should compute the:
   a. mean.   c. mode.
   b. median.   d. standard deviation.

5. If about two-thirds of the cases in a research study fall within 1 standard deviation from the mean, and 95 percent within 2 standard deviations, researchers know that their data form a:
   a. skewed distribution.   c. normal curve.
   b. plot.   d. bar graph.

6. Which of the following exemplifies regression toward the mean?
   a. In his second season of varsity basketball, Edward averaged 5 points more per game than in his first season.
   b. A gambler rolls 5 consecutive "sevens" using her favorite dice.
   c. After earning an unusually low score on the first exam in a class, a "B student" scores much higher on the second exam.
   d. A student who usually gets Bs earns grades of A, C, C, and A on four exams, thus maintaining a B average overall for the class.

7. Which score falls at the 50th percentile of a distribution?
   a. mean   c. mode
   b. median   d. standard deviation

8. If scores on an exam have a mean of 50, a standard deviation of 10, and are normally distributed, approximately 95 percent of those taking the exam would be expected to score between:
   a. 45 and 55.   c. 35 and 65.
   b. 40 and 60.   d. 30 and 70.

9. Joe believes that his basketball game is always best when he wears his old gray athletic socks. Joe is a victim of the phenomenon called:
   a. regression toward the mean.
   b. the availability heuristic.
   c. illusory correlation.
   d. the gambler's fallacy.

10. Five members of Terry's sorority reported the following individual earnings from their sale of raffle tickets: $3, $6, $8, $6, and $12. In this distribution, the mean is _____ the mode and _____the median.
    a. equal to; equal to
    b. greater than; equal to
    c. greater than; greater than
    d. equal to; less than

11. If a distribution has a standard deviation of 0:
    a. it must be very small in size.
    b. it cannot be representative of the population from which it is drawn.
    c. all of the scores in the distribution are equal.
    d. nothing can be determined from the information given.

12. Esteban refuses to be persuaded by an advertiser's claim that people using their brand of gasoline average 50 miles per gallon. His decision probably is based on:
    a. the possibility that the average is the mean, which could be artificially inflated by a few extreme scores.
    b. the absence of information about the size of the sample studied.
    c. the absence of information about the variation in sample scores.
    d. all of the above.

13. Which of the following sets of scores best fits the definition of a normal distribution?
    a. 1, 2, 4, 8, 16, 32
    b. 2, 2, 2, 2, 2, 2
    c. 1, 2, 3, 4, 4, 4, 5, 6, 7
    d. 2, 8, 10, 18, 35

14. Which of the following distributions has the largest standard deviation?
    a. 1, 2, 3   c. 6, 10, 14
    b. 4, 4, 4   d. 30, 31, 32

15. Bob scored 43 out of 70 on his psychology exam. He was worried until he discovered that most of the class earned the same score. Bob's score was equal to the:
    a. mean.   c. mode.
    b. median.   d. range.

16. The four families on your block all have annual household incomes of $25,000. If a new family with an annual income of $75,000 moved in, which measure of central tendency would be most affected?
    a. mean   c. mode
    b. median   d. standard deviation

17. How would you describe a plot depicting a perfect correlation between two sets of scores?
    a. All the points fall on a straight line.
    b. The points are spread randomly about the plot.
    c. All the points fall on a curved line.
    d. It is impossible to determine from the information given.

18. Dr. Numbers passed back an exam and announced to the class that the mean, the median, and the mode of the scores were equal. This means that:

    a. the scores formed a normal distribution.
    b. the distribution had a large standard deviation.
    c. the students did very well on the exam.
    d. all of the above are true.

19. Dr. Salazar recently completed an experiment in which she compared reasoning ability in a sample of females and a sample of males. The means of the female and male samples equaled 21 and 19, respectively, on a 25-point scale. A statistical test revealed that her results were not statistically significant. What can Dr. Salazar conclude?

    a. Females have superior reasoning ability.
    b. The difference in the means of the two samples is probably due to chance variation.
    c. The difference in the means of the two samples is reliable.
    d. None of the above is true.

Essay Question

Discuss several ways in which statistical reasoning can improve your own everyday thinking. (Use the space below to list the points you want to make, and organize them. Then write the essay on a separate sheet of paper.)

Key Terms

Writing Definitions

Using your own words, on a separate piece of paper write a brief definition or explanation of each of the following terms.

1. mode
2. mean
3. median
4. range
5. standard deviation
6. normal curve
7. correlation coefficient
8. regression toward the mean
9. statistical significance

Answers

Describing Data

Section Preview

1. Organizing the data is the first step in constructing a bar graph, which makes the distribution easy to see and interpret. Readers must be cautious in reading graphs, because the graphs can be made to emphasize whatever their creator wishes to emphasize.

2. The mode is the most frequently occurring score in a distribution. The mean, or arithmetic average, is the sum of the scores divided by the number of scores. Although the mean is the most commonly reported measure of central tendency, it is extremely sensitive to unusual scores and therefore is potentially misleading as a representation of the average of a distribution that is skewed. The median is the score that falls at the 50th percentile.

3. The simplest measure of variation is the range, or the difference between the lowest and highest scores in a distribution. As a measure of variation, the range is rather crude because it is based on only the two extreme scores in a distribution. A better gauge of variation is the standard deviation, which is computed as the square root of the average squared deviation of the scores from the mean of the distribution. A symmetrical, bell-shaped distribution forms a normal curve in which the three measures of central tendency are equal, most cases fall near the mean, and fewer

scores fall near either extreme. Furthermore, in a normal distribution roughly 68 percent of the cases fall within 1 standard deviation on either side of the mean, and 95 percent of the cases fall within 2 standard deviations.

4. The correlation coefficient, which can range from +1.00 through 0.00 to –1.00, is a statistical measure of the extent to which two factors vary together and thus how well either predicts the other. A positive correlation means that one set of scores increases in direct proportion to the other. A negative correlation means that one set of scores goes up as the other goes down. The strength of a relationship is indicated by the value of the correlation coefficient. A strong correlation is one that has a coefficient near +1.00 or –1.00. A correlation of 0.00 means that there is no predictive relationship between the sets of scores. While the correlation coefficient reveals whether changes in one variable can be predicted from changes in another variable, it does *not* indicate a cause-and-effect relationship between two variables.

5. Illusory correlation is a perceived correlation that does not actually exist. Believing there is a relationship between two things may make one more likely to notice and recall instances that confirm this belief and contribute to this misperception. Furthermore, because people are sensitive to unusual events, they are likely to notice the occurrence of two such events in close proximity and incorrectly perceive the existence of a correlation between them. Illusory correlations contribute to the illusion that chance events are subject to personal control. This illusion is also fostered by the tendency for unusual events to be followed by more ordinary happenings. Failing to recognize this statistical principle (regression toward the mean) can mislead people into believing that they can control the events in question.

Stepping Through the Section

1. organize; bar graph
2. mean; median; mode
3. mode
4. sum; number
5. 50th
6. skewed; mean
7. low; high
8. range; standard deviation
9. difference between the lowest and highest scores in a distribution
10. crude; is

11. more accurate; takes
12. a. Calculate the deviation between each score and the mean.
    b. Square each deviation score.
    c. Determine the average of the squared deviation scores.
    d. Take the square root of this average.
13. normal curve
14. 68; 95

Since the mean equals 100 and the standard deviation is 15 points, a score of 116 is just over one standard deviation unit above the mean. Since 68 percent of the

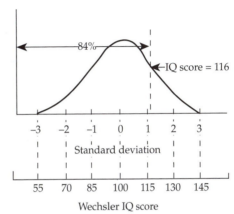

Wechsler IQ score

population's scores fall within one standard deviation on either side of the mean, 34 percent fall between 0 and +1 standard deviation unit. By definition, 50 percent of the scores fall below the mean. Therefore, a score at or above 115 is higher than that obtained by 84 percent of the population (50 percent + 34 percent = 84 percent).

15. correlation coefficient; +1.00; –1.00
16. 0.00; +1.00; –1.00; decreases

An example of a positive correlation is the relationship between air temperature and ice cream sales: As one increases so does the other.

An example of a negative correlation is the relationship between good health and the amount of stress a person is under: As stress increases, the odds of good health decrease.

17. does not give
18. illusory correlation
19. confirm
20. control; chance; regression toward the mean

Making Inferences

Section Preview

1. Although it is tempting to overgeneralize from highly select samples, the most reliable inferences about a population are based on a representative sample. A second important principle is that averages derived from samples with low variability are more reliable than those based on samples with high variability. A third is that averages based on more cases are more reliable than averages based on only a few cases. Generalizing to the population from a small sample with high variability is therefore inadvisable and potentially misleading.

2. When psychologists compare two samples to determine if their difference is statistically significant, they want to know whether the difference is real and not due to chance variation between the samples. When sample averages are reliable, and the difference between the averages for two samples is large, researchers can say that the difference has statistical significance.

Stepping Through the Section

1. fewer; larger

2. low

3. more

4. significance; chance; reliable; large

Progress Test 1

Multiple-Choice Questions

1. **c.** is the answer. The mean is the sum of scores divided by the number of scores. [(2 + 3 + 7 + 6 + 1 + 4 + 9 + 5 + 8 + 2)/10 = 4.7.] (p. A-1)

2. **d.** is the answer. When the scores are put in order (1, 2, 3, 4, 7, 7, 8), 4 is at the 50th percentile, splitting the distribution in half. (p. A-1)

3. **b.** is the answer. The mode is the most frequently occurring score. Since there are more "twos" than any other number in the distribution, 2 is the mode. (p. A-1)

4. **d.** is the answer. The range is the gap between the highest and lowest scores in a distribution. (14 − 1 = 13.) (p. A-3)

5. **d.** is the answer. (p. A-3)

6. **a.** is the answer. (p. A-4)
   b. This situation indicates that the two sets of scores are positively correlated.
   c. Whether a correlation is positive or negative

does not indicate the strength of the relationship, only its direction.
   d. In negative correlations, there *is* a relationship; the correlation is negative because the relationship is an inverse one.

7. **a.** is the answer. (p. A-5)
   b. Regression toward the mean has nothing to do with tests of statistical significance.
   c. In fact, just the opposite is true.
   d. This is true, but not because of regression toward the mean.

8. **c.** is the answer. (p. A-3)
   a. 50 percent of the normal curve falls on either side of its mean.
   b. 68 percent of the scores fall between −1 and +1 standard deviation units.
   d. 99.7 percent fall between −3 and +3 standard deviations.

9. **c.** is the answer. (p. A-4)

10. **d.** is the answer. (p. A-6)

11. **c.** is the answer. (p. A-7)
    a. A statistically significant difference may or may not be of practical importance.
    b. This is often the case when a difference is *not* statistically significant.

12. **c.** is the answer. (p. A-2)

13. **b.** is the answer. (p. A-1)

14. **a.** is the answer. As an average, calculated by adding all scores and dividing by the number of scores, the mean could easily be affected by the inclusion of a few extreme scores. (p. A-2)
    b. The range is not a measure of central tendency.
    c. & d. The median and mode give equal weight to all scores; each counts only once and its numerical value is unimportant.

15. **c.** is the answer. (p. A-3)
    a. A skewed curve is formed from an asymmetrical distribution.
    b. A bimodal curve has two modes; a normal curve has only one.
    d. A bar graph depicts a distribution of scores.

16. **a.** is the answer. The standard deviation is the average deviation in a distribution; therefore, if variation (deviation) is small, the standard deviation will also be small. (p. A-3)

17. **a.** is the answer. (p. A-4)
    b. & c. These are "perfect" correlations of equal strength.
    d. This indicates a much stronger relationship between two sets of scores than does a coefficient of 0.00.

18. **b.** is the answer. (p. A-5)

19. **b.** is the answer. (p. A-5)

Matching Items

1. h (p. A-1)   5. f (p. A-1)   9. c (p. A-1)
2. i (p. A-1)   6. b (p. A-3)   10. a (p. A-1)
3. e (p. A-3)   7. k (p. A-3)   11. d (p. A-3)
4. g (p. A-5)   8. j (p. A-2)

Progress Test 2

Multiple-Choice Questions

1. **b.** is the answer. (p. A-1)

2. **c.** is the answer. The mean is the sum of the scores divided by the number of scores. (60/10 = 6.) (p. A-1)

3. **c.** is the answer. When the scores are put in order (5, 6, 7, 8, 9, 10, 11), 8 is at the 50th percentile, splitting the distribution in half. (p. A-1)

4. **a.** is the answer. (p. A-3)
   b. The range is the difference between the highest and lowest scores in a distribution.
   c. The median is the score that falls at the 50th percentile.
   d. The mode is the most frequently occurring score.

5. **c.** is the answer. (p. A-1)
   a. The mean is the arithmetic average.
   b. The median is the score that splits the distribution in half.
   d. The range is the difference between the highest and lowest scores.

6. **c.** is the answer. The mean, median, and mode are equal to 4. (p. A-1)

7. **d.** is the answer. Since the range is the difference between the highest and lowest scores, it is by definition affected by extreme scores. (p. A-3)
   a. & c. The mean and mode are measures of central tendency, not of variation.
   b. The standard deviation is less affected than the range because, when it is calculated, the deviation of *every* score from the mean is computed.

8. **c.** is the answer, calculated as follows (p. A-3)
   i. The mean = (3 + 1 + 4 + 10 + 12)/5 = 6.
   ii. The deviation scores are $3 - 6 = -3$; $1 - 6 = -5$; $4 - 6 = -2$; $10 - 6 = 4$; $12 - 6 = 6$.
   iii. The squared deviation scores are $-3^2 = 9$; $-5^2 = 25$; $-2^2 = 4$; $4^2 = 16$; $6^2 = 36$.
   iv. The mean of the squared deviation scores is $(9 + 25 + 4 + 16 + 36)/5 = 18$.
   v. The square root of this mean, and the standard deviation of the distribution, is $\sqrt{18}$.

9. **b.** is the answer. Averages derived from scores with low variability tend to be more reliable estimates of the populations from which they are drawn. Thus, a. and c. are incorrect. Because the standard deviation is a more accurate estimate of variability than the range, d. is incorrect. (p. A-6)

10. **b.** is the answer. (p. A-4)

11. **d.** is the answer. A difference that is statistically significant is a true difference, rather than an apparent difference due to factors such as sampling variation, and it is reliable. (p. A-7)

12. **b.** is the answer. A bar graph is based on a data distribution. (p. A-1)

13. **b.** is the answer. (p. A-2)
    a. In fact, just the opposite is true.
    c. Both the mean and the median are based on all the scores in a distribution. The median is based on the number of scores, while the mean is based on the average of their sum.

14. **b.** is the answer. Just as the standard deviation is a measure of variation, so the mode is a measure of central tendency. (pp. A-1, A-3)

15. **b.** is the answer. (p. A-3)
    a. 50 percent of the scores in a normal distribution fall on one side of the mean.
    c. 95 percent fall between –2 and +2 standard deviations.
    d. 99.7 percent fall between –3 and +3 standard deviations.

16. **a.** is the answer. Figures based on larger samples are more reliable. (p. A-6)
    b. & c. These sample characteristics would tend to lower precision.
    d. A test of significance is a determination of the likelihood that an obtained result is real.

17. **c.** is the answer. (p. A-4)

18. **a.** is the answer. The closer the correlation coefficient is to either +1 or –1, the stronger the relationship between the variables. (p. A-4)

19. **d.** is the answer. (p. A-4)

True–False Items

1. T (p. A-1)   6. F (p. A-6)
2. F (p. A-2)   7. F (p. A-2)
3. T (p. A-3)   8. T (p. A-6)
4. T (p. A-4)   9. T (p. A-7)
5. T (p. A-5)   10. T (p. A-6)

Review and Reflect

Multiple-Choice Questions

1. **b.** is the answer. The answer is calculated as follows (p. A-3):

i. The mean = $(3 + 5 + 6 + 2 + 4)/5 = 4$.

ii. The deviation scores are $3 - 4 = -1$; $5 - 4 = 1$; $6 - 4 = 2$; $2 - 4 = -2$; $4 - 4 = 0$.

iii. The squared deviation scores are $-1^2 = 1$; $1^2 = 1$; $2^2 = 4$; $-2^2 = 4$; $0^2 = 0$.

iv. The mean of the squared deviation scores is $(1 + 1 + 4 + 4 + 0)/5 = 2$.

v. The square root of this mean, and the standard deviation of the distribution, is $\sqrt{2}$.

2. **a.** is the answer. Although Jane's individual scores cannot be predicted, over time her scores will fall close to her average. This is the phenomenon of regression toward the mean. (p. A-5)

3. **c.** is the answer. If height and weight are positively correlated, increased height is associated with increased weight. Thus, one can predict a person's weight from his or her height. (p. A-4)
a. Correlation does not imply causality.
b. This situation depicts a negative correlation between height and weight.

4. **d.** is the answer. A small or large standard deviation indicates whether a distribution is homogeneous or variable. (p. A-3)
a., b., & c. These statistics would not give any information regarding the consistency of performance.

5. **c.** is the answer. (p. A-3)
a. In a skewed distribution, the scores are not evenly distributed.
b. A scatterplot is a graph that depicts the nature and degree of relationship between two variables.
d. A bar graph depicts a data distribution.

6. **c.** is the answer. Regression toward the mean is the phenomenon that average results are more typical than extreme results. Thus, after an unusual event (the low exam score in this example) things tend to return toward their average level (in this case, the higher score on the second exam). (p. A-5)
a. Edward's improved average indicates only that, perhaps as a result of an additional season's experience, he is a better player.
b. Because the probability of rolling 5 consecutive "sevens" is very low, the gambler's "luck" will probably prove on subsequent rolls to be atypical and things will return toward their average level. This answer is incorrect, however, because it states only that 5 consecutive "sevens" were rolled.
d. In this example, although the average of the student's exam grades is her usual grade of B, they are all extreme grades and do not regress toward the mean.

7. **b.** is the answer. (p. A-1)
a. The mean is the arithmetic average of the scores in a distribution.
c. The mode is the most frequently occurring score in a distribution.
d. The standard deviation is the average deviation of scores from the mean.

8. **d.** is the answer. 95 percent of the scores in a normal distribution fall between 2 standard deviation units below the mean and 2 standard deviation units above the mean. In this example, the test score that corresponds to -2 standard deviation units is $50 - (2 \times 10) = 30$; the score that corresponds to $+2$ standard deviation units is $50 + (2 \times 10) = 70$. (p. A-3)

9. **c.** is the answer. A correlation that is perceived but doesn't actually exist, as in the example, is known as an illusory correlation. (p. A-5)
a. Regression toward the mean is the tendency for extreme scores to fall back toward the average.
b. The availability heuristic is the tendency of people to estimate the likelihood of something in terms of how readily it comes to mind.
d. The gambler's fallacy is the false perception that the probability of a random event is determined by past events.

10. **c.** is the answer. In this case, the mean, or average (7), is greater than both the mode, or most frequently occurring score (6), and the median, or middle score (6). (p. A-1)

11. **c.** is the answer. (p. A-3)

12. **d.** is the answer. (pp. A-2, A-6)

13. **c.** is the answer. This best approximates a normal distribution because most of the scores are near the mean, fewer scores are at the extremes, and the distribution is symmetrical. (p. A-3)

14. **c.** is the answer. Even without actually computing its value, it is evident that the standard deviation of these three scores will be greater than that in a., b., or d., because the scores in this distribution are much more variable. (p. A-3)

15. **c.** is the answer. (p. A-1)
a. The mean is computed as the sum of the scores divided by the number of scores.
b. The median is the midmost score in a distribution.
d. The range is the difference between the highest and lowest scores in a distribution.

16. **a.** is the answer. The mean is strongly influenced by extreme scores. In this example, the mean would change from $25,000 to $(75,000 + 25,000 + 25,000 + 25,000 + 25,000)/5 = \$35,000$. (p. A-2)

b. & c. Both the median and the mode would remain $25,000, even with the addition of the fifth family's income.

d. The standard deviation is a measure of variation, not central tendency.

17. **a.** is the answer. (p. A-4)

b. This will occur when the correlation coefficient is near 0.00.

c. Correlations are linear, rather than curvilinear, relationships.

18. **a.** is the answer. (pp. A-2, A-4)

b. & c. Neither of these can be determined from the information given.

19. **b.** is the answer. (p. A-7)

a. If the difference between the sample means is not significant, then the groups probably do not differ in the measured ability.

c. When a result is not significant it means that the observed difference is unreliable.

Essay Question

The use of tables and bar graphs is helpful in accurately organizing, describing, and interpreting events, especially when there is too much information to remember and one wishes to avoid conclusions based on general impressions. Computing an appropriate measure of central tendency provides an index of the overall average of a set of scores. Knowing that the mean is the most common measure of central tendency, but that it is very sensitive to unusually high or low scores, can help one avoid being misled by claims based on misleading averages. Being able to compute the range or standard deviation of a set of scores allows one to determine how homogeneous the scores in a distribution are and provides a basis for realistically generalizing from samples to populations. Understanding the correlation coefficient can help us to see the world more clearly by revealing the extent to which two things relate. Being aware that unusual results tend to return to more typical results (regression toward the mean) helps us to avoid the practical pitfalls associated with illusory correlation. Finally, understanding the basis for tests of statistical significance can make us more discerning consumers of research reported in the media.

Key Terms

1. The **mode** is the most frequently occurring score in a distribution; it is the simplest measure of central tendency to determine. (p. A-1)

2. The **mean** is the arithmetic average, the measure of central tendency computed by adding together the scores in a distribution and dividing by the number of scores. (p. A-1)

3. The **median**, another measure of central tendency, is the score that falls at the 50th percentile, cutting a distribution in half. (p. A-1)

Example: When the *mean* of a distribution is affected by a few extreme scores, the **median** is the more appropriate measure of central tendency.

4. The **range** is a measure of variation computed as the difference between the highest and lowest scores in a distribution. (p. A-3)

5. The **standard deviation** is the average amount by which the scores in a distribution deviate from the mean. Because it is based on every score in the distribution, it is a more precise measure of variation than the range. (p. A-3)

6. The **normal curve** is the symmetrical, bell-shaped curve that describes many types of data, with most scores centering around the mean and progressively fewer scores occurring toward the extremes. (p. A-4)

7. The **correlation coefficient** is a statistical measure of how much two factors vary together, and thus how well either predicts the other. (p. A-4)

Example: When the **correlation coefficient** is positive, the two sets of scores increase together. When it is negative, increases in one set are accompanied by decreases in the other.

8. **Regression toward the mean** is the tendency for extreme scores to return back, or regress, toward the average. (p. A-5)

9. **Statistical significance** means that an obtained result, such as the difference between the averages for two samples, very likely reflects a real difference rather than sampling variation or chance factors. Tests of statistical significance help researchers decide when they can justifiably generalize from an observed instance. (p. A-7)

FOCUS ON VOCABULARY AND LANGUAGE

Page A-1: Unaided by statistics, *top-of-the head estimates often misread reality and mislead the public.* Without knowing actual data and numbers (statistics), people may guess at the figures (*top-of-the-head estimates*), which do not reflect the facts (*misreads reality*) and can deceive (*mislead*) the public. The figures generated in this manner are often easy to articulate, such as 10 percent or 50 percent (*a big round number*) and, when repeated (*echoed*) by others, may eventually be believed to be true by most people (*they become public myths*).

Describing Data

Page A-2: Because the bottom *half* of British income earners receive only a *quarter* of the *national income pie*, most British people, like most people everywhere, make less than the mean. Incomes are not normally distributed (they do not follow a bell-shaped curve when plotted as a data distribution), so a better measure of central tendency than the mean (arithmetic average) is either the median (the score in the middle) or the mode (the most frequently occurring score). In Myers's example, half the people account for 25 percent of all the money earned in the country (*national income pie*); in this uneven (*skewed*) distribution, therefore, most people earn below-average wages.

Page A-3: Because it uses information from each score, it [**standard deviation**] better *gauges* whether scores are packed together or dispersed. The most commonly used statistic for measuring (*gauging*) how much scores differ from one another (their variation) is the standard deviation (SD). Using this formula, each score is compared to the mean; the result is an index of how spread out (*dispersed*) the scores are. A relatively small SD indicates that most of the scores are close to the average; a relatively large SD indicates that they are much more variable.

Page A-4: Statistics can help us see what the *naked eye* sometimes misses. When looking at an array of data consisting of different measures (e.g., height and temperament) for many subjects, it is very difficult to discern what, if any, relationships exist. Statistical tools, such as the correlation coefficient and the scatterplot, can help us see clearly what the unaided (*naked*) eye might not see. As Myers notes, we sometimes need statistical illumination to see what is in front of us.

Making Inferences

Page A-6: Data are *"noisy."* Differences between groups may simply be due to random (*chance*) variations (*fluctuations*) in those particular samples. When data have a great deal of variability, they are said to be *"noisy,"* which may limit our ability to generalize them to the larger population. In order to determine if differences are reliable, we should be sure that (a) samples are random and representative, (b) scores in the sample are similar to each other (have low variability), and (c) a large number of subjects or observations are included. If these principles are followed, we can confidently make inferences about the differences between groups.

appendix B

Psychology at Work

Appendix Overview

Research on worker motivation reveals that workers who view their careers as a meaningful calling, those working in jobs that optimize their skills, and those who become absorbed in activities that result in "flow" find work satisfying and enriching. Effective leaders recognize this and develop management styles that focus on workers' strengths and adapt their leadership style to the situation.

Human factors psychologists study the interaction of people and machines and try to find ways to increase safety and productivity.

NOTE: Answer guidelines for all Appendix questions begin on page 482.

Introduction (pp. B-1–B-2)

> David Myers at times uses idioms that are unfamiliar to some readers. If you do not know the meaning of the following words in the context in which they appear in the text, refer to page 485 for an explanation: *drudgery, toil, the daily grind; beeped.*

Introduction Preview

First, skim the introduction. Then read the following objective and, as you read the text, search for the information that will enable you to meet that objective. An answer guideline is provided on page 482.

1. Explain the concept of *flow*, and identify the major subfields of industrial-organizational (I/O) psychology.

Stepping Through the Section

After you have read the section, complete the sentences and answer the questions. As you proceed, evaluate your performance by consulting the answers on page 482. Do not continue with the next section until you understand each answer. If you need to, review or reread the section in the textbook before continuing.

1. According to Freud, the healthy life is filled with _____ and _____ .

2. Most people _____ (have/do not have) a predictable career path, which is one reason that many colleges focus less on _____ and more on _____ .

3. People who are unemployed _____ (report/do not report) lower well-being. People who view their work as a _____ report the greatest satisfaction.

4. Psychologist Mihaly Csikszentmihalyi formulated the concept of _____ , which is defined as a state of focused _____ and diminished awareness of _____ . People who experience this state also experience increased feelings of _____ , _____ , and _____ .

5. The nature of work has changed, from _____ to _____ to _____ _____ .

6. The field of _____-_____ psychology applies

477

psychology's principles to the workplace. The subfield of _____ _____ focuses on employee recruitment, training, and development. Another subfield, _____ _____ , examines how work environments and _____ styles influence worker motivation. A third subfield, _____ _____ _____ , focuses on the design of appliances, machines, and work environments.

Personnel Psychology (pp. B-2–B-7)

> If you do not know the meaning of the following phrase in the context in which it appears in the text, refer to page 485 for an explanation: *what our gut tells us.*

Section Preview

Answer guidelines are provided on page 482.

1. Discuss whether interviews predict performance, and identify four effects that fuel the interviewer illusion.

2. Compare the nature, validity, and reliability of structured and unstructured interviews; describe several performance appraisal methods; and identify several possible errors in performance appraisal.

Stepping Through the Section

Answers begin on page 402.

1. Personnel psychologists have found that the corporate world is generally quite _____ (good/bad) at capitalizing on the strengths of workers. One remedy to this is instituting a _____ selection system which matches strengths to work.

2. (Close-Up) Satisfied and successful people devote less time to _____ _____ than to _____ _____ .

3. Within a matter of seconds, interviewers form impressions of applicants' _____ .

   These impressions tend to be highly _____ (accurate/error-prone).

4. Interviewers tend to _____ (over/under)estimate their interviewing skills and intuition—a phenomenon labeled the _____ _____ .

State four effects that fuel this phenomenon.

5. A more disciplined method of collecting information from job applicants is the _____ _____ , which asks the same questions of all applicants. This method enhances the _____ and _____ of the interview process.

6. Performance appraisal has several purposes, including helping organizations decide _____ , how to appropriately _____ , and how to better harness employees' _____ . Performance appraisal methods include _____ ,

_____ _____ scales,
and _____ _____ scales.

7. One form of bias in performance appraisal is the
_____ _____ , which
occurs when one _____ biases rat-
ings of other work-related behaviors. Another is
the _____ error, which occurs
when raters focus on easily remembered behavior. Two others are the _____ and
_____ errors, in which an evalua-
tor tends to be either too easy or too harsh on
everyone.

Organizational Psychology (pp. B-7–B-11)

> If you do not know the meaning of the follow-
> ing phrases in the context in which they
> appear in the text, refer to page 485 for an
> explanation: *holy grail; exude a self-confident
> "charisma."*

Section Preview

Answer guidelines are provided on page 483.

1. Discuss how managers can create a motivated,
productive, and satisfied workforce.

Stepping Through the Section

Answers are provided on page 483.

1. Positive moods at work contribute to worker
_____ , _____ , and
_____ . Researchers have also
found a positive correlation between measures of
organizational success and employee
_____ , or the extent of workers'
involvement, satisfaction, and enthusiasm.

2. Managers who are directive, set clear standards,
organize work, and focus attention on specific
goals are said to employ _____

_____ . More democratic
managers who aim to build teamwork and mediate conflicts in the work force employ

_____ _____ .

Give several pieces of advice offered in the text to
managers who wish to motivate employees.

3. The most effective style of leadership
_____ (varies/does not vary)
with the situation and/or the person.

4. Effective managers _____
(rarely/often) exhibit a high degree of both task
and social leadership.

5. McGregor refers to managers who assume that
workers are basically lazy and motivated only by
money as _____ managers.
Managers who assume that people are intrinsically motivated in their work are referred to as
_____ managers.

Human Factors Psychology (pp. B-11–B-14)

Section Preview

Answer guidelines are provided on page 483.

1. Explain how psychologists contribute to the
development of machines.

Stepping Through the Section

Answers are provided on page 483.

1. Psychologists who study the importance of considering perceptual principles in the design of machines, appliances, and work settings are called _____

   _____ _____ .

2. Victims of the "curse of knowledge," technology developers who assume that others share their _____ , may create designs that are unclear to others. Another example of failure to consider the human factor in design is the _____ _____ technology that provides embarrassing headsets that amplify sound for people with hearing loss.

Progress Test

Multiple-Choice Questions

Circle your answers to the following questions and check them with the answers beginning on page 483. If your answer is incorrect, read the explanation for why it is incorrect and then consult the appropriate pages of the text (in parentheses following the correct answer).

1. Theory _____ managers tend to adopt a style of _____ leadership.
   a. X; task
   b. X; social
   c. Y; autocratic
   d. Y; directive

2. In almost every industrialized nation, unemployed people report:
   a. better health.
   b. lower well-being.
   c. being bored.
   d. enjoying time to travel.

3. To increase employee productivity, industrial-organizational psychologists advise managers to:
   a. adopt a directive leadership style.
   b. adopt a democratic leadership style.
   c. instill competitiveness in each employee.
   d. deal with employees according to their individual motives.

4. Thanks to _____ , TiVo has solved the TV recording problem caused by the complexity of VCRs.
   a. personnel psychologists
   b. human factors psychologists
   c. organizational psychologists
   d. social psychologists

5. Which of the following was *not* identified as a contributing factor in the interviewer illusion?
   a. The fact that interviews reveal applicants' intentions but not necessarily their habitual behaviors.
   b. The tendency of interviewers to think that interview behavior only reflects applicants' enduring traits.
   c. The tendency of interviewers to more often follow the successful careers of applicants they hired rather than those who were not hired.
   d. The tendency of most interviewers to rely on unstructured rather than structured interviews.

6. Because Alethea is very friendly and likable, her supervisor gives her a positive rating on her overall job performance. By generalizing from these specific traits to a biased overall evaluation, Alethea's supervisor has committed a:
   a. leniency error.
   b. severity error.
   c. halo error.
   d. recency error.

7. Because Brent believes that his employees are intrinsically motivated to work for reasons beyond money, Brent would be described as a(n) _____ manager.
   a. directive
   b. autocratic
   c. Theory X
   d. Theory Y

8. Execuvac Company subscribes to the _____ principle that employees are happier and more productive if they are _____ .
   a. Theory X; given simple tasks and monitored closely
   b. Theory Y; paid enough to fulfill basic needs for food and shelter
   c. Theory Y; allowed to participate in managerial decision making
   d. Theory X; allowed to set their own work hours

9. Which of the following individuals would be characterized as experiencing "flow"?
   a. Sheila, who, despite viewing her work as merely a job, performs her work conscientiously
   b. Larry, who sees his work as an artist as a calling
   c. Darren, who views his present job as merely a stepping stone in his career
   d. Montel, who often becomes so immersed in his writing that he loses all sense of self and time

10. Darren, a sales clerk at a tire store, enjoys his job, not so much for the money as for its challenge and the opportunity to interact with a variety of people. The store manager asks you to recommend a strategy for increasing Darren's motivation. Which of the following is most likely to be effective?
    a. Create a competition among the salespeople so that whoever has the highest sales each week receives a bonus.
    b. Put Darren on a week-by-week employment contract, promising him continued employment only if his sales increase each week.
    c. Leave Darren alone unless his sales drop and then threaten to fire him if his performance doesn't improve.

d. Involve Darren as much as possible in company decision making and use rewards to inform him of his successful performance.

11. For as long as she has been the plant manager, Juanita has welcomed input from employees and has delegated authority. Bill, in managing his department, takes a more authoritarian, iron-fisted approach. Juanita's style is one of _____ leadership, whereas Bill's is one of _____ leadership.
    a. task; social
    b. social; task
    c. directive; democratic
    d. democratic; participative

12. Dr. Iverson conducts research focusing on how management styles influence worker motivation. Dr. Iverson would most accurately be described as a(n):
    a. motivation psychologist.
    b. personnel psychologist.
    c. organizational psychologist.
    d. human factors psychologist.
    e. industrial-organizational psychologist.

Matching Items

Match each term with its definition or description.

Terms

_____ 1. Theory X
_____ 2. Theory Y
_____ 3. personnel psychology
_____ 4. organizational psychology
_____ 5. human factors psychology
_____ 6. task leadership
_____ 7. social leadership
_____ 8. flow
_____ 9. industrial-organizational (I/O) psychology

Definitions or Descriptions

a. state of focused consciousness
b. studies issues related to optimizing behavior in the workplace
c. applies psychological methods and principles to the selection and evaluation of workers
d. goal-oriented leadership that sets standards, organizes work, and focuses attention on goals
e. group-oriented leadership that builds teamwork, mediates conflict, and offers support
f. examines organizational influences on worker satisfaction and productivity
g. assumes that workers are motivated to demonstrate their competence and creativity
h. assumes that workers are lazy and need direction
i. explores how people and machines interact

Key Terms

Using your own words, write on a separate piece of paper a brief definition or explanation of each of the following terms.

1. flow
2. industrial-organizational psychology
3. personnel psychology
4. organizational psychology
5. human factors psychology
6. structured interview
7. task leadership
8. social leadership
9. Theory X
10. Theory Y

Answers

Introduction

Section Preview

1. As described by Mihaly Csikszentmihalyi, flow is a state of involved, focused consciousness that sometimes occurs when a person is immersed in work that optimally engages his or her skills. Industrial-organizational psychology applies psychology to the workplace in order to optimize the behavior of workers. Its major subfields include personnel psychology, which focuses on the best methods of selecting and evaluating workers, and organizational psychology, which explores how work environments and management styles affect worker satisfaction and performance. A third subfield, human factors psychology, investigates how appliances, machines, and work environments can be optimally designed for workers.

Stepping Through the Section

1. work; love
2. do not have; training job skills; enlarging capacities for understanding, thinking, and communicating in any work setting
3. report; calling
4. flow; consciousness; self; self-esteem, competence, well-being
5. farming; manufacturing; knowledge work
6. industrial-organizational; personnel psychology; organizational psychology; management; human factors psychology

Personnel Psychology

Section Preview

1. Interviewers often overestimate their ability to predict the performance of potential employees. This phenomenon, called the *interviewer illusion*, is fueled by the fact that interviews often don't reveal applicants' habitual behaviors; by the tendency of interviewers to more often follow the successful careers of applicants they have hired (rather than those they rejected); by the tendency of interviewers to presume that interview behavior reflects only enduring traits; and by the fact that interviewers' preconceptions and moods do affect their evaluations of job applicants.

2. Unstructured interviews are subject to memory distortions and other forms of bias that undermine their usefulness as predictors of job performance. Structured interviews are more valid and reliable in pinpointing strengths that distinguish high performers in a particular line of work. In a structured interview, the interviewer asks the same job-relevant questions of all applicants, each of whom is also rated on established scales. Irrelevant and follow-up questions are avoided to reduce bias. Among the most frequently used performance appraisal methods are checklists, graphic rating scales, and behavior rating scales. Performance appraisal is subject to several errors, including halo errors, which occur when supervisors' overall evaluation of employees biases their rating of employees' specific job-related behaviors. Evaluators also may err in being too easy (leniency error) or too harsh (severity error) on workers. Recency errors occur when raters focus on easily remembered recent behavior.

Stepping Through the Section

1. bad; strengths-based
2. correcting deficiencies; accentuating strengths
3. likability, self-assuredness, competence; error-prone
4. over; interviewer illusion
   a. Interviews disclose the interviewee's good intentions, which are less revealing than their typical behaviors.
   b. Interviewers tend to follow the successful careers of people they hired and lose track of those they did not hire.
   c. Interviewers mistakenly presume that *how* interviewees present themselves reflects only their enduring traits.
   d. Interviewers' preconceptions and moods influence their perceptions of job applicants.

5. structured interview; validity; reliability

6. whom to retain; reward and pay workers; strengths; checklists; graphic rating; behavior rating

7. halo error; trait; recency; leniency; severity

Organizational Psychology

Section Preview

1. Effective managers assess workers' motives (accomplishment, recognition, affiliation, power, etc.) and adjust their managerial style accordingly. What workers value also varies from culture to culture. Regardless of the managerial style, setting clear objectives, establishing challenging goals, and providing feedback on progress motivate high productivity.

   The appropriate leadership style depends on the situation, the strengths of the manager, and his or her assumptions about employees' motives. Those who excel at task leadership are directive, goal-oriented managers who are good at keeping a group centered on its mission. Those who excel at social leadership take a more democratic approach as they promote teamwork, mediate conflicts, and support their work force. Theory X managers, who assume that workers are basically lazy and extrinsically motivated, monitor employees closely and provide incentives to work harder. Theory Y managers, who assume that workers are intrinsically motivated, encourage employee participation in decision making. Effective managers combine goal-oriented task leadership with group-oriented social leadership, adjusting their managerial style in response to workers' motives.

Stepping Through the Section

1. creativity; persistence; helpfulness; engagement

2. task leadership; social leadership

Effective managers use extrinsic rewards to *inform* employees of their successes and boost intrinsic motivation. They also adjust their managerial style to suit their employees, assessing workers' motives (accomplishment, recognition, affiliation, power), challenging them with clear objectives and specific goals, and rewarding them accordingly.

3. varies

4. often

5. Theory X; Theory Y

Human Factors Psychology

Section Preview

1. Human factors psychologists help to design appliances, machines, and work settings that fit our natural perceptions. Technology developers tend to assume that other people know as much as they do about the product. Psychologists help them to understand human limitations and so to design machines accordingly. Thus, human factors psychologists strive to increase both safety and productivity.

Stepping Through the Section

1. human factors psychologists

2. expertise; assistive listening

Progress Test

Multiple-Choice Questions

1. **a.** is the answer. Because they assume that workers are basically lazy and extrinsically motivated, Theory X managers tend to be task-oriented. (p. B-11)
   c. & d. Theory Y managers tend to be democratic/participative leaders.

2. **b.** is the answer. (p. B-1)

3. **d.** is the answer. As different people are motivated by different things, in order to increase motivation and thus productivity, managers are advised to learn what motivates individual employees and to challenge and reward them accordingly. (p. B-9)
   a. & b. The most effective management style will depend on the situation.
   c. This might be an effective strategy with some, but not all, employees.

4. **b.** is the answer. (p. B-12)
   a. Personnel psychologists apply psychological methods and principles to the selection and evaluation of workers.
   c. Organizational psychologists explore how work environments and management styles affect worker motivation, satisfaction, and productivity.
   d. Social psychologists study how peole think about, influence, and relate to one another.

5. **d.** is the answer. Although unstructured interviews *are* more prone to bias than structured interviews, the text does not suggest that they are used more often. (p. B-5)

6. **c.** is the answer. (p. B-7)
   a. & b. These errors occur when an evaluator tends to be too easy (leniency error) or too harsh on all job applicants (severity error).
   d. This error occurs when an evaluator focuses only on easily remembered recent behaviors.

7. **d.** is the answer. (p. B-11)
   a. Directive managers are likely to favor Theory X assumptions regarding worker motivation.
   b. Although this is not mentioned in the text, it is a characteristic of the task leadership style.
   c. Theory X managers assume that workers are basically lazy, error-prone, and extrinsically motivated by money.

8. **c.** is the answer. (p. B-11)
   a. McGregor identified the two leadership styles—Theory X and Theory Y—but did not specify which was most effective.
   b. Maslow's hierarchy of needs was not directed at a specific task.
   d. Keys studied the role of physiological needs in hunger.

9. **d.** is the answer. (p. B-2)

10. **d.** is the answer. Because Darren appears to resonate with the Theory Y principle that people are intrinsically motivated to work for reasons beyond money, giving him feedback about his work and involving him in participative management are probably all he needs to be very satisfied with his situation. (p. B-11)
    a., b., & c. Creating competitions and using controlling, rather than informing, rewards may have the opposite effect and actually undermine Darren's motivation.

11. **b.** is the answer. (p. B-10)
    a. Bill's style is one of task leadership, whereas Juanita's is one of social leadership.
    c. Juanita's style is democratic/participative, whereas Bill's is directive.
    d. The terms democratic and participative refer to the same style of leadership.

12. **c.** is the answer. (p. B -2)

Matching Items

1. h (p. B-11)   6. d (p. B-10)
2. g (p. B-11)   7. e (p. B-10)
3. c (p. B-2)   8. a (p. B-2)
4. f (p. B-2)   9. b (p. B-2)
5. i (p. B-2)

Key Terms

1. **Flow** is a state of focused consciousness on a task that optimally engages a person's skills, often accompanied by a diminished awareness of self and time. (p. B-2)

2. **Industrial-organizational (I/O) psychology** is a subfield of psychology that studies and advises on issues related to optimizing behavior in workplaces. (p. B-2)

3. **Personnel psychology** is a subfield of industrial-organizational psychology that applies psychological methods and principles to the selection and evaluation of workers. (p. B-2)

4. **Organizational psychology** is a subfield of industrial-organizational psychology that explores how work environments and management styles affect worker motivation, satisfaction, and productivity. (p. B-2)

5. **Human factors psychology** explores how people and machines interact and how machines and physical environments can be adapted to human behaviors and thus to increase safety and productivity. (p. B-2)

6. A **structured interview** is one in which an interviewer asks the same job-relevant questions of all interviewees, who are then rated on established evaluation scales. (p. B-6)

7. **Task leadership** is goal-oriented leadership that sets standards, organizes work, and focuses attention on goals. (p. B-10)

8. **Social leadership** is group-oriented leadership that builds teamwork, mediates conflict, and offers support. (p. B-10)

9. **Theory X** managers assume that employees are basically lazy, error-prone, and extrinsically motivated by money and, thus, should be directed from above. (p. B-11)

10. **Theory Y** managers assume that, under the proper conditions, employees are intrinsically motivated to achieve self-esteem and to demonstrate their competence and creativity. (p. B-11)

FOCUS ON VOCABULARY AND LANGUAGE

Page B-1: *Sometimes work is drudgery, toil, the daily grind.* Work can often be dull, uninspiring, energy consuming, and tiresome (*drudgery, toil, the daily grind*). However, as Myers notes, work is more often a source of happiness (*a blessing*) rather than misery (*a bane*). Getting completely away from the struggle and competitiveness of the job (*the rat race*) will not necessarily bring contentment but, instead, may result in feelings of purposelessness.

Page B-2: When people are *beeped* at random intervals . . . When researchers used pagers to randomly signal subjects (*they were beeped*) and report what they were doing and how they were feeling, those engaged in purposeful activities reported more positive emotions and flow than those who were idle and doing nothing much (*vegetating*).

Personnel Psychology

Page B-5: If there's a contest between *what our gut tells us* about someone and what test scores, work samples, and past performance tell us, we should distrust *our gut*. Subjective judgments (*gut feelings*) based on informal get-acquainted face-to-face meetings (*unstructured seat-of-the-pants interviews*) are very weak predictors of later behavior compared to what test scores, work samples, and previous performance reveal. Thus, we should not rely too much on subjective evaluations obtained (*gleaned*) from unstructured interviews (*we should distrust our gut*).

Organizational Psychology

Page B-7: Conclusive evidence of satisfaction's benefits is, some have said, the *holy grail* of I/O psychology. Finding definitive data that there are real benefits for the organization if employees are satisfied, engaged, and happy workers is one of *the major goals* (*the holy grail*) of I/O psychology.

Page B-10: Effective leaders of laboratory groups, work teams, and large corporations also tend to *exude a self-confident "charisma."* . . . Competent managers who lead groups of people in an effective and productive manner typically exhibit an ability to rely on their own capacities (*exude self-confidence*), project their vision of what needs to be done, and inspire others to follow them (*they have "charisma"*). This type of transformational leadership motivates others to want to belong to the group and to feel a strong commitment to its goal.